YOUR STUDY BIBLE FOR A LIFETIME OF LEARNING

INTRODUCING THE *STANDARD LESSON™ TEACHER'S STUDY BIBLE*

The *Standard Lesson Teacher's Study Bible* uses the full *KJV* Bible and includes over 13,000 lines of commentary derived from 60 years of the #1 bestselling Standard Lesson Commentary,® combined with the most popular study Bible features. This Bible helps adult Sunday school teachers, preachers, and serious students better prepare and learn the most about Bible lessons.

• No other study Bible has study notes from the popular Standard Lesson Commentary.

• Scholarly without being academic, the commentary that accompanies Scripture was prepared by experts but written with the volunteer teacher in mind. It is accurate, reliable, readable and teachable.

• The *King James Version* text is complemented by study notes derived from 60 years of the Standard Lesson Commentary to produce a Bible with helps focused on the "teachable" portions of Scripture—passages from which teachers are most likely to draw lessons for life application.

• In addition to the Standard Lesson Commentary study notes, this Bible includes the most popular features of any study Bible, adding depth and relevance to any lesson.

• This non-dated study Bible can be used during any curriculum year, for a lifetime of teaching and spiritual growth.

> *"Teachers preparing for a Sunday School class, adult Bible fellowship, or small group will find this Bible packed with a wealth of resources for virtually every Scripture passage on which a lesson would likely be based."*
>
> — Jonathan Underwood
> Senior Editor, Standard Lesson Commentary

Standard PUBLISHING

www.standardpub.com

VALUABLE FEATURES

Use the *Standard Lesson Teacher's Study Bible* to prepare for the lessons you are studying and teaching each week.

STUDY NOTES

Study notes, placed alongside Scripture, guide teachers in preparing each class, offering detailed insights from Bible experts and scholars along with additional valuable insights gained from classroom experience by teachers who have used Standard Lesson Commentary.

even this unto you.

16 Nevertheless, whereto we have already attained, *l*let us walk *m*by the same rule, *n*let us mind the same thing.

17 Brethren, *o*be followers together of me, and mark them which walk so as *p*ye have us for an ensample.

18 (For many walk, of whom I have told you often, and now tell you even weeping, *that they are *q*the enemies of the cross of Christ:

3:18, 19 Paul turned up the intensity of his warning. *The enemies of the cross of Christ* can include both Jew and Gentile (1 Corinthians 1:22, 23). The enemies are identified by four characteristics. First, their *end is destruction.* Life will not end well for them. Second, their *God is their belly.* They are not controlled by the Holy Spirit, but by the appetites of the flesh. Third, their *glory is in their shame.* They celebrate that which should embarrass them. Finally, they *mind earthly things.* They live selfishly and materialistically, as if this world is all there is.

"WHAT DO YOU THINK?" QUESTIONS

Discussion questions with "talking points" help teachers guide classes to a deeper understanding of Bible lessons and their application to daily life.

whatsoever things *are* just, whatsoever things *are* pure, whatsoever things *are* lovely, *l*whatsoever things *are* of good report; if *there be* any virtue, and if *there be* any praise, think on these things.

9 *m*Those things, which ye have both learned, and received, and heard, and seen in me, do: and *n*the God of peace shall be with you.

WHAT DO YOU THINK?

In what ways have you seen people willingly accept loss for the sake of Christ? How have things turned out for them?

Talking Points for Your Discussion
- Leaving a high-paying job for the mission field
- Downsizing one's lifestyle so more may be given to kingdom work
- Being ostracized by family members for becoming a Christian
- Other

PRONUNCIATION GUIDE

Simple, clear guide shows how to say those difficult-to-pronounce Bible words and names.

Aaron	*Air*-un.	Abihu	Uh-*bye*-hew.
Aaronic	Air-*ahn*-ik.	Abijah	Uh-*bye*-juh.
Abaddon	Uh-*bad*-dun.	Abilene	*Ab*-ih-leen or
Abana	*Ab*-uh-nuh or		Ab-ih-*lee*-neh.
	Uh-*ban*-uh.	Abimelech	Uh-*bim*-eh-lek.
Abba	*Ab*-buh.	Abinadab	Uh-*bin*-uh-dab.
		Abinoam	Uh-*bin*-oh-am.
		Abishag	

We are committed to serving you by providing excellent resources that inspire, educate, and motivate you in a growing relationship with Jesus Christ. To better serve you, we would appreciate your feedback on this product and others like it. Please tell us about your experience with *Standard Lesson Commentary* (SLC) then fold, tape, and mail this card back, or fax to 513-931-0904. Thank you for giving us the privilege of serving you.

1. SLC offers student take-home papers – Seek® for KJV users and The Lookout® for NIV® users. Do you currently use these? ◯ Yes ◯ No

2. If you do not currently use these, why not? ◯ Was not aware of them ◯ No budget ◯ We don't find the content useful ◯ Other: _____

3. Do you use www.standardlesson.com as a resource? ◯ Yes ◯ No

4. If you do use www.standardlesson.com, what tools do you use on this site?

   Please select all that apply.
   ◯ *In the World* ◯ Standard Lesson PowerPoint® ◯ Standard Lesson Map/Chart
   ◯ Dated Teacher Tips ◯ Reproducible Student Activity Pages

5. Are there additional online resources you would find helpful? _____
   _____
   _____

6. Have you used an eBook version of the SLC? ◯ Apple ◯ Kindle ◯ None
   If yes, did you purchase it instead of or in addition to your printed version?
   ◯ Instead of print ◯ In addition to print

7. Have you used the eCommentary? ◯ QuickVerse ◯ Logos ◯ None

8. Do you use another curriculum with the SLC? ◯ Yes ◯ No

   If yes, what do you use? _____

9. Church Affiliation _____

10. Location of church – City _____ State _____

11. Do you make the adult Sunday school curriculum decisions for your church? ◯ Yes ◯ No

12. How many adults on average participate in your Sunday school class(es)? _____

13. How many classes do you have? _____

14. Role at church – Title _____
    ◯ Paid ◯ Volunteer

15. What is your primary use of the SLC? ◯ I'm a teacher ◯ I'm a student ◯ Personal use

16. Gender ◯ Male ◯ Female

17. Your Age ◯ under 20 ◯ 20-29 ◯ 30-39 ◯ 40-49 ◯ 50-59 ◯ 60-69 ◯ 70 and over

18. Ethnicity _____

Standard®
PUBLISHING

NIV® 2014-15

www.standardpub.com

Standard® PUBLISHING

8805 Governor's Hill Dr. Suite 400
Cincinnati, OH 45249

Attn: SLC Marketing Manager
Standard Publishing
8805 Governor's Hill Dr. Suite 400
Cincinnati, OH 45249

- -

19. Please circle the number that best represents how likely you would be to purchase each potential SLC product.

	very unlikely	unlikely	neutral	likely	very likely
Teen companion to the SLC	1	2	3	4	5
Teen ISSL curriculum	1	2	3	4	5
Children's companion to the SLC	1	2	3	4	5

20. If we introduce an English Standard Version (ESV) of the SLC would you switch from the translation you're currently using? ◯ Yes ◯ No
Which version would you switch from? ◯ KJV ◯ NIV®

21. What top 3 improvements or add-on products would you like to see? _____
_____
_____
_____
_____
_____

Thank you for taking the time to complete this survey. We value your feedback as we work to create great products for your ministry and your life.

Printed in the U.S.A.

Standard® PUBLISHING

www.standardpub.com

ENHANCED BIBLE BOOK INTRODUCTIONS

Each book of the Bible includes introductory commentary on the historical and theological context required for a sound understanding of that book's role in God's Word.

WHAT TO REVIEW BEFORE TEACHING PHILIPPIANS

History of the Church in Philippi (Acts 16:11-40). Paul, Silas, Timothy, and Luke founded the congregation during the second missionary journey. While it was not unusual for the gospel to meet with opposition, hostility in Philippi came from a different source than usual. Leaders of local synagogues and the Jewish leaders often incited the crowds against Paul, but that did not seem to be the case here. In fact, a Jewish presence was minimal. Rather, secular Greek (and obviously anti-Jewish) sentiment fueled persecution.

PRACTICAL QUESTIONS ANSWERED IN PHILIPPIANS

How should church politics be addressed? Assess whether or not it is keeping the gospel from being preached (1:15-18). Ask a mature believer to mediate personality conflicts (4:2, 3).

Is there hope when the world is so uncertain? Hold on to the promise that, for the believer, the best days are always yet to come (1:21).

How can we make sure our church has an impact on our community? Attitude is as important as actions (2:14-16).

TEACHING THROUGH PHILIPPIANS

1. PROCLAIM CHRIST (even in tough times)—1:1-26
"I would ye should understand, brethren, that the things which happened unto me have fallen out rather unto the furtherance of the gospel" (1:12).
2. IMITATE CHRIST (by valuing service more than status)—1:27–2:30
"Look not every man on his own things, but every man also on the things of others" (2:4).
3. TRUST CHRIST (rather than yourself for salvation)—3:1–4:1
"What things were gain to me, those I counted loss for Christ" (3:7).
4. REJOICE IN CHRIST (because victory is ours)—4:2-23
"I have learned, in whatsoever state I am, therewith to be content" (4:11).

Macedonia   Black Sea

• Philippi

Standard LESSON

Teacher's
Study
Bible

A NEW CONVENIENT RESOURCE

FINALLY! A BIBLE THAT INCLUDES ALL THE FEATURES YOU NEED!

Designed for teachers and serious students alike, the *Standard Lesson Teacher's Study Bible* is great for Sunday school, personal study, adult Bible fellowships, and small groups. This Bible contains a wealth of resources for virtually every Scripture on which a lesson would likely be based. Distinctive elements include: study notes from the #1 selling Standard Lesson Commentary, cross-references, discussion questions, in-text maps, Bible book introductions, a comprehensive time line, a pronunciation guide, a concordance, a daily Bible reading plan, *KJV* text, and easy-to-read 10 point Scripture font.

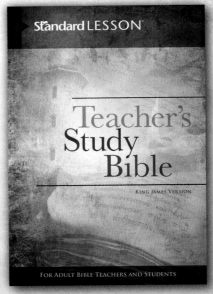

King James Version
DuoTone: $59.99
Binding: Leather, Imitation
ISBN: 978-0-7847-7477-9
Item #: 025610714

King James Version
Hardcover: $49.99
Binding: Casebound
ISBN: 978-0-7847-7478-6
Item #: 025610814

Standard PUBLISHING
www.standardpub.com

2014–2015
SEPTEMBER–AUGUST
NIV®

Standard
LESSON COMMENTARY®

NEW INTERNATIONAL
VERSION®

Edited by
RONALD L. NICKELSON

JONATHAN UNDERWOOD
Senior Editor

VOLUME 21

Standard®
PUBLISHING

Cincinnati, Ohio

IN THIS VOLUME

INDEX OF PRINTED TEXTS

The printed texts for 2014–2015 are arranged here in the order in which they appear in the Bible.

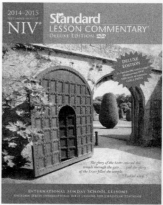

NIV Deluxe Edition

DVD-ROM AVAILABLE!

The *Standard Lesson Commentary®* is available on DVD in the deluxe editions. The DVD contains the full text of both the *KJV Standard Lesson Commentary®* and the *NIV® Standard Lesson Commentary®* powered by QuickVerse® from WORDsearch® Bible Study Software, additional study aids, and a collection of presentation helps that can be projected or reproduced as handouts. Order 020090214 (KJV) or 020080214 (NIV, pictured above). Some 200 additional books and resources are available by FREE download from www.wordsearchbible.com/products/free.

For questions regarding the installation, registration, or activation of the DVD, contact WORDsearch Customer Service at 800.888.9898 or 512.615.9444, Mon–Fri, 8 a.m. to 8 p.m.; or Sat, 10 a.m. to 5 p.m. (Central Time). For problems with the DVD, contact WORDsearch Technical Support at 888.854.8400 or 512.835.6900, Mon–Fri, 9 a.m. to 5 p.m. (Central Time) or by e-mail at Support@WORDsearchBible.com.

Logos users! You can purchase the *Standard Lesson eCommentary* as a download from www.logos.com/standard. This is a separate purchase from the print edition.

CUMULATIVE INDEX

A cumulative index for Scripture passages used in the STANDARD LESSON COMMENTARY
for September 2010–August 2015 is provided below.

SUSTAINING
HOPE

Special Features

Lessons

Unit 1: The Days Are Surely Coming

Unit 2: Dark Nights of the Soul

Unit 3: Visions of Grandeur

QUARTERLY QUIZ

Use these questions as a pretest or as a review. The answers are on page iv of This Quarter in the Word.

Lesson 1

1. Who wanted Jeremiah to write prophecies in a book? (Baruch, God, Hosea?) *Jeremiah 30:2*

2. Following the captivity, Israel was to be ruled by one of its own. T/F. *Jeremiah 30:21*

Lesson 2

1. The new covenant from God was to be similar to the old one. T/F. *Jeremiah 31:31, 32*

2. Where was the new covenant to be written? (stone tablets, hearts, books?) *Jeremiah 31:33*

Lesson 3

1. During the siege of Jerusalem, Jeremiah was a captive of the Babylonians. T/F. *Jeremiah 32:2, 3*

2. Jeremiah made a real estate transaction while imprisoned. T/F. *Jeremiah 32:9*

Lesson 4

1. God promised to provide peace and security after the captivity. *Jeremiah 33:6*

2. During Israel's future restoration, thanks offerings would be given. *Jeremiah 33:11*

Lesson 5

1. Habakkuk stationed himself at a temple gate to await the Lord's answer. T/F. *Habakkuk 2:1*

2. Upon what places did Habakkuk say he would walk? (heights, valleys, old?) *Habakkuk 3:19*

Lesson 6

1. Job desired that his words be written where? (pick two: scroll, heart, sky, rock?) *Job 19:23, 24*

2. Job declared, "I know that my rock lives." *Job 19:25*

Lesson 7

1. Job predicted that wickedness would be broken as a what? (bone, vine, tree?) *Job 24:20*

2. The wicked take advantage of the childless woman and the widow. *Job 24:20b, 21*

Lesson 8

1. After hearing God speak, Job repented in dust and ashes. *Job 42:6*

2. God restored to Job exactly the same amount as he had lost earlier. T/F. *Job 42:10*

Lesson 9

1. In Ezekiel's vision, what filled the temple? (smoke, glory of the Lord, oil?) *Ezekiel 43:5*

2. "The law of the temple" proclaimed an area to be "most holy." *Ezekiel 43:12*

Lesson 10

1. What measuring standard was used in Ezekiel's vision of the altar? (cubit, furlong, ephah?) *Ezekiel 43:13*

2. The temple's altar in Ezekiel's vision was in the shape of a triangle. T/F. *Ezekiel 43:16*

Lesson 11

1. The temple in Ezekiel's vision involved flowing water. T/F. *Ezekiel 47:1*

2. In Ezekiel's vision, certain places were not healed. T/F. *Ezekiel 47:11*

3. Ezekiel's vision includes trees with leaves useful for medicinal healing. *Ezekiel 47:12*

Lesson 12

1. Which tribe of Israel was to be given two portions of land? (Gad, Joseph, Dan?) *Ezekiel 47:13*

2. The western border of the restored land of Israel was to be the _____ Sea. *Ezekiel 47:20*

3. In Ezekiel's vision, all the foreigners will be expelled from the land. T/F. *Ezekiel 47:22*

2-Mediterranean

Lesson 13

1. Zion is another name for Jerusalem in Isaiah's prophecy. T/F. *Isaiah 52:1*

2. Isaiah proclaimed that the feet of the one who brings good news are beautiful. (lips, hands, feet?) *Isaiah 52:7*

QUARTER AT A GLANCE

by Douglas Redford

MUCH OF THE BIBLE is time-bound. It describes life many centuries ago in another part of the world. Certain customs and practices appear very strange to us. We consult commentaries and Bible dictionaries to provide the understanding that we seek.

But there are other portions of the Bible that are timeless. They resonate with us from the moment we read them. Certain themes and the emotions they communicate make an immediate connection, even though we are centuries removed from the times they describe.

To some readers, the prophetic books of the Old Testament, from which this quarter's studies are drawn, are the driest and least relevant portions of Scripture. These books do not resonate at first reading. Yet consider the theme of this quarter: *Sustaining Hope*. While our lessons are concerned with ancient prophets and peoples, they also touch on issues that speak powerfully to people of any time and place.

A People in Turmoil

Most of this quarter's studies are drawn from the period of Old Testament history when the nation of Judah faced the impending judgment of God. Writings of the prophets Jeremiah (lessons 1–4), Habakkuk (lesson 5), Ezekiel (lessons 9–12), and Isaiah (lesson 13) will be under consideration in this regard.

Isaiah was the earliest of these four. He predicted the downfall of Jerusalem and the captivity of Judah over 100 years beforehand. Habakkuk, for his part, observed the rising threat of Babylon and questioned God's justice in allowing such a wicked nation to have its way with his chosen people. Jeremiah lived in Jerusalem at the very time the city was under siege by Babylonian forces. His calls for repentance and reform were not accepted by the people, whose hearts had become too callous to receive his message. Ezekiel experienced firsthand the heartache of the captivity, for he was taken to Babylon in 597 BC in the second part of Babylon's three-stage conquest of Judah.

> *Hope sustained God's people in exile and Job on his ash heap, and hope can yet sustain us today.*

These prophets, however, saw much more than gloom and doom. Each proclaimed a message of hope: a promise that those exiled to Babylon would indeed return home to Judah. God was (and is) the Lord of all nations—not just of his chosen people. His plan cannot be hijacked by any nation or individual.

A Person in Turmoil

While the aforementioned studies focus on national suffering, lessons 6–8 draw our attention to the suffering of an individual. The spotlight is on one of the Bible's most familiar examples in this regard: Job. Though his setting was different, the timeless message of hope was the source of that man's comfort as he confronted his own "exile" on an ash heap. We will see in these lessons the intensity of Job's struggle as he tried to reconcile his pain with his faith in a just God.

Their Hope, Our Hope

Hope sustained God's people in exile and Job on his ash heap, and hope can yet sustain us today. We may not endure the same circumstances as they, but we know that Jesus will return to end our "exile" in this fallen world.

In the meantime, let us take heart from the assurance that "the Scripture cannot be set aside" (John 10:35). And as the prophet Habakkuk so eloquently declared, even though the most adverse circumstances imaginable may arise, "The Sovereign Lord is my strength" (Habakkuk 3:19). This is a timeless truth indeed!

GET THE SETTING

by Lloyd Pelfrey

ONE DEFINITION of the word *hope* is "a feeling or an anticipation that things will somehow be better." Another definition, now considered somewhat archaic, is more in line with the biblical concept of *hope* in that it includes the element of *trust*. Such trust is a confident expectation of the fulfillment of the promises of God.

Judah and National Hope

Solomon died about 930 BC. Not long after that, the 10 northern tribes seceded from the union, retaining the name *Israel* (see 1 Kings 11:30, 31). The 2 southern tribes of Judah and Benjamin became known as *Judah* (see 1 Kings 12:21). The northern nation of Israel was taken into captivity by Assyria about 722 BC; Babylon completed her captivity of Judah in 586 BC. The Lord worked through these events of history to assure that only Judah would become a nation again.

That makes us wonder: What did God do that produced different outcomes for Judah and Israel?

Different methods of captivity. Assyria introduced the two-directional method for dealing with captives. This involved taking people from their home country and settling them in one or more countries elsewhere. People from other areas would in turn be settled in the depopulated area of the first people displaced.

This is exactly what happened to the northern kingdom of Israel in the late eighth century BC. King Sargon II of Assyria boasted that he took 27,290 captives from Israel, and then he forced the mixing of people groups and their gods by resettling foreigners in Samaria (2 Kings 17:23, 24). This mixing demolished any thought of a return for Israel, for others lived in their land. King Nebuchadnezzar, by contrast, used the one-directional approach: the residents of Judah were taken to Babylon, and Judah was left largely uninhabited. This allowed more hope for return.

Prophecies of a return. In about 700 BC, Isaiah's prophecies had amazing content: he said that after a captivity Jerusalem and the cities of Judah would be built and inhabited, that the foundations of the temple would be laid (implying a time when they would be destroyed), and that a person named Cyrus would be the one to accomplish the reconstruction (Isaiah 44:26-28). Isaiah also prophesied that people should flee from Babylon (Isaiah 48:20).

Jeremiah lived 100 years after Isaiah. He prophesied a return after 70 years (Jeremiah 25:12; 29:10), and from Jerusalem he counseled the captives that they should build houses, plant gardens, have families, and seek the welfare of the places where they lived (29:4-7). Later he watched as the Babylonians led captives away and destroyed Jerusalem, and he may have wondered if his prophecies would come to pass.

False prophets tried to hurry God's plan. They said that the return would be within two years and that the vessels of the temple taken to Babylon would be returned (Jeremiah 27:16–28:3). God did not allow his plan to be hurried!

The stirring of the Lord. In God's timing, in October 539 BC, the Persians under Cyrus the Great captured Babylon. The Lord then stirred the mind of Cyrus to proclaim that all the captives in Babylon could return to their native areas; the Lord also prompted many of the exiled Jews to want to return to Jerusalem to rebuild the temple (Ezra 1:1-5). The hope for a return to Judah became a reality, just as God had said.

Sustaining Hope

We must hold to the conviction about three things that abide for now: faith, hope, and love (1 Corinthians 13:13). We say "for now" because hope will be fully realized in Heaven. "Hope that is seen is no hope at all. Who hopes for what they already have?" (Romans 8:24).

THIS QUARTER IN THE WORD

Answers to the Quarterly Quiz on page 2

Lesson 1—1. God. 2. true. **Lesson 2**—1. false. 2. hearts. **Lesson 3**—1. false. 2. true. **Lesson 4**—1. peace. 2. thank. **Lesson 5**—1. false. 2. heights. **Lesson 6**—1. scroll, rock. 2. redeemer. **Lesson 7**—1. tree. 2. widow. **Lesson 8**—1. ashes. 2. false. **Lesson 9**—1. glory of the Lord. 2. holy. **Lesson 10**—1. cubit. 2. false. **Lesson 11**—1. true. 2. true. 3. leaves. **Lesson 12**—1. Joseph. 2. Mediterranean. 3. false. **Lesson 13**—1. true. 2. feet.

LESSON CYCLE CHART

International Sunday School Lesson Cycle, September 2010–August 2016

Year	Fall Quarter (Sep, Oct, Nov)	Winter Quarter (Dec, Jan, Feb)	Spring Quarter (Mar, Apr, May)	Summer Quarter (Jun, Jul, Aug)
2010–2011	The Inescapable God (Exodus, Psalms)	Assuring Hope (Isaiah, Matthew, Mark)	We Worship God (Matthew, Mark, Philippians, 1 & 2 Timothy, Jude, Revelation)	God Instructs His People (Joshua, Judges, Ruth)
2011–2012	Tradition and Wisdom (Proverbs, Ecclesiastes, Song of Solomon, Matthew)	God Establishes a Faithful People (Genesis, Exodus, Luke, Galatians)	God's Creative Word (John)	God Calls for Justice (Pentateuch, History, Psalms, Prophets)
2012–2013	A Living Faith (Psalms, Acts, 1 Corinthians, Hebrews)	Jesus Is Lord (John, Ephesians, Philippians, Colossians)	Undying Hope (Daniel, Luke, Acts, 1 & 2 Thessalonians, 1 & 2 Peter)	God's People Worship (Isaiah, Ezra, Nehemiah)
2013–2014	First Things (Genesis, Exodus, Psalm 104)	Jesus and the Just Reign of God (Luke, James)	Jesus' Fulfillment of Scripture (Pentateuch, 2 Samuel, Psalms, Prophets, Gospels, Acts, Revelation)	The People of God Set Priorities (Haggai, Zechariah, 1 & 2 Corinthians)
2014–2015	Sustaining Hope (Job, Isaiah, Jeremiah, Ezekiel, Habakkuk)	Acts of Worship (Psalms, Daniel, Matthew, Luke, John, Ephesians, Hebrews, James)	The Spirit Comes (Mark, John, Acts, 1 Corinthians, 1–3 John)	God's Prophets Demand Justice (Isaiah, Jeremiah, Ezekiel, Amos, Micah, Zechariah, Malachi)
2015–2016	The Christian Community Comes Alive (Acts)	Sacred Gifts and Holy Gatherings (Pentateuch, Song of Solomon, Hosea, Micah, Gospels)	The Gift of Faith (Mark, Luke)	Toward a New Creation (Zephaniah, Romans)

"God" "Hope" "Worship" "Community" "Tradition" "Faith" "Creation" "Justice"

BUILDING COMMUNITY

Teacher Tips by Wendy Guthrie

WHEN WE CONSIDER the tasks a good teacher performs, factors such as lesson content, preparation, and delivery come to mind. However, there is another element of teaching that often goes unattended, although it is the glue that holds a class together. That element is *community*. The overview below begins a four-part series in this regard. (The remaining parts will address building community through classroom engagement, through shared responsibility, and through community service.)

What Community Is

For most of the twentieth century, the word *community* referred primarily to a group of houses. Today, this word is used more broadly to refer to people who share something in common—think of phrases such as *deaf community* and *retirement community*. The church itself is a community, a people united by shared commitment to the gospel. (Note the similarities between the words *community* and *communion*.) Your class is a community that meets for the common purpose of learning about the Father, Son, and Holy Spirit.

Why Community Is Important

Community fulfills a basic need within each person: the need to be a part of something, to be connected with others. Even those who are very introverted by nature can sense the need for close fellowship with one or two other people.

We recognize that this need is part of our nature as created by God. We see this as early as Genesis 2:18, where God declared, "It is not good for the man to be alone." We see this need throughout the New Testament, which reminds us of the fellowship we do and should have with one another and with Christ (examples: Acts 2:42-47; 1 Corinthians 1:9; Galatians 2:9; and 1 John 1:3, 6, 7).

It is no secret why Christians come together each week: we do so to worship God together, to interact with one another with regard to our shared convictions, to break bread together, etc. Community speaks to mutual support.

How Community Relates to Learning

From an educational perspective, community is the context in which learning takes place. Learning is, at its core, a very social endeavor. We can learn by studying God's Word in private, of course, but the most valuable learning often occurs when we interact with one another (Proverbs 27:17). Each week when your class comes together, your students exchange thoughts and share ideas. They listen to each other (and to you) and respond. They study the Word together and, hopefully, learn something new along the way.

The nature of your class can determine the effectiveness of your teaching. Educational theorists tell us that the most important thing a teacher can do for students is to provide an environment where each feels valued. When they do, they will feel safe to express their flaws and challenges. As this kind of honest sharing takes place, the Word of God is better able to penetrate souls and discern "attitudes of the heart" (Hebrews 4:12).

Creating an environment where your students feel valued can take time. Such an environment is nonthreatening in the sense that students know that their thoughts and concerns will not be treated dismissively. Students learn to trust you and one another as they share their deepest needs, concerns, and doubts.

The building of this kind of environment extends beyond the classroom walls as you and your students become involved in one another's lives. The old adage "I'd rather see a sermon than hear one" applies. Extending class-as-community outside the classroom gives students the opportunity to not only sharpen each other's minds but to challenge each other's actions. Jesus did not have a Sunday-only community of students, and neither should we.

A VISION OF THE FUTURE

DEVOTIONAL READING: Jeremiah 29:10-14
BACKGROUND SCRIPTURE: Jeremiah 30

JEREMIAH 30:1-3, 18-22

¹ This is the word that came to Jeremiah from the LORD: ² "This is what the LORD, the God of Israel, says: 'Write in a book all the words I have spoken to you. ³ The days are coming,' declares the LORD, 'when I will bring my people Israel and Judah back from captivity and restore them to the land I gave their ancestors to possess,' says the LORD."

· ·

¹⁸ "This is what the LORD says:
"'I will restore the fortunes of Jacob's tents
and have compassion on his dwellings;
the city will be rebuilt on her ruins,
and the palace will stand in its proper
place.
¹⁹ From them will come songs of thanksgiving
and the sound of rejoicing.
I will add to their numbers,
and they will not be decreased;
I will bring them honor,
and they will not be disdained.
²⁰ Their children will be as in days of old,
and their community will be established before me;
I will punish all who oppress them.

²¹ Their leader will be one of their own;
their ruler will arise from among them.
I will bring him near and he will come
close to me—
for who is he who will devote himself
to be close to me?'
declares the LORD.
²² "'So you will be my people,
and I will be your God.'"

KEY VERSE

"The days are coming," declares the LORD, "when I will bring my people Israel and Judah back from captivity and restore them to the land I gave their ancestors to possess," says the LORD. —**Jeremiah 30:3**

SUSTAINING HOPE

Unit 1: The Days Are Surely Coming

LESSONS 1–4

LESSON AIMS

After participating in this lesson, each learner will be able to:

1. List three changes the people were to experience after return from exile.

2. Describe God's expectations for his people after the return from exile.

3. Write a prayer expressing joy and thankfulness for being part of the people of God.

LESSON OUTLINE

Introduction
    A. Rebuilding a City
    B. Lesson Background
 I. **Message Transmission** (JEREMIAH 30:1, 2)
    A. To a Man (v. 1)
    B. In a Book (v. 2)
II. **Message Content** (JEREMIAH 30:3, 18-22)
    A. Regarding Land and City (vv. 3, 18)
      Learning from the Past
    B. Regarding Rejoicing and Increasing (v. 19)
    C. Regarding Children and Oppressors (v. 20)
    D. Regarding Leader and Promise (vv. 21, 22)
      Seeking a Better Tomorrow
Conclusion
    A. Rebuilding Jerusalem
    B. Prayer
    C. Thought to Remember

Introduction

A. Rebuilding a City

After a city is destroyed, should it be rebuilt? Historically, a devastated city would be rebuilt if the original reasons for its existence still served. In Bible times, a city needed a location that was defensible; thus cities often were built on elevated locations. This allowed a tremendous tactical advantage because a foreign army was more easily repelled if it had to charge uphill when attacking the city. Cities also needed ready access to food and water; these resources needed to be very close at hand, given the limitations of ancient transportation methods and lack of refrigeration.

Cities were also established in relation to trade routes. A city located at a crossroads of such routes (whether by land or by water) could become a center of commerce. All these reasons were important factors in determining whether a city was rebuilt after being destroyed by war or natural catastrophe.

Another powerful factor for reestablishing a city was religion, a factor that may be difficult for us to understand today. Places deemed to be holy needed to be rebuilt simply because of that fact. Today's lesson looks at a city that met this criteria as well as the others above: the city of Jerusalem —perhaps the most famous city in the history of the world with regard to religion. Jerusalem was destroyed in 586 BC, and the text we will study will help us understand why there was such a strong impetus to rebuild it.

B. Lesson Background

The city of Jerusalem dates to the earliest strands of biblical history. The first mention of Jerusalem in the Bible is in Genesis 14:18 in association with Melchizedek, who is identified as the "king of Salem." (This may be dated to around 2000 BC; compare Hebrews 7:1, 2.) *Salem*—the second half of the word *Jerusalem*— is an ancient word related to *shalom*, the Hebrew word for "peace." It is very likely that the Salem of Melchizedek's day eventually became the Jerusalem of Israel about 1,000 years later, when King David defeated the Jebusites inhabiting the city, taking it as his capital. After this conquest, Jerusalem also began to be known by the designations *Zion* and *the city of David* (2 Samuel 5:5-9; compare Joshua 15:63).

King Solomon, David's son and successor, built a temple in Jerusalem as a permanent "temple of the Lord" to replace the portable tabernacle that had been in use for several hundred years (see 1 Kings 6:1). As a result, the temple became the new home for the ark of the covenant (8:1). The capital city thus became the temple city. The magnificent temple was dedicated around 960 BC. It stood until it was destroyed by the Babylonian army of King Nebuchadnezzar in 586 BC (described in Jeremiah 52).

Jeremiah's 40-year career as a prophet witnessed both sides of that disaster as God used him to warn Judah and its kings of pending divine judgment. God's patience with his people had ended. He spoke (through the prophet) of the problem as a wound that would not heal (Jeremiah 30:12). Even though Judah had had a brief period of religious revival under King Josiah, it did not persist after that man's death (2 Kings 22–25). Jeremiah's message moved from a call for national repentance, to a warning of national disaster by the hand of the Lord, to promise of restoration. The latter is the subject of today's lesson.

The arrangement of material in the book of Jeremiah is not necessarily chronological, so we cannot be sure when the prophecies in Jeremiah 30 should be placed during the prophet's career. They speak of a return from the exile in Babylon, but it is likely that these prophecies are part of a series given before the destruction of the temple in 586 BC. Supporting this conclusion is the fact that the chapter ends on a note that sees the outpouring of God's wrath as something yet to come (Jeremiah 30:23, 24).

I. Message Transmission
(JEREMIAH 30:1, 2)
A. To a Man (v. 1)

1. This is the word that came to Jeremiah from the LORD:

The expression *the word . . . came to Jeremiah from the Lord* or something similar occurs in this book dozens of times (examples: Jeremiah 7:1; 11:1). Sometimes this word of the Lord consists of personal information for Jeremiah (example: 16:1). At other times the word of the Lord directs Jeremiah to do things that have prophetic significance (examples: 13:1-11; 18:1-4). Here, though, what follows is an *oracle*, a message that Jeremiah is intended to deliver to the people of Judah.

> *What Do You Think?*
> How can we know if God is speaking to us today? How is our proof of this same as or different from that in the Old Testament era?
> *Talking Points for Your Discussion*
> • 2 Corinthians 2:12
> • Hebrews 1:1, 2
> • Revelation 22:18, 19
> • Other

B. In a Book (v. 2)

2. "This is what the LORD, the God of Israel, says: 'Write in a book all the words I have spoken to you.

In conjunction with receiving the oracle, Jeremiah is directed to write it *in a book*. A book in Jeremiah's day is a scroll consisting of sheets of parchment sewn together to make a long writing surface that can be rolled up. In Jeremiah 36:4 we find the prophet dictating his message to an associate named Baruch, who writes it "on the scroll." These words are later read by Baruch to the people (36:10). It is possible that this is what is intended here, although Baruch is not mentioned.

HOW TO SAY IT

Babylon	*Bab*-uh-lun.
Baruch	*Bare*-uk or *Bay*-ruk.
Cyrus	*Sigh*-russ.
Jebusites	*Jeb*-yuh-sites.
Jerusalem	Juh-*roo*-suh-lem.
Josiah	Jo-*sigh*-uh.
Melchizedek	Mel-*kiz*-eh-dek.
Nebuchadnezzar	*Neb*-yuh-kud-**nez**-er.
Solomon	*Sol*-o-mun.
Zerubbabel	Zeh-*rub*-uh-bul.

II. Message Content
(JEREMIAH 30:3, 18-22)

A. Regarding Land and City (vv. 3, 18)

3. "'The days are coming,' declares the LORD, 'when I will bring my people Israel and Judah back from captivity and restore them to the land I gave their ancestors to possess,' says the LORD."

The Lord gives Jeremiah a glimpse of the future in a two-part prophecy. First, the people of *Israel and Judah* will suffer another period of captivity. This compares the forthcoming Babylonian exile with Israel's original period of bondage in Egypt, which had come to an end over 800 years earlier. The situation to come will be a forced removal of the people from their homeland to work for their captors. Part of the reason for military conquest in the ancient world is to secure workers to serve the conquering empire (compare Daniel 1:3-5).

Second, Jeremiah sees beyond the period of exile to a time of restoration. This will involve a return of the people to Jerusalem and *the land* around it, real estate that had been promised to their ancestors (see Genesis 13:14, 15; 17:8). A true restoration is in mind when Jeremiah promises that the returnees will *possess* this land, meaning that they will not be merely tenants.

18. "This is what the LORD says:
"'I will restore the fortunes of Jacob's tents
and have compassion on his dwellings;
the city will be rebuilt on her ruins,
and the palace will stand in its proper place.

The lengthy description in Jeremiah 30:4-17 (not in today's text) of the forthcoming captivity and release continues with a very old visual image from Israel's history: *Jacob's tents.* The patriarchs Abraham, Isaac, and Jacob had lived as nomadic people who tended flocks, and their *dwellings* had been tents (see Genesis 25:27). These were not tents such as we might purchase in a sporting goods store today; rather, they were heavy, sturdy affairs made of thick cloth of woven goat hair or tanned animal skins (compare Exodus 26:7). A more luxurious tent might be floored with rugs and have a top high enough to allow people to walk upright inside. Although such tents can be

moved, that is a laborious process done only a few times a year by the nomadic herders. To "pitch their tents" is a Bible way of saying "take up residence" (see Jeremiah 6:3).

There is a double meaning in this regard, however. Jacob was the patriarch whose name was changed to *Israel* (Genesis 32:28); as such he was the father of the 12 tribes of that nation. Symbolically, then, *Jacob's tents* refers to the future dwellings of the nation, not merely those of the past. This is seen in the second half of the verse, which refers to *the city* (Jerusalem) to be *rebuilt on her ruins.* The complete nature of this rebuilding will be shown by the restoration of *the palace* in its rightful place, indicating a reinstitution of the monarchy. This restoration will happen when the Lord fulfills his promise to *restore the fortunes of Jacob's tents.*

> **What Do You Think?**
> What "captivities" today keep Christians from serving God to the extent they ought? What can we do to help eliminate these captivities?
> **Talking Points for Your Discussion**
> - Captivities that those ensnared are aware of
> - Captivities that those ensnared are not aware of
> - 2 Corinthians 10:5

❧ *LEARNING FROM THE PAST* ❧

Colonial Williamsburg® is a re-creation of the capital of colonial Virginia. It is a village that time had ravaged and destroyed, but which has undergone reconstruction, starting early in the twentieth century. Some original buildings have been restored; others have been re-created on their original foundations.

But Colonial Williamsburg is more than a collection of buildings. The "living museum" is staffed by reenactors who dress and speak as the original residents did, in the English of the day. The purpose is to re-create as nearly as possible the spirit of an era. In 1932, John D. Rockefeller, Jr., proposed that the motto of Colonial Williamsburg be, "That the future may learn from the past." In visiting the past at Colonial Williamsburg, tourists are reminded of America's earliest values, both good (such as democracy) and bad (such as slavery).

The Lord's message through Jeremiah regarding the destruction and restoration of Jerusalem has a similar intent. The roots of the Babylonian captivity are found in the Judeans' neglect of their history before God. As we "are being built into a spiritual house" today (1 Peter 2:5), may we never forget the slavery of our past—slavery to sin—lest we return to it. See Romans 6:16-23. —C. R. B.

B. Regarding Rejoicing and Increasing (v. 19)

19. "'From them will come songs of thanksgiving
and the sound of rejoicing.
I will add to their numbers,
and they will not be decreased;
I will bring them honor,
and they will not be disdained.

Jeremiah continues his picture of the future, rebuilt city by describing it as full of happy, thankful people who are prospering and growing in numbers. The prophet foresees this in more than visual terms, for he describes *the sound* of the residents *rejoicing.* The Lord's promise to *bring them honor* means that they will be respected by their neighbors in adjoining nations. A growing population will allow the people to field a capable army. This growth will be a sign of divine blessing, the approval of the all-powerful God of Israel.

C. Regarding Children and Oppressors (v. 20)

20. "'Their children will be as in days of old,
and their community will be established before me;
I will punish all who oppress them.

The presence of children is to be a sign of God's continued blessing. This echoes the vision of Isaiah when he looked forward to an expansion of Israel's tent to house her many children (Isaiah 54:1-3). The fact that *their community will be established before me* signifies a nation unified by a common faith. Jeremiah's point is that Israel is to be resurrected as a true nation, able again to take its place among the other nations. A sign of this is the Lord's promise to *punish all who oppress* his peo-

ple. God's wrath, which results in the destruction of Jerusalem and its temple, will be turned against those who seek to destroy renewed Israel.

D. Regarding Leader and Promise (vv. 21, 22)

21. "'Their leader will be one of their own;
their ruler will arise from among them.
I will bring him near and he will come close to me—
for who is he who will devote himself to be close to me?'
declares the LORD.

Jeremiah finishes the picture of the renewed city by describing its *leader,* who will be native to the nation (*will arise from among them*). This means that *their ruler* will not be an outsider imposed on the people by a foreign power.

It is possible that this prophecy is fulfilled by a person such as Zerubbabel, whom Cyrus the Great will allow to return to Jerusalem from exile in about 538 BC. Zerubbabel and coleader Joshua, the high priest, will return for the purpose of rebuilding the temple, the house of the Lord (Ezra 3:8). Zerubbabel will not be a king, but a governor (see Haggai 2:2) appointed by Cyrus. While Zerubbabel ends up fulfilling some of the characteristics given by Jeremiah, there seems to be more here.

Jeremiah continues his description of this coming ruler by giving spiritual qualifications. The coming ruler will be drawn close to the Lord and will be devoted to him. He will not be just a symbol of the nationalistic hopes of the Jewish people, but a person with a deep, personal relationship with the God of Israel. In this respect the future ruler will be reminiscent of Israel's greatest king, David, who was a man after God's own heart (1 Samuel 13:14; Acts 13:22). Zerubbabel is in the line of David, but he is never seen as a spiritual leader to match David.

While this prophecy is not as specific as others in Jeremiah, it does seem to look forward to the Messiah, God's chosen and eternal king. Its fulfillment will not come until the advent of Jesus, who descends from both David and Zerubbabel. Jesus' rule will extend far beyond the rebuilt city of Jerusalem, for he will be the King of kings and Lord of lords (Revelation 19:16).

❧ SEEKING A BETTER TOMORROW ❧

The 1939 New York World's Fair projected a glowing view of the future. That year was the sesquicentennial of George Washington's inauguration as America's first president, and it seemed like a fitting time to herald America's self-image as a society destined for ever-greater success. The slogan "Building the World of Tomorrow" envisioned a society of great public good, the likes of which had never been seen before.

But the brutality of World War II brought that optimism to a screeching halt. The truth was, "the world of tomorrow" would not be as glorious as predicted. The fair itself demonstrated that fact: its cost was $160 million, but revenues were only $48 million. The Fair Corporation had to declare bankruptcy.

We may build bold structures and hold hopeful exhibitions, but the reality always seems to fall short of the dream. But Jeremiah's vision of a restored Jerusalem was not merely about stone and mortar. It was about a people whose voices praised the Lord and whose hearts exuded the joy of those who lived within the will of God. What will be your role in building up God's people in that regard?
—C. R. B.

22. "'So you will be my people, and I will be your God.'"

This section closes with one of the great promises of the Bible: the possibility of a close relationship between the Lord God and his people. This reminds us of the first captivity, the time the people of Israel spent as slaves in Egypt. When Moses was sent to bring them out to the promised land, he explained the covenant to the children of Israel using the same terms we see here (Exodus 6:7). This is the promise of God's presence among his people, pictured in the law as the Lord walking among them (Leviticus 26:12; quoted in 2 Corinthians 6:16).

Jeremiah uses this promise in other places in his book (Jeremiah 7:23; 11:4; 31:33). It is picked up by the author of Hebrews to describe the new people of God, Christ's church (Hebrews 8:10). Peter applies this to the universal church, consisting of Jew and Gentile who have been formed into a "holy nation," God's own people (1 Peter 2:9, 10).

Often we think of our relationship with God as a private, individual thing. But the consistent picture from the Old and New Testaments gives us the sense of being in relationship with God as we are part of the people of God. Yes, God cares about each and every one of us individually, but his agenda includes forming his followers into a people, a congregation, a new "nation" that transcends national boundaries and ethnic allegiances. As with the promises to Israel of the restoration of their city and its temple, the bigger picture is that of a restored humanity through the work of God's Son, Jesus Christ (Ephesians 2:15).

Conclusion

A. Rebuilding Jerusalem

We wonder how today's prophecy was received by Jeremiah's audience! When they looked around, they did not see a Jerusalem in ruins. They saw no need for rebuilding. Only with a tremendous leap of faith could those folks understand that God's wrath was to destroy their city, and thereby see the promise of future restoration as a message of hope. They had neither the hindsight of our perspective nor the foresight of Jeremiah. They could not conceive of the destruction of the mighty temple that had stood for over three centuries (see Jeremiah 7:4). For this reason, history records they did not heed Jeremiah's call for repentance and for trust in the Lord (17:7).

Many Christians today view events of the twentieth century in the land of modern Israel as necessary fulfillment of various prophecies, and therefore crucial to the outworking of God's plans. The establishment of the modern state of Israel in 1948 was followed by the immigration of hundreds of thousands of Jewish people from all over the world. The Western powers endorsed these moves, partly to atone for the genocide of European Jews by the Nazis.

The city of Jerusalem did not lay in ruins in 1948, but it was nothing like the city promised by Jeremiah and the other prophets. It had no palace for the king, and if it had such a structure, it would have remained empty. It had no temple, for a Muslim shrine stood in its place. It was hardly "Salem," a city of peace, but a place of great tension and sectarian street violence. Some still look to a day when a new temple will be built in Jerusalem to fulfill their understanding of prophecy.

But these are not the concerns of Jeremiah's vision of the future. He speaks of a restored city (Jeremiah 30:18), but he does not mention a restored temple in this chapter. He speaks of the restoration of a king in the line of David (30:9), but not of a new temple of the Lord like Solomon's grand structure. Jeremiah's vision is more like that of Revelation 21, where the apostle John has a vision of the new Jerusalem descending from Heaven. There will be no temple in that perfect

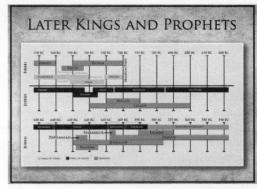

Visual for Lesson 1. *Keep this chart posted throughout the quarter to give your learners a chronological perspective of the prophets being studied.*

city, for the Lord himself will be its temple (Revelation 21:22). That city will be populated by peoples from all nations; it will be a city of great songs of thanksgiving and praise. Jeremiah's promises are not just for the people of Judah facing and looking beyond the Babylonian oppression. They are also for us, the people of God, who look forward to joining our King Jesus in the city prepared for all eternity.

B. Prayer

Lord God, you always have a plan for your people. Your plan may include discipline so that we can be chastened, but restoration is always the final result. May we ever be ready to remain faithful, even in times of great stress and uncertainty. May you heal our wounds and bind us close to you. We pray these things in the name of Jesus our king; amen.

C. Thought to Remember

The pain of exile will give way
to the joy of restoration.

VISUALS FOR THESE LESSONS

The visual pictured in each lesson (see example above) is a small reproduction of a large, full-color poster included in the *Adult Resources* packet for the Fall Quarter. That packet also contains the very useful *Presentation Tools* CD for teacher use. Order No. 020019214 from your supplier.

INVOLVEMENT LEARNING

Enhance your lesson with NIV® Bible Student (from your curriculum supplier) and the reproducible activity page (at www.standardlesson.com or in the back of the NIV® Standard Lesson Commentary Deluxe Edition).

Into the Lesson

Ask learners if they can recall any "good news, bad news" jokes that used to be so popular, and allow them to share a few. If no one remembers any, tell the following one: *Doctor:* "I have some good news and I have some bad news." *Patient:* "What's the good news?" *Doctor:* "The good news is that the tests you took showed that you have 24 hours to live." *Patient:* "That's the good news? What's the bad news?" *Doctor:* "The bad news is that I forgot to call you yesterday!"

Make the transition to the lesson by saying, "In today's text Jeremiah has some really great news for the Israelites that also contains some really bad news. Let's find out what he had to say."

Into the Word

Early in the week, recruit someone to play the part of Jeremiah in an interview. Give him in advance a copy of the Lesson Background and the following interview questions with Scripture references: "What is your family background?" (Jeremiah 1:1); "What made you decide to become a prophet?" (1:4, 5); "Did you have any hesitation about being a prophet?" (1:6); "What assurances did the Lord give you?" (1:7, 8); "Have you enjoyed being a prophet?" (20:7-10); "What personal sacrifice did the Lord ask you to make?" (16:2); "What major disaster did you prophesy that happened during your time as prophet?" (chap. 52); "What good news were you able to speak to the people to give them hope?" (Jeremiah 30:1-3, 18-22 [today's text]).

Alternative: Ask a learner to play the part of the interviewer, while you answer as Jeremiah.

Option 1. If your class is smaller, divide it in half and give each half one of the following assignments on handouts. If your class is larger, form learners into small groups and give one of the two assignments to each, with two or more groups receiving the same assignment.

About the People—Read Jeremiah 30:3, 18a, 19, 20, 22. 1. What was the nature of the punishment to come? 2. How was Jeremiah's prophecy to give hope to God's people in spite of the coming disaster? 3. What would be the attitude of the people when they returned home? 4. What hopeful picture does Jeremiah present of the Israelites' future relationship to God?"

About the City of Jerusalem and the Ruler—Read Jeremiah 30:18b, 21. 1. What changes was Jerusalem to undergo? 2. What is implied by the fact that the palace would be rebuilt? 3. After being under domination by foreigners, what would be the nationality of the people's future ruler? 4. What would be the relationship of this ruler to God?

Ask groups to share discoveries with the class as a whole; expected responses are noted in the commentary. At appropriate points, probe deeper by asking, "Why is this important to us today?"

Option 2. Distribute copies of the "Good Days Are Coming" activity from the reproducible page, which you can download. Have learners work in pairs to see who can solve the puzzle the quickest. As you confirm each answer, compare and contrast the disaster that was to come on the people with the reasons they were to have for hope.

Into Life

Ask learners to share times when they felt like outsiders. Responses may include visiting a foreign country, attending a spouse's family reunion, or visiting a different church. Ask how those experiences compare with what it was like before and after they became part of the family of God. Discuss implications.

Distribute the "Bad Days Are Departing" activity from the reproducible page, to be completed as indicated. You can form learners into pairs or small groups to share their expressions of grateful prayer.

HOPE FOR
THE FUTURE

DEVOTIONAL READING: Hebrews 8:1-7, 13
BACKGROUND SCRIPTURE: Jeremiah 31

JEREMIAH 31:31-37

31 "The days are coming," declares the LORD,
    "when I will make a new covenant
with the people of Israel
    and with the people of Judah.
32 It will not be like the covenant
    I made with their ancestors
when I took them by the hand
    to lead them out of Egypt,
because they broke my covenant,
    though I was a husband to them,"
                        declares the LORD.
33 "This is the covenant I will make with the
        people of Israel
    after that time," declares the LORD.
"I will put my law in their minds
    and write it on their hearts.
I will be their God,
    and they will be my people.
34 No longer will they teach their neighbor,
    or say to one another, 'Know the LORD,'
because they will all know me,
    from the least of them to the greatest,"
                        declares the LORD.

"For I will forgive their wickedness
    and will remember their sins no more."
35 This is what the LORD says,
he who appoints the sun
    to shine by day,
who decrees the moon and stars
    to shine by night,
who stirs up the sea
    so that its waves roar—
    the LORD Almighty is his name:
36 "Only if these decrees vanish from my
        sight,"
    declares the LORD,
"will Israel ever cease
    being a nation before me."
37 This is what the LORD says:
"Only if the heavens above can be
        measured
    and the foundations of the earth below
        be searched out
will I reject all the descendants of Israel
    because of all they have done,"
                        declares the LORD.

KEY VERSE

"The days are coming," declares the LORD, "when I will make a new covenant with the people of Israel and with the people of Judah." —**Jeremiah 31:31**

PS46

SUSTAINING HOPE

Unit 1: The Days Are Surely Coming

LESSONS 1–4

LESSON AIMS

After participating in this lesson, each learner will be able to:

1. Tell some ways the new covenant was to be different from the old covenant.

2. Explain the significance of the term *covenant* in the context of God's relationship with his people.

3. Make plans to renew his or her personal covenant relationship with God.

LESSON OUTLINE

Introduction

A. The Newer, Better Covenant

A mortgage is a binding agreement between a lender (such as a bank) and the person or persons obtaining the mortgage. It has obligations and benefits for both parties. The potential homeowners obtain the funds necessary to buy a house, while the lender benefits by receiving the loan back with interest. Not long ago, my wife and I refinanced the mortgage on our home. We did this to obtain a lower interest rate and therefore lower our monthly payments. This required lots of documentation, signing of paperwork, more paperwork, waiting, and finally notification that the new loan had been approved. Our old mortgage was finished, and our new mortgage was in effect. In this case, newer was better.

Covenants in the Bible also feature agreements that express or imply obligations and benefits between parties. The Old Testament sometimes speaks of covenants made between two people, such as the one between Laban and Jacob (Genesis 31:43-53). The most important covenants in the Bible, though, are those between God and people. They are both like and unlike human-to-human covenants in various ways. This week's lesson will address God's covenant with Old Testament Israel and look at his promise through Jeremiah of a new covenant—a better one.

B. Lesson Background

The first mention of *covenant* in the Bible is in reference to promises the Lord made to Noah (Genesis 6:18; 9:8-17). This is followed by other God-to-human covenants: with Abram (Abraham) and his descendants Isaac and Jacob (Genesis 15:18; Exodus 2:24; 6:5), with the people of Israel after their departure from Egypt (Exodus 19:3-6), and with King David (Psalm 89:3). The covenants after Noah reflect the progress of the people of God from a family group headed by Abraham to a developed nation with a king, land, capital city, and temple. As such, these covenants are interrelated while having distinctive elements.

There is a big picture to keep in mind: the God of Israel was known as the one who kept his covenant (Deuteronomy 7:9; Nehemiah 1:5; Daniel 9:4). This distinguished him from the fictitious gods of other nations, gods who were fickle and might withhold blessings on a whim. Their worshippers believed these deities needed constant appeasement, even by means of the horrible act of child sacrifice. The God of Israel, by contrast, promised sure blessings in exchange for faithful obedience to the clearly established terms of the covenant. To obey God's commandments was to keep the covenant. Unfortunately, the kings and people of Israel and Judah frequently disobeyed, thereby violating the terms of the covenant.

We should note God's covenants to be one-sided affairs in a couple of ways. First, God establishes the terms of his covenants; there are no give-and-take negotiations in this regard. Second, God always keeps his side of his covenants. Humans may fail, but God's promises are always true. The weakness of the covenant to Old Testament Israel was never on the part of God, but on the part of the covenant people. The relentless cycle of sin, sorrow, supplication, and salvation proved that people needed a new covenant.

Jeremiah 31 mostly speaks of a time of restoration. Such restoration was not to come until after 538 BC, the year the exile ended. The prophet pictures this restoration as a great parade of the "remnant of Israel" returning from all directions. This throng is not a victorious army, but includes pregnant women, the blind, and the lame, all weeping with joy (31:7-9). This sets the tone for Jeremiah's broader vision of a new covenant.

HOW TO SAY IT

Abraham	*Ay*-bruh-ham.
Abram	*Ay*-brum.
Hebrews	*Hee*-brews.
Isaac	*Eye*-zuk.
Israel	*Iz*-ray-el.
Jacob	*Jay*-kub.
Jeremiah	Jair-uh-*my*-uh.
Judah	*Joo*-duh.
Laban	*Lay*-bun.
Noah	*No*-uh.
Sabaoth (*Hebrew*)	*Sab*-a-oth.

I. New Covenant Promised
(JEREMIAH 31:31, 32)
A. The Future (v. 31)

31. "The days are coming," declares the LORD,
"when I will make a new covenant with the people of Israel and with the people of Judah.

The book of Jeremiah includes perspectives of the past, present, and future. The verse before us is clearly a look into the future. The promise of *a new covenant* might seem to have some reference to the return of the Jews from exile, since the covenant-breaking that led to their exile means that something has to change. Although God promises to establish this covenant *with the people of Israel and . . . Judah*, the New Testament makes clear that Jeremiah's vision of the future extends far beyond the time of Jerusalem's destruction and rebuilding in the sixth century BC.

The term *new covenant* is found only here in the Old Testament, although the idea of a new or renewed covenant is found in other verses (see Isaiah 42:9, 10; Jeremiah 50:4, 5). *New covenant* is a key concept, and the verse before us is a key passage in connecting the Old Testament with the New Testament. At the last supper, Jesus used this concept to describe the significance of his coming death: "This cup is the new covenant in my blood" (Luke 22:20; compare 1 Corinthians 11:25).

The connection between old and new covenants is seen clearly in Hebrews 8:8-13, where the author quotes Jeremiah 31:31-34 as his key text to explain the Christian system (compare Hebrews 10:16, 17). Consideration of Jeremiah's words leads to the sweeping statement, "By calling this covenant 'new,' he has made the first one obsolete" (Hebrews 8:13).

God's firmly established intention to make a new covenant is seen in the verse before us in the *I will* statement, the first of six in today's text.

❧ WHEN NEW REALLY IS BETTER ❧

New is better . . . or is it? We're used to being bombarded with advertisements telling us that this year's version of a product is "new and improved," when perhaps it has been given no more than a face-lift. That "all new" automobile may have strikingly different styling on the outside while keeping last year's power train underneath. Most likely, the price will be "new" but not necessarily "improved"!

Sometimes we may even question whether something needs to be "new." Mattress stores advertise sales so they can clear out inventory to make room for "next year's models." But is there really that much difference in mattresses from one year to the next?

By contrast, when the Lord says something will be "new," he really means it! The new covenant was not merely a restyled version of the old one. The old covenant was sealed by the sacrificial blood of animals, which dealt with the sin problem only temporarily; the new one has been sealed by the sacrificial blood of the Son of God (Hebrews 10:1-18), which deals with the sin problem permanently. What a difference! —C. R. B.

B. The Past (v. 32)

**32. "It will not be like the covenant
I made with their ancestors
when I took them by the hand
to lead them out of Egypt,
because they broke my covenant,
though I was a husband to them,"
declares the LORD.**

Before God (through Jeremiah) explains the promised new covenant, he speaks of Israel's older covenant. This was the one mediated by Moses after God rescued the nation from slavery in Egypt. God upheld his side of this covenant, but the Israelites did not. Instead, they repeatedly broke it. This covenant-breaking began in a most shocking way even while Moses was on the mountain receiving the terms of the covenant, the law. (See Exodus 32:1-8.) Incredible!

Jeremiah includes a beautiful way of describing how God originally intended this covenant relationship to be understood. The Lord is pictured as a faithful *husband to them*, implying Israel to be his beloved wife. This touches on a couple of ways the prophets speak of the relationship between God and Israel. Sometimes the prophets refer to idolatrous worship of false gods as *adul-tery* (see Jeremiah 3:9; Ezekiel 23:37), the violation of a marriage. Other times the prophets use the love a husband has for his wife as a way to depict God's love for Israel (see Isaiah 54:5; Hosea 2:19, 20; compare Revelation 21:2, 9). The point in the verse before us is that God has been a faithful husband in the covenant, but the Israelites have behaved like an unfaithful wife.

What Do You Think?
Which Scripture do you find most useful in helping you maintain covenant faithfulness to Jesus? Why?
Talking Points for Your Discussion
- 1 Corinthians 11:25
- Galatians 3:13, 14
- Ephesians 5:8
- Hebrews 10:26-29
- Revelation 19:7; 21:2, 9
- Other

II. New Covenant Described
(JEREMIAH 31:33, 34)

A. Hearts and Minds (v. 33)

**33a. "This is the covenant I will make with
the people of Israel
after that time," declares the LORD.
"I will put my law in their minds
and write it on their hearts.**

Jeremiah returns to his discussion of God's covenant to come. In so doing, he shifts to an image of the future by telling the reader that he is passing along something that will be realized *after that time*. In that regard, he reveals the second of the Lord's "I will" promises: *I will put my law in their minds and write it on their hearts.*

The prophet intends us to understand the phrases on either side of the word *and* to be parallel or equivalent in picturing God's law being internalized. This is a vivid contrast with the old law, which is written on stones and parchment (Exodus 31:18; Deuteronomy 4:13; etc.). God intended that the old law should make its way into hearts (Deuteronomy 32:46; Psalm 37:31; etc.), but that never seemed to happen for the vast majority of Israelites.

In Jeremiah's day, the ark of the covenant is a repository for the stone tablets of Moses (2 Chronicles 5:10); a central purpose of the Jerusalem temple is that of a place where the ark rests (see 1 Chronicles 28:2). But in the future, believers themselves will become what we could call "personal arks of the covenant" as we house God's laws in our hearts. God's expectation is that of an inner code that stands at the core of our being. This involves the ministry of the Holy Spirit (see 2 Corinthians 3:3). The emphasis changes from obeying the law to producing the fruit of the Spirit (Galatians 5:22, 23).

As Christians, we do not place ourselves back under the law, for that would be a return to bondage. "Christ has set us free" (Galatians 5:1; compare Romans 2:28, 29; 7:6).

> **What Do You Think?**
> What can you do to make your heart more receptive to having God's Word written on it?
> *Talking Points for Your Discussion*
> ▪ Regarding habits, people, places, and things to embrace
> ▪ Regarding habits, people, places, and things to avoid

33b. "I will be their God, and they will be my people.

The third "I will" statement is seen here (compare Jeremiah 30:22 from last week's lesson). This is to be the essence of the new covenant as it was intended to be with the old. Under the new covenant, God creates a people for himself by writing his law on their hearts and in their minds in calling them out of spiritual bondage to sin rather than out of a physical bondage in Egypt. He calls people into the marvelous light of knowledge of him and relationship with him (2 Corinthians 4:6).

B. Least and Greatest (v. 34a)
34a. "No longer will they teach their neighbor,
or say to one another, 'Know the Lord,'
because they will all know me,
from the least of them to the greatest,"
declares the Lord.

What will personal relationships be like in the new-covenant situation? Jeremiah presents a perfect state of affairs: no one is needed to teach a knowledge of the Lord because everyone (*from the least of them to the greatest*) already has that knowledge. All of our neighbors know. All of our relatives know. They all know!

This prediction raises questions since we understand that a teaching function exists under the new covenant (Matthew 28:19, 20; Romans 12:7; etc.). One interpretation proposes that this looks to the time after Jesus' second coming, when our presence with God in Heaven yields our fullest knowledge of him. Another interpretation proposes that Jeremiah's prediction contrasts the need for human mediators under the old covenant (priests of the tribe of Levi) with the direct access to God that people have under the new covenant (1 Thessalonians 4:9; Hebrews 4:16; 10:19-22; 1 John 2:27).

Either way, the time of the new covenant will be an era when the people of God include more than the peoples of ancient Israel and Judah. Knowledge of God will spread to peoples of all nations and languages (Revelation 7:9).

> **What Do You Think?**
> What more can you do personally to help spread the gospel to peoples of all nations and languages?
> *Talking Points for Your Discussion*
> ▪ In the exercise of spiritual gifts
> ▪ In reevaluation of financial priorities
> ▪ Other

C. Forgive and Forget (v. 34b)
34b. "For I will forgive their wickedness and will remember their sins no more."

This partial verse features the fourth and fifth "I will" statements of the Lord. Some students are puzzled by the latter: is it possible for God to delete certain of his memories in order to *remember their sins no more* permanently? That is not what this text is saying, and we can better understand if we take these two "I will" statements as parallel expressions of a single thought: for God, "forgiving" and "not remembering" are the same thing. He no longer holds our sins against us.

This does not come about because we have offered the proper sacrifice in a temple or prayed a certain prayer; forgiveness under the new covenant is not a reaction by God to something we do. It happens at God's initiative, an act of grace freely given to us by our Lord. Our forgiveness is possible because Jesus, God's Son, bears our sin (Isaiah 53:4). As the sacrificial Lamb of God, Jesus takes away the sin of the world (John 1:29); this is what opens the gate for our forgiveness.

> **What Do You Think?**
> What wrongs against you do you find particularly difficult to forgive? What will you do to overcome this problem?
> *Talking Points for Your Discussion*
> ▪ Broken promises
> ▪ Betrayal
> ▪ Character attacks
> ▪ Other

III. New Covenant's Permanence
(JEREMIAH 31:35-37)
A. Source (v. 35)

35. This is what the LORD says,
he who appoints the sun
to shine by day,
who decrees the moon and stars
to shine by night,
who stirs up the sea
so that its waves roar—
the LORD Almighty is his name:

Having contrasted the old and new covenants to explain how people will relate to God, Jeremiah now begins describing the new covenant's permanence. Its permanence is based on the fact that the maker of the covenant is none other than the Creator of the universe. The phrase *the Lord Almighty* is the Hebrew expression "Lord of Sabaoth," which literally means "the Lord of the heavenly hosts of armies" (see Romans 9:29; James 5:4). We are reminded here of the line "Lord Sabaoth, his Name, from age to age the same" from Martin Luther's hymn "A Mighty Fortress Is Our God."

To reflect on the creation of sun, moon, stars, and sea is to reflect on the eternal nature of God as Creator. Jeremiah also underlines the continuing orderliness of God's creation. In predictable ways, the sun lights the day, while the moon and stars light the night. The waves of the sea continue to be measured and controlled by the Lord of creation. God is in control, even when our lives are chaotic and don't seem to make sense.

> **What Do You Think?**
> When was a trying time that consideration of creation led you to a greater appreciation of the Creator? How do you pass this lesson along?
> *Talking Points for Your Discussion*
> ▪ During a spiritual crisis
> ▪ During a financial crisis
> ▪ During a health crisis
> ▪ Other

B. Promise (vv. 36, 37)

36. "Only if these decrees vanish from my sight,"
declares the LORD,
"will Israel ever cease
being a nation before me."

The text notes the orderliness of God's creation to undergird a promise: the likelihood of God's abandoning *Israel* is as likely as his allowing the orderliness of nature's patterns to vanish. It is like saying, "Just as you can depend on the sun continuing to shine, you can depend on me to remember Israel—and that is forever."

37. This is what the LORD says:
"Only if the heavens above can be measured
and the foundations of the earth below
be searched out
will I reject all the descendants of Israel
because of all they have done,"
declares the LORD.

The Lord's commitment to Israel is now illustrated in another way. God promises that the day when humans are able to measure *the heavens above* and search out *the foundations of the earth below* is when he will renege on his covenant relationship with *the descendants of Israel*. We may think that such measurements are possible in our scientific, technological age. But if science has taught us anything, it is that the universe is impossible to measure and its size is beyond human comprehension. It seems that the more we learn about the cosmos, the more we realize the limitations of our knowledge!

The same is true of our knowledge of the earth itself. For the original hearer of Jeremiah's oracle, the idea of exploring the depths of the oceans is unthinkable. But even as we use various submersibles to explore those depths today, every increase in knowledge brings with it a realization that there is so much more that we do not know. God's commitment to the descendants of Israel is as certain as our inability to know everything.

❧ *The Certainty of God's Promises* ❧

Jeremiah's audience would have been astounded at what we know about God's creation. Think of Mount Everest towering 29,000 feet above sea level, its height more than matched by the depth of the Mariana Trench in the Pacific Ocean. How surprised they would have been to learn that the universe is populated by as many as 70 sextillion stars—that's 7 followed by 22 zeros!

In essence, God said through Jeremiah, "If the time ever comes when you can accurately measure the scope of the creation, that will be the day when I will no longer keep my promises to you." We have discovered various facts about the world and the universe, but even the "fact" of 70 sextillion stars is just a rough order of magnitude estimate. It will undoubtedly change as scientific instruments and methods improve.

It's safe to say that we will never in this life know all the facts about creation. God's promises are just as certain.   —C. R. B.

Conclusion

A. Old and New Covenants Together

We should remember that speaking of an Old Testament and a New Testament does not imply a "bad" covenant and a "good" covenant. The New Testament depends on the foundation of the Old Testament to make its claims. It is the sacrificial system of the old covenant that allows us to understand the atoning, sacrificial death of Jesus—a central doctrine of the Christian faith. The Scripture

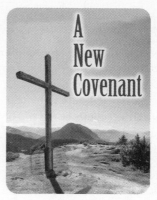

Visual for
Lesson 2

Point to this visual as you discuss the superiority of the new covenant to the old.

of the earliest church was the Old Testament, and the New Testament authors quote from it hundreds of times. We are people of the new covenant, but the old covenant is still of inestimable value (see Romans 15:4; 1 Corinthians 10:11).

When we put Jeremiah 31:31-37 alongside Romans 4:16 and 9:6-8, we see the old covenant being replaced by a new covenant that is not based on law and biological descent, but on faith. This expands the covenant people to include the possibility of every person regardless of tribe or nation.

When we read the new covenant promises in light of the eternity of God, the Lord Almighty, we have the complete picture of an eternal people of God. They accept his offer to write his laws on their hearts; they accept his promise of forgiveness of sins through Jesus. There will never again be a need to send God's people into exile to punish them and cure them of sinful idolatry. The new covenant is the final covenant, and this is the covenant Christians embrace today.

B. Prayer

Mighty God, please keep shaping our hearts. Keep forgetting our sin. Keep accepting us as your people. We pray this in the name of Jesus, who made the new covenant come to life; amen.

C. Thought to Remember

The greatest blessing of all
is to be part of the new covenant!

INVOLVEMENT LEARNING

Enhance your lesson with NIV® Bible Student (from your curriculum supplier) and the reproducible activity page (at www.standardlesson.com or in the back of the NIV® Standard Lesson Commentary Deluxe Edition).

Into the Lesson

Ask learners to open their Bibles to the end of Malachi, which is adjacent (perhaps with an intervening page) to the beginning of Matthew. Ask, "What do we know about the two major parts of the Bible?" Jot responses on the board.

Probe deeper by asking, "Why is one part called the *Old Testament* and the other the *New Testament*?" If no one does so, point out that another name for *testament* is *covenant*. Say, "The Old Testament tells about God's covenant with Abraham, Isaac, Jacob, and their descendants—the nation of Israel. The New Testament is about God's new covenant with all who believe in his Son Jesus. There are important differences between the two covenants, as is explained in today's lesson text."

Alternative. Before learners arrive, place in chairs copies of the "Differences Between Old and New" activity from the reproducible page, which you can download. Do not discuss results at this time; instead, begin by saying, "Understanding the differences between the old and new covenants can be puzzling. Let's read what Jeremiah has to say on the subject."

Into the Word

For an oral reading of the text, divide the class in half, with one group representing the *Old* and the other representing the *New*. Ask learners to read the lesson text aloud, with members of the *New* group reading verses 31, 33, 34 in unison and the *Old* group reading verses 32, 35-37 in unison.

Option 1. Distribute the following questions on handouts: 1. Who drew up the terms of the covenant? 2. Why was a new covenant necessary? 3. Where is God's law to be written under the terms of the new covenant? 4. What changes in the way people "know the Lord" under the new covenant? 5. What is the sign of God's assurance that he will keep his promise? 6. How does all this give you confidence?

Allow a few minutes for completion, either individually or in small groups. Call for answers after learners finish, pausing after each to allow discussion. Make sure to discuss why we should be grateful that we live under the new covenant. *Answer sources: 1, verse 31; 2, verse 32; 3, verse 33; 4, verse 34; 5, verses 36, 37. Responses to question 6 may vary from individual to individual.*

Option 2. If you used the "Differences Between Old and New" puzzle to introduce the lesson, allow learners to discuss their answers now. Then ask, "What were some limitations of the old covenant?" *(Possible responses: needed to obey many rules, required continual animal sacrifices, etc.)* "What changed under the new covenant?" *(Possible responses: covenant is open to all who accept Jesus, depends on faith not law, Jesus' sacrifice is sufficient, etc.)*

Into Life

Have learners pair off to discuss this question: "What would it be like to be in a gathering of Christians where the emphasis is on legalism rather than grace?" As some learners will want to share actual experiences in this regard, caution them not to use real names. After a few minutes, ask learners to share stories about being part of a group that exhibits grace and forgiveness.

Alternative. Distribute copies of the "Identify the Covenant" activity from the reproducible page. After learners have picked either *old* or *new* for each quote, ask, "What are the dangers of falling back into old covenant thinking, speaking, and behaving?" and "How can doing so damage our relationships with others? with God?"

As learners depart, give each a cross cut from a large index card. Say, "I encourage you to write on your cross a commitment to God to renew your covenant relationship with him, a commitment that includes your intention to practice grace and mercy rather than judgment and condemnation."

ANTICIPATION OF A NEW FUTURE

DEVOTIONAL READING: Isaiah 12
BACKGROUND SCRIPTURE: Jeremiah 32

JEREMIAH 32:1-9, 14, 15

¹ This is the word that came to Jeremiah from the LORD in the tenth year of Zedekiah king of Judah, which was the eighteenth year of Nebuchadnezzar. ² The army of the king of Babylon was then besieging Jerusalem, and Jeremiah the prophet was confined in the courtyard of the guard in the royal palace of Judah.

³ Now Zedekiah king of Judah had imprisoned him there, saying, "Why do you prophesy as you do? You say, 'This is what the LORD says: I am about to give this city into the hands of the king of Babylon, and he will capture it. ⁴ Zedekiah king of Judah will not escape the Babylonians but will certainly be given into the hands of the king of Babylon, and will speak with him face to face and see him with his own eyes. ⁵ He will take Zedekiah to Babylon, where he will remain until I deal with him, declares the LORD. If you fight against the Babylonians, you will not succeed.'"

⁶ Jeremiah said, "The word of the LORD came to me: ⁷ Hanamel son of Shallum your uncle is going to come to you and say, 'Buy my field at Anathoth, because as nearest relative it is your right and duty to buy it.'

⁸ "Then, just as the LORD had said, my cousin Hanamel came to me in the courtyard of the guard and said, 'Buy my field at Anathoth in the territory of Benjamin. Since it is your right to redeem it and possess it, buy it for yourself.'

"I knew that this was the word of the LORD; ⁹ so I bought the field at Anathoth from my cousin Hanamel and weighed out for him seventeen shekels of silver."

· ·

¹⁴ "This is what the LORD Almighty, the God of Israel, says: Take these documents, both the sealed and unsealed copies of the deed of purchase, and put them in a clay jar so they will last a long time. ¹⁵ For this is what the LORD Almighty, the God of Israel, says: Houses, fields and vineyards will again be bought in this land."

AGREEMENT FOR SALE AND PURCHASE OF REAL ESTATE

KEY VERSE

For this is what the LORD Almighty, the God of Israel, says: Houses, fields and vineyards will again be bought in this land. —**Jeremiah 32:15**

SUSTAINING HOPE

LESSON AIMS

After participating in this lesson, each learner will be able to:

1. Relate the details of how Jeremiah came to possess his cousin Hanameel's field.

2. Explain why it was so unusual and dramatic for Jeremiah to buy Hanameel's field.

3. State one thing he or she will do in the coming week that is based on hope and not circumstances.

LESSON OUTLINE

Introduction

A. Relatives, Property, and Prison

My wife and I have moved often during our adult years, usually far from family. The result is that we are not close to our various aunts, uncles, and cousins. While there are many people like us in America and Canada, there are also many who have close ties with relatives. In Nebraska, where I now teach, I have students from small towns whose parents, siblings, cousins, etc., mostly live within a few miles of each other. For better or for worse, this has never been my experience.

Sometimes we may assume that our own experiences of family connections (or lack thereof) are pretty much everyone else's, and we are surprised to learn otherwise. Our experiences in this regard may carry over into our study of Old Testament prophets, perhaps causing us to assume that their situations were like ours, only to discover the opposite (compare Jeremiah 16:2; Ezekiel 24:15-18; Hosea 3:1).

Other than the assistance of a certain Baruch, who appears on the scene in Jeremiah 32, the prophet Jeremiah seems to have been all alone as he confronted the sins of his people. Residents of his hometown even plotted to kill him (1:1; 11:21-23). But as these images become fixed in our minds, today's lesson offers the surprising twist of a cousin who appeared on the scene while the prophet was imprisoned.

The astonishing reason for the visit: the cousin wanted Jeremiah to buy a piece of property that was behind enemy lines during a war! It is often said of unusual historical accounts, "You can't make this stuff up." Relatives, property, and prison —all are part of the extraordinary circumstances of our lesson.

B. Lesson Background: Right of Redemption

Today's lesson involves "redemption" of a parcel of land, so some background on that concept is in order. The *right of redemption* within the Law of Moses was a provision designed to keep family properties intact. The land of Canaan, the promised land, had been given to the Israelites by the Lord. Since possession of plots of land was to be seen as a sacred trust, the law made provision for redeeming property that had been sold outside the family. This was something like the modern "right of first refusal," but stronger.

Israelite families retained ultimate rights over land they had sold, rights set forth in Leviticus 25:23-28. If economic hardship necessitated selling a parcel of land, such land was first to be offered to other family members. There was even a sense that a relative who had the means to "redeem" this property (buy it from the distressed family member) was obligated to do so to keep the land in the family. The seller retained the right of repurchase if his finances improved, but at current market value (compare Leviticus 25:15, 16). All unredeemed land was to revert to the original family owners every 50 years, when a year of jubilee was observed.

Overall, the intended effect was to tie people to the land so that an ongoing possibility of economic prosperity could be retained for every family in Israel. From a modern perspective, it placed severe limits on land speculation practices as a means to accumulate wealth.

C. Lesson Background: Anathoth

Jeremiah's hometown of Anathoth (Jeremiah 1:1) was a village in the tribal area of Benjamin, about three miles north-northeast of Jerusalem. Anathoth was a Levite town, a convenient residence for workers in the Jerusalem temple. The priestly tribe of Levi had no tribal area of its own, so its villages and pasture lands were within the territories of other tribes (see Joshua 21:1-4, 17,

HOW TO SAY IT

Anathoth	*An*-uh-thoth.
Babylon	*Bab*-uh-lun.
Babylonians	Bab-ih-*low*-nee-unz.
Baruch	*Bare*-uk or *Bay*-ruk.
Canaan	*Kay*-nun.
Hanamel	*Han*-uh-meel.
Levites	*Lee*-vites.
Nebuchadnezzar	*Neb*-yuh-kud-**nez**-er.
Shallum	*Shall*-um.
Zedekiah	Zed-uh-*kye*-uh.

18). Levites also had the right of property redemption (Leviticus 25:32, 33).

We don't know much about Anathoth, but a close study of the Old Testament yields two facts. First, its residents were opposed to Jeremiah's messages (Jeremiah 11:21-23). Second, people from Anathoth are among those who returned from exile to reestablish their town (see Ezra 2:23; Nehemiah 11:32). That will take place in 538 BC, some 49 years in the future as our text opens.

I. Living Under Siege
(JEREMIAH 32:1-5)
A. Imprisoned Prophet (vv. 1, 2)

1. This is the word that came to Jeremiah from the LORD in the tenth year of Zedekiah king of Judah, which was the eighteenth year of Nebuchadnezzar.

The siege of Jerusalem begins in the ninth year of Zedekiah's reign (Jeremiah 39:1), and Jeremiah receives a *word . . . from the Lord* a few months after that. Enough time has passed for the siege to cause desperate conditions within the city. The siege ultimately lasts 18 months, so we can date this *word* to 587 BC (39:1, 2). This aligns with *the eighteenth year of Nebuchadnezzar,* who ascended to the throne of Babylon in 605 BC (see 25:1).

Zedekiah ends up being the last true *king of Judah.* He had been placed on the throne by Nebuchadnezzar in 597 BC when the Babylonians had conquered (but not destroyed) Jerusalem (see 2 Kings 24:17). Zedekiah has foolishly rebelled against his Babylonian overlords (see 24:20), and he is about to pay the price for that misstep.

2. The army of the king of Babylon was then besieging Jerusalem, and Jeremiah the prophet was confined in the courtyard of the guard in the royal palace of Judah.

For Jerusalem to be besieged means that the Babylonian army surrounds it with encampments and patrols. This is to prevent supplies and reinforcements from entering the city, although the encirclement may be porous enough to allow individuals to slip through here and there. In principle, the residents of the city cannot escape.

Jeremiah is in disfavor with the royal court during the siege, with imprisonment resulting. His confinement *in the courtyard of the guard in the royal palace of Judah* means that he is being given somewhat favorable treatment by not being thrown into a dungeon or cistern (compare Jeremiah 38:1-13).

> **What Do You Think?**
> What parallels do you see between Jeremiah's situation and that of the church today? Why is such an awareness important?
> *Talking Points for Your Discussion*
> ▪ Acts 8:1-3
> ▪ 2 Corinthians 1:8; 7:5; 11:28
> ▪ Hebrews 10:34
> ▪ Other

B. Angry King (vv. 3-5)

3. Now Zedekiah king of Judah had imprisoned him there, saying, "Why do you prophesy as you do? You say, 'This is what the Lord says: I am about to give this city into the hands of the king of Babylon, and he will capture it.

We see the reason for Jeremiah's imprisonment as King Zedekiah quotes the prophet's inflammatory words back to him. The king has been listening, and he is not pleased. Therefore Jeremiah has been separated from the people so that he cannot continue to tell them that Jerusalem will fall. Such a prediction is viewed as demoralizing and perhaps treasonous. More specifically, though, the king is offended by the prophecy in three ways.

First, Jeremiah has not been saying merely that the army of Nebuchadnezzar will win, but that the city will be delivered to that pagan king by the Lord. The prophet's clear message is that the God of Israel is now on the side of the Babylonians. Although this is not a new message (see Jeremiah 20:4), it seems to remain incomprehensible to the city residents in general and Zedekiah in particular. Will their Lord not only abandon them but actively work against them? Unthinkable!

4. "'Zedekiah king of Judah will not escape the Babylonians but will certainly be given into the hands of the king of Babylon, and will

speak with him face to face and see him with his own eyes.

Second, Jeremiah's message offends King Zedekiah in predicting that the king himself will be captured and brought into the very presence of *the king of Babylon*. Zedekiah thus finds the prophet's words threatening for him personally. We can look ahead to Jeremiah 39:5-7 and 52:1 to see how horrific this meeting will be (compare 2 Kings 25:7).

5. "'He will take Zedekiah to Babylon, where he will remain until I deal with him, declares the Lord. If you fight against the Babylonians, you will not succeed.'"

The third offensive element of the prophecy is that Zedekiah himself is to be taken *to Babylon* as a war prize for display. This will indeed happen (2 Kings 25:7; Jeremiah 52:11), the last we hear of Zedekiah. The Bible has no kind words for him (see 2 Chronicles 36:11-16).

> **What Do You Think?**
> What have you learned from the witness of godly people who remained steadfast in the face of opposition?
> *Talking Points for Your Discussion*
> ▪ In use of discretion or tact (Daniel 2:14)
> ▪ In knowing when or if to speak up (Amos 5:13)
> ▪ In remaining focused (Nehemiah 6:3)
> ▪ In understanding the nature of the opposition (Acts 23:6-8)
> ▪ Other

❧ ATTACKING THE MESSENGER ❧

In ancient times, a king's response to hearing bad news might be to punish, even kill, the messenger. The king's subjects were thereby warned not to bring unwanted news to the ruler.

Sometimes, however, the one who brings bad news actually deserves less than favorable treatment. An ancient example is the case of the man who brought David the news of Saul's death; the problem was that the messenger himself had killed Saul (2 Samuel 1:1-16). A modern example is the case of Bradley Birkenfeld, who blew the whistle a few years ago on UBS, the bank that employed him. The bank had helped thousands of rich Americans hide billions of dollars in secret Swiss bank accounts to avoid paying American taxes. The U.S. government awarded Birkenfeld $104 million for being a whistle-blower. However, Birkenfeld was convicted of complicity in his firm's fraudulent activities and spent 30 months in prison as a result.

Jeremiah had a message from God that King Zedekiah didn't like. The king reacted by imprisoning the messenger. But God's Word cannot be silenced. As God's messengers today, which do we fear more: an evil culture's reaction to us because of our message, or God's displeasure for failing to deliver that message?　　　　　—C. R. B.

Visual for Lessons 3 & 8. *Use this visual as a backdrop for your discussion of the question associated with verse 14, below.*

II. Buying Distressed Property
(Jeremiah 32:6-9)

A. Lord's Prediction (vv. 6, 7)

6. Jeremiah said, "The word of the Lord came to me:

Although King Zedekiah has turned against Jeremiah, the Lord has not abandoned him. The prophet continues to receive *the word of the Lord* even while imprisoned. This time it is not a word for the king or the nation, but a personal word for the prophet himself.

7. "Hanamel son of Shallum your uncle is going to come to you and say, 'Buy my field at Anathoth, because as nearest relative it is your right and duty to buy it.'

The Lord advises Jeremiah that he is soon to receive a visitor, a cousin named Hanamel. We can assume that both Hanamel and his father Shallum (Jeremiah's uncle) are also priests who live in nearby Anathoth (Jeremiah 1:1) and work in Jerusalem under normal circumstances. They may be both proud of and embarrassed by their famous relative, for while Jeremiah has the ear of the king, he also is despised by those in his hometown (see 11:21; 20:10).

Hanamel is not coming to denounce Jeremiah though. He is coming on a matter of family business, to request that Jeremiah purchase a piece of property in his hometown in accordance with the law concerning the right of redemption

(see the Lesson Background). This is an extraordinary moment, filled with irony. Jerusalem is under siege, its very existence threatened. Nearby Anathoth will also suffer the ravages of the plundering Babylonians (if it hasn't already). This is almost like the driver of a car asking his passenger to buy the car as they plunge off a cliff in it together!

B. Astonishing Request (vv. 8, 9)

8. "Then, just as the Lord had said, my cousin Hanamel came to me in the courtyard of the guard and said, 'Buy my field at Anathoth in the territory of Benjamin. Since it is your right to redeem it and possess it, buy it for yourself.'

"I knew that this was the word of the Lord;

Hanamel indeed comes to Jeremiah *in the courtyard of the guard*. It's likely that people from surrounding villages have taken refuge within the walled city of Jerusalem as the enemy army approached, and Hanamel may be one of them. If he is coming from Anathoth instead, how he gets past the besieging Babylonians is unknown. But it is not impossible for an individual to sneak through siege lines and/or bribe a sentry to be let into a besieged city.

Details are lacking, but the basic situation is clear. A field owned by Hanamel is available for purchase. This is probably because of economic distress being suffered by Hanamel's family. The fact that Hanamel risks "guilt by association" by being seen in the company of cousin Jeremiah seems to indicate that there is no other relative who has the means or the desire to buy this property. The context indicates that Hanamel comes with a certain amount of family pressure: to purchase this field is not only Jeremiah's right, it is his duty.

Hanamel's offer poses a challenge to the personal faith of the prophet. Jeremiah knows that the field is worthless in the short term, for obvious reasons. The faith question is whether Jeremiah truly believes that the Lord will bring his people back from exile to restore the land.

Jeremiah does not expect this to happen in his lifetime (see Jeremiah 29:10). So to accept Hanamel's offer will be an investment beyond that. Jeremiah has no children to inherit the parcel, but he does have relatives whose descendants might benefit from this audacious act, after return from exile (see Ezra 2:23; Nehemiah 11:32).

> *What Do You Think?*
> When responding to a challenge that involves monetary expenditure, how do you determine whether you are acting in *faith* or *foolhardiness*?
> *Talking Points for Your Discussion*
> - Regarding churches that incur debt for a building program
> - Regarding Christians who pledge monthly support for a missionary or cause
> - Other

9. ". . . so I bought the field at Anathoth from my cousin Hanamel and weighed out for him seventeen shekels of silver."

The *seventeen shekels of silver* Jeremiah pays Hanamel for the purchase are not 17 silver coins, but an exact weighing of certain silver objects, perhaps in a type of bullion (see v. 10, not in today's text). We do not know where Jeremiah obtains this silver, but he must have it accessible within the city since the transaction takes place while he is imprisoned. This purchase is made not with a promissory note but with hard assets, which Jeremiah may need for buying food during the siege. Hanamel is asking (demanding) a lot from his cousin!

The weight of 17 shekels equates to perhaps 7 ounces, but it is impossible to know either the purchasing power of this amount of silver at this time or the market value of Hanamel's field. It makes sense, though, to assume that this is the standard valuation of this parcel of land under normal circumstances. What makes the price seem exorbitant from our perspective is the impending devastation of Jerusalem and its environs. That anyone would buy this field at any price is surprising, much less a guy in prison who is out of favor with the king and his people!

> *What Do You Think?*
> How do you decide when faith demands immediate action or calls for careful waiting?
> *Talking Points for Your Discussion*
> - In a financial crisis
> - In a health crisis
> - In a church crisis
> - In a family crisis
> - Other

III. Preserving the Proof
(JEREMIAH 32:14, 15)
A. Safe-Deposit Jar (v. 14)

14. "This is what the LORD Almighty, the God of Israel, says: Take these documents, both the sealed and unsealed copies of the deed of purchase, and put them in a clay jar so they will last a long time.

The transfer of property is made with the proper documentation (Jeremiah 32:10-12, not in today's text). The *copies of the deed of purchase* (what we would call a title deed) are placed in a container that is then sealed with wax. This provides a moisture-free environment that will preserve the documentation as long as the seal remains intact. The *clay jar* container may be similar to those found containing the Dead Sea Scrolls, some of which had been preserved for over 2,000 years by the time of their discovery.

This safekeeping is in accordance with both protocol and the direction of *the Lord Almighty, the God of Israel.* The use of this long-form reference to the Lord bestows great solemnity on the occasion.

B. Long-Term Investment (v. 15)

15. "For this is what the LORD Almighty, the God of Israel, says: Houses, fields and vineyards will again be bought in this land."

We end with the great promise of this story: the land will be restored. People will again live in the houses. Fields will be planted and harvested. Vineyards will be cultivated.

Jeremiah will not live to see that day, and he knows it (again, see Jeremiah 29:10). Yet the prophet proves his faith both in word and in deed in this remarkable act.

❧ THE PRACTICE OF FARSIGHTEDNESS ❧

When we speak of having 20/20 eyesight, we refer to the ability to see clearly at 20 feet what should normally be seen clearly at that distance. That quality of vision is commonly thought to be the ideal. Working against this ideal are several types of vision defects, one of which is *farsightedness:* a condition of vision being more blurry for near objects than for those at greater distance.

Figuratively, however, *being farsighted* is the positive ability to foresee the future. Only God's prophets had such an ability in an error-free sense! When investing, choosing a marriage partner, teaching our children biblical virtues, etc., we cannot foresee events that will work against our choices and efforts.

Jeremiah had the level of prophetic farsightedness that God intended him to have, and the prophet trusted God with any future that he (Jeremiah) was not privileged to foresee. In so doing, he set an example for us. We practice farsightedness when we believe the New Testament's statements about our future. Such farsightedness reveals itself in behavior when we surrender temporary things to gain that which is eternal. —C. R. B.

Conclusion

A. Faith That Overpays

Personal confession: I am an easy mark for girls selling Girl Scout cookies. If I have any cash in my wallet, I will always buy a box when I see them at a table as I leave the supermarket. I know I am overpaying, that similar cookies are available in the store for half the price. But I always buy them anyway. Why? Because I have faith in their organization and the good things it does in the lives of these youngsters. I never seek a discount. I just pay.

It would be easy to see Jeremiah's actions as foolish. What sense did it make for an unmarried, childless man, stuck in prison and facing the calamity of war, to buy property? Even if he wanted to honor his family's obligation to redeem the property, couldn't he have paid much less? No one would have criticized Jeremiah for driving a hard bargain (or avoiding any bargain) in his circumstances, would they? To think this way misses the point: paying—even overpaying—is an act of faith, a testimony to the long-term commitment of the Lord to his nation.

Faith can be expensive when it comes to money. Faith impels us to send money to agencies for the relief of people we will never see. Faith brings us to give money for a building project we may never personally enjoy. Faith results in financial support of ministries at a level that may cause us to go without things that make our lives more comfortable.

Handling of money can also indicate a lack of faith. May we take heart from Jeremiah's courageous example of faith, trusting God with our hearts and our money.

B. Prayer

O Lord, give us hearts of faithful generosity that look beyond our own needs to the needs of others. We ask this in the name of Jesus, who gave his life for us; amen.

C. Thought to Remember

Hope acts in faith in God's promises.

INVOLVEMENT LEARNING

Enhance your lesson with NIV® Bible Student (from your curriculum supplier) and the reproducible activity page (at www.standardlesson.com or in the back of the NIV® Standard Lesson Commentary Deluxe Edition).

Into the Lesson

Ask which learners have ever purchased property. After a show of hands, ask for a few volunteers to share their stories about the pros and cons considered before the purchase and then tell what was the deciding factor. Then say, "In today's text Jeremiah has good reasons for not buying property, yet he decided to do it anyway. Let's find out why."

Alternative. Distribute copies of the "Counterintuitive" activity from the reproducible page, which you can download. Have learners pair off and race to see which pair can complete the activity first. You can award a small prize for the pair that is the slowest to complete the task; expect learners to note how counterintuitive it is to do that! Then say, "God asked Jeremiah to do something that didn't make sense from a human standpoint. Let's see what it was."

Into the Word

Distribute poster board and markers to small groups. Half the groups will have *Pro* at the top of their poster boards; the other half will have *Con* on theirs.

Give each *Pro* group a copy of the Lesson Background: Right of Redemption, along with a handout of the following instructions and questions: Read through the questions and references from Jeremiah 32. Use the information you discover to come up with compelling reasons why Jeremiah *should* buy his cousin's property, listing them on the poster board. 1. How did Jeremiah know ahead of time that his cousin would ask him to buy property (vv. 6, 7)? 2. In what sense did Jeremiah have a duty to purchase the land (v. 8; see Lesson Background)? 3. What did Jeremiah do about the offer to purchase and why (vv. 8b, 9a)? 4. What did the purchase cost the prophet (v. 9b)? 5. How were the purchase documents preserved (v. 14)? 6. What message by means of an object lesson was the Lord conveying to his people (v. 15)?

Give each *Con* group a handout with the following instructions and questions: Read through the following questions and references from Jeremiah 32 and other chapters as noted. Use the information you discover to come up with compelling reasons why Jeremiah *should not* buy his cousin's property, listing them on the poster board. 1. With what country was the nation of Judah at war (v. 2a)? 2. What was happening to Jerusalem, the nation's capital (v. 2a)? 3. Where was Jeremiah residing and why was he there (vv. 2b-5)? 4. What had Jeremiah prophesied concerning the outcome of the war (vv. 3-5)? 5. Did Jeremiah have any children to inherit the property he purchased (16:2)? 6. How had the residents of the prophet's hometown of Anathoth treated him (11:21-23)?

Allow the *Con* groups time to share all the logical reasons for not making the purchase before asking the *Pro* groups to share reasons in favor of the purchase. Briefly discuss why Jeremiah decided to buy the land when it was counterintuitive to do so. Help learners see how the result was an object lesson to the people that they would return once again to their land.

Into Life

Option 1. Pair learners to answer the following questions, which you have reproduced on handouts: "Was there ever a time when you followed God's leading when it didn't make sense to your family or friends? How did things turn out?" After several minutes, ask for volunteers to share their stories with the whole group. Close with prayer that your learners will have the courage to follow God's leading, wherever it takes them.

Option 2. Distribute copies of the "Could You Do It?" activity from the reproducible page for learners to work on individually. Discuss results as a class or in small groups. This can be a take-home activity if time is short.

FUTURE PEACE AND JOY

DEVOTIONAL READING: Jeremiah 9:17-24
BACKGROUND SCRIPTURE: Jeremiah 33

JEREMIAH 33:1-11

¹ While Jeremiah was still confined in the courtyard of the guard, the word of the LORD came to him a second time: ² "This is what the LORD says, he who made the earth, the LORD who formed it and established it—the LORD is his name: ³ 'Call to me and I will answer you and tell you great and unsearchable things you do not know.' ⁴ For this is what the LORD, the God of Israel, says about  the houses in this city and the royal palaces of Judah that have been torn down to be used against the siege ramps and the sword ⁵ in the fight with the Babylonians: 'They will be filled with the dead bodies of the people I will slay in my anger and wrath. I will hide my face from this city because of all its wickedness.

⁶ "'Nevertheless, I will bring health and healing to it; I will heal my people and will let them enjoy abundant peace and security. ⁷ I will bring Judah and Israel back from captivity and will rebuild them as they were before. ⁸ I will cleanse them from all the sin they have committed against me and will forgive all their sins of rebellion against me. ⁹ Then this city will bring me renown, joy, praise and honor before all nations on earth that hear of all the good things I do for it; and they will be in awe and will tremble at the abundant prosperity and peace I provide for it.'

¹⁰ "This is what the LORD says: 'You say about this place, "It is a desolate waste, without people or animals." Yet in the towns of Judah and the streets of Jerusalem that are deserted, inhabited by neither people nor animals, there will be heard once more ¹¹ the sounds of joy and gladness, the voices of bride and bridegroom, and the voices of those who bring thank offerings to the house of the LORD, saying,

"Give thanks to the LORD Almighty,
    for the LORD is good;
    his love endures forever."

For I will restore the fortunes of the land as they were before,' says the LORD."

KEY VERSE

"I will restore the fortunes of the land as they were before," says the LORD. —**Jeremiah 33:11**

SUSTAINING HOPE

LESSON AIMS

After participating in this lesson, each learner will be able to:

1. Describe the condition of Jerusalem during the siege, and tell what Jeremiah predicted about the city's future.

2. Explain the terminology Jeremiah used to indicate the renewed condition of Jerusalem.

3. Help design a worship service that celebrates hopefulness, healing, and forgiveness from God.

LESSON OUTLINE

Introduction

A. What Does Joy Sound Like?

I just read of a woman who was arrested for celebrating too loudly at her daughter's graduation. When her girl crossed the stage and received her diploma, the mother apparently did a lot of whooping and hollering! The stone-faced authorities—later heavily criticized—maintained that the crowd had been warned against excessive celebration. Therefore they thought it appropriate to have this woman handcuffed and led away at this moment of family triumph.

Does this sound a bit like the Pharisees at the triumphal entry of Jesus? The crowds, shouting lots of *hosannas* and *hallelujahs*, were in a frenzy as Jesus rode into Jerusalem. But the grumpy Pharisees demanded that Jesus calm them down and cut the noise. Jesus answered these melancholy men with a wonderful rebuke: if the crowds were quieted, "the stones will cry out" (Luke 19:40). Heartfelt joy is hard to suppress!

I have participated in scores of high school and college graduation exercises, and it is common for family members to go a little overboard when their graduate crosses the stage. They are proud! In some cases, this is the first family member to graduate, a historic moment. Sometimes they are acutely aware of the great cost and effort that was necessary for this achievement, facts that make their expressions of joy just that more exuberant.

This week's lesson sketches a citywide celebration of joyous praise and worship. There is no video or audio available, of course, so we will need to imagine the prophesied joy to get the full impact.

B. Lesson Background

We recall from last week's lesson that Jeremiah was detained at a courtyard prison connected with King Zedekiah's palace as the Babylonians besieged Jerusalem. The prophet's situation and the reason for it still hold. Jeremiah's imprisonment seems to have been as much about taking him out of the public square as about any treasonable offense. The besieged city was on edge, and the king did not want that prophet exacerbating the morale problems.

Jeremiah had been serving as a prophetic voice in Jerusalem for some 40 years at the time of today's lesson (587 BC), so he was a well-known figure in the city. Although he was never popular because of his dire warnings and harsh condemnations, his longevity attests to some degree of acceptance by the people (compare Jeremiah 26:16). He was not easily silenced.

I. Present Distress
(JEREMIAH 33:1-5)
A. Maker of All (vv. 1-3)

1. While Jeremiah was still confined in the courtyard of the guard, the word of the LORD came to him a second time:

Although the book of Jeremiah is not arranged in strict chronological fashion, this chapter builds immediately on the events of chapter 32 (last week's lesson). Jeremiah is still *confined in the courtyard of the guard,* seemingly a more comfortable billet for a prisoner who has some favor with the king (compare Jeremiah 32:2; 37:16, 21; 38:6-13). Last week we saw Jeremiah receive forewarning of the surprise visit of a relative; that was the first time *the word of the Lord came to him,* in comparison with this *second time.*

2. "This is what the LORD says, he who made the earth, the LORD who formed it and established it—the LORD is his name:

The message to Jeremiah begins with an emphasis on God as *he who made the earth.* This is highlighted in three ways. First, Jeremiah is reminded that God *formed it,* referring to his initial creative act in Genesis (the Hebrew word for *formed* is the same as used in Genesis 2:8, 9, 19). Second, the prophet is reminded that God has *established* his

HOW TO SAY IT

Assyrians	Uh-*sear*-ee-unz.
Babylonians	Bab-ih-*low*-nee-unz.
Judean	Joo-*dee*-un.
Pompeii	Pahm-*pay*.
Sabaoth *(Hebrew)*	*Sab*-a-oth.
Vesuvius	Veh-*soo*-vee-us.
Yahweh *(Hebrew)*	*Yah*-weh.

creation. This has the sense of putting things in their proper places and sustaining the orderliness of creation (compare Jeremiah 10:12; 51:15). This description of creation is tied with the Lord's wisdom in Proverbs 3:19.

Third, God reinforces all of this by giving *his name* in such a way that there should be no mistakes in attributing the creation to him. This is the divine name of God, revealed to Moses at the burning bush (Exodus 3:14-16), sometimes transliterated as "Yahweh." Its threefold use in the verse before us stresses the identity of the Creator.

3. "'Call to me and I will answer you and tell you great and unsearchable things you do not know.'

This verse seems like a personal message to the prophet in that the verb *call* is singular as are the three occurrences of *you.* It is like saying, "You, Jeremiah, I'm talking to you. *Call to me and I will* give you a personal answer." When we remember what we just read in the previous verse, we have something quite amazing: the Creator of all things is singling out one person to receive an invitation! The Lord is a personal God who pays personal attention to those who call on his name.

The one who created everything has the power, of course, to reveal *great and unsearchable things.* The Lord's knowledge is unlimited, while ours is limited. He can add to our knowledge at his discretion, which is what he is about to do for Jeremiah.

B. Executor of Wrath (vv. 4, 5)

4. "For this is what the LORD, the God of Israel, says about the houses in this city and the royal palaces of Judah that have been torn down to be used against the siege ramps and the sword

At the time of this prophecy, Jerusalem is many months into its 18-month siege by the Babylonian army. Not only are food supplies cut off, so also are sources of building materials. As the engineers of the Judean army ponder how to reinforce the city's defenses, they are forced to use material at hand.

The result is that the destruction of the city begins before the Babylonians breach the walls: *the houses* of both kings and people are demolished to provide stone and timbers for counteracting, in various ways, the effects of *the siege ramps and the sword* (the latter representing the soldiers who rush up the ramps) of the Babylonians. The city leaders have decided to hold out as long as possible, even if this means citywide destruction at their own hands (see Isaiah 22:10).

5. ". . . in the fight with the Babylonians: 'They will be filled with the dead bodies of the people I will slay in my anger and wrath. I will hide my face from this city because of all its wickedness.'"

When the houses of Jerusalem are completely cannibalized (including stone flooring), only holes in the ground will remain. Ironically, these holes will make convenient places for mass graves for the coming slaughter. The dead houses will be inhabited by *the dead bodies of the people.*

All this results from the *fight with the Babylonians,* but more importantly, Jeremiah knows that the Lord himself is behind the looming disaster. Ultimately, God is the one who slays the Jerusalemites in *anger and wrath.* Deaths will result because the Lord has hidden his *face from this city,* exactly as predicted in Deuteronomy 31:16-18; 32:30. God is not embracing the Babylonians as his new people, but is using them as an instrument of destruction in his plan to punish Israel and cleanse it from *all its wickedness.*

What Do You Think?

How can we help others make it through a time of prolonged stress? What difference does it make, if any, if the problem stems from their own poor decisions?

Talking Points for Your Discussion
- Regarding financial issues
- Regarding health issues
- Regarding relationship issues
- Other

II. Future Joy
(JEREMIAH 33:6-11)
A. Healing to Be Granted (vv. 6, 7)

6. "'Nevertheless, I will bring health and healing to it; I will heal my people and will let them enjoy abundant peace and security.

Jeremiah's word from the Lord now turns from the immediate future to a time several decades hence: the time of Jerusalem's restoration. The prophet has already predicted that "this whole country will become a desolate wasteland, and these nations will serve the king of Babylon seventy years" (Jeremiah 25:11). When that time is up, God will heal. The wickedness that characterizes the society of Jerusalem after King Josiah is an illness of the soul that only God can cure (compare Hosea 5:13).

The healing remedy is not a physical salve or medicine but *abundant peace and security.* In this context, peace is more than the absence of war, but is personal prosperity and contentment. Most of all, there will be peace with God, a restoration of relationship that calms the souls of the people of Israel. The pain of exile is the cleansing process that must occur prior to this healing.

The restoration of Jerusalem and the rebuilding of its temple in the latter half of the sixth century BC will fulfill many aspects of this prophecy. Yet Jeremiah's words look further ahead, to a kingdom of peace inaugurated by the Messiah, the Prince of Peace. His future government will usher in an era of endless peace and eternal righteousness (compare Isaiah 9:6, 7). In its complete fullness, this is a future time even for us.

❧ DRASTIC STEPS FOR HEALING ❧

It's cancer! It seems we're hearing those dreaded words more and more these days. Whatever the reason for the seeming increase in the frequency of this diagnosis, the good news is that medical science continuously develops new treatments.

However, those improved approaches bring with them their own bad news: radical surgery, chemotherapy, and/or radiation treatments may leave a patient debilitated for months as the body tries to recover. Those going through such prolonged agony may wonder whether it is really worth it.

The kingdom of Judah was extremely ill, sick with a cancer of the spirit. The patient was dying! If the nation was to be cured, it would take a severe dose of a divinely prescribed treatment, the prolonged agony of which lasted 70 years. What can we do, individually and collectively, to make sure that God does not have to take drastic measures to cure spiritual ills today within the church today? See Revelation 2:5. —C. R. B.

7. "'I will bring Judah and Israel back from captivity and will rebuild them as they were before.

This is a surprising, comprehensive vision of the future. In Jeremiah's day, the northern tribes of Israel are long gone, having been dispersed by the Assyrians over a century earlier. Only the tribe of Judah, its ally the tribe of Benjamin, and a few Levites (such as Jeremiah) seem to be left. Yet God promises a complete restoration, as he will *bring Judah and Israel back from captivity*. The full contingent of the tribes of Israel is to return to their land *as they were before*. This reflects on a time like that of King David, when all of Israel was united, blessed, and protected by the Lord.

From our perspective of 27 centuries after Jeremiah's day, and having received the revelation of the New Testament, we can see that this has not happened. Therefore we should understand this prophecy to be far-reaching as it looks to a time when all God's people will be united. This includes Jews and Gentiles who are united through the peace brought about by Jesus (see Ephesians 2:11-16). The people of God in the new Jerusalem will be of every tribe and nation (Revelation 3:12; 5:9; 21:2).

B. Iniquity to Be Cleansed (v. 8)

8. "'I will cleanse them from all the sin they have committed against me and will forgive all their sins of rebellion against me.

The combination of "health and healing" in verse 6 with *cleanse* that we see here may call to mind the intricate procedures necessary in order to be considered cleansed of defiling diseases (Leviticus 14:1-32). Judah's problem is not diseases of the body, but sins of the spirit. This spiritual sickness can be healed only by God's act of forgiveness. This verse makes clear that the sin is wholly the fault of the people and that the forgiving is wholly an act of grace by the Lord. God's punishment is a cleansing punishment to eliminate the cause of his wrath: the people's sin and desire to commit sin.

> **What Do You Think?**
> What lessons do you learn from Bible characters who experienced or did not experience renewal after sin or failure?
> *Talking Points for Your Discussion*
> - David (Psalm 51)
> - Judas (Matthew 27:3-5)
> - Peter (John 21:15-19)
> - Other

C. God to Be Honored (v. 9)

9. "'Then this city will bring me renown, joy, praise and honor before all nations on earth that hear of all the good things I do for it; and they will be in awe and will tremble at the abundant prosperity and peace I provide for it.'

The word *it* refers to Jerusalem. Jeremiah's vision foresees not a city of ruined houses full of dead bodies but a place of *praise and honor*. This will not happen in secret, but will be noticed by *all nations on earth*. The future blessings of the Lord will cause these nations to *be in awe*, trembling when they see God's outpouring of *prosperity and peace*.

The history of Israel is a remarkable testimony to the protection and blessing of God. This is in

Visual for Lesson 4. *Use this visual to remind learners that "release from" something implies at the same time "release to" something else.*

contrast with numerous long-forgotten nations of the ancient world that were more powerful than Israel at one time or another. Jeremiah's continuing vision for Israel is that of destruction followed by restoration.

D. Desolation to Be Reversed (vv. 10, 11)

10. "This is what the LORD says: 'You say about this place, "It is a desolate waste, without people or animals." Yet in the towns of Judah and the streets of Jerusalem that are deserted, inhabited by neither people nor animals, there will be heard once more

If one visits the ruins of an ancient city today and no crowds of tourists are present, it is amazing how quiet the place is. For example, Ephesus—once bustling with commerce and the sound of children laughing—now yields only the sounds of birds, etc. Having existed in such a state of decay for so long, it's difficult to imagine that city ever returning to even a quarter of its former glory.

Jerusalem and its surrounding villages are to be depopulated, *without people or animals* (compare Isaiah 64:10; Jeremiah 6:8; 7:3). Silence will reign. City and countryside will lie desolate until the Lord sees fit to restore them. Yet Jeremiah is allowed to see beyond a destroyed and deserted Jerusalem (next verse).

11a. "'... the sounds of joy and gladness, the voices of bride and bridegroom,

The silent ruins of Jerusalem described above stand in sharp contrast with *the sounds of joy and gladness* depicted here. A wedding celebration is a beloved image of Jeremiah's day. Weddings are public, outdoor events that involve singing, dancing, and music. Even in a larger city like Jerusalem, the joyous sounds of a wedding can be heard across neighborhoods. The people of Jeremiah's world work very hard, and when they take time to celebrate something, such as a marriage, they party loudly. Jeremiah prophesied previously that the Lord will "bring an end to the sounds of joy and gladness and to the voices of bride and bridegroom in the towns of Judah and the streets of Jerusalem" (Jeremiah 7:34). Even so, that joyous sound will be heard once again!

11b. "'. . . and the voices of those who bring thank offerings to the house of the LORD, saying,

"Give thanks to the LORD Almighty,
  for the LORD is good;
  his love endures forever."

The prophecy now connects the joy of a wedding (v. 11a) with a worship song, one that is traditional and beloved by the people of Israel. It is a variation on Psalm 107:1: "Give thanks to the Lord, for he is good; his love endures forever." (This is very similar to Psalm 106:1.)

We trace this praise pattern back at least as far as the time of David, some 400 years before Jeremiah (1 Chronicles 16:34), repeated in Solomon's time (2 Chronicles 5:13; 7:3). These lines are likely used in worship services in a responsive fashion, with a leader singing the first line and the choir or congregation responding with the second line. The most extensive example of this is Psalm 136.

Such a worship liturgy is comforting to the people of Israel. Not surprisingly, they find themselves unable to sing this way after being taken captive to Babylon (see Psalm 137:4). But these lines will be one of the first things the people sing when they return (Ezra 3:11).

As noted in lesson 2, the expression *Lord Almighty* reflects the Hebrew "Lord of Sabaoth" or "Lord of the heavenly hosts of armies" (see Romans 9:29; James 5:4). That power is coupled with his goodness as evidenced by his abundant provisions for his people. The fact that *his love endures forever* implies that God's wrath is temporary. Even as the besieged people of Jerusalem stare doom and destruction in the face, they can still count on the eternal power, goodness, and mercy of God. Today's word from Jeremiah looks beyond the gruesome scene of a destroyed city to the joyous scene of a city restored for, and able to, worship.

❧ WHAT SHOULD STAY DEAD ❧

Mount Vesuvius erupted on August 24, AD 79. The largest city destroyed that day was Pompeii, six miles southeast of the mountain. Ironically, the eruption came just one day after people living in the mountain's shadow had celebrated a festival dedicated to Vulcan, the Roman god of fire—including the fire that comes from volcanoes!

Pompeii lay silent and buried until 1748. Excavations since then have uncovered the ruins of that once-thriving community. Artwork and buildings, frozen in time for centuries, reveal a typical first-century Roman city that embraced "debauchery, lust, drunkenness, orgies, carousing and detestable idolatry" (1 Peter 4:3).

Was the destruction of AD 79 God's wrath on that city for those sins? We don't know, because God has not told us. But he *has* told us about Jerusalem, destroyed as predicted, when his wrath erupted against it. Unlike Pompeii, however, God brought Jerusalem back to life. Sounds of joy again rang in the city's streets when God brought his people back there.

God specializes in bringing the dead back to life, and the resurrection of Jesus ensures our own. As we await that great day, however, may we take care to remain "dead to sin" (Romans 6:11). Some things should stay dead.   —C. R. B.

11c. "'For I will restore the fortunes of the land as they were before,' says the LORD."

The time of the predicted celebration will come when Jews are allowed to return from their cap-tivity to restore Jerusalem. Only then will they be able to "bring thank offerings to the house of the Lord" (v. 11b), implying that that structure will have been rebuilt. That must be accompanied by spiritual renewal; there is no value in restoring the temple, priests, altars, and sacrifices unless the people's hearts are directed toward the Lord.

> **What Do You Think?**
> What specific kind of captivity has the Lord delivered you from for which you will offer praise today?
> *Talking Points for Your Discussion*
> - Captivity of an addiction
> - Captivity of a wrong attitude
> - Captivity of a destructive relationship
> - Captivity of physical infirmity
> - Other

Conclusion
A. Our Praise

The author of Hebrews picks up on Jeremiah's image: "Through Jesus, therefore, let us continually offer to God a sacrifice of praise—the fruit of lips that openly profess his name" (Hebrews 13:15). We do not need a sacrificial system involving animals and grain. Our sacrifice was made once for all by Jesus, our Savior (7:27).

We are heirs to Jeremiah's vision of a joyous future when we sing praises and acknowledge the goodness of God. We don't need a designated structure where we praise the Lord (John 4:21, 23). Rather, "where two or three gather in my name, there am I with them" (Matthew 18:20). May we lift our joyous praises with a loud voice as we worship the Lord, who is good and whose love endures forever!

B. Prayer

Lord God Almighty, you are good to us! You have erased the desolation of sin through your Son, and our joy in that must not be silenced. May your love endure forever. In Jesus' name; amen.

C. Thought to Remember

Praise God for peace with him!

INVOLVEMENT LEARNING

Enhance your lesson with NIV® Bible Student *(from your curriculum supplier) and the reproducible activity page (at www.standardlesson.com or in the back of the* NIV® Standard Lesson Commentary Deluxe Edition*).*

Into the Lesson

Announce a pop quiz, asking learners to jot answers as you verbalize the following true/false questions. Assure your learners that they will score their own results when finished: 1. An Old Testament book is named after Jeremiah *(true)*. 2. Jeremiah warned his people that they would be taken into captivity by the Greeks *(false)*. 3. Jeremiah passed along good news in addition to bad news *(true)*. 4. God told Jeremiah not to marry *(true)*. 5. Both king and people honored Jeremiah for his prophecies *(false)*. 6. At the end of last week's lesson, Jeremiah was in prison *(true)*.

After discussing results, say, "In today's lesson, Jeremiah is still in prison, where he is receiving a message of hope from God for the people. But first, let's consider what life under siege is like."

Alternative. Several days before class, make two copies of "The Siege of Jerusalem" script from the reproducible page, which you can download. Give one copy each to two learners (preferably a man and a woman) to be ready to perform the skit for the class. Stress to your two actors that the script need not be memorized; they are free to ad-lib within the spirit of the script.

As narrator, introduce the skit by verbalizing the first line on the script as a cue for your actors to enter. After the skit, ask learners the following questions, pausing between each for discussion: 1. What did you learn about the conditions in Jerusalem during the siege? 2. Thinking of the people's desperation, do you think they were receptive to a message from Jeremiah about future joy and prosperity? Why, or why not?"

Either of the above activities will serve as a transition to the Into the Word segment.

Into the Word

Read Jeremiah 33:1-5 aloud and discuss what life under siege was like for the residents of Jerusalem. (If you used the *alternative* above, compare and contrast the text with the artistic license of the skit.) *Option:* Expand this discussion by considering Isaiah 36:12 and Jeremiah 19:9.

When you are ready to discuss verses 6-11, distribute to learners pictures of the following six items: a hospital, a building in the process of construction, a bar of soap, money, a "ghost town," and a wedding. Some learners will receive more than one picture if your class is smaller than six; duplicate pictures will be needed for classes larger than six.

Read Jeremiah 33:6-11 aloud. As you pause after each verse, ask, "Who has a picture of this?" The pictures should be discussed in the order given above to match verses 6-11 in sequence. Discuss how the picture illustrates the verse at hand.

Option. After discussing verses 6-11, say, "Close your Bibles for a quick test of recall." Then distribute the "Make the Connection" activity from the reproducible page as a matching exercise. Discuss results.

Into Life

Lead a discussion on how verses 1-5 compare and contrast with our bondage to sin before accepting Christ. Follow this by comparing and contrasting verses 6-11 with our situation after accepting Christ. Then ask, "If we were to plan a worship service based on verses 6-11, what would we include?" Jot responses on the board. (This can be a small-group exercise.)

Wrap up by saying, "This morning we have many reasons to thank God for his blessings to us in delivering us from our captivity to sin. Please join me in praising God." Then lead the class in singing a familiar worship song or hymn of joyful praise (possibilities: "Praise Him, Praise Him," "Give Thanks to the Lord," "O For a Thousand Tongues," etc.). Close with a time of prayer that allows learners to express thanksgiving for their eternal salvation.

Yet I Will Rejoice

Devotional Reading: Psalm 56:8-13

Background Scripture: Job 1; Psalm 56; Habakkuk 1–3

Habakkuk 2:1-5

¹ I will stand at my watch
  and station myself on the ramparts;
I will look to see what he will say to me,
  and what answer I am to give to this
    complaint.
² Then the LORD replied:
"Write down the revelation
  and make it plain on tablets
  so that a herald may run with it.
³ For the revelation awaits an appointed
    time;
  it speaks of the end
  and will not prove false.
Though it linger, wait for it;
  it will certainly come
  and will not delay.
⁴ "See, the enemy is puffed up;
  his desires are not upright—
  but the righteous person will live
    by his faithfulness—
⁵ indeed, wine betrays him;
  he is arrogant and never at rest.
Because he is as greedy as the grave
  and like death is never satisfied,
he gathers to himself all the nations
  and takes captive all the peoples."

Habakkuk 3:17-19

¹⁷ Though the fig tree does not bud
  and there are no grapes on the vines,
though the olive crop fails
  and the fields produce no food,
though there are no sheep in the pen
  and no cattle in the stalls,
¹⁸ yet I will rejoice in the LORD,
  I will be joyful in God my Savior.
¹⁹ The Sovereign LORD is my strength;
  he makes my feet like the feet of a deer,
  he enables me to tread on the heights.

Key Verse

I will rejoice in the LORD, I will be joyful in God my Savior. —**Habakkuk 3:18**

SUSTAINING HOPE

Unit 2: Dark Nights of the Soul

LESSONS 5–8

LESSON AIMS

After participating in this lesson, each learner will be able to:

1. Describe the dialogue between Habakkuk and God.

2. Paraphrase Habakkuk 3:17, 18 using non-agricultural terms.

3. Identify some seemingly negative condition in his or her life and make a statement of commitment of "yet I will rejoice in the Lord" in spite of that condition.

LESSON OUTLINE

Introduction

A. Silent Nights

Still living with mom and dad three years after graduating from college. Didn't get that raise—again. Chronic pain persists. Expenses still exceeding income. Rejected by another potential employer. Reconciliation with an estranged relative seems impossible. The rich seem to keep getting richer, and the poor seem to keep getting poorer. Where is the light load and abundant life that Jesus promised?

Most people feel that way at one time or another. For some, it happens only periodically. For others, it feels like the very rhythm of their lives. We who follow Jesus know that we have eternal life. But how should we process our earthly woes in the meantime? What might God say were he to speak directly to us during times of frustration and doubt?

Though God may seem silent during our darkest nights, we realize when we open the Bible that he is not. God speaks to us through prophets such as Habakkuk. That man stared doubt in the face, questioned God, and received answers. In today's lesson we sample a slice of that conversation and discuss its abiding relevance.

B. Lesson Background

Habakkuk probably ministered in the final decade of the seventh century BC, although some date his prophetic ministry to as early as 630 BC. Those closing decades of the seventh century BC saw God's people under stress. The northern kingdom of Israel had been destroyed by the Assyrians in 722 BC as God's judgment on his people's idolatry, social injustice, and unholy political alliances came to fruition. The people of the southern kingdom of Judah did not learn from that "visual aid," and the same sinful patterns became their norm.

In Habakkuk 1:2-4, the prophet cries out about the violence, injustice, and wide-scale abandonment of God's laws that resulted in the trampling of Israelites by the wicked. The prophet pleaded as one who had been crying out to God for a long time without receiving an answer. In Habakkuk 1:5-11, God answered. Not only was he aware of the sins of his people, he planned to use the Babylonians to level the southern kingdom of Judah just as the Assyrians had done to the northern kingdom of Israel.

Habakkuk was not comforted by that answer. He complained that the Babylonians were far more treacherous than the Israelites, and that they were known for trampling the righteous (Habakkuk 1:12-17). How could a holy God use such a wicked people as his instrument of correction? As our text opens, we find Habakkuk awaiting an answer to that question.

I. Overview
(HABAKKUK 2:1-3)
A. Prophet's Expectations (v. 1)

**1. I will stand at my watch
and station myself on the ramparts;
I will look to see what he will say to me,
and what answer I am to give to this
complaint.**

Habakkuk 1 ends with the prophet complaining that it seems beneath God to use a very unrighteous empire like Babylon to punish the Israelites, who are relatively less unrighteous. The prophet brings this complaint to a close in the verse before us as he stations and braces himself for God's response.

The language here is that of military defense. For surveillance purposes, ancient cities rely on watchmen stationed on high towers that may or may not be part of city walls. These elevated positions offer the best view of the distant horizon from which invading armies might approach.

Habakkuk addresses God with boldness in chapter 1, and God's response in verses 5-11 (see the Lesson Background) is jolting. As far as the prophet is concerned, however, this issue is not

HOW TO SAY IT

Assyrians	Uh-*sear*-ee-unz.
Babylonians	Bab-ih-*low*-nee-unz.
Gethsemane	Geth-*sem*-uh-nee (*G* as in *get*).
Habakkuk	Huh-*back*-kuk.
Plutarch	*Plu*-tark.

settled, and his counterresponse appeals to God's holy character (1:12, 13). Habakkuk is no fool—he knows that God's rejoinder will be equally bold, if not more so.

❧ OF WATCHTOWERS AND WARNINGS ❧

In 2003, archeologists found a rare treasure about 22 miles southeast of Amsterdam. It was the foundation of a wooden watchtower that the Romans had built along the Rhine River, perhaps about AD 50. The tower may have been one of many such structures, built at intervals as a means of spotting trouble along the river. Soldiers stationed in the towers could signal each other for reinforcements to meet threats to Rome's control over the region. The tower's foundation survived because a Roman road was built over it later.

The prophet Habakkuk recognized his role in Judah as a spiritual watchman on a tower, ready to signal God's desires for, and warnings to, the people of Judah (compare Ezekiel 3:17; Hosea 9:8). While God did not tell Habakkuk the day or hour of Judah's demise, he gave the prophet a clear vision of what was to come.

Habakkuk's message comes from a time even more ancient than that of the Roman ruins, yet the message remains intact in a way the ruins do not. The message reminds us that God has plans, and he expects us to watch for those plans to unfold. See Matthew 24:42; 25:13.   —C. R. B.

B. God's Response (vv. 2, 3)

**2. Then the LORD replied:
"Write down the revelation
and make it plain on tablets
so that a herald may run with it.**

The nature of God's response reveals that he does not regard Habakkuk as a foe. God has a message that the prophet is to write in such a way that *a herald*, or courier, may run to deliver it to others. Couriers in a military context do not bear weapons, but news. They move quickly from the battlefront to the homeland to provide status updates to those anxiously awaiting reports. Without the wireless communication we have today, such couriers are a vital element for communication in the ancient world.

3. "For the revelation awaits an appointed time;
    it speaks of the end
    and will not prove false.
Though it linger, wait for it;
    it will certainly come
    and will not delay."

The herald of verse 2 is to bring good news for God's people. *The revelation* at issue is a prophetic vision, a word from God.

God's judgment (explained below) will be decisive. Its timing might not be as people expect or desire, but it will come at just the right time. When it does come, it will be clear that God is keeping his word. Though that word may seem to delay, giving the impression that God isn't paying attention, it will certainly come at just the right time.

This is often a hard truth for God's people to accept. We trust that God is in control and that he works all things out for the good of those who love him (Romans 8:28), but we want results *now*! Yet God's Word to us is the same as to Habakkuk: be patient and trust that God will act at just the right time in just the right way (compare Hebrews 10:37; 2 Peter 3:9). Certainly God can act in ways that conform to our desired timetables. But that would not be in our best interest, since God has knowledge of things that we do not. God always works in the best interest of his people. We may not be able to see it now, but in the end it will be clear that God's ways are higher and better than ours.

What Do You Think?
  When was an occasion that 20/20 hindsight
    demonstrated God's timetable to be superior to
    yours? What did this experience teach you?
Talking Points for Your Discussion
  ▫ When planning a career change
  ▫ When planning a family event
  ▫ Other

II. The Two Paths
(HABAKKUK 2:4, 5)
A. Pride, Part 1 (v. 4a)
4a. "See, the enemy is puffed up;
    his desires are not upright—

God distinguishes between two types of people, who represent two ways of living. One type walks the path of pride. Those on this path strive to elevate themselves regardless of what that might mean for others. There are few empty seats of power in this world (compare Mark 10:42), and those in such seats exercise authority over many areas of life.

To exalt oneself often involves taking power away from another who currently exercises it. Sometimes vacancies open up as others move on, die, etc. In such cases, there are usually several persons who are suitable replacements, so they jockey for the winning position.

Those who focus on winning the proverbial rat race above all else appear to be on top of the world, at least for a little while. Yet they are not right with God. In exalting themselves to places of prominence, they may have had to abandon God's justice. They may regard their neighbors as competitors for resources rather than as fellow image bearers of God—image bearers they have been sent to serve. Unbeknownst to the power-grabbers, they are doomed to come crashing down from whatever height they have managed to achieve by their own strength. These self-exalted ones are obviously not God's people.

B. Faith (v. 4b)
4b. ". . . but the righteous person will live by his faithfulness—

God's true people are described as *the righteous*. They are the ones who are in a right standing with God because they live according to the standards that God has established. It is not as if they have earned their right standing through works; rather, it is that they seek first God's standards. They have dedicated their lives to God's justice—a justice that has to do with how one treats one's neighbors, cares for the poor, and makes decisions that affect the wider community. To be that kind of person requires faithfulness.

It is interesting to note that here the opposite of pride is not humility, as one might expect. Rather, the opposite of prideful people are those who live by faith (compare Romans 1:17; Galatians 3:11; Hebrews 10:38). Faithfulness implies a steadfastness that demonstrates unwavering commitment over time, regardless of the external pressures. Steadfast faithfulness is the life to which God calls his people. The words *faith* and *faithfulness* include a wide range of dispositions, including belief, trust, and godly actions. Faithfulness is connected with righteousness also in 1 Samuel 26:23; Psalm 96.13; 143:1; Isaiah 11:5; etc.

Such faith or faithfulness is therefore characterized by patient endurance. Pride and patience are also contrasted as opposites in Ecclesiastes 7:8. The proud rush to get results for themselves, regardless of the costs.

This fact puts into proper perspective the impatience that Christians sometimes demonstrate. "I hate waiting," we may complain (inwardly if not outwardly) when others are slowing us down on the road or in the checkout line at the store. We are unhappy that others are ahead of us, messing up our timetable! If we resort to driving on the shoulder in a traffic jam, we are further saying that our "need" to get through is more important than that of others stuck in the same situation.

The righteous serve faithfully and diligently, even when they can see no positive results, whether immediately before them or on the distant horizon. God promises to exalt the faithful in due time.

> **What Do You Think?**
> How has God confirmed his presence and strength for you during hardships when others might have questioned both?
> *Talking Points for Your Discussion*
> - In a family matter
> - In a church conflict
> - In your job
> - Psalm 23
> - Other

C. Pride, Part 2 (v. 5)

**5. ". . . indeed, wine betrays him;
he is arrogant and never at rest.
Because he is as greedy as the grave
and like death is never satisfied,
he gathers to himself all the nations
and takes captive all the peoples."**

After pausing to describe righteous living, God returns to a discussion of the nature of those who are proud. Such people are attracted to intoxicating beverages. This attraction may be most evident at parties hosted and attended by those who are upwardly mobile and striving to make names for themselves (compare 1 Samuel 25:2-11, 36; Esther 1:1-11; Daniel 5:1-4). We should not automatically equate this with the kind of drinking typical of those who misuse alcohol to numb themselves to their troubles.

Prideful people are never satisfied. Their desires are as all-consuming as death itself seems to be. The word *grave* is translated "hell" in other versions of the Bible. The Hebrew behind this is a vague word that probably signifies "the abode of the dead" in a general sense. Therefore this is not necessarily the place of eternal torment for the wicked as we understand Hell to be today. The Jews of Habakkuk's day do not have as clear a view of the afterlife as we now possess with the New Testament.

Death never seems to have its fill. It wants and expects to consume everything; it will not be satisfied until it does! So it is with proud people. "Death and Destruction are never satisfied, and neither are human eyes" (Proverbs 27:20). Whatever name prideful people manage to make for themselves will not be enough; they will eventually want to make it greater still. As with the wine they choose to misuse, the proud eventually become addicted to glory grabbing.

In the same way, the kings and kingdoms of this world want to conquer more and more, until all people belong to their dominion. Imperialism cannot tolerate a fixed border. It is by expanding their borders that kingdoms acquire new wealth that enables them to keep building and expanding. The Greek historian Plutarch (AD 46–120) notes that "Alexander [the Great] wept when he heard . . . that there was an infinite number of worlds, and to his friends asking him if any accident had befallen him, he returns this answer: 'Do not you think it a matter worthy of lamentation, that, when there is such a vast multitude of them, we have not yet conquered one?'"

Such kingdoms eventually overreach, spreading themselves too thin. This inevitably leads to their downfall because they lack the resources to protect their ever-expanding boundaries. Pride often seems to be its own death sentence, although God also punishes self-ambition. That punishment is spelled out in the fivefold woes in Habakkuk 2:6-20 (not in today's text).

> **What Do You Think?**
> When was a time you saw pride end up being "its own death sentence"? How did you grow spiritually from that experience?
>
> *Talking Points for Your Discussion*
> - Regarding pride of accomplishment (Daniel 4:28-33)
> - Regarding pride of position (Acts 12:21-23)
> - Regarding national pride (Jeremiah 48:29, 30)
> - Other

III. The Way of Faith
(Habakkuk 3:17-19)

A. Times of Scarcity (v. 17)

**17. Though the fig tree does not bud
and there are no grapes on the vines,
though the olive crop fails
and the fields produce no food,
though there are no sheep in the pen
and no cattle in the stalls,**

As we leap forward to verse 17, we see that Habakkuk has received God's message loud and clear. So the prophet drops his inquiry and submits to God's timing.

Habakkuk recognizes that there will be times in life when nothing appears to be going well. He illustrates such times with reference to the primary indicators of economic well-being in his day: the status of crops and livestock. When these falter, nothing else seems to go well. Borrowing will ensue as loans have to be taken out. Property ownership will be on the line as it serves as a guarantee against a loan gone bad. A succession of bad years creates a downward spiral in this regard.

We may experience the same thing today in the form of rising bills coupled with declining purchasing power due to inflation, rising responsibility coupled with declining health, etc. In marital vows we symbolize the ups and downs of life in terms of "for richer or poorer, in sickness and in health." Whatever terms one uses, Habakkuk acknowledges the reality that even under God, life does not always go well for us. The next two verses reveal the prophet's attitude toward this reality.

B. Times of Rejoicing (vv. 18, 19)

**18, 19. . . . yet I will rejoice in the Lord,
I will be joyful in God my Savior.
The Sovereign Lord is my strength;
he makes my feet like the feet of a deer,
he enables me to tread on the heights.**

Habakkuk has moved from complaint to praise. He recognizes that God alone is his *Savior* and the source of his *strength*, and this is good news indeed. What strength do we have against the storms of this life, whether of financial ruin, natural disasters, overpowering enemies, or pending death? God triumphs over them, and he extends that victory to those who call on him.

> **What Do You Think?**
> What spiritual help can your church provide to those facing physical hardship? What will be your part in this?
>
> *Talking Points for Your Discussion*
> - Counseling resources within your church
> - Counseling resources among neighboring churches
> - Prayer chains vs. personal availability for prayer support
> - Proper use of Romans 8:28
> - Other

Jesus was born into a life of poverty, was tossed about by a raging sea, was assailed by religious and political enemies, and stared death in the face all the way to the cross. Yet he submitted to the conditions of humanity, trusted in God, and waited for God's deliverance. His victory is ours as well.

Though Habakkuk never knew Jesus, he knew Jesus' Father and trusted him. Habakkuk confessed God's unique ability to grant the sure-footedness like that of *deer* that *tread on the heights,* places that Habakkuk could never ascend by himself.

❧ REJOICING IN BAD TIMES ❧

The summer of 2012 was a time when so-called global warming became real to many people. The scientific fact or fiction of global warming will continue to be debated for some time, but that summer was unquestionably among the hottest and driest that most Americans had ever seen.

Some feared that the Dust Bowl era of the 1930s might be repeating itself. The year 2012 wasn't as bad at that, but the extreme heat and drought raised the specter that a time of extended scarcity lay ahead. Farmers lost crops and livestock, others whose livelihoods depend on the farming industry suffered, and the general populace experienced higher food prices as a result.

It is natural, of course, to ask "Where is God?" during such times. Of greater importance, however, is the question "How will I praise God?" when disaster looms. The answer Habakkuk proposed is still valid. Those who trust God can rejoice in the midst of trials, because they know God is their refuge. Even when life brings us low, God will give us the strength to walk "on the heights" of faith. —C. R. B.

Conclusion

A. Pride or Faith?

The battle was over before it began. Yet, Habakkuk was never truly at war with God, though the prophet directed frustrations to him. That itself was an act of faith. Rather than brood over Israel's misfortunes, Habakkuk verbalized his concerns to the only one powerful enough to do something about them.

God was not threatened by Habakkuk's complaint. He responded with grace, with good news. In our day, God has spoken good news to us through his Son (Hebrews 1:1, 2).

Jesus lived out the perfect example of patiently trusting in God alone. We see such trust in his prayer in the Garden of Gethsemane, "Not my will, but yours be done" (Luke 22:42), and in his final words on the cross, "Father, into your hands I commit my spirit" (23:46). Before that, Jesus had encouraged people not to strive to elevate themselves by taking seats of honor at banquets, but to wait for the host's invitation (14:7-11). How much better it is to be elevated by God than by one's own pride!

The Babylonians of this world will continue to elevate themselves. May we model for them a better way, the better way that Habakkuk learned and Jesus exemplified. It is the way that looks up in faith, no matter the circumstances.

B. Prayer

Powerful God, we voice to you our concerns because we know you care. We thank you for tolerating our prideful impatience; please replace it with a godly faithfulness that looks up to you during every storm of life. We ask this in Jesus' name; amen.

C. Thought to Remember

Patiently rely on God's strength.

Visual for Lesson 5. *Use this visual as a discussion starter by pointing to it as you ask, "What other images of 'lack' could you put here?"*

INVOLVEMENT LEARNING

Enhance your lesson with NIV® *Bible Student (from your curriculum supplier) and the reproducible activity page (at www.standardlesson.com or in the back of the* NIV® *Standard Lesson Commentary Deluxe Edition).*

Into the Lesson

Have the one-word question *Why?* displayed on the board. Ask, "If you could ask God one *why* question, what would it be?" Allow several responses; be prepared to give one yourself. (*Option:* Compare and contrast these with *why* questions in the Bible, such as those found in Judges 6:13; 21:3; and Jeremiah 5:19.)

After brief discussion, introduce as the context for today's study the question of Habakkuk 1:13b: "[Lord,] why are you silent while the wicked swallow up those more righteous than themselves?"

Into the Word

Display this completion statement: *Because the Lord God _____, I will _____.* Ask how the blanks should be filled in according to the prophet's outlook as seen in the first and last verses of today's lesson text. (Possible responses: "Because the Lord God is the one with the power to answer my question, I will be ready to listen to that answer" [for 2:1] and "Because the Lord God is the source of my strength, I will go where he enables me to go" [for 3:19].) Ask, "What is the relationship between what goes in the two blanks?" If learners do not do so, point out the relationship between acknowledging God's sovereignty and our responsibility to submit to his purposes.

Say, "Let's now take a look at Habakkuk 2:2-5 in light of that relationship." Using the lesson commentary, work your way through verses 2-4 to explore further connections between God's sovereignty and human responsibility. When you get to verse 5, be sure to discuss where and why that connection is missing.

To explore the implications of Habakkuk 3:17, 18, distribute the following on handouts: *Even if the _____ does not _____, the _____ yields no _____, and there are no _____ in the _____, I will still rejoice in the Lord!*

Say, "Habakkuk uses the agricultural terminology familiar to him, but let's see how you would complete his thoughts using words of some other vocational or cultural context." After a few minutes, ask for volunteers to read their completed statements. Here is an example, if the class needs it: "Even if the inflation rate does not fall below 4 percent, the stock market yields no positive returns, and there is no money in the bank, I will still rejoice in the Lord!"

Pose these questions for deeper discussion: 1. Why is it important to rejoice in the Lord when things are going very badly? 2. How was Habakkuk able to rejoice in the midst of painful circumstances? 3. What can we learn from him?

Into Life

Option 1. Give each learner another copy of the fill-in-the-blank statement drawn from Habakkuk 3:17, 18, with these directions: "It's time to personalize Habakkuk's 'no matter what' for your particular circumstances. But this is indeed *personal*, so it's take-home work for you to consider. Think about the hard things in your life right now. Will you commit to having a 'no matter what' faith? What will cause you to stick with it?"

Option 2. Distribute copies of the "Running with the Revelation" activity from the reproducible page, which you can download. Have learners complete this in small groups or pairs. Stress the importance of the last word in the instructions: *personally.* Say, "This means that gospel messages through social media don't count since it's too easy to hide behind such an impersonal communication method."

Option 3. Distribute copies of "The Old Is New Again!" activity from the reproducible page. This exercise calls for personalized responses, so you will need to evaluate the nature of your class to determine whether this should be in-class or take-home work.

I KNOW THAT MY REDEEMER LIVES

DEVOTIONAL READING: 1 Chronicles 16:28-34
BACKGROUND SCRIPTURE: Job 19; Psalm 57

JOB 19:1-7, 23-29

¹ Then Job replied:

² "How long will you torment me
and crush me with words?

³ Ten times now you have reproached me;
shamelessly you attack me.

⁴ If it is true that I have gone astray,
my error remains my concern alone.

⁵ If indeed you would exalt yourselves
above me
and use my humiliation against me,

⁶ then know that God has wronged me
and drawn his net around me.

⁷ "Though I cry, 'Violence!' I get no response;
though I call for help, there is no
justice."

· · · · · · · · · · · · · · · · · ·

²³ "Oh, that my words were recorded,
that they were written on a scroll,

²⁴ that they were inscribed with an iron tool
on lead,
or engraved in rock forever!

²⁵ I know that my redeemer lives,
and that in the end he will stand on the
earth.

²⁶ And after my skin has been destroyed,
yet in my flesh I will see God;

²⁷ I myself will see him
with my own eyes—I, and not another.
How my heart yearns within me!

²⁸ "If you say, 'How we will hound him,
since the root of the trouble lies in him,'

²⁹ you should fear the sword yourselves;
for wrath will bring punishment by the
sword,
and then you will know that there is
judgment."

KEY VERSE

I know that my redeemer lives, and that in the end he will stand on the earth. —**Job 19:25**

SUSTAINING HOPE

Unit 2: Dark Nights of the Soul

LESSONS 5–8

LESSON AIMS

After participating in this lesson, each learner will be able to:

1. Summarize Job's reply to Bildad.

2. Explain how Job's confidence in his "redeemer" affects our understanding of his complaint.

3. Express faith in the Redeemer, Jesus, and tell how that faith helps in times of trial.

LESSON OUTLINE

Introduction

A. Guilty Until Proven Innocent?

The legal concept of *presumption of innocence* (also known as *innocent until proven guilty*) goes back many centuries. It means that the burden of proof is on the prosecution to show that the accused is guilty beyond a reasonable doubt before a conviction can be secured. Although this principle lets some guilty parties off the hook, it is one of the best safeguards to keep innocent people from being unjustly convicted.

Going back centuries more, we see that God himself gave Israel laws to protect the innocent. Within the Ten Commandments is the law against bearing false witness (Deuteronomy 5:20). When violated, the penalty to be placed on the false witness was to be the very consequence that he or she was willing to see the innocent undergo (19:16-21). Two witnesses were required to secure a conviction (19:15).

Job believed in this kind of justice. One problem, as far as Job could tell, was that his friends were not extending the benefit of the doubt to him. After evaluating his sorry state, they seemed to presume him guilty until proven innocent.

We may go through times when it seems that we are being punished for no reason. We are frustrated, we pour out our hearts to God and friends, and still nothing changes. People around us may think we deserve what we are getting. They become desensitized to our situation. But we are not willing to give up, holding out hope that God will do something about the problem. That's where Job was in today's text.

B. Lesson Background

Though he lived a righteous life—righteous enough to receive a divine endorsement in that regard (Job 1:8)—Job experienced terrible adversity. God, unbeknownst to Job, was in the process of disproving Satan's contention that Job lived an upright life only because God had blessed and prospered him (1:9, 10). God then granted Satan permission to test Job. Would great disaster cause Job to crumble and curse God to his face as Satan claimed (1:11)?

The bulk of the book of Job features conversations between Job and the friends who came to console him. Their dialogue was different from the one between God and Satan. Job and his friends shared the simplistic view that bad things happen only (or primarily) to bad people. According to that view, if you want to know whether people are righteous or not, all you have to do is see how well they are faring. Are they thriving? They must be doing right. Are they suffering? They must be doing wrong.

Since the friends saw that Job was suffering terribly, they assumed he was guilty of some grave offense (example: Job 4:7, 8). Perhaps Job would have agreed under normal circumstances. But Job was the one suffering, and he could recall no wicked action or set of habits that warranted the magnitude of his downfall. Job had no defense other than his own claim of innocence.

We don't know when Job lived. One proposal places him in the twentieth or nineteenth century BC. This is based on the description of Eliphaz (one of Job's friends) being "the Temanite" (Job 2:11). Abraham's grandson Esau (also known as *Edom*; see Genesis 25:30; 36:1, 8) had a grandson named Teman (Genesis 36:11). Teman is mentioned as a place within the territory of Edom (Jeremiah 49:7, 20; compare Ezekiel 25:13; Amos 1:12; Obadiah 8, 9). The length of Job's life (Job 42:16) fits this period of time (Genesis 25:7; 35:28).

Job is mentioned by name in Ezekiel 14:14, 20 and James 5:11, so we are certain that he is not a fictional character.

HOW TO SAY IT

Bildad	*Bill*-dad.
Edom	*Ee*-dum.
Eliphaz	*El*-ih-faz.
Esau	*Ee*-saw.
Ezekiel	Ee-*zeek*-ee-ul or Ee-*zeek*-yul.
Messiah	Meh-*sigh*-uh.
Obadiah	O-buh-*dye*-uh.
Teman	*Tee*-mun.
Temanite	*Tee*-mun-ite.
Zophar	*Zo*-far.

I. Job's Complaint
(JOB 19:1-7)

A. Repeated Reproach (vv. 1-3)

1, 2. Then Job replied:
"How long will you torment me
and crush me with words?

At this point, Job has been "counseled" by Eliphaz twice, Bildad twice, and Zophar once. These three friends are remembered for giving Job bad advice, since God later rebukes them (Job 42:7). But they have good intentions, at least at first (2:11). Initially, these three had wept: "When they saw him from a distance, they could hardly recognize him; they began to weep aloud, and they tore their robes and sprinkled dust on their heads" (2:12). They may have gone down in history as the greatest comforters of all time had they only kept their mouths shut (2:13).

Yet Job's friends eventually open their mouths, and it is all downhill from there. Though much of what they say is true and appropriate in certain circumstances, their misperception of Job's situation leads them into error. The friend to speak most recently is Bildad, although Job's response in the verses before us is not necessarily aimed only at him. Job seems to address the friends' collective failure to say anything helpful; what they have to say is causing Job even more pain. Their words torment him, violating his dignity.

What Do You Think?
What can we do to minimize the possibility that our counsel to a fellow Christian merely makes things worse?
Talking Points for Your Discussion
▪ Knowing when to refer to someone with more advanced counseling skills
▪ "Giving advice" vs. "providing counsel"
▪ Developing listening skills
▪ Understanding the situation
▪ Other

3a. "Ten times now you have reproached me;

Job's three friends have responded to him a total of five times at this point in the book of Job.

So the phrase *ten times* is not intended to be a precise count, but a hyperbole (compare Genesis 31:7; Numbers 14:22).

3b. ". . . shamelessly you attack me.

However modest Job's friends Eliphaz, Bildad, and Zophar were when they first arrived, they have now become quite bold. It is one thing to slip up a time or two and offer bad counsel, but these friends have been relentless in their unfair reproaches.

What Do You Think?

When was a time that someone's counsel only made your situation worse? What did you learn from that experience?

Talking Points for Your Discussion

- During a serious illness
- After a financial setback
- During a crisis of faith
- Other

❧ FRIENDS LIKE . . . YOU? ❧

Well-meaning friends may occasionally give us advice that demonstrates a lack of understanding of our circumstances. Their remarks may cut us to the heart as their attitude makes us question their friendship. That's when we wonder, *With friends like these, who needs enemies?*

We may also wonder if such friends are actually *frenemies*—people who pretend to be friends but are actually enemies. A biblical example of such a person is found in 2 Samuel 15:32-37; 16:15–17:16, where an advisor to King David pretended to be loyal to the king's son who was attempting to gain the throne by force.

A key difference between a clumsy but well-meaning friend and a frenemy is that of *motive*. Whatever their flaws, Job's inept friends did seem to have his best interests at heart. That factor is important as we examine our own motives in our helping interactions with others.

Even so, possessing good motives is no guarantee that we will not do more harm than good when a friend needs a shoulder to cry on. As we ponder the errors of Job's friends, how do we avoid repeating them?   —C. R. B.

B. Remaining Innocent (vv. 4-7)

4. "If it is true that I have gone astray,
my error remains my concern alone.

At first glance, this might be seen as a confession of sorts on Job's part, as if he is finally willing to admit that he has sinned and that his sin is his problem. This is not the correct interpretation, however, because there is no evidence elsewhere that Job ever gives up his plea of innocence. In his final words to his friends, he will say "I will maintain my innocence and never let go of it" (Job 27:6).

Job is maintaining, rather, that any sin on his part is his business and his alone. His friends have no good reason to besiege him as they have. They have been playing God (see Job 19:22a).

5, 6. "If indeed you would exalt yourselves
above me
and use my humiliation against me,
then know that God has wronged me
and drawn his net around me.

Job knows that his friends will not accept his plea of innocence, given his experience with them thus far. So Job shifts the attention back to the mutually shared conviction that good things should happen to good people and bad things to bad people.

Since Job knows that he has done nothing to deserve his tragedy, then he must conclude that this normal cause-and-effect system has broken down. The implication is that God, who is the author of that system, has broken his own rules. There seems to be no other explanation available to Job for God's having *wronged* him.

Job is starting to speak out of his depth. It is one thing to claim innocence when one is indeed innocent or to wonder why normal cause and effect does not seem to apply. It is another thing, however, to claim to know God's role in this apparent anomaly when God has not specifically revealed that role.

God does indeed reveal his role and that of Satan to the reader in Job 1:1–2:7, but Job does not have this information. Job will be rebuked later by God for speaking out of turn about him (Job 38–41), although Job's words are more truthful than those of his friends (42:7).

7. "Though I cry, 'Violence!' I get no response; though I call for help, there is no justice."

Job intensifies his defense. We may see "crying out" language so often in the prophets, psalms, and other parts of Scripture that we can become numb to the desperation it signals for the original plaintiffs. Let us pause to absorb the full force of this verse. It is as if Job, having been beaten and bruised, is crying "Help!" in the middle of the public square.

But no one notices his need for assistance and vindication. Though Job might plead his case before many judges, he cannot find one to render a judgment in his favor. Verses 8-22 (not in today's text) vividly paint Job's sense of desperation and alienation.

II. Job's Hope
(JOB 19:23-27)

A. Written Record (vv. 23, 24)

23. "Oh, that my words were recorded, that they were written on a scroll, that they were inscribed with an iron tool on lead, or engraved in rock forever!

Job does not give up. Though he despairs of getting a fair hearing from anyone of his time, he pines for some sort of permanent record that will preserve his case for a future day (compare Psalm 102:18). The fact that we have the book of Job available to us means that Job gets his wish! Job's record has been preserved, and later generations can consider his case and render a proper verdict.

"'Tis pleasant, sure, to see one's name in print. A Book's a Book, altho' there's nothing in't." That quaint (and somewhat cynical) bit of verse by Lord Byron (1788–1824) speaks to the human desire to be known. And, it seems to us, if that knowledge can be passed along in our own words, so much the better! That way we will have more assurance that history will deal with us in a way we think it should rather than as some revisionist prefers.

Historical revisionism is popular and never-ending. For example, the life of Abraham Lincoln probably has been subjected to more revisionism than any other American hero. He has been claimed as inspiration by numerous advocates of opposing perspectives: communists and anti-communists, liberals and conservatives, both sides of the twentieth-century temperance movement —the list goes on and on. If Lincoln's life had not been cut short by assassination, perhaps he would have had time to write an autobiography that would have curtailed so much revisionism.

But wait—isn't historical revisionism also a danger in autobiographies? Indeed it is, and perhaps more so! But since God is the ultimate author of the book of Job, we are assured that what we read is truth. Job speaks properly, but he also says things that need correction (see lesson 8). As we consider all this, we keep in mind that the only book that really counts to be named in is "the book of life" (Revelation 3:5). Let us dedicate ourselves to God's work in such a way that his record of our lives will show deeds of "gold," not those of "straw" (1 Corinthians 3:11-15).   —C. R. B.

B. Living Redeemer (vv. 25-27)

25. "I know that my redeemer lives, and that in the end he will stand on the earth.

The original thrust of verses 25-27 can be missed if we read them only in Christian hindsight. That hindsight includes our firm grasp regarding the nature of Christ's redemption and our clear hope for the resurrection of the dead. However, the concept of a redeeming Messiah probably is unknown to Job if he lives during or just after the time of Abraham, when salvation-history is just being

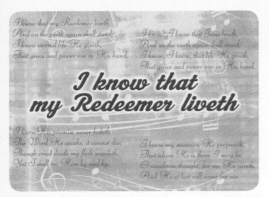

Visual for Lesson 6. *Display this visual as you distribute copies of the "Waiting for a Redeemer" activity from the reproducible page (see p. 56).*

inaugurated. Also, belief in the resurrection of the dead is not common until much later (compare Job 7:7-10; Hebrews 11:19), and even then not in pagan thought (Acts 17:32).

Before we attempt to come to grips with this passage's original, primary meaning, we acknowledge that it is quite possible that God desires the modern reader to see a secondary meaning as well: Jesus came to redeem all God's people, and that includes Job. Affirming this secondary meaning does not mean we should ignore the original, primary meaning of verses 25-27. Secondary meanings in Scripture always use primary meanings as their points of departure. Skipping over original, primary meanings will cause us to miss the richness of the secondary meanings.

An investigation into what Job intends to convey by his two statements here in verse 25 should explore what he understands a *redeemer* to be. For the ancient Israelites, who come after Job, the word *redeemer* is a technical term with concrete associations. It will come to be associated first and foremost with the "kinsman redeemer" role that is to play a vital part in maintaining Israel's economic system (see Leviticus 25:25, 48; Numbers 5:8; Ruth 4:4-6; Jeremiah 32:6, 7).

But if Job lives before the time of Moses (see the Lesson Background), this concept is unknown to him, having not yet been revealed by God. Job apparently does not expect to experience vindication in his lifetime, but perhaps after death.

Even so, it is not clear who Job imagines will appear as his redeemer. Some translations, such as the 1984 edition of the NIV®, capitalize that word, which makes it seem like it must refer to God. But there are no upper and lowercase letters in the original language. It is possible that Job thinks God himself will be the one to redeem him. But Job holds God responsible for his misfortune, so perhaps Job is thinking of a nondivine heavenly advocate who will serve as an intermediary between him and God (compare Job 16:18-21; 33:23, 24).

What Do You Think?
 When was a time you were able to "release" your concern to God by focusing on the fact that he is still in control? How did things turn out?
Talking Points for Your Discussion
 ▪ When a loved one was dying
 ▪ When unemployed
 ▪ During a church crisis
 ▪ Other

26, 27. "And after my skin has been destroyed,
 yet in my flesh I will see God;
I myself will see him
 with my own eyes—I, and not another.
 How my heart yearns within me!"

These two verses are very difficult to interpret, partly because it is not clear whether the first half of verse 26 begins a new thought or concludes the thought of verse 25. There are three main lines of interpretation.

Possibility 1: If all of verses 26 and 27 belong together as a unit of thought, then Job may be anticipating a resurrection from the dead, when he will see God and be vindicated. Assuming that Job lives about the time of Abraham, Hebrews 11:19 indicates awareness in that time frame of the possibility of resurrection. However, the characters in the book of Job seem to presume in various places that death is final (Job 3:11-19; etc.). Job himself says "one who goes down to the grave does not return" (7:9; compare 10:19-22). Job may be pondering the possibility of resurrection in 14:14, 15, but the rest of that chapter is pessimistic in that regard.

Possibility 2: Some interpreters focus on the fact that ancient people believed that the dead exist as disembodied spirits known as *shades* (compare 1 Samuel 28:13). Even if Job does not believe in resurrection, he may believe that after death he will exist as a shade when he sees God. However, this theory doesn't account for Job's statement that he will see God *in my flesh.* Shades by definition do not have flesh.

Possibility 3: If the first seven words of verse 26 complete the thought of verse 25, then Job believes that his redeemer will vindicate him eventually after Job dies (*after my skin has been destroyed*). The second half of verse 26 then combines with verse 27 to form a different unit of thought: Job would rather not wait until he is dead before being vindicated. He wishes to see God before dying, while still in the flesh. In other words, Job wants to be vindicated firsthand, not through someone else long after he is gone.

The statement *How my heart yearns within me!* speaks to Job's emotional and spiritual longing.

III. Job's Warning
(Job 19: 28, 29)
A. Continued Blame (v. 28)
28. "If you say, 'How we will hound him,
since the root of the trouble lies in him,'

Job returns to addressing his three accusers (*you*) directly. The statement Job attributes to them can also be seen as a rhetorical question along the lines of "Why should we not continue to persecute him, since the root of the problem is to be found within Job himself?" Thus Job is resigned to the fact that the three friends are not going to be moved by his pleas of innocence.

What Do You Think?
How can we be sure not to impugn another for *tunnel-vision stubbornness* when he or she is really exhibiting *thoughtful tenacity*?
Talking Points for Your Discussion
- Seeking third-party input
- Awareness of presuppositions
- Other

B. Eventual Judgment (v. 29)
29. ". . . you should fear the sword yourselves;
for wrath will bring punishment by the sword,
and then you will know that there is judgment."

Since Eliphaz, Bildad, and Zophar will not pursue justice on Job's behalf, he warns them that they should watch their own backs. Those who persecute the innocent will eventually experience judgment themselves. Though Job protests that justice is not being rendered to him, he believes that it will indeed be visited on his inept counselors.

Conclusion
A. Hope

Perhaps the most significant contribution of today's passage is Job's resilience in reaching for hope when there seemed to be no hope. That Job did so even as he suspected God to be his opponent is itself a sort of statement of faith in God. Though God was to blame in Job's eyes, that man's view of God was not so negative as to see God failing to mete out eventual justice for both Job and his persecutors. Though God, from Job's perspective, was tormenting him, that man did not believe that God had stepped out of character to such an extent as to neglect upholding justice on some level.

This gives us all the more reason to hope! When it seems as though our world is falling apart, we can draw strength from the fact that we have Jesus and his promise of resurrection—something Job did not have. If Job could find faith resources in his day and situation, then all the more should we be able to do so! Though we should not echo all of Job's sentiments, we can live out his tenacity in the face of despair. We cling to Christ in our darkest hours.

B. Prayer

Lord God, we thank you for the example you have given us in your servant Job. Strengthen our feeble faith that we may face the trials of our lives with equal resilience. In Jesus' name; amen.

C. Thought to Remember
Hold on to hope. Hold on to Jesus.

INVOLVEMENT LEARNING

Enhance your lesson with NIV® Bible Student (from your curriculum supplier) and the reproducible activity page (at www.standardlesson.com or in the back of the NIV® Standard Lesson Commentary Deluxe Edition).

Into the Lesson

Draw an outline of a man's torso and head on the board. Also draw concentric red circles on it, as if it were a target. Label the outline clearly as *BAD GUY*. Give each arriving learner a sheet of paper crumpled into a ball (possibly wrapped in a rubber band). As class begins, say, "Throw your weapon at the bad guy!" After the bombardment, say, "Now, doesn't that feel better?"

After allowing for brief responses, note, "That is like what happened to Job. His friends had labeled him as a *bad guy,* pummeling him with accusations of being an unrepentant sinner. His accusers no doubt felt some level of self-satisfaction. They had tried to straighten out 'Job the sinner'! Our text today is part of Job's response, uttered in frustration and despair."

Option. Before the above, place in chairs copies of the "Moving from Pain to Hope" activity from the reproducible page, which you can download. Learners can begin working on this as they arrive.

Into the Word

Note that Job's frustration vents itself in hard and harsh questions. Then distribute handouts with the following instructions and questions: "Look at today's text and identify a verse or two that relates to each question—each of which is a paraphrase or implication."

1. "What kind of friend will stand beside me and stand up for me?" 2. "Is everybody here deaf?" 3. "How can I get this all recorded so the future will remember me?" 4. "What is it to you if I have sinned?" 5. "Why have you pursued me with the idea that it's all my fault?" 6. "How many times will you repeat the same indictments?" 7. "Do you think you will escape the punishment of God's wrath?" 8. "Why do you feel superior to me?" 9. "Who do you think is in the wrong here: God or me?" 10. "How long will your accusations go on?"

Allow five or six minutes, then read the questions and ask for matches. Learners can work on this individually or in small groups. Expected responses, not to be included on the handouts are 1, verse 25; 2, verse 7; 3, verses 23, 24; 4, verse 4; 5, verse 28; 6, verse 3; 7, verse 29; 8, verse 5; 9, verse 6; 10, verse 2.

Alternative. Pose the questions orally for class-wide responses. This approach may be appropriate if your class is smaller.

Option. Have learners complete in small groups the "When Friends Turn Bad" activity from the reproducible page. This will help personalize the truths of the text as learners ponder what good friends should and should not do when aiding the suffering.

Into Life

Write on the board the words *Tragedy* and *Redemption*. Ask, "How do these two words relate to one another regarding Job's expression of faith?" Jot responses on the board.

Then ask, "How do these two concepts relate to one another regarding your own faith?" Again, jot responses on the board. Finally ask, "How does one's sense—or how *should* one's sense—of a Redeemer help us in times of great challenge and anxiety?" The desired responses should relate to a sense of "being valued" and "bought back" by someone who cares deeply. Use this to lead into a discussion of Jesus as Redeemer.

Option. Distribute copies of the "Waiting for a Redeemer" activity on the reproducible page. Then have the class sing the first verse and refrain of "I Know That My Redeemer Liveth"; the words are included in the activity.

As learners depart, encourage them to use the activity for reflection in the week ahead on how the truth of Job's hope in the midst of great personal stress is all the more their own hope in the New Testament era.

I WILL CALL ON GOD

DEVOTIONAL READING: Jeremiah 14:14-22
BACKGROUND SCRIPTURE: Job 5; 24; Psalm 55:12-23

JOB 24:1, 9-12, 19-25

¹ "Why does the Almighty not set times for judgment?
Why must those who know him look in vain for such days?"

· ·

⁹ "The fatherless child is snatched from the breast;
the infant of the poor is seized for a debt.
¹⁰ Lacking clothes, they go about naked;
they carry the sheaves, but still go hungry.
¹¹ They crush olives among the terraces;
they tread the winepresses, yet suffer thirst.
¹² The groans of the dying rise from the city,
and the souls of the wounded cry out for help.
But God charges no one with wrongdoing."

· ·

¹⁹ "As heat and drought snatch away the melted snow,

so the grave snatches away those who have sinned.
²⁰ The womb forgets them,
the worm feasts on them;
the wicked are no longer remembered
but are broken like a tree.
²¹ They prey on the barren and childless woman,
and to the widow they show no kindness.
²² But God drags away the mighty by his power;
though they become established, they have no assurance of life.
²³ He may let them rest in a feeling of security,
but his eyes are on their ways.
²⁴ For a little while they are exalted, and then they are gone;
they are brought low and gathered up like all others;
they are cut off like heads of grain.
²⁵ "If this is not so, who can prove me false
and reduce my words to nothing?"

KEY VERSE

As for me, I call to God, and the LORD saves me. —**Psalm 55:16**

SUSTAINING HOPE

Unit 2: Dark Nights of the Soul

LESSONS 5–8

LESSON AIMS

After participating in this lesson, each learner will be able to:

1. Summarize Job's view of reality regarding the existence of evil.

2. Compare and contrast the evils Job observed in his day with the evils of today.

3. Prepare an answer to the common question, "If God exists and is good, then why is there so much evil in the world?"

LESSON OUTLINE

Introduction

A. The Problem of Evil

Theodicy is a technical term that means "defense of God's goodness and power in view of the existence of evil." For some, this definition brings up a logical dilemma that keeps them from placing faith in the God of Scripture. According to this dilemma, skeptics say that there are three statements that cannot all be true at the same time: *God is good, God is all-powerful,* and *evil exists.* Skeptics say that it's a case of "you can pick any two to be true, but not all three."

This line of thought allows the skeptic to propose that (1) if evil exists and God is good, then God is not powerful enough to do anything about the evil or else he would; or (2) if God is all-powerful and evil prevails, then it means that God must not be good, or else he would use his power to end evil; or (3) if God is both good and all-powerful, then evil must not really exist—it's an illusion.

Let's take for granted that evil does indeed exist; it is not a figment of our imagination. Must we then choose between Proposal 1 and Proposal 2? It seems as though something has to give.

Christian thinkers have long wrestled with questions of theodicy and have suggested various answers. The book of Job is a valuable resource in this regard. In last week's lesson, we saw Job wrestling with the issue of the suffering of innocent people. This week he ponders the issue of the prosperity of the wicked.

B. Lesson Background

The background of this week's lesson is the same as last week's, so that information need not be repeated here. We can add that in the interim between Job 19 (last week) and Job 24 (this week), Job has undergone two more rounds of counseling —one by Zophar (chap. 20) and one by Eliphaz (chap. 22).

The friends' counsel did not comfort Job. They said he was guilty of wrongdoing that deserved to be punished. They accused him of pride in being unwilling to confess his guilt. They called him to heed time-tested wisdom, to repent of evil, and get right with God so God could prosper him again.

Zophar seems to have taken the response in Job 19:28, 29 as a personal insult (20:3). In turn, Job viewed Zophar's rejoinder as mockery (21:3) and falsehood (21:34). When it was Eliphaz's turn, he accused Job of great wickedness (22:5-9), the cure being repentance (22:21-30).

In reaction, Job expressed his wish to gain access to God's presence so he (Job) could plead his case and be acquitted (Job 23:3-7). Job then confessed that it was impossible to do so (23:8, 9) and that he was powerless to do anything about God's plans for him (23:13, 14). Today's text offers us another part of Job's reaction.

I. Injustice Thrives
(JOB 24:1, 9-12)
A. Job's Question (v. 1)
1. "Why does the Almighty not set times for judgment?
Why must those who know him look in vain for such days?"

This verse begins by making two important statements about God. First is the recognition that all things are laid bare before God. Nothing is hidden. This is important for Job, because the fact that God can see all things means that he is fully aware of all injustice.

Second, Job's reference to God as *the Almighty* emphasizes his unlimited power. Not only does God see all the wrongs of this world, he also has the ability to do something about them.

In Job's eyes, knowledge and ability mean responsibility. This is why he expresses puzzlement in the second half of the verse. Those who know who God is—how powerful and aware he is—expect to see evidence of his justice in the world around them. They expect to see firsthand the days when God brings the wicked to justice and

HOW TO SAY IT

Bildad	*Bill*-dad.
Demjanjuk	Dem-*yan*-yuk.
Eliphaz	*El*-ih-faz.
theodicy	the-*ah*-duh-see (*the* as in *thief*).
Zophar	*Zo*-far.

restores the righteous. Job does not see this happening, and he wonders why not. If God does not do something, the wicked will continue in their ruthless ways as Job predicts in the next section.

> **What Do You Think?**
> Is it true that "knowledge and ability mean responsibility" to do something? Why, or why not?
> *Talking Points for Your Discussion*
> - Defining the terms
> - Defining limits
> - Other

B. Wicked Oppression (vv. 9-12)
9. "The fatherless child is snatched from the breast;
the infant of the poor is seized for a debt.

One's place in society is often secured through one's father. To be fatherless in the ancient Near East is therefore to be quite vulnerable. *The fatherless* are often the first to be taken advantage of.

The fatherless who have not lost their mothers still have a certain degree of parental protection. It is thus an act of ruthless cruelty to remove the fatherless *from the breast* of the mother. Taken literally, this means removing an infant from his or her parental life support. Taken more generally, it means severing infants from their best chance for proper integration into society. Either way, to do so is to cut children off from any sense of security, even to the point of jeopardizing their lives.

The phrase *is seized for a debt* tells us why an evil person would do such a thing. As today, someone in the ancient world who incurs debt will often have to provide some sort of collateral as security for the loan (examples: Genesis 38:17, 18; Job 24:3; Proverbs 20:16; 27:13). Foreclosure by seizing the collateral is often to strip the poor of what little resources they have remaining (compare Deuteronomy 24:6). If a poor widow puts up her child as collateral, her situation must be desperate indeed!

A child seized this way may end up in slavery. A widow whose children are taken may end up without support in old age. But the wicked don't care!
10. "Lacking clothes, they go about naked;
they carry the sheaves, but still go hungry.

These references also may have to do with collateral. If the *clothes* or *the sheaves* of grain that are taken as a loan guarantee are not returned, the poor will *go about naked* and be *hungry*. The wicked are those who allow (or cause) this to be the case when it is in their power to do otherwise. On a purely contractual level, it is within their right to keep such a pledge, but only a cruel person would actually do so. (When the Law of Moses comes to be, after Job's day, God will strictly forbid such practices; see Exodus 22:26; Deuteronomy 24:12, 13, 17.)

There are other ways the wicked inflict damage on the poor, both in Job's era and today. They do so by giving unreasonably low wages, by monopolizing resources, by bribing judges and witnesses in court, by price fixing, etc. The wicked who are particularly devious can come up with intricate plans for taking advantage of the poor. Lending money at high interest rates and manipulating circumstances so the poor cannot pay it back is an example. The wicked can then take the debtor to court to seize possessions and property (compare Mark 12:40; James 2:6). Later the wicked may go after the children, with the entire household of a poor family becoming indentured.

What Do You Think?
  How do the wicked of Job's day compare and
    contrast with the wicked of today? Why is this
    question important?
Talking Points for Your Discussion
  ▪ Ways they are similar
  ▪ Ways they are different

11. "They crush olives among the terraces; they tread the winepresses, yet suffer thirst.

It is one thing to lack resources during a flagging economy when few others are thriving. It is another thing to be surrounded by wealth and to have no share in it. Job is describing the latter case. Though the poor are manufacturing olive oil and treading grapes for others, they are not able to enjoy the fruit of their labors. They go thirsty while they toil arduously to produce these two liquids, watching others reap all the benefits. This is the kind of injustice that God's people will be called to oppose later (compare Deuteronomy 24:19-22; 25:4).

12. "The groans of the dying rise from the city,
and the souls of the wounded cry out for help.
But God charges no one with wrongdoing."

There is abundant evidence in our world, as in Job's, that things are not going well. The cries of the afflicted rise to God on a daily basis. Surely he who sees all also hears all! God cannot be oblivious to the sorry state of the poor.

Yet God is doing nothing as far as Job can tell. In particular, God does not assign blame to the guilty parties. If he did, there would be evidence of that as well. But the wicked do not cry out under divine discipline since they seem to receive none (compare Malachi 3:15). Only the poor cry out in desperation.

What Do You Think?
  What are some ways our church can "comfort the
    afflicted and afflict the comfortable," as the old
    saying goes?
Talking Points for Your Discussion
  ▪ Regarding ways to be a conscience of the
    community
  ▪ Regarding methods of interchurch cooperation
  ▪ Regarding sermon topics
  ▪ Other

❧ HELPLESS OBSERVERS ❧

Those of us who heard that a plane had struck the World Trade Center on 9/11 probably thought at first, *What a horrible accident!* We knew that airplanes sometimes fly into buildings by accident (pilot error, mechanical malfunction, etc.). But we came to realize that it was no accident as the events of that day unfolded. Recorded phone calls and radio transmissions allow us to hear yet today "the groans of the dying rise from the city."

We feel so helpless in the face of such tragedies wrought of evil intent. In our helplessness, we may wonder, *Since God has foreknowledge of all events, why didn't he act to prevent the terrorists' actions?*

We should keep a few things in mind as we grapple with this question. First, God may indeed prevent hundreds of evil actions every day, but we are unaware of these because they never happen. Second, God may turn the question around and wonder why *we* don't do something to act as his instrument to prevent or counteract evil (compare Judges 6:13, 14; Ezekiel 22:30). Third, we may be unsatisfied with his answers, prompting us to further question his ways (see the book of Habakkuk).

Above all, we keep in mind that we live in a fallen world. It is a world where God himself suffered the greatest tragedy in history: the judicial murder of his innocent Son. Whatever our suffering, God's has been greater. —C. R. B.

Call on God

Visual for Lesson 7. *Use this visual to start a discussion about how a reliance on God by a country's founders sets a tone for future generations.*

II. Justice Prevails
(JOB 24:19-25)
A. Destiny of the Wicked (vv. 19, 20)

19. "As heat and drought snatch away the melted snow,
so the grave snatches away those who have sinned.

After pining over God's apparent inaction, Job now acknowledges the ultimate fate of the wicked (*those who have sinned*). The verse before us reads like a proverb in that regard as it compares the fate of the wicked with the effects of the relentless heat of the sun. Rain does not fall year-round in Job's area of the world. Much falls in the winter; in higher elevations, precipitation takes the form of snow. Melting snow then fills the streambeds (Job 6:15-17a), which dry up in hot weather (6:17b).

The fate of *the melted snow* thus makes a good parallel with the fate of the wicked. Though they appear to thrive, the grave eventually overtakes them as it does everyone else. There is no escape.

❧ GETTING AWAY WITH MURDER? ❧

Some historians think John Demjanjuk (1920–2012) literally got away with murder. Demjanjuk lived in obscurity in the U.S. from 1952 until 1986, when he was deported to Israel to stand trial for his alleged role in the Nazi holocaust. But his subsequent conviction in 1988 for war crimes was overturned in 1993. He was charged anew

in 2001, deported to Germany in 2009 to stand trial, and was convicted there in 2011 on 27,900 counts of accessory to murder. This conviction was annulled, however, because Demjanjuk died before his appeal could be heard. Thus John Demjanjuk was legally innocent at his death.

The true nature of John Demjanjuk's involvement in the holocaust may never be known in this world. But God knows.

God's judgment does not always come immediately or as soon as we would prefer. That can be a good thing, because it gives us time to repent. And before we cry out that someone is "getting away with murder," we should remember that God knows what murder is like because it happened to his Son—and it was our sins that put him on the cross. The wicked of this world will indeed "get theirs." But before we pray too quickly for that to happen *right now*, we remember that before we accepted Christ we were part of them.—C. R. B.

20. "The womb forgets them,
the worm feasts on them;
the wicked are no longer remembered
but are broken like a tree.

The grave does not treat *the wicked* kindly. They will be forgotten by the living (compare 2 Chronicles 21:20). Of course, the bodies of all the dead, both good and evil, undergo decay. But the evil dead do not leave a legacy that is worth remembering, except perhaps as a bad example!

This is a sober warning. Though everyone in Job's day, as today, realizes that the grave awaits them, the righteous will at least be remembered fondly (compare Hebrews 11:4). They leave a legacy for future generations to celebrate and imitate. The wicked, by contrast, do not.

B. Intervention of God (vv. 21-24)

21. "They prey on the barren and childless woman,
and to the widow they show no kindness.

Job reflects further on the misdeeds of the wicked. Here they are seen to be guilty of mistreating two categories of vulnerable women. *The barren and childless* woman has no sons to perpetuate the family legacy and provide support during old age (compare Ruth 4:15). *The widow* has no husband to protect her (compare 1 Timothy 5:5).

The wicked know how to exploit such women. Without protectors or advocates, they are easy targets. Without a support network to help with harvesting, etc., they eventually get into debt, which calls for loans (perhaps at exorbitant interest rates), which opens doors to further economic abuse when such loans cannot be repaid (Luke 20:46, 47).

22. "But God drags away the mighty by his power;
though they become established, they have no assurance of life.

The wicked, who are *the mighty* in the eyes of the world, get a taste of their own medicine when they encounter God's *power.* No matter how secure the wealthy wicked think themselves to be, God has ways of exposing and defeating their arrogance (compare Luke 12:16-20).

23. "He may let them rest in a feeling of security,
but his eyes are on their ways.

The ways of the wicked may go unhindered for a while. They may sleep well at night and have no anxiety going into the next day. They may feel secure because they've developed a system that appears to be working for them. Their delusions of invulnerability grow each time they commit fraud and get away with it.

But God can and does see. Though it seems as if the wicked are getting away with murder, God is taking note. The wicked of all eras live as if they are accountable to no one but themselves. But they are wrong, and their error is going to cost them dearly.

24. "For a little while they are exalted, and then they are gone;
they are brought low and gathered up like all others;
they are cut off like heads of grain.

When God eventually intervenes, the wicked will see how fleeting ill-gotten prosperity really is. Their triumph is revealed to be only temporary as *they are brought low.*

Some students think that a problem for Job is the idea of "eventually." Doesn't that seem like piecemeal justice—a little here sooner and a little there later? What about a great day of final judgment when all wrongs are set right?

This takes us back to the question of Job 24:1: "Why does the Almighty not set times for judgment? Why must those who know him look in vain for such days?" Job seems to desire something like "the day of the Lord," a topic that comes to be addressed in the prophets (Isaiah 13:6; Joel 2:1; etc.). If this is what Job really wants, it seems to be nowhere in sight! The justice he sees is piecemeal in nature.

> *What Do You Think?*
> What faith lessons have you learned from experiencing the kinds of injustice that may not be made right until Jesus returns?
> *Talking Points for Your Discussion*
> - As a victim of violent crime
> - As a victim of theft
> - As a victim of medical malpractice
> - As one wrongfully accused
> - Other

C. Challenge to Friends (v. 25)

25. "If this is not so, who can prove me false and reduce my words to nothing?"

Concluding his response to Eliphaz, Job asks who can refute him. This is a rhetorical question, of course. No one can, because there remains no evidence that the wicked fare any better against death than anyone else.

The challenge of verses 19-25 is that this section sounds more like what the friends have been saying and less like what Job has been saying thus far. Throughout his observations, Job has been pointing out the injustices of this world while his friends have been directing him toward God's justice. Why all of a sudden would Job at this point (seemingly) change his position?

Various answers to this question have been proposed. Some suggest that this section was originally spoken by one of Job's friends and that the manuscripts must have gotten jumbled at some point, with the speech being mistakenly reassigned to Job. Since Bildad's reply in this third cycle of speeches is very short (only the six verses of Job 25) and Zophar doesn't give a third speech at all, the suggestion is that today's section really belongs to one of those two. The problem with this view is that there is no concrete evidence that a manuscript jumbling has taken place. It remains speculative. Another, equally speculative solution is to say that the final editor of the book inserted this poem here.

Two other views leave the speech on Job's lips. One is that Job is throwing the words of his friends back at them. In other words, he is mocking them for saying such things as if he is unaware or oblivious to this line of thought. Of course Job knows the way things normally are! But his point —which the three friends miss—is that his situation is not normal. He is not a wicked man. He has not ravaged the poor, yet he is being treated as if he has.

The other view is that Job is calling out for God to bring justice. Job is affirming the way things should be because he hopes that God will hear him and return his situation to "normal."

What Do You Think?
What are some ways to help victims of injustice focus on the ultimate justice that Jesus will bring when he returns?
Talking Points for Your Discussion
- Things to encourage victims to say or do
- Things to encourage victims not to say or do
- Things to do for the victims

Conclusion
A. Untamed God

The problem of *theodicy*, with which we began, remains a challenge for our thinking about God. Our passage has affirmed God's power, affirmed God's justice, and affirmed the reality of suffering. Humans may not understand how to affirm all three of these at the same time, but Scripture does not hesitate to do so. God cannot be contained by the logical boxes that we create, and we are too small to build boxes that can even come close (compare Isaiah 55:9).

All of this is for the good. As children, we could not understand why our parents wouldn't let us eat ice cream before bed, why they were allowed to stay up late, and why one sibling was allowed to do something that another was not. It all seemed unfair from our perspective, no matter how hard we tried to wrap our minds around it. We truly comprehend only after we grow up.

In 1 Corinthians 13:12, the apostle reminds us that now we "know in part." When Christ returns and his kingdom comes in its fullness, then we will have answers to questions that are currently beyond us. In the meantime, we are to trust that the one in control has our best interests at heart. We do not have all the answers now, but we can rest assured that God does.

Job was not privileged at the time to know what was really going on (see Job 1:1–2:7), but he had the wherewithal to invoke God's justice. Even when the fulfillment of that justice is not within sight, we can call on it in response to our pain (see Psalm 119:126). God is able and willing to handle the hurts and frustrations of his children.

B. Prayer

O Lord, we thank you for the witness of Job. As we sense his pain, we realize that others suffer worse than we do. As you gave Job the strength to endure, so also give us strength until your Son returns in glory to set all things right. In Jesus' name; amen.

C. Thought to Remember
Cling to God's justice.

INVOLVEMENT LEARNING

Enhance your lesson with NIV® Bible Student *(from your curriculum supplier) and the reproducible activity page (at www.standardlesson.com or in the back of the* NIV® Standard Lesson Commentary Deluxe Edition*).*

Into the Lesson

Have displayed on the board the outline of a newspaper. Have the phrase *TODAY'S NEWS* at the top to resemble a newspaper title. Below the title, have the main headline reading WHERE IS GOD IN ALL THIS? Give each learner a half sheet of paper as you ask them to write a sentence or two about something they heard or saw this past week that they considered bad news. Collect the papers after a few minutes; read them aloud as you affix them underneath the headline on the board.

As you finish, say, "As we see all the bad news around us, it's natural to ask, 'Where is God in all this?' That is Job's cry in today's lesson."

Into the Word

Have a learner read Job 24:1, 9-12 aloud and another read 24:19-25. Comment that these verses emphasize a fundamental complaint of Job: *Where is God when he is needed?*

Give each learner a bookmark-size (perhaps 1½" x 5") piece of poster board featuring the word *INJUSTICE* vertically down the left-hand side. Form learners into pairs or small groups to make an acrostic from the word, using ideas from the text, with the letters of *injustice* as the first letters of the resulting words.

After learners finish, have them share results with the class as a whole. Jot responses on the board; ask for explanations and verse references where appropriate. Some possible results are *Inactivity*, an accusation that God isn't doing anything; *Noise*, representing the vocal groans arising from the distressed; *Jubilation*, representing the attitude of the wicked; *Unclothed*, depicting the status of the poor; *Suffering*, for the general status of the disenfranchised; *Times*, for Job's question in verse 1; *Inadequate*, summarizing the status of food for the poor; *Callous*, summarizing the behavior of the rich toward the poor; and *Elimination*, as Job notes the ultimate outcome for the wicked. (Many other entries are possible, of course.)

Suggest that learners put in their Bibles the bookmarks they have created, for future reference as they read and ponder the concerns and truths of the book of Job.

Into Life

Option 1. Prepare in advance a video for your class. The video will feature an actor dressed in Bible-times clothing, seated at a table. He will present the following monologue slowly and emphatically, incorporating Psalm 73.

Monologue: "Ah, good ol' Job. He and I have something in common. I am Asaph, writer of some of the psalms. When I saw the success of the wicked and the distress of the righteous, I became upset. But then God set me straight, as he did Job. Listen to what I wrote. [Actor reads Psalm 73:1-22.] Yes, I was thinking and acting like a dumb animal. [Actor reads Psalm 73:23-28]. Ah, Job. There *is* justice. God is there, and he will not let sin win. I must tell all his deeds, as I am doing today. What about you, you whom God holds in his hand?"

As the video concludes, say, "When we reflect on the whole of God's promises and activities, we must conclude—as did Job and Asaph—that God will indeed bring about complete justice. But as we pray for that to happen, we are thankful that God does not always mete out justice immediately for our misdeeds. His grace allows us time to repent. Praise the Lord!" Read 2 Peter 3:9.

Options 2 and 3. Distribute copies of the "What Job Saw; What I See" activity and/or the "What God Sees" activity from the reproducible page, which you can download. Have learners complete one or both as indicated. Depending on the nature of your class, learners can work individually or in small groups. Discuss results.

THINGS TOO WONDERFUL FOR ME

DEVOTIONAL READING: Galatians 1:11-19
BACKGROUND SCRIPTURE: Job 42; Psalm 86

JOB 42:1-10

¹ Then Job replied to the LORD:

² "I know that you can do all things;
   no purpose of yours can be thwarted.

³ You asked, 'Who is this that obscures my
      plans without knowledge?'
   Surely I spoke of things I did not
      understand,
   things too wonderful for me to know.

⁴ "You said, 'Listen now, and I will speak;
   I will question you,
   and you shall answer me.'

⁵ My ears had heard of you
   but now my eyes have seen you.

⁶ Therefore I despise myself
   and repent in dust and ashes."

⁷ After the LORD had said these things to Job, he said to Eliphaz the Temanite, "I am angry with you and your two friends, because you have not spoken the truth about me, as my servant Job has. ⁸ So now take seven bulls and seven rams and go to my servant Job and sacrifice a burnt offering for yourselves. My servant Job will pray for you, and I will accept his prayer and not deal with you according to your folly. You have not spoken the truth about me, as my servant Job has." ⁹ So Eliphaz the Temanite, Bildad the Shuhite and Zophar the Naamathite did what the LORD told them; and the LORD accepted Job's prayer.

¹⁰ After Job had prayed for his friends, the LORD restored his fortunes and gave him twice as much as he had before.

KEY VERSE

I know that you can do all things; no purpose of yours can be thwarted. —**Job 42:2**

SUSTAINING HOPE

Unit 2: Dark Nights of the Soul

LESSONS 5–8

LESSON AIMS

After participating in this lesson, each learner will be able to:

1. Tell how Job responded after God spoke to him and to Eliphaz.

2. Explain why Job needed to "repent" (v. 6) in light of God's declaration that Job had spoken truth (v. 7).

3. Offer an intercessory prayer for someone experiencing a physical or spiritual crisis.

LESSON OUTLINE

Introduction

A. Running Off at the Mouth

As children, we were warned of the dangers of "running off at the mouth." Despite the warning, we eventually learned the lesson the hard way.

An example is found in a memorable scene in the 1995 romantic comedy *The American President*, in which a lobbyist shows off in front of a colleague by speaking bold words against the president of the United States. Unbeknownst to her, the president walks into the room and listens in on the last part of her rant against him. The lobbyist is mortified when she realizes that the president has overheard her. Had she known he was there, she would not have run off at the mouth as she did.

Many of us have experienced something like this as we have spoken about others behind their backs only to learn that they were listening in all along. How much more problematic, then, to say incorrect things about God, who actually *is* listening at all times and in all places! That's the situation Job found himself in.

B. Lesson Background

We are nearing the end of the book of Job, and a lot has happened since the previous lesson. Bildad was the last of Job's three friends to speak (in chap. 25), and that only briefly—six verses. He added nothing new to the friends' case against Job, so Job continued to assert his innocence while waxing eloquent on the nature of God (chap. 26–31).

Job was then followed by a man named Elihu (chap. 32–37). Elihu is not mentioned until this point in the book and is not mentioned again after he finishes speaking. Neither Job nor God responded to Elihu's thoughts. The man just mysteriously showed up, offered his thoughts, and disappeared.

Then God finally spoke (Job 38:1–40:2). Posing a series of rhetorical questions, God accused Job of lacking knowledge. The gist of God's line of questioning was that he and not Job was the one who established and sustained creation. God then invited Job to respond (40:2). Job declined to answer, merely citing his own unworthiness to do so (40:3-5).

God was not satisfied with Job's reaction. Job was not going to get off the hot seat that easily! God demanded a real answer, rejected Job's accusations, and reminded Job that he could not justify or save himself, for no human could stand up even to creatures God had made—creatures such as Behemoth and Leviathan (Job 40:6–41:34). Job was required to answer for what he had said.

I. Job Responds
(Job 42:1-6)
A. Humility (vv. 1-3)

1, 2. Then Job replied to the Lord:
"I know that you can do all things;
no purpose of yours can be thwarted.

Job begins by acknowledging God's power—God can do whatever he wills.

This response does not contradict anything Job has said previously. All along he has expressed disappointment that God does not do anything to right the wrongs that he and others suffer. This disappointment would not be appropriate if Job believes that God lacks the ability to do something about injustice.

What Do You Think?
How should our knowledge of the fact that God knows all things affect our daily life?
Talking Points for Your Discussion
- Regarding thoughts
- Regarding words
- Regarding actions

---

3. "You asked, 'Who is this that obscures
my plans without knowledge?'
Surely I spoke of things I did not
understand,
things too wonderful for me to know.

Job paraphrases God's question to him in Job 38:1, 2, then responds to it. We may wonder why God is confronting Job so forcefully, since God himself has affirmed Job's truthfulness in 42:7. Despite that affirmation, there are several times throughout Job's speeches when he oversteps his

bounds. He has not cursed God in response to his suffering (compare 1:11; 2:5, 9, 10), but he certainly has called God's justice into question (see especially 9:15–10:7).

Job has been correct in claiming to be innocent and in rejecting the simplistic cause-and-effect "wisdom" of his friends. Even so, he is wrong to pretend to know about God's role in his misfortune and that of other oppressed persons. Though God does not let Job in on his conversation with Satan, God's forceful expression of his role as Creator of the universe alongside Job's comparative smallness—even before nonhuman creatures—is enough to remind Job of his proper place.

It is interesting that God takes this approach. Why not tell Job what has been happening behind the scenes? Why not do a little "image management" by placing the blame on Satan where it belongs? Why not explain that this was all a test to resolve the bigger question of Job 1:9-11?

Were God to lay out all the facts, there would be no room for faith. God is concerned that humans know their place in relation to him. Were God to share the specifics of his debate with Satan, Job may be satisfied for the time being, but later he probably would want new explanations for new injustices encountered. God would then find himself in a position of perpetually explaining himself.

We see an example of such a cycle starting with regard to the prophet Habakkuk. God's

HOW TO SAY IT

Behemoth	*Bee*-heh-moth or Beh-*hee*-moth.
Bildad	*Bill*-dad.
Elihu	Ih-*lye*-hew.
Eliphaz	*El*-ih-faz.
Leviathan	Luh-*vye*-uh-thun.
Naamathite	*Nay*-uh-muth-ite.
patriarchal	pay-tree-*are*-kul.
Shuah	*Shoe*-uh.
Shuhite	*Shoe*-hite.
Sinai	*Sigh*-nye or *Sigh*-nay-eye.
Temanite	*Tee*-mun-ite.
theophany	the-*ah*-fuh-nee (*the* as in *thief*).
Zophar	*Zo*-far.

answer to that man's first complaint about injustice (Habakkuk 1:1-11) leads the prophet to ask yet another question (1:12–2:1). After God's second reply (2:2-29), he puts the brakes on further queries by telling the prophet in a polite way to shut up (2:20).

God therefore chooses not to explain himself to Job, but rather to remind him that the Creator is not answerable to his creation. When doubts arise, we need to reflect on God's majesty and avoid questioning his way of running the world, lest we end up having to say *Surely I spoke of things I did not understand.*

> **What Do You Think?**
> How does God rebuke people today? Why is it
>   important to consider this question?
> *Talking Points for Your Discussion*
> - In moments of pride
> - In moments of bitterness
> - In moments of envy
> - Other

❧ MISDIRECTED ANTAGONISM ❧

The darkest moment of my 30-plus years of marriage was after an interstate move. My husband was deliriously happy with his new dream job. I was miserable in my attempt to rebuild my life from scratch.

My mind grew darker, and I blamed my husband for choosing his own happiness above mine. Eventually, the fact that I had been a part of the decision confronted me. What's more, I can see looking back that the move was an answer to years of prayer to be able to move closer to family.

The truth is, I knew my husband hadn't moved us capriciously. The truth is, we made the decision together with much prayer. The truth is, I was angry with God. But since there is no way to be right when at odds with God, I had transferred my dissatisfaction to an easier target. Job was wrong in questioning God's ways. But Job acted more nobly than did I—at least he was honest in naming his primary antagonist. If you're angry with God today, confess your anger to him. Don't take it out on someone else!   —V. E.

B. Repentance (vv. 4-6)

4. "You said, 'Listen now, and I will speak;
   I will question you,
   and you shall answer me.'

Job now quotes God from the beginning of God's second speech at Job 40:7; this is where God refuses Job's nonanswer of 40:3-5. Job has tried to dodge God's question by acknowledging his own vileness. Though Job is right in that regard, this does not absolve him of responsibility for his words.

5. "My ears had heard of you
   but now my eyes have seen you.

Job acknowledges that his encounter with God exceeds all previous experiences. In the past, Job had only heard of God. Job undoubtedly has had conversations with friends and family who have speculated about God. Most people in the ancient world believe in a deity or, more likely, multiple gods. Many ancient people acknowledge that humans are creatures, that the world is the product of divine activity, and that the world works in such a way that good actions produce good results and bad actions produce bad results. Yet such knowledge is incomplete.

If Job lives in patriarchal times (that is, prior to about 1800 BC; see the Lesson Background to lesson 6), it means that God has only begun to reveal himself to Abraham's descendants. The exodus from Egypt, the receiving of the law at Sinai, etc., are centuries in the future. There is so much about God that people do not know before the events of God's self-revelations noted in the book of Genesis.

The absence of those revelations does not inhibit people from speculating about God or attempting to explain his involvement in human affairs, however. In being confronted by the self-revealing God, Job is seeing him in a brand-new light.

Even so, we should be careful not to press too literally the statement *now my eyes have seen you.* Exodus 33:20 says that no one can see God's face and live. Those who are said to see God are likely seeing a *theophany* (meaning "appearance of God"; see Genesis 32:30; Isaiah 6:1). It is not clear what exactly Job sees as God addresses him.

Job 38:1 and 40:6 simply state that God speaks to Job "out of the storm." Perhaps Job sees dark clouds with flashes of lightning. Whatever Job sees, it changes him.

6. "Therefore I despise myself and repent in dust and ashes."

Job ultimately responds the only way one ought to respond after speaking out of turn about God: he repents. Sitting *in dust and ashes* is an outward sign of repentance in the ancient Near East (examples: Ezekiel 27:30; Jonah 3:6). Posturewise, this may not be much of a change for Job, since he's been sitting in ashes since Job 2:8. However, he is no longer lamenting his situation in general or protesting God's injustices; instead, Job despises himself.

What Do You Think?

What are some ways people express repentance today? How do these compare and contrast with using "dust and ashes"?

Talking Points for Your Discussion
- 2 Chronicles 7:14
- Ezra 10:1
- Ezekiel 18:21
- 2 Corinthians 7:10
- Other

This does not mean that Job hates himself in the same way he hates what has happened to him. Rather, he regrets having spoken against God. He realizes his rightful place with relation to God, and he determines to move forward with a proper perspective. Such abhorrence is analogous to Jesus' teaching that those who follow him must hate their parents (Luke 14:26). Jesus is calling people to view their parents in their proper place with relation to God. Though unbelievers might place their earthly families before all other loyalties, believers will place God first in all things.

II. God Rebukes
(JOB 42:7-9)
A. Anger and Truth (v. 7)

7. After the LORD had said these things to Job, he said to Eliphaz the Temanite, "I am angry with you and your two friends, because you have not spoken the truth about me, as my servant Job has.

Having corrected Job, God now turns to Job's friends. Only Eliphaz is named in this verse. But *your two friends* means that Bildad and Zophar, mentioned by name in verse 9, are included in the rebuke. Elihu (chap. 32–37) is left out of the rebuke—he seems to be ignored altogether. The fact that Eliphaz is identified as *the Temanite* likely means he is a descendant of Esau (see the Lesson Background of lesson 6).

God's anger is now turned toward these men because they have misrepresented God even worse than Job has. It is clear above that Job has misspoken about God in attributing to him injustices. Yet Job is right in claiming that his devastation is not the result of wrongdoing on his part. He is right in challenging the notion that one can determine unrighteous behavior in himself merely by observing the fact that he is not prospering. In this regard, Job has been correct in accusing his friends of lying about his condition (Job 13:4); Job correctly interprets their lies as flattery that speaks "wickedly" and "deceitfully" on behalf of God (13:7).

This means that Job is closer to knowing God than are Eliphaz, Bildad, and Zophar. Paradoxically, to know God is to know that we cannot completely figure him out. "'For my thoughts are not your thoughts, neither are your ways my ways,' declares the Lord. 'As the heavens are higher than the earth, so are my ways higher than your ways and my thoughts than your thoughts'" (Isaiah 55:8, 9). Job has the healthier sense of distance from God. Job's friends, by contrast, presume to know God's ways so well that they think they can speak authoritatively on his behalf (compare Job 33:14-16).

B. Sacrifice and Prayer (v. 8)

8. "So now take seven bulls and seven rams and go to my servant Job and sacrifice a burnt offering for yourselves. My servant Job will pray for you, and I will accept his prayer and not deal with you according to your folly. You have not spoken the truth about me, as my servant Job has."

Job's friends have attempted to shame him, but now it is they who are to be shamed in Job's presence! The commanded sacrifice of *seven bulls and seven rams* will be quite expensive, indicating the severity of the friends' sins. By having Job's friends ask Job to invoke God's blessing upon them, the friends will be admitting that Job is their superior; "without doubt the lesser is blessed by the greater" (Hebrews 7:7).

It will not be enough for the friends to apologize to Job; they must show by their actions that he was right and not they. *Seven* is a significant number in the Bible in various contexts (see Genesis 2:2, 3; 7:4, 10; 8:10; 21:27-31; etc.).

❧ THE SAME BOAT ❧

My husband's family moved to the suburbs of Kansas City in the 1970s and found a local church where they could participate and grow. After a short time, however, a conflict arose and the minister was pressured to leave the church. My husband's family stopped attending church altogether as a result. My father-in-law didn't believe that the ungracious behaviors he had witnessed were Christlike. I have seen conflicts arise within church families many times. Sadly, the outcome is too often a parting of the ways, with most being emotionally if not spiritually battered.

Job and his friends did not hold back in expressing their viewpoints, everyone hoping to see Job's situation eased. Each had some things right, other things wrong. When God showed up and made things clear, each person had to undergo divine correction. God restored the relationship between Job and his friends, delivering blessings through the hands of former sparring partners.

Our relationship with God is the most important one we have. Our relationships with one another are precious to him and beneficial to us as well. Even when we are on opposite sides of an issue, we frail children of dust are more alike than we would like to believe. Conflicts often seem unavoidable. In their resolution, forgiveness and reconciliation are worth pursuing (1 Corinthians 1:10; Philippians 4:2).

We are in the same boat, the boat of God's forgiving grace. —V. E.

C. Action and Acceptance (v. 9)

9. So Eliphaz the Temanite, Bildad the Shuhite and Zophar the Naamathite did what the LORD told them; and the LORD accepted Job's prayer.

The friends are not too proud to obey. They have encountered God, and this experience must affect them deeply. *Eliphaz*, whose designation *the Temanite* refers to a place known as a center of wisdom (Jeremiah 49:7), learns that he is not so wise after all. We easily imagine *Bildad the Shuhite* (see "Shuah" in Genesis 25:2; 1 Chronicles 1:32) and *Zophar the Naamathite* (location uncertain, possibly a town in northern Arabia) meekly complying as well.

We see no "I told you so" attitude on the part of Job. Realizing that the issue is not "the man Job compared with his friends" but "humans compared with God," Job heeds God's instructions to the letter on behalf of those who had condemned him relentlessly. God is pleased to accept Job's intercession.

> **What Do You Think?**
> How do we know if and when our repentance is acceptable to God?
> *Talking Points for Your Discussion*
> - Psalm 51:17
> - Matthew 11:20-24
> - Luke 19:8, 9
> - 2 Corinthians 7:9, 10
> - Other

III. God Restores
(JOB 42:10)

10. After Job had prayed for his friends, the LORD restored his fortunes and gave him twice as much as he had before.

It is interesting to observe that God does not restore Job's *fortunes* until after he intercedes on behalf of his persecutors. The reasons are not stated. Perhaps to double Job's wealth without Job first being reconciled to his friends would be to leave Job embittered toward them. Such bitterness could prevent Job from fully enjoying the blessings God subsequently lavishes on him.

The story comes full circle as Job receives *twice as much as he had before.* Job originally had 7,000 sheep, 3,000 camels, 500 yoke of oxen, 500 donkeys, and many servants, which made him "the greatest man among all the people of the East" (Job 1:3). To double all this results in an incredible fortune (42:12).

This new prosperity doesn't simply fall from the sky, however. God brings many people to Job who lavish him with gifts (Job 42:11). Of course, there is no way to replace Job's original children, but he receives a number of sons and daughters at least equal to before (42:13-15). Part of the *twice as much* blessing in this regard is seen in the fact that Job lives another 140 years, enabling him to see four generations of offspring (42:16).

Conclusion

A. Awesome God

The final chapter of Job teaches two important lessons, and we must be careful not to allow the second lesson to negate the first one. The first lesson is that we must never think that we fully understand God. Job and friends learned the hard way that it is easy to slip into dangerous speaking patterns in this regard. We can become so comfortable with God that we lose our "reverent distance" from him—distance that results from awe. True, we are in God's image, but in important ways he is not like us. He is not our personal buddy as some well-meaning Christian songs misrepresent him.

This does not mean that we should say nothing about God or fail to speak on his behalf. As readers of Scripture, we are able to echo God's words in new situations. Yet even as we do so, we exercise caution. Much of what Job's friends said echoes sentiments that God's Word itself expresses in Proverbs and elsewhere. A word about God that is appropriate to one situation is not necessarily appropriate to all situations.

We therefore exercise discretion. Before pronouncing a "thus says the Lord" in a new situation, we ought to read the Scriptures together and ask God's Spirit to lead us into an understanding as to whether this or that passage applies in our specific situation.

The second lesson is that God is just, and he will ultimately restore the fortunes of his people (James 1:12). God did not leave Job in the ditch. From the beginning, God cared for him. This does not mean, however, that all believers will be restored in this lifetime. Some die in painful misery. We cannot predict when God will or will not restore people in this life, so we must never turn Job's restoration into a promise for all people as if it always happens in all situations. As one commentator said, God cannot be domesticated.

B. Prayer

Father, we thank you for the reminders of this lesson. We must be speechless when confronted with your majesty even as you commission us to speak your Word on your behalf. May we speak of you properly always. In Jesus' name; amen.

C. Thought to Remember

Speak on God's behalf—but think first.

Visual for Lessons 3 & 8. *Start a discussion by pointing to this visual as you ask, "In what area of your life do you most need this reminder today?"*

INVOLVEMENT LEARNING

Enhance your lesson with NIV® Bible Student (from your curriculum supplier) and the reproducible activity page (at www.standardlesson.com or in the back of the NIV® Standard Lesson Commentary Deluxe Edition).

Into the Lesson

Put an empty chair labeled *Witness Stand* at the front of your learning area, facing the class. As class begins, put a large doll or stuffed toy labeled *Job* in the chair. Say, "Let's take a brief trip to what we will call 'the divine courtroom' of Job 38–41. Here we have a record of God's questioning Job on the witness stand."

Quickly turn your attention to your "Job" as you ask, "Job, where were you when the earth and everything in it was created? Tell the court, Job, what do you know about the origin of light and darkness? Can you explain that for the court? Job, how do you control the weather systems of the world? How successful, Job, are you at controlling the wild beasts? Are you the one who made the eagle fly? Job, how does your power and glory compare to that of the Almighty? How about Behemoth and Leviathan, Job—are they fully in your control? What tricks have you taught them?" (Make sure to move through the questions rapidly, with a possible aside of "Speak up; I can't hear you" and/or "Cat got your tongue?" once or twice.)

Note that God confronts Job with hard questions that cannot be answered other than with a weak "I was not" or "I cannot." Since your class will find the "interrogation" a bit laughable, say, "Although our courtroom scene appears a bit silly, there was no humor or silliness in the original occasion. In it God was putting an end to the foolishness of those who considered themselves wise!"

Into the Word

Write on the board *Talking to God . . . and Listening*. Say, "God had overheard the incessant back and forth of Job and his friends. Finally, he stepped into the conversation. It was time to listen to God, instead of just talking about him."

Continue: "Based on what we've heard in our courtroom scene, what did Job and his friends need to hear or be reminded of about God?" After a time of free response and discussion, say, "Now let's see how Job's response in 42:1-6 confirms that he actually listened to God."

Immediately read those six verses aloud. Ask learners to share their impressions of the appropriateness of (1) the content of Job's response, (2) the humility he displayed, and (3) the nature of repentance evident in the face of the absolute superiority of God's wisdom and power.

After discussion, say, "Although Job's response isn't necessarily what we would call prayer, what essential elements of prayer do you see in his reaction?" Anticipate responses such as "Prayer must confess our own inadequacy and God's sovereignty" and "Prayer should include repentance." Then ask, "How is our listening to God different from Job's?" If no one does so, point out that we listen to God first and foremost through Scripture, which Job probably did not have available to him. Discuss the relationship between this kind of listening and prayer.

Option. Distribute copies of the "Job's God, Our God" activity from the reproducible page, which you can download. Form learners into small groups to complete as indicated.

Into Life

Give each learner a small envelope that contains eight strips of paper measuring ¾" x 5". As learners examine the contents, say, "This is a do-it-yourself prayer chain. Write a friend's name on a strip daily in the week ahead, looping and fastening each strip as you go. After seven days, put your own name on the eighth strip. Let your completed chain remind you of how much stronger we are when we pray for one another, as Job did for his friends."

Alternative. Instead of the above, distribute copies of the "BFWP" activity on the reproducible page. You can have learners work on this during a few minutes of quiet time or take it home for completion later.

God's Glory
Fills the Temple

DEVOTIONAL READING: Psalm 138
BACKGROUND SCRIPTURE: Ezekiel 40:1–43:12

EZEKIEL 43:1-12

[1] Then the man brought me to the gate facing east, [2] and I saw the glory of the God of Israel coming from the east. His voice was like the roar of rushing waters, and the land was radiant with his glory. [3] The vision I saw was like the vision I had seen when he came to destroy the city and like the visions I had seen by the Kebar River, and I fell facedown. [4] The glory of the LORD entered the temple through the gate facing east. [5] Then the Spirit lifted me up and brought me into the inner court, and the glory of the LORD filled the temple.

[6] While the man was standing beside me, I heard someone speaking to me from inside the temple. [7] He said: "Son of man, this is the place of my throne and the place for the soles of my feet. This is where I will live among the Israelites forever. The people of Israel will never again defile my holy name—neither they nor their kings—by their prostitution and the funeral offerings for their kings at their death. [8] When

they placed their threshold next to my threshold and their doorposts beside my doorposts, with only a wall between me and them, they defiled my holy name by their detestable practices. So I destroyed them in my anger. [9] Now let them put away from me their prostitution and the funeral offerings for their kings, and I will live among them forever.

[10] "Son of man, describe the temple to the people of Israel, that they may be ashamed of their sins. Let them consider its perfection, [11] and if they are ashamed of all they have done, make known to them the design of the temple—its arrangement, its exits and entrances—its whole design and all its regulations and laws. Write these down before them so that they may be faithful to its design and follow all its regulations.

[12] "This is the law of the temple: All the surrounding area on top of the mountain will be most holy. Such is the law of the temple."

KEY VERSES

The glory of the LORD entered the temple through the gate facing east. Then the Spirit lifted me up and brought me into the inner court, and the glory of the LORD filled the temple. —**Ezekiel 43:4, 5**

Sustaining Hope

Unit 3: Visions of Grandeur

Lessons 9–13

Lesson Aims

After participating in this lesson, each learner will be able to:

1. Summarize what Ezekiel saw regarding the return of God's glory to the temple.

2. Explain how Ezekiel's description of God's glory filling the temple and of God's expectations applies to Christians as God's holy "temples" today.

3. Identify and "put away" (v. 9) one habit that doesn't belong in the temple of the New Testament era.

Lesson Outline

Introduction

Introduction

A. God Amidst the Rubble

On Sunday, May 22, 2011, an EF-5 tornado, the most severe kind, devastated nearly one-third of the city of Joplin, Missouri. "It was a searing scene straight from the book of Revelation," said one account of the damage.

Yet from the aftermath there emerged numerous testimonies of faith, hope, and love from the Christians there, from those firmly committed to the "kingdom that cannot be shaken" (Hebrews 12:28). God worked through their relief efforts. God was there.

The prophet Ezekiel also lived through a disaster, though it was not of the natural kind such as we classify the results of a tornado to be. The disaster he witnessed was the invasion of his homeland of Judah by the Babylonians under King Nebuchadnezzar, who ravaged the land and took thousands of its citizens (including Ezekiel himself) captive to Babylon. There on foreign soil, about a thousand miles from home, Ezekiel witnessed something else: dramatic visions conveying a message that God was still in control. His Word had lost none of its power. The captive people needed to hear and believe this. God was there.

B. Lesson Background: Ezekiel's Times

The Babylonians conducted a series of three deportations against Judah in the years 605, 597, and 586 BC (2 Kings 24:1–25:21). Daniel was taken captive in the first of these (Daniel 1:1-6), while Ezekiel the "priest, the son of Buzi" was taken captive in the second (Ezekiel 1:1-3).

Of interest is the mention of the "thirtieth year" in Ezekiel 1:1, which apparently is a reference to Ezekiel's age at the time he received God's call. This age is noteworthy, since it was the age at which Levites (the tribe from which all priests came) began their sacred service to the Lord (Numbers 4:46, 47), perhaps after first serving a five-year apprenticeship (8:24).

God had special plans for Ezekiel: this priest was destined to be a prophet of the Lord to the exiles in Babylon (Ezekiel 2:1–3:6, 10-15). Ezekiel's name means "God strengthens" or "God makes hard"—quite appropriate given the circumstances of his ministry (compare 3:7-9).

At the point in the book of Ezekiel where our lesson begins, that man had been serving as the Lord's prophet in Babylon to a people who had been in exile some 25 years. The date noted in Ezekiel 40:1 calculates to 573 BC.

A certain "man," introduced in 40:3, served as a kind of tour guide for Ezekiel throughout the visions of Ezekiel 40–48. The visions involved the prophet's being taken "to the land of Israel and set . . . on a very high mountain" (Ezekiel 40:2). It was there he saw the "man whose appearance was like bronze; he was standing in the gateway with a linen cord and a measuring rod in his hand" (v. 3).

This individual may well have been an angelic being of some kind. He commanded Ezekiel to watch carefully everything he was about to be shown, because the prophet was to declare all he saw to the house of Israel (Ezekiel 40:4). The experience shares certain parallels with what the apostle John was told in Revelation 1:3, 19.

C. Lesson Background: Foreshadowing

The four lessons from Ezekiel in this unit of study come from the final portion of that book, where the prophet received visions of a restored temple. A crucial question is how these chapters should be interpreted. Should this temple blueprint be viewed in terms of a literal, earthly fulfillment, or should it be taken as symbolic of something else?

HOW TO SAY IT

Athaliah	Ath-uh-*lye*-uh.
Baal	*Bay*-ul.
Babylon	*Bab*-uh-lun.
Babylonians	Bab-ih-*low*-nee-unz.
Euphrates	You-*fray*-teez.
Ezekiel	Ee-*zeek*-ee-ul or Ee-*zeek*-yul.
Judah	*Joo*-duh.
Kebar	*Kee*-bar.
Levites	*Lee*-vites.
messianic	mess-ee-*an*-ick.
Nebuchadnezzar	*Neb*-yuh-kud-***nez***-er.
Sinai	*Sigh*-nye or *Sigh*-nay-eye.

As elaborate and detailed as the blueprint of Ezekiel's temple is, it does not appear that the envisioned temple was ever considered as a pattern to be followed by those who returned from Babylonian captivity in 538 BC. Nothing of Ezekiel's temple vision is mentioned in any of the Bible books from the post-exilic period.

The position taken here is that the content of Ezekiel's temple visions is best interpreted in other than a literal "hewn stone" way. Many Old Testament practices and institutions (such as the sacrificial system and the high priesthood) involve the concept of *foreshadowing*. God's presence in Ezekiel's visionary temple can be understood as foreshadowing his presence in the temple of the new covenant—his church, made up of individuals ("living stones") who comprise a dwelling place for his Spirit (1 Peter 2:4, 5; compare 1 Corinthians 3:16, 17; 6:19, 20; Ephesians 2:19-22).

I. Seeing a Vision
(Ezekiel 43:1-5)
A. Movement of God's Glory (vv. 1-4)

1. Then the man brought me to the gate facing east,

The man is the one noted in the Lesson Background. For Ezekiel to be situated at *the gate [of the temple] facing east* is crucial. The reason for this is seen in the next verse.

2. . . . and I saw the glory of the God of Israel coming from the east. His voice was like the roar of rushing waters, and the land was radiant with his glory.

To this point, Ezekiel has been given the opportunity to view the layout of the new temple and to hear a description of its dimensions (Ezekiel 40–42). Now, however, his experience becomes more personal—and intensely so as he sees *the glory of the God of Israel coming from the east.*

For Ezekiel to see the glory of the Lord in this regard must be contrasted with what the prophet had witnessed earlier in Ezekiel 8–11. There he had been taken on a very disturbing tour of the current temple in Jerusalem to see some of the disgusting and offensive practices that the leaders of God's people were engaging in. Clearly, the

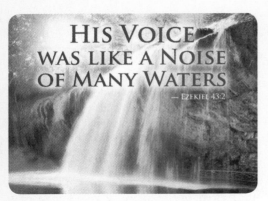

HIS VOICE WAS LIKE A NOISE OF MANY WATERS

— EZEKIEL 43:2

Visual for Lesson 9. *Start a discussion by pointing to this visual as you ask, "How is this verse like and unlike Psalm 19:1-4?"*

Lord could no longer reside amidst such unholy surroundings. In the climax of that earlier vision, Ezekiel saw the most disheartening scene imaginable: the glory of the Lord departing from the temple and moving eastward from it (Ezekiel 10:18, 19; 11:22, 23).

We can only imagine the prophet's thrill at seeing the glory return! The accompanying voice of the Lord *like the roar of rushing waters* is reminiscent of the prophet's first vision (Ezekiel 1:24; compare Revelation 1:15; 14:2; 19:6).

Also as a result of the Lord's return, *the land* shines with God's glory. The Hebrew word translated *land* can also be rendered as "earth" (as it is in Ezekiel 34:6; 35:14), so we are uncertain whether the scope of Ezekiel's vision is limited to the promised land as such or embraces the entire world. One can imagine the prophet being heartened in particular by his homeland's being restored, since it was in a state of spiritual and physical disarray the last time he saw it.

3. The vision I saw was like the vision I had seen when he came to destroy the city and like the visions I had seen by the Kebar River, and I fell facedown.

Ezekiel recalls his previous experiences in beholding the glory of the Lord, giving those experience in reverse order. The first vision preceded the Lord's call to that man to be his prophet in Ezekiel 2:1-8. That vision had occurred *by the Kebar River,* which is an irrigation canal of the Euphrates

River in Babylonian territory (1:3). A group of the captives from Judah, including Ezekiel, live somewhere in the vicinity of this canal (3:15).

The second vision of the Lord's glory was of its aforementioned departure from the temple. Ezekiel describes this as the time *when he came to destroy the city,* referring to Jerusalem's destruction by God's decision. Ezekiel's reaction of falling on his face is noted in connection with the earlier visions (Ezekiel 1:28; 3:23; 9:8; 11:13).

❧ *IMAGINING GOD'S GLORY* ❧

I think in words, meaning that I don't often get pictures in my mind. This is just normal for me. But never do I want to visualize scenes more than when I read Scripture passages that describe God and his glory. I have talented friends who not only visualize well, but express themselves through art and photography. Their works have brought me great joy.

A friend responded to my challenge to depict Genesis 1:2: "And the Spirit of God was hovering over the waters." Amazingly, a photograph he took of a river at first light captured a mass of sparkles glimmering above the water. Of course, I would not say that he captured an image of the Spirit of God. But he did capture a beautiful scene that inspired me to imagine God's glory.

God's glory is beyond human comprehension. We can sense Ezekiel's struggle in that regard as he falls facedown. When was the last time that an awareness of God's presence and blessing caused you to do likewise?   —V. E.

> *What Do You Think?*
>   Which aspect of creation best helps you imagine the glory of God in difficult times? in good times? Why?
> *Talking Points for Your Discussion*
> ▪ Very large things (the solar system, etc.)
> ▪ Things of intermediate size (trees, etc.)
> ▪ Very small things (molecular structures, etc.)

4. The glory of the LORD entered the temple through the gate facing east.

Ezekiel is careful to note again the entry of the Lord's glory into *the temple* through *the gate fac-*

ing east—the direction toward which the glory had earlier departed. Of all the directional words in the book of Ezekiel, *east* seems to be the most important, occurring more than 50 times. Its first use is in Ezekiel 8:16, where a couple of dozen men "with their backs toward the temple of the Lord and their faces toward the east" commit idolatry as they worship "the sun in the east." How appropriate, then, for the Lord's glory to return from that direction!

B. Movement of God's Prophet (v. 5)

5. Then the Spirit lifted me up and brought me into the inner court, and the glory of the LORD filled the temple.

The phrase *the Spirit* refers to the Holy Spirit. On previous occasions, Ezekiel uses the phrase *lifted me up* in describing the Spirit's influence on his ministry (see Ezekiel 3:12, 14; 8:3; 11:1, 24). Now the Spirit takes the prophet from the gate on the eastern side of the temple *into the inner court*, from which vantage point the prophet is able to see more clearly how *the glory of the Lord* fills *the temple*. The scene is reminiscent of how God's glory filled Solomon's temple at its dedication (1 Kings 8:10, 11).

II. Hearing a Message
(EZEKIEL 43:6-9)

A. Promise and Prediction (vv. 6, 7)

6. While the man was standing beside me, I heard someone speaking to me from inside the temple.

The vision takes a turn as Ezekiel hears a voice from somewhere *inside the temple*. Given the contents of the verses that follow, the speaker is clearly the Lord. *The man*, referring to Ezekiel's tour guide (see the Lesson Background), remains stationed beside the prophet.

7. He said: "Son of man, this is the place of my throne and the place for the soles of my feet. This is where I will live among the Israelites forever. The people of Israel will never again defile my holy name—neither they nor their kings—by their prostitution and the funeral offerings for their kings at their death.

The Lord addresses Ezekiel with the phrase *Son of man* dozens of times throughout this book. The phrase does not have messianic significance for Ezekiel as it does for Jesus; it simply highlights Ezekiel's humanness and, consequently, his need to depend on the Lord to carry out the prophetic ministry.

The Lord, who has entered this new temple, declares his intentions for the structure: it is to be *the place of my throne and the place for the soles of my feet*. The presence of the holy God demands holiness from those who claim to be his people, so *prostitution* is forbidden. Variations of the words *prostitution* and *adultery* are used often in this book figuratively to signify the worship of other gods—idolatry (see especially Ezekiel 16 and 23). This amounts to God's people breaking covenant with their "husband," the Lord (compare Jeremiah 31:32; Ezekiel 16:32). At the same time, literal prostitution is known to be part of the practices of those who worship fictitious gods such as Baal.

> *What Do You Think?*
> In what ways does spiritual adultery manifest itself today? How do we guard against this?
> *Talking Points for Your Discussion*
> - Matthew 12:39; 16:4
> - James 4:4
> - Other

The reference to *the funeral offerings for their kings at their death* (also v. 9, below) apparently describes the practice of burying kings near the temple. Their graves become some of the "high places" where idolatrous ceremonies are carried out (compare Psalm 78:58). Many kings of Judah are buried in Jerusalem, perhaps near the temple area. This is near enough that the Lord expresses that his holiness must no longer be compromised by such corrupting influences.

B. Defilement and Destruction (v. 8)

8. "When they placed their threshold next to my threshold and their doorposts beside my doorposts, with only a wall between me and them, they defiled my holy name by their

detestable practices. So I destroyed them in my anger.

Their threshold . . . and their doorposts most likely refer to those of the royal palace. The proximity of the royal palace to the temple is reflected in the account of the overthrow of Athaliah, the wicked queen of Judah, in 2 Kings 11. Verses 13-16 there imply that the distance between the two buildings is not great. Ezekiel notes that only a wall separates the two.

Such closeness blurs the distinction between what is holy and what is not. This seems to make it easier to accept idolatrous practices that amount to abominations that defile God's holy name. God will not tolerate this, and he has judged the people (*destroyed them*) in that light.

What Do You Think?
In what areas of life have you seen Christians put that which is secular too close to (or in place of) the sacred? What guardrails can we erect to prevent this?
Talking Points for Your Discussion
▪ Regarding entertainment choices
▪ Regarding secular spirituality
▪ Regarding attitudes toward money
▪ Other

C. Practice and Presence (v. 9)

9. "Now let them put away from me their prostitution and the funeral offerings for their kings, and I will live among them forever."

God reiterates his requirements. His holy presence in the new temple requires a holy people. Practices that result in his judgment must be *put away*.

III. Conveying a Message
(Ezekiel 43:10-12)
A. Confronting Sins (v. 10)

10. "Son of man, describe the temple to the people of Israel, that they may be ashamed of their sins. Let them consider its perfection,

We may wonder how Ezekiel's showing the blueprint for *the temple to the people of Israel* and

having them *consider its perfection* will have the effect of their being *ashamed of their sins*. Perhaps the description is to impress on the people what they lost through the destruction of Solomon's temple some 13 years earlier, in 586 BC. They must acknowledge that they have no one to blame but themselves for that disaster. Or perhaps they will realize how unworthy they are to be in the Lord's presence as they see the temple's majestic design.

What Do You Think?
What role should being ashamed of sin play in Christian messages today? Why?
Talking Points for Your Discussion
▪ Regarding evangelistic messages to unbelievers
▪ Regarding discipling messages to believers
▪ Other

B. Conforming to a Plan (v. 11)

11. ". . . and if they are ashamed of all they have done, make known to them the design of the temple—its arrangement, its exits and entrances—its whole design and all its regulations and laws. Write these down before them so that they may be faithful to its design and follow all its regulations.

If the people respond to seeing the temple plan by being *ashamed of all they have done*, then Ezekiel is to go into much greater detail about the temple and various facets of its operation. The prophet is to write all of this information *before them* so that they will be accountable for following the pattern and regulations faithfully.

Do the people exhibit the shame necessary for Ezekiel to convey the design as he is told? There is no record that this happens, yet the plan is recorded in his book.

It may be helpful here to consider the symbolic interpretation of Ezekiel's temple vision that is suggested in Lesson Background: Foreshadowing. Ezekiel earlier uttered prophecies of foreshadowed blessings associated with the new covenant in Christ (Ezekiel 34:23, 24; 36:26, 27; 37:24-28). In the last of these passages, the prophet declares God's promise to "put my sanctuary among them forever" (37:26). God also promises the presence of his Holy Spirit "in you" (36:27; the *you* is plural).

That kind of intimacy may be the point of Ezekiel's description here: those who are ashamed of their sins will enjoy a close relationship with God as he himself dwells within them and they then become his temple. Such language is very much a part of the New Testament (1 Corinthians 3:16, 17; 6:19, 20; Ephesians 2:19-22; 1 Peter 2:4, 5).

C. Closing Statement (v. 12)

12. "This is the law of the temple: All the surrounding area on top of the mountain will be most holy. Such is the law of the temple."

This regulation contrasts with the people's failure to respect sacred territory as noted in verse 8, above. All the area around the temple is to be considered *most holy*. This is reminiscent of the holiness associated with Mount Sinai (Exodus 19:12, 13).

From a new-covenant perspective, this verse conveys how passionate God is for the holiness of his house or temple—the church. All of life is to be lived in a holy manner for God's glory (1 Corinthians 10:31).

What Do You Think?

What connections do you see between the law of Ezekiel's idealized temple and that of the temple of the New Testament era?

Talking Points for Your Discussion

* 1 Corinthians 3:17; 6:19
* Ephesians 2:21
* Hebrews 12:14
* 1 Peter 1:15, 16; 2:5
* 1 John 3:24
* Other

❧ *REDECORATING* ❧

My daughter loves the abundance of home decorating programs on television. OK, I think they're fun too. There's just something about taking a space that's dated or cluttered and making it fresh again. What is amazing to me is that it's not always the new things you bring in that make a difference as much as the old things you "retire." This reminds me of a thought of A. W. Tozer:

To God, our thoughts are things. Our thoughts are the decorations inside the sanctuary where we live. . . . If you would cultivate the Spirit's acquaintance, you must get hold of your thoughts and not allow your mind to be a wilderness in which every kind of unclean beast roams and bird flies. You must have a clean heart.

The Old Testament temple regulations were designed to keep the temple holy. Sin defiled the Old Testament temple, angered God, and brought forth his wrath. Sin defiles us today and grieves the Holy Spirit, who lives within us. What "redecorating" do you need to do to keep the temple holy?   —V. E.

Conclusion

A. Under Construction

When encountering road construction while driving, most of us become at least a little frustrated with the waiting that results. But we eventually come to an "End Construction" sign. I often think that that is exactly what I would like to have happen in my life: end construction —permanently!

Being "under construction" provides a helpful way to think about the Christian life: we are always "works in progress." Whether we have been Christians for 60 days or 60 years, there is always room to grow. We may not be guilty of the specific practices cited by Ezekiel, but we can be guilty of spiritual adultery nonetheless. Consider James 4:4: "You adulterous people, don't you know that friendship with the world means enmity against God?"

God's presence filled both Solomon's temple and Ezekiel's visionary temple. Is he welcome in ours?

B. Prayer

Holy God, let us never forget that we are your temple. May we welcome your Spirit to live within us as an honored guest. In Jesus' name; amen.

C. Thought to Remember

God's glory is in a temple,
and Christians are that temple.

INVOLVEMENT LEARNING

Enhance your lesson with NIV® Bible Student *(from your curriculum supplier) and the reproducible activity page (at www.standardlesson.com or in the back of the* NIV® Standard Lesson Commentary Deluxe Edition*).*

Into the Lesson

As learners arrive, give each an index card. Say, "Describe on your card the most incredible thing you have ever witnessed, either in a dream or in real life. It can be something either positive or negative. Do not be specific in identifying the circumstances and context."

After two minutes, have learners swap cards and see whether the partner can guess whether the description is from a dream or real life. After a minute, ask, "How easy was it to guess the event as belonging to a dream or to real life? Why?" Then say, "If you had difficulty in deciding, you're in good company, as Peter experienced the same difficulty in Acts 12:9! Today's lesson is about a visionary experience of the prophet Ezekiel that should find realization in our lives."

Into the Word

Before learners arrive, have the following headings and accompanying Scripture references written on the board: *Context* (Ezekiel 40:1-4) / *Seeing a Vision* (Ezekiel 43:1-5) / *Hearing a Message* (Ezekiel 43:6-9) / *Conveying a Message* (Ezekiel 43:10-12). Divide the class into four groups and assign each a heading and accompanying reference. Ask groups to identify positive and negative elements from their assigned texts.

After groups finish, summarize for the class the information in the two Lesson Backgrounds. Then allow a time of whole-class sharing of the information the groups gleaned; jot responses on the board for use in the Into Life segment.

Expect responses to include the following: *Context group*—positive elements of God's revelation and Ezekiel's privilege; negative elements of captivity and smitten city. *Seeing group*—positive elements of God' glory and Ezekiel's privilege; negative element of a destroyed city. *Hearing group*—positive elements of God's promise to "live among" and emphasis on his "holy name"; negative elements of past sin and unholiness. *Conveying group*—positive elements of law, regulations, and holiness; negative elements of shame and sin.

Discuss the possibility that today's passage is a foreshadowing of life under the new covenant, where no inanimate, physical temple is needed. *Option:* Ask four learners in advance to come prepared to debate this proposition: *The fulfillment of Ezekiel's vision of a new temple is intended to happen in a spiritual way.* One team of two learners will affirm the proposition, while the other team of two learners will deny it. Obviously, the four learners you select should be some of your biblically "sharper" ones. Research the Internet to discover various formats such a debate can take.

Into Life

Assign the following passages to four groups, one passage each: 1 Corinthians 3:16, 17; 1 Corinthians 6:19, 20; Ephesians 2:19-22; 1 Peter 2:4, 5. Say, "Let's spend some time considering the significance of 'temple' and 'spiritual house' for the new-covenant era. Your task is to examine the list of positive and negative elements from today's text that we jotted on the board, to determine which can be connected in some way with your assigned passage. See if you can find other Scripture passages that are relevant to this topic." *Option:* Distribute Bible handbooks and concordances for use as research tools.

Call for conclusions after a few minutes; someone may have discovered 2 Corinthians 6:16 to be relevant, so be prepared to discuss that reference as well. Discuss ways to make both the individual "temple" of one's self and the collective "temple" of the church more holy in the coming week. *Option:* As a lead-in to that discussion, distribute copies of "Temple Building: A Choral Reading" from the reproducible page, which you can download. Assign the various parts and perform as indicated.

THE ALTAR
OFFERS HOPE

DEVOTIONAL READING: Psalms 130, 131
BACKGROUND SCRIPTURE: Ezekiel 43:10–46:24

EZEKIEL 43:13-21

13 "These are the measurements of the altar in long cubits, that cubit being a cubit and a handbreadth: Its gutter is a cubit deep and a cubit wide, with a rim of one span around the edge. And this is the height of the altar: 14 From the gutter on the ground up to the lower ledge that goes around the altar it is two cubits high, and the ledge is a cubit wide. From this lower ledge to the upper ledge that goes around the altar it is four cubits high, and that ledge is also a cubit wide. 15 Above that, the altar hearth is four cubits high, and four horns project upward from the hearth. 16 The altar hearth is square, twelve cubits long and twelve cubits wide. 17 The upper ledge also is square, fourteen cubits long and fourteen cubits wide. All around the altar is a gutter of one cubit with a rim of half a cubit. The steps of the altar face east."

18 Then he said to me, "Son of man, this is what the Sovereign LORD says: These will be the regulations for sacrificing burnt offerings and splashing blood against the altar when it is built:

19 You are to give a young bull as a sin offering to the Levitical priests of the family of Zadok, who come near to minister before me, declares the Sovereign LORD. 20 You are to take some of its blood and put it on the four horns of the altar and on the four corners of the upper ledge and all around the rim, and so purify the altar and make atonement for it. 21 You are to take the bull for the sin offering and burn it in the designated part of the temple area outside the sanctuary."

KEY VERSE

At the end of these days, from the eighth day on, the priests are to present your burnt offerings and fellowship offerings on the altar. Then I will accept you, declares the Sovereign LORD. —**Ezekiel 43:27**

SUSTAINING HOPE

Unit 3: Visions of Grandeur
LESSONS 9–13

LESSON AIMS

After participating in this lesson, each learner will be able to:

1. Tell how the altar in Ezekiel's temple vision was to be prepared and purified for use in worship.

2. Explain why the altar—and a sanctified altar—was so important for the people to be acceptable to God.

3. Give thanks for the once-for-all sacrifice of Jesus, which makes us acceptable to God.

LESSON OUTLINE

Introduction
A. What's Behind the Door?

The TV game show *Let's Make a Deal* offers contestants the opportunity to trade something they have or a particular item they've won for something else that is hidden perhaps behind a door or under a box. The contestant has to decide whether or not to "make a deal" for the hidden item.

The deal often proves to be a good one because that which is behind the door or under the box is quite valuable. But at other times the prize is a "zonk," the deal clearly a bad one. The word picture of *a door* is often used to describe an opportunity to serve the Lord in a particular place. The Bible uses that picture in 1 Corinthians 16:8, 9; 2 Corinthians 2:12; Colossians 4:3; and Revelation 3:8. When a door opens, however, sometimes there is something behind it that we do not anticipate.

Imagine Ezekiel, nearing his thirtieth birthday (Ezekiel 1:1), eagerly anticipating the opportunity to carry on the noble family tradition by serving as a priest in the temple (see Numbers 4:46, 47). Then picture his plans shattered as mighty Babylon enforces her will on Judah. Ezekiel finds himself shoved through an open door to end up in a pagan land. The door he preferred, the one that led to service in the temple, was slammed shut.

Yet God had plans for his would-be priest. Ezekiel may have been separated from the temple of the Lord in Jerusalem, but he was not separated from the Lord himself. As described in Ezekiel 1, God came to him in pagan territory in an awe-inspiring vision to call him to be a prophet to his captive people. And when the magnificent temple vision that we are currently studying was granted to Ezekiel, he saw himself fulfilling a priestly role in that temple in a way he never could have imagined. God closed one door on Ezekiel, but he opened another—taking Ezekiel's ministry in a magnificently unexpected direction.

B. Lesson Background

Today's lesson text picks up where last week's ended. Therefore the background is the same, and that information need not be repeated here. But since today's text introduces the new element of a restored altar of sacrifice, some observations on its predecessors are in order.

A vital part of the Old Testament system of worship was the altar. Altars are mentioned in connection with Noah (Genesis 8:20), Abraham (12:7, 8; etc.), and Jacob (35:1-7). After the Israelites emerged as a nation from Egypt, God prescribed exact specifications for an altar of burnt offerings (Exodus 27:1-8; not to be confused with the altar for burning incense in 30:1-10; 39:38). The portable altar of burnt offerings was superseded by the temple's altar, which was more than 50 times larger by volume (2 Chronicles 4:1).

Over the centuries that followed, the temple's altar underwent episodes of desecration, rededication, removal, and repair until the destruction of Jerusalem in 586 BC. The altar was rebuilt as a first priority after return from exile in 538 BC (Ezra 3:1-3). But the account of that reconstruction does not claim to fulfill Ezekiel's vision of a new altar, received in 573 BC (Ezekiel 40:1). Fulfillment was to come later (today's lesson).

I. Features of the Altar
(Ezekiel 43:13-17)
A. Height and Horns (vv. 13-15)

13a. "These are the measurements of the altar in long cubits, that cubit being a cubit and a handbreadth:

As today's text opens, Ezekiel is receiving instructions from the Lord himself, since he is the most recent speaker mentioned (see Ezekiel 43:7). The altar in the temple of Ezekiel's vision was mentioned in passing in Ezekiel 40:47 as being "in front of the temple." Now come the details.

The measurements of the altar will be described in the verses to follow in terms of *long cubits*. A regular cubit is the distance between the elbow and the tip of one's middle finger; this is about 18 inches in biblical times. The regular cubit becomes a long cubit when adding *a handbreadth*. The measure of a handbreadth is about 3 inches. So a regular cubit of 18 inches plus a handbreadth of 3 inches totals the 21 inches of the long cubit.

13b. "Its gutter is a cubit deep and a cubit wide, with a rim of one span around the edge.

The specifications start at the *gutter*, or base, of the altar. The phrase *its gutter is a cubit deep* refers to height; therefore the base is to be about 21 inches tall.

At first glance, the phrase *a cubit wide* seems to indicate a width of 21 inches as well. But investigation of verses 13-17 indicates that the base actually is to measure 18 cubits (about 31 feet, 6 inches) by 18 cubits, or 18 cubits square. The single cubit under consideration in the verse before us refers instead to the area of the base that is not covered by the section above it.

The idea seems to be that this one-cubit perimeter will serve as a receptacle for the blood of sacrificial animals. This idea is supported by the phrase *with a rim of one span around the edge.* A span is the width of a spread-out hand from the tip of the thumb to the tip of the little finger, about 9 inches. The rim of this size is probably an upward projecting lip that is around the base to provide added protection against any blood spilling out from the altar.

> **What Do You Think?**
> What lessons should we draw and not draw from God's precise requirements for the building of the altar? Why?
> *Talking Points for Your Discussion*
> ▪ Regarding the nature of God himself
> ▪ Distinguishing *detailed blueprint* from *artist's conception* in implementing New Testament imperatives
> ▪ Other

13c, 14a. "And this is the height of the altar: From the gutter on the ground up to the lower ledge that goes around the altar it is two cubits high, and the ledge is a cubit wide.

The verse divisions at this point are not the best since the last line of verse 13 really goes with verse 14, which introduces the remaining parts of the description as that description moves upward. Having just specified one measurement for *the gutter* (base) of the altar, the Lord proceeds to describe the section immediately above it.

That next section above the base is called *the lower ledge*. Its height of *two cubits* calculates to about 3 feet, 6 inches. (*Up to the lower ledge* means to the top of that ledge.) As above, *a cubit wide* refers to the perimeter of this section that is not covered by the next section upward. The overall horizontal dimensions of this section seem to be 16 cubits (about 28 feet) by 16 cubits, or 16 cubits square, as context indicates.

14b. "From this lower ledge to the upper ledge that goes around the altar it is four cubits high, and that ledge is also a cubit wide.

The upper ledge is the next section upward. Its height of *four cubits* calculates to about 7 feet. (*To the upper ledge* means to its top.) The meaning of *a cubit wide* for the upper ledge is the same as for the lower ledge.

15a. "Above that, the altar hearth is four cubits high,

The altar hearth is the topmost part of the structure; this is where offerings are to be made to the Lord. When adding its height of about 7 feet to the other parts, the overall height of the structure is 11 long cubits, or about 19 feet, 3 inches. This makes it more than 4 feet taller than the altar of Solomon's temple, and nearly 15 feet taller than the altar for the tabernacle described in Exodus 27:1-8 (see the Lesson Background). The height of the new altar is all the more striking given the fact that Ezekiel's vision rarely addresses the height of anything!

15b. ". . . and four horns project upward from the hearth.

The top of the altar also features *four horns*. These upward projections will be at the corners if the altar of the tabernacle is a precedent in this regard (see Exodus 27:2; 38:2). These horns will make the altar even higher than the 19 feet, 3 inches noted above. But dimensions of the horns are not given, so we do not include the horns in the height calculation. The horns of previous altars seem to have provided temporary refuge to those who came and lay hold of them after committing an act considered punishable by death (Exodus 21:12-14; 1 Kings 1:50, 51; 2:28-34).

B. Area and Stairs (vv. 16, 17)

16. "The altar hearth is square, twelve cubits long and twelve cubits wide.

Additional details about *the altar hearth* are now revealed. Still using the long cubit measurement of 21 inches, this topmost part is 21 feet square. The area of the top is thus calculated to be 441 square feet.

17. "The upper ledge also is square, fourteen cubits long and fourteen cubits wide. All around the altar is a gutter of one cubit with a rim of half a cubit. The steps of the altar face east."

Verse 14 noted that the altar as a whole has two parts called *ledges*—a lower ledge and an upper ledge. Like the lower ledge just below it, the size of the upper ledge allows a cubit to be exposed on all sides; this exposed area is referred to here as *a gutter*. We may think of this as a trough to catch spills, particularly since it features a *rim* (a lip or upturned edge).

Since the altar is 11 long cubits (or 19 feet, 3 inches) high, steps will be an obvious necessity for any priest officiating there and offering a sacrifice. Earlier regulations prohibited steps from being attached to an altar in order to prevent indecent exposure (Exodus 20:24-26). This issue was addressed later by requiring priests to wear certain undergarments (Exodus 28:42, 43; Leviticus 6:10; compare Ezekiel 44:18).

The requirement that *the steps of the altar face east* may connect with a problem encountered by Ezekiel earlier when he saw men "with their backs toward the temple of the Lord and their faces toward the east," who were "bowing down to the sun in the east" (Ezekiel 8:16). Placing steps on the east side results in priests facing west as they ascend to offer sacrifices to the Lord—a symbolic turnaround.

HOW TO SAY IT

Babylon	*Bab*-uh-lun.
Ezekiel	Ee-*zeek*-ee-ul or Ee-*zeek*-yul.
Judah	*Joo*-duh.
Levites	*Lee*-vites.
Sinai	*Sigh*-nye or *Sigh*-nay-eye.
Zadok	*Zay*-dok.

The length and width of the next two sections downward (the lower ledge and the base) are not provided. But the given length and width dimensions of verses 16, 17 and the given sizes of the exposed perimeters of verses 13, 14, 17 let us see the pattern: the lower ledge is 16 cubits by 16 cubits (see v. 14a), and the base is 18 cubits by 18 cubits. Thus an overhead view would give the appearance of 4 concentric squares, with a footprint of about 992 square feet.

❧ *Precision Matters!* ❧

If you have ever fought through the icy winds of a blizzard, you may have wondered why God positioned the sun so far away. If you have ever suffered through an extended heat wave, you may have wondered why God placed the sun so close. Earth's average distance from the sun is a little over 92,955,800 miles; when combined with the effects of our planet's 23.4° axial tilt, that is the right distance to keep everything within the proper temperature range. Our atmosphere remains in place because the correct level of power of the Earth's magnetic field prevents cosmic radiation from stripping it away.

These and other factors allow us to thrive. We may find ourselves uncomfortable from time to time, but God has designed a home for us that meets our needs. We have only to compare Earth's conditions with those of Venus, Mars, etc., to be convinced that *precision matters*.

As we work through our lesson for today, the details that God prescribed for the altar may seem tedious. But these details remind us that God is ever orderly and never capricious. Can we say the

same thing about our prayer life? our giving pattern? our worship attendance? Think it over—when you have between 1.000 and 2.000 minutes to do so.
—V. E.

II. Dedication of the Altar
(EZEKIEL 43:18-21)
A. Animal Chosen (vv. 18, 19)

18. Then he said to me, "Son of man, this is what the Sovereign LORD says: These will be the regulations for sacrificing burnt offerings and splashing blood against the altar when it is built:

Having been told the measurements of the altar, Ezekiel is now given *the regulations* concerning the dedication of the altar to the Lord's service. Regarding the phrase *Son of man,* see comments on Ezekiel 43:7 from last week's lesson.

19. "You are to give a young bull as a sin offering to the Levitical priests of the family of Zadok, who come near to minister before me, declares the Sovereign LORD.

It is noteworthy that each of the next three verses begins with a *you are to* command to Ezekiel. This means that the prophet himself is to take part in the consecration ceremony. What a thrilling moment for one whose priestly aspirations had seemingly been quashed by the Babylonian dominance of Judah! Ezekiel is depicted as having the privilege to fulfill priestly duties in another, far more magnificent setting.

Ezekiel's envisioned participation in this ceremony reminds us of what happened when God established his covenant with Israel at Mount Sinai after the exodus from Egypt. At that time, Moses was commanded to carry out a similar ceremony in consecrating the altar of the tabernacle (Exodus 29:36, 37; Leviticus 8:14-17). Ezekiel's action may be seen as foreshadowing the new covenant established by Jesus, which is in keeping with the interpretation of these chapters proposed in the previous lesson.

What Do You Think?

Considering how the ancient Jews were to make special preparations for the altar, what preparations should we make before offering our "sacrifice of praise" to God (Hebrews 13:15)?

Talking Points for Your Discussion
- Mental preparations
- Spiritual preparations
- Physical preparations

Related to this interpretation is the question of whether Ezekiel ever participates in an actual dedication of an altar when the exiles return to the promised land from Babylon in 538 BC. We have no record of Ezekiel's making the trip. If he is 30 years old in 597 BC (see lesson 9), then he would be almost 90 when the first group of captives return. What is described in this passage, then, is not a prophecy that Ezekiel ever sees fulfilled in his lifetime, but is, as Christopher Wright suggests, "a visionary 'compensation' to the prophet himself for the fact that he had never been able to serve as a priest in the Jerusalem temple before its destruction."

Ezekiel will not be alone in this task, but is to be assisted by *the Levitical priests of the family of Zadok.* Zadok, long dead by Ezekiel's day, was a Levite whose lineage is traced to Aaron, Israel's first high priest, through Aaron's son Eleazar (1 Chronicles 6:50-53). Zadok served as a priest under David (2 Samuel 8:17), and he supported Solomon as the successor to David (1 Kings 1:38-45).

Of most importance for the present study, Zadok became the first high priest in Solomon's temple (1 Kings 2:35). The fact that the descendants (*family*) of Zadok are included in this dedication ceremony thus provides an important link with the dedication of Solomon's temple, where Zadok served.

A young bull as a sin offering is the required offering according to the Law of Moses (Leviticus 4:3). The purpose of the offering is stated in the next verse.

❧ GOD OFFERS HOPE ❧

In early 2011, the British government issued a report stating that "scientists believe recent natural disasters were not an aberration, but the beginnings of a new kind of future in which mega-disasters are going to be more frequent." The envisioned disasters are predicted to create humanitarian crises on a scale heretofore unseen. Increasing urbanization and climate change will be contributing factors.

Some Christians have expressed their expectation of divinely ordained catastrophes as they take note of the sobering trends in hate crimes, child abuse, human trafficking, abortion, etc. We rejoice in the fact that God "is patient with you, not wanting anyone to perish, but everyone to come to repentance" (2 Peter 3:9). Yet we wonder how long God will stand by patiently while morality spirals downward.

The events of Ezekiel's day were indeed catastrophic, as ordained by God. His patience had reached its end. But despite all outward appearances, God was not finished with his people; he had a plan for their renewal. Despite how things look on the news reports and in our personal situations, God is not finished with us either. His plan for our renewal—even the renewal of all creation—is already underway through the work of his Son, Jesus. He is the one who has opened a door of reconciliation, a door that is open as long as we are breathing.   —V. E.

B. Blood Sprinkled (v. 20)

20. "You are to take some of its blood and put it on the four horns of the altar and on the four corners of the upper ledge and all around the rim, and so purify the altar and make atonement for it.

The blood from the bull is to be placed on specifically designated portions *of the altar* to *purify* and *make atonement for it.* This reflects the earlier altar dedication of Leviticus 8:15.

C. Carcass Burned (v. 21)

21. "You are to take the bull for the sin offering and burn it in the designated part of the temple area outside the sanctuary."

The handling of *the sin offering* we see here is in accordance with the Law of Moses (see Exodus 29:14; compare Leviticus 4:21; 8:14-17; 9:10, 11; 16:27). The last six verses of Ezekiel 43, which are not in today's lesson text, describe the rest of the dedication ceremony.

Conclusion

A. Their Hope

While the details we have read today may seem rather tedious and mundane, they were very hopeful and heartening to Ezekiel and the people of God who received this message originally. The destruction of the temple and the sacred area where sacrifices could be offered to the Lord had been emotionally devastating. Add to this the sad state of the people exiled far from the promised land, and we see a picture of near hopelessness.

Hope blossomed anew as Ezekiel saw the vision of a restored temple with restored worship of the Lord. Ezekiel's audience could understand that their captivity was not "a period" in the plan of God, marking an end; it was rather "a comma," just a pause. God had other, greater plans for his people. He certainly was not finished with them.

B. Our Hope

Hebrews 13:10 states, "We have an altar from which those who minister at the tabernacle have no right to eat." That writer wants to impress upon his readers the superiority of life in Christ.

But what is this altar of which the author of Hebrews speaks? If we think of an altar's primary purpose as sacrifice, then perhaps the altar in Hebrews is the cross, where Jesus sacrificed his life as the ultimate sin offering. As Hebrews 13:11, 12 goes on to say, "The high priest carries the blood of animals into the Most Holy Place as a sin offering, but the bodies are burned outside the camp. And so Jesus also suffered outside the city gate to make the people holy through his own blood."

If Ezekiel's vision of an altar brought hope to him and to God's people, how much more does the altar of the book of Hebrews bring hope—the hope of sins forgiven, the hope of new beginnings, the hope of eternal life!

C. Prayer

Father, we thank you for not leaving us to perish in our sin and despair. You have provided in the sacrifice of your Son the way by which sin can be atoned for permanently. May we never forget that the perfect, once-for-all, fully sufficient sacrifice of Jesus at the cross is what allows eternal life in your presence. In Jesus' name we pray; amen.

D. Thought to Remember

The cross of Christ
is the altar and anchor of our hope.

Visual for Lesson 10. *Start a discussion by pointing to this visual as you ask, "How does the cross of Christ make us acceptable to God?"*

INVOLVEMENT LEARNING

Enhance your lesson with NIV® Bible Student (from your curriculum supplier) and the reproducible activity page (at www.standardlesson.com or in the back of the NIV® Standard Lesson Commentary Deluxe Edition).

Into the Lesson

Begin by asking learners to share times when their plans had to change, for better or for worse. After three or four responses, say, "We talked last week about Ezekiel's priestly lineage. For many years, he probably had been looking forward to serving as a priest for Israel. But any plans he had in that regard were dashed when the Babylonians invaded Judah and took him captive. In today's lesson we see further how God's plans for that man changed, as we examine a specific part of the temple vision God gave him while in exile."

Into the Word

Prepare in advance 13 sentence strips with the following phrases, 1 per strip: (1) long-cubit measure: 1 cubit + 1 handbreadth = 21" (v. 13a); (2) the gutter of the altar: 1 cubit [high] (v. 13b); (3) rim: 1 span (v. 13b); (4) from gutter to lower ledge: 2 cubits (v. 14a); (5) from lower ledge to the upper ledge: 4 cubits (v. 14b); (6) the altar hearth: 4 cubits (v. 15a); (7) top of altar: 4 horns (v. 15b); (8) altar hearth: 12 cubits long by 12 cubits wide (v. 16); (9) the upper ledge: 14 cubits long by 14 cubits wide (v. 17a); (10) rim of upper ledge: ½ cubit (v. 17b); (11) gutter: a cubit about (v. 17c); (12) stairs: on the east side (v. 17d); (13) instructions for the dedication: young bull for an offering, priests descended from Zadok, etc.

Cut each strip in two after the colon. Affix the first parts of the 13 strips to the board; spread out the remaining parts randomly on a table. Say, "One of the most important items in the Old Testament system of worship was the altar of burnt offerings. Let's see what God had in mind for a new altar."

Have learners take turns reading aloud the nine verses of the lesson text. Then have everyone gather around the table where you have the strips spread out; ask learners to match them to the ones on the board. (This can be a whole-group exercise for smaller classes; larger classes can divide the work among small groups.) Check matches for accuracy.

Conclude by saying, "You may be thinking at this point that our matching activity was rather tedious. We keep in mind, however, that we serve a God who is very specific when it comes to issues of holiness. The altar was to be sacred, and it was imperative that it be respected as such."

Option. Before beginning this segment of study, distribute copies of the "Ezekiel's Altar" exercise from the reproducible page, which you can download. This can serve as a visual aid as learners work through the details of the lesson.

Into Life

Say, "Today we've looked at the detail for the dimensions of the new altar and instructions for purifying it. If Ezekiel's vision was a foreshadowing of the messianic era of Jesus, then we should spend some time connecting the dots between Ezekiel 43:19-21 and the New Testament."

Assign learners the following passages: (1a) Colossians 1:19, 20; (1b) Hebrews 9:12-14; (2a) Hebrews 5:4-6; (2b) Hebrews 7:11-17; (3a) Hebrews 9:27, 28; (3b) Hebrews 10:11-13. Ask for 1a to be read aloud, immediately followed by 1b; pause to ask for connections with Ezekiel 43:19-21 (expected response: v. 20 notes the need for blood). Do the same for 2a and 2b (expected response: v. 19 notes that priests had to be of a certain lineage), then for 3a and 3b (expected response: v. 21 notes that the offering was for sin).

Option 1. To consider further the implications of Jesus as our high priest, distribute copies of the "Our Great High Priest" activity from the reproducible page. This can be a whole-class exercise as you move down through the letters.

Option 2. Distribute copies of the "New Testament Priestly Duties" activity from the reproducible page. You can use this either for whole-class brainstorming or as a take-home exercise.

WATER FROM THE
SANCTUARY GIVES LIFE

DEVOTIONAL READING: Psalm 1
BACKGROUND SCRIPTURE: Ezekiel 47:1-12

EZEKIEL 47:1-12

[1] The man brought me back to the entrance to the temple, and I saw water coming out from under the threshold of the temple toward the east (for the temple faced east). The water was coming down from under the south side of the temple, south of the altar. [2] He then brought me out through the north gate and led me around the outside to the outer gate facing east, and the water was trickling from the south side.

[3] As the man went eastward with a measuring line in his hand, he measured off a thousand cubits and then led me through water that was ankle-deep. [4] He measured off another thousand cubits and led me through water that was knee-deep. He measured off another thousand and led me through water that was up to the waist. [5] He measured off another thousand, but now it was a river that I could not cross, because the water had risen and was deep enough to swim in—a river that no one could cross. [6] He asked me, "Son of man, do you see this?"

Then he led me back to the bank of the river. [7] When I arrived there, I saw a great number of trees on each side of the river. [8] He said to me, "This water flows toward the eastern region and goes down into the Arabah, where it enters the Dead Sea. When it empties into the sea, the salty water there becomes fresh. [9] Swarms of living creatures will live wherever the river flows. There will be large numbers of fish, because this water flows there and makes the salt water fresh; so where the river flows everything will live. [10] Fishermen will stand along the shore; from En Gedi to En Eglaim there will be places for spreading nets. The fish will be of many kinds—like the fish of the Mediterranean Sea. [11] But the swamps and marshes will not become fresh; they will be left for salt. [12] Fruit trees of all kinds will grow on both banks of the river. Their leaves will not wither, nor will their fruit fail. Every month they will bear fruit, because the water from the sanctuary flows to them. Their fruit will serve for food and their leaves for healing."

KEY VERSE

Swarms of living creatures will live wherever the river flows. There will be large numbers of fish, because this water flows there and makes the salt water fresh; so where the river flows everything will live.

—**Ezekiel 47:9**

SUSTAINING HOPE

Unit 3: Visions of Grandeur
LESSONS 9–13

LESSON AIMS

After participating in this lesson, each learner will be able to:

1. List characteristics of the river flowing from the temple.

2. Explain how the word pictures of river and water become used as a way of describing new covenant blessings in Christ.

3. Write one meditation daily in the week ahead that reflects on the nature of the living water available in Christ.

LESSON OUTLINE

Introduction

A. Water

Some years ago, the church building where I worship experienced water damage. A leak occurred in the baptistery, which was located behind the stage in the sanctuary and directly above the kitchen in the fellowship hall below. By the time anyone noticed what was happening, water had poured through the ceiling panels in the kitchen and had spread out into the fellowship hall. What a mess!

As part of his temple vision, the prophet Ezekiel saw water flowing from under the threshold of the temple. This water, however, did not do any damage—quite the opposite! This water became the source of life and productivity in the places where it flowed. The imagery of life-giving water is frequent in the Bible.

Water is necessary to all life on this planet, of course. That is one reason the Bible uses it so often to portray spiritual life and abundance. Jesus spoke this way of the Holy Spirit, who was to come following Jesus' ascension into Heaven (John 7:37-39). Unlike some figurative language in Scripture, this one is not at all difficult to grasp.

B. Lesson Background

Today's lesson text takes us into another part of the prophet Ezekiel's temple vision. Beginning with chapter 40 and extending through chapter 48, the end of the book, Ezekiel presents the future in the context of worship from the glorious, perfect temple of God. This description of the new temple constitutes about 20 percent of the entire book of Ezekiel. Therefore, understanding the meaning and significance of the vision is crucial if we are to appreciate this great book fully.

Between Ezekiel 43:21 (where last week's lesson ended) and 47:1 (where this week's begins), Ezekiel received details concerning (1) the officials to serve in the temple, (2) allotment of land, and (3) instructions regarding offering procedures for the Passover and other special days. As chapter 47 opens, we see Ezekiel having been brought back to the entrance of the idealized temple.

I. Rising Water
(Ezekiel 47:1-7)
A. Initial Flow (vv. 1, 2)

1. The man brought me back to the entrance to the temple, and I saw water coming out from under the threshold of the temple toward the east (for the temple faced east). The water was coming down from under the south side of the temple, south of the altar.

The man likely refers to Ezekiel's companion (perhaps an angel) who has been guiding the prophet's visionary temple-tour from the beginning (Ezekiel 40:3). Previously, the man had taken Ezekiel to the temple's "portico" (40:48, 49) and "entrance" (41:1, 2). Now they are back again at *the entrance to the temple*.

On arrival, Ezekiel witnesses a bizarre sight: *water coming out from under the threshold of the temple toward the east.* We think of a threshold as the small gap between the bottom of a closed door and the floor. For some reason, the flow of water from this narrow gap is from *under the south side of the temple.* (South is to Ezekiel's right if he is facing east, watching the water flow away from the door). Apparently the waters are flowing in a southeasterly direction. We will see why shortly.

2. He then brought me out through the north gate and led me around the outside to the outer gate facing east, and the water was trickling from the south side.

Ezekiel's guide leads him through *the north gate* for the prophet to have a different perspective on the flowing water. They cannot leave by the eastern gate because that gate has already been closed (Ezekiel 44:1, 2). Circling around by means of the northern gate may help the two avoid the flow of the water. They then proceed to go around *the outer gate facing east*, where they are able to resume watching the movement of the water.

B. Increasing Depth (vv. 3-6)

3. As the man went eastward with a measuring line in his hand, he measured off a thousand cubits and then led me through water that was ankle-deep.

The man proceeds to lead Ezekiel *eastward,* in the direction toward which the waters are flowing, and even into the waters themselves. The man has a certain *measuring line in his hand.* This may be the same "linen cord" that is mentioned at the beginning of the vision (Ezekiel 40:3).

After the man measures *a thousand cubits,* he and Ezekiel find themselves in water that is up to the ankles. In this case the cubit is most likely the standard cubit of 18 inches in length; therefore, it is not the "long cubit" of 21 inches used in the temple measurements in Ezekiel 43 (last week's lesson).

Measured according to the standard cubit, 1,000 cubits is the equivalent of about 1,500 feet, a little short of three-tenths of a mile. The shallow water is about 6 inches deep.

4. He measured off another thousand cubits and led me through water that was knee-deep. He measured off another thousand and led me through water that was up to the waist.

As the two walk farther, the depth of the waters increases. The measuring line is used to determine distance, but the depth of the water is determined as Ezekiel's guide leads him into the water itself. *Knee-deep* water is 18 to 20 inches. Depth *up to the waist* is about 3 feet.

5. He measured off another thousand, but now it was a river that I could not cross, because the water had risen and was deep enough to swim in—a river that no one could cross.

As the fourth thousand-cubit segment is measured off, the waters become *a river* too deep to wade. The shallow flow that escapes from under a door of the temple has become a mighty stream. Just as there is no natural explanation for the

HOW TO SAY IT

Arabah	*Are*-uh-buh.
En Eglaim	En *Egg*-lay-im.
En Gedi	En *Gee*-dye (*g* as in *got*).
Ezekiel	Ee-*zeek*-ee-ul or Ee-*zeek*-yul.
Jerusalem	Juh-*roo*-suh-lem.
Mediterranean	*Med*-uh-tuh-*ray*-nee-un.
messianic	mess-ee-*an*-ick.

source of the water behind the door, there is no natural explanation for the stream's increasing depth. The power of God must be escalating its volume.

❧ *Too Much of a Good Thing?* ❧

Water is an inescapable necessity of life. We all know that we cannot live without it.

We also know that there can be "too much of a good thing." Flooding causes massive destruction and death yearly. I live in a city that is on a major river, and I know all too well how excessive rain can create flood conditions.

Every few years people who live on the river's edge have their homes washed away by flood waters. Folk here still talk about the flood of 1937, when the river crested 28 feet above flood stage. Of course, that flood pales in comparison with the one in Genesis 7.

When it comes to God's living water, there can never be too much! Ankle-deep is fine, knee-deep is better, and waist-deep better still. When it becomes too deep to wade, we can swim! The rainbow reminds us of God's promise never again to destroy the world by flood (Genesis 9:12-17). The cross and empty tomb remind us of "the river of the water of life" that awaits us in Heaven (Revelation 22:1, 2).   —J. B. N.

6. He asked me, "Son of man, do you see this?"

Then he led me back to the bank of the river.

Having witnessed the waters emerging from the temple go from a depth of a few inches to a depth uncrossable, without resorting to swimming, the man asks Ezekiel, *Son of man, do you see this?* The question may be posed as an exclamation of wonder: "Son of man, look at this! Isn't this something?"

It is an amazing sight indeed, especially when one considers that the setting is a "very high mountain" (Ezekiel 40:2). Only an act of the Lord can enable water to flow in the manner described in such a setting (compare Isaiah 41:18).

We may compare the scene unfolding before the prophet with what he witnessed earlier in the valley of dry bones (Ezekiel 37:1-14). There a vast

array of dry, lifeless bones, seemingly beyond all hope of living again, suddenly yet methodically came together. As they did so, they received all the necessary components for living human bodies. The prophet watched in stunned amazement as "a vast army" came into being (37:10). The vision of a mountaintop featuring much water is no less spectacular. As the guide brings Ezekiel back to *the bank of the river,* the prophet is about to behold even more stunning sights.

Regarding the phrase *Son of man,* see commentary on Ezekiel 43:7 in lesson 9.

> *What Do You Think?*
> How can water, in its various contexts, illustrate the character of God?
> *Talking Points for Your Discussion*
> ▪ The depth of an ocean (Psalm 24:1,2; etc.)
> ▪ The flowing of a river (Isaiah 48:18; etc.)
> ▪ The placid stillness of a lake (Psalm 23:2; etc.)
> ▪ The refreshment of a cool spring (Isaiah 43:20)
> ▪ Other

C. Innumerable Trees (v. 7)

7. When I arrived there, I saw a great number of trees on each side of the river.

From his new vantage point on the riverbank, Ezekiel is treated to a scene of many *trees on each side of the river.* Ezekiel, being as familiar with this region as he is, knows that something of God is happening. This river is bringing life to the area. (Compare Psalm 107:35: "He turned the desert into pools of water and the parched ground into flowing springs.")

II. Reviving Water
(Ezekiel 47:8-12)
A. Extraordinary Change (v. 8)

8. He said to me, "This water flows toward the eastern region and goes down into the Arabah, where it enters the Dead Sea. When it empties into the sea, the salty water there becomes fresh.

Ezekiel's guide now offers further explanation of the waters, both in terms of flow and effect. As the water flows eastward (also v. 1) and *goes down into the Arabah,* or desert, it ends up in *the Dead Sea.* The city of Jerusalem lies at almost exactly the same latitude as the northernmost tip of the Dead Sea. Therefore, the waters flowing from Jerusalem's temple toward this body of water have to flow a bit to the south as well as east in order to empty *into the sea* rather than end up connecting with the Jordan River (see comment on v. 1, above).

The Dead Sea has been known for centuries as just that—dead, because its salt concentration is 5 to 10 times greater than that of normal ocean water. Yet this once-stagnant water *becomes fresh* because of the waters flowing from the temple. Ezekiel has previously seen dead bones come to life; now he sees dead waters transformed to support life (next verse).

What Do You Think?

In addition to dry bones and salty water, what other images—biblical and otherwise—strike you powerfully as illustrations of one's spiritual deadness before coming to Christ? Why?

Talking Points for Your Discussion

▪ Images of deadness tied to human behavior (air pollution, etc.)
▪ Images of deadness tied to forces of nature (tornadic devastation, etc.)
▪ Images tied to cultural expressions ("dead as a doornail," etc.)

B. Abundant Fish (vv. 9, 10)

9. "Swarms of living creatures will live wherever the river flows. There will be large numbers of fish, because this water flows there and makes the salt water fresh; so where the river flows everything will live.

A consequence of the transformation that occurs *where the river flows* is that marine life is able to exist and flourish where it previously could not, especially in the once "dead" sea. We could say that the River of Life has created the Sea of Life. Fish, which could not have survived in the overly salty waters of the old Dead Sea, are now described as existing in *large numbers.*

Fresh water will yield abundant life in the formerly brackish water and on the land that is near the water.

10a. "Fishermen will stand along the shore; from En Gedi to En Eglaim there will be places for spreading nets.

Who can imagine that a fishing industry will thrive in the vicinity of the Dead Sea? Yet here are fishermen standing on its shore *from En Gedi to En Eglaim*!

The oasis of En Gedi, about 22 miles south-southeast of Jerusalem, is located about halfway down the western shore of the Dead Sea (compare Joshua 15:62). The location of En Eglaim is uncertain; some suggest it may be situated on the central eastern shore of the Dead Sea. If so, this indicates that the fishing trade flourishes on both sides of the Dead Sea. The impression is that boats are unnecessary because fish are so abundant that they can be caught from shore.

What Do You Think?

What should others see in our reactions to receiving unexpected blessings from God? Why?

Talking Points for Your Discussion

▪ Reactions toward God
▪ Reactions toward the blessings themselves
▪ Reactions in how we use the blessings to benefit others
▪ Other

10b. "The fish will be of many kinds—like the fish of the Mediterranean Sea.

This half verse speaks to variety. Fish are known to be very plentiful in *the Mediterranean Sea.* Imagine—fishermen being able to catch as many varieties of fish in the Dead Sea as they can in the Mediterranean!

The bumper crop of fish ensures a never-ending food supply for the new Jerusalem, the source of the River of Life. The use of the word *kinds* calls to mind the language of the creation account in Genesis 1:21, 24, 25.

C. Exception Noted (v. 11)

11. "But the swamps and marshes will not become fresh; they will be left for salt.

This verse notes an exception to the abundance of life. *The swamps and marshes* will not be affected by the life-giving waters; salty, brackish water will remain there.

The reason for this is not given. One theory is that a source of salt is necessary because salt is required for certain offerings (Ezekiel 43:24; compare Leviticus 2:13). Another theory is that these places remain in their unhealthy state as a reminder that one must be near the River of Life to have its benefits.

What Do You Think?

Why do many people prefer to seek spiritual water from sources other than God?

Talking Points for Your Discussion

- Psalm 63:1
- Job 15:16
- Jeremiah 2:13
- Other

D. Abundant Fruit (v. 12)

12. "Fruit trees of all kinds will grow on both banks of the river. Their leaves will not wither, nor will their fruit fail. Every month they will bear fruit, because the water from the sanctuary flows to them. Their fruit will serve for food and their leaves for healing."

Ezekiel's "tour guide" now returns to a description of the trees that were seen earlier in the vision (v. 7). Here they are described as *fruit trees of all kinds*. That *their leaves will not wither, nor will their fruit fail* speaks to the fact that the fruit will not be susceptible to disease or anything else that would make it inedible.

The prediction that *every month* the trees *will bear fruit* shows that these trees are quite unlike ordinary trees, with their dormant cycles. The continual fruitfulness of such trees results from the unique properties of the water that flows *from the sanctuary*.

The leaves of the trees have life-giving properties as the water does (see v. 9). All this reminds us of the presence of "the tree of life" in the Garden of Eden (Genesis 2:9), only here there are numerous "trees of life"!

⅔ WHAT TREES DO ⅔

A careful study of trees reveals some amazing facts. For one, trees are a perfect counterpart to human life in that they take in carbon dioxide, which we breathe out as a waste product, and turn it into oxygen, which we need to live. In one season, a mature leafy tree can produce as much oxygen as 10 people will inhale for the entire year! That's one reason why tropical rain forests are so important to the world's ecosystem.

Trees also interact with water in surprisingly beneficial ways, such as slowing storm water runoff so it can be absorbed into the ground. One source estimates that a single, fully grown Colorado blue spruce can intercept more than 1,000 gallons of water annually in this way. This helps replenish underground aquifers.

Ezekiel, of course, was not aware of modern scientific facts such as these. But he knew life when he saw it. And the trees lining the river in his vision not only represented life, they also witnessed to the blessings of food and medicinal applications.

This can be a prayer stimulus: the next time you glance out a window and see a tree, pause to thank God for his provisions for life, both immediate and eternal.   —J. B. N.

Conclusion
A. Living Water Now

The introduction to lesson 9 proposed that Ezekiel's temple vision should be understood as using certain images or word pictures to prophesy coming blessings under the new covenant through Jesus. Under that covenant, every Christian is pictured as a temple of God's Spirit.

The most significant of the word pictures found in today's passage is *water*. The Old Testament uses water imagery to convey the message that God's "water of life" is never stagnant, but always available, active, and life-giving (Psalms 1:3; 36:8; 84:5, 6; Isaiah 12:3; 41:18; 43:19; 66:12; Jeremiah 31:9).

Jesus used the imagery of water on various occasions to depict the abundant life he came to bring. When he attended the Feast of Tabernacles in Jerusalem, he declared, "Let anyone who is thirsty come to me and drink. Whoever believes in me, as Scripture has said, rivers of living water will flow from within them" (John 7:37, 38; compare 4:10, 14). Jesus was not quoting a single, particular Old Testament passage, but the general message derived from several passages, including our text for today.

Interestingly, the climax of the Feast of Tabernacles featured the pouring out of water as part of the symbolism. It was in such a setting—perhaps during the pouring-out ceremony itself—that Jesus made his promise of living water. Christopher Wright notes that the water-pouring ceremony at this feast in Jesus' day "was already interpreted in various Jewish traditions as a symbolic anticipation of the messianic outpouring of the Spirit in fulfillment of various Scriptures, including Ezekiel 47:1-9."

The apostle John goes on to explain, "By this [Jesus] meant the Spirit, whom those who believed in him were later to receive" (John 7:39). This means that we can enjoy right now the benefits of the spiritual refreshment that come from the Holy Spirit.

B. Living Water for Eternity

We see Ezekiel's vision reaching its clearest and ultimate fulfillment in the book of Revelation. There the apostle John was shown "the river of the water of life, as clear as crystal, flowing from the throne of God and of the Lamb down the middle of the great street of the city. On each side of the river stood the tree of life, bearing twelve crops of fruit, yielding its fruit every month. And the leaves of the tree are for the healing of the nations" (Revelation 22:1, 2).

John saw a certain river as the source of life, just as Ezekiel saw. Trees on either side of John's river were fruitful, just like Ezekiel's. And the leaves of the trees that John saw were a source of healing, again just like Ezekiel's. Such parallels indicate how Ezekiel's great temple vision should be understood.

It does not appear that the temple layout shown to that prophet was ever intended to be followed by the exiles who returned from Babylon or by any other group of God's people. Since the vision portrays something unique and miraculous in nature, we must allow God himself to declare how its fulfillment is to be understood.

That is what the New Testament does for us. It points to a fulfillment that is initiated by Jesus' first coming and climaxed by his second coming. At Jesus' return, his holy city will become inhabited for eternity by his people. It is a city "whose architect and builder is God" (Hebrews 11:10).

What Do You Think?
Through which conduit is God's living water affecting you most powerfully right now? Why?
Talking Points for Your Discussion
- The conduit of God's Word
- The conduit of fellow believers (the church)
- The conduit of God's Spirit
- Other

C. Prayer

Father, thank you for the living water that continues to bring healing and hope to our lives. May we never separate ourselves from it, and may we as your people point others to it as well. We praise you for sending Jesus, who makes this living water available. In his name we pray; amen.

D. Thought to Remember

Let the living waters
flow through you!

Visual for Lesson 11. *Point to this visual as you ask, "Which of the seven images best illustrates the living water Christ offers? Why?"*

INVOLVEMENT LEARNING

Enhance your lesson with NIV® Bible Student (from your curriculum supplier) and the reproducible activity page (at www.standardlesson.com or in the back of the NIV® Standard Lesson Commentary Deluxe Edition).

Into the Lesson

Announce a game to see how many benefits and problems your learners can name that are related to the use of water in its liquid and solid (ice) forms. Allow one minute of silent reflection for learners to think of answers before you start.

Begin the game by pointing to a learner at random as you say one of these four phrases: *liquid benefit, liquid problem, solid benefit,* or *solid problem.* That person has five seconds to come up with an answer in that regard. He or she then gets to call on another person while voicing one of the four phrases. Jot responses on the board to make sure they are not repeated. When learners run out of answers, say, "Although water isn't always beneficial in either form, today's lesson uses an image of water that is of great benefit."

Into the Word

Today's lesson format will be guided instruction through the text. Ask for volunteers to read the text aloud, as it is sectioned off below. Some discussion starters are suggested, but it will be important to follow each discussion starter with this question: "What impact could this section of text have had on the original readers, who were exiled in Babylon?" Expected and possible responses are in italics.

Verses 1, 2: Identify the source of the water and to which direction it flows. *(The temple is the immediate source, but learners may note that God must be the ultimate source. The water flows eastward. Original impact: Exiles made aware that the temple is to be renewed in some sense, etc.)*

Verses 3-5: Explain what is happening in the progression of these three verses. *(The flowing water gets deeper and deeper as the distance increases. Original impact: This must be supernatural, since there is no river in that area.)*

Verses 6, 7: Identify a result of the river flowing. (*Trees begin to be visible.* ***Original impact:***

Presence of trees implies a reversal of homeland devastation.)

Verses 8-10: Explain the effect the flowing river has on things in its path. *(The waters of the Dead Sea become fresh, able to sustain a fishing industry.* ***Original impact:*** *Implies more than the homeland merely reverting to its status before the exile; this is a supernatural improvement to the area.)*

Verse 11: Specify what does not happen as a result of the presence of the new river. *(Certain areas remain salty.* ***Original impact:*** *See the commentary for two possibilities.)*

Verse 12: Explain the relationship between the river and the trees. *(River makes it possible for the trees to grow; trees in turn provide a continual source of food and medicine.* ***Original impact:*** *Divine healing of both land and people.)*

Conclude this segment by asking learners how today's text reminds them of other sections of Scripture. *(Possible responses are Genesis 2:8-10 and Revelation 21:1, 2; 22:1-3.)* Use the texts from Revelation as a transition to Into Life.

Option. For deeper study, distribute copies of the "A River Runs Through Scripture" activity from the reproducible page, which you can download. Discuss insights after completing in small groups.

Into Life

Ask learners what similarities they see between today's text and Revelation 21:1, 2; 22:1-3; jot observations on the board. Make sure to note these two similarities if learners do not do so: *both rivers are sources of life* and *both visions point to a fulfillment that was initiated by Jesus' first coming and will culminate at his second coming.* Discuss the hope these verses have for Christians today and compare that with the way the readers in Ezekiel's day may have reacted.

Option. Distribute the "A Meditation for Others" activity from the reproducible page as a take-home exercise.

INHERITANCE MARKS A NEW BEGINNING

DEVOTIONAL READING: Psalm 51:1-13
BACKGROUND SCRIPTURE: Ezekiel 47:13-23; Acts 2:37-47

EZEKIEL 47:13-23

¹³ This is what the Sovereign LORD says: "These are the boundaries of the land that you will divide among the twelve tribes of Israel as their inheritance, with two portions for Joseph. ¹⁴ You are to divide it equally among them. Because I swore with uplifted hand to give it to your ancestors, this land will become your inheritance.

¹⁵ "This is to be the boundary of the land:

"On the north side it will run from the Mediterranean Sea by the Hethlon road past Lebo Hamath to Zedad, ¹⁶ Berothah and Sibraim (which lies on the border between Damascus and Hamath), as far as Hazer Hattikon, which is on the border of Hauran. ¹⁷ The boundary will extend from the sea to Hazar Enan, along the northern border of Damascus, with the border of Hamath to the north. This will be the northern boundary.

¹⁸ "On the east side the boundary will run between Hauran and Damascus, along the

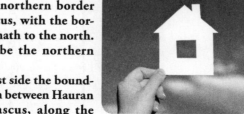

Jordan between Gilead and the land of Israel, to the Dead Sea and as far as Tamar. This will be the eastern boundary. ¹⁹ "On the south side it will run from Tamar as far as the waters of Meribah Kadesh, then along the Wadi of Egypt to the Mediterranean Sea. This will be the southern boundary.

²⁰ "On the west side, the Mediterranean Sea will be the boundary to a point opposite Lebo Hamath. This will be the western boundary.

²¹ "You are to distribute this land among yourselves according to the tribes of Israel. ²² You are to allot it as an inheritance for yourselves and for the foreigners residing among you and who have children. You are to consider them as native-born Israelites; along with you they are to be allotted an inheritance among the tribes of Israel. ²³ In whatever tribe a foreigner resides, there you are to give them their inheritance," declares the Sovereign LORD.

KEY VERSE

Peter replied, "Repent and be baptized, every one of you, in the name of Jesus Christ for the forgiveness of your sins. And you will receive the gift of the Holy Spirit." —**Acts 2:38**

Sustaining Hope

Unit 3: Visions of Grandeur
LESSONS 9–13

LESSON AIMS

After participating in this lesson, each learner will be able to:

1. Identify the recipients of the inheritance in Ezekiel's vision.

2. Compare and contrast the tribal divisions of Ezekiel 47 with those of Joshua 13–21, and explain the differences.

3. List two "strangers" (v. 23) living in his or her midst who need help for a new beginning and make a plan to help them attain this.

LESSON OUTLINE

Introduction

A. Inheritance Squabbles

No matter what family you belong to, serious issues always seem to present themselves when an estate is to be divided and distributed. Conflict arises as to who is to receive what and how much. Nothing seems fair, especially to a family member who is not in line to receive any inheritance whatsoever—even when the deceased has left a detailed will. Family members have been known to grab all there is to grab of the estate, whether it be money, land, or personal possessions. I am certain that at least 80 percent of the readers of this commentary can identify with this scenario.

The sharing of the unearned, inherited wealth that could follow is often the furthest thing from anyone's mind. But if there is any instance where such sharing is to be considered, should it not be in a context of having received unearned assets (compare Matthew 10:8)? Ancient Judah was exiled from her land in the sixth century BC; God's people had lost their inheritance due to national idolatry and other sins. Ezekiel offered hope to an exiled people through divine vision of an inheritance renewed and restored. It was an unearned inheritance, to be shared with the "foreigners" (strangers) who lived among the Judeans.

B. Lesson Background

Today's lesson text picks up where last week's left off. Therefore the background is the same, and that information need not be repeated here. Even so, more can be said about the literary context.

Our text belongs to the larger block of Ezekiel 40–48. The form is that of a divine vision in apocalyptic style. This block as a whole is a counter-vision to the disaster of Ezekiel 8–11, where God's glory departed from the temple in Jerusalem: the Lord's glory returned to a new "temple," in 43:1-5 (lesson 9). There God was again enthroned as king over his people (43:7; compare 34:23-31; 37:26-28). The promise of restoration to the land (20:42) was seen as being fulfilled in a divine vision by a detailed look at the new temple and in the division of the land among the 12 tribes of Israel (chap. 47 and 48).

The literary structure of Ezekiel 40–48 is important. References to a "city" bookend this segment (see 40:2 and 48:30-35), and the city is ultimately called "The Lord is there" (48:35). After a preamble in 40:1-4, the text falls into three parts: (1) 40:5–43:27, the Lord's return to reside in the new temple; (2) 44:1–46:24, Israel's proper response to the holy "portion of the land" in their midst; and (3) 47:1–48:29, apportionment of the newly healed land among the 12 tribes within idealized boundaries, with resident "foreigners" sharing. This larger context will help us discern the proper interpretation and application of today's text.

I. The Inheritance
(EZEKIEL 47:13, 14)
A. Two Portions for Joseph (v. 13)

13. This is what the Sovereign LORD says: "These are the boundaries of the land that you will divide among the twelve tribes of Israel as their inheritance, with two portions for Joseph.

The land is to be distributed *among the twelve tribes of Israel*, with the particular notice that a double portion is to be given to Joseph. This reflects the fact that Joseph had two sons, Ephraim and Manasseh (Genesis 48:1-22), whose descendants formed two tribes of those names.

This peculiarity means that the listing of Israel's (Jacob's) 12 sons—whose names became tribal

HOW TO SAY IT

apocalyptic	uh-*paw*-kuh-**lip**-tik.
Beersheba	Beer-*she*-buh.
Berothah	Bee-*row*-thah.
Damascus	Duh-*mass*-kus.
Ephraim	*Ee*-fray-im.
Euphrates	You-*fray*-teez.
Hamath	*Hay*-muth.
Hauran	*Hah*-you-rawn.
Hazar Enan	*Hay*-zawr *Ee*-nan.
Hazer Hattikon	*Hay*-zer *Hat*-ih-kahn.
Hethlon	*Heth*-lawn.
Jeroboam	Jair-uh-*boe*-um.
Manasseh	Muh-*nass*-uh.
Sibraim	Sib-*ruh*-im.

designations—adds up to 12, since the tribe of Levi does not inherit land. Compare a "normal" listing of the 12 tribes in Genesis 49:13-28 with variant listings in Deuteronomy 33:6-25 and Revelation 7.

By this time in Israel's history (about 573 BC, per Ezekiel 40:1), a regathering of the 12 tribes seems impossible. But God has promised that a "remnant" will return (Isaiah 10:20-22), that he will indeed regather his people (Jeremiah 23:3; Ezekiel 34:11-16). The return of a remnant will be fulfilled literally, but it is also symbolic for a greater fulfillment as we shall see.

B. Equal Divisions (v. 14)

14. "You are to divide it equally among them. Because I swore with uplifted hand to give it to your ancestors, this land will become your inheritance.

This text confronts the reader with a surprise: each tribe is to receive an equal share of land. Such an idea was unrealistic in the beginning because of the differing sizes of the tribes and their needs (compare Numbers 32:1-5; Joshua 14–19). Yet even taking tribal size and need into account, the land was apportioned originally by lot (Numbers 26:55, 56; 33:54; Joshua 14:2). Not so here.

Even today, an uplifted hand is the gesture accompanying an oath (compare Deuteronomy 32:40). God is said to have made such an oath, promising this land to the patriarchs (compare Exodus 6:8 with Genesis 12:7; 13:14-17; 15:7-20). The people who have lost everything are promised a new inheritance (see Ezekiel 45). They will experience a new temple (40:1–43:11), a new law (43:12), a new land (today's lesson), along with a new city (48:30-35).

II. The Boundaries

(EZEKIEL 47:15-20)

A. North Side (vv. 15-17)

15. "This is to be the boundary of the land: "On the north side it will run from the Mediterranean Sea by the Hethlon road past Lebo Hamath to Zedad,

The vision describes Israel's borders beginning with the northern side in a complex description across three verses. The descriptions will then move clockwise—east, south, and west. These descriptions are patterned after Numbers 34:1-12.

The northern boundary begins with *the Mediterranean Sea* near *Hethlon*, a place we cannot identify today. Comparison can be made with Numbers 34:7-9, but the difficulty remains as that text gives "Mount Hor" instead of Ezekiel's *the Hethlon road*. The town or district of *Zedad* is probably to be identified with the modern name *Sedad*, or *Sadad*.

The Hebrew word for *boundary* (also translated "border" in Ezekiel 47:16, next) can also mean "territory" (as in 48:2-8). Thus the difficulty of determining the exact location of *the boundary* is increased. Our best guess is that Zedad is the northernmost point of the new tribal boundaries.

❧ AN IMMOVABLE, UNCROSSABLE BOUNDARY ❧

The deed to the parcel of land I own lists the state, the county, the township, the fractional range, the section, and a definite point located in the subdivision. The property lines are measured in feet, and the directions are given in degrees and minutes. All this is depicted on a plat map. I don't think the location and size of my property could be described with more precision!

It has not always been so. On the American frontier, it was common for properties to be recorded with reference to geographical features. "Beginning at the willow tree on the north bank of Cedar Creek, go west 239 feet to an oak tree, then north 356 feet to a large stone . . ." Confusion resulted when unscrupulous people cut down trees or moved rocks! To help prevent this in the Northwest Territory, the U.S. Congress passed the Land Ordinance of 1785, which established official surveyors.

The Old Testament has been described as "a book of boundaries." Many boundaries therein are physical (example: Psalm 104:9); others are spiritual in nature (examples: Leviticus 10:10; Ezekiel 44:23). The problem was that people had an evil tendency to try to move (or remove) both kinds of boundaries (examples: Job 24:2; Ezekiel 22:26). Today's text shows us that God has the right to redraw boundaries. He also moved boundaries for the New Testament era (examples: Mark 7:19; Colossians 2:16, 17). But God also has established for eternity a boundary that is not only immovable but uncrossable (see Luke 16:26; Revelation 21:27; 22:14, 15). Make sure you're on the desirable side of it—no fence straddling permitted!   —J. B. N.

> ### What Do You Think?
> How do we respond to cultural attempts to move or remove boundaries set by God?
> *Talking Points for Your Discussion*
> - Regarding moral boundaries
> - Regarding ethical boundaries
> - Regarding boundaries that separate truth from falsehood
> - Others

16. ". . . Berothah and Sibraim (which lies on the border between Damascus and Hamath), as far as Hazer Hattikon, which is on the border of Hauran.

Since there are no natural boundaries (river names, etc.) for the northern description, place names are used, and many are difficult to determine. *Berothah* (meaning "cypress grove") is probably 30 miles north-northwest of *Damascus*. The other named towns are probably nearby. *The border of Hauran* is an area located within modern Syria. See the next verse regarding *Hamath*.

17. "The boundary will extend from the sea to Hazar Enan, along the northern border of Damascus, with the border of Hamath to the north. This will be the northern boundary.

Scholars locate *Hazar Enan* (meaning "village of springs") 70 miles northeast *of Damascus* (compare Numbers 34:9, 10). *Hamath* ("fortress") is a major city-state about 100 miles north of Damascus. As vague as this description of the northern border is to us, we should note that this border is much farther north than the land actually controlled by the Israelites in history—"from Dan to Beersheba" (2 Samuel 3:10).

God did promise to Abraham land "from the Wadi of Egypt to the great river, the Euphrates" (Genesis 15:18). But because of unfaithfulness, Israel came close to controlling this territory only twice: once under David and Solomon (see 2 Samuel 8:1-12; 1 Kings 8:65; 1 Chronicles 13:5; 2 Chronicles 7:8) and once under Jeroboam II (see 2 Kings 14:25). In describing this idealized northern area as he does, Ezekiel is leaving room for the 12 tribes to receive roughly equal strips of land down to the southern border.

B. East Side (v. 18)

18. "On the east side the boundary will run between Hauran and Damascus, along the Jordan between Gilead and the land of Israel, to the Dead Sea and as far as Tamar. This will be the eastern boundary.

There is less uncertainty for the modern reader regarding the description of *the east side*. But still *the boundary* is described in regional terms: *Hauran, Damascus,* and *Gilead*. We should think in terms of the northernmost point of the eastern boundary extending from *Hauran* south until it reaches the latitude of the Jordan River, where it then extends westward to touch that river. The river then becomes, along with the Dead Sea, the majority of the eastern border. The eastern border terminates at *Tamar* (also known as "Tadmor" in 1 Kings 9:18), located near the southern extremity of the Dead Sea.

This description cuts out the Transjordan tribal settlements of Numbers 34:1-12. The Transjordan was not part of the original promise of land; the two and a half tribes that originally settled there are described in Ezekiel's vision as located elsewhere (see Ezekiel 48:4, 6, 27).

C. South Side (v. 19)

19. "On the south side it will run from Tamar as far as the waters of Meribah Kadesh, then along the Wadi of Egypt to the Mediterranean Sea. This will be the southern boundary.

Visual for Lesson 12. *Have this visual on display as you introduce the question below regarding today's key verse, Acts 2:38.*

The southern boundary begins at Tamar (see v. 18, above) and moves southwest through the ancient site of *Meribah Kadesh* (Numbers 20:13, 14, 24; 27:14). It then follows *the Wadi of Egypt* (see also Numbers 34:5 and Joshua 15:4) *to the Mediterranean Sea*. The river noted (today known as Wadi el-Arish) serves as a natural boundary between Egypt and Canaan.

D. West Side (v. 20)

20. "On the west side, the Mediterranean Sea will be the boundary to a point opposite Lebo Hamath. This will be the western boundary.

The Mediterranean Sea clearly marks the entire western boundary from Egypt (v. 19) all the way to the northern border, which is located *opposite Lebo Hamath* (see v. 16, above; compare Numbers 34:6). So we have moved in this vision from the most uncertain (to us) of the border descriptions to the most certain.

III. The Imperative
(EZEKIEL 47:21-23)
A. Regarding the Twelve Tribes (v. 21)

21. "You are to distribute this land among yourselves according to the tribes of Israel.

The verse before us reiterates the preamble in Ezekiel 47:13, 14. The book goes on to assign equal strips of land, with seven tribes north of the strip reserved for the holy city and sanctuary

(48:1-7) and five tribes south of it (48:23-29; compare 45:1-8). The tribal arrangements seem to place the more favored tribes, the ones descending from Jacob's wives Leah and Rachel, closest to the sanctuary; the less favored tribes, descending from Jacob's concubines Bilhah and Zilpah, are farther away (compare Genesis 35:23-26).

> **What Do You Think?**
> How does today's key verse of Acts 2:38 and its context speak to our inheritance from God in the New Testament era?
> *Talking Points for Your Discussion*
> - Regarding what is inherited
> - Regarding who can inherit
> - Regarding when the inheritance happens
> - Regarding the basis of the inheritance
> - Other

B. Regarding Outsiders (vv. 22, 23)

22. "You are to allot it as an inheritance for yourselves and for the foreigners residing among you and who have children. You are to consider them as native-born Israelites; along with you they are to be allotted an inheritance among the tribes of Israel.

We come to a key point of this lesson: *inheritance . . . for the foreigners residing among* the Israelites. These foreigners are the resident aliens living in their midst. Such a person is listed alongside "the fatherless and the widow" in Ezekiel 22:7 and "the poor and needy" in 22:29—people vulnerable to abuse and oppression. Israel is to protect such people because the Israelites know what it is like to be foreigners in another land (see Leviticus 19:33, 34; Deuteronomy 10:19; 26:5; Isaiah 52:4; Psalm 105:23).

If we are correct in seeing Ezekiel 40–48 as being a divine vision set in apocalyptic style, then we must see it fulfilled in Christ. As Ezekiel saw a wholly new temple with God's glorious presence returned, so Jesus is that "new temple" (John 2:18-22) and Christians make up a "new temple" on earth (Ephesians 2:19-22). The living water that flows from the temple in Ezekiel 47:1-12 (last week's lesson) is understood as fulfilled in the new

covenant era, when people of every ethnic group can call on the Lord for forgiveness of sin and the gift of the Holy Spirit (Acts 2:38).

> **What Do You Think?**
> How do we determine what and when to share and not share with others? How can we improve our discernment in this area?
> *Talking Points for Your Discussion*
> - Regarding what and when to share:
>   1 Samuel 30:21-25; Matthew 25:34-40; Mark 7:9-13; 2 Corinthians 8:13, 14; Hebrews 13:2; 1 Timothy 5:3-8; 1 John 3:18
> - Regarding what and when *not* to share:
>   Matthew 7:6; 25:1-13; 2 Thessalonians 3:10; 1 Timothy 5:9-13

❧ ALIENS (NOT THE KIND FROM OUTER SPACE) ❧

A major problem facing America today is that of *undocumented immigrants*, also referred to as *illegal aliens*. The U.S. spends huge amounts of money to control its southern border against the arrival of such persons. The ongoing debate as to how to handle this problem is quite heated at times!

The U.S. is not alone in this challenge. Brazil and Chile face this problem, and even Mexico has to deal with unauthorized immigration from various South American countries, the Caribbean, and even Asia. The list goes on and on. One organization reports that there may be between 25 and 30 million illegal aliens throughout the world.

In Ezekiel's vision, *illegal aliens* is a contradiction in terms when seen from the vantage point of spiritual fulfillment in the New Testament era. God welcomes everyone to join his people! How welcoming is your church in this regard? See Acts 10:34, 35 and Revelation 7:9.   —J. B. N.

23. "In whatever tribe a foreigner resides, there you are to give them their inheritance," declares the Sovereign LORD.

A foreigner is not to be oppressed or exploited in any way for any reason. The injunction to grant foreigners *their inheritance* within the tribes where they are living is pure compassion.

The apostle Paul in his day spends much time and effort to bring Jews and Gentiles together into one family. He argues that faith or faithfulness is the mark of the new people of God; because of that, Abraham is the father of all who believe (see Romans 4:11, 16). How we treat those among us who are different in various ways speaks volumes as to the quality of our Christian faith. How can any of us elevate ourselves above another in light of the fact that "all have sinned and fall short of the glory of God" (3:23)? Therefore we are to "accept one another, then, just as Christ accepted you, in order to bring praise to God" (15:7).

Conclusion

A. New Beginnings

The Old Testament gives us many examples of new beginnings. In Exodus 32, God's newly freed people worshipped a golden idol (bull image), even while Moses was receiving the Ten Commandments, the second of which forbade that very act. God came close to destroying the people and starting over with Moses (Exodus 32:10), but Moses intervened and God relented (32:11-14). After this incident God would forever be known as "the compassionate and gracious God, slow to anger, abounding in love and faithfulness, maintaining love to thousands, and forgiving wickedness, rebellion and sin" (34:6, 7).

Jonah was told to proclaim judgment against the Ninevites, who were considered the greatest of sinners in his day. After God's "persuasion," Jonah did preach to them, but to his consternation they repented. Jonah became angry because he knew that God was compassionate (Jonah 4:2). Not only did God allow new beginnings for his own people, he also offered new beginnings for the Gentile pagans, the "foreigners."

Sometimes people did not accept God's offer of a new beginning. Such was the case for the northern kingdom of Israel as told through the prophet Hosea. God instructed him to marry "a promiscuous woman" (Hosea 1:2). After three children were born, each given symbolic names, Hosea's wife left him for a life of prostitution slavery. Hosea bought her back at the Lord's insistence and waited to see if she would be faithful (3:1-3). The implication is that Hosea's wife never truly returned to faithfulness, a sad imitation of Israel. The northern kingdom of Israel was destroyed in 722 BC.

Isaiah cried out for a new beginning for an exiled people (Isaiah 40–66). This was fulfilled in the ultimate sense by the suffering servant, Jesus (53:11, 12). He delivered us from slavery to sin by his atonement on the cross (Romans 3:25).

Jeremiah's prophecies are mostly judgmental in nature. But in the section called "Book of Consolation" (chap. 30–33), the prophet noted God's offer of a radical new beginning: a new covenant whereby everyone could know the Lord intimately and know that their sins have been forgiven (Jeremiah 31:31-34). A new beginning indeed!

King David, a man after God's own heart, sinned greatly by committing adultery and murder. But he confessed his sin, and Nathan assured him that "the Lord has taken away your sin" (2 Samuel 12:13). Even though David suffered the consequences for those sins the rest of his life, he did indeed experience a new beginning. He could write, "Create in me a pure heart, O God, and renew a steadfast spirit within me" (Psalm 51:10). With this accomplished, David wanted to share his new beginning (see Psalm 51:13). So should we!

B. Prayer

Heavenly Father, teach us to share your blessings with the "foreigners" among us, to help them have a new beginning just as you have given us a new beginning in Christ. In Jesus' name; amen.

C. Thought to Remember

Your inheritance in Christ
can be everyone else's as well.

INVOLVEMENT LEARNING

Enhance your lesson with NIV® Bible Student (from your curriculum supplier) and the reproducible activity page (at www.standardlesson.com or in the back of the NIV® Standard Lesson Commentary Deluxe Edition).

Into the Lesson

Say, "Suppose you got a call from a lawyer on Monday morning informing you that a relative had died and left you a large amount of money. What would you do with it?" Jot responses on the board. Then say, "In today's lesson we will look at the part of Ezekiel's vision where Israel was promised an inheritance that probably no one expected."

Option. Place in chairs copies of the "New Inheritance" activity from the reproducible page, which you can download, for learners to begin working on as they arrive. This will provide familiarization with the text before the Bible study begins. As an alternative, use the "New Beginnings" activity from the reproducible page to set the theme of today's study.

Into the Word

As teacher, research in advance the locations mentioned in today's text. Also research Ezekiel 48:1-7, 23-29 (not in today's text) to determine which tribes were to be given which areas of land; prepare strips of paper with the names of the tribes.

Draw on the board an outline of the borders of Old Testament Israel and the immediately surrounding areas. (*Option:* Distribute handouts of this outline; learners can use this as a note taker.) Ask a volunteer to read Ezekiel 47:13, 14 to establish the overall distribution of the inheritance.

Say, "Ezekiel's vision establishes God's intent to grant once again the land that he promised to Abraham's descendants. This would have seemed unbelievable to those living in Ezekiel's time, since the people had been in exile 25 years at that point (Ezekiel 40:1). Let's dig deeper to discover more detail about God's intent." Ask a learner to read Ezekiel 47:15-21 slowly. As the reading proceeds, point out geographical references on your sketch, interrupting the reading as needed.

Distribute handouts that depict in map form the original tribal allotments according to Joshua

13–20. (Since many Bibles have these allotments depicted in a map section in the back, draw learners' attention to that as well.)

Divide the class into four small groups. Distribute assignments regarding tribal allotments as follows: *Group 1*—Dan, Asher, Naphtali (Ezekiel 48:1-3); *Group 2*—Manasseh, Ephraim, Reuben (Ezekiel 48:4-6); *Group 3*—Judah, Benjamin, Simeon (Ezekiel 48:7, 23, 24); *Group 4*—Issachar, Zebulun, Gad (Ezekiel 48:25-28). Say, "Read your assigned text; then on your handout draw the new tribal boundaries over the top of the old tribal boundaries. Be sure to consult Ezekiel 47:13-20 as appropriate." (Larger classes can form more groups with fewer tribes and verses to research each; smaller classes can do the reverse.)

Call for conclusions after groups finish. As the groups report their findings tribe by tribe, affix the paper strips noted above to your map outline that is on the board. Discuss differences between old and new tribal allotments.

Say, "In addition to the locations and sizes of the new allotments, Ezekiel's vision notes inheritance for the 'foreigners' living among the Israelites." Read Ezekiel 47:22, 23 aloud. Use the commentary to establish why these two verses are important for Christians. Discuss why inheritance for "foreigners" would have been surprising for the original readers (compare Acts 10:45; 11:18) as a transition to the Into Life segment.

Into Life

Ask learners to identify "foreigners" in your area; jot responses on the board (example: someone newly arrived in town). Have the class suggest ways to reach them with the gospel. Follow this by having learners suggest ways such "foreigners" can be made to feel welcome in your church.

Option. If you did not use the "New Inheritance" activity earlier, distribute it now as a take-home exercise.

GOOD NEWS BRINGS REJOICING

DEVOTIONAL READING: Psalm 42:5-11
BACKGROUND SCRIPTURE: Isaiah 52:1, 2, 7-12; Psalm 33

ISAIAH 52:1, 2, 7-12

¹ Awake, awake, Zion,
  clothe yourself with strength!
Put on your garments of splendor,
  Jerusalem, the holy city.
The uncircumcised and defiled
  will not enter you again.
² Shake off your dust;
  rise up, sit enthroned, Jerusalem.
Free yourself from the chains on your neck,
  Daughter Zion, now a captive.

· ·

⁷ How beautiful on the mountains
  are the feet of those who bring good
    news,
who proclaim peace,
  who bring good tidings,
  who proclaim salvation,
who say to Zion,
  "Your God reigns!"
⁸ Listen! Your watchmen lift up their voices;
  together they shout for joy.
When the LORD returns to Zion,
  they will see it with their own eyes.
⁹ Burst into songs of joy together,
  you ruins of Jerusalem,

for the LORD has comforted his people,
  he has redeemed Jerusalem.
¹⁰ The LORD will lay bare his holy arm
  in the sight of all the nations,
and all the ends of the earth will see
  the salvation of our God.
¹¹ Depart, depart, go out from there!
  Touch no unclean thing!
Come out from it and be pure,
  you who carry the articles of the LORD's
    house.
¹² But you will not leave in haste
  or go in flight;
for the LORD will go before you,
  the God of Israel will be your rear guard.

KEY VERSE

How beautiful on the mountains are the feet of those who bring good news, who proclaim peace, who bring good tidings, who proclaim salvation, who say to Zion, "Your God reigns!" —**Isaiah 52:7**

SUSTAINING HOPE

Unit 3: Visions of Grandeur
LESSONS 9–13

LESSON AIMS

After participating in this lesson, each learner will be able to:

1. Summarize the content of Isaiah's "good news."

2. Explain how today's passage is fulfilled by Christ and the preaching of the gospel.

3. List seven songs and/or hymns that reflect themes in today's text; sing one each day in a time of devotion in the week ahead.

LESSON OUTLINE

Introduction
  A. Rejoicing in Part
  B. Lesson Background
 I. New Reality (ISAIAH 52:1, 2)
  A. Garments (v. 1a)
    Dressing Up for God
  B. Holiness (v. 1b)
  C. Position (v. 2)
 II. New Message (ISAIAH 52:7-10)
  A. Messenger Proclaims (v. 7)
  B. Watchmen Shout (v. 8)
  C. Jerusalem Rejoices (v. 9)
  D. Nations See (v. 10)
 III. New Exodus (ISAIAH 52:11, 12)
  A. Bearing the Vessels (v. 11)
  B. Protected by God (v. 12)
    Better Than a Testudo!
Conclusion
  A. Rejoicing in Full
  B. Prayer
  C. Thought to Remember

Introduction

A. Rejoicing in Part

It was April 9, 1865 (Palm Sunday), when General Robert E. Lee stepped into the parlor of the Wilmer McLean house at Appomattox Court House to surrender his Army of Northern Virginia to General Ulysses S. Grant. Following the formalities of surrender, Union soldiers in the field shouted in exultation. But Grant put a stop to that. A time of rejoicing would be allowed, but not at that particular moment. The surrender of one Confederate army didn't mean the end of the war; there was much yet to be done.

There is a certain parallel between that incomplete celebration and the end of the Babylonian exile. The remnant of Israel was allowed to return home to rebuild their society, city, and temple (Ezra 1). They would rejoice in doing so (Ezra 3:11-13; 6:16; Nehemiah 8:12, 17; 12:43), but rejoicing in the fullest sense could not occur until the Messiah came in fulfillment of all that Isaiah and other prophets predicted.

As Christians, we know that we live in a "now, but not yet" situation with respect to victory. Christ has paid the penalty for our sins through the cross, and for this we rejoice. But our joy is tempered by continuing struggles with sin (1 Peter 1:6). Even so, ultimate victory is certain; future rejoicing will be boundless (Revelation 19:7).

B. Lesson Background

Today's text is part of Isaiah's message of hope expressed to people who were yet to be exiled to Babylon (Isaiah 40–55). A voice cried for a highway to be constructed from Babylon to Jerusalem for the return of God as king (40:3-5). Jerusalem/Zion was predicted to be the focal point of the good news (40:9). Not only Judah but also the whole Gentile world was to have occasion to rejoice (41:21–42:17). Through a series of servant songs (42:1-9; 49:1-7; 50:4-9; 52:13–53:12; 61:1-4), the prophet sketched God's plan of redemption for the nations. It was to be God's special servant who would rescue God's world!

In Isaiah, the term *servant* can refer to different persons or groups in different contexts. The nation of Israel was called to be a servant to the world, but refused (see Isaiah 42:18-24; compare 6:9, 10). In spite of that, God decided to create a new exodus for his people (43:14-21). From political oppression, God delivered his people by means of Cyrus (44:28; 45:1). That man was a servant for God's purposes. Babylon could no longer hold God's people in captivity (48:20, 21).

But there was to be deliverance even greater than the one that came through Cyrus—a spiritual deliverance announced in the first servant song (Isaiah 42:1-9). The servant mentioned here was prophesied not only to restore the preserved of Israel, but also to be a "light for the Gentiles" (49:6). This servant was to suffer in so doing (50:6).

Rejoicing would finally come to Jerusalem when good news was announced (Isaiah 52:7-12). However, the reason for rejoicing—the basis of the great salvation, and the hope for the future—is not revealed until the servant song of Isaiah 52:13–53:12. There the "righteous servant" is predicted to "justify many, and he will bear their iniquities" (53:11). In this way the entire world would be invited to enter into the kingdom of God. A new David would rule over this kingdom (55:3, 4). This servant, whom we now know to be Jesus, would be king! This is the fitting context for our lesson, which immediately prefaces one of Isaiah's servant songs, as it falls on this first Advent Sunday.

I. New Reality
(ISAIAH 52:1, 2)
A. Garments (v. 1a)

1a. Awake, awake, Zion,
clothe yourself with strength!
Put on your garments of splendor,
Jerusalem, the holy city.

Earlier, the Israelites blamed God for lack of action and appealed to him with a double imperative: "Awake, awake, arm of the Lord, clothe yourself with strength!" (Isaiah 51:9). But it is not God who is asleep—it is Jerusalem. In our text the prophet uses the very same verb *awake* in the same form as in 51:9.

Zion must wake up to a new reality! In spite of Israel's call in the first exodus to be a "trea-

sured possession . . . a kingdom of priests and a holy nation" (Exodus 19:5, 6), she never fulfilled God's desire in that regard. Despite Israel's having the priestly house of Aaron, the royal dynasty of David, etc., the world does not see the true character of God through his people.

Now God is calling the exiles to be part of a second exodus in order to fulfill the original mandate. Zion is to awake to new clothing that will become her strength. She can finally discard the filthy rags of sin and idolatry that led her into exile in the first place, leaving with new garments of beauty and strength (compare Exodus 28:2).

We should note that the parallelism we see in this half verse is typical of Hebrew poetry: *clothe yourself with strength* is parallel to and synonymous with *put on your garments of splendor*. Likewise, *Zion* is parallel to and synonymous with *Jerusalem*. Thus there is only one action and subject involved, not two.

❧ DRESSING UP FOR GOD ❧

My siblings and I did not get new clothes very often when growing up. Like most people I knew, I usually wore hand-me-downs; any item of clothing, either purchased or handmade, that was outgrown was subject to being passed on to a sibling who could wear it. We had what we needed, but it was still a happy day when the mail-order catalog arrived. My sisters and I would turn its pages eagerly as we admired the pictures of new sweaters and skirts, daydreaming of new outfits for school.

Even better than the arrival of a catalog was the arrival of outfits that my mother actually ordered. My sisters and I would race to the mailbox each day in anticipation of that package. Those crisp new clothes made us feel so special!

Perhaps this feeling of being special was part of what God had in mind for the Israelites when Isaiah spoke of their "garments of splendor" to come. New and beautiful clothing causes people to see themselves in a new light.

God has new clothing in mind for us as well, clothing fit for eternity (see Revelation 3:4, 5). Until that time, we wear different clothing: the armor of God (Ephesians 6:10-17). Along with that we clothe ourselves with Christ and everything he expects of us as Christians (Romans 13:14; Galatians 3:27; Colossians 3:12; 1 Peter 5:5). Make sure you're properly dressed for the day!   —C. M. W.

B. Holiness (v. 1b)

1b. The uncircumcised and defiled will not enter you again.

What causes exile was expressed by Isaiah earlier: "See how the faithful city has become a prostitute!" (Isaiah 1:21). After full judgment and a purging of dross, Jerusalem is once again to be pronounced as "the City of Righteousness, the Faithful City" (1:25, 26). The "garments of splendor" of verse 1a above refer to a new character of holiness in this regard.

As a result, *the uncircumcised and defiled* cannot enter this renewed city (compare Isaiah 35:8-10; Revelation 21:27). The new reality is that the renewed people of God will be "Holy to the Lord," as was written on the golden plate on the front of Aaron's turban (Exodus 28:36, 37). How that is to happen is revealed in the servant song that begins in Isaiah 52:13, just after the end of today's text.

C. Position (v. 2)

**2. Shake off your dust;
rise up, sit enthroned, Jerusalem.
Free yourself from the chains on your neck,
Daughter Zion, now a captive.**

When we place this verse alongside Isaiah 47:1, we see the prophet contrasting the Babylonian captors with the exiles who are to return: "Go down, sit in the dust, Virgin Daughter Babylon; sit on the ground without a throne, queen city of the Babylonians. No more will you be called tender or delicate." What a reversal as the exiles shake from themselves the dust of humiliation!

This verse features a play on words regarding two terms that sound almost alike in Hebrew but mean the opposite: *shevi* for *sit enthroned* and *sheviyya* for *captive*. This highlights for the original reader the startling change in status to come for the exiles—from captivity to royalty (see Psalm 113:7, 8)! The remnant of Israel will be in a position to fulfill God's desire of Exodus 19:5, 6.

II. New Message
(ISAIAH 52:7-10)

A. Messenger Proclaims (v. 7)

**7. How beautiful on the mountains
are the feet of those who bring good
news,
who proclaim peace,
who bring good tidings,
who proclaim salvation,
who say to Zion,
"Your God reigns!"**

Isaiah 52:7-12 is a brief recapitulation of 40:1-21. Indeed, the entire message of 40:1–52:12 is how God as king is returning to Zion. The salvation he brings is complete, as depicted in the fourth servant song, Isaiah 52:13–53:12.

The scenario builds anticipation for a great rejoicing by first announcing runners (*those*), who are to bring the messages we see in the verse before us. Watchmen then pass along the good news (v. 8, next), the immediate result being that the whole city of Jerusalem rejoices with loud singing (v. 9). Finally, all nations see this great salvation, implying that many will join in the rejoicing (v. 10).

Very few people have beautiful feet in a literal sense. However, a messenger who runs to deliver good news can be described as having beautiful feet even if those feet are covered in dust, calloused, bruised, and cut from the run. The nature of the news is described with the words *peace, good tidings,* and *salvation.* All of these concepts converge in the thunderous expression *Your God reigns!* (see Psalms 93:1; 96:10; 97:1).

Peace is the familiar Hebrew word *shalom.* The war is over! There are no more enemies at the gate. Wholeness of life prevails, and people can truly say *Shalom!* to one another. The word *good* occurs seven times in Genesis 1 to describe the creation of the world; *salvation* is more than just the salvation of humans, since all creation is to be saved (see Romans 8:18-25). Only when goodness is restored to everything can we rejoice fully in salvation.

We note in passing that the word *salvation* is a play on Isaiah's own name, which means "salvation of God." God is finally coming back to Zion to reign as king, to bring peace, goodness, and salvation to his people, even to the whole world. Israel will continue to rejoice over the fact that God reigns (see Psalm 98:1-3).

> **What Do You Think?**
> What attitudes and actions in your life need the most help in your witness to the reign of God? What corrective action will you take?
> *Talking Points for Your Discussion*
> ▪ For witness to fellow Christians
> ▪ For witness to unbelievers

B. Watchmen Shout (v. 8)

8. Listen! Your watchmen lift up their voices; together they shout for joy.
When the LORD returns to Zion, they will see it with their own eyes.

Here we have an image of watchmen on the walls receiving the news of the runners of verse 7, above. (The historical account of 2 Samuel 18:19-33 offers us a good picture of how this works.) After receiving the news, the watchmen are predicted to join their voices together as if in a choir. The phrase *with their own eyes* refers to eyewitnesses' clarity of sight (see Jeremiah 32:4). In addi-

tion to the runners' bearing of good news, what the watchmen will see is God's coming as king, which is described in the servant song of Isaiah 52:13–53:12 that follows. This is what all the shouting is about!

C. Jerusalem Rejoices (v. 9)

9. Burst into songs of joy together, you ruins of Jerusalem,
for the LORD has comforted his people, he has redeemed Jerusalem.

As will the watchmen, the inhabitants of Jerusalem shall break forth in singing as a choir. This type of singing is the mark of a redeemed people (see Isaiah 26:1; 49:13). Such rejoicing occurs on top of the *ruins of Jerusalem.*

This predicts a spiritual renewal of Jerusalem. Since Isaiah 49:1, the prophet has switched topics from political restoration to the greater spiritual restoration. Only the forgiveness of sin and reconciliation to God can bring true comfort to the people (see 51:3, 12; 57:18; 61:2; 66:13). It is the impending advent of God himself that motivates this exuberant singing. Indeed, the Redeemer of 49:7, 26; 54:5, 8 will rescue his people (see 51:11; 63:9). The faithful still expect this centuries after Isaiah's day (see Luke 2:38).

> **What Do You Think?**
> How do we best help fellow Christians who seem to live joyless lives of despair and pessimism in spite of all that there is to praise God for?
> *Talking Points for Your Discussion*
> ▪ As they deal with physical problems
> ▪ As they deal with family conflicts
> ▪ As they deal with financial difficulties
> ▪ As they deal with spiritual struggles
> ▪ Other

D. Nations See (v. 10)

10. The LORD will lay bare his holy arm in the sight of all the nations,
and all the ends of the earth will see the salvation of our God.

What began in Isaiah 40:10 with reference to the arm of the Lord, which is his power to save, is to be fulfilled in full view *of all the nations.* We may think of a homespun idiom of God "rolling up his sleeves" to *lay bare his holy arm* for accomplishing this salvation (Isaiah 51:5; 63:5; compare Exodus 6:6; 15:16). God's plan of salvation has included all nations from the outset (see Genesis 12:3; Isaiah 42:6; 49:6).

For the nations to *see the salvation of our God* means that they experience it. A foretaste of this salvation is first given in Cyrus's decree for the Judeans to return to their homeland. This is nothing, however, compared with the great salvation visible when Jesus is crucified and rises from the dead three days later. All of this is done in history *in the sight of all*; as the apostle Paul testifies before Agrippa, "It was not done in a corner" (Acts 26:26).

III. New Exodus
(ISAIAH 52:11, 12)
A. Bearing the Vessels (v. 11)
11. Depart, depart, go out from there!
Touch no unclean thing!
Come out from it and be pure,
you who carry the articles of the LORD's
house.

Once again we have a double imperative—this time *depart, depart*—given to God's people who respond to his call. If Israel is to be a holy nation, she must do two things, one negative and one positive: *touch no unclean thing* and continually *be pure* (compare 2 Corinthians 6:17). The Lord's wrath is gone (Isaiah 51:17-23), and his people are established as a holy nation (52:1, 2). All this imagery is to prepare Isaiah's original readers for a new exodus, for now God's people must *carry*

HOW TO SAY IT

Babylon	*Bab*-uh-lun.
Chaldeans	Kal-*dee*-unz.
Cyrus	*Sigh*-russ.
shalom *(Hebrew)*	shah-*lome*.
shevi *(Hebrew)*	sheh-*vee*.
sheviyya *(Hebrew)*	sheh-vee-*yaw*.
testudo *(Latin)*	tess-*too*-doe.
Zion	*Zi*-un.

the articles of the Lord's house. While many commentators view this as leaving Babylon with the vessels of the temple (Ezra 1:7-11), the context of Isaiah persuades us to view it otherwise, as our next verse reveals.

B. Protected by God (v. 12)
12. But you will not leave in haste
or go in flight;
for the LORD will go before you,
the God of Israel will be your rear guard.

The prophet concluded his references to Cyrus and Babylon in Isaiah 48:20, 21. There Isaiah referred to Israel as fleeing from the Babylonians as in the first exodus from Egypt (compare Exodus 14:5). While exodus themes are used, they are employed now to refer to the spiritual deliverance that consists in dealing with the root of Israel's problem: sin and its devastating results.

Haste is not necessary as it was in the first exodus (Exodus 12:11, 33, 34). *The God of Israel* establishes his kingship over his people as one who goes before them as well as acting as their *rear guard* in the pilgrim journey of life (see Numbers 10:25; Joshua 6:9; also Exodus 13:21). The new exodus is to take place in order for the renewed people of God to be his once again. The suffering servant of Isaiah 52:13–53:12 takes upon himself the "punishment" that brings "peace" (53:5). By means of this substitutionary atonement, God's people, made up of all the nations, are set free from sin bondage.

❧ *BETTER THAN A TESTUDO!* ❧

Roman historian Cassius Dio (AD 150–235) relates a striking picture of a Roman military formation called *testudo,* which is Latin for "tortoise shell." When ordered to assume this formation, heavily armed Roman soldiers would close ranks and hold their shields in such a way as to form a tight "wall" and "roof" against arrows.

The formation worked quite well in that regard, even providing protection for baggage animals and lightly armed soldiers who were clustered in the middle of the formation. When properly arranged, this formation was strong enough to hold the weight of horses and wagons so those could cross terrain that was otherwise impassable to them.

But every military formation has weaknesses as well as strengths, and enemy armies figured out ways to defeat Roman troops arrayed in testudo formation. Not so with the Lord's protection! He knows where we've been and where we're headed. He knows who is attempting to hinder our service. He is the guard no enemy can defeat. Our task is to remain in him. Rejoice that God is our protection (see Psalm 5:11)! There is none better!
—C. M. W.

What Do You Think?
How have you sensed the Lord's protection over the years? Is his protection more apparent to you in hindsight? Why, or why not?
Talking Points for Your Discussion
- Regarding spiritual protection
- Regarding physical protection
- Regarding protection of relationships
- Other

Conclusion
A. Rejoicing in Full

Sometimes we find ourselves in situations that seem hopeless, where reasons for rejoicing seem few and far between. We wonder how deliverance will come about, if at all. The problem may involve church conflicts, work difficulties, health issues—the list goes on and on. So, where is any reason for rejoicing? Romans 5:2-5, 10, 11 has the answer:

Through whom we have gained access by faith into this grace in which we now stand. And we boast in the hope of the glory of God. Not only so, but we also glory in our sufferings, because we know that suffering produces perseverance; perseverance, character; and character, hope. And hope does not put us to shame, because God's love has been poured out into our hearts through the Holy Spirit, who has been given to us. . . . For if, while we were God's enemies, we were reconciled to him through the death of his Son, how much more, having been reconciled, shall we be saved through his life! Not only is this so, but we also boast in God through our Lord Jesus Christ, through whom we have now received reconciliation.

The apostle Peter offers further reasons for joyous praise in 1 Peter 2:9:

You are a chosen people, a royal priesthood, a holy nation, God's special possession, that you may declare the praises of him who called you out of darkness into his wonderful light.

Obviously, Peter thinks we can be the people God wants us to be. We are indeed "a holy priesthood, offering spiritual sacrifices" (1 Peter 2:5). What a privilege! What a reason for rejoicing to the fullest!

The great battle for our souls was fought and won at the cross. Peace has been declared (Romans 5:1). Like the ancient exiles who long ago had to be awakened from their spiritual sleep, "the hour has already come for you to wake up from your slumber, because our salvation is nearer now than when we first believed" (Romans 13:11). Rejoice!

B. Prayer

Heavenly Father, God of all hope, we thank you for the good news we have through our Lord Jesus Christ, for the peace, goodness, and salvation we experience each and every day through him. May our joy cause us to exclaim again and again, "Our God reigns!" In Jesus' name; amen.

C. Thought to Remember
Our God reigns!

Visual for Lesson 13. *Start a discussion by pointing to this visual as you ask, "How has God blessed you with hope most recently?"*

INVOLVEMENT LEARNING

Enhance your lesson with NIV® *Bible Student (from your curriculum supplier) and the reproducible activity page (at www.standardlesson.com or in the back of the* NIV® *Standard Lesson Commentary Deluxe Edition).*

Into the Lesson

Have learners call out titles of favorite praise songs and/or hymns. After each response, ask why it is a favorite. After a few minutes, say, "Music can minister to our souls in ways different from prayer, the spoken word, etc. Often a song or hymn becomes a favorite because it speaks of deliverance we can identify with."

Note that today's lesson text promised God's deliverance of the ancient Judeans from the tough situation of Babylonian captivity. Say, "It's difficult to sing songs of joy in such times, as Psalm 137:1-4 makes clear. [Read that passage aloud.] But even in situations where we find it hard to sing, we can meditate on those parts of God's Word that strengthen our faith that God will deliver. Today's text is one that did so for the ancient Judeans, and can still do so for us today."

Option. Place in chairs copies of the "Action!" crossword puzzle from the reproducible page, which you can download, for learners to begin working on as they arrive. This will create familiarity with the text before the lesson proper begins.

Into the Word

Using the Lesson Background, summarize the context of today's lesson. Then read the entirety of the lesson text aloud. Discuss how ancient Judeans in captivity may have reacted on being reminded of Isaiah's assertions and challenges, which were delivered before the captivity even began.

After the reading and discussion, ask a learner to come up front to serve as a scribe; he or she will jot learners' ideas on the board in the exercise to follow. Say, "As we work through today's text, let's be alert for themes that we think should be put to music. [Scribe's name] will write your ideas on the board as you call them out. Please keep your thematic suggestions succinct—four words per theme at the most. I will pause at appropriate points to give you a chance to respond."

Read aloud today's text again, pausing at obvious points (major punctuation marks, etc.) for learner responses. Some possible responses (among many) are as follows: *verse 1*–wake up / strong in the Lord / unstained; *verse 2*–rise up / captive no more; *verse 7*–beautiful feet, beautiful message / share the good news / our God reigns; *verse 8*–be God's watchman / sing to be heard; *verse 9*–joy in the Lord / God has redeemed us / sing together; *verse 10*–our God is powerful / our God is holy / our God saves; *verse 11*–leave sin behind / sinful no more; *verse 12*–God is our protection / never alone.

When learners run out of ideas, say, "Now let's consider which of these themes already have been put to music. Name some praise songs and/or hymns with these themes." Possible responses (among many) are "Our God Reigns," by Leonard E. Smith; "Joy to the World," by Isaac Watts; "Redeemed, How I Love to Proclaim It!" by Fanny Crosby; and "The Lord's Salvation," by Rich Mullins. (*Option:* Depending on the nature of your class, distribute Christian songbooks and/or hymnals to aid learners in responding. Ideally, these resources should have topical and/or Scripture indexes.)

Say, "As the ancient Judeans were to become a 'new people' after exile, we too become a 'new people' in God as we leave behind the captivity of sin. Our songs should reflect this!"

Into Life

Say, "God's rescue of the Judeans was a foreshadowing of our rescue from sin." Note that Isaiah 52:7 is quoted in Romans 10:15 and that Isaiah 52:11 is quoted in 2 Corinthians 6:17. Close by having the class sing "In Christ Alone," by Getty and Townend (or pick another appropriate song if your learners are not familiar with that one).

Option. Distribute copies of the "Sing!" activity from the reproducible page. Have learners fill it out by using the listing on the board and class discussion as thought prompts.

ACTS OF
WORSHIP

Special Features

Lessons

Unit 1: In Awe of God

Unit 2: Learning to Pray

Unit 3: Stewardship for Life

Unit 1 (Spring): The Pledge of God's Presence

QUARTERLY QUIZ

Use these questions as a pretest or as a review. The answers are on page iv of This Quarter in the Word.

Lesson 1

1. Hebrews says that in these last days God has spoken to us by his _____. *Hebrews 1:2*

2. Jesus has inherited a _____ that is "superior" to that of the angels. *Hebrews 1:4*

Lesson 2

1. We should always come into God's presence with quiet reverence. T/F. *Psalm 95:1, 2*

2. The psalmist describes us as the people of God's what? (pasture, hills, rock?) *Psalm 95:7*

Lesson 3

1. The angel described the place where the Savior was born as the town of _____. *Luke 2:11*

2. The shepherds waited until morning to go to see the infant Jesus. T/F. *Luke 2:15, 16*

Lesson 4

1. Just before he walked on the water, Jesus was alone to _____. *Matthew 14:23*

2. Which disciple asked to walk on the water with Jesus? (John, Judas, Peter?) *Matthew 14:28*

Lesson 5

1. Jesus taught his disciples to pray because one of them asked him to do so. T/F. *Luke 11:1*

2. Prayer is to involve asking, seeking, and what? (finding, knocking, kneeling?) *Luke 11:9, 10*

Lesson 6

1. Jesus prayed that his disciples would be what? (one, happy, tripled?) *John 17:11*

2. In his great prayer, Jesus noted that he had kept all his disciples from straying. T/F. *John 17:12*

Lesson 7

1. Hebrews teaches that Jesus was tempted like we are but he did not _____. *Hebrews 4:15*

2. Jesus is a high priest after the order of whom? (Aaron, Melchizedek, Levi?) *Hebrews 5:6*

3. Hebrews teaches that Jesus learned obedience by the things he suffered. T/F. *Hebrews 5:8*

Lesson 8

1. James prescribes singing songs by whom? (the happy, the sick, the elders?) *James 5:13*

2. According to James, sins should be confessed only to God. T/F. *James 5:16*

Lesson 9

1. Daniel believed that eating the king's food would defile him. T/F. *Daniel 1:8*

2. Seeing fasting done secretly, the heavenly Father rewards openly. T/F. *Matthew 6:17, 18*

Lesson 10

1. Jerusalem and _____ are the cities named in the parable of the good Samaritan. *Luke 10:30*

2. The parable of the good Samaritan includes an innkeeper. T/F. *Luke 10:34, 35*

Lesson 11

1. Jesus promised that he would return in glory along with "all the _____." *Matthew 25:31*

2. The great judgment will separate sheep from what? (cattle, goats, donkeys?) *Matthew 25:32*

Lesson 12

1. In spiritual warfare, our primary battle is against evil people. T/F. *Ephesians 6:12*

2. "The sword of the Spirit" is what? (flaming arrow, the Word of God, prayer?) *Ephesians 6:17*

Lesson 1 (spring)

1. John the Baptist saw Jesus and said, "Look, the _____ of God." *John 1:29*

2. John's God-given mission was to baptize people with the Holy Spirit. T/F. *John 1:33*

Note: *The first lesson of spring is placed as the final lesson of winter because the winter quarter has only 12 Sundays while the spring quarter has 14.*

QUARTER AT A GLANCE

by Mark S. Krause

STYLES AND ACCESSORIES of worship have changed a great deal over the last 30 years. Organs have been replaced by guitars and drums. Stained glass windows and fixed pews have given way to high-tech lighting and stackable chairs. The church's music in many places is now new songs almost every week in place of familiar hymns from centuries past.

Worship styles and accessories may change, but the essence of worship does not. Worship is the recognition of the greatness and glory of God by our humble adoration and submission to him. There is a growing awareness in the church today that worship involves much more than what we do in a church setting on Sunday morning.

Unit 1: In Awe of God

The lessons of this quarter examine biblical teachings of various aspects of worship. First will come a consideration of Scriptures that emphasize the basis for worship: God's absolute worthiness to receive it. The author of Hebrews begins his book with a marvelous description of the Father and the Son, showing both to be worthy of our adoration. Numerous Old Testament texts come together to create a powerful picture of the Son, whom the angels themselves worship.

Worship by angels is seen clearly in the third lesson, the famous account of the heavenly host saying, "Glory to God in the highest heaven" in the presence of the shepherds near Bethlehem (Luke 2:14). Rounding out our studies will be lessons that address God's worthiness to receive worship in light of his roles in creation and commanding the forces of nature.

Unit 2: Learning to Pray

A second aspect of worship that deserves careful study is the matter of prayer. We do not worship an abstraction, but the living God. This means we can communicate directly with God in our times of personal and corporate worship. Prayer is a fundamental element to effective worship. In that regard, we will examine what Jesus taught his disciples about prayer and how Jesus himself prayed.

Another lesson in this unit takes the element of intercessory prayer a step further in considering Jesus as our high priest, the one who intercedes for us eternally in Heaven. A lesson from James will encourage us to use prayer in practical, daily ways within the church community.

Unit 3: Stewardship for Life

The fact that worship is more than what we do on Sunday morning means that worship includes how we live daily. This unit addresses this reality in terms of stewardship, the way we use the resources and opportunities that God gives to us. We can choose to be selfish and live only for ourselves, but that does not glorify God in any sense of worship. Worship is necessarily tied to service for God and service to others.

In this light, our studies will consider the beloved parable of the good Samaritan, a story told by Jesus to answer the question, "Who is my neighbor?" This unit also includes a lesson that examines Jesus' depiction of the final judgment,

> *Worship styles and accessories may change, but the essence of worship does not.*

where those who had served the needy are commended as having served Jesus himself. The other two lessons address honoring God via dietary restrictions and preparation for spiritual warfare.

Worship begins with recognition of the greatness of God, is developed through our prayers to God, and is acted out through our service for God and others. The studies of this quarter will enrich your sense of worship so that you live each day in the acknowledged presence of God.

GET THE SETTING

by Jon Weatherly

WORSHIP IS one of those words that many Christians use but few seem to understand. We use the word to refer to our Sunday services, or perhaps just to the time when we sing on Sunday. But why should such things be called *worship*, and is there anything to the idea of worship besides those things?

This quarter's lessons will bring into focus a key biblical truth: for God's people in the Bible, worship was the celebration of God's mighty deeds of salvation. In worship, God's people remembered, recited, and reenacted the ways that he had acted in history to deliver and bless his people. By a variety of means, biblical Israel and the first-century church expressed wonder, awe, thanks, and dependence on the God who had done great things for his people in the recent and distant past.

God's deeds of the past were the foundation of biblical worship, but God's deeds in the present were biblical worship's first floor. Recognizing what God had done for his people in the past meant identifying oneself with those people. So for the faithful of the Bible, when God delivered Israel from Egypt, he did not merely deliver *them*; he delivered *us*.

In worship the past becomes the present. The worshipper joins with those who witnessed God's deeds firsthand, claiming their blessings like God's people in the past. In worship the Bible's story becomes the worshipper's story. In worship, God's faithfulness to his people in the past enables his people in the present to put their complete trust in him.

Worship that celebrates God's mighty deeds can never be dull or routine. Take prayer as an example. Knowing what he has done for his people in the past, biblical worshippers could pray in anticipation of what he will do in the present and the future: bringing his kingdom into the world (Luke 11:1-13), empowering his people and mak-

ing them one (John 17:6-12), and meeting needs of his praying people, just as he had in the past (James 5:13-18). Like them, we celebrate that God became one of us in Christ, so we pray knowing that with deep understanding Christ makes known to the Father our every need (Hebrews 4:14–5:10).

Worship that celebrates God's mighty deeds is never confined to special days or times. It finds its way into every act and every moment. God created the world for his people's provision, so they receive even the simplest of foods with thanksgiving; refraining from food, they celebrate their dependence on him (Daniel 1:5, 8-17; Matthew 6:16-18). Living in a world filled with deep need, they give of themselves to meet those needs (Luke 10:25-37; Matthew 25:31-46), always celebrating the way that in Christ God gave himself for them.

If the setting of biblical worship is the mighty deeds of God, then the very center of that setting is the greatest of God's mighty deeds: sending of the Son to become a human—living, dying, rising, and ascending to the Father's right hand—it was all on behalf of God's stubborn, sinful people. Though he arrived as a poor child in a feeding trough for animals, Heaven's angel army acclaimed him as Savior and Lord (Luke 2:8-20).

Among his people, he lived as one with authority unlike any other, teaching, serving, and saving as only God could. His command of nature's elements was but one demonstration of his authority, all exercised for the benefit of his followers (Matthew 14:22-33). After all, who can command the sea if not the one who made it (Psalm 95:5)? Jesus' supreme greatness over all provided security for the first Christians in the presence of God, just as it does for us (Hebrews 1:1-9).

How does one worship such a God? With humble dependence, radical generosity, and persistent trust—the very things that Christ showed his people. He is indeed a very great God (Psalm 95:3)!

THIS QUARTER IN THE WORD

Answers to the Quarterly Quiz on page 114

Lesson 1—1. Son. 2. name. **Lesson 2**—1. false. 2. pasture. **Lesson 3**—1. David. 2. false. **Lesson 4**—1. pray. 2. Peter. **Lesson 5**—1. true. 2. knocking. **Lesson 6**—1. one. 2. false. **Lesson 7**—1. sin. 2. Melchizedek. 3. true. **Lesson 8**—1. the happy. 2. false. **Lesson 9**—1. true. 2. true. **Lesson 10**—1. Jericho. 2. true. **Lesson 11**—1. angels. 2. goats. **Lesson 12**—1. false. 2. the Word of God. **Lesson 1 (spring)**—1. Lamb. 2. false.

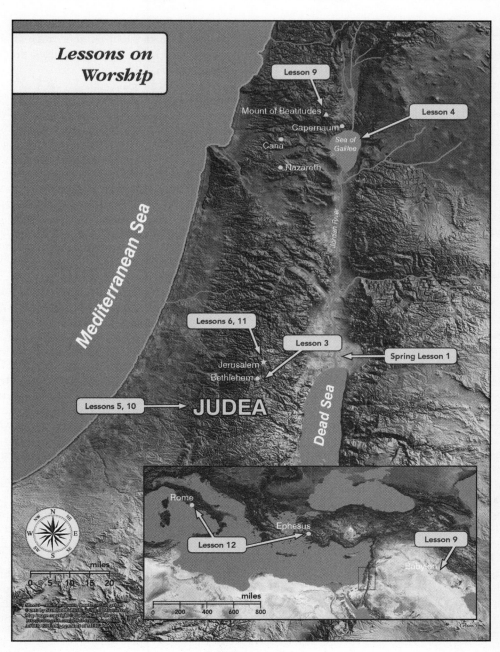

Lessons on Worship

Lesson 9

Lesson 4

Mount of Beatitudes

Capernaum

Cana

Sea of Galilee

Nazareth

Mediterranean Sea

Jordan River

Lessons 6, 11

Lesson 3

Spring Lesson 1

Jerusalem

Bethlehem

Lessons 5, 10

JUDEA

Dead Sea

N

NW NE

W E

SW SE

S

miles

0   5   10   15   20

Rome

Ephesus

Lesson 9

Lesson 12

Babylon

miles

0   200   400   600   800

CLASSROOM ENGAGEMENT

Teacher Tips by Wendy Guthrie

THE FIRST ARTICLE of this four-part series introduced the idea of community as the context in which learning takes place. This installment will focus on using certain teaching strategies to promote learner engagement, which helps to build community within the classroom.

A Comprehensive Process

Learning should be viewed as a comprehensive process that involves not just the head but heart and hands as well. Lesson preparation and delivery should take this into account. Students need information to ponder and reflect upon (head), but they also need input that interacts with their emotions (heart). It is head and heart together that will challenge learners to some sort of action (hands).

A Personal Process

Because learning involves more than just the intellect, teachers must find ways to make it relevant to the learner—to help the learner attach the information from class to his or her previous knowledge and experiences. One way to do this is to use current events or past personal experiences as an introduction to the lesson.

For example, in a lesson on the birth of Jesus (Lesson 3 of this quarter), you the teacher might begin by having a couple tell their story of being surprised and alarmed to have a child born in an unanticipated environment (in the car on the way to the hospital, etc.). If a couple with a personal story such as this is not available to relate it, a learner (or you) can share a similar story about someone you know personally.

Using this method activates learning on an emotional level as well as on an intellectual level. The lesson becomes personalized to the learner rather than being just a collection of facts or verses the teacher thinks are important. Lessons that become emotionally and personally relevant prompt the learner to make application to his or her life, thus better assuring changed thinking and behaviors.

An Engaging Process

Using strategies that promote problem-solving, cooperative learning, and personal reflection will also help to build fellowship among a class of learners. Rather than relying on lecture or questions and answers as the main vehicle for dispensing biblical information, a teacher could use the following scenario for a lesson on James 5:13-18 (Lesson 8 of this quarter): Begin by showing the class pictures of people in need of prayer or needing to pray for the various reasons listed in the text. Say that there are people like this in every church (the problem).

Next, propose a prayer ministry where church members make personal visits to those in need of prayer or who need help praying. Have students brainstorm the pros and cons of this idea and record their responses on the board. Then divide students into groups and assign portions of the text to each, asking groups to defend or refute the proposal as they combine the pros and cons with what they see in the text (cooperative learning). Finally, give each learner an index card on which he or she will identify the biblical strengths and weaknesses of your original proposal (personal reflection).

A Growing Process

When learners struggle together to solve problems, they become connected to one another and begin to trust each other with their own flaws and shortcomings. Trust builds community, and community helps each learner to grow in his or her walk with God. Teachers who use strategies that engage learners in not only the knowledge of Scripture but also in its emotion and action will accomplish the goal of the gospel.

WORSHIP CHRIST'S MAJESTY

DEVOTIONAL READING: 1 Timothy 1:12-17
BACKGROUND SCRIPTURE: Hebrews 1

HEBREWS 1:1-9

¹ In the past God spoke to our ancestors through the prophets at many times and in various ways, ² but in these last days he has spoken to us by his Son, whom he appointed heir of all things, and through whom also he made the universe. ³ The Son is the radiance of God's glory and the exact representation of his being, sustaining all things by his powerful word. After he had provided purification for sins, he sat down at the right hand of the Majesty in heaven. ⁴ So he became as much superior to the angels as the name he has inherited is superior to theirs.

⁵ For to which of the angels did God ever say,

"You are my Son;
    today I have become your Father"?

Or again,

"I will be his Father,
and he will be my Son"?

⁶ And again, when God brings his firstborn into the world, he says,

"Let all God's angels worship him."

⁷ In speaking of the angels he says,

"He makes his angels spirits,
    and his servants flames of fire."

⁸ But about the Son he says,

"Your throne, O God, will last for ever and
        ever;
    a scepter of justice will be the scepter of
        your kingdom.
⁹ You have loved righteousness and hated
        wickedness;
    therefore God, your God, has set you
        above your companions
    by anointing you with the oil of joy."

KEY VERSE

The Son is the radiance of God's glory and the exact representation of his being, sustaining all things by his powerful word. —**Hebrews 1:3**

ACTS OF WORSHIP

Unit 1: In Awe of God
LESSONS 1–4

LESSON AIMS

After participating in this lesson, each learner will be able to:

1. List ways in which Jesus is superior to angels.

2. Explain the significance of Jesus' superiority to angels.

3. Help plan a Christmas season worship service that emphasizes the majesty of Jesus.

LESSON OUTLINE

Introduction
  A. Let Me Draw You a Picture
  B. Lesson Background
I. God's Self-Expression (HEBREWS 1:1-3)
  A. Revelation Before Christ (v. 1)
  B. Revelation in Christ (v. 2)
    Is God Speaking to Me?
  C. Revelation Through Christ (v. 3)
II. Superior to Created Beings (HEBREWS 1:4-9)
  A. Name Above Angels' (vv. 4, 5)
  B. Worthy of Worship (vv. 6, 7)
    Angelic Work, Visible and Otherwise
  C. Rules in Heaven (vv. 8, 9)
Conclusion
  A. No Comparison
  B. Prayer
  C. Thought to Remember

Introduction

A. Let Me Draw You a Picture

When we're lost, verbal directions over the phone can be helpful, but the visual aid of a map or a GPS device offers a fuller picture. Written instructions for assembling a bicycle are necessary, but they can be hard to follow without diagrams. Most cookbooks include not only recipes but also pictures of the finished product. Visual illustrations go a long way toward making things clearer, especially when discussing difficult concepts.

Before Jesus came, God told people about himself through prophets, angels, dreams, etc. Sometimes these revelations included visual aids (examples: Genesis 28:12; Exodus 4:1-7). As a visual aid, however, Jesus was in a class by himself. His earthly life was a visible manifestation of God's invisible nature. To see Christ was to see God (John 14:9). Our passage today applies the visual-aid principle to help us understand the significance of Christ and his work.

B. Lesson Background

The book of Hebrews is shrouded in mystery, and scholars have debated its authorship, date, and audience. Was it written by Paul? Luke? Apollos? Barnabas? Timothy? even by Priscilla? Was it written before or after the destruction of the temple in AD 70? Does the traditional title "Hebrews" suggest the first readers to have been Jewish Christians primarily or even exclusively?

Not in doubt, however, is the fact that the author of Hebrews wishes to show Christ's superiority. Who the prophets, the angels, etc., were and what they revealed about God pale in comparison with who Christ is and what he in himself has disclosed about God. The implications of this are profound, as we shall see.

I. God's Self-Expression
(HEBREWS 1:1-3)

A. Revelation Before Christ (v. 1)

1. In the past God spoke to our ancestors through the prophets at many times and in various ways,

The author begins the discussion of Christ's superiority by sketching a background of divine communication *to our ancestors*. They were the ancients who lived in the time of great prophets such as Moses, Isaiah, Elijah, and Jeremiah. God's communication through such prophets took various forms as he spoke as circumstances required.

By the time of Jesus' birth, Jews widely acknowledged that no new prophet had arisen for almost four centuries, since the time of Malachi. No prophet had brought God's complete message, and the death of a prophet would require God to find new spokespersons periodically. This state of affairs took a dramatic turn with the arrival of Christ (next verse).

B. Revelation in Christ (v. 2)

2. . . . but in these last days he has spoken to us by his Son, whom he appointed heir of all things, and through whom also he made the universe.

The author proceeds to highlight the difference between the prophets and Jesus by noting two unique aspects of Christ's identity. First, Jesus is naturally the heavenly Father's *heir* because Jesus is God's *Son*. Since God has only one Son (John 3:16), the Father's entire estate belongs to Christ —Jesus doesn't have to divide the inheritance with anyone. This being the case, *all things* that God has also belong to Christ. No prophet could make such a claim, and certainly no prophet knew the heavenly Father in the way that his own Son does.

Second, God created the physical realm through Christ (compare Colossians 1:16). Many readers

HOW TO SAY IT

Apollos	Uh-*pahl*-us.
Barnabas	*Bar*-nuh-bus.
Elijah	Ee-*lye*-juh.
Isaiah	Eye-*zay*-uh.
Jeremiah	Jair-uh-*my*-uh.
Malachi	*Mal*-uh-kye.
Messiah	Meh-*sigh*-uh.
Moses	*Mo*-zes or *Mo*-zez.
Septuagint	Sep-*too*-ih-jent.
Zechariah	Zek-uh-*rye*-uh.

of the New Testament are familiar with John 1:1-5, which speaks of Christ as "the Word" regarding his role in creation. This builds on an ancient Jewish metaphor that uses God's *word* or *wisdom* as a symbol for his active, personal involvement in human affairs (Proverbs 8). First-century Jews believe that God engages and influences the world through his divine Word, which essentially signifies his personal will and creative power. Thus, in Genesis 1 God created the physical universe simply by speaking everything into existence ("God said, 'Let there be . . .'"); it was by his Word that he made everything.

But that view is incomplete without Jesus. As the eternal Word who "was with God," and "was God" (John 1:1), Christ is the one through whom the Father made everything; thus Jesus was actively involved in our world from the very beginning, not just when he came to earth. Obviously, no prophet could have made such a claim.

> *What Do You Think?*
> What is one thing you have learned from the revelation through Jesus that you did not learn from studying the Old Testament prophets?
> *Talking Points for Your Discussion*
> ※ Regarding God's love, compassion, and grace
> ※ Regarding God's wrath and judgment
> ※ Other

❧ IS GOD SPEAKING TO ME? ❧

Since "in these last days [God] has spoken to us by his Son," does that mean he does not speak to us in any other way? I often hear fellow believers say something like "I think God is trying to nudge me in a certain direction. But how do I know it's him—and not just me trying to convince myself that it really is God?"

Good question! To answer it, we should ask ourselves a few more questions. First of all, does the perceived nudge violate Scripture? Obviously, God is never going to tempt you to do something sinful (James 1:13). Second, what do you expect to gain from the perceived nudge? Are you expecting to be better paid, publicly honored, etc., or do you see God opening a door to a thankless service that

Visual for
Lessons 1 & 4

Have this visual on display as you pose the discussion question associated with verse 4.

will glorify only him? Third, what is your level of passion for the direction of the nudge? God wants to give us the desires of our hearts in his service (see Psalm 37:4). Finally, what is the opinion of mature believers who know you well? Their counsel may make you aware of blind spots, etc., that you need to address first (Proverbs 15:22; 20:18).

God will not speak to you in terms of allowing you to add to the Scriptures. He has taken care of all that through his Son (compare Revelation 22:18, 19). But God may indeed speak to you in terms of opening doors of ministry opportunity (compare 2 Corinthians 2:12). Take the steps above as you watch for them! —D. C. S.

C. Revelation Through Christ (v. 3)

3a. The Son is the radiance of God's glory and the exact representation of his being, sustaining all things by his powerful word.

This verse makes statements that affirm Jesus is set apart from every other figure in religious history. The fact that Christ is *the radiance of God's glory* connects Jesus with God in a unique way. God's glorious nature is made known to us through Christ as *the exact representation* of God's invisible being. The Greek word translated *representation* gives us the English word *character*; this is not in the sense of a cartoon character but in the sense of a symbol. Characters of this kind stand for other things or concepts. For example, an arrow symbol may stand for "direction" in a sign that tells us

which way to go. When Jesus walked the earth, he was a physical representation of the invisible God; thus Jesus pointed the way to God. We can know about the unseen God by knowing Christ.

Christ was not only active in creating the universe (v. 2, above), he continues to be active in sustaining it. All things have been created through Christ, and all things are now held together *by his powerful word.* Jesus is therefore not simply another great religious teacher or prophet. Those prophets spoke for God; Christ was God speaking. Such a special person is clearly able to do special things, two of which are noted next.

3b. After he had provided purification for sins, he sat down at the right hand of the Majesty in heaven.

The one able to create and sustain the universe also has the power to purge sin. This refers to Jesus' death, to his self-sacrifice. This theme is developed in greater detail later in this book (see especially Hebrews 9:11–10:18); what we have here is only an introduction to this topic.

Jesus' subsequent ascension to the highest position of honor in Heaven is noted frequently in the New Testament (Mark 16:19; Acts 2:33-36; Ephesians 1:20; etc.). This happened after Christ had voluntarily suspended his divine power and privileges to die for our redemption (Philippians 2:6-9) and rise again. The same cannot be said of any other being, prophet or otherwise.

II. Superior to Created Beings
(HEBREWS 1:4-9)

A. Name Above Angels' (vv. 4, 5)

4. So he became as much superior to the angels as the name he has inherited is superior to theirs.

The verse before us introduces the main theme of Hebrews 1: Christ's superiority to angels. This is no small claim! The word *angel* means "messenger" in everyday usage of ancient Greek. Throughout the Old Testament, angels are portrayed as messengers of God who enjoy direct access to his divine presence and have special knowledge of his hidden affairs (examples: Genesis 19:1-21; 2 Samuel 14:20; Judges 13; Zechariah 1:14-17).

The Law of Moses was itself delivered by angels (see Acts 7:38; Galatians 3:19). Since no sinful human can stand in God's holy presence, the angels communicated the terms of God's covenant to Moses, who in turn passed that law on to the Israelites. Hebrews 2:2 affirms this line of thinking. But despite their exalted position, angels still cannot tell us as much about God as Christ has. While angels have direct access to God (Luke 1:19), they are not one with God as Christ is.

We can sum up by saying that Christ's authority is superior to that of the angels for two reasons: his position and his nature. In terms of position, verse 3 has just indicated that Christ was exalted to the highest place in Heaven, the right hand of God, after faithfully fulfilling his calling. In setting aside his rights and dying for our sins, Christ was forever elevated to the highest position of honor.

Regarding Christ's nature, it is important to stress that his authority is not simply a result of his good works—he did not earn a high place with God by dying on a cross. That honor was already Christ's by his very nature, as the author of Hebrews proceeds to stress. Christ's authority is a function of his eternal birthright—he is greater than the angels not only because he did a greater work than they could do but also because he has inherited a superior *name* from his Father. This name, a name of authority, is revealed in the next two verses.

What Do You Think?

Which description or title of Jesus is your favorite? Why? How does it reveal his superiority?

Talking Points for Your Discussion
- Immanuel (Matthew 1:23)
- The Word (John 1:1)
- Christ or Messiah (John 1:41)
- Son of God (Mark 1:1)
- Son of Man (John 12:23)
- Other

5a. For to which of the angels did God ever say,
"You are my Son;
today I have become your Father"?

The book of Hebrews takes the form of a series of mini-sermons. The author's technique is often to cite an Old Testament passage then discuss its implications for understanding Christ's superiority. Verses 5-9 of our lesson text follow this pattern.

The quotation we see here is from Psalm 2:7. This verse appears in a coronation psalm—a song to be sung during worship ceremonies at the crowning of a new king in Israel. The psalmist stresses that God will prosper the new king in his reign, despite attacks from enemies (Psalm 2:2-4). Israel's king will be like a son to God, enjoying God's full protection and guidance while being exalted over other earthly rulers; this happens because of the heavenly Father's divine blessing. This sets the theme for the other quotations: Christ is not like the angels in merely being God's messenger or servant, but rather he is his *Son*.

Elements of these Old Testament citations should not be taken too literally. Specifically, *today I have become your Father* does not imply that Christ came into being only after he was conceived. To use a double negative, there was never a time when Christ did not exist. Hebrews 1:2, 3 has already established that Christ and God are one, so that seeing Christ is seeing the Father. The prophecies cited here in verse 5 therefore do not refer to Christ's nature but rather to his title: he enjoys the status of God's unique *Son*, with all the rights and privileges that pertain to it.

What Do You Think?

How will or should Jesus' absolute superiority affect your service to him in the week ahead?

Talking Points for Your Discussion
- At work or school
- At home
- In intercessory prayer
- In worship
- Other

5b. Or again,
"I will be his Father,
and he will be my Son"?

The second quotation is from 2 Samuel 7:14 (parallel is 1 Chronicles 17:13). This originally referred to God's promise to David that his throne would be secure after that man's death. David's son—first literally Solomon and then figuratively descendants who served as kings of Israel—was to be God's son as well, also enjoying God's protection. The author of Hebrews applies this concept to sketch Christ's relationship with God as the Father's true *Son*. As such, Christ's "name" (Hebrews 1:4, above) and status in Heaven are far superior to that of angels.

B. Worthy of Worship (vv. 6, 7)

6. And again, when God brings his firstborn into the world, he says,
"Let all God's angels worship him."

Having contrasted Christ's nature and status with that of angels, the author turns to some implications, again citing Old Testament passages. The first of these implications is indicated in the verse before us: Christ is not only superior to angels but also worthy of their worship.

A quick review of Psalm 97:7, the passage cited, reveals an interesting difference between the language of the original text and its application here. Psalm 97 stresses God's unique power and majesty, calling all people to submit to him. In the course of this exhortation, the psalmist highlights the folly of worshipping idols rather than the true King of kings. To stress God's absolute authority, the psalmist calls even the false gods of the pagans to bow down before him: "worship him, all you gods" in the original setting.

Many centuries after this psalm was written, a Greek translation known as the Septuagint was produced for use by Jews who lived outside Israel and who spoke Greek as their primary language. In this version, the word *gods* was changed to *angels* here. One theory for the change is that the ancient translators feared that some readers might take Psalm 97:7 to imply that pagan gods actually exist. Their substitution of *angels* for *gods* still stressed God's superiority to all spiritual beings. The author of Hebrews cites this Greek translation of Psalm 97:7 to emphasize this very point: the angels in Heaven do not compete with Christ in any way as they themselves submit to him in worship. Modern translations of the Old Testament are based on the Hebrew text (which reads *gods* rather than *angels*), with the result that Psalm 97:7 reads differently from Hebrews 1:6 today.

Since Christ is of one nature and glory with God and shares in his Father's eternal reign, then Christ should be worshipped not only by angels but also by humans. This especially applies to those who have been purified of sins by his death (Hebrews 1:3, above).

What Do You Think?

Which aspect of Jesus' life illustrates to you most strongly his superiority to angels? Why? How does this influence your view of angels?

Talking Points for Your Discussion

- Regarding Jesus' incarnation in general and birth in particular
- Regarding Jesus' temptations in the wilderness
- Regarding Jesus' resurrection and ascension
- Other

---

7. In speaking of the angels he says,
"He makes his angels spirits,
and his servants flames of fire."

The author now cites Psalm 104:4 to stress further Christ's superiority to angels. Psalm 104 describes God's majesty by noting his power over that which he created. The angels, like humans and the elements of nature, have been created by God, who makes everything to serve his purposes. Christ, by contrast, is uncreated and eternal.

❧ ANGELIC WORK, VISIBLE AND OTHERWISE ❧

We've all heard dramatic stories of angelic intervention for the deliverance of God's people. Missionaries tell stories of sadistic rebel troops who will not go near the huts where God's servants are hiding because of the "glowing guards" at the entrance. A young woman was not accosted by a mugger (later captured) on a street at night because of the "two large men" walking behind her—although she had been walking alone.

Visible angelic activities, if that is indeed what happened in the above cases, may be the rare exception, however. Perhaps God prefers that the vast majority of angelic activity remain hidden. Later in Hebrews, the writer reminds his readers, "Do not forget to show hospitality to strangers, for by so doing some people have shown hospitality to angels without knowing it" (13:2).

Whether considering the visible intervention of angels or their invisible acts of behind-the-scenes ministry, Jesus is superior. The angels of Heaven receive their orders from him. As we praise God for the work of his angels on our behalf, we also remember Paul's caution: "Do not let anyone who delights in false humility and the worship of angels disqualify you" (Colossians 2:18).   —D. C. S.

C. Rules in Heaven (vv. 8, 9)

8, 9. But about the Son he says,
"Your throne, O God, will last for ever and
     ever;
  a scepter of justice will be the scepter of
     your kingdom.
You have loved righteousness and hated
     wickedness;
  therefore God, your God, has set you
     above your companions
  by anointing you with the oil of joy."

The author now cites Psalm 45:6, 7 to contrast the angels with Christ even further. While the angels are created beings who act only on God's instructions, Christ, as God's Son and heir, has been granted an eternal throne and reign. In its original context, Psalm 45 was a royal wedding song, performed at wedding ceremonies for Israel's kings. Following the theme that the king enjoys special protection as God's "son," the psalmist compares him with God himself: Israel's kings were to reign forever under God's protection, enforcing justice and calling people to obey God's law (in theory, if not reality).

But what the psalmist meant theoretically the author of Hebrews takes for reality: Christ, as God's ultimate *Son*, has a permanent throne. Christ will reign on that throne *for ever and ever* because God the Father has set him above everyone else in Heaven, including the angels.

One final detail in this quotation is not to be missed: when God the Father anoints God the Son, the Father literally makes the Son to be *Christ* since the Greek word *Christ* means "anointed one," as does its Hebrew equivalent *Messiah*. Jesus was not self-anointed for his mission. Rather, he was anointed by the Father for that mission—the most important mission in history! (See Luke 4:18.)

What Do You Think?
  Which imagery in Hebrews 1:8, 9 speaks most
     strongly to you regarding Jesus' authority in
     your life? Why?
Talking Points for Your Discussion
  ▪ Throne
  ▪ Scepter
  ▪ Anointed
  ▪ Other

Conclusion
A. No Comparison

Western culture shows a curious fascination with angels. Charms, pendants, bumper stickers, decorative figurines, and Christmas ornaments bearing images of angels are readily available. Numerous books and websites promise to help the reader get in touch with a "guardian angel" or to harness the power of angels in everyday life.

While the Bible does teach that angels are real and active, it is important to stress that they should not be viewed as objects of devotion, etc. (see Revelation 19:10; 22:9). The fact that Christ receives their worship in Heaven underlines his unique status: he relates to God and reveals God in ways like no other. As the very image of God himself, and as the one who is exalted in Heaven because he died for our sins, Christ and no angel deserves our worshipful praise.

B. Prayer

Father, let our knowledge of Christ's glory and yours compel us to serve and worship him. In the name of your Son we pray, amen.

C. Thought to Remember

Christ is worthy of our worship.

VISUALS FOR THESE LESSONS

The visual pictured in each lesson (example: page 124) is a small reproduction of a large, full-color poster included in the *Adult Resources* packet for the Winter Quarter. That packet also contains the very useful *Presentation Tools* CD for teacher use. Order No. 020029214 from your supplier.

INVOLVEMENT LEARNING

Enhance your lesson with NIV® Bible Student (from your curriculum supplier) and the reproducible activity page (at www.standardlesson.com or in the back of the NIV® Standard Lesson Commentary Deluxe Edition).

Into the Lesson

To introduce both today's study and the quarter's theme, prepare seven flash cards with the following words, one each, with initial letters highlighted in some way: *Praise / Intercession / Humility / Submission / Rejoicing / Obeisance / Whom*. Reveal each card briefly to your group, in the order given above, then affix it to the board so it remains visible. Once all seven are posted in the same order revealed, ask, "Who has figured out the significance of these seven words?"

Someone should soon note the word *worship* when the initial letters are considered in reverse order. When someone does so, say, "And that is today's lesson challenge: 'Worship Christ's Majesty'!" Continue: "As I point to each word again, tell me how each concept relates to worship." Do so in the same order; saving the *W* (*whom*) for last will allow a transition to the idea that Jesus is to be the object of our worship, not angels.

Option. Before class begins, place in chairs copies of the "Messengers" activity from the reproducible page, which you can download. Learners can begin working on this as they arrive.

Into the Word

Give each learner a sheet of paper featuring a clock face, centered, with only the hours 1 through 12 within. Refer to verse 1 of the lesson text and say, "For the hours 1 through 6 on this clock, I'm going to name six Old Testament prophets. As I do, write their names as spokes that extend outward from the hour designations." Then name Moses, Micah, Isaiah, Zechariah, Daniel, and Hosea.

After everyone has written the names, ask for volunteers to read Genesis 3:15; Micah 5:2; Isaiah 53:3-10; Zechariah 9:9; Daniel 7:13, 14; and Hosea 11:1 to give a context of prophetic revelations of the Christ who was to come. Do not let this section drag out.

Then say, "Now look at Hebrews 1:2-4 for hours 7 through 12. As you read those verses, write one characteristic or accomplishment noted for Christ beside each of the six remaining hour designations on your clock." Allow four or five minutes, then call for responses. (Focusing on verbs, the expected responses are *being the exact representation; sustaining all things; purified our sins; sat down; superior to the angels; has inherited a superior name.*) Discuss. *Option:* Form learners into small groups or study pairs for this part.

Then say, "The author of Hebrews goes on to affirm a number of reasons why Jesus is superior to angels. What are some of those?" Jot answers on the board and discuss as learners respond. If learners need help, ask questions such as, "What does the end of verse 6 indicate?" and "What is the difference noted as to their roles in verses 7, 8?"

Into Life

Form learners into four groups to plan a worship service featuring the theme, "O Worship the King." *The Song Group* will select relevant hymns and/or praise songs on the majesty of Jesus. *The Prayer Group* will write an invocation as a call to worship and a prayer of benediction. *The Communion Group* will develop a communion meditation on the subject "Jesus Is the Worthy Lamb" from Revelation 5:12 and other appropriate passages. *The Sermon Group* will outline a sermon with the title "A Face Like the Sun," using one or more of these texts: Matthew 17:1-8; Mark 9:2-8; Luke 9:28-35; John 1:14; 2 Peter 1:16-18.

If your class is smaller, use only the first three groups. When groups finish, collect the ideas, discuss, and promise to pass them along to those who plan your congregation's worship services.

Option. Distribute copies of the "It's Time!" activity from the reproducible page. Since this involves personal reflection, you may wish to distribute it as take-home work.

MAKE A JOYFUL NOISE

DEVOTIONAL READING: 1 Kings 8:54-62
BACKGROUND SCRIPTURE: Psalm 95

PSALM 95:1-7A

¹ Come, let us sing for joy to the LORD;
  let us shout aloud to the Rock of our
  salvation.
² Let us come before him with thanksgiving
  and extol him with music and song.
³ For the LORD is the great God,
  the great King above all gods.
⁴ In his hand are the depths of the earth,
  and the mountain peaks belong to him.

⁵ The sea is his, for he made it,
  and his hands formed the dry land.
⁶ Come, let us bow down in worship,
  let us kneel before the LORD our Maker;
⁷ for he is our God
  and we are the people of his pasture,
  the flock under his care.

KEY VERSE

Come, let us sing for joy to the LORD; let us shout aloud to the Rock of our salvation. —**Psalm 95:1**

ACTS OF WORSHIP

Unit 1: In Awe of God

LESSONS 1–4

LESSON AIMS

After participating in this lesson, each learner will be able to:

1. List some reasons to praise God.

2. Compare and contrast the elements of worship cited in Psalm 95 with his or her own worship experience.

3. Use the lesson's seven verses, in turn, in daily devotions in the week ahead.

LESSON OUTLINE

Introduction
  A. Spurned Invitations
  B. Lesson Background
 I. Exhortation to Sing (PSALM 95:1-5)
  A. What to Do (vv. 1, 2)
    Joyful Abandon
  B. Why to Do It (vv. 3-5)
 II. Exhortation to Worship (PSALM 95:6, 7a)
  A. Postures to Take (v. 6)
    The Standing Posture
  B. Reasons for Reverence (v. 7a)
Conclusion
  A. What Is Worship?
  B. Prayer
  C. Thought to Remember

Introduction

A. Spurned Invitations

He was a new preacher in town, and he was going door-to-door in the community for several purposes: to introduce himself to the residents, to invite them to come to the church where he preached, and to do what he could to lead people to salvation in Christ. He had recently earned a doctorate, so his introductory remarks included that bit of information. His get-acquainted comments were usually like this: "Hello, I'm Dr. Jones. I'm the new preacher at Main Street Church, and I would like to invite you to come and worship with us."

The new preacher was unable to finish his introduction at one particular home when the man who opened the door interrupted as soon as he heard the word *doctor*. The man's reply (modified) was "No one here is sick!" as he slammed the door. The invitation was rudely spurned, even before it could be fully expressed. What if that man later called on that minister, whom he had treated so discourteously, to pray on his behalf? Would the minister say, "Sorry! You did not come when I invited you, so I am rejecting your counterinvitation. You had no time for God or me earlier. Why should I give you my time now?"

Certainly, no caring Christian would respond in such a way! Even so, Jesus spoke of a time to come when a spurned invitation would remain just that (see Matthew 22:2-14; Luke 14:16-24). *The great invitation of the Old Testament* is a designation often given to Isaiah 55:1-3, which bids a person to "come . . . buy . . . without money and without cost. . . . listen, that you may live." Jesus offered one of the great invitations of the New Testament when he said, "Come to me, all you who are weary and burdened, and I will give you rest" (Matthew 11:28).

The verb *come* appears three times in the verses of today's lesson. The verbs in the Hebrew are different each time, and there are different purposes in the invitations, as we shall see. We do well to keep in mind, however, that the invitation inherent in the word *come* is, as TV commercials say, "a limited-time offer."

B. Lesson Background

Most editions of the Bible group the 150 chapters of the book of Psalms into five subdivisions: 1–41, 42–72, 73–89, 90–106, and 107–150. These subdivisions are usually designated as *books* themselves. It is often noted that this five-book arrangement is a reminder of the first five books of the Bible by Moses—the Pentateuch. Each of the first four books in Psalms concludes with a brief doxology, and the fifth book utilizes all of Psalm 150 as a doxology that is a fitting close for the Psalter as a whole.

The superscriptions featured at the beginning of many psalms provide the names of authors, historical occasions that prompted the psalm in view, and/or musical instructions. Psalm 54 offers an example of a superscription that has all three components. At the other end of the spectrum are the 34 so-called *orphan psalms*, which have no superscription. Psalm 95, from which today's text is drawn, is one of these.

Some suggest that the orphan status of Psalm 95 makes it especially suited to the Messianic era, and this thought may be reinforced by the fact that this psalm is quoted in Hebrews 3:7-11, 15; 4:3, 5, 7 (which attributes this psalm to David). Psalm 95 is recognized as having two major parts, and the text for our lesson is the first part. This part is not quoted in the New Testament.

I. Exhortation to Sing

(PSALM 95:1-5)

A. What to Do (vv. 1, 2)

1. Come, let us sing for joy to the LORD; let us shout aloud to the Rock of our salvation.

The use of the word *come* is an imperative, and it is one of three different words translated this way in today's text. The word here is usually translated "walk," so the idea is to walk so as to come and do something.

The command to come is immediately followed by an exhortation for an action: singing. The words *let us* encourage everyone to participate in a song of joy, not a psalm of grief or sorrow in which penitent tears may flow.

The people of the Middle East have always loved to sing songs characterized by exuberance; they only need an occasion to break forth into such song. An example is the song that was sung when the Israelites crossed the Red Sea by a mighty miracle (Exodus 15:1-18). Another event was when women sang of the military exploits of David and Saul (1 Samuel 18:7). Breaking forth into a victory song is the natural thing to do in such cases.

The singing that is encouraged here is to be directed toward *the Lord*, and it is fitting to recognize that human accomplishments result from the Lord's enabling. How essential it is to recognize that the Lord is the source of power and strength! The apostle Paul does just that when he says, "I can do all this through him who gives me strength" (Philippians 4:13).

The astute reader will notice that the words of the latter part of the verse before us are very similar in meaning to what has just been stated for the first part: *let us sing* is parallel with *let us shout aloud,* while *the Lord* is parallel with *the Rock of our salvation* (compare Deuteronomy 32:15; 2 Samuel 22:47; Psalm 89:26). Such parallelism is characteristic of Hebrew poetry. The Western mind may look on it as redundant, but it is a delight to the person of the Middle East to repeat a thought by using different words and phrasing.

What Do You Think?

When do you find it appropriate to sing joyous worship songs/hymns rather than those more solemn in nature? When the reverse? Why?

Talking Points for Your Discussion
- Special times of the year
- In worship services
- When experiencing challenges or blessings
- Other

The exhortation for loudness can be used for sounding an alarm (example: Joel 2:1) or shouting during battle (example: Joshua 6:16). Those are not times for timidity or uncertain sounds, and neither is the occasion at hand!

The *salvation* in view is not defined, so its general meaning could fit any situation of triumph. It could be the fact that the Lord saved Israel from the

Egyptians in the days of Moses or that there had been a recent military victory. The superscription of Psalm 18 identifies the salvation discussed in that psalm as being that of David's deliverance "from the hand of all his enemies and from the hand of Saul." But there is no superscription to Psalm 95 to help us identify the salvation in view here.

> **What Do You Think?**
> During what times or seasons of life do you reflect most deeply on the certainty of your salvation in Christ? Why is that?
> *Talking Points for Your Discussion*
> - When facing temptation
> - When facing disappointment
> - When dealing with uncertainty
> - Other

Some may point to verses such as this to justify extreme loudness in contemporary worship. But we should be cautious in seeing a precedent. The song after the crossing of the Red Sea, the singing of the women when they praised David, and the singing at the temple all had two things in common: the singing was outside and there was no electronic amplification. Both facts imply limitations on decibel levels that often do not apply today. Some parts of the temple may have had a roof, but the sides were open as hundreds sang and played their instruments (2 Chronicles 29:30).

2. Let us come before him with thanksgiving and extol him with music and song.

The word *come* is used again, but it is not the same Hebrew word for *come* as was used in verse 1. The word here has the idea of walking at the head of a procession, or being in front (compare Psalm 68:25). It marks a progression in that the person who receives the invitation in verse 1 is now encouraged to take the lead in coming before the Lord *with thanksgiving*. Any time is a good time to express such thoughts. Being thankful is not to be confined to one holiday each year.

❧ JOYFUL ABANDON ❧

As a former resident of St. Louis, I have many friends there who are ardent fans of the city's professional baseball team. One of my friends has a season ticket for a seat near first base. Sometimes the TV cameras capture her—and not by accident. She is so exuberant and expressive! Sometimes I suspect she expends more energy during the game than the players do. She experiences as much joy as anyone there. One year she was on crutches when her team made it to the playoffs. While she needed assistance in getting to her seat, she still attended. She is a true fan.

We are designed to worship God, and that means much more than being his "fan." We have a God who is good, every day. He is always faithful, always loving, always with us, always giving us reasons to abandon ourselves in worship of him. We praise him best when we allow ourselves to be focused fully on the grandeur of who he is.

Certainly, there are times when measured, reflective approaches to God are appropriate. But when was the last time you found yourself so wrapped up in praise of him that you were simply lost in the love of the one who gave his Son so that you might live eternally? —V. E.

B. Why to Do It (vv. 3-5)
3a. For the LORD is the great God,

The transitional word *for* prepares to give reasons for the joyful music. Many cultures of the psalmist's day believe that the outcome of a war is determined by the nation that has the greater god. Israel often scored victories against great odds, and Israel's God was definitely greater (example: Exodus 12:12).

Israel was defeated at other times, but those occasions were usually judgments by God when Israel had gone after other gods. The defeats were a part of God's plan as he disciplined his people to accomplish his purposes through them.

3b. . . . the great King above all gods.

The second half of verse 3 reinforces the first half. The mention of *gods* is not a reference to angels nor is it meant to imply that other gods actually exist in any form except in imaginations and carvings of stone and wood (compare Psalms 82:1; 136:2; Galatians 4:8). Referring to the God of Israel as *the great King* (compare Psalm 48:2; Matthew 5:35) and as being *above all gods* (compare Psalms 96:4; 97:9; 135:5) are early affirmations for what Jesus will say when he boldly proclaims that all power belongs to him (Matthew 28:18).

4. In his hand are the depths of the earth, and the mountain peaks belong to him.

Other so-called gods are imagined as ruling different areas—to be the god of the sea, of the mountains (compare 1 Kings 20:23, 28), over a certain city or nation (11:33), etc. The God of Israel, however, is infinitely greater.

The Hebrew behind the phrase *the depths of the earth* is used only here in the Old Testament, so the exact meaning is uncertain. But since the phrase *the mountain peaks* refers to the highest places on earth, it is logical to conclude that *the depths of the earth* refers to the lowest (compare Job 38:16).

These two opposites are thus all encompassing. God rules everything. No matter where you may go, the Lord is already there—under the sea, on top of Mount Everest, with astronauts in a space laboratory, or anywhere in the universe. Similar thoughts are given expression by King David in Psalm 139.

Visual for Lesson 2

Have this visual on display as you pose the second discussion question associated with verse 7a.

> **What Do You Think?**
> What experience with the grandeur of nature gives you the greatest sense of God's presence and power? Why is that?
>
> *Talking Points for Your Discussion*
> - In a deep place (Grand Canyon, etc.)
> - On a high place (Pike's Peak, etc.)
> - During a specific season (winter, etc.)
> - Other

5. The sea is his, for he made it, and his hands formed the dry land.

Again the psalmist (David) contrasts two opposites. This time the contrasts are *the sea* and *the dry land*. Two things are stated about the sea: that it belongs to the Lord and that he made it. This again is parallelism since to create something implies ownership of what has been created.

We don't want to miss the intent: this verse introduces the element of creation as another reason that God is to be praised in song. *Made* and *formed*, words from the creation account of Genesis, are used. Water is simply a part of God's cre-

ating the heavens and the earth in Genesis 1:1, 2; dry land is said to "appear" as the waters were "gathered to one place" (1:9). In the verse before us, however, *the sea* is said to be *made*, and *the dry land* is said to be *formed*. New perspectives are therefore developed in this poetic description of creation (compare Psalm 104:5-9).

Given our modern scientific discoveries, we should have even more reason to sing praise to the God who made the heavens and the earth! This becomes all the more significant as we combine this fact with John 3:16, that God so loved the world—the people who inhabit this speck in the universe—that he sent his one and only Son for the salvation of those who believe in him.

II. Exhortation to Worship
(PSALM 95:6, 7a)
A. Postures to Take (v. 6)
6. Come, let us bow down in worship, let us kneel before the LORD our Maker;

The flow of thoughts about the greatness of God leads to two things. First, the third invitation to *come* is given. The Hebrew is different from the *come* of either verse 1 or verse 2. The Hebrew word for *come* in the verse before us involves opposites, for it may mean "to come" or "to go," depending on the context. The use of three different words for *come* should leave no doubt as to the psalmist's intent: all this is a decisive invitation to approach

God for a specific reason. That reason, the second feature of this verse, is *worship*.

The biblical concept for genuine worship is that of submission, the idea of giving honor to deity. The invitation therefore is for bowing and kneeling—postures of submission—before the Lord. Such is the appropriate response to the one who has made everything. Anyone who may be tempted to feel superior can find the cure by bowing and kneeling before Almighty God.

The words of the Old and New Testaments associated with *worship* are words that depict bowing, humbly entreating, or doing obeisance. One suggestion is that this type of worship may be done by touching the floor with the forehead while on hands and knees. It is a demonstration that we are nothing when we compare ourselves with God.

The verse under consideration is one of many Old Testament examples of falling before God. Revelation 4:10; 19:4, 5 provide New Testament examples. We keep in mind that true worship is primarily an attitude of the heart. When the heart is right before God, then it is appropriate also to stand and praise him (Exodus 33:10; 2 Chronicles 20:19). The worship leader who says "Let's all stand and worship" is usually giving an invitation for people to stand and sing, and we know what this leader means. Eventually the dictionaries may include singing as a definition for *worship*.

The phrase *the Lord our Maker* has drawn two interpretations: (1) that God is the one who created people in general or (2) that God made the nation of Israel in particular. The former idea comes from the thoughts expressed in the previous verses of Psalm 95; the latter sense is found in the next verse below (compare Deuteronomy 32:6). God took a slave people that had never existed as a nation, but only as the descendants of a man named Israel. In Exodus 3:16, the distinction begins to appear between Israel as a nation in contrast with identification as a family. This designation becomes definite at the time of the fifth plague (Exodus 9:4), when Israel is contrasted with Egypt.

❧ THE STANDING POSTURE ❧

One recent December I was visiting my parents for my birthday. They live near a college town, and Handel's *Messiah* was being performed on campus that year. I had never been to a live performance of that composition, so I was delighted when they suggested we attend with their minister and his wife.

The conductor presented the history of the oratorio along with some interesting anecdotes about the composer. In these opening remarks, he said that the Hallelujah Chorus (which concludes the second of the oratorio's three parts) often evokes a strong response: some will feel led to stand; others will then feel uncomfortable, not knowing how they should respond. He gave the audience freedom to decide as they would . . . to stand or not.

I had heard the Hallelujah Chorus countless times, but what happened caught me off guard nonetheless. There was something different about being present at a live performance of it. When the piece began, something stirred inside of me and many others there. I stood, as did at least half of the audience. I was moved to reverence, awe, and tears as this piece struck me more viscerally than my own national anthem. Indeed, this felt to me like we were experiencing a kingdom anthem. Standing just seemed to be the right posture of worship for this occasion!   —V. E.

B. Reasons for Reverence (v. 7a)

7a. . . . for he is our God
and we are the people of his pasture,
the flock under his care.

Two reasons are given for the exhortations to worship. First, worship is the reasonable thing to do considering all that the Lord has done as *our God*. In part, worship is a proclamation based on the fact that God has fulfilled the promises that

HOW TO SAY IT

Ezekiel	Ee-*zeek*-ee-ul or Ee-*zeek*-yul.
Galatians	Guh-*lay*-shunz.
Messiah	Meh-*sigh*-uh.
Moses	*Mo*-zes or *Mo*-zez.
Pentateuch	*Pen*-ta-teuk.
Psalter	*Saul*-tur.

he made to the patriarchs. He promised many nations from their descendants (Genesis 17:4), but only one of them is the special covenant nation—the nation of Israel. Through that nation the Messiah would come at just the right time in history (Galatians 4:4). Israel was therefore a nation with privileges. At a later time, a prophet reminds the northern nation of Israel of the fact that it was the nation that God had specially chosen (Amos 3:2), so Israel was to be punished because of its sins. There is peril in privilege.

The second reason for worship is similar to the first, but it uses familiar imagery of agriculture to make the point: *we are the people of his pasture.* The Bible frequently uses the analogy of a shepherd and his sheep to illustrate the special relationship between God and his people (examples: Psalm 23; 74:1; 79:13; 80:1; 100:3; Isaiah 40:11; Ezekiel 34:12-14; Hebrews 13:20).

What Do You Think?

In what ways is your church a visible manifestation of God's shepherding care? What more can it do in this regard?

Talking Points for Your Discussion

- Through church leaders
- Through specific ministries
- Other

It is a blessing to be in the care of the one who said, "I am the good shepherd. The good shepherd lays down his life for the sheep" (John 10:11). How appropriate for Christians to join together to sing to him and to worship him who is our shepherd!

What Do You Think?

What hymns or worship songs are especially meaningful to you in expressing themes found in today's psalm? Why is that?

Talking Points for Your Discussion

- Music with the theme of God as Savior
- Music with the theme of God as King
- Music with the theme of God as Creator
- Music with the theme of God as Shepherd
- Other

Conclusion

A. What Is Worship?

Several years ago, an article in a certain journal described worship as "shouting praises to God, banging on drums and cymbals, jamming on electric guitars, dancing, waving, laughing," and other emotional actions. A preacher who read the article commented that that description sounded more like what Elijah witnessed at the contest on Mount Carmel (1 Kings 18:26-29).

Worship is not easy to define to everyone's satisfaction, as the "worship wars" in some churches attest! Since a form of the word *worship* is used approximately 80 times in the New Testament, then surely the New Testament has explicit words of instruction about worship for the assembled church, doesn't it? The answer may surprise you: the New Testament never explicitly describes the church as coming together to worship or says that an assembly of Christians is a "worship service." (The closest situations are in Acts 13:1, 3 and 1 Corinthians 11:17-21; 14:23-25.)

Today's lesson should lead us to conclude that worship is at least reverence, including acts that demonstrate reverence, directed toward God. What is of the utmost importance is the heart of the individual. Is he or she in submission to God when singing or praying? This focus on the individual does not establish an exemption from being in a weekly assembly. The one who deliberately forsakes the assembly when he or she could attend does not have a truly submissive heart (compare Hebrews 10:25).

May we worship together to declare the worth of God! He is a God indeed above all gods because he is the maker of all.

B. Prayer

Heavenly Father, thank you for the worship emphasis of Psalm 95! May I be in submission to you in all that I do because of your greatness. Grant that I may join with other believers in singing your praises. In Jesus' name, amen.

C. Thought To Remember

God, and no other, is worthy of worship.

INVOLVEMENT LEARNING

Enhance your lesson with NIV® Bible Student *(from your curriculum supplier) and the reproducible activity page (at www.standardlesson.com or in the back of the* NIV® Standard Lesson Commentary Deluxe Edition*).*

Into the Lesson

Write this statement on the board before class begins: *Worship is always a response to God's worthiness, or it is not worship at all.* Cover the statement so that it cannot be seen.

Begin class by saying, "Our study is about a call to worship. It is a reasoned and reasonable call as the psalmist invites us to join him in affirming the worthiness of God. In that light, I propose that [reveal the hidden statement]." Ask, "In what ways is this statement true?" Jot learner responses on the board and discuss. Note that the word *worship* relates directly to worthiness.

Into the Word

Read today's text aloud. Then distribute handouts of, or otherwise display, the following list of names and descriptors of God: 1. Good shepherd; 2. Creator of mankind; 3. Savior; 4. King; 5. Creator of the earth; 6. Lord; 7. God of gods. Say, "Let's look at today's text and note a verse or verses where the psalmist states or implies these names and descriptors of God." Work through the list item by item, jotting responses on the board. *(Expected responses: 1–verse 7; 2–verse 6; 3–verse 1; 4–verse 3; 5–verse 5; 6–verses 1 and 3; 7–verse 3.)*

Alternative. Instead of the above, distribute copies of the "What and Why" activity from the reproducible page, which you can download. Have learners complete this individually or in pairs. It should take no more than three minutes.

Next, have a vocal or instrumental soloist (whom you have invited in advance) sing or play an appropriate portion of each of the following compositions. When you signal your musician to pause, ask learners to match to a verse what was sung or played: A. "Down in the Valley with My Savior I Would Go"; B. "There's Within My Heart a Melody"; C. "I Will Enter His Gates"; D. "O Worship the Lord in the Beauty of Holiness"; E. "O Worship the King"; F. "Joyful, Joyful, We Adore Thee"; G. "God, Who Made the Earth"; H. "The Lord Is My Shepherd." *(Expected matches: A–verse 4; B–verse 2; C–verse 2; D–verse 6; E–verse 3; F–verse 1; G–verse 5; H–verse 7.)*

Of course, you may wish to choose other songs or hymns that are more familiar to your class. As each verse is identified with a composition, you will have an opportunity to offer further insights. *Option:* If you choose an instrumentalist over a vocalist, you can add a "name that tune" procedure similar to the old television game show of that title.

Into Life

Read Romans 12:1 aloud. Then invite learners to complete the following stimulus statements in light of that verse as you read them:

1. He gives reason for joy; therefore let us ____.
2. He is the rock of our salvation; therefore let us ____.
3. He is the great king; therefore let us ____.
4. He controls all of earth's elements; therefore let us ____.
5. He is worthy of worship; therefore let us ___.
6. He is our shepherd; therefore let us ____.
7. He is our Creator; therefore let us ____.
8. He is the only God who is a true God; therefore let us ____.

Distribute handouts that list the seven verses of today's text next to the seven days of the week, one each. Leave space between each pair of entries for learners to write a brief devotional thought each day of the week to come as they reflect on the associated verse. Say, "If you wish, send each day's thoughts to me via e-mail, and I will combine them to send to all class members."

Distribute copies of the "'Old 100th' and I" activity from the reproducible page. Ask volunteers to share with the class responses to the questions thereon. If time is short, this can be a take-home activity for personal reflection.

GIVE GLORY
TO GOD

DEVOTIONAL READING: Psalm 19
BACKGROUND SCRIPTURE: Luke 2:1-20

LUKE 2:8-20

8 And there were shepherds living out in the fields nearby, keeping watch over their flocks at night. 9 An angel of the Lord appeared to them, and the glory of the Lord shone around them, and they were terrified. 10 But the angel said to them, "Do not be afraid. I bring you good news that will cause great joy for all the people. 11 Today in the town of David a Savior has been born to you; he is the Messiah, the Lord. 12 This will be a sign to you: You will find a baby wrapped in cloths and lying in a manger."

13 Suddenly a great company of the heavenly host appeared with the angel, praising God and saying,

14 "Glory to God in the highest heaven,
and on earth peace to those on whom
his favor rests."

15 When the angels had left them and gone into heaven, the shepherds said to one another, "Let's go to Bethlehem and see this thing that has happened, which the Lord has told us about."

16 So they hurried off and found Mary and Joseph, and the baby, who was lying in the manger. 17 When they had seen him, they spread the word concerning what had been told them about this child, 18 and all who heard it were amazed at what the shepherds said to them. 19 But Mary treasured up all these things and pondered them in her heart. 20 The shepherds returned, glorifying and praising God for all the things they had heard and seen, which were just as they had been told.

KEY VERSE

The shepherds returned, glorifying and praising God for all the things they had heard and seen, which were just as they had been told. —**Luke 2:20**

Graphic: Dorling Kindersley RF / Thinkstock

ACTS OF WORSHIP

Unit 1: In Awe of God

LESSONS 1–4

LESSON AIMS

After participating in this lesson, each learner will be able to:

1. Describe how God's glory was revealed in the story of the Bethlehem shepherds.

2. Compare and contrast the reactions of first-century individuals and groups regarding the news of Christ's birth with each other and with modern reactions.

3. Commit to sharing one's own wonder at the birth of Christ with an unbeliever.

LESSON OUTLINE

Introduction
  A. Baby Portrait: Awesome and Lowly
  B. Lesson Background
I. Exalted Announcement (LUKE 2:8-14)
  A. Quiet Night (v. 8)
  B. Blaze of Glory (vv. 9, 10)
  C. Startling Information (vv. 11, 12)
  D. Angelic Chorus (vv. 13, 14)
    No Aurora Borealis!
II. Submissive Response (LUKE 2:15-20)
  A. Immediate Obedience (v. 15)
  B. Amazing News (vv. 16-18)
  C. Quiet Reflection (v. 19)
    A New Interpretive Grid
  D. Joyful Celebration (v. 20)
Conclusion
  A. Quite a Contrast!
  B. Prayer
  C. Thought to Remember

Introduction

A. Baby Portrait: Awesome and Lowly

People love baby pictures. Announce that a baby has been born, and people will immediately ask, "Do you have pictures?" We carry them in our wallets and purses. We share them through social media. We frame and hang them in our homes.

Years later we look at those pictures and ask ourselves, "Was he ever really that small?" "When did she get all grown up?" We hold in our minds the contrast between the tiny, helpless baby and the growing child or grown adult that the baby has become.

The story of Jesus' birth can call up similar feelings. When we think of the infant Jesus at Christmas, we are awestruck that God was entering the world in that child. The Creator chose to enter his creation as a human baby, one as weak and vulnerable as any other. That baby grew up in a lowly setting to demonstrate amazing power that could belong only to God. Yet he also chose to surrender himself to his enemies and die a tortuous death.

Today's text exemplifies this contrast. As we gain in our understanding here, we will move closer to comprehending what God has really done for us through Jesus Christ.

B. Lesson Background

Our lesson text is part of a much larger story of Jesus' conception and birth in Luke 1 and 2. Luke weaves this story in with his account of John the Baptist's conception and birth. Both births were announced by an angel, accomplished by God's miraculous power, and accompanied by wonders that God performed. Both children were announced to be God's future instruments. But Jesus stands supreme in this pairing. He is God's Son (Luke 1:32a), the promised king (1:32b, 33), virgin born (1:35), the Lord (1:43), and the source of the salvation (2:30). To him alone the glory of God belongs.

But as Jesus was born against the backdrop of Roman imperial power, there was another who claimed glory. Caesar ruled much of the world and had ordered it to pay him taxes (Luke 2:1).

Some said that the true glory in the world was that of Rome's political, military, and economic power. Of such glory Jesus and his family had none. Shut out from ordinary living quarters for humans, the newborn Jesus lay in a manger, a feeding trough for animals (2:7).

Where was true glory to be found—in the palaces of Caesar or the manger of Bethlehem?

I. Exalted Announcement
(LUKE 2:8-14)
A. Quiet Night (v. 8)

8. And there were shepherds living out in the fields nearby, keeping watch over their flocks at night.

The scene opens with a sight familiar to all who live in the area. Most people in the biblical world make their living in agriculture, and the herding of sheep and goats is prominent in their economy. Many famous people in Israel's history were shepherds, including the patriarchs Abraham, Isaac, and Jacob as well as the great King David.

Yet as common as it is to herd sheep, shepherds receive a measure of scorn from some. Because shepherds commonly stay out at night with their herds, some religious teachers view them with suspicion since nighttime is associated with thievery (compare Jeremiah 49:9; 1 Thessalonians 5:2). At the very least, the commonness of herding sheep does not impart prestige on shepherds.

B. Blaze of Glory (vv. 9, 10)

9. An angel of the Lord appeared to them, and the glory of the Lord shone around them, and they were terrified.

HOW TO SAY IT

aurora borealis	uh-*roar*-uh boar-ee-*a*-lus (*a* as in *mad*).
Bethlehem	*Beth*-lih-hem.
Caesar	*See*-zer.
Gabriel	*Gay*-bree-ul.
Hosea	Ho-*zay*-uh.
Isaiah	Eye-*zay*-uh.
Pax Romana *(Latin)*	*Pahks* Ro-*mah*-nah.

To this ordinary scene comes a most extraordinary event. *An angel of the Lord* is a heavenly messenger of God. This is now the third appearance of an angel in Luke's story line: Gabriel had announced John the Baptist to be the prophet of the great king (Luke 1:11) and Jesus as the king himself (1:26-33). Now an angel is about to make an announcement to a band of humble shepherds.

Luke describes an illumination of the nighttime scene. Such light can come only from God, who calls light into existence (Genesis 1:3). The typical reaction to the appearance of an angel is fear (Judges 6:22, 23; Luke 1:11, 12; Acts 10:3, 4). God's heavenly messengers express the power and majesty of God, so the shepherds' reaction of being *terrified* is understandable.

10. But the angel said to them, "Do not be afraid. I bring you good news that will cause great joy for all the people.

This heavenly messenger does not come in judgment but in mercy. So he tells the shepherds to *not be afraid* (compare Luke 1:13, 30). The angel brings *good news,* like the prophet Isaiah's promise of good news for the suffering people of God (see Isaiah 40:9; 52:7; 61:1). The joyous news is not just for the shepherds but also for all who await the fulfillment of God's promises.

We notice that this glorious message *for all the people* is first given to ordinary, lowly shepherds. God's glory works that way.

> *What Do You Think?*
> What are some ways the Christmas season renews your hope? Why is that?
> *Talking Points for Your Discussion*
> - In preparing for the season, at home or church
> - In observing family or church traditions
> - In recalling memories of Christmases past

C. Startling Information (vv. 11, 12)

11. "Today in the town of David a Savior has been born to you; he is the Messiah, the Lord.

Birth announcements typically proclaim an addition "to our family" or something similar. This one is different. This announcement is of a birth that is *to you,* as if the new baby is of the family or families of the shepherds!

Visual for
Lesson 3

Keep this map posted for the rest of the quarter to give your learners a geographical perspective.

The birth has taken place in Bethlehem, but the angel designates the little village as *the town of David* instead. This is not a secret code, for the shepherds know immediately that the reference is to Bethlehem (see v. 15, below). The angelic designation is a reminder that the birthplace is the home of Israel's great king, the one to whom God made a promise of a descendant whose throne would endure forever (1 Chronicles 17:11-14). That long-awaited promise is now coming to fulfillment.

The angel calls the newborn child *a Savior*. We are familiar with that term for Jesus in designating him as the one who saves from sin. But for the shepherds, this term may sound at first like a title that the Romans give to their successful rulers. But the Scriptures call God the Savior of his people (Isaiah 43:3; Hosea 13:4; etc.). Is this child to be a rival to Caesar for the title of Savior?

The angel adds that this Savior is *the Messiah,* a Hebrew word meaning "anointed one"; therefore this is the designation of God's king. The further designation *the Lord* expresses supreme authority. Rome insists that Caesar is the only king and lord, but for the people of Israel the true king is none other than God himself (notice the irony in John 19:15). Therefore only God can be rightly called *Lord* in the ultimate sense. This child brings with him the authority of God himself!

12. "This will be a sign to you: You will find a baby wrapped in cloths and lying in a manger."

Now comes the great contrast. The announced Savior/Messiah/Lord will be identified with *a sign* indicating which newborn child is the right one. But the sign also indicates the kind of king the child will be. The sign is not that the child is to be found *wrapped in cloths* (what older translations call "swaddling clothes"); to be wrapped that way is just normal procedure. A nonbiblical work written a century or two before Jesus reflects this normalcy: "I was nursed with care in swaddling cloths. For no king has a different beginning of existence" (Wisdom of Solomon 7:4, 5; contrast Ezekiel 16:4). Therefore to be wrapped in cloths is nothing unique as a sign.

The unique sign, rather, is that this child lies *in a manger,* a feeding trough for animals. No lodging is available for the family (Luke 2:7), so Joseph and Mary have taken shelter with animals, perhaps in one of the caves near Bethlehem used as a stable. The promised king, the powerful Lord and Savior, is born in the lowliest of circumstances!

> *What Do You Think?*
> In what format do you find the retelling of the Christmas story especially meaningful? Why?
> *Talking Points for Your Discussion*
> - Children's Christmas program
> - Christmas Eve service
> - Family gatherings
> - Live nativity scene
> - Television or movie
> - Other

D. Angelic Chorus (vv. 13, 14)

13. Suddenly a great company of the heavenly host appeared with the angel, praising God and saying,

The solitary angel is now joined by a great choir of angels. Or more specifically it is an army of angels since the term that is translated *host* typically refers to armies. Heaven's army, so much more powerful than any human army, now joins in praise to God for the king who lies in an animal's feeding trough.

14. "Glory to God in the highest heaven, and on earth peace to those on whom his favor rests."

Who is worthy of glory? Only God—the true God who is sending his Son as a human infant who lies in a manger. God is supreme, above all who pretend to have authority or power. The highest glory can belong only to him.

In sending his Son, God is bringing his supreme blessing to humanity. Earth has been filled with turmoil, violence, and fear ever since our first parents rebelled against God. Now God promises to restore his peace to the troubled earth.

For the shepherds living under Roman occupation, the angelic note of praise strikes another contrast. The *Pax Romana*, or "Roman peace," is what Rome claims to give its subjects. Now true peace, God's peace, is near—not through Caesar but through God's anointed one.

What Do You Think?

How can your church better promote the peace Christ brings?

Talking Points for Your Discussion

- In distinguishing Christ's peace from the peace that the world tries to achieve
- By use of social media
- Through Christmas programs
- Other

The *peace* of God, sing the angels, come to those who submit to the reign of the king whom God is sending. These people have God's *favor*. The decision to submit to Christ is what will result in peace.

❧ No Aurora Borealis! ❧

The year 2012 witnessed what was called "the world's best light show." Due to an increase in solar activity, the aurora borealis (the Northern Lights) appeared with greater than usual intensity, as pulsating curtains of color danced across the night sky during February and March. One could sign up for "aurora alarms" to be notified when auroras reached certain levels of visibility. Savvy travel agents marketed cruises to locations where viewing would be optimal.

Yet we may safely presume that even the best view of the auroras could not compare with the glory of the Lord on the night of the angelic mes-

sage. This is sharpened by the fact that the unsophisticated men to whom the angels appeared had never used a telescope, had never seen the sky pierced by searchlights, and had never heard voices or music through electronic amplification. To describe their experience as overwhelming seems so inadequate. No wonder they rushed to the baby (see the next verse)!

Our response each Christmas should be the same: hurry to Jesus. To contemplate the wonder of the aurora borealis is a marvelous thing. To embrace the one who created the aurora borealis is infinitely better still. See John 1:3.   —V. E.

II. Submissive Response
(LUKE 2:15-20)

A. Immediate Obedience (v. 15)

15. When the angels had left them and gone into heaven, the shepherds said to one another, "Let's go to Bethlehem and see this thing that has happened, which the Lord has told us about."

As the angels depart *into heaven*, the story shifts from the message of the angels to the response of the shepherds. The shepherds, now alone in the scene, speak in a way that confirms their immediate submission to the angelic message: *Let's go* expresses urgency—"We must go!" They affirm their intent to do exactly as the angel has instructed. This reveals trust in the truthfulness of the angel's message. That message is the Lord's message.

The shepherds as ordinary people have no power, riches, or prestige to lose in recognizing that God's promised king has come into the world (contrast Mark 10:21, 22). They are ready, eager to see what God has done. They are ready to receive the peace that God is delivering to his people.

B. Amazing News (vv. 16-18)

16. So they hurried off and found Mary and Joseph, and the baby, who was lying in the manger.

The shepherds' words are confirmed by their actions—they go to Bethlehem as quickly as they can. What the shepherds see is exactly what the angel said they would see. The angelic appearance was not a hallucination. What the shepherds heard predicted by the angel is what they now see with their own eyes.

Luke introduced Mary and Joseph earlier as ordinary folk, subject to the whims of those in power. So the two have come to Bethlehem to pay taxes, perhaps on a piece of farmland that Joseph has inherited (Luke 2:1-5, not in today's text). With no guest lodging available, this humble, devoted pair now make do with other shelter as their newborn lies in a trough used to feed farm animals.

The baby . . . lying in a manger is the sign of which the angel spoke. God's promised king, the Messiah, the Lord, the world's Savior, is designated by such lowliness. He will not rule like Caesar or any other earthly ruler. He will rule in lowliness, as the servant of all. And it begins here —in a feeding trough.

17. When they had seen him, they spread the word concerning what had been told them about this child,

Throughout his two volumes of the Gospel of Luke and the Acts of the Apostles, the author emphasizes that when people see what God has done in Christ, they share the news with others (examples: Luke 7:16, 17; Acts 8:4). The angel has brought "good news that will cause great joy" to the shepherds (Luke 2:10, above). Now, having seen the child about whom the angel spoke, they feel compelled to tell others. The shepherds are witnesses of what God has just done. There will be many more eyewitnesses in the years ahead regarding Jesus' ministry, death, and resurrection.

What Do You Think?

When were times you had to share good news immediately with others? If none of these involved the message of the gospel, why not?

Talking Points for Your Discussion

- Among members of your immediate family
- Among members of your extended family
- At work or school
- Other

---

18. . . . and all who heard it were amazed at what the shepherds said to them.

Like others who have heard the stories surrounding the conception and birth of John the Baptist, those who hear the shepherds' story display amazement at this message (compare Luke 1:65, 66). The people are uncertain about its meaning. Have these shepherds truly seen and heard angels? How can a poor infant sleeping in a feeding trough be God's promised king? How can anyone so weak challenge the power of Caesar? How can God bring peace to his people by such a means as this?

Years later, Jesus' disciples will wonder whether it is really Jesus who appears before them alive after he dies the death of a criminal on a cross (Luke 24:41). Indeed, God can bring peace to his people by such a means as this! In his Son's submissive lowliness, his obedience to the mission of the cross, God triumphs over all the powers that hold the world in the grip of evil. It is indeed an amazing message, but it is a true message.

C. Quiet Reflection (v. 19)

19. But Mary treasured up all these things and pondered them in her heart.

The best informed of the witnesses is Jesus' mother, Mary. She had received the angel Gabriel's first message about the pending birth of her child (Luke 1:26-38). She had heard Elizabeth, her relative, exalt her child as "Lord" (1:43-45). Mary had herself praised God for what he was promising to do (1:46-55).

But even for Mary, the events are not yet entirely clear. Why does she find herself in a stable? Why do shepherds come in from the fields at night to see her child? How will her child take his place as God's king? We easily imagine such questions going through Mary's mind as she struggles to put everything together, to make sense of it all.

Luke will later note that Mary keeps memories in her heart of amazing things associated with Jesus' childhood (Luke 2:51). Her puzzlement will be greatest when, as Simeon will prophesy, her heart is pierced with a sword of grief at Jesus' death (2:35). Jesus' death will become the lowest point of his lowly calling that begins in the manger. But the cross is to be answered by the triumph of the resurrection, demonstrating that God is truly victorious through Jesus' voluntary weakness. This is what Mary and all who follow Jesus must come to understand.

> **What Do You Think?**
> How are you like and unlike others regarding the kinds of experiences you ponder most in your heart? Why is this question important?
>
> *Talking Points for Your Discussion*
> - During times when God seems closest (Christmas, personal victories, etc.)
> - During times when God seems distant (personal or national tragedies, etc.)
> - Other

❧ *A New Interpretive Grid* ❧

I have a friend named Ron whose background growing up was Reform Judaism. He tells the story of his father's conversion to Christianity on discovering the love of Jesus. After accepting Christ, the father shared the good news with other family members and even with Ron's friends.

Ron, a teenager at the time, was somewhat annoyed at his father's zealous new ways. One day when Ron found himself home alone, he decided to get to the bottom of this lifestyle change. He took his father's Bible and sat down. He read the entire book of Matthew, and, as Ron said, "I just knew it was true."

Some converts like to say that their lives were "wrecked" by God. That is because when we collide with the love of Jesus, we can never go back to business as usual. But in the process of wrecking our old way of seeing life, in destroying our old interpretive grid, God provides us with a new one, a better one.

Joseph, Mary, the shepherds, those whom the shepherds told, my friend Ron—all received a new way of looking at life, a new interpretive grid. Like them, we will not comprehend everything at first. Like Mary, we may have to ponder at length. But ultimately our response can be like hers as we treasure every touch from God.   —V. E.

D. Joyful Celebration (v. 20)

20. The shepherds returned, glorifying and praising God for all the things they had heard and seen, which were just as they had been told.

The shepherds have made the angel's message their own. As the angel army praised God, now the shepherds do as well. What the angel had promised, the shepherds have verified. They truly have become witnesses of God's work.

The shepherds' praise and worship will characterize the lives of Jesus' followers after his resurrection and ascension (Acts 2:47). The shepherds show no concern regarding their low status in the eyes of the world. God has reached out to them in their lowliness through the lowliness of his Son. That changes all of life, to the glory of God.

Conclusion
A. Quite a Contrast!

The contrast in today's passage is between the power of the world and the lowliness of the Son of the almighty God. That contrast is the contrast of the ages! If we know Jesus, we can never think of life in the same way again. Life can never be about becoming powerful, wealthy, or important. It can only be about seeking and embracing the lowliness of Jesus Christ, thereby giving our lives in service for the sake of others who need to follow him as well.

Perhaps we feel like shepherds, alone in the night, ignored by others. If so, we can know that the angelic message is for us, that Christ comes for us. We can and should join the shepherds in joyfully sharing that good news.

B. Prayer

Our mighty, all-powerful God and Father, we are in awe that you sent your Son into the world in such a lowly estate. We are most of all in awe that in Jesus you gave your Son in death for us. Empower us to live as reflections of his lowly service that others might hear and believe. In Jesus' name, amen.

C. Thought to Remember
Share the news!

INVOLVEMENT LEARNING

Enhance your lesson with NIV® Bible Student (from your curriculum supplier) and the reproducible activity page (at www.standardlesson.com or in the back of the NIV® Standard Lesson Commentary Deluxe Edition).

Into the Lesson

In advance, ask learners to bring Christmas cards that feature images of shepherds; bring several yourself as well. Arrange the assembled cards for all to see, but wait until later in the lesson to comment on them.

Prepare in advance an official-looking letter, possibly with a gold seal, fancy ribbon, etc. Produce it with a flourish; read the contents dramatically: "Dear citizen, One of the privileges of living in our country is to speak of good things to others as we witness those good things happening. You are hereby summoned to the address 1 King David Street in Bethlehem to witness a marvelous event. Your job will be to listen, see, and speak of what you have seen and heard. We expect, good citizen, that you will relay the truth, the whole truth, and nothing but the truth."

Comment: "That authoritative summons is similar to the one that came to the shepherds of Luke 2. It is a summons to us as well! Let's see how and why."

Into the Word

Have two learners read the text aloud, alternating readers with each verse. *Alternative:* Play a video clip of a dramatic reading of the text (easy to find on the Internet).

After the reading, distribute copies of the following closed-Bible, true/false quiz to test recall. Assure learners that they will score their own results; you will not collect them. 1. The text says that the angels were singing. 2. The shepherds were initially afraid. 3. The angel(s) said to look for a baby named *Jesus*. 4. The shepherds were to recognize the correct baby by the sign of a dove descending on him. 5. The shepherds' flock was said to include goats as well as sheep. 6. The shepherds were to find the baby lying in a manger. 7. The shepherds went to Bethlehem to find the baby. 8. The shepherds were stricken dumb (unable to speak) because they expressed skepticism at the angelic announcement. 9. The shepherds were introduced to Magi from the East, who were in attendance with Mary, Joseph, and the baby. 10. The angel described the location of the newborn as "the fortress of David." *(Answers: 1–false; 2–true; 3–false; 4–false; 5–false; 6–true; 7–true; 8–false; 9–false; 10–false.)*

After discussing results of the quiz, draw learners' attention to the Christmas cards displayed earlier. Ask, "What artistic license do you see compared with what the text actually says?" One or more cards may invite further discussion of question 9 of the true/false quiz.

Option. If your learners would benefit from a study on the role of shepherds in biblical times, distribute copies of the "Good and Not So Good Shepherds" activity from the reproducible page, which you can download.

Into Life

Ask, "Do you suppose there were people in or near Bethlehem who heard the shepherds' story but did not believe that the baby born there was anyone special?" Assuming some will respond in the affirmative, ask, "Does that mean the shepherds were failures as messengers of the gospel?" Assuming a negative response, say, "So what is keeping us from proclaiming the good news of incarnation of the Savior?"

If an awkward silence ensues, let it "hang in the air" for at least 10 seconds before continuing: "Christmas offers excellent opportunities to discuss with unbelievers the subject of Jesus' divinity and what his arrival means. Why not do so this week?" Offer a prayer for wisdom and strength for class members to speak out about Jesus this week.

Option. Distribute copies of the "A New Task" activity from the reproducible page as a take-home reflection exercise. It will challenge your learners to follow in the shepherds' footsteps.

WORSHIP
GOD'S SON

DEVOTIONAL READING: Mark 9:15-24
BACKGROUND SCRIPTURE: Matthew 14:22-36

MATTHEW 14:22-36

22 Immediately Jesus made the disciples get into the boat and go on ahead of him to the other side, while he dismissed the crowd. 23 After he had dismissed them, he went up on a mountainside by himself to pray. Later that night, he was there alone, 24 and the boat was already a considerable distance from land, buffeted by the waves because the wind was against it.

25 Shortly before dawn Jesus went out to them, walking on the lake. 26 When the disciples saw him walking on the lake, they were terrified. "It's a ghost," they said, and cried out in fear.

27 But Jesus immediately said to them: "Take courage! It is I. Don't be afraid."

28 "Lord, if it's you," Peter replied, "tell me to come to you on the water."

29 "Come," he said.

Then Peter got down out of the boat, walked on the water and came toward Jesus. 30 But when he saw the wind, he was afraid and, beginning to sink, cried out, "Lord, save me!"

31 Immediately Jesus reached out his hand and caught him. "You of little faith," he said, "why did you doubt?"

32 And when they climbed into the boat, the wind died down. 33 Then those who were in the boat worshiped him, saying, "Truly you are the Son of God."

34 When they had crossed over, they landed at Gennesaret. 35 And when the men of that place recognized Jesus, they sent word to all the surrounding country. People brought all their sick to him 36 and begged him to let the sick just touch the edge of his cloak, and all who touched it were healed.

KEY VERSES

When they climbed into the boat, the wind died down. Then those who were in the boat worshiped him, saying, "Truly you are the Son of God." —Matthew 14:32, 33

ACTS OF WORSHIP

Unit 1: In Awe of God
LESSONS 1–4

LESSON AIMS

After participating in this lesson, each learner will be able to:

1. Describe how people reacted to and interacted with Jesus in light of the miraculous powers he demonstrated.

2. Explain why worship is the natural reaction to Jesus.

3. Identify one specific way to approach worship with a greater sense of awe and make a plan to do so.

LESSON OUTLINE

Introduction
A. Self-Reliance vs. Christ-Reliance

What kind of person do you want to be in hard times? We probably would like to be strong, tough, able to take what life gives and keep going. We admire those who face hardship with firm resolve, who keep going to prevail because of their deep well of inner determination.

Our heroes are like that: the gallant soldier, the dynamic businessperson, the athlete who performs under pressure in the big game, the bystander who puts life on the line to save someone else. We admire the rugged individual. We celebrate those who seem to do great things on their own.

Perhaps we celebrate self-reliance because we want to run our lives by ourselves. We prefer to live life our way. So we honor those who seem to do great things on their own, and we aspire to be such people ourselves.

But the Bible shines a very different light on this issue. The great people of the Bible were not self-reliant. They were not distinguished by the depth of their inner resources. No, the great people of the Bible were distinguished by something else, call it *God-reliance* or *Christ-reliance*. They were people who reacted—although imperfectly on occasion—to hard times not with personal resolve but with reliance on God's goodness, love, and power. Today's text is an example.

B. Lesson Background

Matthew, Mark, and John place the account of today's text (absent from Luke) after the account of the feeding of the 5,000. Jesus' power was very much on display in that feeding, but so was the disciples' limitation in their thinking even though it was by then the third year of Jesus' public ministry (Matthew 14:15-17).

Our lesson is set on the Sea of Galilee, which is actually a freshwater lake—compare the designation "the Lake of Gennesaret" in Luke 5:1—that is about 13 miles long and 8 miles wide. It is in the north of Israel's territory, and much of Jesus' ministry took place around this lake.

In 1986, the remains of a boat from the time of Jesus were discovered buried in the mud near the shore of the Sea of Galilee. Excavated and now on display, the boat is probably typical for the time. It measures 27 feet in length and 7.5 feet at its widest point. It could have been propelled with oars, a sail, or both.

Such boats were quite safe when the weather was fine. But storms can arise quickly on this lake. Because its western coastline features steep hills, a storm blowing in from that direction, from the Mediterranean Sea, might be seen by boaters only when it is nearly upon them. A small boat hit by high winds is in a perilous condition, even on such a small lake.

The situation in today's text was not the first time the disciples had encountered danger on the water. Earlier they had faced a storm while Jesus slept in their little boat, and he had responded to their cries by speaking the storm to stillness (Matthew 8:23-27). The episode in today's text differs in that Jesus was not initially present as danger presented itself. Even so, our text raises the question of whether the disciples (particularly Peter) would exercise trust in the power of Jesus. (Mark 6:45-52 and John 6:16-21 are parallel accounts of today's text.)

I. Dismissal for Solitude
(MATTHEW 14:22, 23)
A. Sending Away (v. 22)

22. Immediately Jesus made the disciples get into the boat and go on ahead of him to the other side, while he dismissed the crowd.

After feeding *the crowd* in the wilderness, Jesus sends everyone away. Jesus also directs his 12 disciples to go across the lake in a boat. This deliberate step shows us that the events to follow are no accident. The disciples go into danger, but they go with Jesus' guidance and protection.

B. Being Alone (v. 23)

23. After he had dismissed them, he went up on a mountainside by himself to pray. Later that night, he was there alone,

A reason for sending everyone away, even the 12, is revealed: Jesus wants solitude *to pray*. It is a remarkable part of this story that the Jesus who

exercises the almighty power of God nevertheless prays earnestly and at length to God the Father. This paradox is critical to our understanding of Jesus. He is the divine Son of God, to whom all authority is given (Matthew 28:18). He does mighty deeds that demonstrate a power that can belong only to God (9:6, 7). Yet Jesus consistently and willingly submits to God the Father in prayer; the Father's will must prevail (26:39, 42). If Jesus, the almighty Son of God, willingly submits to God the Father, how much more should we, who have no real power or authority, do the same?

> **What Do You Think?**
> Under what circumstances have you found prayer in solitude to be more appropriate than prayer in a group? Why is that?
> *Talking Points for Your Discussion*
> - Regarding the past (repentance for sin, praise for blessing, etc.)
> - Regarding the present (current events, etc.)
> - Regarding the future (decisions to make, etc.)

The fact that Jesus is now *alone* indicates that he is successful in persuading everyone to depart—most by foot homeward, the 12 by boat. Evening comes as Jesus is left by himself. Any trouble on the boat will be compounded by the darkness now settling over the lake.

II. Walking on Water
(MATTHEW 14:24-27)
A. Difficult Situation (v. 24)

24. . . . and the boat was already a considerable distance from land, buffeted by the waves because the wind was against it.

Matthew gradually takes us into the danger that the disciples face, almost as if we ourselves are experiencing the onset of the storm in the darkness. The boat is far from land, near the middle of the lake (compare Mark 6:47). The waves beat against the boat as if tormenting it. Perhaps the boat is taking on water faster than the disciples can bail.

The wind, usually a friend to sailing vessels, is an enemy as it impedes progress on the journey.

On their own without Jesus present, the disciples can only bail and row.

B. Startling Appearance (v. 25)

25. Shortly before dawn Jesus went out to them, walking on the lake.

If you are using the 1984 edition of the NIV, the text says "during the fourth watch of the night" instead of the 2011 edition's *shortly before dawn*. Both indicate the same thing: the time period from approximately 3 a.m. to 6 a.m. By this time, the disciples must be exhausted, having struggled against the storm for hours. While they may have hoped for some act of deliverance, we can speculate that at this point their hopes are fading, if not gone altogether.

But then Jesus comes to them in a most exceptional manner: *walking on the lake.* Matthew describes this incredible action with the simplest of phrases, saying in a few words that Jesus is doing something that no one else can. In the exodus, God had parted the waters of the Red Sea to allow his people to escape their enemies. But here is an action without compare. At the point of the disciples' exhaustion and hopelessness, the Lord comes to reassure and rescue.

C. Fearful Reaction (v. 26)

26. When the disciples saw him walking on the lake, they were terrified. "It's a ghost," they said, and cried out in fear.

Jesus' walking on the water seems to be the last thing that the disciples expect to see! Not knowing what to make of the sight, the disciples are freshly alarmed. They assume that anyone who walks on or above water cannot be a flesh-and-blood human, so they conclude that they are seeing *a ghost*. First a storm, now an apparition (compare Luke 24:37)! Little wonder that they cry *out in fear*. They feel assaulted from both the physical and spiritual realms.

HOW TO SAY IT

Galilee	*Gal*-uh-lee.
Gennesaret	Geh-*ness*-uh-ret (*G* as in *get*).
Mediterranean	*Med*-uh-tuh-**ray**-nee-un.

D. Comforting Response (v. 27)

27. But Jesus immediately said to them: "Take courage! It is I. Don't be afraid."

Jesus does not delay in revealing to the disciples the unexpected truth: they see not a disembodied spirit but their Lord. Therefore they can *take courage* in the midst of the storm. There is no more reason to be fearful, either of the storm that continues or certainly of the one who walks on the water to join them.

As Jesus identifies himself to the disciples in this instance, they are (or should be) learning what Jesus will assure them of after his resurrection: "And surely I am with you always, to the very end of the age" (Matthew 28:20b). They may feel that they are alone, but the Christ who will give his life for them will also remain with them in every circumstance, even when they cannot see him.

❧ THE NAVY HYMN ❧

The Navy Hymn, properly titled "Eternal Father, Strong to Save," is a musical benediction for seafarers. The wording has undergone various adaptations over the years, but the original lyrics of 1860 included, in the second verse, an appeal for safety to "Christ . . . Who walked'st on the foaming deep," with apparent allusion to today's text.

The foaming deep can indeed be perilous! Just off the Outer Banks of North Carolina is the so-called Graveyard of the Atlantic, where thousands of ships have sunk because of bad weather. Over in the Pacific Ocean, a typhoon during World War II sank three American warships, damaged many others, and took 790 lives in the process—causing almost as much damage to the fleet as a major naval battle would have. The apostle Paul mentions that he suffered shipwreck three times (2 Corinthians 11:25), and those didn't include his shipwreck of Acts 27.

The terror of the disciples during the storm on the Sea of Galilee is not hard to imagine! But in the moments of our greatest fear, we do well to remember that we serve the one who created all the forces of nature in the first place. When we sense our fears begin to rise, may they always give way to prayer and faith.

—J. B. N.

III. Test of Faith

(MATTHEW 14:28-32)

A. Request, Response, Result (vv. 28-30)

28. "Lord, if it's you," Peter replied, "tell me to come to you on the water."

The story now shifts to one disciple's reaction to Jesus' self-revelation. While the storm rages, Peter, who often seems to take the lead among the 12, asks Jesus to give the command to join him on the water. The phrase *if it's you* might make us think that Peter is uncertain whether this truly is Jesus. But in this context *if* is like *because*: if it is you, Lord (and it certainly is), then order me to join you.

We might wonder why Peter asks for such a thing. In the context of the Gospel of Matthew, it is probably best to see that Peter is asking to share in Jesus' work and authority. Already Jesus had sent the disciples out to preach, with authority to heal and cast out demons (Matthew 10:1). They are already sharing in his ministry, and they desire to reign with him (20:20-22). Peter's request is the product of an ambition, but it is a sacred ambition: to stand with his Lord in the Lord's kingly work.

29. "Come," he said.

Then Peter got down out of the boat, walked on the water and came toward Jesus.

Jesus grants Peter's request. And just as has been the case before, when Jesus commands his followers to do something, he also grants them the power to carry it out. Therefore, Peter does the seemingly impossible: walking *on the water* just as Jesus is doing.

30. But when he saw the wind, he was afraid and, beginning to sink, cried out, "Lord, save me!"

Peter begins his adventure with confident obedience to Jesus. But as he steps out farther, he is distracted by the strength of the wind. Peter's fear returns, and as it does, he begins to sink. Just as the disciples had called out "save us" when they had been in a storm before (Matthew 8:25), now Peter does so again. This desperate cry, stripped of all self-reliance and pride, is the essence of faith in Jesus, especially when that faith is troubled by doubt. Even so, Peter's faith is defective, as our next verse shows.

B. Rescue, Return, Reverence (vv. 31-33)

31. Immediately Jesus reached out his hand and caught him. "You of little faith," he said, "why did you doubt?"

Jesus' responds to Peter instantly and decisively. As he does on other occasions, Jesus makes physical contact with the one whom he delivers (Matthew 8:3, 15; 9:29; 14:36; 17:7; 20:34).

With the rescue comes a rebuke. Jesus chides Peter as one *of little faith,* as Jesus had done to the disciples collectively when stilling another storm (Matthew 8:26) and as he will do again in a context of a more peaceful journey on the lake (16:8). Peter's doubt in the midst of the storm reveals that his confidence in Jesus can be shaken (see also 26:69-75). Even when the disciples see Jesus after his resurrection, doubt will infect some of them (28:17). Doubt is a powerful, pervasive disposition, especially when faith is challenged in times of trouble (compare James 1:6).

When we are guilty of defective faith, we can remember what Jesus does in the passage before us. Yes, Peter's faith is weak. Under stress, he is plagued by doubt. But Jesus rescues Peter anyway! Peter's weak faith is still sufficient to call out to Jesus for help. Jesus responds even to weak faith. When we recognize this, we realize that our relationship with Jesus depends on how

Visual for
Lessons 1 & 4

Point to this visual as you ask, "What storm of life has Jesus helped you through recently?"

ready we are to recognize our weaknesses and rely on his strength. That extends to trusting that in his strength he can overcome our doubts and worries.

32. And when they climbed into the boat, the wind died down.

Only as Jesus comes to the boat, still escorting Peter to safety, does the storm end. The disciples are now assured that they are utterly safe. We note that Jesus does not rescue Peter by calming the storm, as in Matthew 8:26; rather, Jesus rescues Peter while the storm still rages. Jesus does not always calm the storms of life, but he is always there to rescue or calm us in one way or another.

What Do You Think?

When was a time that Jesus calmed you rather than the storm you were in at the time? How did things eventually turn out?

Talking Points for Your Discussion
- During a personal or family crisis
- During a work crisis
- During a church crisis
- Other

On the two occasions that Jesus quiets storms on the Sea of Galilee, he does what the psalmist famously had said can be done only by God (Psalm 107:28-30). Those who are in danger from the storm cry out to God for deliverance.

But notably on this occasion, the disciples come to a point of deliverance even before the storm is stilled, since Jesus' protection has been assured all along, even while he was separated from them. The disciples now receive a demonstration of that wonderful fact. As the wind at last ceases, their real condition—living under the sure protection of Jesus—becomes clear.

❧ WALKING WITH JESUS ❧

Some years ago, a friend pointed out an interesting part of the text we are studying: we don't know how far Peter walked on the water before losing faith. Perhaps it was only a foot or two, perhaps it was several yards, perhaps even farther before he needed Jesus' help. And after Jesus "caught him," how did Peter get back to the boat?

Three possibilities occur to me. One is that Jesus picked Peter up and carried him back. Somehow that doesn't seem likely. Another possibility is that Jesus held on to Peter's hand and dragged him through the water until they reached the boat. That seems even more unlikely.

A third possibility is that Peter, holding on to Jesus' hand, walked back to the boat—which means he was once again walking on top of the water. It is intriguing to think of Peter walking out several yards, sinking, being rescued by Jesus, then once more walking on the water as he accompanied Jesus side by side back to the boat.

What a picture of trust, and what a challenge to us! When we hold Jesus' hand and walk side by side with him in faith, we can do things that otherwise would be impossible. Our faith may (and probably will) falter at times. Those are the very times to cry out to Jesus for help. As we do, we will find him right there with us, "to the very end of the age" (Matthew 28:20). —J. B. N.

33. Then those who were in the boat worshiped him, saying, "Truly you are the Son of God."

As the storm stills, the disciples react to all that they have just experienced. They thought themselves to have been in acute danger for their lives. They have struggled on their own up to the limits of their strength and endurance. They have witnessed Jesus demonstrate power available only to God. They have seen him empower one of their number to join him in his sovereign control of the deep. To what conclusion does all of this drive them?

They can conclude nothing less than that Jesus is utterly unlike any other. For the Jewish people of Jesus' time, the phrase *Son of God* first means that Jesus is God's promised king, the great Son of David. Certainly the disciples are affirming at least that much here. Jesus has shown his kingly authority in what he had just accomplished.

But questions undoubtedly remain: Just how great a king is Jesus? How can he exercise powers that the Scriptures attribute to God alone? The disciples will continue struggling to understand. Peter—whose mind-set probably is typical of the others—will again confess Jesus as God's Son (Matthew 16:16), will waver in submission to him (16:22), and will desert and deny him (26:56, 69-75). Greater understanding will come when Jesus rises from the dead.

But in this particular moment, their expression is full even if their understanding is not complete as they fall in worship of Jesus. In so doing, they affirm his supreme authority, just as they will when he is risen from the dead (Matthew 28:17).

IV. Healing the Sick
(MATTHEW 14:34-36)
A. Jesus Recognized (vv. 34, 35)

34, 35. When they had crossed over, they landed at Gennesaret. And when the men of that place recognized Jesus, they sent word to all the surrounding country. People brought all their sick to him

Gennesaret is a village on the northwestern shore of the Sea of Galilee. Jesus' ability to heal is well established by this time since he is in the third year of his public ministry. No doubt word has gotten around that he has just fed thousands in a wilderness area, in something of a parallel to God's providing manna to Israel in the wilderness during the exodus. Little wonder that *all the surrounding country* reacts by bringing the sick to Jesus!

B. Wholeness Results (v. 36)

36. . . . and begged him to let the sick just touch the edge of his cloak, and all who touched it were healed.

Chapters before, a woman who had sought Jesus had touched *the edge of his cloak* in faith and was healed of her 12-year illness (Matthew 9:20-22). Now many others are similarly healed. We are impressed by their faith. But the emphasis here is just as much, if not more so, on the one who has the power to see that people are healed. The one who has just demonstrated power over the forces of nature now uses his power for all who come to him. Truly there is no one like him.

What Do You Think?
How do Jesus' miracles strengthen your faith even though you didn't witness them firsthand?
Talking Points for Your Discussion
- Regarding control over the forces of nature
- Regarding healings
- Other

Conclusion
A. Coming to Jesus

Like the disciples in the storm, Jesus seems absent from our lives at times. During such times, we may feel that we have no one to rely on but ourselves.

But our own power will fail in the end. We will find ourselves in situations that we simply cannot handle. We will admit that we cannot add a single day to our lives by our own efforts. Like others who have realized their deep need for his power, we have to abandon ourselves to his strength. That's when faith grows.

B. Prayer

Almighty God, grant us the sense of your presence when we feel alone. Manifest your sovereign power when we are weak. Remind us always that your power is that of the cross, power that overcomes our darkest moments. In Jesus' name, amen.

C. Thought to Remember

God's power is greater than our weak faith.

INVOLVEMENT LEARNING

Enhance your lesson with NIV® Bible Student (from your curriculum supplier) and the reproducible activity page (at www.standardlesson.com or in the back of the NIV® Standard Lesson Commentary Deluxe Edition).

Into the Lesson

Download a short video clip from the Internet on the subject "storm at sea." As class begins, show that clip with the sound turned up. At the same time, have a strong-voiced reader read Psalm 107:24-30 over the sound. If such a visual presentation is not possible, use instead an audio recording of a strong rain and windstorm as the verses are read. Then comment, "Few things are more frightening than a storm at sea . . . especially in a small, crowded boat. Today's text is a picture of just such an event. Let's take a look and listen!"

Alternative. Ask students, "Have you ever been in a dangerous weather situation where you feared for your life?" Allow a few learners to share their stories, but don't let this drag out. Then ask, "Did praying and calling out to God for help come naturally to you in that situation? If so, in what way did God assist you?" Make a transition as you say, "In today's text the disciples were afraid of Jesus just as much as of the bad weather, if not more so. Let's find out why."

Into the Word

Have the text read aloud. Then ask, "What do you see Jesus doing in these verses that impresses you?" Make a list of the responses, which should include (1) authoritative directions to the apostles and to the assembled crowd, (2) isolating himself for prayer at a hectic time, (3) walking on the water in violation of the laws of nature that he himself had put into place at creation, (4) calm encouragement in the face of the apostles' fear, (5) allowing Peter's impromptu request, (6) saving response to Peter's cry for help, (7) changing storm to calm as he entered the boat, (8) accepting worship, (9) continuing a busy healing ministry after the incident on water, and (10) granting healing by mere contact with his clothing. During your discussion, ensure that learners do not focus on 3, 6, 7, and 10 to the exclusion of the others.

Alternative. Distribute copies of the "Power in Person" from the reproducible page, which you can download. Have learners work in pairs to complete it. Then lead a discussion of the two questions at the end.

Option. Begin the Into the Word segment by distributing copies of the "Around the Sea" activity from the reproducible page. Have learners work on it in pairs; provide concordances and Bible dictionaries for their research as appropriate. Discuss results, noting especially the feeding of the 5,000 just preceding the events of today's text.

Into Life

Option 1. Distribute handouts with this heading: *To prepare myself for the storms of the week ahead, I will ponder these accounts of God's demonstrations of power.* Have seven blank lines below the heading. Ask, "As you read the heading of this handout, what incidents come to mind?" Let learners suggest several, even if only of events without including Scripture references. If they need a start, say, "I think of God's parting of the Red Sea in Exodus 14 to escape the 'storm' of pursuers."

Whether or not your class has time to complete the seven lines, recommend that learners (1) do Bible research later this afternoon to identify texts that remind them of God's power and (2) enter the references to them on the handouts for meditation in private daily worship.

Option 2. Give each learner a handout with these four stimulus statements: 1. Life is like the Sea of Galilee in that both _____. 2. I have a wavering faith like that of Peter since I _____. 3. The mighty works of Jesus awe me when I _____. 4. The strong hand of Jesus that rescued Peter from the water is the same hand that will _____. Ask learners to complete each statement in some personal fashion. If not too personal for the nature of your class, ask for volunteers to share their completions. Be prepared to give your own.

Jesus' Model for Prayer

Devotional Reading: Psalm 103:1-13
Background Scripture: Luke 11:1-13

Luke 11:1-13

[1] One day Jesus was praying in a certain place. When he finished, one of his disciples said to him, "Lord, teach us to pray, just as John taught his disciples."

[2] He said to them, "When you pray, say:

"'Father,
hallowed be your name,
your kingdom come.
[3] Give us each day our daily bread.
[4] Forgive us our sins,
for we also forgive everyone
who sins against us.
And lead us not into temptation.'"

[5] Then Jesus said to them, "Suppose you have a friend, and you go to him at midnight and say, 'Friend, lend me three loaves of bread; [6] a friend of mine on a journey has come to me, and I have no food to offer him.' [7] And suppose the one inside answers, 'Don't bother me. The door is already locked, and my children and I are in bed. I can't get up and give you anything.' [8] I tell you, even though he will not get up and give you the bread because of friendship, yet because of your shameless audacity he will surely get up and give you as much as you need.

[9] "So I say to you: Ask and it will be given to you; seek and you will find; knock and the door will be opened to you. [10] For everyone who asks receives; the one who seeks finds; and to the one who knocks, the door will be opened.

[11] "Which of you fathers, if your son asks for a fish, will give him a snake instead? [12] Or if he asks for an egg, will give him a scorpion? [13] If you then, though you are evil, know how to give good gifts to your children, how much more will your Father in heaven give the Holy Spirit to those who ask him!"

Key Verse

He said to them, "When you pray, say: "'Father, hallowed be your name, your kingdom come.'"

—Luke 11:2

ACTS OF WORSHIP

Unit 2: Learning to Pray

LESSONS 5–8

LESSON AIMS

After participating in this lesson, each learner will be able to:

1. Summarize Jesus' teaching about how and why to pray.

2. Give a modern example that illustrates the need for persistence in prayer.

3. Write a personalized version of the model prayer.

LESSON OUTLINE

Introduction

A. Praying More

A few years ago, the Pew Forum conducted a research poll to determine how common it was for adherents of various religious groups in America to pray at least daily. Overall, 58 percent of Americans reported being daily pray-ers. The two groups with the highest percentage of folks who claimed to do so were the Jehovah's Witnesses (at 89 percent) and the Mormons (at 82 percent). Why would those two groups have the highest percentage of those who claim to pray daily?

I'm sure there are many reasons that may be proposed, but here is my theory: those two groups both teach and expect their people to pray daily (even multiple times per day). Do we? Do we see the need to teach people to pray? Should we *expect* people to pray, even incorporating some accountability into the practice? Today's lesson gives us insights into Jesus' prayer practices. It also shows how Jesus included learning to pray as a part of the training of his disciples.

B. Lesson Background

The Gospel of Luke has an emphasis upon prayer, with proportionally more references to that subject than any other Gospel. Various people are presented in Luke as persons of prayer (examples: Luke 1:13; 2:37). This emphasis continues in Luke's second book, Acts, where the early Christian community is frequently presented as being engaged in prayer (see Acts 1:14; 2:42; 4:31; 6:4).

The preeminent prayer-person in the Gospel of Luke is Jesus himself. Jesus prayed at his baptism (Luke 3:21), before the choosing of the 12 disciples (6:12), at the time of Peter's confession (9:18-20), on the Mount of Transfiguration (9:28, 29), as a motivation for cleansing the temple (19:45, 46), and during his agony in the garden (22:41).

The immediate context of today's lesson on prayer is that of Jesus' final journey to Jerusalem, where he would be arrested, crucified, buried, and resurrected (Luke 9:51). This fateful journey and its aftermath occupy about 60 percent of the Gospel according to Luke.

I. Request and Response

(LUKE 11:1-4)

A. Observing the Master (v. 1)

1. One day Jesus was praying in a certain place. When he finished, one of his disciples said to him, "Lord, teach us to pray, just as John taught his disciples."

This situation before us is the only biblical record of an occasion where a disciple comes to Jesus with a request to be taught how to pray. Luke is not long on details here, but we can determine what is happening by piecing things together. Jesus is traveling with his group of disciples toward Jerusalem (see the Lesson Background). His group includes the 12 chosen to be apostles (Luke 6:13) as well as others (10:17). The entourage perhaps includes women (8:1-3). They have stopped at an unnamed *certain place*, likely a village on the way to Jerusalem (compare 10:38). Perhaps the time of day is morning, and Jesus pauses for a time of prayer before the group resumes its trek.

There may be some prayers offered as a group, but we easily imagine that eventually Jesus is the only one still praying. His disciples wait for him to finish, and then one of them expresses a request probably shared by the group at large: *Lord, teach us to pray.*

But there is something unsaid here. As observant Jews, don't they already know how to pray? Their parents had taught them to pray as youngsters. They had been in synagogues for hundreds of prayer services and have heard the elders of their communities pray many times. Don't they already know how to pray?

Perhaps by this time the one making the request has become aware of Jesus' prayer pattern from numerous occasions (Luke 5:16; 6:12; 9:18, 28). The disciple has noticed that the content, context, and length of Jesus' prayers are different

HOW TO SAY IT

Deuteronomy	Due-ter-*ahn*-uh-me.
Galilean	Gal-uh-*lee*-un.
Jerusalem	Juh-*roo*-suh-lem.
Pentecost	*Pent*-ih-kost.

from what that disciple experienced before meeting him. If so, what the requester is really saying is "Lord, teach us how to pray as you do."

Implied here is that there is a method, a structure to Jesus' prayers that would be helpful for his disciples to know. The one making the request mentions John the Baptist (now deceased; see Luke 9:9). Some of Jesus' disciples had been disciples of John the Baptist (see John 1:35-37). Those present who had been in the latter group may be interested in comparing and contrasting John's prayer method with that of Jesus.

What Do You Think?

In what areas have you seen the most improvement in your prayer life? How can you use your experience to help others in their prayer lives?

Talking Points for Your Discussion

- Setting aside enough time for prayer
- Establishing an appropriate place for prayer
- Establishing a set of themes for prayer
- Dealing with distractions
- Other

B. Providing the Model (vv. 2-4)

2. He said to them, "When you pray, say:
"'Father,
hallowed be your name,
your kingdom come.

What follows may be seen as Luke's version of the Lord's Prayer, which is better known to us in the version given in Matthew 6:9-13. The similarities and differences between the two versions show us that Jesus probably teaches this prayer on more than one occasion and with variations. The differences indicate that the exact wording is not as important as the general pattern and the emphasis. There is no magic in repeating the words of the Lord's Prayer, but there is great power in the thoughts being expressed within it.

The opening word, *Father,* establishes the basis for prayer. Prayer, by definition, is directed to God. As Christians, we do not pray into the void in the hope that someone somewhere will be listening. Rather, we pray in faith as we address the Creator of the universe, the God of Heaven.

Following the address, the prayer features several petitions. A petition in prayer is simply a request, and here we must be careful. What are proper things to ask God for, and what are improper? We must resist treating prayer as if we were on the lap of the department store Santa, giving him our Christmas wish list. As one author has said, "God is not a cosmic catalogue, and prayer is not placing an order."

The first petition Jesus mentions is *hallowed be your name*. The word *hallowed* is an older expression that simply means "holy." This petition in modern words would be "Let your name be holy." This is a commitment to the Third Commandment: "You shall not misuse the name of the Lord your God, for the Lord will not hold anyone guiltless who misuses his name" (Exodus 20:7). When we pray the way Jesus is teaching, we are making a commitment to be a guardian of God's holiness among men and women, a commitment to not misuse God's holy name.

❧ THE HALLOWED NAME ❧

I remember an occasion in high school when a fellow student knocked a girl's books off her desk. The irate girl started to use profanity, but caught herself before she actually did so. In the process she wound up saying, "God . . . bless you!" It was obvious she wasn't really asking God to bless that person.

All too often our own speech patterns do the same thing. Many people want to keep their speech pure, but they use euphemisms that communicate a different effect. Think of how many times we have heard someone say, "Gosh, darn it!" or something similar.

Taking the Lord's name in vain means using it lightly, flippantly, or in a curse. Some who would never use God's name in a curse will use the flippant "OMG!" nonetheless. This is a serious issue. May we vow today to use God's name only and always reverently.   —J. B. N.

The second petition is *your kingdom come*. This expresses the desire for the establishment of God's kingdom, God's reign, God's sovereign rule in our lives and in our world.

What Do You Think?

How might prayer for God's kingdom to come be answered by your own actions in that regard?

Talking Points for Your Discussion

- At work or school
- At home
- In "the marketplace of ideas"
- Other

A footnote of the NIV has the third petition: "may your will be done on earth as it is heaven." This is in a footnote because only some manuscripts of Luke have it. But since this petition is indeed found in Matthew's version of the Lord's Prayer, there is no doubt that it is authentic to Jesus. By praying this we ask that God's will be carried out in all things, particularly in our personal lives. Together, the second and third petitions are twins. To pray for the establishment of God's kingdom is to pray for the carrying out of God's will.

3. "Give us each day our daily bread.

This is the fourth petition. Some students see a certain distinction between *each day* here and "today" in Matthew 6:11, but both focus on the hand to mouth existence of most who live in the first century. Those of us today who do not experience this kind of existence may have greater difficulty recognizing our daily dependence on God for essential needs, but we must do so! We are not to pray, "Lord, would you be my safety net when I can't provide quite enough on my own?" Rather, our prayer should admit our dependence on God for food, for clothing, for shelter, for health—for everything we need on a daily basis.

What Do You Think?

When was a time that you felt most sharply the need to rely on God daily for an essential? How did you grow spiritually from this experience?

Talking Points for Your Discussion

- Regarding food
- Regarding housing
- Regarding transportation
- Regarding health
- Other

4a. "Forgive us our sins,
   for we also forgive everyone who sins
      against us.

The fifth petition is unlike the others because it is conditional: as we ask for God's forgiveness, we promise to be forgiving people. In Matthew's version, this is the only petition to receive a clarifying comment from Jesus (Matthew 6:14, 15). There we are told that if we fail to forgive others, then we should not expect God to forgive us (compare Mark 11:25).

This petition for forgiveness is tied to the previous petition for "daily bread": as we ask for the daily necessities to meet our daily needs, we also ask for daily forgiveness for our daily sins. We are asking that both our physical and our spiritual needs be met on a daily basis.

This connection gives us insight into the fact that Jesus intends his model prayer to be a daily guide, not just something said in church on Sunday morning. Remember that at this time Jesus is without a permanent home, dependent upon the generosity of friends for food and lodging (Luke 9:58). It is in this context that Jesus teaches his disciples to pray to God on a daily basis to supply their needs, believing that God will do so.

4b. "And lead us not into temptation.'"

This, the sixth petition, may seem strange given the fact that "God cannot be tempted by evil, nor does he tempt anyone" (James 1:13). The problem is relieved when we realize that the Greek word translated *temptation* does not always mean "enticement to commit sin." It can also mean "testing" (as translated in Luke 8:13) or "trials" (as translated in Luke 22:28; James 1:2; 1 Peter 1:6; 2 Peter 2:9).

A seventh petition, *but deliver us from the evil one,* is found in a footnote of the NIV because only some manuscripts of Luke have it. Matthew 6:13 assures us that it is authentic to Jesus.

II. Seeking and Receiving
(LUKE 11:5-10)

A. Testing a Friendship (vv. 5-8)

5, 6. Then Jesus said to them, "Suppose you have a friend, and you go to him at midnight and say, 'Friend, lend me three loaves of bread; a friend of mine on a journey has come to me, and I have no food to offer him.'

Unlike the setting of the Lord's Prayer in Matthew's Gospel, Luke follows the prayer with several parable-type teachings to explain the nature of praying to God. The image is that of a villager who receives an unexpected visitor *at midnight.* The situation is tied with the prayer's request for "daily bread" in Luke 11:3, above. The one who is knocking apparently has no bread for emergencies. This may be because his household practice is to bake or buy only enough bread for family needs on a daily basis.

This daily plan is now disrupted because his need for bread cannot wait until morning. His failure to provide a meal for his visitor would be a grave social error of inhospitality. So he asks for *three loaves,* probably because his entire family will participate in this midnight meal.

7. "And suppose the one inside answers, 'Don't bother me. The door is already locked, and my children and I are in bed. I can't get up and give you anything.'

The neighbor does not respond well to the interruption of his sleep! He resists by noting that his household is bedded down for the night. He does not want to wake everyone up (although the pounding on the door already has done so). Therefore it is not realistic for him to come to the door and help—he *can't get up.* But he can if he really wants to. His *I can't get up* is actually *I don't want to get up.*

8. "I tell you, even though he will not get up and give you the bread because of friendship, yet because of your shameless audacity he will surely get up and give you as much as you need.

The resolution of the story is that the awakened one does finally get up and supplies the needed bread. Why? Jesus explains that it is not *because of friendship* but *because of your shameless audacity.* The awakened neighbor meets the need because he knows his breadless neighbor will not give up pounding on his door until the request is granted. The best and quickest way for the homeowner to resume his sleep is to grant the request.

The point applies to prayer. Persistence in prayer is important (compare Luke 18:1-8). Prayer is a laying bare of the heart before God. If a request is not worth repeating as a daily petition, it may be deemed as whimsical or unimportant. Prayer that is persistent and personal is powerful in God's eyes. Needs are daily, therefore our practice of prayer must be ongoing, never taking for granted the gracious provision of God.

We should take care here, though. Persistence in prayer is not effective because we somehow wear God down, as may a child who repeatedly asks her mother for a candy bar while shopping. The mother may say "No" a dozen times but finally give in just to stop the whining. That's not how it works with God. Persistence in prayer is a test for us, not for him.

B. Persisting in Asking (vv. 9, 10)

9, 10. "So I say to you: Ask and it will be given to you; seek and you will find; knock and the door will be opened to you. For everyone who asks receives; the one who seeks finds; and to the one who knocks, the door will be opened.

Jesus describes the process of petitioning God in prayer with three related verbs. To *ask* is easily understood as a request, the way we normally understand prayer. To *seek* takes this a step further and implies persistence in prayer, working hard to get an answer. To *knock* refers to the parable above, the man in need who boldly knocks on his neighbor's door at midnight.

All this forms part of Jesus' teaching his disciples how to pray. A prayer must be expressed, it must be expressed repeatedly, and it must be expressed boldly. If we want to pray like Jesus, this is the pattern!

❧ PERSEVERANCE IN PRAYER ❧

More than 35 years ago, a professor colleague was telling me of a time he was filling the pulpit for a church in a rural area. An elderly woman was chatting with him after one sermon, and she remarked that she had been puzzled for a long time over Paul's comment about "perseverance" in prayer in Ephesians 6:18. (This word appears in older translations such as the *King James Version*; the *New International Version* offers the translation "keep on" instead.) Not being familiar with some finer points of the English language, she was mistaking the word *persevere* for *preserve*.

She had wrongly resolved her puzzlement by means of her experience with canning fruit into *preserves*, a process that allows the fruit to be stored for a lengthy period of time before consumption. Through that experience she had concluded that what Paul meant was that we are to *preserve* in prayer—that is, lay up a surplus that can be used later in time of need.

But that wasn't what Paul had in mind, and it was not what Jesus was teaching in today's text either. Prayer is not a commodity that can be preserved (stored up) in some way. Rather, it is something to be practiced over the long haul to keep us in the habit of calling on the one who is able to meet our need. May we persevere in the knocking of prayer! And may we thereby be preserved in our work for him.

—J. B. N.

What Do You Think?
What are some things that hinder persistence in prayer? How do we overcome these?
Talking Points for Your Discussion
- Things of a spiritual nature
- Things of a physical nature

III. Material and Spiritual
(LUKE 11:11-13)

A. Earthly Fathers Provide (vv. 11, 12)

11, 12. "Which of you fathers, if your son asks for a fish, will give him a snake instead? Or if he asks for an egg, will give him a scorpion?

When the devil tempted Jesus to turn a stone into bread to quell hunger (Luke 4:3), Jesus answered by quoting Deuteronomy 8:3, thereby invoking the principle that humans must have more than physical food to be whole. But no Scripture teaches that we don't need physical food! This is how our bodies work, and parents are responsible to provide the necessary food for their children.

In this regard, Jesus offers examples of dietary food staples from a Galilean village. To respond to a child's request for food with a snake or a scorpion would be downright malevolent. No loving parent would do either! Even parents who fail in many things will naturally try to provide adequate food for their children, even going hungry themselves so their children may eat.

B. Heavenly Father Provides (v. 13)

13. "If you then, though you are evil, know how to give good gifts to your children, how much more will your Father in heaven give the Holy Spirit to those who ask him!"

We have just seen two potential human responses to requests: the neighbor who initially says "no" and a father who could give dangerous creatures. In both cases, even flawed human beings (who *are evil*) manage to do the right thing. Jesus' point is that if imperfect humans are able to give the right things when requested, how much greater our situation is when we petition the heavenly Father!

Visual for Lesson 5

Point to this visual as you ask, "What responsibility do we have to teach the next generation to pray?"

> **What Do You Think?**
> What was an occasion that God gave you something better than what you had asked for, but you didn't realize it at the time? How did you grow spiritually from this experience?
> *Talking Points for Your Discussion*
> ▪ Employment opportunity
> ▪ Major purchase
> ▪ Choice of college
> ▪ Other

This brings us full circle to the opening address of the Lord's Prayer (Luke 11:2), namely requests made to God himself. And although Jesus does not elaborate here, he points to the greatest gift of all: the Father's gift of *the Holy Spirit*.

This foreshadows Peter's dramatic sermon in Luke's second book, Acts, where Peter repeats the promise of "the gift of the Holy Spirit" (Acts 2:38). God gives daily sustenance to those who ask. God forgives those who ask. And God will give his Holy Spirit according to the conditions that Peter said he would.

Conclusion
A. Growing in the Holy Spirit

From this wonderful text in Luke 11 we learn we should pray with structure, with persistence, and with expectations. We should not expect prayer to be something we do naturally or easily. It is something we learn to do, just as we learn to sing praise songs or learn how to study the Bible effectively. Learning to pray is a central part of being a disciple of Jesus Christ. God is a giving God, but we are to ask in prayer. "You do not have because you do not ask God" (James 4:2).

God will not force his gifts on us. God's Holy Spirit does not come upon us like an overbearing alien presence that invades us. We do not lose our identity, even our free will. We enjoy this gift as we yield to God's Holy Spirit, and this is something we learn to do more and more as we grow in Christ.

B. Prayer

Father God, we believe you will meet our daily needs, both the physical and spiritual. Grant us the continued presence of your Holy Spirit in our lives, molding us to be as you would have us. We pray these things in the name of the one who taught us to pray, Jesus, your Son, amen.

C. Thought to Remember
Never forget to pray.

INVOLVEMENT LEARNING

Enhance your lesson with NIV® Bible Student (from your curriculum supplier) and the reproducible activity page (at www.standardlesson.com or in the back of the NIV® Standard Lesson Commentary Deluxe Edition).

Into the Lesson

Display models of cars, houses, people, etc. (Perhaps you have a crafter in your class who builds models and would be pleased to bring some; an easier route is to construct models from Lego® material.) Ask, "What do these items all have in common?" The expected response is that all are models of something else.

Point out that as models each is intended to bring to mind a greater reality. Suggest that the model for prayer in today's text is also designed to point to a greater reality: the existence of God, who is the recipient of prayer. Say, "Prayer implies and affirms that God *is* and that he is powerful and good. How does the concept of prayer do that?" Jot responses on the board. If no one mentions it, add the idea that prayer is self-deceiving and foolish if it doesn't take as its point of departure the existence of the powerful and good God.

Into the Word

Distribute handouts that feature two columns with six lines under each. Title the first column *Element* and the second one *Reality*. The first column should include the following portions of today's text on the six lines as indicated: 1. Father / 2. hallowed be your name / 3. your kingdom come / 4. Give us each day our daily bread / 5. forgive us our sins / 6. lead us not into temptation. Leave the lines under the second column blank.

At the bottom of the handout, have these words/phrases: *atonement, enemy, eternity, holiness, grace, reign, relationship, submission, sustenance, weaknesses.* Ask learners to write on each blank line one of these words/phrases that they think best matches the line on the left; choices may be used once, more than once, or not at all.

After a few minutes, ask volunteers to read and defend their matches; learners may make good cases for different picks. Encourage discussion of differing choices among learners.

Next, distribute handouts of the following questions: 1. How do you react to inopportune requests from friends? 2. When was the last time you did something for a friend that you really did not want to do? 3. What was the most startling "substitution" you received from a family member after having requested something else? 4. What was a request that you honored that was very happily received? 5. When was a time you made a request that the other party thought to be unreasonable? 6. When was a time you made an excuse while turning down a friend's request?

Discuss as a class by asking for volunteers to respond. Since the answers for some may be embarrassing, don't put anyone on the spot. Be prepared to answer each question personally if learners do not volunteer to do so.

After discussion, say, "Now, let's relate these questions to verses 5-13 of our text." For each question, read it aloud and ask for its relationship to something in Jesus' remarks. Give hints as needed; as an example, for question 3 you could say, "Look at the gifts in verses 11 and 12!"

Alternative. Distribute copies of the "Types and Principles" activity from the reproducible page, which you can download. Have learners complete in study pairs.

Into Life

Option 1. Comment, "The model prayer suggested by Jesus is simply and profoundly that: a model. It is not necessary or even desirable to repeat its exact words time after time. Our prayers should be personal as they reflect his model." Give each learner a copy of the model, leaving spaces between words to allow such personalizing.

Option 2. Use the "Jesus, Man of Prayer" activity from the reproducible page to help your learners evaluate their prayer lives as indicated.

Jesus' Prayer for His Disciples

DEVOTIONAL READING: **John 15:1-11**
BACKGROUND SCRIPTURE: **John 17:1-26**

John 17:6-21

6 "I have revealed you to those whom you gave me out of the world. They were yours; you gave them to me and they have obeyed your word. 7 Now they know that everything you have given me comes from you. 8 For I gave them the words you gave me and they accepted them. They knew with certainty that I came from you, and they believed that you sent me. 9 I pray for them. I am not praying for the world, but for those you have given me, for they are yours. 10 All I have is yours, and all you have is mine. And glory has come to me through them. 11 I will remain in the world no longer, but they are still in the world, and I am coming to you. Holy Father, protect them by the power of your name, the name you gave me, so that they may be one as we are one. 12 While I was with them, I protected them and kept them safe by that name you gave me. None has been lost except the one doomed to destruction so that Scripture would be fulfilled.

13 "I am coming to you now, but I say these things while I am still in the world, so that they may have the full measure of my joy within them. 14 I have given them your word and the world has hated them, for they are not of the world any more than I am of the world. 15 My prayer is not that you take them out of the world but that you protect them from the evil one. 16 They are not of the world, even as I am not of it. 17 Sanctify them by the truth; your word is truth. 18 As you sent me into the world, I have sent them into the world. 19 For them I sanctify myself, that they too may be truly sanctified.

20 "My prayer is not for them alone. I pray also for those who will believe in me through their message, 21 that all of them may be one, Father, just as you are in me and I am in you. May they also be in us so that the world may believe that you have sent me."

KEY VERSES

My prayer is not for them alone. I pray also for those who will believe in me through their message, that all of them may be one, Father, just as you are in me and I am in you. May they also be in us so that the world may believe that you have sent me. —**John 17:20, 21**

Acts of Worship

Unit 2: Learning to Pray
Lessons 5–8

Lesson Aims

After participating in this lesson, each learner will be able to:

1. List some specific things that Jesus prayed for on behalf of his disciples.

2. Explain how one can be "in the world" but not "of the world."

3. Commit to correcting one area of his or her life that is out of harmony with that for which Jesus prayed.

Lesson Outline

Introduction

A. A Scripture for All Churches

While ministering in Los Angeles, I was invited to participate in a community service for the Week of Prayer for Christian Unity, to be held in January. This was organized by the Roman Catholic congregation in our neighborhood, and other participants included ministers from Lutheran, Episcopal, Methodist, Presbyterian, and Congregational churches. Including my own, there were seven Christian traditions represented. The result was a very impressive service that included the formalities of robes, processions, etc. I was asked to be the Scripture reader.

Much to my surprise, the text chosen to be read was from John 17. I was startled to discover that Jesus' prayer for unity was not just the possession of my own church tradition; the others all cared about church unity too! Today's lesson will look at this important prayer, offered up by Jesus on his last night before his death. It is a prayer that reveals his earnest desire that his followers be one.

B. Lesson Background

All four Gospels have an account of Jesus' dining with his disciples on the night before his crucifixion. We traditionally call this meal *the last supper*. It was held in "a large room upstairs" (Mark 14:15; Luke 22:12), probably an enclosed rooftop space of a borrowed house.

The synoptic Gospels (that is, Matthew, Mark, and Luke) give us few details about the last supper beyond that of the group eating from a common loaf and drinking from a common cup. Those three accounts focus on Jesus' teaching regarding the great abiding symbolism in those two elements: remembrance of his body and blood given as a sacrifice for sin. The Gospel of John, written after the other three Gospels, does not cover the loaf and cup teaching, presumably because the author had nothing to add to the accounts of the others. Instead, John provides details of the last supper that the other three Gospel writers do not.

These additional details fall into two broad groupings. One is what we call *the upper room discourse* of John 13–16; the other broad grouping is what is called *the high priestly prayer of Jesus* of John 17. Today's lesson comes from this section.

In the opening section of the prayer in John 17:1-5 (not in today's text), Jesus mentioned things that had been themes up to that point: his completion of the work the Father had given him (compare 5:36); his mission of bringing eternal life to the world (compare 6:40); and that the time for him to be glorified had come (compare 12:23).

I. Prayer for Disciples
(JOHN 17:6-19)
A. Given to Christ (v. 6)

6. "I have revealed you to those whom you gave me out of the world. They were yours; you gave them to me and they have obeyed your word.

In the verse before us, Jesus continues to review important aspects of his ministry. A purpose throughout that ministry has been to reveal (make known) in both word and deed the nature and purpose of God the Father to the disciples (compare John 1:18; 14:9).

Jesus also prays thankfully for his disciples, those who have kept faith with him. Jesus sees the Father's hand in their selection, for they are the ones *whom you gave me out of the world*. Being entrusted to Jesus, they have remained faithful, for they have kept the Father's *word*. This does not include Judas Iscariot (see John 17:12, below), who has long been recognized as unfaithful (6:70, 71; 12:4-6). At this point in time, Judas has already departed from the group (13:26-30).

B. Taught by Christ (vv. 7, 8)

7, 8. "Now they know that everything you have given me comes from you. For I gave them the words you gave me and they accepted them. They knew with certainty that I came from you, and they believed that you sent me.

HOW TO SAY IT

Ephesians	Ee-*fee*-zhunz.
Judas Iscariot	*Joo*-dus Iss-*care*-ee-ut.
synoptic	suh-*nawp*-tik.

Jesus continues to reaffirm the foundational aspects of his ministry. At the core is the disciples' conviction that it is the Father who has sent Jesus (*knew with certainty that I came from you*). Jesus refers to this sending numerous times in this Gospel (examples: John 5:23; 8:42; 16:30), so much so that Jesus' primary identity in this book can be said to be the Son sent by the Father (see 10:36). But Jesus is not sent merely to go on a journey. He has a mission to accomplish: to bring people to faith (John 20:31) so that they too may be sent out (17:18 [below]; 20:21).

One of the boldest expressions of this is found in Jesus' *bread of life discourse* of John 6:25-59. In this sermon, Jesus tells his followers, "The work of God is this: to believe in the one he has sent" (v. 29). The conviction that Jesus comes from the Father requires Jesus' followers to understand that his teachings are from the Father as well. There is no separation between the mission and message of Jesus in the purposes of God the Father.

C. Glory to Christ (vv. 9, 10)

9, 10. "I pray for them. I am not praying for the world, but for those you have given me, for they are yours. All I have is yours, and all you have is mine. And glory has come to me through them.

Jesus' prayer focuses on the disciples gathered in the upstairs room; by extension, we may see ourselves included as well (see v. 20, below). The gathered group is characterized in three ways here. First, they are given to Jesus by the Father. Jesus does not see his disciples as a random group of accidental followers. They have found him and he them for a purpose established by the Father himself.

Second, Jesus' disciples belong both to him and to the Father (*all I have is yours, and all you have is mine*). There is a common identity. For the Jewish disciples in the upstairs room to follow Jesus is not a rejection of the God of their forefathers, for they are one and the same God.

Third, the disciples' purpose is to glorify Jesus (and the Father). Circumstances may cause the purpose of being a follower of Jesus to be muddled at times, but we should always return to this touchstone: we are called to bring glory to the name of Christ. We serve to glorify him, and we do so by our lives of service.

> **What Do You Think?**
> What are some practical ways we can bring glory to Christ?
> *Talking Points for Your Discussion*
> - In personal choices and habits in public
> - In a family context
> - In the workplace
> - Other

❧ Yours? Mine? Ours? ❧

My wife and I have been married for over 50 years. That does not make us experts on marriage, but we have learned a few things along the way. One is that we have to think of the family as a unit, not as individual pieces, on most issues. That has certainly been the case regarding finances.

Not everyone learns this lesson. When the wife of a friend began to take Social Security early, she insisted this was "her money" and she could spend it as she wished. My friend suggested that since they didn't need it for daily expenses, most of it ought to be invested until they both retired and needed the extra income. She didn't want to do that. So he suggested that she take "her money" and pay "her share" of the mortgage, utilities, and groceries. She didn't want to do that either. This led to harsh words, hurt feelings, and extra tension. It didn't destroy their marriage, but it did create some difficulties.

In marriage it is often best when *yours* and *mine* simply become *ours*. The church is the bride of Christ. All we have should be seen as his. God and Christ are one. What is God's is Christ's; what is Christ's is God's. What a model of heavenly harmony and unity!   —J. B. N.

D. Protection (vv. 11, 12)

11. "I will remain in the world no longer, but they are still in the world, and I am coming to you. Holy Father, protect them by the power of your name, the name you gave me, so that they may be one as we are one.

Jesus is returning to the Father (John 14:2; 16:28). Jesus will physically leave the disciples with his coming death, resurrection, and ascension, but the power of the Father to keep them will remain. Jesus points to more than spiritual protection; he also points to unity, *that they may be one.*

This is not just unity of a common church membership or group identity that comes from meeting together. Jesus prays to the Father that his followers may have oneness *as we are one* (also John 10:30). This is the deep spiritual unity of the Father and Son, something beyond easy explanation. This is the unity that the church of Jesus Christ our Lord should have even today with its millions of disciples (see also 17:21, below).

> **What Do You Think?**
> What are some symptoms of Christian disunity? How can we overcome this problem?
> *Talking Points for Your Discussion*
> - Between individual Christians
> - Within a congregation
> - On a national level

12. "While I was with them, I protected them and kept them safe by that name you gave me. None has been lost except the one doomed to destruction so that Scripture would be fulfilled.

Jesus' prayer remembers that he has kept his disciples safe, not allowing them to stray from their faith in him and not allowing them to disintegrate into factions of disunity (John 6:39; 18:9). There is one exception, though: *the one doomed to destruction.* This is Judas Iscariot, whose unfaithfulness and treachery is seen as a fulfillment of Scripture (see John 13:18, quoting Psalm 41:9) and thus is part of the Father's plan for the ministry of Jesus. Even among the closest disciples, there will be those who fall away by their own volition.

E. Joy (v. 13)

13. "I am coming to you now, but I say these things while I am still in the world, so that they may have the full measure of my joy within them.

Jesus' pending transition from being in the world to being fully reunited with the Father is again emphasized. There are great horrors ahead for Jesus and his followers, but for Jesus the present moment is a time of joy. The journey home has begun, and he looks forward joyfully to the final destination, not the road he must travel to get there. He wants this joy to be shared among his disciples. He desires a sustaining joy that will transcend the many hard things they will be called to endure shortly, for their anguish will be transformed into joy (see John 15:11; 16:20).

F. Hatred (v. 14)

14. "I have given them your word and the world has hated them, for they are not of the world any more than I am of the world.

John tells us at the outset of his Gospel that "the Word became flesh and made his dwelling among us" (John 1:14). This means that Jesus the man has revealed the Word of God, has given God's message of truth to his disciples. Since Jesus is *not of the world* but sent by the Father, the acceptance of his message makes his followers *not of the world* either.

They (we) experience the world's hatred as a result (see John 1:11; 15:18, 19). The world is in rebellion against God, and it hates those who are reconciled to him. The world is at odds with God's truths, and it hates those who embrace them. The world rejects holiness, and it hates those who practice godliness. Part of being a follower of Jesus is to endure the scorn and hatred of many who are sold out to the world and its selfish standards.

> *What Do You Think?*
> How should we respond when the world expresses its hatred toward us?
> *Talking Points for Your Discussion*
> - Situations calling for passive acceptance
> - Situations calling for a response of defense
> - Situations calling for a pushback response

G. Sanctification (vv. 15-19)

15. "My prayer is not that you take them out of the world but that you protect them from the evil one.

Although Jesus prays for protection for his followers, he does not pray for their extraction. He wants his troops to have the best spiritual armor possible, but he is not calling for them to be withdrawn from the theater of war. Recognizing the adversary, Jesus asks that God keep his followers *from the evil one*, echoing his final petition in the Lord's Prayer (Matthew 6:13). Satan is this adversary, warned about earlier (John 8:44). The danger of the devil is not so much the physical harm he might do to Jesus' disciples, but the spiritual damage he may exact by enticing us to follow him.

16, 17. "They are not of the world, even as I am not of it. Sanctify them by the truth; your word is truth.

As in John 17:14 above, Jesus' prayer reminds those overhearing it that his followers *are not of the world*, and again he gives the basis for such assertion: *I am not of it.* The world, the human realm in rebellion against God, is not the permanent home for those who follow Christ and love God. Their (our) protection in this hostile environment is to be sanctified, to be made holy.

A key aspect of the concept of holiness is to be separated from sin, to be set apart for the Lord's service. The chief component of this sanctification is to possess the truth, as embodied in God's Word. It is this word of truth that frees us from the world (John 8:32). Following God's Word sets us apart in terms of different, holy behavior and thinking. Believing God's Word gives victory over the deceptions of the world, the wily tricks of the evil one (see Ephesians 6:11).

> *What Do You Think?*
> How can we demonstrate that God's truth has set us apart without that manifestation becoming a "holier than thou" barrier to evangelism?
> *Talking Points for Your Discussion*
> - In personal lifestyle choices
> - In relationships
> - In responses to difficult people and situations
> - Other

18, 19. "As you sent me into the world, I have sent them into the world. For them I sanctify myself, that they too may be truly sanctified.

Jesus finishes this section of the prayer by summarizing his disciples' mission and tying it very closely to that of his own. Jesus sends them (us) into the world as he was sent by God. He prays for their (our) sanctification just as he prays for his own. They (we) are mission-driven, holy soldiers, sent into an unbelieving world to testify for him and of him (see John 21:24).

We should end this section with some reflection on our churches and ourselves. These are among the last words of Jesus before his death, so they take on great significance for us. Are we so attached to the world that we cannot claim to be "not of the world"? Are we so enmeshed in the things of the world that we cannot claim to be sanctified, set apart from the world? Do we see God's Word as a freeing truth that allows us to resist the temptations of the world?

II. Prayer Inclusion
(JOHN 17:20, 21)
A. Who (v. 20)

20. "My prayer is not for them alone. I pray also for those who will believe in me through their message,

Jesus now leaves no doubt regarding whom his prayer includes; his prayer extends far beyond the circle of disciples gathered in an upstairs room (see comment on John 17:19, above). In so praying, Jesus discloses his plan for the future, his reason for sending his disciples into a realm that hates him and them: prophetically, there will be other disciples *who will believe in me through their message.* The multitude of the saved in Heaven will be exponential multiplication of Jesus' disciples (Revelation 7:9).

❧ CONVEYING A MESSAGE ❧

A diplomatic ambassador occupies a unique position of responsibility. His or her duties involve conveying the interests of the home country to the government of the host country. The ambassador should know the language of the host country well, otherwise misunderstandings can occur easily. These can be very damaging to the interests of the home country.

There was one particular incident when the French government conveyed to Great Britain a message containing the French word *demandon*. That word was improperly translated "demand," and the British government was incensed that the French would use such language! The difficulty was soon straightened out, for the French word really means "request" or "ask." The ideas overlap, but there are important nuances to consider.

We are ambassadors of Christ (2 Corinthians 5:20, 21). If we are to convey Christ's message to our culture effectively, we must be able to present it in language that the culture understands, without causing needless offense in the process (1 Corinthians 10:32, 33). There are times, of course, when one government must firmly inform another of its concerns, concerns that cannot be watered down. So it is with us as ambassadors of Christ (1 Corinthians 1:23; 1 Peter 2:8). It is only through the uncompromised message of Christ that the world can be saved.   —J. B. N.

B. Why (v. 21)

21. ". . . that all of them may be one, Father, just as you are in me and I am in you. May they also be in us so that the world may believe that you have sent me."

This section of the prayer ends with a grand crescendo, a celebration of unity. The one who reads the Gospel of John up to this point should be convinced of the essential, indivisible unity between the Father and Son (see John 6:46; 10:30, 38; etc.). Now there is a vision of many who join in this unity through faith. The unity of the followers of Christ is both a goal of the church and a witness to the world of the legitimacy of their faith.

When the church presents a united front of faith, its message of calling God's wayward children back to him through Jesus becomes powerful and effective. When the church is divided and preaches narrow, self-serving messages, its impact is minimized, just as the church's great adversary desires. Satan gains victory not only as individual Christians stumble and sin but also when churches divide and splinter. How can the world be united in faith when churches in the same neighborhood won't even speak to one another?

What Do You Think?
What are some practical ways to foster the type of unity among believers that Christ envisions?
Talking Points for Your Discussion
- On an individual level
- On a congregational level
- Among congregations within a community
- Other

Conclusion

A. Essential Unity

In the early 1800s, a transplanted Scotch-Irish clergyman on the American frontier of western Pennsylvania was disciplined for extending Christian fellowship to believers who were not part of the sectarian heritage of his group. He was confronted by the harsh reality of European divisions of the church that were retained by some immigrants in their new homeland.

This man, Thomas Campbell (1763–1854), had been studying the issue of division of the church from the perspective of the Bible. He concluded that passages such as John 17 taught that Christ desired unity for his followers. If this was so, reasoned Campbell, then dividing the church was contrary to the will of its Lord and therefore a sinful act. To participate knowingly in things that caused division in the church was to commit sin.

Campbell expressed his convictions when he wrote that the church on earth was "essentially, intentionally, and constitutionally one." By this he meant that there was unity in *the essence* of the church, in its commitment to Jesus Christ of those saved by faith in him. There was unity *in the intentionality* of Christ, who intended his church to be one as evidenced by his prayer in John 17.

Further, there was a *constitutional* unity of the church, as Campbell thought in terms of the U.S. Constitution, a written document that unified the many states and peoples of America. For the church, Campbell's idea of a constitution was the Bible, particularly the New Testament.

Campbell believed the church could be united if it recognized its essential oneness in Christ, if it recognized that division in the church was a sin-

ful violation of Christ's intention, and if it recognized the New Testament as the authoritative guide for all matters of Christian faith and practice. In the 205 years since Campbell wrote his thoughts, we have seen some steps toward Christian unity, but other developments have worked against unity even more so.

Those who love Christ and his words are (or should be) deeply troubled by this disunity, especially when it resorts to name-calling or elitist dismissal of those with whom we disagree. May we never be satisfied with a divided church, whether that be disunity within a congregation or the divisions we see between congregations. May we long for and work toward a united church, unified under the lordship of Jesus Christ in adherence to his Word. Such a church can then produce a unified witness to an unbelieving world.

B. Prayer

Father, we are humbled by our inclusion in your great creation of the church by your Son, Jesus. Convict us to extend fellowship to other Christians while remaining true to your Word as revealed to us in the Scriptures. Empower us as instruments of your will to foster unity among believers everywhere. We pray this in the name of the one Lord of the church, Jesus Christ, amen.

C. Thought to Remember

Christ intended his church to be united.

Visual for Lesson 6. *Point to the various elements of the license plate in this image as you discuss, in turn, their significance for the Christian.*

INVOLVEMENT LEARNING

Enhance your lesson with NIV® Bible Student (from your curriculum supplier) and the reproducible activity page (at www.standardlesson.com or in the back of the NIV® Standard Lesson Commentary Deluxe Edition).

Into the Lesson

Ask learners to call out the names of churches within a three-mile radius (if you are in an urban or suburban environment) or a six-mile radius (if you are in a rural environment). After jotting all responses on the board, ask, "What do these churches have in common?" After several responses, ask, "How do they differ?"

This brief discussion of similarities and differences will set the stage for studying Jesus' prayer for unity. Be careful not to let this discussion become accusatory or demeaning; keep it objective. To lead into the Bible study, say, "Jesus had some important things to say about unity among his followers. Let's see what they are."

Into the Word

Divide the class into three groups and give each a handout with one of the following three assignments. Include a copy of today's lesson text on the handouts. *Action Group:* Make a list of statements from Jesus' perspective that declare 'I [have performed some action on behalf of the disciples].' *Realized Consequences Group:* Make a list of statements regarding what had been the good consequences for the disciples as a result of Jesus' actions. *Anticipated Consequences Group:* Make a list of statements that reflect the expected, future good results for the disciples as a result of Jesus' actions.

Allow groups a few minutes to finish, then ask a spokesperson for the *Action Group* to read its list. Challenge learners who are not in the *Action Group* to look for the biblical basis for each entry as it is called out. Repeat the procedure for the remaining two groups. For the *Action Group*, expect entries such as "I have revealed you to them" (v. 6) and "I have given them your word" (v. 14). For the *Realized Consequences Group*, expect entries such as "they have obeyed your word" (v. 6) and "they believed" (v. 8). For the *Anticipated Consequences Group*, expect entries such as "that they also might

be sanctified" (v. 19) and "that all of them may be one" (v. 21). If the groups do a good job, this will give a comprehensive look at the text.

Alternative. Distribute copies of the "What to Pray For" activity from the reproducible page, which you can download. Have learners work on this in pairs or small groups.

Next, note the concept in verse 11 of being protected by the name of the heavenly Father. Have Deuteronomy 28:9, 10 read aloud. Note that in these verses God says that his name's being attached to his people will result in fear on the part of those who do not carry his name. Assign some or all of the following passages to be read aloud: Genesis 26:25; Exodus 34:5; Numbers 6:27; 2 Kings 5:11; Psalm 5:11; Psalm 9:10; Psalm 116:4; Proverbs 18:10; Malachi 1:14b. Explain that one must carry the name of God and his Son with both great humility and great strength. Ask, "How does a sense of the power of God's name encourage you?" Discuss.

Into Life

Stress that being in harmony with the world makes one to be out of harmony with God. Discuss how Christians tend to have problems in this area. *Option:* Distribute copies of the "Otherworldly" activity from the reproducible page. Have learners complete it as indicated.

Have someone with computer skills prepare for each class member a small "banner" with an ornate frame of stars and planets. The banner is to feature these words: *In the world, but not of it. How will that change my day?* Distribute as you say, "Put this in a place where you will see it each morning. Ponder the thought throughout the day as you decide how you are in the world but not of it."

Return to the list of churches from the Into the Lesson segment and discuss what your church can do to help bring about the unity for which Christ prayed. Conclude with prayer in that regard.

Jesus' Intercession for Us

Devotional Reading: Psalm 107:1-15
Background Scripture: Hebrews 4:14–5:10

Hebrews 4:14-16

¹⁴ Therefore, since we have a great high priest who has ascended into heaven, Jesus the Son of God, let us hold firmly to the faith we profess. ¹⁵ For we do not have a high priest who is unable to empathize with our weaknesses, but we have one who has been tempted in every way, just as we are—yet he did not sin. ¹⁶ Let us then approach God's throne of grace with confidence, so that we may receive mercy and find grace to help us in our time of need.

Hebrews 5:1-10

¹ Every high priest is selected from among the people and is appointed to represent the people in matters related to God, to offer gifts and sacrifices for sins. ² He is able to deal gently with those who are ignorant and are going astray, since he himself is subject to weakness. ³ This is why he has to offer sacrifices for his own sins, as well as for the sins of the people. ⁴ And no one takes this honor on himself, but he receives it when called by God, just as Aaron was.

⁵ In the same way, Christ did not take on himself the glory of becoming a high priest. But God said to him,

"You are my Son;
today I have become your Father."

⁶ And he says in another place,

"You are a priest forever,
in the order of Melchizedek."

⁷ During the days of Jesus' life on earth, he offered up prayers and petitions with fervent cries and tears to the one who could save him from death, and he was heard because of his reverent submission. ⁸ Son though he was, he learned obedience from what he suffered ⁹ and, once made perfect, he became the source of eternal salvation for all who obey him ¹⁰ and was designated by God to be high priest in the order of Melchizedek.

Key Verse

For we do not have a high priest who is unable to empathize with our weaknesses, but we have one who has been tempted in every way, just as we are—yet he did not sin. —**Hebrews 4:15**

ACTS OF WORSHIP

Unit 2: Learning to Pray
Lessons 5–8

LESSON AIMS

After participating in this lesson, each learner will be able to:

1. Tell how Aaron and Melchizedek are significant to Jesus' role of high priest.

2. Explain the need for Jesus to be "a great high priest."

3. Praise God for giving us the perfect intercessor.

LESSON OUTLINE

Introduction

A. Embracing Change

In his influential 1962 book *Diffusion of Innovations,* author Everett Rogers sought to explain the rates at which new ideas and technology spread. At one extreme of his scale are the *innovators* (2.5 percent of the people) and *early adopters* (13.5 percent). As those labels suggest, people in these categories readily embrace change. At the other end of the scale are the *laggards* (16 percent). A motivational speaker described these as people who buy push-button phones only because rotary-dial phones are no longer available!

We see both extremes—and everywhere in between—in the pages of the New Testament as people are confronted with the new covenant brought by Jesus. Even after embracing the change, some eventually abandoned what they had previously accepted. The people being addressed in the book of Hebrews seem to have been Jewish Christians who were wavering in this regard (Hebrews 3:12; 5:11–6:12; 10:32-35; etc.).

Central to the message of Hebrews is the fact that while the Jewish system was good for its intended purposes, it had to be superseded by the new, Christian system, which was far superior in every way. But what about the Jewish priesthood? Didn't priests, especially the high priest, perform vital functions? There had been high priests for centuries and centuries, all the way back to Aaron, the brother of Moses. How were the functions of this priesthood to be covered in the new system? The author of Hebrews provided the answer.

B. Lesson Background

Outside the book of Hebrews, the man Melchizedek is mentioned by name in only two places in the Bible: Genesis 14:18 and Psalm 110:4. Genesis 14 notes this man's encounter with Abram (Abraham) after the latter had won a small military victory. As Abraham and his men returned home, they were met by "Melchizedek king of Salem," who brought them bread and wine, plus a blessing for Abraham. In turn, Abraham gave that king a tenth of the spoils of the battle.

Melchizedek was more than a king, however, for Genesis 14:18 refers to him as a "priest of God Most High." This is the first time in the Bible the term *priest* is used. Here was a priest who had nothing to do with Aaron or the tribe of Levi (from which all Israelite priests descended), for he predated both by hundreds of years!

Regarding Psalm 110, Jesus identified himself as one of the two Lords in the opening line "The Lord says to my Lord" (see Matthew 22:41-45), and Psalm 110:1b-3 goes on to describe his kingly authority. Then Psalm 110:4 declares "The Lord has sworn and will not change his mind: 'You are a priest forever, in the order of Melchizedek.'"

Leadership in ancient Israel was typically understood to be vested in the three offices of *prophet*, *priest*, and *king*. Usually those were distinct functions that did not overlap (compare 2 Chronicles 19:11; 26:16-20). But there were exceptions. Ezekiel was both a prophet and a priest (Ezekiel 1:3). King David performed the functions of a priest on one occasion (2 Samuel 6:16-18), as did King Solomon (1 Kings 8:62-64). Jesus ended up being the ultimate exception, as we shall see.

The author of Hebrews (whose identity is not conclusively known) is a master of the Old Testament, knowing well all the data on Melchizedek. The author presents the data with regard to Jesus using a technique called *typology* as he draws on patterns from the Old Testament to understand the events and people of the New Testament.

I. Son of God
(HEBREWS 4:14-16)
A. Hold Firmly (v. 14)

14. Therefore, since we have a great high priest who has ascended into heaven, Jesus the Son of God, let us hold firmly to the faith we profess.

The author has already mentioned Jesus as a *high priest* twice by this point, but without elaboration (Hebrews 2:17; 3:1). The verse before us marks the beginning of the explanation.

The author begins by assuring the readers that understanding Jesus as a high priest will contribute to our confidence to *hold firmly to the faith*

we profess in him. That which we profess refers to deeply held beliefs, convictions so dear that our lives are guided by them.

❧ MAKING ADJUSTMENTS . . . OR NOT ❧

Whenever a presidential candidate is defeated in a U.S. election, there are always voices on the losing side that call for their political party to "get back in touch" or "move to the political center" to recover. The same happens when control of a house of congress changes hands. Elections in other countries draw similar wails from the losing side.

Others of the losing party, however, will counter that their side lost precisely because their candidate moved to the center, thereby alienating the party's base (whether that base be conservative-right, liberal-left, or something else). Therefore, they argue, the party's future should be entrusted anew to the party's base, which will hold firmly to the core principles. Every national election seems to go this way.

The history of the Christian faith illustrates much the same. Whenever Christian influence is on the decline, some will say that the problem is that the church is failing to adjust to cultural trends. Others will assert just the opposite: that Christian influence has declined precisely because the church has compromised itself to cultural trends, losing God's blessing in the process.

Occasionally, the proper voice is heard: the church can change its *methods* but never its *message*. Our message—the faith we profess—is that Jesus is the Christ, the Son of the living God. Is that still what you profess?   —C. R. B.

We are told two things about the high priesthood of Jesus in this verse. First, it is *great*, mean-

HOW TO SAY IT

Abraham	*Ay*-bruh-ham.
Abram	*Ay*-brum.
Levi	*Lee*-vye.
Levites	*Lee*-vites.
Levitical	Leh-*vit*-ih-kul.
Melchizedek	Mel-*kiz*-eh-dek.
Nehemiah	*Nee*-huh-**my**-uh.

ing it is a high priesthood that exceeds the Jewish version in every way. Second, we have a high priest *who has ascended into heaven*. No Jewish high priest is ever described this way. The description indicates that Jesus is in the heavenly realm as he continues to function as high priest. Both Jewish and Christian thought understand Heaven to contain the perfect, ultimate temple of the Lord (see Psalm 11:4; Revelation 11:19). The risen Jesus is positioned to work as high priest in a realm compared with which the temple of earthly Jerusalem is but an inferior copy (see Hebrews 8:5).

B. Approach Confidently (vv. 15, 16)

15. For we do not have a high priest who is unable to empathize with our weaknesses, but we have one who has been tempted in every way, just as we are—yet he did not sin.

Our *high priest* in Heaven is not some heavenly being like an angel who has had no experience of being human. Jesus, however, "became flesh and made his dwelling among us" (John 1:14). If he had not been made human, then he would not have experienced death as humanity does. If Jesus had not been made human, then he would not have died for our sins (Hebrews 2:9). Yet even being fully human, Jesus differed from all of us in that *he did not sin*. Fully human, yet unstained by sin—this is the combination necessary for the perfect, eternal high priest.

16. Let us then approach God's throne of grace with confidence, so that we may receive mercy and find grace to help us in our time of need.

When in need of help, a normal impulse is to approach someone who knows us and is in a position to assist. The one in Heaven who understands our needs on our terms is Jesus, our heavenly advocate (1 John 2:1). While on earth, Jesus revealed himself to be a person of mercy and of grace (see Acts 10:38). This is why we may approach him *with confidence*, for he has already promised to be with us and supply our needs (Matthew 28:20).

Knowing that we are invited to bring our needs before our heavenly advocate, who intercedes for us as ultimate high priest, is a key element of prayer. If we do not *receive mercy and find grace to help us*

in our time of need, it is because we have not asked.

II. Order of Melchizedek
(HEBREWS 5:1-10)

A. Purpose of a High Priest (vv. 1-3)

1. Every high priest is selected from among the people and is appointed to represent the people in matters related to God, to offer gifts and sacrifices for sins.

The author draws on common understandings with his readers to portray the traditional roles and functions of the high priest. Such a person is *selected from among the people,* meaning he is an ordinary human being who comes from those whom he serves. The fact that he *is appointed to represent the people in matters related to God* means that his defined function is to serve as a mediator (a go-between) for the rest of the people in their relationship with the Lord.

One way high priests serve as mediators is by administering *gifts*. These are the various offerings that people bring to the temple, including the tithe of produce from the land (see Deuteronomy 12:5, 6). Such gifts serve the practical function of supporting the Levites who work in the temple and the high priest and his associates who perform religious duties there (and had done so in the temple's predecessor, the tabernacle; see Numbers 18:21; Deuteronomy 18:1; Nehemiah 13:10).

Second, the high priest offers *sacrifices for sins.* This includes the ritual sacrifice of animals as atonement for the sins of the nation and for individuals (see Leviticus 9:15-22). This has been the primary function of the Jerusalem temple, a sort of "sacrifice factory" where thousands of animals are slaughtered every year according to the expectations of the Law of Moses. Later, the author of Hebrews will make the point that despite this massive shedding of animal blood, the result is ineffective in actually removing the sins of the people (Hebrews 10:11).

2a. He is able to deal gently with those who are ignorant and are going astray,

The author continues by offering a personal element of the high priesthood. The ministry of offering sacrifices for sins is an act of dealing *gently with those who are ignorant,* those who know their relationship with God is damaged by sin but have no idea how to address the problem. These folks, who *are going astray,* need such help.

> **What Do You Think?**
> How can Christ's compassion serve as a model for us as we interact with others?
> *Talking Points for Your Discussion*
> - Regarding people who anger us
> - Regarding people whose views and lifestyles challenge ours
> - Regarding people in authority over us
> - Regarding Christians who have backslidden
> - Other

2b, 3. . . . since he himself is subject to weakness. This is why he has to offer sacrifices for his own sins, as well as for the sins of the people.

The fact that the high priest *himself is subject to weakness* means that he too is in need of sacrifice for his personal sins. This puts him in the peculiar position of needing to serve as his own high priest in the matter of atoning sacrifice for sins (Leviticus 9:7; 16:6). He is at the top of the Levitical and priestly hierarchy. There is no super-duper high priest to do this work for him. Even if there were, who then would offer the sacrifices for *that* person?

B. Appointment of a High Priest (vv. 4-6)

4. And no one takes this honor on himself, but he receives it when called by God, just as Aaron was.

The victors of wars or coups in the ancient world often were those most ruthless and cunning. They would gather followers, consolidate power by conquest or intimidation, and be accepted as the monarch of the people. In so doing, they heaped earthly honors on themselves. Priests in general and the high priest in particular were a different matter. No Israelite was to become high priest through military action. The high priest was not to be a self-made man, but a qualified person appointed by God. He was to be from the tribe of Levi and from Aaron, one of Levi's descendants (see Exodus 28:1; Leviticus 16:32; 1 Chronicles 23:6, 13; 2 Chronicles 35:14; Nehemiah 10:38).

History shows, however, that appointment to be high priest could come about because of politics. This happened frequently during the time between the Old and New Testaments. Even during Jesus' day, the Romans chose Annas and Caiaphas to be high priests (compare Luke 3:2; John 18:13). Although history reveals human maneuvering in the succession of high priests, the people believed these men to be appointed and approved by God. High priests were not to be elected or gain office by killing their rivals.

5, 6. In the same way, Christ did not take on himself the glory of becoming a high priest. But God said to him,

"You are my Son;
today I have become your Father."
And he says in another place,
"You are a priest forever,
in the order of Melchizedek."

The pieces of the author's argument come together in quotations of Psalm 2:7 and 110:4. Jesus did not come to earth to seize the office of high priest as an act of human ambition. He never served in the capacity of high priest in the Jerusalem temple, something impossible for a man born into the tribe of Judah. He was, rather, chosen and appointed by God to be a high priest of a superior nature, a priest *in the order of Melchizedek.*

> **What Do You Think?**
> In what ways can the fact that Jesus is the unique and eternal priest inform our reaction to other faiths and worldviews?
> *Talking Points for Your Discussion*
> - Regarding the "all religions are the same" view
> - Regarding the "we all serve the same God" view
> - Regarding denial of the existence of sin
> - Other

The author identifies in Jesus the promises of Psalm 110 for the one who, from the psalmist's perspective, was yet to come. Melchizedek had been both king and priest in the days of Abraham (see the Lesson Background and Hebrews 7:1). Thus the combination of kingly and priestly roles in Jesus follows the pattern of Melchizedek, not the pattern of Judaism, which separates those roles.

After the author of Hebrews identifies Jesus firmly with Melchizedek, he goes on to describe that ancient worthy as "without father or mother, without genealogy, without beginning of days or end of life" (Hebrews 7:3). This establishes that no genealogical record exists for Melchizedek. Such a record is important for the priesthood of Israel (see Nehemiah 7:63, 64), yet here is a man who existed before the nation of Israel did, a man whose priesthood no devout Jew questions! There is no evidence that Melchizedek's priesthood was hereditary, gained by being the son of an earlier priest; Jesus is in this pattern. Furthermore, Jesus is qualified to be *a priest forever* on the basis of his "indestructible life" (Hebrews 7:16), his victory over death by self-resurrection.

❧ "I'M THE GREATEST" ❧

"It's what I came here to do. I'm now a legend. I'm the greatest athlete to live." Those are the proud words of Usain Bolt after winning gold medals for 100- and 200-meter sprints at the 2012 London Olympics. "Lightning" Bolt, as he is known, is regarded by many to be the fastest man alive, and his boast was apparently intended to make sure everyone knows it.

Of course, Bolt is not the first athlete to have a high opinion of himself. Former heavyweight boxing champion Muhammad Ali also boasted of being "the greatest." A problem with this kind of boasting is that sooner or later someone else will be seen to be "greater" as time takes its toll.

Jesus did not come to earth to take upon himself the honor of being "the greatest" (compare Mark 10:45). His role as our great high priest was bestowed on him by God the Father. One lesson for followers of Jesus is to serve God in the humility Jesus demonstrated and let the Father bestow any accolades (compare Job 1:8).   —C. R. B.

C. Perfecting of Our High Priest (vv. 7-10)

7. During the days of Jesus' life on earth, he offered up prayers and petitions with fervent cries and tears to the one who could save him from death, and he was heard because of his reverent submission.

The author now reveals intimate knowledge of Jesus' prayer life. All four Gospels note that Jesus prayed to the Father, but this author adds that Jesus was entreating the one who had the power to *save him from death*. Jesus must have prayed many times in the way this verse describes, but one occasion of note is his time of prayer in the garden (see Matthew 26:39; Mark 14:36; Luke 22:42).

The Greek word translated *reverent submission* is also translated "reverence" in Hebrews 12:28, and it should be understood in that manner here. Therefore Jesus' prayers were heard not because he feared death but because he had the proper attitude of personal surrender to God. This is another quality that makes Jesus the ideal person to be our high priestly intercessor in prayer.

> *What Do You Think?*
> How do we approach God boldly in prayer (v. 16) yet also with godly fear?
> *Talking Points for Your Discussion*
> ▪ The role of motive
> ▪ The role of confidence
> ▪ The role of persistence
> ▪ Other

8. Son though he was, he learned obedience from what he suffered

This book's opening lines celebrate God's speaking through "his Son" (Hebrews 1:2a). Jesus is further celebrated as the one who creates and sustains all things, and who is "the exact representation" of his Father (1:2b, 3). Despite these lofty qualities and qualifications, there were things the Son had to learn as a human through obedience. As Leon Morris puts it, Jesus "learned obedience by actually obeying" (compare Luke 2:51, 52). In the context at hand, Jesus' obedience is tied with *what he suffered,* a reference to the events leading up to and including his horrific death on a Roman cross (see Hebrews 13:12; 1 Peter 4:1).

9. . . . and, once made perfect, he became the source of eternal salvation for all who obey him

We are now provided an important perspective on the value and result of Christ's obedient suffering. The text does not say that Christ lived through pain to become stronger or wiser, nor does it insinuate that Jesus was ever imperfect in his divine nature. Rather, the writer is saying that the sufferings Christ endured made him *perfect* as in "completely tested and qualified" in some sense.

The sense intended is revealed in the phrase *became the source of eternal salvation*. The next few chapters will expand on this, making the point that Jesus' obedience all the way to the cross qualifies him as the all-sufficient, perfect sacrifice for human sin (see Hebrews 7:27; 9:12).

10. . . . and was designated by God to be high priest in the order of Melchizedek.

This brings our lesson back to the beginning point. The first Christians to read this—probably those of Jewish background who may be thinking of abandoning their new faith to return to Judaism—should ponder carefully the significance of Jesus' priesthood. Why go back to the imperfect and sometimes corrupt priesthood of Levi and Aaron when a *high priest in the order of Melchizedek* has come?

Conclusion

A. Needing a Priest

There have been many times in my ministry when a visitor to my church asked to see a priest. On one occasion, a young man met me after the Sunday service and said, "Father, I need to confess." I quickly realized that he was coming from a Roman Catholic background, and he wanted someone to hear his confession as a Catholic priest might do. I told him that I was not a priest, but that I would be glad to talk and pray with him. We did just that in my office. His problem was that he was getting married that week, but he still had strong feelings of attraction for a woman other than his fiancée. In his own way, he was suffering in his attempt to be righteous.

Rugged individualism is not the Christian way when it comes to spiritual matters. We all need someone to listen to us and to pray for us. This is partly why a specialized category of priests is valued in some branches of Christianity. But in the New Testament era we do not need this kind of priest to make intercession. We are all priests (1 Peter 2:9), and we all can pray for each other —something Paul asked his readers to do for him (see Ephesians 6:19). Even so, we ultimately and always rely on Jesus, our faithful and eternal high priest, to intercede for us at the very throne of God.

B. Prayer

Father, thank you for sending your Son to serve as the perfect sacrifice for our sins, to be the perfect and eternal high priest on our behalf. As we look to him, may we never be tempted to go back to old ways. We pray this in Jesus' name, amen.

C. Thought to Remember

We have a perfect and eternal high priest.

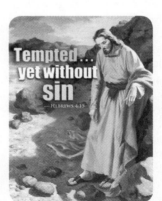

Visual for Lesson 7

Point to this visual and refer to Matthew 4:3, 4 as an example of Jesus' sinlessness.

INVOLVEMENT LEARNING

Enhance your lesson with NIV® Bible Student (from your curriculum supplier) and the reproducible activity page (at www.standardlesson.com or in the back of the NIV® Standard Lesson Commentary Deluxe Edition).

Into the Lesson

Display these groups of letters: *EIMORSSTUY* and *CHIMEEELZKD*. Say to half your class, "See if you can rearrange the first set of letters to form an important word for today's study." To the other half say, "See if you can rearrange the second set of letters to reveal a proper noun that is important for today's study." If no solutions are forthcoming after a few minutes, provide a hint that both words start with *M*. Provide further clues of your own devising until the solutions *mysterious* and *Melchizedek* are reached.

Comment that Melchizedek certainly has an aura of mystery about him as you ask two learners to read aloud Genesis 14:17-20 and Psalm 110:1-4, one each. Note that the latter is a psalm by King David regarding the priesthood of the coming Messiah. Then say, "Now let's see how this mysterious Melchizedek helps us understand Jesus."

Into the Word

Distribute handouts featuring three columns that have the headings *Melchizedek / Aaron / Jesus Christ*. Ask learners to enter applicable statements and facts under the appropriate column headings as you read aloud the 13 verses of the lesson text; pause after each verse to allow learners to ponder their entries.

Example: after you read Hebrews 4:15, learners should make the entry "did not sin" under the column for Jesus. Some facts will be entered in more than one column. Enhance the discussion by also reading other texts of your choice for which learners will make entries on their handouts as well. Some excellent possibilities are Genesis 14:18; selected verses of Exodus 28, 29 that deal with the appointment of priests; and Psalm 110:4.

After you finish reading the texts, ask learners to share their entries. Be prepared to resolve differences. (*Option:* use small groups to have learners compare their entries and resolve differences.)

Next, ask learners to focus on the word *order* in Hebrews 5:6, 10 as you say, "Let's do a synonym brainstorm. What synonyms come to mind for the noun *order* as you see it used in these two verses?" Jot responses on the board. Responses should reflect the ideas of *class* (as in *classification*) and *category* (as in *categorization*). After discussing why it is appropriate for the author of Hebrews to see Jesus and Melchizedek as being classified together, ask, "In what ways does Jesus stand alone as a 'category of one'?" Responses should reflect the uniqueness of Jesus' person (God's only Son, etc.) and work (only he can save us from sin's penalty, etc.).

Option. Begin this segment by having learners complete the "Mega High Priest" activity on the reproducible page, which you can download. Adding this exercise will result in an extra look at Jesus regarding his priestly role.

Into Life

Give each learner a stick-on label upon which they will write *JIMGHPH!* After a brief time of speculation about the meaning, say that the letters stand for *Jesus Is My Great High Priest, Hallelujah!* Suggest posting it in a conspicuous place (refrigerator, etc.) for several days as a reminder of the lesson's great truth and our necessary response of praise and thanksgiving. Some learners may prefer to wear the label for a day to draw the attention of the curious; this will provide opportunity to describe the good news of what Jesus has done and is doing on our behalf.

Option. Distribute copies of the "Priest? Who, Me?" activity from the reproducible page; have learners work in pairs to complete it. Use it to lead a discussion on ways to serve as priests.

Note that our use of the phrase *in Jesus' name* to conclude prayers is, in part, our affirmation of his priestly intercession on our behalf. Offer a closing prayer of praise and thanksgiving for Jesus' ministry as our high priest.

POWERFUL
PRAYER

DEVOTIONAL READING: Lamentations 3:52-58
BACKGROUND SCRIPTURE: James 5

JAMES 5:13-18

¹³ Is anyone among you in trouble? Let them pray. Is anyone happy? Let them sing songs of praise. ¹⁴ Is anyone among you sick? Let them call the elders of the church to pray over them and anoint them with oil in the name of the Lord. ¹⁵ And the prayer offered in faith will make the sick person well; the Lord will raise them up. If they have sinned, they will be for-given. ¹⁶ Therefore confess your sins to each other and pray for each other so that you may be healed. The prayer of a righteous person is powerful and effective.

¹⁷ Elijah was a human being, even as we are. He prayed earnestly that it would not rain, and it did not rain on the land for three and a half years. ¹⁸ Again he prayed, and the heavens gave rain, and the earth produced its crops.

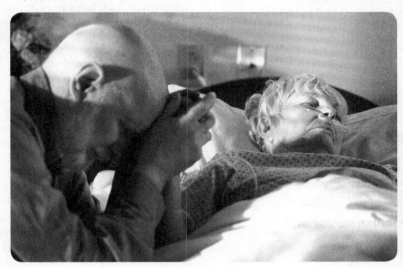

KEY VERSE

Confess your sins to each other and pray for each other so that you may be healed. The prayer of a righteous person is powerful and effective. —James 5:16

Acts of Worship

Unit 2: Learning to Pray
Lessons 5–8

Lesson Aims

After participating in this lesson, each learner will be able to:

1. Summarize what James says about prayer, confession, intercession, and faith.

2. Compare and contrast James's assertion about the power of a righteous person's prayer with one's own prayer experience.

3. Commit to greater involvement in praying for others.

Lesson Outline

Introduction

A. Timely Prayer

Bernard of Clairvaux (1090–1153) wrote, "Anyone who wishes to pray must choose not only the right place but also the right time." Bernard was an abbot of a medieval monastic community, and part of his responsibility was teaching the brothers of his house to pray. Daily routine was the rule in his environment, and prayers were offered multiple times, at specific hours. Bernard's rigid schedule for prayers may not be suitable for us, but his advice about the timing of prayer still rings true.

The noise of the world seems to drown out opportunities for prayer. We are too busy, too stressed, or too tired to take time to pray. Peter Marshall, who served as the U.S. Senate Chaplain from 1947 until his untimely death in 1949, once offered this prayer for that body: "Forgive us for thinking that prayer is a waste of time and help us to see that without prayer, our work is a waste of time." The advice within that prayer applies to a group far larger than just elected officials. It applies to us. The Christian should be a person of prayer. The church should be a community of prayer. Yet too often we have allowed prayer to be crowded from our worship services and our lives.

James wraps up his letter by discussing the necessity of timely prayer. He has lessons for us on both the purpose of prayer and the power of prayer. This is the focus of this week's lesson.

B. Lesson Background

The book of James is unlike any other book of the Bible in certain respects. Although it begins like a letter, it reads more like a sermon, speaking with firm authority. It is loosely organized, jumping from topic to topic with little connecting material. It is also intensely practical, showing relatively little interest in doctrinal principles or formulations. The author is interested in conduct; he teaches his readers *how* they should live as Christian believers in a world that is often hostile to Christian values.

There are several men named *James* in the New Testament, but most scholars believe the author of this book is the James who was the half brother of Jesus (Matthew 13:55; Mark 6:3). According to church tradition, this James became the leader of the church in Jerusalem a few years after the resurrection of Jesus (Acts 12:17; 15:13; 21:18; Galatians 2:9), serving in this role until his death sometime in the AD 60s. He was given the moniker *James the Just* because of his constant pleas for justice for his people. Although he was a Jewish Christian in the predominantly non-Christian, Jewish city of Jerusalem, he was respected by all the people for his integrity. A second-century church historian records that James went to the temple daily to pray and spent so much time on his knees that they "became [calloused] like that of a camel's."

A word from James, then, seems a fitting end to this month's lessons on prayer. In his little letter that we divide into five chapters, prayer is the final subject of his teaching, a position of importance and urgency that we should not ignore.

I. Call for Prayer
(JAMES 5:13-15)
A. Asking (v. 13a)

13a. Is anyone among you in trouble? Let them pray.

The author's Jewish heritage admits a central place for prayer, and prayer is an essential for the first-century Jewish Christians. Therefore we should not be surprised at James's attention to this matter. Here he begins to set forth his thoughts on prayer in terms of the first of four categories of people who need to pray or be prayed for. The prayer strategy for each group is different.

The first group consists of those *in trouble,* literally "those who suffer bad things." James's advice for these people is that they should pray. At first glance, this recommendation seems so generic as to be of little practical value. But since it serves as the pattern or template for what follows, we should pay attention.

This half verse features the most common verb in the New Testament for praying (used more than 80 times), and it embraces the sense of "asking." The person with overwhelming life troubles should not be a passive sufferer but an asker, one

who asks God for help. We should not be passive sufferers but active in lifting our issues to God in prayer. This echoes the teachings of Jesus, who counseled his disciples to "Ask and it will be given to you" (Matthew 7:7). The first step in dealing with personal challenges is to ask for God's help.

B. Singing (v. 13b)

13b. Is anyone happy? Let them sing songs of praise.

The status of the second group, the *happy,* may seem at first glance to be unrelated to prayer needs. The word translated *happy* is seldom used in the New Testament (elsewhere only in Acts 27:22, 25). It has the sense of strong, positive passions; it is the opposite of being apathetic. The happy person is one who is cheerful, whose heart is bursting with optimism. James's tone is different here than a few verses earlier, where he commanded that there be mourning instead of laughter (James 4:9).

Songs directed to God can be thought of as "musical prayer" or "prayer set to music." James is teaching that times of high spirits are also times to pray. If you are happy, then *sing songs* of prayerful praise to God, the ultimate source of your happiness. Don't spoil the moment by artificially depressing yourself, but don't neglect prayer in the midst of good times either.

❧ PRAISE IN PRAYER ❧

We're used to seeing people pray in bad times. We remember the droves of people who flocked to churches after the terrorist attacks of 9/11. When a gunman slaughtered 20 children in Newtown, Connecticut, in 2012, the churches of the area were filled with people praying. It's easy to get

Visual for
Lesson 8

Point to this visual as you ask, "What examples of powerful prayer in the Bible can you recall?"

cynical and chalk all this up to the old "no atheists in foxholes" syndrome, but even the most devout Christians can be driven to their knees when circumstances overwhelm. James says it's perfectly appropriate to pray when we're hurting.

On the other hand, James tells us it's also appropriate to offer joyful praise when we are happy. This seems to be much of the appeal of contemporary praise services. Younger people (and many older Christians as well) enjoy offering vibrant praise to God when they are happy. James strongly commends the practice.

One important benefit of singing praise to God in "up" times is that we will avoid being guilty of practicing spare-tire religion: used only in emergencies. You're not guilty of that, are you?

—C. R. B.

C. Healing (vv. 14, 15a)

14, 15a. Is anyone among you sick? Let them call the elders of the church to pray over them and anoint them with oil in the name of the Lord. And the prayer offered in faith will make the sick person well; the Lord will raise them up.

James's third group regarding prayer is the *sick*. Different Greek verbs are behind the two translations of *sick* in this verse and a half, and the distinction is worth investigating.

The Greek verb translated *sick* in the first instance occurs 33 times in the New Testament. It is used in various places to describe those who

are "diseased" as we typically think of today in terms of bacterial or viral infections (example: John 4:46, 52). But it is also used to describe other physical infirmities, as in John 5:3, where the verb is translated "disabled," with further clarification "the blind, the lame, the paralyzed." Paul uses this verb to refer to the "weak brother or sister" (literally: "the [one] being weak"), specified as one with a "weak conscience," in 1 Corinthians 8:11, 12. As Paul uses this same verb in 2 Corinthians 11:21; 13:4, 9, he is not talking about a physical disease.

By contrast, the Greek verb translated *sick* in the second instance in the text before us is quite rare in the New Testament. It is used elsewhere only in Hebrews 12:3, there translated "weary."

All this has caused interpreters to wonder whether James is referring to physical, psychological, or spiritual deficiencies. To set this up as "either this or that" is to create a false choice, however. Folks who are seriously ill in body or otherwise physically impaired will often be psychologically and/or spiritually weakened at the same time. Debilitating illness can be accompanied by paralyzing depression, which can result in (or from) "not wanting to be a burden" on others while needing help and care. Debilitating illness also can be accompanied by weakened faith; this can take the form of feeling abandoned by God.

These factors may cause people to feel isolated or to want to be left alone—to hole up in their homes and gut it out by themselves. Yet this is precisely the time when the sick person should *call the elders of the church*, asking for help from those who are appointed to be shepherds of the flock (Acts 20:28).

The elders can do two things. First, they *pray over* the ill person, showing that they care for the suffering one and that God is present and cares too. This is the act of intercessory prayer (praying

HOW TO SAY IT

Baal	*Bay*-ul.
Elijah	Ee-*lye*-juh.
Jezebel	*Jez*-uh-bel.
Zarephath	*Zair*-uh-fath.

for one another) so valued by Paul (see Romans 15:30).

Second, the elders can anoint this sick person *with oil.* This is an act of care, for olive oil is seen to have cleansing and healing properties in the first century (see Luke 10:34). But there is more than that here since the elders are to anoint the sick person *in the name of the Lord.* This implies not a medical approach to healing but a spiritual one. To anoint an ill person in this manner is the physical counterpart of praying to the Lord for healing (see Mark 6:13).

There is nothing magical here. Both the anointing and the reception of the anointing are acts of faith, faith that leaves the healing to God, not to special properties of the oil. Does this mean that anointing with oil by church elders always produces healing? Does it mean that a lack of healing indicates defective elders or improper oil? *No* and *no.* Praying and anointing do not guarantee healing, but they bring the dire needs of the ill brother or sister before the throne of the Lord, imploring God to act with mercy for this beloved lamb of the church. They claim a promise that God is a God of healing (Jeremiah 33:6) and that Jesus is our Savior who bears our diseases (see Matthew 8:17).

As one who has served as a minister, I have often gathered elders to pray for and anoint a church member who was ill. Did this ever result in instantaneous healing? No. Did some of these persons get worse, even die? Yes. But the visitation and interaction showed a struggling, fearful, isolated person that we cared and that God cared too. More than once, a recovered person has told me, "It felt like I began to get better from that day."

What Do You Think?
What are some other ways our congregation can respond in an organized way to needs that can be met only through the intervention of others?
Talking Points for Your Discussion
- Regarding physical illness or infirmity
- Regarding mental disorders
- Regarding financial need
- Other

D. Forgiving (v. 15b)

15b. If they have sinned, they will be forgiven.

James presents a fourth issue to be addressed by prayer: the need for forgiveness. This issue arises from the previous scenario of having elders make a visit to one in need of prayer. We all need forgiveness, of course, but think of that homebound person with hours upon hours to reflect on life's twists and turns. This person's illness is not helped by ongoing self-examination and self-recrimination, which can turn ugly with regret.

If death is near, the person with a burden of unresolved guilt is in no condition to face it alone. The illness being suffered may be the result of sinful behavior (example: a person's liver is failing because of alcoholism), although that is not always the case (compare John 9:1-3). It may be too late to reverse the physical malady without God's miraculous intervention, but it is not too late to be released from past sins that need forgiveness.

This is spiritual healing of the highest order, to realize and experience the love of the leaders of the church and the Christ they represent no matter what sins lie in the past. This is to leave the soul at rest, even as the disease continues to ravage the body.

What Do You Think?
What are some ways our church can assist those who feel burdened by past sin?
Talking Points for Your Discussion
- "My hardship is God's punishment for past sin"
- "My sin is so serious it cannot be forgiven"
- "My past choices have led others into sin"
- Other

II. Sharing in Prayer
(JAMES 5:16-18)

A. Confessing (v. 16)

16a. Therefore confess your sins to each other

James now supplies a missing piece to the promise of forgiveness of sins that is discussed in the previous verse: such forgiveness is to be accompanied by confession of our sins. These are sins that need to be acknowledged so they can be forgiven.

The fact that "the elders of the church" are being called for in James 5:14 to minister to an afflicted member in their charge causes some to wonder if the confession of sins is to be made to those leaders only regarding the phrase *to each other,* or if public confession is in view. A biblical case can be made for instances calling for both private and public confession of sins; passages such as Matthew 18:15-17 and Acts 19:18 can help us sort out what kinds of situations call for which manner of confession.

Looking at James 5:19, 20 (not in today's text), we note that the task of guiding an erring one back to the truth is a pastoral responsibility not restricted to elders only. We also realize that while there may need to be reconciliation between individuals on matters of sin (Matthew 5:23, 24; 6:12, 14), forgiveness in the ultimate sense must come from God (see Psalm 32:5; 1 John 1:9). Therefore no church member, elder or otherwise, can bestow forgiveness on God's behalf. Rather, those who hear a confession of sins serve as facilitators to get those sins out of the hidden life of the suffering person so he or she can be eligible to claim the promise of forgiveness (Proverbs 28:13).

In any case, those who hear confessions of sins should be persons of discretion. They will not allow details to leak out as juicy gossip.

What Do You Think?

What could be some practical guidelines to make confession of sin as useful as possible for spiritual restoration and healing?

Talking Points for Your Discussion
- In one-on-one settings
- In group settings
- In situations of church discipline
- Other

❧ CONFESSION: GOOD FOR THE SOUL? ❧

"Confession is good for the soul." At least that's the way we usually hear this old Scottish proverb, which dates back at least to the seventeenth century. In its original form it says, "Ane open confessione is good for the soul." What's the difference, and which kind is James talking about?

An open confession seems to be one made publicly, or at least to everyone who has been harmed by the sin of the one confessing. That's certainly not the kind of remorse we've become used to hearing in the public square these days. Rather than "I confess that I lied about my opponent's record," a politician may say something like "I'm sorry if anyone is offended by what I said." The latter is really a *statement of regret* not an *admission of guilt* that we expect a genuine confession to be.

James is telling us that the kind of confession that is effective is one that genuinely acknowledges the sin one has committed. Such confession seeks forgiveness from all those harmed by the sin, not least of whom is God. —C. R. B.

16b. . . . and pray for each other

Personal, private prayer is a great thing, but the church also needs interactive, informed, and engaged prayer among its members. We are most effective in praying for each other when we have awareness of the real need. Think about it: Is it better to pray for a fellow Christian who says she is "struggling," or who admits she is "struggling with her alcoholism"? Is it better to pray for a brother who says he is "down right now," or who admits he is depressed because he has been "out of work for three months"? Again, such information should be guarded so that the community of faith is also a community of trust. We note that *pray for each other* is the positive part of the prohibitions "do not slander one another" (James 4:11) and "don't grumble against one another" (5:9).

16c. . . . so that you may be healed.

In the context of what James has said above, this may be taken either as physical healing or the healing of the soul. (The word translated *healed* is used both ways in the New Testament; see Luke 8:47; John 12:40; etc.) The praying community is a caring community, and this makes for a community of healing. Prayer is too great a gift to be limited to our individual needs and practices.

16d. The prayer of a righteous person is powerful and effective.

This statement is almost proverbial. Although James will follow this statement with an example from the life of Elijah the prophet, this is not to limit powerful prayers to biblical heroes. The *righteous person* in this context may be a very ordinary member of the church who has proven faithful in word and deed. In the larger context of James, this is the person whose faith is not dead, but active and thriving (James 2:26). This is the person who has already confessed his or her own sins, sought and received forgiveness, and lives a life of righteousness in God's sight (although this does not mean "without sin"). There are folks like this in almost every church, believers whose power for prayer may be largely untapped.

B. Waiting (vv. 17, 18)

17. Elijah was a human being, even as we are. He prayed earnestly that it would not rain, and it did not rain on the land for three and a half years.

James uses an incident from the career of Elijah as a case study in the power of prayer: the prophet's role in causing a lengthy drought in Israel as a sign to that nation and its wicked king (see 1 Kings 17:1). Elijah's character increased the effectiveness of his prayer.

There is another part to this story that, while untold by James, is familiar to his Jewish-Christian readers: that of the widow of Zarephath and her son (1 Kings 17:7-16). Elijah's prayers caused the widow's limited resources of oil and flour to be replenished miraculously during the drought, and Jesus refers to this in Luke 4:25, 26. Later, the prayer intercession of Elijah even brought the son back to life (1 Kings 17:20-22). This parallels many things James is teaching in his discussion about the role of elders and other righteous people regarding prayer in the life of the church.

18. Again he prayed, and the heavens gave rain, and the earth produced its crops.

James skips ahead to tell the end of the story of Elijah and the long drought. After a dramatic contest between that man and Queen Jezebel's prophets of Baal, Elijah prayed for rain. The result was that the drought was broken by a heavy deluge (1 Kings 18:41-45). James wants us to understand that our prayers for the spiritually and physically ill in our congregations can be like that. We can be Elijahs in their midst, and our prayers can bring spiritual and physical relief.

Conclusion
A. God's Working Through Prayer

It seems to me that a wrong way of thinking about prayer is that *prayer works*. This treats prayer as if it were some type of energy we can tap, a power we can wield and control. Imagine prayer working like that: every time we ask God for anything and end the prayer "in Jesus' name," we immediately receive what we ask for. In that case, prayer would be like rubbing Aladdin's lamp, and God would be no more than a powerful genie.

Consider a different way of thinking about prayer: not as a power we tap, but as a privilege we exercise. It is not that *prayer works*, but that *God works through prayer*. God actively listens to the prayers of his people to bring needed healing of the body, of the soul, and of the community.

Prayer requires an active role from us. We pray about our own needs and those of others. Prayers are not magical words that activate a cosmic force for our benefit. Rather, they are personal entreaties to God, our Lord and Master who hears and answers in accordance with his will.

B. Prayer

Lord God, may we take our eyes off of ourselves and turn them to you when we pray. Be powerful in our lives to bring the healing we need. We pray with faith, believing you both hear and care. In the name of Jesus our Lord, amen.

C. Thought to Remember

Be a person of prayer.

INVOLVEMENT LEARNING

Enhance your lesson with NIV® Bible Student *(from your curriculum supplier) and the reproducible activity page (at www.standardlesson.com or in the back of the* NIV® Standard Lesson Commentary Deluxe Edition*).*

Into the Lesson

Begin by sharing a story about something you did that was foolish or embarrassing but not sinful. Then remark, "The old saying is that 'confession is good for the soul.' Does anyone else want to share an embarrassing moment that you brought upon yourself?"

After responses, make a transition by saying, "Whether confessing such things is good for us is debatable. But James instructs that confessing sins is proper. And he's talking about more than just confessing them to God, as we will see."

Alternative. Distribute copies of the "Principle for Prayer" activity from the reproducible page, which you can download. Say, "In this maze of letters is a fundamental principle about prayer and its value, which we find in James 5:16. See if you can discern it without looking at that verse."

After a reasonable amount of time, say, "Try to think of someone you know who is an effective pray-er. How does his or her life match the principle you discovered?" After discussion, make a transition by saying, "James has much to teach us about when, why, and how we are to pray."

Into the Word

Point out that James uses a procedure that involves posing a rhetorical question followed by God's prescription. Form learners into study pairs to complete the following, which you have prepared on handouts titled *Prayer Questions and Answers*: 1. What are some occasions for prayer? 2. Whom can you ask to pray for you? 3. What does confession have to do with prayer? 4. What can we learn from Elijah's prayer life? 5. What can or should we expect in God's answers to our prayers?

Discuss conclusions as a class. After stressing the principle stated in the second sentence of verse 16, say, "While we are moving to verse 17, I want to introduce the hero of the story James refers to there. Here is a man of prayer: Elijah!" Before class, recruit a person to play the role of Elijah to deliver the following monologue:

Friends, I am glad to be present with you today. The last time I stood on the earth, I was privileged to be with the Lord Jesus on his mountain of transfiguration. Earlier, I had been represented well in the person of John the Baptist, the one who came calling for repentance.

My prophetic ministry started with a prediction of a drought to evil King Ahab when I said, 'As the Lord, the God of Israel, lives, whom I serve, there will be neither dew nor rain in the next few years except at my word.' Well, for three and a half years, Ahab learned of the power of God behind my prophecy. There was no rain. To him, I was the troubler of Israel. To God, he was the troubler. At the end of a prayer contest on Mount Carmel, his priests of Baal demonstrated the lack of power of a pagan's false god. God then responded to my prayer by lifting the drought. And did it rain! The prayer of a righteous person is powerful and effective. Believe it!

After "Elijah" departs, direct learners to 1 Kings 17, 18 and ask, "Of all the examples of effective pray-ers of the Old Testament, what are some reasons why James chose this one?" Responses should reveal insight regarding prayer and the one praying.

Option. Distribute copies of the "Powerful Prayers and Pray-ers" activity from the reproducible page at this point. This will offer further examples of what the name of the exercise implies.

Into Life

Distribute handouts with the following stimulus questions, perhaps arranged artistically:

Whom do I know who has had a recent joyful success? has a persistent physical malady? has a sin that continues to beset? What can and should I pray about for each person I have named? When will I do it?

Encourage learners to complete their handouts within the next day or two, then pray for God's blessing for each person listed.

FEASTING AND FASTING

DEVOTIONAL READING: 2 Chronicles 7:11-18
BACKGROUND SCRIPTURE: Daniel 1; Matthew 6; 9:9-17

DANIEL 1:5, 8-17

5 The king assigned them a daily amount of food and wine from the king's table. They were to be trained for three years, and after that they were to enter the king's service.

. . . .

8 But Daniel resolved not to defile himself with the royal food and wine, and he asked the chief official for permission not to defile himself this way. 9 Now God had caused the official to show favor and compassion to Daniel, 10 but the official told Daniel, "I am afraid of my lord the king, who has assigned your food and drink. Why should he see you looking worse than the other young men your age? The king would then have my head because of you."
11 Daniel then said to the guard whom the chief official had appointed over Daniel, Hananiah, Mishael and Azariah, 12 "Please test your servants for ten days: Give us nothing but vegetables to eat and water to drink. 13 Then compare our appearance with that of the young men who eat the royal food, and treat your ser-

vants in accordance with what you see." 14 So he agreed to this and tested them for ten days.
15 At the end of the ten days they looked healthier and better nourished than any of the young men who ate the royal food. 16 So the guard took away their choice food and the wine they were to drink and gave them vegetables instead.
17 To these four young men God gave knowledge and understanding of all kinds of literature and learning. And Daniel could understand visions and dreams of all kinds.

MATTHEW 6:16-18

16 "When you fast, do not look somber as the hypocrites do, for they disfigure their faces to show others they are fasting. Truly I tell you, they have received their reward in full. 17 But when you fast, put oil on your head and wash your face, 18 so that it will not be obvious to others that you are fasting, but only to your Father, who is unseen; and your Father, who sees what is done in secret, will reward you."

KEY VERSES

When you fast, put oil on your head and wash your face, so that it will not be obvious to others that you are fasting, but only to your Father, who is unseen; and your Father, who sees what is done in secret, will reward you. —Matthew 6:17, 18

Acts of Worship

Unit 3: Stewardship for Life

Lessons 9–12

Lesson Aims

After participating in this lesson, each learner will be able to:

1. Identify the difference(s) between Daniel's refusal of certain foods and what Jesus meant when he discussed fasting.

2. Relate the biblical ideal of fasting to the life of discipline.

3. Participate in a 24- or 36-hour fast.

Lesson Outline

Introduction

A. Faith and Food

As a teacher at a Bible college, I have noticed that students are interested in food! This interest causes those who take Old Testament classes to ask a lot of questions about the dietary restrictions of the ancient Israelites. Leviticus 11 sets forth many such restrictions, but God did not wait for the nation of Israel to become a reality before he gave guidelines about food.

The subject of food restrictions is mentioned as early as Genesis 2, where God commanded Adam that he could eat from any tree in the garden except "the tree of the knowledge of good and evil" (2:16, 17). Since only trees are mentioned, this has caused some to conclude that God intended for Adam and Eve to eat only nuts and fruit from trees and the seeds of plants. The instruction for Noah in Genesis 9:3, however, causes most to conclude that the initial diet also included green herbs.

After the great flood, God declared that "everything that lives and moves about will be food for you" (again, Genesis 9:3). An important restriction was that meat with the blood still in it was not to be eaten (9:4). With the advent of the Law of Moses, God placed limitations on the foods that an Israelite could eat. Many of the animals used for sacrifices were eaten, and guidelines in this regard were given. The only purpose stated for the complex restrictions for the Israelites was that they were to "distinguish between the unclean and the clean" (Leviticus 11:47). The Israelites had to evaluate whatever they ate or did each day against that standard.

Today we have great freedom of food choice under the new covenant according to Mark 7:19; Romans 14:14; 1 Corinthians 8:8; 10:25; and Colossians 2:16. The few restrictions are noted in Acts 15:20, 29; Romans 14:1-4, 15, 20, 21; and 1 Corinthians 8:13. Is a person somehow superior by being a vegetarian or a vegan? No—that is merely a personal choice. It is not mandated by God; consequently, it should not be mandated by others (1 Timothy 4:3-5). Even so, the Bible has things to say about dietary choices for today.

B. Lesson Background: Daniel

The first part of our lesson comes from Daniel 1. The year was 605 BC, and Daniel and others had been taken from Jerusalem to Babylon as hostages by King Nebuchadnezzar. To the Babylonians, having the best and brightest (Daniel 1:4) as hostages would weaken the resolve in Judah to rebel, and the captives would be taught to respect the power of Babylon. Jehoiakim, the king of Judah, evidently had decided to surrender rather than resist, and the subjugation was symbolized by royal captives being taken to Babylon (2 Kings 24:1; 2 Chronicles 36:5-7; Daniel 1:3).

After making the 900-mile trip, some captives were selected to be immersed in Babylonian culture. This involved a three-year program in receiving the best education that Babylon could provide (Daniel 1:3-5). The indoctrination undoubtedly included being taught Babylonian literature, history, mathematics, astronomy, and religion. Would the Hebrew captives remain true to their religious convictions in the process, or would they compromise those beliefs? Daniel and his three friends chose their battles wisely in this regard, one of which involved dietary choices.

C. Lesson Background: Matthew

Our text from the book of Matthew is part of the Sermon on the Mount, which spans Matthew 5:1 to 7:29. Our three verses from this section establish an interesting comparison with Daniel 1 in that both are about dietary restrictions and the witness that results from observing such restrictions. The Sermon on the Mount was given during Jesus' first Galilean tour. The name of the mountain is not given, but tradition places it just to the northwest of the Sea of Galilee.

HOW TO SAY IT

Aramaic	Air-uh-*may*-ik.
Ashpenaz	*Ash*-pih-naz.
Azariah	Az-uh-*rye*-uh.
Babylon	*Bab*-uh-lun.
Babylonian	Bab-ih-*low*-nee-un.
Hananiah	Han-uh-*nye*-uh.
Jehoiakim	Jeh-*hoy*-uh-kim.
Mishael	*Mish*-a-el.
Nebuchadnezzar	*Neb*-yuh-kud-*nez*-er.

I. Decree by Nebuchadnezzar

(DANIEL 1:5, 8-17)

A. King's Directive (v. 5)

5. The king assigned them a daily amount of food and wine from the king's table. They were to be trained for three years, and after that they were to enter the king's service.

As our text opens, *the king* in view is Nebuchadnezzar of Babylon. *Them* refers to all the Jewish captives of Daniel 1:4, not just to Daniel and his three friends noted in 1:6.

Kings or governors customarily provide food for those in their entourage (compare 1 Kings 4:22, 23, 27; Nehemiah 5:17, 18). Such is the case here, but expanded to include the Hebrew "guests." The king includes them because they are what we might call interns. The result of a successful, multi-year internship would be *to enter the king's service.* To have the foods and beverages that are being served to the king is ordinarily considered to be a privilege.

The final exam for the interns after *three years* will be an interview by King Nebuchadnezzar himself (Daniel 1:18-20). Therefore it would seem expedient for those in training to cooperate fully with the program that is prescribed for them!

Verses 6, 7 (not in today's text) narrow the focus to four Hebrew interns in particular, who are renamed by their captors. Their original names give recognition to God in various ways; their new Babylonian names, by contrast, give recognition to pagan deities. The renaming procedure confirms that the four are under the authority of the captors. Interestingly, most Bible readers are more familiar with Daniel's Hebrew name than his Babylonian name while the reverse is true for the other three.

B. Daniel's Decision (v. 8a)

8a. But Daniel resolved not to defile himself with the royal food and wine,

With training under way to make Daniel and his associates into good Babylonians, the Hebrews are confronted with various temptations to compromise their faith. The exact reason for Daniel's decision is not given, only his general resolve *not to defile himself with the royal food and wine*.

The observations in the Lesson Background about food and faith are undoubtedly in play here. Therefore the distinction between clean and unclean meats for an Israelite is probably the major element in the potential defilement that concerns Daniel and his friends. The Babylonians love to eat pork, and the flesh of horses is also consumed (contrast Leviticus 11:1-8, 26). It is also possible that blood is not drained from the meat (see 17:12-14).

In addition, food served to the king is first dedicated to pagan deities. This is not expressly forbidden in the Law of Moses, but a person with Daniel's insight can see that consuming such food and/or the accompanying libations will cause defilement. This issue becomes a sensitive matter in the early days of the church (1 Corinthians 8).

❧ DIETARY RESTRICTIONS ❧

Dietary fads come and go, with some lingering much longer than others. The Cabbage Soup Diet has been around for 30 years or so. Eat all the cabbage soup you want for seven days, but not a drop after that. No bananas are allowed on day one, but you can eat up to eight of them on day four.

Such quirky rules create a mystique that seems to be an integral part of most dietary fads. The Grapefruit Diet stipulates that fruit be eaten with every meal as the key to weight loss—that and the fact that the dieter can't consume more than 1,000 calories per day!

More recently, The Daniel Plan promotes reliance on "plant-based proteins" for weight loss. But when Daniel refused the king's food, his concern was not weight loss but faithfulness to God's law. Things are different under the new covenant as we focus primarily on our spiritual diet (see Colossians 3:2). How amazing and sad it is to see someone follow with fanatical dedication a physical dietary regimen while paying scant attention to all the junk that he or she is feeding to mind and spirit! The basis of our spiritual diet should be

faithfulness to God, whatever that requires us to abstain from.　　　　　　　　　　　　—C. R. B.

> **What Do You Think?**
> How do you apply, if at all, Daniel's concern regarding dietary choices to your life in the New Testament era? Why?
> *Talking Points for Your Discussion*
> ▪ Mark 7:18, 19
> ▪ Romans 14:14-17
> ▪ 1 Corinthians 8
> ▪ Other

C. Daniel's Request (vv. 8b-14)

8b. . . . and he asked the chief official for permission not to defile himself this way.

Daniel presents his request to Ashpenaz, who is named in verse 3. He is *the chief official* responsible for the care of the young captives. When Daniel makes his request, he demonstrates that he is religious and that he has a conscience that governs what he does.

> **What Do You Think?**
> How do we decide which issues and situations call for taking a definite stand for Christ (Acts 5:27-29) and which do not (Matthew 17:24-27)?
> *Talking Points for Your Discussion*
> ▪ In the workplace
> ▪ In athletics
> ▪ In church
> ▪ Other

9. Now God had caused the official to show favor and compassion to Daniel,

Ashpenaz is favorably impressed with Daniel by this time. The word translated *compassion,* which is changed from "sympathy" in the 1984 NIV, is also translated "merciful" and "mercy" in Daniel 9:9, 18, and that is the sense here. The text is clear in describing God to be behind this disposition. As a result, Ashpenaz concludes that Daniel is not trying to make trouble, but that he is sincerely conscientious.

10. . . . but the official told Daniel, "I am afraid of my lord the king, who has assigned

your food and drink. Why should he see you looking worse than the other young men your age? The king would then have my head because of you."

The reaction by Ashpenaz shows that he is a reasonable person. His personality is such that he does not demonstrate his authority by immediately rejecting what Daniel proposes. He is willing to listen to any proposal, but he is also compelled to remind Daniel that dire consequences may result: Ashpenaz could lose his head!

It all comes down to the change in physical appearance that may result from granting a variance of diet. As a high-ranking member of the king's cabinet, Ashpenaz knows that he will be called to account if the appearance of his charges deteriorates, and King Nebuchadnezzar is capable of great rage (see Daniel 2:12; 3:19).

The reference to the fact that there are *other young men* who are ready to begin this special training probably refers to captives or hostages from other countries. Nebuchadnezzar uses this retraining method to hinder rebellions, to increase recognition for his kingdom, and to maintain tax revenues.

11, 12. Daniel then said to the guard whom the chief official had appointed over Daniel, Hananiah, Mishael and Azariah, "Please test your servants for ten days: Give us nothing but vegetables to eat and water to drink.

Daniel does not simply protest and dig in his heels. He has a plan to resolve the situation, and he expresses it *to the guard,* who works for *the chief official* (Ashpenaz).

Daniel's proposal is that he and his friends be allowed to abstain from the king's food and drink for 10 days. During this time they will be on a vegetarian diet. The word translated *vegetables* here is also translated "seeds that are to be planted" in Leviticus 11:37, so the vegetarian diet can include all food products that begin that way. Therefore the diet may include bread (which is made from seeds that are sown) as well as the produce that naturally comes to mind when we hear the word *vegetables.* The request for water as the only source of hydration is intended to exclude alcoholic beverages, as Daniel 1:16 makes clear.

What Do You Think?
Why do some believers seem to have more difficulty than others in making the hard choices of the Christian life?
Talking Points for Your Discussion
- Fear of consequences
- Uncertainty
- Vocational expectations
- Other

13, 14. "Then compare our appearance with that of the young men who eat the royal food, and treat your servants in accordance with what you see." So he agreed to this and tested them for ten days.

A 10-day testing period should reveal the difference between those *who eat the royal food* and those who do not. The plan is very reasonable, and it leaves the final decision to the guard. The hostages probably do not dine in the presence of the king, or this unusual test may result in serious questions or other dire consequences. If the Hebrews are housed separately from others, the test is conducted more easily (and secretly).

D. Test Results (vv. 15, 16)

15, 16. At the end of the ten days they looked healthier and better nourished than any of the young men who ate the royal food. So the guard took away their choice food and the wine they were to drink and gave them vegetables instead.

The special diet produces the desired results for the Hebrews. The guard keeps his part of the agreement, so the young men from Judah continue to maintain the same diet for the entire period of their intensive education and training. We note that while Daniel and his friends are feasting on certain foods they are also fasting from other kinds.

E. God's Rewards (v. 17)

17. To these four young men God gave knowledge and understanding of all kinds of literature and learning. And Daniel could understand visions and dreams of all kinds.

Visual for Lesson 9. *Point to this visual as you ask, "Which of the activities suggested by these images should be nonnegotiable for Christians? Why?"*

The assessment is that the four Hebrews excel in everything they study, with credit to God. It is assumed that the teachers provide periodic status reports on their progress as the four gain *knowledge and understanding of all kinds of literature and learning.*

Daniel, however, ends up with a special gift from God: the ability to know the meanings of *visions and dreams of all kinds.* Some ancient cultures have dream manuals, so Daniel and the others probably receive instruction about such things. Even so, Daniel receives special insights from God that make his knowledge superior to such manuals. This fact prepares the way for the accounts that follow, when Daniel becomes a special prophet of God to King Nebuchadnezzar.

This verse is one of five places in the Hebrew section of the book of Daniel (about half the book is written in Aramaic) where Daniel writes something distinctive: he adds the definite article to the word *God* so that it actually reads "the God" in the original. This is unusual, and it may be that Daniel wants to make a point for any reader who believes in many gods.

II. Declarations by Jesus
(Matthew 6:16-18)
A. Fasting for Display (v. 16)

16. "When you fast, do not look somber as the hypocrites do, for they disfigure their faces to show others they are fasting. Truly I tell you, they have received their reward in full.**

A person's spirituality in Jesus' day is often judged by three things: financial stewardship (Matthew 6:1-4), prayer life (6:5-13), and fasting (6:16-18). In this section of the Sermon on the Mount, Jesus boldly says that some who practice these disciplines are *hypocrites* (compare 6:2, 5). The three practices are not wrong in and of themselves, but the motives of the individuals doing them becomes a problem when the visible piety is merely a desire for personal attention. In each case, Jesus declares that recognition from others is the only *reward* that such hypocrites will receive.

Fasting (abstaining from certain food and drink) is not a major issue in the Law of Moses, being prescribed only yearly, on the Day of Atonement (Leviticus 16:29-31; 23:27; Numbers 29:7; Jeremiah 36:6). Other fasts were added to the calendar to commemorate special events (see Zechariah 7:1-5; 8:19). The case of Esther offers another example of fasting, for she requested a three-day fast before making her uninvited approach to the king (Esther 4:16). In Jesus' day, some Jews observe a custom of fasting two days per week (Luke 18:12).

Fasting may be a natural reaction when a person is sorrowful, for there is no desire to eat. Fasting may accompany intense prayers of the heart (compare Nehemiah 1:4; Daniel 9:3, 4; Luke 2:36, 37). Sometimes fasting precedes ordination to special ministry (Acts 13:1-3).

❧ *Hypocritical Spirituality* ❧

There was a time in the past century when it was customary to wear one's "Sunday best" to church. Often that meant a man's best suit or a woman's nicest dress. It was an unwritten rule: everyone was expected to show reverence to God in this way.

The custom led to some interesting excesses. The approach of Easter became a time for some to splurge on an extravagant new outfit in order to outdo other worshippers in fashionable display. I remember one Christian woman expressing great disdain for this practice. She was vocal in her criticism of the "hypocrisy" of those who participated in the "Easter parade." She found a way to avoid the hypocrisy she abhorred so much: she showed her superior spirituality by wearing her new spring outfit on Palm Sunday rather than Easter Sunday!

The legalistic way in which the lady judged others and was oblivious to the "plank" in her own eye (Matthew 7:3-5) demonstrated itself readily enough. "Spirituality" shown for the purpose of impressing others may accomplish that goal—but only that goal.   —C. R. B.

B. Fasting's Accompaniment (vv. 17, 18a)

17, 18a. "But when you fast, put oil on your head and wash your face, so that it will not be obvious to others that you are fasting, but only to your Father, who is unseen;

Jesus approves fasting as a religious exercise (compare Matthew 9:15), but it should be accompanied by the typical procedures of daily grooming. The goal is to look normal so that others do not know one is fasting. (Then one should avoid pride in the fact that the fasting is being done without others knowing it!) Like so many of Jesus' teachings, this one is nothing new, since hypocritical fasting is condemned in the Old Testament (see Isaiah 58:3-7; Jeremiah 14:12; Zechariah 7:5, 6).

What Do You Think?
 What would be valid reasons for Christians to fast or deny themselves in areas other than food?
Talking Points for Your Discussion
 ▪ In use of finances
 ▪ In use of time
 ▪ In choices of entertainment
 ▪ Other

C. Fasting's Dividend (v. 18b)

18b. ". . . and your Father, who sees what is done in secret, will reward you."

The reward that comes from dedicated fasting is received from the Father, who is fully aware of what is being done even though it is concealed from others. Fasting does have a purpose, but if it is used to try to manipulate God or to earn a reward, then it already has its reward. This is part of seeking "first his kingdom and his righteousness" (Matthew 6:33).

What Do You Think?
 Why can't we make hard and fast lists of spiritual disciplines that are always to be done either secretly or openly?
Talking Points for Your Discussion
 ▪ Matthew 5:14-16; 6:1-4
 ▪ 1 Corinthians 11:1
 ▪ Philippians 3:17
 ▪ 1 Timothy 4:12b
 ▪ Titus 2:7, 8

Conclusion
A. Testing Faith

The feasting and fasting episodes of this lesson may seem unrelated, even opposites. Daniel's feasting on certain foods while fasting from others was designed, in part, to achieve a certain outward appearance. Yet Jesus instructed that one's outward appearance should be unchanged while fasting. Even so, the two episodes have this in common: they represent spiritual tests for the person who eats or does not eat. Daniel was tested regarding the compromise of a core element of his spiritual heritage, and he passed the test. The hypocrites of Jesus' day were tested regarding whose approval was to be sought, and they failed the test.

The Christian will have to work through many tests in his or her spiritual walk, and selective use or nonuse of food may be one type (Romans 14:1-3, 15, 20, 21; etc.). "Trials of many kinds" are certain, and the secret is to rejoice and handle them so as to develop patience or steadfastness (James 1:2-4). Blessings result when we handle trials with the strength God provides. A tested faith is a stronger faith. When eternity begins, we will know the tests were worth it (Revelation 7:17; 21:4).

B. Prayer

Almighty God, I ask for strength to resist the temptations to do good things for wrong reasons. May I successfully pass the tests that are placed before me. In Jesus' name, amen.

C. Thought for Today

Ask God to help you pass the tests.

INVOLVEMENT LEARNING

Enhance your lesson with NIV® Bible Student *(from your curriculum supplier) and the reproducible activity page (at www.standardlesson.com or in the back of the* NIV® Standard Lesson Commentary Deluxe Edition*).*

Into the Lesson

In the week before this lesson, contact your learners to suggest that they abstain from eating breakfast before coming to class. If they are unable to do so for health reasons, ask them if they will refrain from one item, such as a cup of coffee.

Begin class by asking those who participated in the fast to share their reactions. Then say, "We're going to learn from both Daniel and Jesus that there can be spiritual benefits from fasting."

Into the Word

Ask two learners to alternate reading aloud the verses of Daniel 1:5, 8-17; have a third learner read aloud Matthew 6:16-18. Before the text from Daniel is read, say, "Daniel and others had been taken to Babylon as captives. Some, including Daniel, were to be trained to serve in Babylon. During the training period, they encountered a challenge as they were given food that violated their dietary laws as given by God. Let's see how they handled this dilemma." Before the Matthew passage is read, say, "During his Sermon on the Mount, Jesus gave instructions on right ways and wrong ways to fast. Let's see what they were."

After the readings, divide the class into a *Daniel Group,* a *Hypocrite Group,* and a *Disciple Group.* Tell them that you will be conducting interviews of Daniel, a hypocrite in Jesus' time, and one of Jesus' disciples; consequently, each group should select someone to be interviewed according to group designation, then help that person prepare answers to the following questions (distribute on handouts).

Daniel Group: 1. What was the dilemma you faced regarding food? 2. Who else was in this dilemma with you? 3. What were the details of the 10-day test that you suggested to the official in charge of your care? 4. What was the purpose for this selective fast? 5. What was the outcome? (Use Daniel 1:5-17 to prepare.)

Hypocrite Group: 1. Why do you look so sad and miserable? 2. If God's law doesn't require you to fast twice weekly, why do you do so? 3. Do you let other people know you are fasting? 4. What is the reward that you are seeking for fasting? (Use Matthew 6:16-18 and Luke 18:12 to prepare.)

Disciple Group: 1. Why do you look so much better than that hypocrite over there? 2. Since God's law doesn't require you to fast, why do you do it? 3. When you are fasting, why do you keep it to yourself? 4. What benefit do you receive from fasting? (Use Matthew 6:16-18 to prepare.)

Use the following questions to lead a discussion that follows the interviews: 1. What are the differing purposes among the fast Daniel engaged in, the one condemned by Jesus, and the one approved by Jesus? 2. What are the different outcomes that resulted or will result? 3. For those of you who have participated in a fast, what was your purpose for doing so? 4. How were you blessed by the experience?

Into Life

Suggest that your learners consider participating in a 24- to 36-hour fast together. Perhaps there is an individual in your congregation who is experiencing a crisis. You might agree as a class to fast and pray for him or her. Stress that this is voluntary—no "guilt trips" will be imposed for not participating. Also, stress that you realize some may not be able to participate in a fast for health reasons. But also make the point that a partial fast from a specific food item or a favorite activity is also possible.

Option: Distribute copies of the "Follow the Guidelines" checklist from the reproducible page, which you can download, and go over it with your class. Ask for those who have fasted previously to offer further suggestions. Then distribute copies of the "Commitment to Fast" card from the reproducible page to those willing to participate.

SERVING NEIGHBORS, SERVING GOD

DEVOTIONAL READING: Matthew 22:33-40
BACKGROUND SCRIPTURE: Luke 10:25-37

LUKE 10:25-37

²⁵ On one occasion an expert in the law stood up to test Jesus. "Teacher," he asked, "what must I do to inherit eternal life?"

²⁶ "What is written in the Law?" he replied. "How do you read it?"

²⁷ He answered, "'Love the Lord your God with all your heart and with all your soul and with all your strength and with all your mind'; and, 'Love your neighbor as yourself.'"

²⁸ "You have answered correctly," Jesus replied. "Do this and you will live."

²⁹ But he wanted to justify himself, so he asked Jesus, "And who is my neighbor?"

³⁰ In reply Jesus said: "A man was going down from Jerusalem to Jericho, when he was attacked by robbers. They stripped him of his clothes, beat him and went away, leaving him half dead. ³¹ A priest happened to be going down the same road, and when he saw the man, he passed by on the other side. ³² So too, a Levite, when he came to the place and saw him, passed by on the other side. ³³ But a Samaritan, as he traveled, came where the man was; and when he saw him, he took pity on him. ³⁴ He went to him and bandaged his wounds, pouring on oil and wine. Then he put the man on his own donkey, brought him to an inn and took care of him. ³⁵ The next day he took out two denarii and gave them to the innkeeper. 'Look after him,' he said, 'and when I return, I will reimburse you for any extra expense you may have.'

³⁶ "Which of these three do you think was a neighbor to the man who fell into the hands of robbers?"

³⁷ The expert in the law replied, "The one who had mercy on him."

Jesus told him, "Go and do likewise."

KEY VERSES

"Which of these three do you think was a neighbor to the man who fell into the hands of robbers?" The expert in the law replied, "The one who had mercy on him." Jesus told him, "Go and do likewise."

—Luke 10:36, 37

ACTS OF WORSHIP

Unit 3: Stewardship for Life
LESSONS 9–12

LESSON AIMS

After participating in this lesson, each learner will be able to:

1. Summarize the message of Jesus' parable of the good Samaritan.

2. Explain the significance of Jesus' use of a Samaritan in answering the question, "Who is my neighbor?"

3. Identify one person locally who needs "a neighbor" in the sense Jesus uses that term and make a plan to be that neighbor.

LESSON OUTLINE

Introduction

A. Stump the Expert

Have you ever seen a TV game show on which ordinary people try to match wits with experts? It is a format that has proven popular off and on through the years. The rules are different from show to show, but the idea is for the contestant to prove that the so-called expert is not as knowledgeable as one might expect. Since 1992, Apple Inc. has hosted a Stump the Experts segment, in a game show format, at its annual Worldwide Developers Conference.

Of course, game shows often rely on topics that have wide popular appeal but ultimately are of little consequence—things like sports or movies. Or the topic might be certain issues of science or history—the kind of thing a person learns in school but seldom remembers. The important questions of life are not the subject matter of most game shows.

The Gospels show us that some people in Jesus' day tried to play stump-the-expert with him. Appearing sincere, they really were attempting to put Jesus to shame by asking questions he could not answer effectively.

But Jesus always overcame these challenges. In so doing, he fashioned answers that addressed something of greater significance than what the questioners had asked. Jesus was the master of life's most significant questions. Today's text is an example of this, perhaps the most famous of all such examples.

B. Lesson Background

Today's lesson is best understood by first familiarizing ourselves with the characters that appear in it. The text begins with Jesus being confronted with a question from an expert in the law, or what some translations simply call "a lawyer." This refers to someone very different from modern lawyers. This first-century Jewish lawyer was not a legal advocate like a lawyer of today, but was an expert in the Law of Moses—someone who taught that law and its application. We might compare this kind of lawyer with a scholar of the Bible today.

In responding to this expert's challenge, Jesus introduced some typical characters in the form of a story. One was a Jewish priest. As descendants of Aaron (Exodus 29:9), priests offered sacrifices in Israel's temple in Jerusalem. Their duties were sacred to all the Jewish people.

Another character in Jesus' story is a Levite, a member of Israel's tribe of Levi. Levites assisted the priests in the temple (Numbers 3:5-9). Levites might be masons or carpenters who maintained the temple grounds, musicians accompanying worship, janitors who cleaned up after the crowds, or even animal handlers who managed the livestock that was sacrificed (1 Chronicles 23:27-31). The role of Levites was not as distinct as that of the priests, but was nonetheless sacred to the Jews.

In contrast with these two is a Samaritan, who stands at the center of the story. Jews and Samaritans were rivals for the land of Israel and for the claim to be God's people (Luke 9:51-56; John 4:9, 19-22). Assyria deported many people of the tribes of northern Israel in 722 BC and brought captives from elsewhere into the land of Israel. This resulted in intermarriages between those imported captives and the Israelites who remained, those not taken into exile (2 Kings 17; Ezra 4:2, 10). The descendants of such intermarriages became the Samaritans. The designation *Samaria* comes from 1 Kings 16:24.

The "pure blood" Jews viewed Samaritans with disdain. This resulted in antagonism between Samaritans and the Jews who returned from the Babylonian exile after 539 BC (Ezra 4:1-5; Nehemiah 4:1, 2). Jews were afraid of being corrupted by those who were not pure Israelites, so postexilic Jews had few dealings with Samaritans (John 4:9). Jesus' enemies tried to discredit him by labeling him a Samaritan (John 8:48). Thus a Samaritan serves as a perfect foil in Jesus' story, as we shall see.

Today's text is found in a section of Luke in which Jesus is teaching his followers and responding to his critics while making his way slowly and fatefully toward Jerusalem (see Luke 9:51). Jesus had already warned his disciples that he was to be crucified and rise from the dead, something that they could not grasp (9:21, 22, 44). It has been said that the cross casts a shadow over every episode in this section of Luke's Gospel.

I. Great Questions
(LUKE 10:25-29)

A. Inheriting Eternal Life (vv. 25-28)

25. On one occasion an expert in the law stood up to test Jesus. "Teacher," he asked, "what must I do to inherit eternal life?"

From the crowd following Jesus, *an expert in the law* (see the Lesson Background) emerges to pose a question of great significance. There can be no more important issue than that of obtaining *eternal life*! This is not the only time Jesus is asked this question (see Luke 18:18).

Luke notes that the man has an agenda: he is putting Jesus to a test. The lawyer hopes to show Jesus up before the crowd. Should Jesus' answer deviate from established teaching, the expert in the law can criticize Jesus for his ignorance or failure to respect tradition.

What Do You Think?
What questions do unbelievers ask today to test or trip up Christians? How can we prepare ourselves for these?
Talking Points for Your Discussion
- Questions concerning miracles
- Questions about the prevalence of evil
- Questions concerning human origins
- Other

26. "What is written in the Law?" he replied. "How do you read it?"

Jesus responds to the question with questions of his own. Jesus' inquisitor is an expert in the law, so surely he has a good answer already thought out. By first asking the man to answer his own question, Jesus compels the man to go on record before the crowd regarding the all-important question of how to inherit eternal life. The expert in the law also will have to consider whether he is acting on what he believes to be true. The test of Jesus' conformity to established tradition and doctrine becomes a test of the man's sincerity.

27. He answered, "'Love the Lord your God with all your heart and with all your soul and with all your strength and with all your mind'; and, 'Love your neighbor as yourself.'"

The man obviously has thought through this question himself since he has two passages from the Law of Moses as a ready response: Deuteronomy 6:5, commanding love for God, and Leviticus 19:18, commanding love for neighbor. In Jesus' day, many teachers identify these as the central commands of the law (compare Mark 12:28-33). The first demands absolute devotion to the one and only God. The second demands love for neighbor that is based on that devotion to God; if God loves all of his people, then his people must certainly love each other (compare 1 John 3:17).

> **What Do You Think?**
> What are some ways to express love for God in each of the four areas mentioned?
> *Talking Points for Your Discussion*
> - Regarding heart
> - Regarding soul
> - Regarding strength
> - Regarding mind

28. "You have answered correctly," Jesus replied. "Do this and you will live."

Jesus affirms that the man's answer to his own question is correct. Loving God and loving one's neighbor are foundational in the life of the one who belongs to God and who receives God's gift of eternal life.

But is the issue as simple as keeping these two commands? How do we know whether we have kept them well enough? Does God give eternal life only to those who measure up? These questions are important, but we remember that Jesus is being tested. Therefore he leaves such questions unposed and unanswered to see what the expert in the law will do next. The man now has two options: (1) he can shut up or (2) he can continue to push the test. Option 1 would make it appear that he agrees with Jesus, an outcome unacceptable to the man. So he chooses Option 2.

B. Identifying One's Neighbor (v. 29)

29. But he wanted to justify himself, so he asked Jesus, "And who is my neighbor?"

Luke explains the motive for the man's follow-up question: he is attempting *to justify himself.* That is, the expert in the law wants to make himself out to be righteous.

But how can he say that he has loved his neighbor well enough when there are so many potential neighbors to be loved? Does the category *neighbor* include only fellow Israelites? all and only those who keep the law faithfully? only those he sees daily? If the circle can be drawn small enough, perhaps one can say, "Yes, I have truly loved my neighbor." So the lawyer's strategy is to narrow the scope of those who can be called *neighbor*.

> **What Do You Think?**
> What are some ways people try to justify themselves today?
> *Talking Points for Your Discussion*
> - Regarding things they should do but don't
> - Regarding things they shouldn't do but do anyway

❧ QUESTIONS THAT REVEAL ❧

Twenty Questions was a popular game show on radio and TV in the 1940s and 1950s. It grew out of a parlor game in which one person thinks of something and the other players try to guess what it is by asking no more than 20 questions that can be answered only *yes* or *no*. Key to winning the game is careful selection of questions to narrow down possible answers. That requires quick, sharp thinking under game-show pressure.

The law expert's first question, "Teacher, what must I do to inherit eternal life?" was not of the knee-jerk variety, thought up on the spur of the moment in a game-show environment. He obviously had pondered the question well in advance. He also obviously thought that his question (and follow-up questions, if needed) would expose Jesus as a false teacher to the crowd. But as the verbal sparring progressed, it was the man's heart that was revealed.

People still have questions about Jesus today. Some questions come from the lips of sincere seekers. Others originate from evil hearts that only want to discredit. Ultimately our questions about Jesus end up revealing more about us than about him, don't they?
—C. R. B.

II. Compelling Story

(LUKE 10:30-37)

A. Failure (vv. 30-32)

30. In reply Jesus said: "A man was going down from Jerusalem to Jericho, when he was attacked by robbers. They stripped him of his clothes, beat him and went away, leaving him half dead.

To answer the man's question—or to force him to answer his own question—Jesus launches into a dramatic story. Its setting is the familiar geographical feature of the steep, winding road between Jerusalem and Jericho. This route of about 15 miles involves a descent of roughly 3,000 feet as a person travels *from Jerusalem to Jericho*; thus it is appropriate to speak of such a journey as *going down* (contrast "up to Jerusalem" in Luke 18:31; 19:28). The factor of *down* is important, as we shall see.

The *robbers* in the story take advantage of the road's many hiding places to ambush the traveler. They take everything of value, including the man's clothes. To assure that he does not pursue them, they inflict serious injury, leaving him wavering between life and death.

31. "A priest happened to be going down the same road, and when he saw the man, he passed by on the other side.

A priest appears along the road (see the Lesson Background). Surely a priest will assist! But the priest goes to *the other side* of the road.

We might imagine the priest's justification for avoiding the man after seeing him: *The robbers may still be nearby, waiting to ambush another victim—me!* But does the potential danger relieve him of his duty to help? Contact with the man could make the priest ceremonially unclean for a

HOW TO SAY IT

Assyria	Uh-*sear*-ee-uh.
Babylonian	Bab-ih-*low*-nee-unz.
denarii	dih-*nair*-ee or dih-*nair*-eye.
Levi	*Lee*-vye.
Levite	*Lee*-vite.
Samaria	Suh-*mare*-ee-uh.
Samaritan	Suh-*mare*-uh-tun.

period of time, and so unable to perform his duties in the temple. But the priest is traveling *down* the road, meaning toward Jericho and away from the temple. This indicates that he will not need to perform priestly duties for many days. In the end, the priest's inaction is nothing other than failure to extend love as he should.

> **What Do You Think?**
> What reasons do people today give for ignoring someone in need? How do we avoid rationalizing in this regard?
> *Talking Points for Your Discussion*
> ▪ Reasons Christians give
> ▪ Reasons non-Christians give

32. "So too, a Levite, when he came to the place and saw him, passed by on the other side.

The second man to pass is *a Levite*, also set apart for sacred duty (see the Lesson Background). His reaction is the same as the priest's. Neither man is willing to take the risk or undergo inconvenience or expense to help the victim, to act in practical love to save his life. Both pass by, as if nothing has happened.

B. Compassion (vv. 33-35)

33. "But a Samaritan, as he traveled, came where the man was; and when he saw him, he took pity on him.

A Samaritan appears on the scene. This is unexpected because a Samaritan would not normally be traveling to or from Jerusalem, where the Jewish temple is located (see John 4:9, 20 and the Lesson Background). The road that he travels does not lead to Samaritan territory but between two Jewish cities. He is away from his home. Is anyone whom he might meet on this road a "neighbor"? Surely not, if he is a Samaritan and they are Jews!

But Jesus notes that the Samaritan sees the victim and takes *pity on him*. The Samaritan feels deeply the suffering of this fellow human being. That compassion is like that which Jesus demonstrates in Luke 7:13. The Samaritan is demonstrating something that the priest and Levite do not: a response to a needy person like the response of God to needy humanity.

Visual for
Lesson 10

Point to this visual as you ask, "How can we adopt Jesus' viewpoint of 'neighbor' as our own?"

34. "He went to him and bandaged his wounds, pouring on oil and wine. Then he put the man on his own donkey, brought him to an inn and took care of him.

The Samaritan's compassion compels him to act. He approaches the man instead of avoiding him, in contrast with the priest and the Levite. The Samaritan cleanses the man's wounds with olive *oil and wine*, a common medicinal practice of the time (compare Mark 6:13; James 5:14). The Samaritan applies bandages—perhaps made from his own clothing—to the man's wounds and gets *him to an inn*. In short, the one providing aid does everything necessary to render the proper on-scene and follow-on care necessary to reverse the victim's life-threatening condition.

Jesus is therefore describing a great price that the Samaritan pays, both in time and resources, to care for the stranger, who is most likely a Jew. But there's more.

35. "The next day he took out two denarii and gave them to the innkeeper. 'Look after him,' he said, 'and when I return, I will reimburse you for any extra expense you may have.'

When the sun rises *the next day*, the Samaritan continues his journey. But he does not end his compassionate service then and there. Rather, he gives the innkeeper *two denarii*, each equal to a day's wage for a typical laborer (compare Matthew 20:2). This is to pay for the man's continuing care: for food, shelter, and attention to his wounds

and recovery. The Samaritan also promises to return to the inn to pay any additional expenses incurred for the man's recovery. The victim himself has nothing, for the thieves have taken everything of value from him. The Samaritan, owing the man nothing but feeling great compassion for him, acts with extravagant generosity. This is the result of genuine love.

Who loves like that—providing rescue, healing, and sustenance for those in desperate need, on the threshold of death, even for foreigners or enemies? Surely it is obvious to all gathered that the Samaritan's actions reflect the love that God shows to stubborn, rebellious humanity!

C. Application (vv. 36, 37)

36. "Which of these three do you think was a neighbor to the man who fell into the hands of robbers?"

Jesus has told his story in response to the question, "Who is my neighbor?" That question is an attempt to make the command so narrow that the one asking it can hope to keep it well enough to be counted righteous by God.

That question is a poor one to ask, though, when one realizes that loving God and loving one's neighbor are the greatest commandments (Matthew 22:34-40). A better question is, "What must I do to love my neighbor and to love God?" Jesus' story has answered the better question, the one that the expert in the law has not asked. The Samaritan shows how to love one's neighbor. Doing so reflects the love of God, who reaches out generously and graciously to meet our desperate need, a need that we could not meet on our own.

To direct the law expert to the real question, Jesus asks the question we see here. The answer is obvious, but it alters our usual definition of *neighbor*. The neighbors of the victim were not (but should have been) the priest and Levite. Instead, a contemptible Samaritan was the neighbor. He made the (probably Jewish) victim his neighbor, ignoring social boundaries in the process. He recognized his shared humanity with the victim.

37a. The expert in the law replied, "The one who had mercy on him."

The law expert seems reluctant to admit that the Samaritan is the story's hero, given that the response is the indirect *the one who had mercy on him* rather than the direct *the Samaritan was*. Even so, the man still speaks truly of what the Samaritan has done. Mercy in Luke's Gospel is what God shows as he brings salvation in Jesus (Luke 1:50, 54, 72, 78). The Samaritan in the story shows by his actions that he knows God better than those devoted to service in God's temple!

⚘ THE SPIRIT OF THE SAMARITAN ⚘

The designation *good Samaritan* has become part of modern culture. An Internet search for that phrase will yield hits for "Good Samaritan laws," which offer legal protection to those rendering aid to others who are injured. The search will also find a "Good Samaritan Hospital" in cities across the country. There is even a "Good Sam Club" for owners of recreational vehicles!

The compassion of the Samaritan in Jesus' parable strikes a chord even in modern culture. We shouldn't mind this cultural appropriation as long as the sense is not violated. The Samaritan's "goodness" need not be uniquely Christian, but it should be typically Christian.

Think of what you and the members of your church could do that would cause the watching community to label you *good Samaritans*. Does such a mind-set drive your expressions of benevolence in Jesus' name, or are such expressions merely occasional, such as with an annual food drive? Does your compassionate outreach result only from the excess of your blessings, or does it spring from your willingness to risk? —C. R. B.

37b. Jesus told him, "Go and do likewise."

Jesus' response is straightforward. Those who profess to love God are compelled to show active, generous love to those whom God loves. Such love is not based on who the person is or whether the person fits our own definition of *neighbor*. God's love knows no such boundaries (see Matthew 5:45). His love is based not on merit but on grace.

The law expert sees no need to be the object of God's grace. The man wants to make himself righteous, to find a way to understand God's commands so that he can keep them well enough to deserve God's blessing. That is a program doomed for failure. Until the man realizes that his need for God's mercy is as deep as the needs of the victim bleeding on the Jericho road, he will not understand the nature of God's gracious love or how to respond to it.

> *What Do You Think?*
> Is categorizing those in need (elderly, developmentally disabled, etc.) useful in helping us to do as Jesus commanded? Why, or why not?
> *Talking Points for Your Discussion*
> ▪ Benefits of categorizing those in need
> ▪ Drawbacks to categorizing those in need

Conclusion
A. Challenges to Our Thinking

Jesus' story challenges some ways we commonly think about ourselves, others, and God. He challenges the ways we distance ourselves from people who are not like us. He challenges the ways we try to narrow our obligations. He challenges any thinking that pretends one can be good enough to deserve God's favor.

When we read the story of the good Samaritan, it is proper to think that we must be like the Samaritan. But first we need to think of ourselves as the victim in the story. His helpless, near-death condition is our condition when God finds us. Through the sacrifice of his Son, God in his grace and mercy rescues us from eternal death. We love him in response to his gracious love for us. Loving God compels us to love others in the same way, to reach out graciously and generously to those who have need of salvation just as we did.

B. Prayer

Gracious God, remind us of the depth of your love for us, and lead us to let your love flow from our hearts into the lives of others. We pray this in the name of Jesus, who died for us, amen.

C. Thought to Remember

Be a good Samaritan today.

INVOLVEMENT LEARNING

Enhance your lesson with NIV® Bible Student (from your curriculum supplier) and the reproducible activity page (at www.standardlesson.com or in the back of the NIV® Standard Lesson Commentary Deluxe Edition).

Into the Lesson

Distribute copies of the following true/false quiz as learners arrive. Have them work on the quizzes alone or in pairs. 1. The main purpose of Good Samaritan laws is to prevent lawsuits against people who give reasonable assistance to those who are injured, ill, or in peril. 2. Good Samaritan laws usually apply to the on-the-job conduct of professional emergency responders. 3. In most localities, a person who causes another's illness or injury (even unintentionally) is legally required to give aid to the victim. 4. A "duty to rescue" is a circumstance in which a person can be penalized for failing to come to the rescue of another person in danger. 5. Most Good Samaritan or duty-to-rescue laws require a person to use whatever methods they can to rescue someone. (*Answers: 1-T, 2-F, 3-T, 4-T, 5-F.*)

Have learners score their own quizzes. After a brief discussion, say, "Today we'll meet the original good Samaritan."

Alternative. Ask learners to share stories of times when someone came to their rescue. You can also request stories about when they had an opportunity to help and what motivated them to do so. (Be careful not to let this segment drag out with several long-winded stories!) Then say, "Today's parable features both people who refused to help and someone who did. Let's take a closer look at what happened."

Into the Word

Option 1. Enlist four learners to perform with you (as "the reporter") the skit "The Scoop on the Good Samaritan" on the reproducible page, which you can download. You may wish to distribute copies of the script in advance for familiarization, or learners can simply read or ad-lib their parts.

Option 2. Form groups of three to five for stop-and-start storytelling. Have each group select a spokesperson who will help retell the parable of the good Samaritan. Say, "Read Luke 10:25-37 and make a list of the chain of events. After you do so, close your Bibles."

Assign a number to each group, then read the first half of verse 25 aloud. When you finish doing so, call out a group number, which is the cue for the spokesperson of that group to pick up where you left off. After an appropriate length of time (depending on the number of groups you have), interrupt by calling out a new number. Continue in this manner until the parable is complete. Review what was left out, if anything.

After completing either of the above activities, lead a discussion using the following questions: 1. What was the law expert's purpose in asking Jesus the question about eternal life? 2. What was the purpose for asking, "Who is my neighbor?" 3. Why should the original hearers have expected better behavior from the priest and Levite? 4. What excuses might they have used for failing to help? 5. What was so unusual about Jesus' choosing a Samaritan as the hero of the story? 6. How does Jesus turn the law expert's question around at the end? 7. What truth was Jesus communicating?

Into Life

Form learners into small groups if they are not in groups already. Distribute handouts of the following scenario to be discussed within groups: *Panhandler*—You are walking along when a man in shabby clothes approaches to ask for money to purchase a prescription for his bronchitis. Under what circumstances and in what way would you help? What would be a reason to say no? Discuss reasons and excuses we sometimes use to avoid helping a person who appears to be in need.

Ask learners to identify someone who is in difficult circumstances. Brainstorm how your class might be a good neighbor to him or her. Ask for a volunteer to head up the project and make plans to put your best ideas into action.

SERVING
THE LEAST

DEVOTIONAL READING: Psalm 10:12-18
BACKGROUND SCRIPTURE: Matthew 25

MATTHEW 25:31-46

31 "When the Son of Man comes in his glory, and all the angels with him, he will sit on his glorious throne. 32 All the nations will be gathered before him, and he will separate the people one from another as a shepherd separates the sheep from the goats. 33 He will put the sheep on his right and the goats on his left.

34 "Then the King will say to those on his right, 'Come, you who are blessed by my Father; take your inheritance, the kingdom prepared for you since the creation of the world. 35 For I was hungry and you gave me something to eat, I was thirsty and you gave me something to drink, I was a stranger and you

invited me in, 36 I needed clothes and you clothed me, I was sick and you looked after me, I was in prison and you came to visit me.'

37 "Then the righteous will answer him, 'Lord, when did we see you hungry and feed you, or thirsty and give you

something to drink? 38 When did we see you a stranger and invite you in, or needing clothes and clothe you? 39 When did we see you sick or in prison and go to visit you?'

40 "The King will reply, 'Truly I tell you, whatever you did for one of the least of these brothers and sisters of mine, you did for me.'

41 "Then he will say to those on his left, 'Depart from me, you who are cursed, into the eternal fire prepared for the devil and his angels. 42 For I was hungry and you gave me nothing to eat, I was thirsty and you gave me nothing to drink, 43 I was a stranger and you did not invite me in, I needed clothes and you did not clothe me, I was sick and in prison and you did not look after me.'

44 "They also will answer, 'Lord, when did we see you hungry or thirsty or a stranger or needing clothes or sick or in prison, and did not help you?'

45 "He will reply, 'Truly I tell you, whatever you did not do for one of the least of these, you did not do for me.'

46 "Then they will go away to eternal punishment, but the righteous to eternal life."

KEY VERSE

The King will reply, "Truly I tell you, whatever you did for one of the least of these brothers and sisters of mine, you did for me." —Matthew 25:40

ACTS OF WORSHIP

Unit 3: Stewardship for Life
Lessons 9–12

LESSON AIMS

After participating in this lesson, each learner will be able to:

1. List some generous behaviors that King Jesus commends.

2. Contrast acts of benevolence performed by Christians with those performed by secular charities.

3. Volunteer to serve in his or her church's benevolence ministry.

LESSON OUTLINE

Introduction
   A. Seeing Beyond Appearances
   B. Lesson Background
 I. The Scene: Separation (MATTHEW 25:31-33)
   A. Jesus Returns (v. 31)
   B. Nations Gathered (vv. 32, 33)
 II. The Sheep: Invitation (MATTHEW 25:34-40)
   A. Blessing Bestowed (v. 34)
   B. Reason Given (vv. 35, 36)
   C. Questions Asked (vv. 37-39)
   D. Kindness Praised (v. 40)
     The Bigger Picture
 III. The Goats: Dismissal (MATTHEW 25:41-45)
   A. Curse Pronounced (v. 41)
   B. Reason Given (vv. 42, 43)
   C. Question Asked (v. 44)
   D. Neglect Rebuked (v. 45)
 IV. The Result: Eternal States (MATTHEW 25:46)
     Harvest from Spiritual Gardens
Conclusion
   A. Caring for the Needy
   B. Prayer
   C. Thought to Remember

Introduction

A. Seeing Beyond Appearances

"Appearances can be deceiving." "Things are not always what they seem." We have all heard those old sayings. And we can all name situations in which they have proven true. A piece of fruit looks fresh, but inside it is rotten. A book looks interesting, but we discover it is not after reading a few pages. We size a person up by appearances, only to discover later that the person is very different from our first impression.

Appearances are especially deceiving when we assume that the real truth is only what we see with our eyes. As believers in Almighty God and followers of Jesus Christ, we affirm that there is an invisible reality that changes everything. What we see is real and true—when we see rightly. But what we cannot see can be just as real and true, able to change what we understand about what we see. Today's text describes how God will one day show everyone the unseen reality that many miss.

B. Lesson Background

Today's lesson occurs in the context of Jesus' final week in Jerusalem. After delivering a blistering condemnation of the scribes and Pharisees (Matthew 23), Jesus instructed his disciples about the real nature of his reign as king (Matthew 24). Evil would remain active while the good news of God's kingdom was proclaimed to the world. The disciples would face hardship when a great siege would be laid against Jerusalem a generation after Jesus' warning, an event that took place in AD 70.

Such events were not to be identified with the fullness of Jesus' reign as king, however. That would come at an unknown time (Matthew 24:36), a time when he would bring final judgment on the wicked and the full measure of blessing on his people. Until then, Jesus' followers are to remain alert and faithful, like servants who diligently do their master's work while he is away, knowing that he can return at any time (24:45-51; 25:14-30). They must be prepared for the possibility that that return will be long in coming (25:1-13).

While waiting for the full appearance of Jesus' kingdom, his people are to remain utterly devoted.

Today's lesson offers an important contribution to this emphasis.

I. The Scene: Separation
(Matthew 25:31-33)
A. Jesus Returns (v. 31)

31. "When the Son of Man comes in his glory, and all the angels with him, he will sit on his glorious throne.

Jesus sets a scene that resembles a royal court. The king sits on his throne, surrounded by the members of his court. But this is no ordinary royal court. The members of the court are *all the angels* (compare Matthew 16:27). This is the court of Heaven, and the king can be none other than God himself.

But the one who sits on the throne Jesus calls *the Son of Man.* Jesus uses this phrase repeatedly in the Gospels to refer to himself. It appears that he does so to connect himself with the figure of Daniel 7:13, 14, the one whom God sends to destroy the kingdoms of evil.

In referring to himself as the Son of Man and describing himself on the throne of Heaven, Jesus clearly is claiming to be none other than God himself. Yet this picture of power and glory for the Son of Man stands in contrast with other ways that Jesus has spoken of himself with this phrase. As the Son of Man, Jesus is lowly (Matthew 8:20); as the Son of Man, Jesus will suffer and die for his people (17:22, 23).

The glorified Son of Man who sits on the throne and pronounces judgment is the one who comes to earth initially in lowly humanity. He is the one who gives his life on the cross for sinners. He will exercise judgment as that servant-king.

What Do You Think?
What are some ways to demonstrate Christ's reign in our hearts as we await his return?
Talking Points for Your Discussion
- Regarding speech patterns
- Regarding leisure activities
- Regarding professional conduct
- Other

B. Nations Gathered (vv. 32, 33)

32. All the nations will be gathered before him, and he will separate the people one from another as a shepherd separates the sheep from the goats.

The Son of Man is the King of kings. All of humanity is gathered before him—*all the nations,* not just a single nation. Again, there is but one who rules all nations: God himself. The Son of Man rules as Son of God.

Humanity is gathered before the Son of Man for judgment. As judge, he separates them into two groups: one that will receive blessing, one that will receive condemnation. Jesus compares this separation with what a shepherd does after his flocks of sheep and goats have mingled together at pasture. The time comes to separate these two groups, but with a much more momentous result than would be the case for literal sheep and goats (compare Ezekiel 34:17).

33. He will put the sheep on his right and the goats on his left.

Jesus strongly emphasizes the division of the gathered multitude into the two groups noted. This division is crucial to the rest of the story. Ultimately, it expresses the reality of Christ's rule over the world.

And so the scene is set. Jesus' first coming is not for judgment (John 12:47), but his second coming will be. One group, like sheep, stand on the right, the place of favor. On the left are the goats, whose condemnation awaits. As we hear the story, we naturally wonder the basis on which the king separates the flocks.

II. The Sheep: Invitation
(Matthew 25:34-40)
A. Blessing Bestowed (v. 34)

34. "Then the King will say to those on his right, 'Come, you who are blessed by my Father; take your inheritance, the kingdom prepared for you since the creation of the world.

The King begins by offering an invitation to *come.* Those *on his right,* the sheep, are *blessed,* meaning that they receive the king's favor. But note that the king calls this the blessing *by my*

Father. The Son of Man, though reigning as king, nevertheless acknowledges that he submits to God the Father. This king who pronounces blessing on his people knows what it is to be in submission.

The blessing for those on the right is to inherit the kingdom of God. God's kingdom is his promised reign or rule over the world (compare Luke 22:30). While God is always the world's king, his kingdom exists in its fullest measure where he is obeyed, where his will is done. God's objective for all of creation, the purpose he has for the world, is that he rule over a people who belong to him.

Those *on his right* receive the full blessing of God. These are the benefits of his rule that mean peace, protection, and security. Earlier, Jesus had announced that "the kingdom of heaven" belongs to "the poor in spirit" (Matthew 5:3). The king now pronounces the ultimate fulfillment of this promise on this group. *Inheritance* is a vital concept in the Bible (examples: Exodus 15:17; 32:13; Mark 10:17; 1 Peter 1:4).

B. Reason Given (vv. 35, 36)

35. "'For I was hungry and you gave me something to eat, I was thirsty and you gave me something to drink, I was a stranger and you invited me in,

The king now begins to move through a list of six items to explain why the group on his right receives his blessing. He presents himself as having experienced deep, urgent needs, all of which have been met by people of this group. He was starving, and these people gave him *something to eat.* Likewise, when he was in danger of dehydration, they relieved his thirst. As *a stranger,* he had lived in a land foreign to him, without a home. But the people of this group welcomed him with hospitality into their own houses.

Amazingly, the king who sits on the throne represents himself as having been a person of deep need, one without the means to help himself. Somehow he had been utterly at the mercy of other people, utterly in need of the help that they could give.

36. "'I needed clothes and you clothed me, I was sick and you looked after me, I was in prison and you came to visit me.'

The king's list of needs continues, moving to the second half of the list of six. He had lacked adequate clothing, in danger from exposure to the elements. But the people of this group had provided clothing. He had been in a weakened physical condition, in need of someone to help him back to health. Again, these people met that need.

The king even had been thrown *in prison,* a place in biblical times where debtors might be kept to work off their debt at hard labor (Matthew 18:30). Prisons are dark, damp, cold places, and there is little or no provision for clothing, bedding, or food. Only those with friends to visit and provide for them can hope to endure the hardships of an ancient prison. But the king had been aided by those willing to provide for his needs in such a place.

> **What Do You Think?**
> How do we decide which ministries to the needy are best handled at the initiative of individuals vs. which call for a group approach?
> *Talking Points for Your Discussion*
> - Acts 6:1-6
> - 2 Corinthians 8 and 9
> - 1 Timothy 5:16
> - 1 John 3:17
> - Other

C. Questions Asked (vv. 37-39)

37. "Then the righteous will answer him, 'Lord, when did we see you hungry and feed you, or thirsty and give you something to drink?

The group that is to receive the blessing now replies. Those of this group have reflected God's right way in their lives, so Jesus calls them *the righteous.* But they are perplexed and confused. The king is and has been enthroned in Heaven! How could they possibly have helped him in so many ways? They seem to have been entirely unaware of his presence among them.

38, 39. "'When did we see you a stranger and invite you in, or needing clothes and clothe you? When did we see you sick or in prison and go to visit you?'

The righteous continue their queries, noting all six situations that the king has just mentioned.

It is unimaginable to them that they have ever served their king in any of these ways. How could the king ever have been in such needy conditions?

We note that the righteous never say that they have not responded to needs. They have indeed been busy serving those in need. But the righteous imply by their questions that they never have seen the king in such conditions as he mentions. So they express their confusion at length.

D. Kindness Praised (v. 40)

40. "The King will reply, 'Truly I tell you, whatever you did for one of the least of these brothers and sisters of mine, you did for me.'

The king now clears things up as he begins his response with the solemn word *truly*. This is the Greek word *amen*, with which we are so familiar. Jesus often begins weighty statements with this word (examples: Matthew 5:18; 10:15; 16:28). The king, who is Jesus, speaks with certainty!

Point to this visual as you introduce the discussion question associated with verse 36.

> **What Do You Think?**
> Why do we sometimes fail to see our ministry to others as ministry to Jesus himself? How are things different when we do?
> *Talking Points for Your Discussion*
> - Regarding how we allow the attitudes and character of those to whom we minister to affect us
> - Regarding a worldview that draws an improper boundary between the secular and the sacred
> - Other

The king's response focuses on *the least of these brothers and sisters of mine*. This raises the question of identity: does the phrase *brothers and sisters of mine* refer to anyone in need or only to believers in Christ who are in need? Certainly, the church is to extend generosity "to all people" (Galatians 6:10), but the words *of mine* in our text indicate that the *brothers and sisters* in view here are Jesus' disciples, as supported by Matthew 12:48-50; 28:10. They are not just the original disciples of the first century, but "whoever does the will of my Father in heaven" (12:50).

The exact identification of those who are *the least* among such brethren is not specified. It may include those among Jesus' disciples who are most

aware of the depth of their sin; the apostle Paul puts himself in this category (1 Corinthians 15:9; Ephesians 3:8). This is an issue of humbling one's self (compare Matthew 18:4, 5).

Jesus has pronounced as exalted those who are in positions of weakness; they are the ones who are blessed (Matthew 5:3-6). Those who are last shall be first (19:30; 20:16), but that fact will not be fully evident until realized in eternity. Until then, the last and least appear to be just that. Their needs are easy to overlook since they do not draw attention to themselves.

❧ THE BIGGER PICTURE ❧

Hebrews 13:1-3 is interesting to consider alongside today's text.

> Keep on loving one another as brothers and sisters. Do not forget to show hospitality to strangers, for by so doing some people have shown hospitality to angels without knowing it. Continue to remember those in prison as if you were together with them in prison, and those who are mistreated as if you yourselves were suffering.

The second sentence of this passage (that is, v. 2) is occasionally used to explain so-called paranormal encounters. An example of this is a story told by a hitchhiker who found himself running out of daylight as he stood by the side of a road. With little hope of getting to his destination, he says he prayed to God for help. Within a few minutes, a pickup truck stopped, and the driver offered to take the hitchhiker to a bus station and buy him a ticket.

At the destination, the driver then gave the hitchhiker $10 for a meal. The hitchhiker got out of the truck and approached the restaurant. When he turned to wave "thanks," there was no vehicle anywhere in sight. Referring to Hebrews 13:2, his conclusion was that, "I would say I had dealt with an angel that night."

But wait—since the hitchhiker (the man telling the story) was the one who received help *from* a stranger, then that stranger could not have been an angel per Hebrews 13:2, where it is the stranger (the angel) who receives the help! Paranormal or metaphysical considerations aside, the details of the story and its conclusion simply do not match what that Scripture says.

The proper applications of Hebrews 13:1-3 and today's text are similar: we minister to others with a view to the bigger picture. That bigger picture is that of eternity. Let's make sure we see this picture correctly!   —C. R. B.

What Do You Think?

How should reactions by those receiving the help of a benevolence ministry be allowed to influence or not influence future such ministries?

Talking Points for Your Discussion

- Regarding expected and unexpected positive reactions
- Regarding expected and unexpected negative reactions

III. The Goats: Dismissal
(MATTHEW 25:41-45)

A. Curse Pronounced (v. 41)

41. "Then he will say to those on his left, 'Depart from me, you who are cursed, into the eternal fire prepared for the devil and his angels.

The story of those *on his left* reflects the exact opposite of that of those on the right. The king now reverses everything he has just said about the righteous. The righteous are invited to "come" to Jesus; the group here is commanded *depart from me.* The righteous clearly belong to the king and are invited to share his glory; the other group has

no part with the king. The first group is called "blessed"; this one is called *cursed.*

A curse is a pronouncement of judgment, punishment, or condemnation (Galatians 1:8, 9). This group stands under the king's judgment and will receive the punishment that he allots: to share the destiny of *the devil* (the great adversary of God and his people) and the devil's *angels* (those spirit beings who serve him). Their punishment of *eternal fire* allows for no escape or relief (Revelation 20:10). The group on the king's left is completely identified with God's enemies and so will suffer the consequence of having opposed him.

B. Reason Given (vv. 42, 43)

42. For I was hungry and you gave me nothing to eat, I was thirsty and you gave me nothing to drink,

The king begins to name the six services that the group on the left failed to render to him. They have shown contempt for the king by refusing him basic assistance. These people have denied food and drink, essential for everyone, to the one who now announces their eternal fate.

43. I was a stranger and you did not invite me in, I needed clothes and you did not clothe me, I was sick and in prison and you did not look after me.'

The righteous offered hospitality to the king; they cared for him when he was unclothed, ill, or imprisoned. But those on the left did nothing. We can imagine their shock as they listen to this pronouncement.

C. Question Asked (v. 44)

44. "They also will answer, 'Lord, when did we see you hungry or thirsty or a stranger or needing clothes or sick or in prison, and did not help you?'

The accursed respond with confusion similar to that expressed by the righteous. Neither group believes that it has encountered their king in such situations as just described. The accursed address the king as *Lord,* acknowledging his authority. Try as they might, they can imagine no situation in which they had neglected him. Surely had they seen him in need they would have served him!

Jesus has warned his followers that merely calling him *Lord* is not enough (Matthew 7:21-23). Those who confess Jesus as king must do the king's will lest their confession be empty of meaning.

D. Neglect Rebuked (v. 45)

45. "He will reply, 'Truly I tell you, whatever you did not do for one of the least of these, you did not do for me.'

Now the failure of the accursed is clear: when they failed to serve the needs of those around them, they failed to serve the king. Their king is the self-giving servant-king, the king of the cross. He is the one who gave his life for all, meeting deepest needs with an act of generosity that none deserve. They have not honored his gift. They have not followed his example. In neglecting those around them, they neglected him. They have proven themselves ungrateful for his gift, disobedient to his message, insensitive to his presence.

What Do You Think?
How might our efforts to avoid being duped by those falsely presenting themselves in need end up making us guilty of failing to help those genuinely in need? How do we avoid this trap?
Talking Points for Your Discussion
- Reasonable safeguards
- Unreasonable safeguards

IV. The Result: Eternal States
(MATTHEW 25:46)

46. "Then they will go away to eternal punishment, but the righteous to eternal life."

The story ends with a restatement of the eternal destinies of the groups. See also Daniel 12:2 and John 5:29.

❧ *HARVEST FROM SPIRITUAL GARDENS* ❧

Avid gardeners who live in the "snow belt" are known to spend long winter evenings poring over seed catalogs or clicking through gardening sites in the Internet. We know that winter won't last forever, and these exercises allow us to imagine next summer's garden—where we will plant our early tomatoes; what new varieties of beans, peas,

and squash we'll try; and/or which rose we will buy to replace the one that died last summer.

How would our lives change now if we gave that much thought to the spiritual harvest we will reap on the last day? The apostle Paul stressed that "a man reaps what he sows" (Galatians 6:7). This is not salvation by works. Rather, our service to others shows where our hearts lie. Today is the right time to sow some new thoughts in this regard.
—C. R. B.

Conclusion
A. Caring for the Needy

The unseen reality is that Jesus Christ, although invisible to us, is not absent from our world. He rules from on high, and he is present among us wherever people have great need. The ones who serve those who are thought to be "the least" in the eyes of the world serve the Lord who rules over all.

Jesus told the story of today's lesson to help his followers adjust their vision. Seeing only what lies on the surface, they would see nothing exceptional about the needs of people around them. After all, the world has always been filled with needy people. There is nothing unusual in that!

But with the adjustment that this story brings, one can see something else: we still see a world filled with need, but we also remember our Lord who deliberately shared those needs. We remember the Lord who used his divine authority not to serve himself but to meet the needs of others. We remember the Lord who gave his body and shed his blood for needy people like us. And so we can see that in the needy around us, whether their needs are big or small, the Lord himself is present.

What needs will you meet today?

B. Prayer

Father, increase the clarity of our vision! Help us to see those around us through your eyes. Help us to see you in those around us. May our everyday actions reflect and honor your gift to us, given at the cost of your Son's life. In his name, amen.

C. Thought to Remember

See and serve Jesus in others.

INVOLVEMENT LEARNING

Enhance your lesson with NIV® Bible Student (from your curriculum supplier) and the reproducible activity page (at www.standardlesson.com or in the back of the NIV® Standard Lesson Commentary Deluxe Edition).

Into the Lesson

Option 1. As learners arrive, give each a copy of the "Secret Message" activity from the reproducible page, which you can download. Use the answer to introduce the topic of today's study.

Option 2. Ask learners what they did to celebrate Valentine's Day, if anything. After several have shared, say, "Valentine's Day is for showing affection or love to those whom we know will reciprocate. Today we're going to read about a day when we will be evaluated on how well we show love to those who are not necessarily able to reciprocate."

Into the Word

Before class, prepare eight flashcards that can be seen easily by everyone. On the cards have the following phrases, one each: *Visit Prisoners / Clothe the Naked / Preach the Gospel / Feed the Hungry / Give the Thirsty a Drink / Pray for the Lost / Take in Strangers / Visit the Sick.*

Before showing the flash cards, say, "While the Bible mentions many good activities for Christians to do, there are six that Jesus says he will use at the final judgment as criteria to separate sheep from goats. As I show a card, hold 'thumbs up' if you think the activity was one that Jesus mentioned, 'thumbs down' if not." (The "thumbs up" answers are listed in Matthew 25:35, 36.)

Follow with a reading of today's text. Ask two learners to read the parts of the narrator and Jesus. Then divide the rest of the class into "sheep" and "goats" to read those parts in unison. Whether or not you used the "Secret Message" activity to begin class, write on the board the phrase "Each needy person could be Jesus incognito" and discuss how it applies to the text. Ask, "Why does Jesus say that taking care of 'the least of these brothers and sisters of mine' is the same as taking care of him?"

Distribute handouts that feature the word *Point* as the heading of a column on the left and *Counterpoint* as the heading of a column on the right. Have this assertion under the *Point* column: "Today's text establishes that it is our good works that determine whether we are among the 'sheep' who go to Heaven or among the 'goats' who do not." Have the following passages listed under the *Counterpoint* column: Romans 4:1-5; Ephesians 2:8, 9.

Have learners break into small groups or study pairs for discussion in order to reach a conclusion about the truth or falsehood of the *point* statement. After several minutes, give each group time to offer its conclusion. James 2:14-26 will be a key to resolving the tension between point and counterpoint, so you should be prepared to introduce it if one of your learners does not do so. Some learners may also mention 1 Corinthians 3:10-14 and/or 2 Corinthians 5:10, so be prepared to discuss those as well.

Into Life

Early in the week, contact someone who serves on your church's benevolence ministry and ask him or her to speak to the class about various opportunities to serve—either individually, through the benevolence ministry, or through other organizations in your area. If no such speaker is available, present the relevant information yourself. Should your church not have such a ministry, ask learners to share what they have seen done for benevolence in other churches. Then discuss the possibility of starting such a ministry in your church.

Option. Distribute copies of the "Christian and Secular Charities" activity from the reproducible page, to be completed as indicated. Ask learners to share stories about their involvement in any of the Christian charities named, other Christian charities not named, and/or secular charities. Discuss methods and results.

Close with prayer for greater involvement in meeting needs in the name of Jesus.

CLOTHED
AND READY

DEVOTIONAL READING: Colossians 3:12-17
BACKGROUND SCRIPTURE: Ephesians 6:10-20

EPHESIANS 6:10-20

[10] Finally, be strong in the Lord and in his mighty power. [11] Put on the full armor of God, so that you can take your stand against the devil's schemes. [12] For our struggle is not against flesh and blood, but against the rulers, against the authorities, against the powers of this dark world and against the spiritual forces of evil in the heavenly realms. [13] Therefore put on the full armor of God, so that when the day of evil comes, you may be able to stand your ground, and after you have done everything, to stand. [14] Stand firm then, with the belt of truth buckled around your waist, with the breastplate of righteousness in place, [15] and with your feet fitted with the readiness that comes from the gospel of peace. [16] In addition to all this, take up the shield of faith, with which you can extinguish all the flaming arrows of the evil one. [17] Take the helmet of salvation and the sword of the Spirit, which is the word of God.

[18] And pray in the Spirit on all occasions with all kinds of prayers and requests. With this in mind, be alert and always keep on praying for all the Lord's people. [19] Pray also for me, that whenever I speak, words may be given me so that I will fearlessly make known the mystery of the gospel, [20] for which I am an ambassador in chains. Pray that I may declare it fearlessly, as I should.

KEY VERSE

Put on the full armor of God, so that you can take your stand against the devil's schemes.

—Ephesians 6:11

Graphic: Hemera / Thinkstock

ACTS OF WORSHIP

Unit 3: Stewardship for Life
Lessons 9–12

LESSON AIMS

After participating in this lesson, each learner will be able to:

1. Identify the elements of the full armor of God.

2. Explain the significance of each piece of armor in his or her battle against the spiritual forces of evil.

3. Identify one weakness in his or her own spiritual armor and make a plan to correct the deficiency.

LESSON OUTLINE

Introduction
A. The Art of War

Military leaders as well as political and business strategists around the world have been influenced by the teachings of an ancient Chinese general named Sun Tzu. His classic work *The Art of War* offers timeless pearls of wisdom for victory on the battlefield. Deceptively simple in his approach, Sun Tzu consistently emphasizes three principles critical to success: knowing yourself, knowing your enemy, and being prepared for every circumstance, particularly so that you can leverage your strengths against your opponent's weaknesses.

The nature of spiritual warfare requires principles specifically tailored for it, and this is where the apostle Paul provides inspired help. To him, at least three principles are essential to success in our spiritual battles: awareness of the situation, advance preparation, and mutual support during the conflict. Unlike Sun Tzu's principles, each of these has both a physical and spiritual side as we fight our battles on the spiritual plane. Through good stewardship of our spiritual resources, we will win!

B. Lesson Background

Paul wrote his letter to the Ephesians when he was especially conscious of the stakes in the battle between good and evil. Having planted churches across the Roman world over the course of more than two decades, the apostle had been arrested in Jerusalem during a riot (Acts 21:26-35). A corrupt governor refused to resolve his case (24:27), so after sitting in jail for two years Paul appealed to Caesar. This appeal resulted in a trip to Rome to stand trial (25:1-12).

Paul then spent two years under house arrest in Rome, waiting for a hearing before the emperor (Acts 28:30). During this time (about AD 61–63) Paul wrote letters to his churches in cities back east, including the one in Ephesus. Doubtless the circumstances of his arrest and the daily frustrations of his imprisonment led Paul to greater awareness of Satan's schemes and the preparation necessary for defeating them.

I. Situational Awareness
(EPHESIANS 6:10-12)
A. Source of Power (v. 10)

10. Finally, be strong in the Lord and in his mighty power.

The last two chapters of the book of Ephesians focus on ways that true faith in Christ expresses itself in daily living. This includes unity among believers (Ephesians 4:3, 4), speaking truthfully and dealing with people honestly (4:25, 28); extending forgiveness (4:32); avoiding sexual sin (5:3); being a good spouse and parent (5:22-33; 6:4); and demonstrating a strong work ethic (6:5-9). These imperatives are not always easy to carry out, so Paul reminds the reader of the true source of power to be able to do so: *the Lord*.

It may seem impossible to remain consistently faithful to Christ in every (or even any) area of life. From a human perspective, this is indeed the case. Left to our own devices, we cannot become the people God has called us to be. But God has not left us to our own devices. In commanding us to live rightly, he also provides us with the resources to do so. *His mighty power* is available to us in the battle against evil.

B. Source of Opposition (vv. 11, 12)

11. Put on the full armor of God, so that you can take your stand against the devil's schemes.

Paul now introduces an illustration of God's provision for our spiritual protection. Comparing the church with an army, he notes that the Lord has provided armament for his troops, equipping us for spiritual battle. The elements of this armament will be discussed shortly, but first Paul pauses to make two key points about its nature and purpose.

Repeating the thought of verse 10, Paul first stresses that the armament is provided by God himself. God does not leave us defenseless or send us into situations where we are unequipped for success. Our heavenly commander knows that the challenges are difficult, so he prepares us beforehand to succeed. The main question is whether we will avail ourselves of what he provides.

Second, Paul names the enemy and (in v. 12, next) the context in which our armament will be used. The devil is constantly on the prowl, seeking to undermine our faith and commitment (compare 1 Peter 5:8). Since knowing one's enemy is critical to victory, Paul proceeds to elaborate on the true source of our struggles.

> ### What Do You Think?
> What are some of Satan's favorite tactics ("schemes") today? How are these different from his favorite tactics of the past, if at all?
> *Talking Points for Your Discussion*
> - Favorite tactics for use against believers
> - Favorite tactics for use against unbelievers

12. For our struggle is not against flesh and blood, but against the rulers, against the authorities, against the powers of this dark world and against the spiritual forces of evil in the heavenly realms.

People today commonly think of Heaven as the place of God's abode, a place somewhere above the earth, while Satan and his angels live in Hell, a fiery place under the earth. This thinking is reflected in the popular notion that Heaven is "up above" while Hell is "down below."

However, Judaism and other ancient religions taught that good and evil spirits all live in the heavens above the physical world, with human beings living in the bottom layer of a massive cosmic hierarchy. Elsewhere, Paul describes a visionary experience of his own as a trip to "the third heaven" (2 Corinthians 12:2), the place where God himself dwells beyond the sky (the first heaven) and the stars (the second heaven).

A similar outlook is reflected in the verse before us, which envisions Satan and other evil spirits living skyward (*in the heavenly realms*; see also Ephesians 3:10), between the earth and God's abode. From this vantage point, demons can descend to move quickly among humans to threaten and tempt us in various ways (Job 1:7). As "the ruler of the kingdom of the air" (Ephesians 2:2; compare John 14:30), Satan's influence extends from certain high places to the world in which we live.

As a result *flesh and blood* people, including some who have influence over our lives and livelihoods, can serve as tools of Satan to bring the powers of darkness to bear in concrete ways. Of course, such people are not always aware that their actions are serving the devil's purposes, and many do not even believe in Satan at all. This does not change the fact, however, that their actions can present serious challenges to us as believers, challenges that we must be prepared to face. These challenges can take the form of outright threats, persecution, ridicule, and rejection, but also (and more often) of more indirect temptations to join in their sin.

Even so, *flesh and blood* people are never the real enemy. They are victims of the real enemy: Satan. Against him is our struggle.

II. Battle Preparation
(Ephesians 6:13-17)
A. Desired Outcome (v. 13)

13. Therefore put on the full armor of God, so that when the day of evil comes, you may be able to stand your ground, and after you have done everything, to stand.

Because we cannot predict when, where, or how the enemy will strike, we must be ready for conflict at any moment. The goal of such preparation is repeated in the phrases *able to stand your ground* and *after you have done everything, to stand*. No matter what comes our way, we must be prepared to stand against every challenge.

This calls up the mental image of soldiers holding their ground on a battlefield. The ground for which we fight is our faith and faithfulness to a godly lifestyle. The armor that God provides—"the armor of light" (Romans 13:12)—will protect us from assaults on our beliefs and from temptations to sin *when the day of evil comes*.

❧ *Getting Ready for Doomsday?* ❧

As the era of the Cold War dawned, the U.S. started developing a massive nuclear weapons arsenal. Plans for mass evacuation of American cities were developed. Underground shelters got a lot of attention. Doomsday seemed a very real possibility.

That scary period largely passed into history with the fall of the Soviet Union. But in a way, things became even more complicated. We now prepare ourselves against various kinds of terrorism at the hands of religious radicals, against state-sponsored cyber attacks on industries and infrastructure, and against shootings that occur in schools, theaters, and other public places.

Preparedness for such eventualities is important to address. But as Christians, preparedness of a different kind is much more important: preparation for defeating the forces of spiritual darkness that surely and always come our way. Most of the threats we face in this regard are not of the massive, "doomsday" variety. Instead, the threats are largely that of the small, everyday life situations that require the spiritual armor of which Paul speaks. Satan knows how to chip away with hit-and-run, guerilla-style spiritual attacks. Are you prepared to meet these?   —C. R. B.

B. Defensive Armament (vv. 14-17a)

14a. Stand firm then, with the belt of truth buckled around your waist,

Having twice mentioned the armor of God, Paul now proceeds to discuss specific ways for Christians to prepare themselves for conflict with the forces of evil. His list proceeds through standard pieces of equipment issued to Roman soldiers, each piece being associated with an important aspect of Christian living. That which is *buckled around* our *waist* is *the belt of truth*.

The word *truth* emphasizes both the content of our faith (the propositions of the true gospel message) and the way we live out that faith (our lifestyle). We protect ourselves by staying in line with God's will as expressed in his Word. Truth is our defense against Satan's lies (compare John 8:44). By thinking and living in ways consistent with

HOW TO SAY IT

Caesar	*See*-zer.
Ephesians	Ee-*fee*-zhunz.
Ephesus	*Ef*-uh-sus.
Isaiah	Eye-*zay*-uh.
scutum *(Latin)*	*skoo*-tum.

God's truth, we prepare ourselves for periods of trial that would take us along false paths.

What Do You Think?
What are possible reasons for Paul's mentioning truth as the first article of spiritual armor?
Talking Points for Your Discussion
- Considering the benefits of truth
- Considering the liabilities of the absence of truth
- Considering the pitfalls of half truths

14b. . . . with the breastplate of righteousness in place,

Roman armor also includes a *breastplate,* a large leather or metal covering that protects the torso from frontal assault. Paul connects this piece of equipment with *righteousness* (compare Isaiah 59:17). While our righteousness before God ultimately depends on his grace and Christ's death for our sins, Paul refers here to moral conduct and character. We protect ourselves from Satan's assaults by living rightly.

Again, the focus here is not so much on how we behave in the moment of temptation, but rather on the need to prepare for such moments ahead of time. A person who lives rightly on a consistent basis will be better prepared for periods of doubt and temptation than will someone who takes a more casual approach to obedience.

15. . . . and with your feet fitted with the readiness that comes from the gospel of peace.

Paul now moves to the *feet.* The footwear of a soldier isn't really armament as such, but a soldier without proper footwear isn't prepared either for the march to the battlefield or for battle itself. During America's Civil War, for example, Robert E. Lee's offensive of September 1862 into Maryland was greatly hindered because of a lack of proper (or any) footwear for many of his soldiers.

We note that the spiritual footwear of which Paul speaks is not *the gospel of peace* itself, but *the readiness that comes from* that gospel. The meaning of this phrase as structured in the original language is not easy to interpret. What exactly is this *readiness?* In this case, it is the gospel itself that results in our feet being prepared for the day of spiritual battle.

When we allow ourselves to be properly prepared in this regard, we can step out confidently on that day. We can move nimbly and sure-footedly when the foe comes against us (compare Psalm 37:31).

16. In addition to all this, take up the shield of faith, with which you can extinguish all the flaming arrows of the evil one.

This verse evokes two images from ancient warfare to describe our conflict with Satan. The *shield* to which Paul refers is the large, semicylindrical *scutum* (Latin for "shield") of the frontline Roman soldier. These shields can be locked together by soldiers standing shoulder-to-shoulder to form a virtual protective wall of wood and leather.

Paul's application of this imagery makes two key points. First, he portrays *faith* as our protective shield, referring not only to our beliefs in and about God but also to our trust in God's protection. Obedient faith shields us from temptations and difficulties, symbolized as *the flaming arrows* of Satan. Second, the typical Roman use of the *scutum* reminds Paul's readers that there is strength in numbers. As we stand together, we become better able to protect ourselves.

What Do You Think?
How does faith provide protection against the attacks of Satan?
Talking Points for Your Discussion
- Regarding faith's sure foundation
- Regarding the power that faith draws on
- Regarding the hope that faith provides

17a. Take the helmet of salvation

As a helmet provides vital protection to the head, assurance of salvation plays a key role in preparedness for spiritual warfare. Paul also calls this helmet "the hope of salvation" (1 Thessalonians 5:8). In addition to its defensive function, the Roman soldier's helmet has a distinctive style that indicates the wearer's nationality. Similarly, salvation through Christ is the distinctive that indicates where our allegiance lies.

C. Offensive Armament (v. 17b)

17b. . . . and the sword of the Spirit, which is the word of God.

Paul closes the series of analogies by noting the important role of *the word of God,* which functions in the Christian's life as *the sword of the Spirit.* A soldier may use a sword defensively to parry the thrust of an enemy, but a sword is primarily a weapon of attack. Soldiers equipped only with defensive armaments won't win battles!

The Word of God is our sword that ensures victory (compare Hebrews 4:12). It is God's Word that allows us to move forward (Matthew 28:19, 20) as it provides guidance on overcoming difficulties along the way (2 Corinthians 10:4, 5).

What Do You Think?

What are some practical ways to address the challenge of spiritual preparedness in the twenty-first century?

Talking Points for Your Discussion

- Regarding the piece of armament most misunderstood and therefore misused
- Regarding the piece of armament most commonly missing altogether

---

III. Prayer Support
(EPHESIANS 6:18-20)
A. In General (v. 18)

18. And pray in the Spirit on all occasions with all kinds of prayers and requests. With this in mind, be alert and always keep on praying for all the Lord's people.

The armament illustrations above emphasize ways that individual Christians are equipped for spiritual battle. Success on the battlefield, however, also requires a unified effort among individual soldiers and their commanding officers. In a Christian context, one manifestation of unity is found in prayer, the topic to which Paul now turns. This verse makes several important points about the role of prayer.

First, prayer should be frequent and should cover a wide range of concerns. Believers should *always keep on praying* (compare 1 Thessalonians 5:17). Our prayers are to include *requests* for aid against spiritual dangers. The context suggests that Paul is not thinking of prayers for personal desires, but rather of requests for endurance and assistance against trials and temptations—similar to a soldier's call for supplies, reinforcements, etc., during battle.

Second, prayer should be *in the Spirit.* This does not refer to some sort of heavenly language but rather to the channel by which we communicate with God. Paul is envisioning the Holy Spirit as a sort of messenger, carrying requests from the front lines back to the commander of the army, God.

Third, prayer should be offered not only for oneself but *for all the Lord's people.* No soldier can win a war alone—it is a team effort. Similarly, we will be much more successful at resisting the powers of evil when we have the assistance of faithful brothers and sisters in Christ. By praying for one another, we ask God to supply all of us with what we need to keep fighting. If Paul recognized the need to have others pray for him (next verse), who are we to think we can do without such prayers or that others don't need ours?

What Do You Think?

How should our prayers for fellow soldiers in the Lord's army differ from prayers for soldiers in a country's army? Why?

Talking Points for Your Discussion

- Romans 15:30-33
- Ephesians 3:14-21
- 2 Thessalonians 3:1, 2
- 2 Timothy 2:3
- Other

❦ *MUTUAL AID* ❦

Huge fires have ravaged many parts of North America in recent years, especially in the U.S. South and West. When local fire-fighting agencies are overwhelmed by the size of a fire they face, other teams often come from long distances to help. Wildfires may draw fire-fighting teams from other states, even other nations.

The U.S. and Canada have a formal agreement specifying the details of how such circumstances will be managed. The agreement covers how requests for help are to be made, how costs for personnel and equipment will be covered, whether personnel with questionable backgrounds may be used, when and how assistance may be withdrawn, and many other details the average person would never think of.

At a personal level, to "pray in the Spirit on all occasions" means that we do not wait until disaster strikes others before we come to their aid; continual prayer may prevent spiritual disasters from occurring in the first place! Also, we do not need to develop a formalized agreement regarding when and how we shall help, because we already have such a document: the New Testament. It is not something to be consulted only when an emergency arises.   —C. R. B.

B. In Particular (vv. 19, 20)

19. Pray also for me, that whenever I speak, words may be given me so that I will fearlessly make known the mystery of the gospel,

Paul now narrows the focus to prayers for himself personally. As Paul writes this, he is living under house arrest in Rome (see the Lesson Background). These circumstances obviously present him with many temptations to compromise, or at the very least to say whatever would secure his release. Facing the situation head on, Paul does not ask the Ephesians to pray for his freedom, but rather to pray that he will have enough confidence to keep fighting the battle boldly. Such boldness, driven by the Spirit, will serve as yet another weapon in his arsenal.

20. . . . for which I am an ambassador in chains. Pray that I may declare it fearlessly, as I should.

Paul switches metaphors to describe himself as *an ambassador* of a great king, God (compare 2 Corinthians 5:20). But Paul, sent by his king to convert enemies into allies, has become a prisoner of war. These circumstances do not, however, change the terms of his commission: despite being *in chains,* he must fulfill the charge of speaking on behalf of his king.

Even here, the theme of preparation comes to the forefront. An ambassador must be ready at a moment's notice to represent the one who sent him or her. Paul assumes that such moments will come and requests prayers that he will be prepared to speak *fearlessly, as I should.*

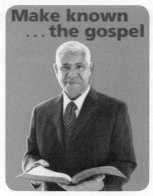

Visual for
Lesson 12

As you discuss verse 19, point to this visual and ask, "What are some ways to fulfill this imperative?"

Conclusion
A. Ready for a Tough Fight

Chuck Norris, a Christian widely known for his prowess in martial arts and his TV and movie career, was once asked about the importance of "thinking like a champion." Norris, a six-time world champion in karate, immediately spoke of mental preparation: "Before Olympians mastered their bodies and sports, they mastered their minds. They've learned how to stay positive, discard distractions, and focus on the present, especially in the midst of adverse conditions."

Similarly, we as Christians must recognize the nature of the preparation that our inevitable spiritual battles call for. We allow Christ to take control of our thoughts as we put on the full armor of God before battle. Those who wait until temptations come before deciding how to prepare are easy prey for the schemes of Satan.

B. Prayer

God, please remind us daily of our need to prepare so we can be faithful to your calling in every situation. Give us the strength and the resources that we need to stand strong against every trial and temptation. In Jesus' name, amen.

C. Thought to Remember

"By failing to prepare, you are preparing to fail."
—Benjamin Franklin (1706–1790)

INVOLVEMENT LEARNING

Enhance your lesson with NIV® Bible Student (from your curriculum supplier) and the reproducible activity page (at www.standardlesson.com or in the back of the NIV® Standard Lesson Commentary Deluxe Edition).

Into the Lesson

Option 1. Invite a current or former member of the military to describe equipment that is provided in basic training and how each piece is used. Ask your presenter to bring pictures as visual aids; he or she should not bring actual weapons to class.

Option 2. Ask learners to share preparations they have made for various emergency situations. These may include power outages, dangerous weather while at home or on the road, home invasion, house fire, car fire, car breakdown, etc.

After either of the above, say, "As important as such preparation is, spiritual preparation to handle Satan's attacks and spiritual danger is more so. Let's see how and why."

Into the Word

Write the following questions on the board before class, but keep them covered until the appropriate point in this segment: "Do you have daily awareness of being in a spiritual battle? Why, or why not?"

Divide your class into three groups of no more than four learners each. Give each group a handout with one of the assignments below. (If you end up with more than three groups, distribute duplicate assignments.)

Situational Awareness Group. Read Ephesians 6:10-12 and discuss the following: 1. Who are the commanding generals in the struggle between good and evil? 2. Who are the soldiers for each side? 3. Why should God's soldiers feel confident about victory? 4. Who is *not* our enemy?

Battle Preparation Group. Read Ephesians 6:13-17 and discuss the following: 1. Why is the Christian able to stand on the day of battle? 2. In what ways do truth, righteousness, faith, and salvation protect us? 3. What is the connection between readiness and footwear? 4. Which element of our spiritual armament has more than a defensive function? Why?

Prayer Support Group. Read Ephesians 6:18-20 and discuss the following: 1. Why is it important for soldiers of the Lord to stay on the alert? What can happen if we don't? 2. How is it possible to pray "on all occasions"? 3. In what ways were the Ephesians' prayers for Paul providing assistance to him? 4. What does Paul's request for prayers for him to "declare [the gospel] fearlessly" rather than for release from imprisonment say to us about what our own prayer priorities should be?

As groups appear to begin winding up their discussions, reveal the questions on the board. Ask groups to discuss these after they have answered the questions on their handouts. Call for volunteers to share their groups' conclusions. Then lead a general discussion on how to be more aware daily of being involved in a spiritual battle.

Into Life

Option 1. Lead a discussion regarding typical ways Satan attacks Christians today and how those attacks can be defeated. Here are some possible discussion questions: 1. What would be an example of an untrue "flaming arrow" accusation that Satan might throw at a Christian? 2. How can we anticipate those arrows in advance so they have no force when they come? 3. How can such an attack be made to boomerang on Satan to prove him the liar that he is?

Option 2. Distribute copies of the "Arm Yourself!" activity from the reproducible page, which you can download. Have learners complete this in their previous groups. Learners may make a good case for more than one answer to each entry. You may wish to ask groups to suggest a Scripture verse that can be used to fight off each attack listed, thereby demonstrating proper use of the sword of the Spirit.

Option 3. Distribute copies of the "Weapon Maintenance" activity as a take-home exercise for self-evaluation.

THE LAMB OF GOD

DEVOTIONAL READING: **Joel 2:23-27**
BACKGROUND SCRIPTURE: **John 1:29-34**

JOHN 1:29-34

²⁹ The next day John saw Jesus coming toward him and said, "Look, the Lamb of God, who takes away the sin of the world! ³⁰ This

is the one I meant when I said, 'A man who comes after me has surpassed me because he was before me.' ³¹ I myself did not know him, but the reason I came baptizing with water was that he might be revealed to Israel."

³² Then John gave this testimony: "I saw the Spirit come down from heaven as a dove and remain on him. ³³ And I myself did not know him, but the one who sent me to baptize with water told me, 'The man on whom you see the Spirit come down and remain is the one who will baptize with the Holy Spirit.' ³⁴ I have seen and I testify that this is God's Chosen One."

> **Special note!**
> The winter quarter has only 12 Sundays while the spring quarter has 14. This quirk of the calendar requires that the first lesson of next quarter be printed here for production purposes.

KEY VERSE

I have seen and I testify that this is God's Chosen One. —**John 1:34**

Graphic: Standard Publishing

THE SPIRIT COMES

Unit 1 (Spring): The Pledge of God's Presence

LESSONS 1–5

LESSON AIMS

After participating in this lesson, each learner will be able to:

1. Summarize John the Baptist's identification and testimony about Jesus.

2. Explain the significance of John the Baptist's description "Lamb of God."

3. Prepare a brief testimony about Jesus that can be used to help an unbeliever come to faith in Christ.

LESSON OUTLINE

Introduction

A. The Water and the Dove

In modern culture, particularly since the days of the war in Vietnam, the image of a dove has come to serve as a symbol of peace. This symbol was popularized before that by Pablo Picasso, who was commissioned to design a logo for the meeting of the 1949 First International Peace Conference, in Paris. Following his lead, the dove was widely adopted as a symbol for anti-war movements.

Those living in the first-century AD also saw the dove as symbol of peace, but for a very different reason. In Roman culture, the olive branch was often used to represent Eirene, the goddess of peace (think of the word *irenic*). Some Roman coins bore an image of Eirene holding an olive branch. Imagery of this kind doubtless reminded the earliest Jewish Christians of the story of Noah. As the waters of the great flood began to recede, Noah sent birds from the ark to see if they could find dry land. On the third attempt, one of Noah's doves returned to the ark carrying a freshly plucked olive branch (Genesis 8:9-12).

The meaning for the earliest Christians was that peace with God had been restored after the flood, a parallel to eternal peace with God available because of the death of Christ. Consequently, the comforting image of a dove carrying an olive branch was often painted on the walls of burial catacombs and inscribed on sarcophagi in the early centuries of the church. This reminded mourners of hope beyond the grave. Yet Noah and Picasso are not the only sources for the popular connection between doves and peace, as today's lesson reveals.

B. Lesson Background: John's Identity

The ministry of John the Baptist opened a significant chapter in the history of God's communication with humanity. For almost 400 years, no prophet had risen in Israel to speak God's word to the people. The last of the great Hebrew prophets, Malachi, ended his book by predicting that the prophet Elijah would one day reappear to call people to remember the Law of Moses (Malachi 4:4-6).

As years, decades, and centuries passed, this promise seemed less and less certain. One can readily understand why John the Baptist's controversial ministry in the wilderness around the Jordan River area, near the very place where Elijah himself had ascended to Heaven in a fiery chariot (compare 2 Kings 2:7-12 with John 1:28), aroused popular interest. John's simple attire (compare 2 Kings 1:8) and sparse diet of locusts and honey (Mark 1:6; Matthew 3:4)—ritually clean food (Leviticus 11:22; 20:24)—complemented his message of repentance and call to justice (Matthew 3:7-10; Luke 3:10-14).

All this led at least some of John's contemporaries to speculate that Elijah himself had indeed returned, a speculation that John denied in the literal sense of being Elijah reincarnated (John 1:21; compare Matthew 11:13, 14; 17:10-13; Luke 1:13-17). Instead, John the Baptist openly identified himself as "the voice of one calling in the wilderness" (John 1:23) that was predicted in Isaiah 40:3. This identification stressed his role as the forerunner to the Lord's appearance. John's designation as "the Baptist" is helpful to us for not confusing him with the apostle John, who wrote the Gospel from which today's lesson is drawn.

C. Lesson Background: John's Baptism

While modern readers of the Bible may be most captivated by John the Baptist's diet, attire, and radical message, a most distinctive feature of his ministry was the fact that he baptized people in water (Matthew 3:11; Mark 1:8; Luke 3:16; John

HOW TO SAY IT

Bethany	Beth-uh-nee.
Columbidae	Kuh-lum-buh-dee.
Eirene	Eye-ree-nee.
Elijah	Ee-lye-juh.
Isaiah	Eye-zay-uh.
Levites	Lee-vites.
lustrations	luhs-tray-shunz.
Malachi	Mal-uh-kye.
Messiah	Meh-sigh-uh.
ornithologist	ore-nuh-thaw-luh-jist.
Pharisees	Fair-ih-seez.

1:26). Ritual or ceremonial washings (known as *lustrations*) as a means of removing impurities from hands, eating utensils, and even the entire body were common in first-century Judaism (Mark 7:1-4; Luke 2:22; John 2:6; 3:25; compare Leviticus 11:32; 14:8, 9; 15:4-12, 16-22, 25-27; Ezekiel 36:25). Faithful Jews, desiring to avoid anything that might make them "unclean" in God's sight, would wash themselves regularly in running streams or pools of water. John, however, gained notoriety for washing *other* people, a practice unheard of at the time.

Since washing with water was viewed as a sign of self-purification, then almost by definition it would not occur to Jews that one person could wash another—no person could secure another person's purity that way. For John the Baptist, however, water baptism represented the cleansing of the soul that came through genuine repentance (Luke 3:3; Matthew 3:11; compare Ephesians 5:26; Titus 3:5).

Such repentance was critical in view of the fact that God was soon to establish his kingdom on earth. John associated this event with the coming of a figure much greater than himself (Mark 1:7; Acts 13:25). This figure to come would baptize people not with water but rather "with the Holy Spirit and fire" (Matthew 3:11; Luke 3:16), symbols of a much deeper and more thorough cleansing from sin.

Within the larger context of his baptizing ministry, John also baptized Jesus himself. The first three Gospels mark Jesus' baptism as the beginning of his public ministry (see especially Luke 3:21-23). Jesus' baptism, not recorded in the Gospel of John, had already occurred at the point in time of today's lesson (see Matthew 3:13-17; Mark 1:9-11). The location as our text opens is "at Bethany on the other side of the Jordan" (John 1:28).

I. Observations
(JOHN 1:29-31)
A. Lamb That Saves (v. 29)

29. The next day John saw Jesus coming toward him and said, "Look, the Lamb of God, who takes away the sin of the world!

The next day means that what we are reading happens immediately after John the Baptist's interaction with the priests, Levites, and Pharisees noted in John 1:19-27. John, seeing Jesus, clarifies that Jesus is in fact the person of whom John has been speaking in verses 26, 27. While the author of this Gospel does not specify the audience of the observation before us, it seems likely that John the Baptist is sharing this information with several of his own disciples, at least two of whom later become followers of Jesus (John 1:35-37).

> **What Do You Think?**
> What have you found to be effective and ineffective ways to introduce others to Jesus?
> *Talking Points for Your Discussion*
> - Through visible lifestyle choices
> - In personal, one-on-one conversations
> - In group settings
> - Other

The title that John the Baptist bestows on Jesus is essential for understanding Christ's identity and mission. At first glance, the phrase *the Lamb of God* may seem to associate Jesus with the sacrificial lambs used in the celebration of Passover. Paul uses this image to so describe Jesus in 1 Corinthians 5:7, with specific reference to the purifying effects of Christ's death, and John may be thinking along similar lines.

However, the Passover lamb was not understood to be a sacrifice for sin in its original context. Rather, it is eaten as the main course of the Passover dinner, where it functions as a reminder of God's rescue of the Israelites from slavery in Egypt—rescue that involved the lamb's blood (Exodus 12:21-27). Many commentators therefore suggest that John is referring not to Exodus 12 but to Isaiah 53, a famous passage that describes the coming Messiah as God's suffering servant. Foreseeing Christ's ministry, Isaiah says that he is to be "led like a lamb to the slaughter" (v. 7).

Whether John the Baptist is referring to the Passover lamb or to the Suffering Servant as lamb, the essential point is the same: Christ will be able to effect a total elimination of sin and its consequences through his death.

B. Man Who Surpasses (v. 30)

30. "This is the one I meant when I said, 'A man who comes after me has surpassed me because he was before me.'

The past tense verb *said* indicates that John the Baptist has previously spoken of his own status with regard to that of Christ. We see this prior declaration at John 1:15. Further, at 1:27 John the Baptist stresses his own unworthiness to untie the sandals of the other one, who is now on the scene (compare Mark 1:7).

In the Greek text, John the Baptist's comment takes the form of a saying that seems paradoxical on the surface, but reveals a deeper meaning once its various terms are correctly understood. More literally, John 1:15 and 1:30 read, "The man coming behind me has become ahead of me because he was before me." If someone is ahead of John, how can that person also be coming behind him?

The meaning is clear, however, when John the Baptist's language is understood in terms of the eternal nature of Christ. Jesus comes *after* John in the sense that Jesus' ministry begins after John's ministry is already well under way—John preaches first, and Jesus preaches second. This is only natural in view of John's role as Jesus' forerunner. But even though Jesus starts his ministry after John does, Jesus *was before* John because of Christ's preexistence (see John 1:1, 2). John preaches about the coming of a superior one, and Jesus is that person. While Jesus the man comes after John the Baptist in time, Jesus the Word existed before time itself.

There can be no question, then, about Jesus' authority. As a prophet, John the Baptist speaks the very words of God; Jesus, as the Word become flesh, is God himself.

> **What Do You Think?**
> What are some proper ways to view ourselves as we meditate on Christ's preexistence?
> *Talking Points for Your Discussion*
> - Relative to his authority
> - With regard to servanthood
> - Regarding recognition and honor
> - Other

Michael J. Fox starred as teenager Marty McFly in the 1985 science-fiction comedy *Back to the Future*. The teen's much older, eccentric friend was modifying a car to be able to travel through time. Marty accidentally triggered the time-travel mechanism, and he ended up 30 years in the past.

Arriving in his hometown in the year 1955, when his (future) parents are teenagers, Marty's presence interrupts the chain of events that is to cause those two to be attracted to each other. Marty then sets out to repair the damage that his arrival has caused so that he will eventually be born. Through a convoluted and fanciful plot as such films are forced to use, Marty accomplishes his goal. Eventually, he is able to travel "back to the future."

John the Baptist's expression of his status with regard to that of Jesus can seem as convoluted as a time-travel movie! It requires careful thinking, and John's audience may receive our sympathy if they did not immediately comprehend his description of Jesus as being both "before" and "after" him. Which of us is capable of fully understanding Jesus' eternal existence, even with our better historical perspective? Even so, Jesus' factual response to his opponents was "'Very truly I tell you, before Abraham was born, I am!'" (John 8:58). The great *I am* still *is.*   —C. R. B.

C. Revealed to Israel (v. 31)

31. "I myself did not know him, but the reason I came baptizing with water was that he might be revealed to Israel."

I myself did not know him indicates that up to a certain point John the Baptist had not known Jesus to be the one to come. The remainder of this verse sheds light on the ministry of John the Baptist by revealing an important detail: his own uniqueness in *baptizing with water* (see the Lesson Background) is connected with his larger work of preparing people for the Messiah. In other words, John's baptism helps make it possible for Christ to *be revealed to Israel* by getting people ready to recognize and receive Jesus.

This verse also suggests that John has been told by God that the identity of the Messiah was to be revealed to John through his baptizing—that somehow John would recognize the Christ in the context of that baptizing ministry. Such a recognition takes place in the special sign that occurs when John baptizes Jesus (next two verses).

II. Testimony
(John 1:32-34)
A. Identification (v. 32)

32. Then John gave this testimony: "I saw the Spirit come down from heaven as a dove and remain on him.

Speaking with his own disciples sometime after he had baptized Jesus, John recounts what happened and explains the significance of what he saw. The reference to *a dove* lines up with the accounts of Jesus' baptism in Matthew, Mark, and Luke.

Correlating the data from all four Gospels, the following sequence emerges: (1) Jesus came to the Jordan River from Galilee and asked John to baptize him (Matthew 3:13; Mark 1:9); (2) John initially resisted, arguing that he should be baptized by Jesus rather than vice versa (Matthew 3:14); (3) Jesus insisted that he had to be baptized in order "to fulfill all righteousness" (Matthew 3:15); (4) John relented and baptized Jesus in the Jordan River (Matthew 3:15; Mark 1:9; Luke 3:21); (5) after Jesus came out of the water, John *saw the Spirit come down from heaven as a dove and remain on him* (compare Matthew 3:16; Mark 1:10; Luke 3:22);

Visual for Lesson 1 (spring)

Point to this visual as you introduce the discussion question associated with verse 34.

and (6) after the dove landed on Jesus, a voice from Heaven declared Jesus to be "my Son, whom I love" (Matthew 3:17; Mark 1:11; Luke 3:22).

While the fourth Gospel bypasses many of these details, it provides important insights on key elements of the event nonetheless. First, this Gospel makes clear that the descent of the dove was a special sign (see next verse below) seen by John the Baptist. Since Matthew 3:16 and Mark 1:10 specify only Jesus ("he") as seeing the dove, we wonder if anyone else has been privileged to see this sign at Jesus' baptism; Luke 3:22 may imply an answer of *yes* in describing the Spirit's descent "in bodily form like a dove." In any case, the focus here is on what John the Baptist has seen and what that signifies.

What Do You Think?

In what ways is the presence of God's Spirit in the lives of Christians like and unlike the presence of the Spirit on Jesus at his baptism?

Talking Points for Your Discussion

- Similarities
- Dissimilarities

❧ THE POWER OF IMAGERY ❧

It's a good thing that today's passage doesn't describe the Spirit descending from Heaven like a pigeon! I don't know how first-century readers would have reacted to pigeon imagery, but modern readers probably would have negative thoughts. We know how pigeons have adapted themselves to our urban environments. The messy creatures roost on and besmirch monuments and fountains. They befoul city sidewalks and park benches. Yuk!

Doves, on the other hand, draw from us positive thoughts. Both ancient and modern peoples associate doves with peace (see the lesson's Introduction). Doves are more likely to take up residence in rural areas, reminding us of humanity's pastoral history. Given a choice between pigeon imagery or dove imagery, wouldn't we all choose the latter?

But now here's a catch: *pigeons and doves are both members of the family Columbidae, and to an ornithologist they are pretty much the same bird!* Even in the pages of the Bible, doves and pigeons are rather interchangeable (see Leviticus 1:14;

12:6, 8; 14:22; 15:14; Luke 2:24; etc.). But do those facts change our emotionally driven preference? Probably not! Such is the power of imagery.

We can also notice that God did not select a bird of prey such as a hawk to symbolize the divine presence on and approval of Jesus at his baptism. Those possible alternatives say something too about the selection of a dove to represent the Holy Spirit. What might that be?   —C. R. B.

B. Affirmation (vv. 33, 34)

33. "And I myself did not know him, but the one who sent me to baptize with water told me, 'The man on whom you see the Spirit come down and remain is the one who will baptize with the Holy Spirit.'

John, as the prophetic forerunner for Jesus, is specially chosen to bear witness to Christ's identity. The dove serves as a special sign in that regard. Although John will request clarification later (Matthew 11:2, 3), Jesus is in fact the one he has been waiting for. The descent of *the Spirit* as a dove, a unique event, is designed to reveal to John that the promise of "one who comes after me" (John 1:27) is fulfilled in Jesus.

John the Baptist carefully connects this sign with previous revelation from God regarding what the one on whom the Spirit (signified by the dove) remains will do: Jesus is the one who is to baptize *with the Holy Spirit*. But what does this mean?

Many commentators relate this baptism with the Spirit to the events of the Day of Pentecost, some seven weeks after Jesus' death and resurrection; Jesus himself seems to make this connection in Acts 1:5. On that day, the disciples' empowerment by the Holy Spirit to speak in tongues is accompanied by "tongues of fire" (Acts 2:3). At the end of Peter's sermon to the crowd, he encourages those present to "repent and be baptized," promising that those who did so would "receive the gift of the Holy Spirit" (Acts 2:38).

One can readily argue, then, that Christ does indeed offer baptism with the Holy Spirit not long after his death, burial, resurrection, and ascension. This implies that baptism in the Holy Spirit refers to the gift of the indwelling Spirit promised at John 7:37-39; 14:15-18.

However, another reading of John 1:33 understands baptism with the Spirit in a more general sense (compare John 15:26). Old Testament prophets had promised that God would pour out his Spirit on all peoples in the last days, the time of the Messiah (see Isaiah 32:15; 44:3; Ezekiel 36:24-27; Joel 2:28-32 [quoted in Acts 2:16-21]). Closer to Jesus' day, a similar theme is reflected in several of the Dead Sea Scrolls, which envision a time when God's Spirit purifies the righteous of all sin, preparing them to enter his holy presence.

If John is referring to these ideas, then baptism with the Spirit refers to the totality of Jesus' ministry and its effects on those who hear his message: "When he comes, he will prove the world to be in the wrong about sin and righteousness and judgment" (John 16:8). Put another way, John the Baptist may be referring less to a single, specific event (Acts 2) than to the overall effect of Jesus' work: people are made holy.

One implication is clear either way: while John the Baptist himself can offer only a preliminary cleansing, Jesus comes to offer a complete cleansing of the soul—one that produces holiness in those who believe and repent in contrast with those who do not.

What Do You Think?
What changes in your life are most evident as you move from unholiness to holiness? Why is that?
Talking Points for Your Discussion
- Incremental changes
- Drastic, sudden changes

---

34. "I have seen and I testify that this is God's Chosen One."

Jesus refers to himself as "the Son of Man" in many places throughout the fourth Gospel, usually leaving different designations to others (compare John 1:49; 11:27; 19:7; 20:31). The 1984 NIV has John the Baptist saying "the Son of God" here while the 2011 NIV has him saying *God's Chosen One*, based on different manuscripts. His affirmation *I have seen* alludes again to his own witness of the Spirit's descent upon Jesus. John the Baptist is portrayed as the ultimate witness to Jesus in the fourth Gospel. This witness is most profound at John 3:30, where John informs his disciples that he is glad to see Jesus' influence become greater than his own because, ultimately, Christ "must become greater; I must become less."

What Do You Think?
What are some specific ways for Christians to bear witness to Christ daily?
Talking Points for Your Discussion
- In the workplace
- Among family members
- In social settings
- While participating in athletic events
- Other

Conclusion

A. Pivotal Figures

A *pivotal figure* can be thought of as someone who stands at the crossover point between two periods of history and is instrumental in bringing about the transition from one to the other. An Old Testament example is Samuel. As the last of the judges (Acts 13:20) and the first of the prophets (Acts 3:24), he played a key role in Israel's transition to monarchy (1 Samuel 8–10).

John the Baptist is no less a pivotal figure, his ministry signaling that a transition was underway. In a sense, this "voice calling in the wilderness" was both the last of the Old Testament prophets and the first of the New Testament prophets. His testimony still rings forth today: Jesus is "the Lamb of God, who takes away the sin of the world" (John 1:29). May we proclaim this until Jesus, the final and ultimate pivotal figure, presents himself at his glorious second coming.

B. Prayer

God, may our lips offer the same testimony of John the Baptist: that Jesus is your Son. May that testimony cause us to serve you ever more faithfully as we fulfill your calling for us. In Jesus' name, amen.

C. Thought to Remember
Testify to the Christ!

INVOLVEMENT LEARNING

Enhance your lesson with NIV® Bible Student *(from your curriculum supplier) and the reproducible activity page (at www.standardlesson.com or in the back of the* NIV® Standard Lesson Commentary Deluxe Edition*).*

Into the Lesson

Form learners into pairs to answer one or more of the following riddles (use handouts): 1. Does the law allow a man to marry his widow's sister? 2. What word doesn't belong in this group: *that, hat, what, mat, cat, sat, pat, chat*? 3. Two men are in a desert. They both wear backpacks. One of the men is dead, and his backpack is closed. The guy who is alive has his backpack open. What is in the dead man's pack? 4. Two girls have the same parents and were born at the same hour of the same day of the same month, but they are not twins. How is this possible? *(Answers: 1. No, if he has a widow then he's dead, and dead people can't get married. 2. What—it doesn't rhyme with the others. 3. A parachute that didn't open. 4. They were not born in the same year.)*

Congratulate those who came up with the correct answers, perhaps awarding a token prize. Then say, "There is also something of a riddle that John the Baptist sets forth in today's text. Let's see if we can also solve that one."

Into the Word

Form learners into groups of three or four. Ask each group to select a spokesperson who will answer questions as John the Baptist. Give half the groups interview questions about John's identity, the other half interview questions about Jesus' identity. Make available appropriate portions of the lesson commentary (including the Lesson Background) to help groups with their research.

John's Identity Group(s). Answer the following questions as John the Baptist would: 1. When the priests and Levites came to see you, at first you told them who you were not. So, who are you not? 2. How would you describe your mission? 3. You seem to be an important prophet, so why do you say Jesus "has surpassed" you? 4. Whose idea was it for you to preach repentance and baptize people? 4. Why do you do what you do?

Jesus' Identity Group(s). Answer the following questions as John the Baptist would. 1. Why do you refer to Jesus as "the Lamb of God"? 2. How is it possible for a mere man to take away the sin of the entire world? 3. We know that you are six months older than Jesus, so how can you say he was before you? 4. When did you realize Jesus' identity? What happened to make that identity clear? 5. If you were to summarize Jesus' identity in three words, what would those words be? Why?

Option. Before the interviews, distribute copies of the "Identity Check" activity from the reproducible page, which you can download. Say, "Let's take a closed-Bible pretest to see how much we already know about the identities of Jesus and John the Baptist. When we're finished, you will score your own quiz; I will not collect them. Work quickly!" Discuss correct answers as a class. This should be easy for most, but the interviews that follow will allow a closer look at both identities as you work through the text.

After groups finish preparing, rotate among them to have spokespersons answer the questions.

Into Life

Say, "John the Baptist came baptizing in order that Jesus 'might be revealed to Israel.' We have a similar duty to make Jesus known where we live. As I mention some different types of people who are Christians, help me brainstorm ways that each one can help others know about Jesus." Then name the following, pausing after each so that witnessing techniques can be suggested: a superstar athlete; a loving wife and mother; an elderly Sunday school teacher; a person with a disability; a successful business owner; a skillful artist.

Option. Distribute copies of the "Will You Testify?" activity from the reproducible page. Encourage learners to write out their own testimony per the instructions. Explore proper uses and potential misuses of testimonials.

THE SPIRIT
COMES

Special Features

Lessons

Unit 1: The Pledge of God's Presence

Unit 2: The Community of Beloved Disciples

Unit 3: One in the Bond of Love

QUARTERLY QUIZ

Use these questions as a pretest or as a review. The answers are on page iv of This Quarter in the Word.

Lesson 2*

1. There were two disciples named Judas. T/F. *John 14:22*

2. *The Advocate* is another name for whom? (John the Baptist, Jesus, Holy Spirit?) *John 14:26*

Lesson 3

1. To "prove the world to be in the wrong about sin" is the job of the Advocate. T/F. *John 16:7, 8*

2. Another name for the Holy Spirit is the Spirit of what? (man, truth, Heaven?) *John 16:13*

Lesson 4

1. The risen Jesus showed the disciples his what? (pick two: feet, hands, side, back?) *John 20:20*

2. Jesus _____ on the disciples to give them the Holy Spirit. *John 20:22*

Lesson 5

1. For Jesus' triumphal entry, the disciples made him a saddle from palm branches. T/F. *Mark 11:7*

2. The people cried "Hallelujah!" as Jesus approached Jerusalem. T/F. *Mark 11:10*

Lesson 6

1. On which day did Jesus rise from the dead? (first, second, third?) *1 Corinthians 15:4*

2. Paul called himself "the least of the apostles." T/F. *1 Corinthians 15:9*

Lesson 7

1. The one who hates his brother is a murderer. T/F. *1 John 3:15*

2. We must love in what ways? (pick two: word, tongue, actions, truth, fear?) *1 John 3:18*

Lesson 8

1. There is no what in love? (regret, challenge, fear?) *1 John 4:18*

2. We must love God before God will love us. T/F. *1 John 4:19*

Lesson 9

1. The letter of 2 John is written to the _____ chosen by God. *2 John 1*

2. False teachers should still receive hospitality so as to win them over to the truth. T/F. *2 John 10*

Lesson 10

1. The one who does evil has not seen whom? (God, Gaius, Diotrephes?) _____. *3 John 11*

2. John prefers writing a letter over a face-to-face visit. T/F. *3 John 13, 14*

Lesson 11

1. There are different kinds of gifts, but the same Spirit. T/F. *1 Corinthians 12:4*

2. The manifestation of the _____ is given for the common good. *1 Corinthians 12:7*

Lesson 12

1. The parts of the body that are weaker are expendable. T/F. *1 Corinthians 12:22*

2. God set whom first in the church? (apostles, prophets, teachers?) *1 Corinthians 12:28*

Lesson 13

1. The Holy Spirit came on the Day of _____. *Acts 2:1*

2. Tongues in worship services require what? (coordination, interpretation, toleration?) *1 Corinthians 14:13*

3. Paul spoke in tongues more than all the Corinthians. T/F. *1 Corinthians 14:18*

Lesson 14

1. Without love, we are _____. *1 Corinthians 13:2*

2. The greatest of faith, hope, and love is _____. *1 Corinthians 13:13*

Note: The first lesson of spring is placed as the final lesson of winter because the winter quarter has only 12 Sundays while the spring quarter has 14.

QUARTER AT A GLANCE

by Mark S. Krause

CHRISTIANS ARE BLESSED to enjoy the fulfilled promise of the indwelling presence of the Holy Spirit. The New Testament has much to say about the Spirit, with references or allusions in nearly every book.

The Gospel accounts of Jesus' life are interwoven with such references (Matthew 1:18; etc.). Jesus himself was described as being full of the Holy Spirit (Luke 4:1). John the Baptist promised that Jesus would baptize with the Holy Spirit (Mark 1:8). The majority of the lessons of this quarter will examine, from various angles, facts and issues concerning the promise, nature, presence, and role of the Holy Spirit.

The Pledge of God's Presence

Most of the lessons for March include teachings about the Holy Spirit as promised to be sent to empower Jesus' disciples after his departure. Four of the unit's five lessons are drawn from the Gospel of John, one of the premier books of the New Testament for understanding the person and work of the Spirit.

Despite Jesus' wonderful pledge of the Holy Spirit to be God's presence among believers, teaching about the Holy Spirit is often either neglected or controversial in many churches today. Some Christians are wary of those who claim the Holy Spirit to be actively involved in their lives. Others cannot comprehend why all Christians are not experiencing the power of the Holy Spirit daily. Such controversy should not cause us to shy away from study of the Spirit, however, but the opposite!

The Community of Beloved Disciples

Our second unit of study looks at first-century Christians as they related to one another in community. The Holy Spirit was active and influential in this context, and lessons 7 and 8 of this quarter address this fact explicitly.

The text for those two lessons (and for two of the other three lessons of this unit) are from the pen of John, the only living apostle at the time when he wrote. John's letters reveal the struggles of Christians of the late first century AD. Much like us, they were trying to be faithful and hopeful in a hostile and challenging environment. Like them, we make our existence more difficult if we ignore or spurn the work of the Spirit in our lives and our congregations.

One in the Bond of Love

The four lessons of our final unit are largely drawn from 1 Corinthians 12–14, three of the most important chapters in the Bible when it comes to learning about the Holy Spirit. The church in Corinth was both a dynamic place where the activity of the Spirit was evident and a troubled place where misunderstandings and personal conflicts threatened the unity of the body.

To correct this, Paul taught the Corinthians that excitement over gifts of the Spirit was no substitute or excuse for a lack of love or disunity. The presence of the Holy Spirit was essential, but so was human cooperation with him.

> *Controversy should not cause us to shy away from study of the Spirit.*

The next to last lesson of this unit allows us to compare and contrast the issue of speaking in tongues in Corinth with the manifestation of the Spirit via tongues on the Day of Pentecost. The Holy Spirit's presence in the church and in the lives of believers has been a reality for nearly 2,000 years. Churches come and go, membership roles change year by year, but the Holy Spirit is the same today as he was at creation (Genesis 1:2), on the Day of Pentecost (Acts 2), and when he fills our lives today (Ephesians 5:18).

GET THE SETTING

by Mark S. Krause

ONE BIG DIFFERENCE between the Old and New Testaments is the promise and presence of the Holy Spirit. While the Old Testament speaks occasionally of the power and ministry of God's Spirit (examples: Psalm 51:11; Isaiah 61:1), the New Testament portrays the ministry of Jesus as being saturated by the Holy Spirit (see Luke 4:1) and shows the Spirit's presence to be a defining characteristic of the first-century church (Acts 5:3, 32; 6:5; 9:31; 13:2; etc.).

But what about the pagan world of New Testament times, those Greeks and Romans not influenced by any Old Testament teaching about God's Spirit? How did they view the spiritual realm and the powers that inhabited it? This is an important subject because the first-century church found itself bumping up against wrong beliefs that needed to be countered.

Important Words

Two important Greek words should be considered at the outset of our inquiry. The first is *pneuma,* usually translated "spirit(s)" in the New Testament. By itself this word is neutral; whether a spirit is good or bad depends on context (example: the "impure spirit" of Mark 1:23).

The other Greek word is *daimonion,* translated "demon(s)" in the New Testament. Pagans sometimes used this word to refer to their gods. The New Testament authors see demons and impure (or evil) spirits as the same thing (examples: Luke 8:2, 29). The pagan and Christian understandings have a point of agreement in realizing these to be unseen spiritual beings capable of exerting power over humans. First-century Judaism affirmed this as well (examples: Matthew 11:18; Mark 3:22).

Great Contrast

Beyond that singular point of agreement, however, lies a significant difference between Christian and pagan views of the spirit world. A Greek man living in Ephesus would certainly believe in spiritual beings, but he did not necessarily see them in categories of polar opposites (good vs. bad; angelic vs. demonic; etc.). To him, these powerful beings had a mixed moral nature similar to that of humans.

Pagans who attempted to interact with spirit beings did so in the hope of enticing them into doing something of benefit. There was no desire to be controlled by spirits in such interactions because spirit beings could not be trusted fully due to their mixed moral nature. Rather, interactions were attempts to exert control over the spirit beings.

Corrective Teaching

Paul, in dealing with former pagans, understood the lure of attempting to interact with spirit beings. Such forces were enemies, not potential helpers, and Christians were engaged in warfare against them (Ephesians 6:12). This is why he warned against attempts to mix "the cup of the Lord" with "the cup of demons" (1 Corinthians 10:21).

Understanding this context helps us appreciate the radical contrast Christianity offered with its message of a singular Spirit of God (Ephesians 4:4)—a Spirit as different from the multitude of "impure spirits" or "demons" as can be imagined! Rather than see the Holy Spirit as a power that a human might control (Acts 8:18, 19), the Christian message introduced the world to a Spirit whose presence and control was to be invited and welcomed (Galatians 5:25). Those indwelt by the Holy Spirit had the power and strength to become holy and pleasing to God.

Our lessons for this quarter examine several New Testament passages that teach us about the blessings we enjoy through the presence and ministry of the Holy Spirit in our lives. With all the wrong understandings of spirit beings and spirituality in our world today, this message is more urgent than ever!

THIS QUARTER IN THE WORD

Mon, Mar. 2	Is There No Balm in Gilead?	Jeremiah 8:18-22
Tue, Mar. 3	No One to Comfort Me	Lamentations 1:17-21
Wed, Mar. 4	Here Is Your God!	Isaiah 40:1-10
Thu, Mar. 5	This Is My Comfort	Psalm 119:49-64
Fri, Mar. 6	The Shepherd's Comfort	Psalm 23
Sat, Mar. 7	When the Advocate Comes	John 15:18-26
Sun, Mar. 8	An Advocate with You Forever	John 14:15-26
Mon, Mar. 9	Where There Is No Revelation	Proverbs 29:12-18
Tue, Mar. 10	The Lord Has Closed Your Eyes	Isaiah 29:8-14
Wed, Mar. 11	Speak, for Your Servant Is Listening	1 Samuel 3:1-10
Thu, Mar. 12	A Trustworthy Prophet of the Lord	1 Samuel 3:11-21
Fri, Mar. 13	I Commit My Spirit	Psalm 31:1-8
Sat, Mar. 14	Worship in Spirit and Truth	John 4:21-26
Sun, Mar. 15	The Spirit of Truth Will Guide You	John 16:4b-15
Mon, Mar. 16	The Holy Spirit Speaks	Mark 13:5-11
Tue, Mar. 17	Gentiles Receive the Holy Spirit	Acts 10:39-48
Wed, Mar. 18	Full of the Spirit and Faith	Acts 11:19-26
Thu, Mar. 19	Joy in the Holy Spirit	Romans 14:13-19
Fri, Mar. 20	Power from the Holy Spirit	Acts 1:4-8
Sat, Mar. 21	Be Filled with the Spirit	Ephesians 5:15-21
Sun, Mar. 22	Receive the Holy Spirit	John 20:19-23

Mon, May 18	Made You Hear God's Voice	Deuteronomy 4:32-40
Tue, May 19	A Small Member, Great Boasting	James 3:1-5
Wed, May 20	All Languages, One Loud Voice	Revelation 7:9-12
Thu, May 21	We Hear in Our Own Languages	Acts 2:8-13
Fri, May 22	They Shall Prophesy	Acts 2:14-21
Sat, May 23	Excel in Your Gifts	1 Corinthians 14:6-12
Sun, May 24	Building Up Others	Acts 2:1-7, 12; 1 Corinthians 14:13-19
Mon, May 25	Love and the Knowledge of God	Hosea 6:1-6
Tue, May 26	Abounding in Steadfast Love	Jonah 3:10–4:11
Wed, May 27	Keep in Step with the Spirit	Galatians 5:19-26
Thu, May 28	Increasing Love for One Another	2 Thessalonians 1:1-5
Fri, May 29	Love and Steadfastness	2 Thessalonians 3:1-5
Sat, May 30	Filled with the Fullness of God	Ephesians 3:14-21
Sun, May 31	Love Never Ends	1 Corinthians 13

Answers to the Quarterly Quiz on page 226

Lesson 2—1. true. 2. Holy Spirit. Lesson 3—1. true. 2. truth. Lesson 4—1. hands, side. 2. breathed. Lesson 5—1. false. 2. false. Lesson 6—1. third. 2. true. Lesson 7—1. true. 2. actions, truth. Lesson 8—1. fear. 2. false. Lesson 9—1. lady. 2. false. Lesson 10—1. God. 2. false. Lesson 11—1. true. 2. Spirit. Lesson 12—1. false. 2. apostles. Lesson 13—1. Pentecost. 2. interpretation. 3. true. Lesson 14—1. nothing. 2. love.

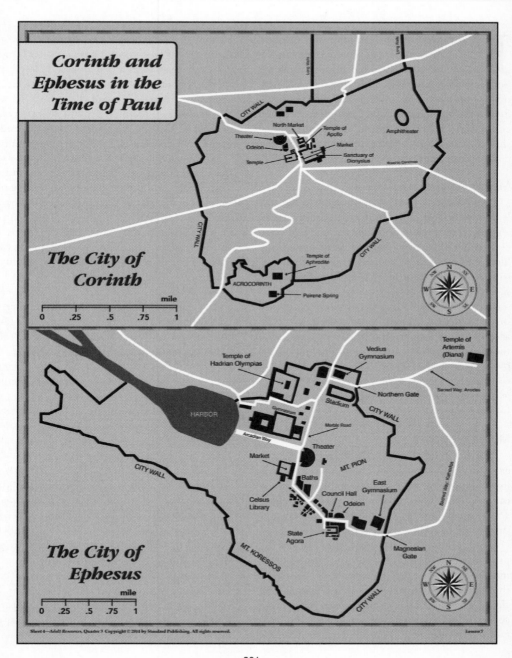

Corinth and Ephesus in the Time of Paul

The City of Corinth

CITY WALL

North Market

Theater

Odeion

Temple

Temple of Apollo

Market

Sanctuary of Dionysius

Amphitheater

Long Walls

Long Walls

Road to Cenchrea

CITY WALL

CITY WALL

Temple of Aphrodite

ACROCORINTH

Peirene Spring

N E S W

mile

0   .25   .5   .75   1

The City of Ephesus

Temple of Hadrian Olympias

Vedius Gymnasium

Temple of Artemis (Diana)

Sacred Way: Anodos

Gymnasium

Stadium

Northern Gate

CITY WALL

HARBOR

Marble Road

Arcadian Way

Theater

Market

Baths

MT. PION

Celsus Library

Council Hall

East Gymnasium

Odeion

Sacred Way: Kathodos

State Agora

Magnesian Gate

MT. KORESSOS

CITY WALL

CITY WALL

N E S W

mile

0   .25   .5   .75   1

Lesson 7

SHARED RESPONSIBILITY

Teacher Tips by Wendy Guthrie

HAVING ADDRESSED the role of classroom engagement last quarter, we now move to the issue of shared responsibility in building community. This installment, the third of our four-part series, focuses on the responsibility of class members to build community because community is, by definition, something that is shared. Community helps achieve our mutual goal as it fosters mutual support and mutual trust.

Mutual Goal

Every Sunday your class comes together to learn about God. This common purpose creates a partnership bond among the members of your class and with the Holy Spirit. This partnership ideally helps to equip "people for works of service, so that the body of Christ may be built up" (Ephesians 4:12).

A learning context that encourages each member to participate actively in discussions, to accept accountability for personal Bible study, etc., will more readily achieve the desired goal of mature disciples of Jesus. When a classroom becomes community, we are providing the opportunity for learners to become vessels whom God can mold for his purposes.

Mutual Support

Transforming class into community makes it easier for learners to get involved in one another's lives. The teacher who is intent on building community will promote and encourage such interaction outside of class. Fellowship and mutual support go hand in hand (Acts 2:42-47; etc.).

Holding monthly class socials is one way to promote community fellowship among class members. Another way is to create a class forum through social media or e-mail. This should be a closed site where class members can post prayer concerns, spiritual struggles, and personal victories. It can also be a place where class members encourage one another on a daily basis by posting inspirational or scriptural messages. Such media allow students to practice biblical fellowship as they carry one another's burdens (Galatians 6:2), share in spiritual victories (Romans 1:12) and personal joys (Philemon 7), and encourage one another (1 Thessalonians 4:18). This is the essence of the bonds of mutual support in community.

Note that you, the teacher, can only *foster* such mutual support—you cannot create it yourself. The idea of community dictates a shared responsibility on the part of students; indeed, they will play the major part in making it work. As they help build community, they will find themselves tearing down walls of fear and isolation as those walls are replaced by the support of fellowship.

Mutual Trust

The more your learners trust one another, the better they will function as a unified whole rather than as individual parts. Learners provide themselves opportunities to help one another grow in biblical understanding as they participate in creating community by embracing the shared responsibility of engaged learning. As they do, they will find themselves working together to implement biblical solutions to personal and congregational problems. Struggling together in this way challenges individualistic ways of thinking.

Students become better connected with one another as they interact in such ways outside of class. In so doing, they grow to trust one another with personal flaws and shortcomings. The result will be continued growth in spiritual attributes, fulfilling Jesus' desire that his disciples mature in thought and action (Ephesians 4:11-16).

Mutual trust both builds and is built by community in a positive cycle of reinforcement. But wait—what about service? Isn't that a vital part of building community? Indeed it is, and that will be the topic of our final installment, next quarter.

March 8
*Lesson 2

ANOTHER
ADVOCATE

DEVOTIONAL READING: Psalm 23
BACKGROUND SCRIPTURE: John 14:15-26

JOHN 14:15-26

¹⁵ "If you love me, keep my commands. ¹⁶ And I will ask the Father, and he will give you another advocate to help you and be with you forever—¹⁷ the Spirit of truth. The world cannot accept him, because it neither sees him nor knows him. But you know him, for he lives with you and will be in you. ¹⁸ I will not leave you as orphans; I will come to you. ¹⁹ Before long, the world will not see me anymore, but you will see me. Because I live, you also will live. ²⁰ On that day you will realize that I am in my Father, and you are in me, and I am in you. ²¹ Whoever has my commands and keeps them is the one who loves me. The one who loves me will be loved by my Father, and I too will love him and show myself to them."

²² Then Judas (not Judas Iscariot) said, "But, Lord, why do you intend to show yourself to us and not to the world?"

²³ Jesus replied, "Anyone who loves me will obey my teaching. My Father will love them, and we will come to them and make our home with them. ²⁴ Anyone who does not love me will not obey my teaching. These words you hear are not my own; they belong to the Father who sent me.

²⁵ "All this I have spoken while still with you. ²⁶ But the Advocate, the Holy Spirit, whom the Father will send in my name, will teach you all things and will remind you of everything I have said to you."

> *Special note!*
> The winter quarter has only 12 Sundays while the spring quarter has 14. This quirk of the calendar requires that the first lesson of this quarter be printed as the final lesson of last quarter for production purposes.

KEY VERSE

The Advocate, the Holy Spirit, whom the Father will send in my name, will teach you all things and will remind you of everything I have said to you. —**John 14:26**

THE SPIRIT COMES

Unit 1: The Pledge of God's Presence

LESSONS 1–5

LESSON AIMS

After participating in this lesson, each learner will be able to:

1. Summarize Jesus' promise of the Holy Spirit.

2. Explain the link between the presence of the Holy Spirit and living in loving obedience to Christ.

3. Write a prayer of thanks to God for the presence of the Holy Spirit in his or her life.

LESSON OUTLINE

Introduction
 A. Abandoned!
 B. Lesson Background
 I. Promise of the Spirit (JOHN 14:15-17)
 A. Initial Requirement (v. 15)
 B. Firm Promise (vv. 16, 17)
  The God Who Is There
 II. Assurance by the Son (JOHN 14:18-24)
 A. Presence (v. 18)
 B. Life (v. 19)
 C. Knowledge (v. 20)
 D. Obedience (v. 21)
  Loved
 E. Clarification (vv. 22-24)
 III. Purpose of the Spirit (JOHN 14:25, 26)
 A. Son's Present Message (v. 25)
 B. Spirit's Future Ministry (v. 26)
Conclusion
 A. Abandoned? Never!
 B. Prayer
 C. Thought to Remember

Introduction

A. Abandoned!

"Sorry, I have to leave now." Words like these have broken many hearts. Someone goes off to war, a dear friend moves far away, an elderly loved one passes on. There is likely a sad embrace, a final farewell, and cold reality sets in: abandoned!

For some, it is even worse. By one estimate, there are over 100 million people in our world who are faced with the harsh reality of being left as orphans. War, famine, and disease have no respect for the plight of little children. Parents are stripped from their lives; they are left all alone. They have little hope unless someone steps in to help. They feel—and often really are—abandoned (Lamentations 5:3).

For most of three years, Jesus had been the constant companion of his chosen 12. They had left everything to follow him. But he was about to leave them. What would the sheep do if they were abandoned by their shepherd?

B. Lesson Background

Jesus came to reveal God to humanity. Jesus was the Word who "was God"; he was the Word who "became flesh" (John 1:1, 14). He was the Lamb of God who came to take away the sins of the world (1:29). As the Gospel of John progresses, we see an increasing emphasis on the divine identity of Jesus. He was accused of "making himself equal with God" (5:18). He exhibited the power to raise the dead and the authority to pronounce judgment (5:21, 22). He said, "I and the Father are one" (10:30). His miracles confirmed that his claims were true (10:36-38).

The climax of Jesus' claims came in the upper room in the final week before his death. There Jesus told his disciples that no one could come to the Father except through him (John 14:6). Even more stunningly he said, "Anyone who has seen me has seen the Father" (14:9). Truly God was present with his people! But Jesus also had an unpleasant shock to give his disciples that night: he was leaving. Just when they were realizing that they had God's presence in their very midst, it seemed that they were about to lose it!

It was in this setting that Jesus promised to send another advocate—the Holy Spirit. From the very beginning of Jesus' ministry, the Spirit had had an active role. The Spirit had descended as a dove to Jesus at his baptism (John 1:32). Nicodemus had been told of the need to be born of water and the Spirit in order to enter God's kingdom (3:5). The woman at the well in Samaria learned that those who would worship God acceptably must worship "in the Spirit and in truth" (4:24). Although the Holy Spirit had not yet been given, Jesus promised that one day the Spirit would be granted to all believers (7:39). And on a Thursday night in an upper room, Jesus made final preparations for that to be possible.

I. Promise of the Spirit
(JOHN 14:15-17)
A. Initial Requirement (v. 15)
15. "If you love me, keep my commands.

Interwoven with the promises of the coming Spirit is Jesus' insistence that if we love him we must keep his commands. Love for Jesus must be more than a fleeting emotion. The Bible meaning of *love* includes loyalty and commitment. That is the kind of love Jesus meant when he said the greatest commandment is to love God with all one's heart, soul, and mind (Matthew 22:37). We owe this kind of love to Jesus as God's Son. Nothing less will do.

Love is at the core of our relationship with God and Jesus, and true love requires obedience. That is why Jesus repeats this concept of obedience in verse 21 and again in verses 23, 24 here in John 14. Real believers don't just *believe*; they *obey*.

A tragic footnote must be added to these words of Jesus. When he says *if you love me,* he is keenly aware that not all of his disciples do, in fact, love him. Only minutes before, Jesus had dismissed

HOW TO SAY IT

Judas Iscariot	*Joo*-dus Iss-***care***-ee-ut.
Nicodemus	*Nick*-uh-***dee***-mus.
Samaria	Suh-*mare*-ee-uh.
Thaddaeus	Tha-*dee*-us.

Judas Iscariot out into the night to do what he was determined to do—betray his Lord to the temple authorities (see John 13:21-30). Believers will always show by their actions their response to Jesus' fateful words *if you love me.*

What Do You Think?
How does love for God compare and contrast with love in human to human relationships?
Talking Points for Your Discussion
- Ways they are similar
- Ways they are different

B. Firm Promise (vv. 16, 17)
16. "And I will ask the Father, and he will give you another advocate to help you and be with you forever—

Jesus has already told his disciples that he will be with them only a little while longer (see John 13:33). As they puzzle over the meaning of those alarming words, Jesus makes the promise we see here. The Father always hears the Son (see 11:41, 42), and this prayer will be answered. *Another advocate*, by Jesus' personal request, will soon be given.

But who will this advocate be and what will he do? The main difficulty with the Greek word being translated is its potentially wide range of meanings. Older translations of the Bible render this word as "Comforter" (*King James Version*) and "Helper" (*New American Standard Bible*). This word is often found in legal settings to refer to someone who goes to court with another to help plead a case. (The same Greek word appears in 1 John 2:1, where the NIV translates it *advocate*, referring to Jesus.) In a general sense, such a one might promise, "If you're ever in trouble, I'll be there for you."

So then as Jesus announces that he is leaving, he also promises that someone else will come and replace him. Furthermore, Jesus' replacement is going to be with the disciples forever. In the Old Testament, the Spirit of God came upon individuals somewhat sporadically and temporarily (examples: Judges 14:6, 19; 15:14). But for believers in Christ, the indwelling Spirit remains continually (see Acts 2:38; Ephesians 1:13, 14).

When I was a newlywed, panic would grip me when my husband said he needed to travel. I had lived with my family before marrying, and I had never lived alone. On those long nights on my own, my untamed imagination created miserable thoughts of things that could happen: fire, burglaries, physical attacks. To add to this, I was concerned that something might happen to him.

Years later, I read an article about prayer that suggested a time of quiet focus on the Lord. This was a new concept to me. I had thought prayer was offering up a list of needs, giving thanks, etc. (Similarly, I've been better at talking than listening in my human interactions). The suggestion was not to empty your mind in terms of trying to create a blank chalkboard, but to set aside concerns, considering instead the magnificence of the One who can handle them all. This refocus brought a keen awareness of God's nearness. He had been there all along, just waiting for me to notice (Psalm 46:10).

I still miss my husband when he travels. But now I enjoy the opportunity for extra time to be in the company of the God who is there. —V. E.

17. ". . . the Spirit of truth. The world cannot accept him, because it neither sees him nor knows him. But you know him, for he lives with you and will be in you."

God's Spirit is *the Spirit of truth* because God himself is always true. God cannot lie (see Hebrews 6:18), and his Word is truth (see John 17:17). This same Spirit moved the men who wrote the prophecies of the Old Testament (see 2 Peter 1:21) to write infallible truth. Now the Spirit is coming to the disciples and to the church (compare John 15:26; 16:13).

But the Spirit will not indwell the people of *the world*—they *cannot accept him.* God sends the Spirit into the hearts of those who are redeemed (see Galatians 4:6), not into the hearts of worldly people. Only the children of God have the Spirit of God, and only those who are led by the Spirit are his children (see Romans 8:14).

Jesus assures his disciples that they know the Spirit of truth. This must be puzzling to the disciples, but things will become much clearer to them

after Jesus ascends to Heaven and the Day of Pentecost comes (see Acts 2:1-4).

What Do You Think?

When was a time your realization of the Spirit's presence made the difference in how things turned out? How did you grow spiritually from this experience?

Talking Points for Your Discussion

- Regarding a moral dilemma
- Regarding a counseling situation
- Regarding a family crisis
- Other

II. Assurance by the Son
(JOHN 14:18-24)
A. Presence (v. 18)

18. "I will not leave you as orphans; I will come to you.

Jesus fully understands that his disciples may feel like *orphans,* forlorn and alone, after he departs, so he is preparing for this. Just as God the Father had promised that he would never leave or forsake the children of Israel (see Deuteronomy 31:6), now God the Son makes a similar promise to his disciples. The children (see John 13:33) are not being abandoned.

The promise *I will come to you* has drawn three interpretations: (1) it refers to Jesus' second coming (John 14:3), (2) it refers to the gift of the Holy Spirit (14:16, 17, 26), or (3) it refers to Jesus' resurrection (20:19, 26). Based on what Jesus says in John 14:20 (below), the third proposal is probably the best.

B. Life (v. 19)

19. "Before long, the world will not see me anymore, but you will see me. Because I live, you also will live.

On the very next day, Good Friday, Jesus will be crucified and buried. Never again does the unbelieving world see him alive. (Individual exceptions to this statement include appearances to his half-brother James, who previously did not believe in him, and to Saul of Tarsus; compare Mark 3:21; 6:3; John 7:5; Galatians 1:19; 1 Corinthians 15:5-8.) After his resurrection, Jesus will appear repeatedly to his disciples, in both small and large groups (see also John 16:16).

Jesus' resurrection will give new hope to disciples: *because I live, you also will live.* His forthcoming victory over death will mean victory for all who follow him. His resurrection will mean that they can live—really live—a whole new kind of life even while they are still on earth.

What Do You Think?

In what ways have you benefitted from lengthy personal time with another? How has that experience been an example for you?

Talking Points for Your Discussion

- Regarding a grandparent
- Regarding a parent
- Regarding a friend
- Regarding a teacher
- Other

C. Knowledge (v. 20)

20. "On that day you will realize that I am in my Father, and you are in me, and I am in you.

Jesus has already discussed his relationship with his Father (John 14:7-11). However, the disciples' understanding of this relationship is not yet what it should be. The greater understanding will come on a certain day when they *will realize that I am in my Father.*

But when exactly is *that day*? Bible students have proposed three possibilities: (1) the day Jesus rises from the dead (John 2:22), (2) the day when Jesus is glorified (12:16), or (3) the day when the Holy Spirit comes (16:12-15). The strongest case probably can be made for the day of Jesus' resurrection given the last part of John 14:19, just considered above: "because I live, you also will live."

This signifies, as noted by G. R. Beasley-Murray, that Jesus "comes at Easter to be reunited with his disciples and to lift to a new plane his relationship with them." The transformation of that relationship seems to be the intent of the phrases *you are in me, and I am in you.* Jesus addresses the significance of this more fully in John 14:23, 24 (below) and in John 17.

D. Obedience (v. 21)

21. "Whoever has my commands and keeps them is the one who loves me. The one who loves me will be loved by my Father, and I too will love them and show myself to them."

Jesus repeats the importance of keeping of his commands (see v. 15, above; compare John 15:10). His teachings are not mere suggestions or general guidelines for an improved life; they are, rather, directives from the Lord to his servants. It is by keeping the Lord's commands that his servants show that they love him (compare 1 John 5:3, lesson 8; and 2 John 6, lesson 9). True discipleship must be more than mere lip service (compare Luke 6:46: "Why do you call me, 'Lord, Lord,' and do not do what I say?")

True love is to be modeled on the Father's own love for us: always loyal and committed. The harmonious oneness between Father and Son is so profound that to be loved by one is to be loved by the other. The result for the disciples in being so loved is that Jesus plans to *show* himself to them. This certainly happens after Jesus' resurrection (John 20:19-29; 21:1-14).

❧ LOVED ❧

While in high school, I worked with a classmate at a trendy clothing store for women. This young lady had caught the eye of the star quarterback at the state university. She loved to talk about her handsome beau, who was regularly featured in the media. The team was on a roll, and the fans relished every win.

One day she told me that she had gone to meet him at the airport as the team returned from a victorious away game. But she had been unable to get near the plane because of the sea of screaming fans present. As the players deplaned, the crowds pressed in.

Her guy, however, was on the lookout for her. He used his powerful frame to snatch her up and carry her through the chaotic mass of humanity. She told of the thrilling experience with such detail and delight that I could literally feel the excitement with her.

Those in Christ are not just faces in the crowds on planet Earth. We are held up by the powerful, loving arms of our Creator. How can we not be exhilarated when we pause to think of life in the Spirit of the living God?! —V. E.

E. Clarification (vv. 22-24)

22. Then Judas (not Judas Iscariot) said, "But, Lord, why do you intend to show yourself to us and not to the world?"

Judas Iscariot has already departed to betray Jesus at this point (John 13:26-30). But there is another man named Judas among the 12 apostles (Luke 6:16; Acts 1:13); this Judas is also known as Thaddaeus (Matthew 10:3; Mark 3:18).

Jesus has just stated that "Before long, the world will not see me anymore, but you will see me" (v. 19), and Judas is struggling to understand what this means; so he asks for clarification. Jesus' answer follows.

What Do You Think?

When in a crisis situation, how do you know when it's better to voice your concerns rather than remain quiet?

Talking Points for Your Discussion

- Regarding the nature of the crisis
- Regarding who is "in charge"
- Regarding the personalities of those present
- Regarding the presence or absence of opponents
- Other

---

23. Jesus replied, "Anyone who loves me will obey my teaching. My Father will love them, and we will come to them and make our home with them.

For the third time (see vv. 15, 21, above), Jesus emphasizes that those who love him must obey him. This time it is stated not as a command but as a simple fact. Whoever really loves the Lord will do whatever he says.

When followers do obey their Lord, two things are promised to follow. First, the Father *will love them*. Second, both the Father and the Son *will come to them* and will make their *home with them*. The word translated *home* is the same that is translated "rooms" in John 14:2. In both places the emphasis is on the intended permanence of the dwelling place.

Therefore as Jesus departs to prepare the place of John 14:2, he is also making the believer to be a home or dwelling place for him. The role of the Holy Spirit in this abiding is addressed in verses 25, 26, below.

24. "Anyone who does not love me will not obey my teaching. These words you hear are not my own; they belong to the Father who sent me.

After saying that those who love him will keep his commands, Jesus now states the flip side of this same truth: whoever does not love him will not obey his teaching. After all, how can someone truly love Jesus but ignore what he says?

These commands are not just from Jesus; they are in fact those of the Father (compare John 7:16; 14:10). God has sent his Son to deliver the Father's message and to show the Father's love. Therefore, to disregard Jesus is to disregard God.

III. Purpose of the Spirit
(John 14:25, 26)

A. Son's Present Message (v. 25)

25. "All this I have spoken while still with you.

Jesus has spoken many things to his disciples this night. He has instituted the Lord's Supper, has demonstrated a servant spirit by washing their feet, and has taught them about the coming of an advocate. While he is yet with them, he has even more to teach. But their minds are able to absorb only so much (compare John 20:9). Even so, there is more to come, as the next verse shows.

B. Spirit's Future Ministry (v. 26)

26. "But the Advocate, the Holy Spirit, whom the Father will send in my name, will teach you all things and will remind you of everything I have said to you."

Jesus now summarizes the forthcoming ministry of *the Advocate* (see discussion on meaning of which on v. 16, above), who is also known as *the Holy Spirit*. This is God's own Spirit, who will soon be sent to the apostles in the name of Jesus.

Jesus also adds information about what the apostles can expect the Holy Spirit to do. First, he *will teach you all things.* This will become the basis of the inspiration of the men who will write the New Testament. Things that they do not know will be taught to them by the Holy Spirit. Like the prophets of old they will be moved by the Spirit to write Scripture.

The Spirit will also remind them of things previously seen and heard. Since two of those present, namely Matthew and John, will later write Gospels of Jesus' life, it will be vital for them to be able to recall accurate details of what they have witnessed. Even as they write decades later, their thoughts on the life of Jesus will be clear and correct.

In an indirect way, the work of the Spirit to teach and to remind is a promise to all of us. First through Scripture and then through his indwelling presence, the Spirit leads us toward the truth and to recall it. The Spirit is our helper, indeed!

Visual for Lesson 2. *Start a discussion by pointing to this visual as you ask, "How is the presence of the Spirit of Truth a source of peace to you?"*

What Do You Think?
When was a time that recall of a Scripture helped you make a right choice? What did you learn from this experience?

Talking Points for Your Discussion
- When you needed comfort
- When you needed boldness or confidence
- When you needed to resist temptation
- Other

Conclusion
A. Abandoned? Never!

The disciples in the upper room were startled, even frightened, to hear that their shepherd was going to leave them. They did not really understand about the good shepherd laying down his life for his sheep (see John 10:11), and they certainly did not want to be left alone. Their lack of understanding was still evident at the empty tomb (20:9), and again at the ascension (Acts 1:6). But was their Lord going to abandon them? Never!

One of the most precious promises in the Bible, stated in both the Old and New Testaments, is God's promise not to abandon his people (see Joshua 1:5; Hebrews 13:5). Even though we walk through the darkest valley, our shepherd is with us (Psalm 23:4). Even if a cruel cross should slay our shepherd, he rises again and is always with us. We are not forsaken.

As we are reminded each Christmas season, one of the names of Jesus is *Immanuel,* which means "God with us." That truth transcends the miracle of the incarnation in the first century to become true for believers in every generation. When Jesus was no longer to be present on earth physically, he promised the Holy Spirit to be sent as God's own presence within us. Because we have this divine presence, we are never abandoned.

B. Prayer

Father, we thank you for your promise that you will never leave us. Help us sense your constant presence as you dwell in our hearts. May we show you our love every day through our obedience. In the name of Jesus, amen.

C. Thought to Remember
We have the promised Spirit of God.

VISUALS FOR THESE LESSONS

The visual pictured in each lesson (see example above) is a small reproduction of a large, full-color poster included in the *Adult Resources* packet for the Spring Quarter. That packet also contains the very useful *Presentation Tools* CD for teacher use. Order No. 020039215 from your supplier.

INVOLVEMENT LEARNING

Enhance your lesson with NIV® Bible Student (from your curriculum supplier) and the reproducible activity page (at www.standardlesson.com or in the back of the NIV® Standard Lesson Commentary Deluxe Edition).

Into the Lesson

Give an index card to each learner, each card having one of the following references: Deuteronomy 31:6; Joshua 1:5; Hebrews 13:5; Isaiah 41:17; Psalm 23:4. (Create duplicate cards as needed for your class size.) Say, "Please look up the Scripture on your card, read it silently, and summarize the passage on the back of the card."

After a few minutes, call for passages and summaries to be read aloud. After all are read, note what the passages have in common: God's promise not to forsake his people. Say, "One of God's characteristics is his faithfulness in keeping promises. Today, we will examine a vital promise he made for the New Testament era."

Into the Word

Review quickly the events in the upper room found in John 13:1–14:14 that preface today's lesson. The Lesson Background will be useful for this.

Have volunteers take turns reading the verses of today's text aloud. Then form three groups with these assignments: *Group A*—Summarize what Jesus promised concerning the Holy Spirit; *Group B*—Identify the relationship between the presence of the Holy Spirit and a Christian's obedience to Christ; *Group C*—Identify the relationship of the world to Father, Son, and Holy Spirit.

When groups are ready, have them present their conclusions, which should include the following: *Group A*—1. When Jesus leaves, God will send "another advocate," the Spirit of truth, to dwell with the disciples permanently (vv. 16, 17). 2. Therefore disciples will not be abandoned (v. 18). 3. The disciples will realize the nature of the connection between them, God the Father, and God the Son (v. 20). 4. The Holy Spirit will teach all things to the disciples and remind them of everything Jesus said (v. 26).

Group B—1. Those who love Jesus obey his commands (vv. 21, 23). 2. Whoever loves Jesus is loved by God (v. 21). 3. Whoever loves Jesus will be loved by the Father (v. 23a). 4. God's love is shown through the abiding of his Spirit (v. 23b).

Group C—1. The world cannot accept the Spirit of truth "because it neither sees him nor knows him" (v. 17). 2. The world will no longer be able to see Jesus, but his followers will see him (v. 19). 3. Those of the world do not know God; therefore, they will not obey Jesus' teachings (v. 24).

As groups share findings, clarify their observations with information from the commentary (examples: relationship between love and obedience in vv. 15, 21, 23; significance of the various roles of the Spirit in vv. 16, 17, 26; interrelatedness of God, Christ, and the disciples in v. 20).

Option: Distribute copies of the "The Promised Spirit" activity from the reproducible page, which you can download. Have learners work on this in pairs to provide a focused look at verses 16, 17, 26. Conclude by discussing which activities of the Spirit are for all Christians of any era vs. which activities were only for the first-century apostles.

Into Life

Ask learners to identify the Spirit's functions from the text; jot these on the board as they are called out. (Learners will be better prepared to do this if you have used the optional activity above.) Then invite learners to identify how the Spirit has acted in those ways in their own lives or in the church as a whole. Be prepared to share personally in this regard. Challenge learners as appropriate by asking, "How do you know that was the Holy Spirit at work?"

Option: Distribute copies of the "A Prayer of Thanks" activity from the reproducible page. Depending on the nature of your class and the time remaining, you can use this either to conclude the class session or as an exercise for learners to complete later in private.

THE SPIRIT OF TRUTH

DEVOTIONAL READING: **1 Samuel 3:1-10**
BACKGROUND SCRIPTURE: **John 16:4b-15**

JOHN 16:4B-15

4b I did not tell you this from the beginning because I was with you, 5 but now I am going to him who sent me. None of you asks me, 'Where are you going?' 6 Rather, you are filled with grief because I have said these things. 7 But very truly I tell you, it is for your good that I am going away. Unless I go away, the Advocate will not come to you; but if I go, I will send him to you. 8 When he comes, he will prove the

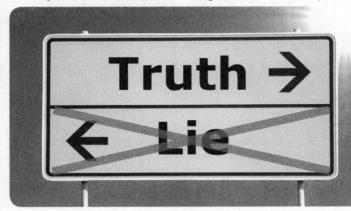

world to be in the wrong about sin and righteousness and judgment: 9 about sin, because people do not believe in me; 10 about righteousness, because I am going to the Father, where you can see me no longer; 11 and about judgment, because the prince of this world now stands condemned.

12 "I have much more to say to you, more than you can now bear. 13 But when he, the Spirit of truth, comes, he will guide you into all the truth. He will not speak on his own; he will speak only what he hears, and he will tell you what is yet to come. 14 He will glorify me because it is from me that he will receive what he will make known to you. 15 All that belongs to the Father is mine. That is why I said the Spirit will receive from me what he will make known to you."

KEY VERSE

Very truly I tell you, it is for your good that I am going away. Unless I go away, the Advocate will not come to you; but if I go, I will send him to you. —**John 16:7**

THE SPIRIT COMES

Unit 1: The Pledge of God's Presence

LESSONS 1–5

LESSON AIMS

After participating in this lesson, each learner will be able to:

1. Describe the work of the Holy Spirit.

2. Explain the significance of the apostles' receiving truth from the Holy Spirit.

3. Make a plan to read the entire Bible, inspired of God's Spirit, in the year 2015.

LESSON OUTLINE

Introduction

A. Exposed!

Adam and Eve knew what it was like to be exposed. After they sinned against the Creator by eating the forbidden fruit, they knew both their guilt and their nakedness. For them, the blessing of the presence of God became a threat. They tried to hide themselves from the very one who wanted their companionship. They did not want to be exposed.

Other people have also been exposed throughout history—sometimes for the better, but usually for the worse. For those who lived in the days of Noah, exposure meant that God knew their profound wickedness; the result was destruction by water. For young David, on the other hand, exposure meant that God knew the inherent goodness of his heart (see Acts 13:22). David welcomed being exposed that way before the Lord, even saying, "Search me, God, and know my heart" (Psalm 139:23).

Whether we like it or not, the hearts of all are exposed before God (Hebrews 4:13). This sounds frightening because we know our own sins and failures all too well. It can be something of a challenge, then, for Christians to welcome the presence of God's Spirit into every facet of their lives. Do we really want God taking notice of our every thought, action, or conversation? As Jesus teaches in this lesson, the indwelling of the Spirit is nothing to be feared.

B. Lesson Background

Jesus gathered with his 12 apostles in the upper room on a Thursday night for a meal to celebrate the Passover. The heart of Judas Iscariot was exposed during the meal, and Jesus dismissed him into the night to carry through with his evil designs (see John 13:27). To the 11 who remained, Jesus promised that the Father would send the Holy Spirit (John 14:26, last week's lesson). They were not to be left to fend for themselves.

This promise to send an Advocate, repeated in John 15:26, was the prelude to Jesus' final promises in this regard in John 16. The disciples were to face difficult times. They would be rejected and persecuted by their own people—some of whom would even kill the apostles, thinking that they were "offering a service to God" (John 16:2). To face such challenges in Jesus' absence, the disciples needed to know that they still had the reality of God's presence backing them up.

I. Coming of the Spirit
(JOHN 16:4b-7)

A. Preparation and Grief (vv. 4b-6)

4b. "I did not tell you this from the beginning because I was with you,

Jesus has taught his disciples many things during his three years with them. He has spoken about righteousness, about his own divine authority, and about the nature of the kingdom of Heaven. He has worked many miracles; he has spoken many parables. But he has not taught his disciples very much about the persecutions to come (*this*) of verses 2-4a.

The disciples have not needed information on this thus far because Jesus' physical presence has served as something of a lightning rod to draw opposition to himself and away from the disciples. Neither is there a record of the disciples having been taught much about the Holy Spirit thus far (part of the subject of *this*; see John 15:26).

Now, however, the time approaches for Jesus to depart. Therefore Jesus informs the disciples what will be happening to them all too soon.

> *What Do You Think?*
> When was a time you gave someone information that was "too much, too soon"? What did you learn from this experience?
> *Talking Points for Your Discussion*
> - Regarding information given to a child
> - Regarding information given to a teenager
> - Regarding information given to an adult

5. ". . . but now I am going to him who sent me. None of you asks me, 'Where are you going?'

As Jesus prepares to leave his disciples, he chides them for not asking where he will be going. Actually, Peter had asked Jesus about this earlier in the evening (John 13:36). But Peter's question shows that he is not really interested in *where*; what he cares about is *why* he cannot go with Jesus (13:37). Similarly, Thomas has complained on this same evening that the disciples do not know where Jesus is going (14:5), but his question is more of a protest than a genuine query regarding *where*.

So the gentle accusation of Jesus stands. None of the disciples has shown that they really care about where Jesus is going; they only care about being left behind and alone. They fail to grasp how great a thing it actually will be for Jesus to return to his Father (John 14:28). If they could understand this, they would rejoice for their master.

6. "Rather, you are filled with grief because I have said these things.

Jesus easily recognizes the apostles' sorrow (also John 16:22). The one they have faithfully followed for three years will no longer be there to lead them. The one they have come to know as their Lord and as the Messiah sent from God is being taken from them. The more Jesus tries to prepare them for his departure, the sadder they seem to become. It is perhaps understandable, yet still regrettable, that they cannot see beyond their pending loss of Jesus' physical presence. They do not yet understand that the coming of the Advocate will be a wonderful benefit.

B. Promise and Sequence (v. 7)

7. "But very truly I tell you, it is for your good that I am going away. Unless I go away, the Advocate will not come to you; but if I go, I will send him to you."

In spite of the disheartened reaction of the disciples, Jesus is determined to tell them the truth they need to hear. *It is for your good*—a beneficial thing—for Jesus to go away. If he were to stay with them in the flesh, he could not provide for them the new, divine presence of *the Advocate*—the Holy Spirit (John 14:26).

As Jesus has just explained, the Advocate will bring to them a new dimension of the presence of God (see John 14:16-18, last week's lesson). Jesus counteracts their sorrow with a solemn promise: *I will send him to you*. The Spirit will not be an impersonal force or a feeling; he will be the personal presence of God himself.

II. Work of the Spirit
(JOHN 16:8-11)
A. Regarding Sin (vv. 8, 9)

8. "When he comes, he will prove the world to be in the wrong about sin and righteousness and judgment:

The Holy Spirit will have two primary theaters of operation *when he comes*. As will be seen in later verses, he will have an important ministry in the lives of Jesus' disciples. He will also have a crucial ministry to the unbelieving world, as stressed by the verse before us.

Regarding the latter, Jesus explains that the work of the Spirit will be to prove unbelievers *to be in the wrong* in three areas: *sin*, *righteousness*, and *judgment*. To *prove* in the sense intended here means to convince people of their guilt by exposing all the truth. Therefore, one important role of the Spirit of truth (John 14:17; 15:26) is to impress truth upon the minds of unbelievers so they can see their need to repent. The Spirit does this work through the inspired Word of God (Hebrews 4:12).

In each of the three areas noted, the Spirit will attempt to make the world accept that a problem exists and that people must embrace God's solution for that problem. The Spirit will bring people under conviction—if they will allow it. Jesus' ministry has had this as its focus (John 7:7; 15:22); the Spirit will pick up where Jesus leaves off after he departs.

> **What Do You Think?**
> How does knowing about the Holy Spirit's ministry of reproof to the world affect you personally?
> *Talking Points for Your Discussion*
> ▪ Regarding your attitude toward sin
> ▪ Regarding your attitude toward righteousness
> ▪ Regarding your attitude toward judgment
> ▪ Other

9. ". . . about sin, because people do not believe in me;

Jesus offers further explanation of the three problem areas noted in verse 8, above. The first—

and most obvious—area that the Spirit must address is *sin*. All have sinned (see Romans 3:23), but not all will admit the truth of that fact. The Spirit's aim is to make people aware of their guilt; he will usually work through believers to accomplish this aim (John 15:26, 27). The problem is sin, and the first step is for the Spirit to bring the world under conviction of that ugly reality.

The solution for the problem of sin is faith in Jesus. God has promised to forgive the sins of all who believe in Christ, following the biblical plan of salvation. But most people *do not believe in* him (John 5:38; 6:36, 64; 7:5; 10:26; 12:37), so their problem remains. It is the difficult challenge given to the Spirit to bring these rebellious people under conviction. They are sinners, and the only remedy is to rely on Jesus. Until they accept the reproof of the Spirit and admit both their problem and God's solution, they are lost.

❧ CLARIFYING AGENT ❧

Sometimes the water of a diligently maintained swimming pool can become cloudy. Filters and sanitizers are doing their job, but many types of particulates are so tiny that they cannot be caught by filters. Fortunately, there are products that can help. Flocculants and clarifiers essentially cause the tiny particles to glob together, becoming big enough for a filter to capture them or for them to grow heavy enough to settle to the bottom to be vacuumed out, leaving clear water behind.

Satan muddied the simple command of God in the Garden of Eden and so deceived humanity; he uses various techniques to stir up confusion yet today. The Holy Spirit, by contrast, works through God's Word to convict our hearts, clarifying the sin within us. When we perceive what he is doing as we study that Word, we may sense a restraint when we are about to err. During that same study, we may also sense his peace as a green light to continue when we are headed down the right path.

We can improve the purity in our lives by growing in sensitivity to the Spirit's presence. We can die to self by choosing to align ourselves with God's will. As we submit to him, he can help us filter out the sinful things that we otherwise might not be able to detect without his help.   —V. E.

B. Regarding Righteousness (v. 10)

10. ". . . about righteousness, because I am going to the Father, where you can see me no longer;

The second area of the Spirit's reproof is *righteousness*, a word appearing in John's Gospel only here and in verse 8, above. To be righteous in the sense intended here means "being absolutely in the right." Failure to be righteous will mean condemnation as guilty sinners when the time comes to stand before the eternal judge.

The unbelievers of both Jesus' day and ours prefer to define righteousness on their own terms; this often involves comparisons with others, as in Luke 18:11 (see also Romans 10:3; Titus 3:5). But self-defined and world-defined righteousness is condemned in Isaiah 64:6: "All of us have become like one who is unclean, and all our righteous acts are like filthy rags." Even though someone may be "better than the next guy," that kind of righteousness is never good enough.

The solution for always-deficient attempts to be righteous by one's own effort is acceptance of Jesus and his payment of the penalty for our sins at the cross. The Holy Spirit is to continue the work of Jesus in bringing this message to the world after Jesus returns to the Father. Again, the Holy Spirit will accomplish this work through Jesus' followers (Matthew 28:19, 20; John 13:35; 1 John 4:12).

> *What Do You Think?*
> What are some ways you think the Holy Spirit was working through Christians to reach you before you became a Christian?
> *Talking Points for Your Discussion*
> ▪ Through a family member
> ▪ Through a colleague at work or school
> ▪ Other

C. Regarding Judgment (v. 11)

11. ". . . and about judgment, because the prince of this world now stands condemned.

As the world holds false, self-deceiving views about righteousness, so also the world holds false views of judgment—the third area of the Spirit's reproof. The world has falsely judged Jesus to be demon-possessed and insane (John 10:20). The world's false judgments are based on appearances (7:24) and worldly ideals (8:15).

Regarding their own status, many people do not really accept the fact that they will face judgment after death (compare Hebrews 9:27) or if judgment does happen that somehow they will escape the penalty for their sins. The work of the Spirit of truth will be to rid the world of such wishful thinking and to impress on people the truth of inevitable judgment.

The solution for the problem of the world's faulty judgments and faulty views of God's judgment lies in the fact that the devil—*the prince of this world*—is judged and condemned at the cross (John 12:31). "The god of this age" (2 Corinthians 4:4), "the ruler of the kingdom of the air" (Ephesians 2:2) is dethroned by Jesus' crucifixion and glorification. The Holy Spirit will work to convict the world of the fact that evil will not prevail and that all who are on the side of Satan will share his final defeat (Matthew 25:41). Believers in Jesus can take courage in the fact that their accuser is and will be condemned (Revelation 12:10, 11); no one will be able to press a case against us!

> *What Do You Think?*
> What attitudes prevail today that illustrate the need for the Holy Spirit's ministry of reproof?
> *Talking Points for Your Discussion*
> ▪ Modern attitudes toward sin
> ▪ Modern attitudes toward righteousness
> ▪ Modern attitudes toward judgment
> ▪ Other

III. Testimony of the Spirit
(JOHN 16:12-15)
A. About Truth (vv. 12, 13a)

12. "I have much more to say to you, more than you can now bear.

The disciples are no doubt struggling to understand what Jesus has just said. Their minds simply cannot comprehend and embrace so much so quickly. But Jesus has even more that he needs to tell them. So much is about to happen: his arrest and trials, his scourging and crucifixion, his burial and resurrection.

How can they understand the need for all this? How can they bear the anguish of watching these events unfold? And afterward, how can they put it all together into a coherent message to proclaim to the world? Indeed, they are presently incapable of processing all this truth.

13a. "But when he, the Spirit of truth, comes, he will guide you into all the truth. He will not speak on his own; he will speak only what he hears,

There will be help in the near future for the struggling apostles. Jesus has promised the coming of the Advocate, also known as *the Spirit of truth* (John 14:17; 15:26). The Spirit will come to them on the Day of Pentecost (see Acts 2:1-4), during and after which he will guide them *into all the truth*. What the apostles do not now know will be taught to them; what they do not now understand will be made clear. Consequently, a man like Peter, who has so much trouble accepting the plan for Jesus to die (see Matthew 16:22), will stand before thousands and proclaim the gospel. Enemies of the gospel will be startled that he and John, "unschooled, ordinary men" (Acts 4:13), speak with such confidence.

The Holy Spirit, like Jesus himself, will faithfully speak as he has been sent to speak. *He will speak only what he hears* from Jesus (see John 16:14, 15, below) as he teaches the apostles. Everything to be spoken by the Spirit of truth will be truth.

What Do You Think?

What can we do to make ourselves better vessels through whom the Holy Spirit can teach others?

Talking Points for Your Discussion
- Regarding study of God's Word
- Regarding recognition and stewardship of opportunities to be a vessel
- Regarding various priorities
- Other

B. From Jesus (vv. 13b-15)

13b. ". . . and he will tell you what is yet to come.

The Spirit of truth will also reveal to the apostles the truth about what the future holds. This will help them not to be caught off guard when certain events come to pass. As the apostles write various books of the New Testament, they will demonstrate their knowledge of things to come. The truths of future events spoken by the Spirit are thus conveyed to all believers.

❧ *FLATLAND* ❧

A fascinating little book called *Flatland,* by Edwin A. Abbott, takes readers on an amazing mental journey. Written from the viewpoint of a character named Square, who is quite literally a square, the book portrays life in his two-dimensional realm.

Square visits Lineland, a one-dimensional realm, where he attempts to enlighten its inhabitants with facts of two dimensions. But residents of Lineland have no conceptual grid through which to process this information. Square himself is then visited by Sphere from Spaceland, a realm of three dimensions. Sphere attempts to expand Square's view of reality, and this time it is Square who is unable to comprehend!

During Jesus' last days on earth, he laid the groundwork to prepare his followers for what was coming. Nonetheless, he knew that they did not grasp the fullness of the information. Weighed down by the heaviness of his message and their own defective conceptual framework (compare Luke 24:21a; Acts 1:6; etc.), they did not have the proper interpretive grid through which to process the plan God was enacting. Even so, Jesus promised them that he would send the Spirit, who would guide them in the truth.

Like the characters in *Flatland* who were visited by beings from more complex realms, we have received first God's Son and then the Holy Spirit who bring us truth about a greater reality. They introduce us to a new way of living in preparation for eternal life in that greater reality. Will we believe and obey, or will we disbelieve and reject?
—V. E.

HOW TO SAY IT

Immanuel	Ih-*man*-you-el.
Isaiah	Eye-*zay*-uh.
Judas Iscariot	*Joo*-dus Iss-*care*-ee-ut.

14. "He will glorify me because it is from me that he will receive what he will make known to you.

Jesus' earthly ministry glorifies the Father (John 7:18; 14:13; 17:4), and the task of the Holy Spirit will be to put the spotlight on Jesus and to glorify him. It will not be the work of the Holy Spirit to glorify himself. The Spirit will be sent by the authority of Jesus (see John 16:7, above) and will faithfully represent the one who sends him. The Spirit will be given the message from Jesus, and then he will reveal it to the apostles. The teaching of the Holy Spirit will be the Word of Christ.

The humility to be seen in the work of the Holy Spirit is a remarkable thing. Even though the Spirit is part of the triune God, he sees no need to exalt himself. This same humility is seen many times in Jesus as well. Jesus has said that he can do nothing by himself, but only what the Father shows him (see John 5:19). Jesus also has said that he speaks only what the Father has taught him (8:28). Like the Spirit, Jesus does not take credit for doing everything on his own. What a model of humility!

15. "All that belongs to the Father is mine. That is why I said the Spirit will receive from me what he will make known to you."

Jesus speaks of the essential unity of *the Father*, the Son, and *the Spirit*. Everything that belongs to the Father also belongs to the Son (compare John 17:10). All their knowledge and truth are also available to the Spirit. As he is instructed, the Spirit will make this divine knowledge available.

The phrase *will make known to you* must refer primarily to the apostles since the Holy Spirit's role in John 14:26; 15:27 is directed to those who have been with Jesus during his earthly ministry (the apostle Paul being the notable exception). It is in the sacred Scriptures written by such men that divine truth is passed on to each succeeding generation of believers. The Spirit of truth will inspire the writing of the Word of truth.

Conclusion

A. The Pledge of God's Presence

From the beginning, God has taken steps to be present with humanity. In the case of Adam and

Visual for Lesson 3. *Start a discussion by pointing to this visual as you ask, "How will you let the reality of the Spirit's presence cause joy for you this week?"*

Eve, this presence was first a blessing and later a threat. As long as they obeyed God, his presence was a great blessing. When they disobeyed, however, his presence exposed their shame.

God is present with his people. In the desert wilderness, God dwelt in the tabernacle's "Most Holy Place." God was also present when the temple was built in Jerusalem. When Jesus was born, God became present in a different way, a physical way. One of the designations prophesied for Jesus was *Immanuel*: "God with us" (Isaiah 7:14). For those in Palestine who believed in Christ, this physical presence was a wonderful thing. For those who rejected him, it became their condemnation.

Today God is yet present in his world. The presence of God is expressed through his Spirit. The presence of the Spirit is a threat to those who resist the Spirit's threefold reproof regarding sin, righteousness, and judgment. But for those who embrace the promises of Jesus, the indwelling Spirit is a source of comfort, strength, and truth. And so it shall be until Christ returns.

B. Prayer

Father, thank you for sending the Spirit! Help us to accept his reproof and to learn his truth. May our lives show that we are gratefully aware of his presence. In the name of Jesus, amen.

C. Thought to Remember

The Spirit of truth still guides God's people.

INVOLVEMENT LEARNING

Enhance your lesson with NIV® Bible Student (from your curriculum supplier) and the reproducible activity page (at www.standardlesson.com or in the back of the NIV® Standard Lesson Commentary Deluxe Edition).

Into the Lesson

Before learners arrive, write these references on the board: Exodus 13:21; 1 Kings 8:10, 11; Ezekiel 43:7; Matthew 1:23. After learners are settled, say, "We started last week's lesson by looking at some passages that showed us God's promise not to forsake his people and the ultimate fulfillment of that promise. Let's continue in that vein."

Ask for volunteers to read aloud the passages referred to on the board, then discuss the fact that there is a long history behind God's promise not to abandon his people. Make a transition by saying, "Last week we learned of Jesus' promise of the Holy Spirit's presence. Today we'll examine the role of the Spirit in a bit more detail."

Into the Word

Prepare in advance seven sentence strips with the following phrases in very large lettering, one phrase per strip: *Reproves the world with regard to sin. / Reproves the world with regard to righteousness. / Reproves the world with regard to judgment. / Guides into all truth. / Gives his own instruction. / Confirms past rather than future events. / Glorifies himself.* Draw two columns on the board, one headed *True* and the other headed *False.* Mix the sentence strips so the true and false statements are not grouped together (in the order above, the first four are true, the last three are false). Say, "I'm going to show you a phrase concerning the Holy Spirit. Identify each one as true or false."

Proceed to hold up each strip and read it aloud. When learners indicate their answer, affix it to the board under the corresponding heading. Do not discuss at this time. If learners are unsure, place the strip to straddle the two columns.

When all strips are placed, say, "Now let's check our responses with the lesson text." Ask two volunteers to alternate reading the verses of the text aloud. Pause after every two or so verses to check the class responses to the statements. Correct the

placement of any strips. Continue in this manner until all of the lesson text has been read; then have learners work together as a class or in small groups to make the three false statements true. (Corrections: speaks what he hears from Jesus instead of "gives his own instruction," v. 13a; tells what is yet to come, not "confirms past rather than future events," v. 13b; brings glory to Jesus rather than "glorifies himself," v. 14.)

Pose these questions for discussion: 1. Generally speaking, why was and is the coming of the Holy Spirit important for believers? *(The Spirit would take the apostles and all Christians to the next level of spiritual maturity.)* 2. What was the significance of the apostles' receiving truth from the Spirit? *(What they did not previously know the Spirit was to teach to them and, through the apostles, us.)*

Alternative: Instead of the discussion questions, distribute copies of the "Work of the Spirit" activity from the reproducible page, which you can download. Have learners work on this in small groups; discuss results as a class.

Into Life

Say, "We've touched on three areas of the Holy Spirit's responsibility: reproving the world with regard to sin, righteousness, and judgment. Let's spend the rest of our time looking at those three areas." Divide learners into three groups; give each group one of the following collections of Scripture references on handouts: *Sin*—Romans 2:12; 3:23; 6:23; 1 Corinthians 15:56; James 1:15. *Righteousness*—Romans 5:19; 8:10; 2 Corinthians 5:21; Galatians 3:6; 1 John 2:1. *Judgment*—Acts 17:31; Romans 2:5, 16; 1 Peter 4:5; Hebrews 10:31. Have groups discuss the significance of their assigned passages with regard to daily living. Allow time for whole-class sharing of implications.

Option: Distribute copies of the "Bible Reading Plan" activity from the reproducible page as learners depart.

THE SPIRIT
OF PEACE

DEVOTIONAL READING: Romans 14:13-19
BACKGROUND SCRIPTURE: John 20:19-23; Acts 1:4-8; 2:1-4

JOHN 20:19-23

¹⁹ On the evening of that first day of the week, when the disciples were together, with the doors locked for fear of the Jewish leaders, Jesus came and stood among them and said, "Peace be with you!" ²⁰ After he said this, he showed them his hands and side. The disciples were overjoyed when they saw the Lord.

²¹ Again Jesus said, "Peace be with you! As the Father has sent me, I am sending you." ²² And with that he breathed on them and said, "Receive the Holy Spirit. ²³ If you forgive anyone's sins, their sins are forgiven; if you do not forgive them, they are not forgiven."

KEY VERSE

With that he breathed on them and said, "Receive the Holy Spirit." —**John 20:22**

THE SPIRIT COMES

Unit 1: The Pledge of God's Presence

LESSONS 1–5

LESSON AIMS

After participating in this lesson, each learner will be able to:

1. Retell what happened when the resurrected Jesus first stood among his disciples in Jerusalem.

2. Explain the connection between the resurrection and the apostles' commission to effect the forgiveness of sins.

3. Affirm the ministry to which he or she has been sent by the risen Christ.

LESSON OUTLINE

Introduction

A. Commemorative Items

Type the phrase "commemorative items" into an Internet search engine and the resulting hits will number in the millions! Clearly, the business of commemorating people, places, events, achievements, etc., is huge. Products available for purchase range from mass-produced items that are intended to address the collective consciousness of a nation (first moon landing, etc.) down to single-copy, personalized tokens intended for just one recipient (job promotion, etc.).

Were we to count the number of commemorative items in our homes right now, we would probably be surprised that we have so many. Over the years we may find ourselves tossing out various items of this nature; some achievements or transitions that we once thought to be important to mark end up being seen as relatively minor in the broader contexts of our lives.

And then there are the commemorative items that we might prefer never to have received in the first place: those physical and emotional scars that remind us of past trauma of some sort. Even so, the existence of such scars is evidence of victory over (or at least survival of) the trauma.

Today's passage notes two "commemorative items" that served as proof of Jesus' own victory over adversity. The first were the physical wounds he had received during the crucifixion; these bore witness both to God's power and Jesus' authority. The second was and is the disciples themselves—from the first generation of disciples to believers today. The fact that believers in every generation continue to proclaim him serves a powerful confirmation of his victory over the grave. Jesus' defeat of death lives on in the witness of those who accept the facts of history.

B. Lesson Background

Today's brief passage brings the Gospel of John full circle in many respects. The writer prefaces his account of Jesus' ministry with an episode involving John the Baptist. When a delegation from the religious authorities in Jerusalem questioned him about his identity, he explained that he was simply preparing the way for someone much more worthy than himself (John 1:19-27).

The next day, John the Baptist told two of his disciples that Jesus was the one they had been waiting for. He predicted that Jesus would baptize people not with water but with the Holy Spirit (John 1:29-34, lesson 1). Jesus himself affirmed this promise of Holy Spirit—bestowal when he invited those present at the Festival of Tabernacles to "come to me and drink," promising that "rivers of living water" would "flow from within them" (John 7:37, 38); the Gospel writer then immediately explains that Jesus was referring to the forthcoming gift of the Holy Spirit, who would be granted only after Jesus had been glorified.

The night before the crucifixion, Jesus repeated several times the promise of the granting of the Holy Spirit. Jesus told his disciples of his pending departure (John 14:2-4, 19, 25, 28; 16:5-7, 16, 28), while assuring them that he would send the Advocate, the Spirit of truth, to be with them (14:16-18, lesson 2; 15:26, 27; 16:7-14, lesson 3).

The disciples were confused by such statements (John 14:5; 16:17, 18), not least because it seemed impossible that God's Messiah could be killed. Their expectation was challenged dramatically by the events of Jesus' arrest, trials, torture, and crucifixion. Whatever they had expected the Messiah to be, none of it seemed reconcilable with the horrific fact of Jesus' death. That experience seemed to dash any hope that the promises of John the Baptist and Jesus would be fulfilled. If those two could not avoid death at the hands of earthly authorities, then how could anyone believe their statements about a baptism with the Spirit, the sending of the Spirit of truth, etc.?

Of course, the cross was not the end of the story, and our passage today shows the beginning of the fulfillment of John the Baptist's prophecy and Jesus' promises regarding the Holy Spirit. The

HOW TO SAY IT

Emmaus	Em-*may*-us.
Gethsemane	Geth-*sem*-uh-nee (*G* as in *get*).
Magdalene	*Mag*-duh-leen or Mag-duh-*lee*-nee.
Sanhedrin	*San*-huh-drun or San-*heed*-run.

episode described in John 20:19-23 is recorded in a different form in Luke 24:36-43, which sheds helpful light as we consider the significance of the momentous occasion that was at hand.

I. Peace and Joy
(JOHN 20:19-21a)
A. Comforting Greeting (v. 19)

19a. On the evening of that first day of the week, when the disciples were together, with the doors locked for fear of the Jewish leaders, Jesus came and stood among them

Our passage opens on a scene of confusion and turmoil for the disciples. *On the evening of that first day of the week* refers to the Sunday following Jesus' crucifixion and death (John 20:1). That morning Mary Magdalene and several other women (Mark 16:1) had discovered Jesus' tomb to be empty (John 20:2). Mary had rushed to report this to two of Jesus' disciples, who ran to the tomb to see for themselves (20:3-10). Mary had remained near the tomb after those two departed, and the risen Jesus had appeared to her. She quickly reported this incident to the disciples (20:11-18).

Additional testimony had been provided by two disciples who encountered on that same day a mysterious figure while they walked on the road from Jerusalem to the village of Emmaus. Eventually learning that they had encountered Jesus himself, these two, like Mary, immediately went to the house where the apostles were gathered in order to report their experience (Luke 24:13-35). Clearly, this first Sunday after Jesus' death is filled with astonishing reports and puzzling questions.

Any hope the disciples may reap from these strange reports, however, is tempered by their ongoing *fear of the Jewish leaders*. When Jesus was arrested in the garden of Gethsemane, he had successfully negotiated the disciples' freedom in exchange for his own cooperation (John 18:1-12). In a scuffle, however, Peter had attacked one of the high priest's servants with a sword. This incident did nothing to detract from the possibility that the authorities could view Jesus' followers as rebels or terrorists. Thus the perceived need to hide to avoid arrest.

The Gospel writer draws attention to this seclusion to highlight the remarkable nature of what now happens: although the doors are closed, Jesus suddenly appears in the room where his bewildered followers are huddled.

What Do You Think?

What fears lead Christians to hide allegiance to Christ today? How do we correct this problem?

Talking Points for Your Discussion

- At work or school
- At home
- In the public square
- Other

19b. . . . and said, "Peace be with you!"

On one level, Jesus' greeting simply addresses the disciples' frazzled nerves. Having witnessed Jesus' gruesome death a few days previously and now seeing their crucified master standing before them, it's not hard to imagine their state of mind! Luke 24:37 describes it as being one of fear as they assume that they are seeing "a ghost." Narrowly speaking, then, *Peace be with you* seems to be Jesus' attempt to put the disciples at ease (compare Luke 24:36-38).

Similar greetings are used by angels as they appear unexpectedly (as Jesus does here) to startled onlookers. Angels may preface their message with a reassurance, probably because their appearance is terrifying (Daniel 10:12; Mark 16:5, 6; Luke 1:13, 30). In John's account of the resurrection, Jesus' statement *Peace be with you* also sets an important theme for the remainder of the discussion: Jesus is fulfilling his promise that believers will have peace after his death and return to the Father (John 14:27; 16:33).

What Do You Think?

What are some ways to be an instrument in bringing the peace of Christ to various people?

Talking Points for Your Discussion

- To fellow believers
- To unbelieving relatives
- To unbelieving coworkers
- Other

B. Compelling Evidence (v. 20)

20. After he said this, he showed them his hands and side. The disciples were overjoyed when they saw the Lord.

At first glance, one might wonder how a close look at Jesus' gruesome death wounds can alleviate the disciples' fears. Details in Luke's account add clarity: when Jesus appears, the disciples think they are seeing a disembodied spirit. So Jesus shows them the distinctive marks from the crucifixion to prove that it is really him in the flesh. He also proceeds to eat as further proof that he is risen bodily from the dead (Luke 24:36-43).

These details establish that the resurrected Jesus is not an apparition or a collective hallucination but is the same person who recently had been tortured, crucified, and buried. The Jesus who appears on the first Easter is the same who had died on the first Good Friday, proof positive that death is conquered.

John's account of this encounter is more concise than Luke's, but adds a significant detail: Jesus shows the disciples not only *his hands*, which bear the marks of the crucifixion nails, but also his *side* (see also John 20:25, 27). John alone among the writers of the four Gospels mentions that the soldiers pierced Jesus' lifeless body with a spear as he hung on the cross; they did this to ensure that he was dead (19:31-34).

Confronted with such unique and overwhelming physical evidence, the disciples' fear quickly turns to joy as they realize that their master is indeed alive. This fulfills Jesus' prediction of John 16:20, 22.

C. Confirming Statement (v. 21a)

21a. Again Jesus said, "Peace be with you!

Having convinced the disciples of his identity, Jesus again extends his peace to them. The repetition of this phrase is important. As noted above, Jesus had promised the disciples just before his death that they would receive a special peace that could not be shaken even in the face of the world's persecutions and hatred (John 16:33). Jesus' double exhortation *Peace be with you* thus serves as a fitting introduction for the events that immediately follow.

❧ LIFTING OUR GAZE ❧

As I write this, the headlines scream of North Korea's nuclear tests, a child killed in a shooting, and a flu outbreak that could reach epidemic proportions—and it's not even a big news day! Fear seems to be everywhere. We fear losing jobs, houses, and relationships. We worry about the cost of gas, of food, and of health care. We are afraid to speak our beliefs. The list goes on and on.

The world was not a kinder, gentler place in Jesus' day. There was grinding poverty and low life expectancy. There was slavery. There was injustice in government. Jesus' disciples suffered a brutal blow to their expectations when he was killed (Luke 24:21a). But Jesus shocked his followers by presenting himself alive. His return demonstrated a victory different from what they had expected. And he returned with a message: *Peace.*

The message is the same for us today. Sure, we can read the headlines and acknowledge economic distress, crime, and injustice. But there is an unseen, higher reality: the peace of Jesus. But we will miss it unless we lift our gaze off of our fallen world and onto him.   —V. E.

II. Peace and Mission
(JOHN 20:21b-23)
A. Task Stated (v. 21b)

21b. "As the Father has sent me, I am sending you."

In this Gospel, Jesus regularly refers to himself as the one whom the Father has sent into the world to share the good news (John 5:23, 36, 37; 6:44,

57; 8:16, 18, 42; 10:36; 12:29; 14:24; 17:21, 25). This theme is intensified by Jesus' frequent references to himself as "the Son"—one who bears the king's full authority because he, the Son, is heir to the throne. As God's unique Son who has been sent to represent the Father, Jesus possesses unique powers and privileges. These include the ability to reveal God, to pass judgment on those who reject his Word, and to grant eternal life to those who accept him (examples: John 5:19-29; 17:2, 3).

The Father has sent the Son, but soon the Son must return to the Father (John 13:1; 14:12, 28; 16:10, 17, 28). Who, then, will carry God's message after Jesus' departure from the world? The last phrase in the verse before us provides the answer: as the Father had sent Jesus into the world to proclaim his message, Jesus now sends his disciples into the world to continue that proclamation.

Although the disciples have not anticipated that Jesus' story would play out the way it has and will, he has already begun to prepare them for their own role in God's plan. Jesus initiated this preparation long before his crucifixion and continued it right up to the night of his arrest. After washing the disciples' feet in the upper room, he had urged those men to exhibit the same spirit of sacrificial love. He then had told them that anyone who receives their teaching and example will be accepting the words of Christ himself (John 13:12-20).

Later that same evening, Jesus had informed the disciples that they would be working alongside the Spirit to testify on Jesus' behalf. Since much of Christ's teaching concerns his identity, the disciples will be extending that same message (John 15:26, 27). Jesus, in his magnificent prayer for his disciples just before his arrest, had asked the Father to grant his followers strength and courage to fulfill their mission in the face of the world's hostility.

As the Father has sent Jesus into the hostile world, so now Jesus is sending the disciples (John 17:16-18). As Jesus has been sent into the world as God's ambassador, Jesus in turn sends forth the disciples as his ambassadors. The Father has empowered the Son's ministry in a unique way, and Jesus will grant the Spirit to the disciples to empower their ongoing witness (lessons 2 and 3).

What Do You Think?

When you sense that Jesus is sending you, how do you evaluate the validity of that impression?

Talking Points for Your Discussion

- Role of Scripture
- Role of counsel of other Christians
- Role of your life situation
- Other

❧ HEARING AND PROCLAIMING RIGHTLY ❧

The website kissthisguy.com is an archive that chronicles misunderstood lyrics from popular songs. Sometimes the misunderstanding is quite comical!

God sent Jesus to earth to proclaim the saving message of the gospel. In turn, Jesus now sends us into the world with that same message. But proclaiming that message rightly requires first that we hear it rightly. If we think it is our duty to convince others to "clean up their act"—as if proper behavior will put a person in a right standing before God—then we have misheard the gospel. If we believe we have to convince our neighbors of the proper way to vote, then we have misunderstood Jesus. If we proclaim a "health and wealth" gospel, then we have badly misinterpreted the New Testament.

Surely it is a weighty task to make certain that we proclaim the gospel message correctly! Who are we, sinful as we are, to carry on such a work? How can we complete such an important task? We can do it through the power of the Holy Spirit. What God calls us to do, he enables us to accomplish. —V. E.

B. Spirit Bestowed (v. 22)

22. And with that he breathed on them and said, "Receive the Holy Spirit.

After signaling the disciples' work to come, Jesus proceeds to breathe on them for the purpose of conveying *the Holy Spirit*. But wait—isn't the Holy Spirit bestowed on the Day of Pentecost, when all of the disciples "were filled with the Holy Spirit and began to speak in other tongues" (Acts 2:4)?

There are several theories that attempt to harmonize these two records. One proposal is that the first granting of the Spirit here in John 20:22 is a "sprinkling" while the second granting of the Spirit in Acts 2 is a "saturation."

Another theory is that John's account refers to what is sometimes called the indwelling of the Spirit—the constant experiences of comfort, conscience, and strength for service that Christians experience through the Spirit's continual and empowering presence. Acts 2:1-4, for its part, is said to refer to a rare situation in which the Spirit comes upon the disciples in a way that he sometimes came upon certain people in the Old Testament to grant special power or ability needed to meet the needs of a specific situation (examples: Judges 3:10; 6:34; 1 Samuel 10:10). The rarity of this kind of empowerment by the Holy Spirit, even in the first century AD, is said to be supported by Acts 11:15, where Peter describes the Spirit's actions of Acts 10:44-47.

These are just two possible answers among several proposals! What is crucial to recognize is that Jesus does not give his disciples their mission without also providing them the power to succeed. Genesis 2:7 tells us that God formed Adam's body from the dust and then "breathed into his nostrils the breath of life." The first chapter of John's Gospel picks up this theme by portraying Jesus as the creative Word of God, who brought everything, including human beings, into existence at the Father's command (John 1:1-4). John goes on to portray Jesus as the one who gives eternal life to those who believe in him (3:16; 5:21-26), and here in John 20 Jesus provides a new empowerment for the kind of life the disciples are to live. As the Father had worked through Christ to give physical life to Adam, Christ now works through the Spirit to empower his followers.

C. Authority Granted (v. 23)

23. "If you forgive anyone's sins, their sins are forgiven; if you do not forgive them, they are not forgiven."

Some are troubled by this verse, but we should remember that Jesus is speaking to his chosen apostles. They will become his personal representatives in this world. As Jesus came to deal with the problem of sin, the apostles will also continue this ministry of liberation. As the apostles share the message of the gospel, they can, under Christ's authority, assure those who accept the gospel message that they are forgiven. The apostles are to announce the forgiveness that God offers. When people hear the gospel, they either accept it or reject it. Accepting the gospel means forgiveness of sin; rejecting the gospel means the opposite.

Some students see here an extended application to church leaders beyond those of the first-century apostles. As the church grows, it will become necessary for her members to maintain a doctrine and lifestyle in line with Jesus' message; this verse is thought to confirm the fact that Christ will work with the human leadership of the church as long as they operate in harmony with his own mission and under the guidance of the Spirit. Sometimes it will be necessary to expel an errant member to protect the church's purity and bring that individual to repentance. In such cases, Christ, through the Holy Spirit, will affirm the prayerful decision of the majority.

If this teaching seems unusual to us in view of our experience in the church today, we should recall that it is consistent with what Jesus teaches the disciples before his death (see Matthew 18:15-20; compare v. 18 there with John 20:23; compare also 1 Corinthians 5 and 2 Corinthians 2:5-11). The Spirit thus not only empowers the proclamation of Christ's message but also provides wisdom for ensuring that the church remains pure.

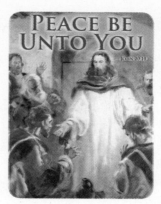

Visual for
Lesson 4

Point to this visual as you introduce the discussion question that is associated with verse 21a.

ultimate testimony to Christ's authority is seen in the reversal of the judgments of Rome and the Jewish Sanhedrin in Jesus' resurrection from the dead. That's power!

In certain ways, Christ's relationship with the Father is a pattern for our own role as ambassadors for Christ. Like Jesus, we are not citizens of this world; we belong to another kingdom. Like Jesus, we are sent to act as God's spokespersons. Also like Jesus, we can expect to be rejected and ridiculed. Christ guides our witness through the Holy Spirit. The Spirit of truth is our peace and power as we fulfill our mission.

What Do You Think?
In what other ways does being an ambassador for Christ compare and contrast with being an ambassador of a nation?
Talking Points for Your Discussion
- Points of similarity
- Points of difference

Conclusion

A. Ambassadors for God

An ambassador is someone designated to represent officially the positions of a nation. By definition, an ambassador's authority is derivative: ambassadors speak on behalf of those who send them. Jesus, as God's Son, bore this type of authority. He had been sent by God to speak on the Father's behalf. As such, the Son's words were God's Word, carrying eternal consequences.

Jesus' divine power underlines this point; he could do things that others simply could not. The

B. Prayer

Father, how often we look only to our own strength! Please help us to walk confidently in the knowledge that your Spirit provides everything we need to fulfill our calling as Christians. In Jesus' name, amen.

C. Thought to Remember
God's Spirit enables.

INVOLVEMENT LEARNING

Enhance your lesson with NIV® Bible Student (from your curriculum supplier) and the reproducible activity page (at www.standardlesson.com or in the back of the NIV® Standard Lesson Commentary Deluxe Edition).

Into the Lesson

Begin by showing learners a picture of a scar that is presentable (that is, not in some way offensive). Discuss briefly the nature of the scar. Say, "We all have scars that remind us of trauma we've undergone. Many scars are visible, some are not. Every scar we bear—physical or emotional—is a mark of survival. In today's lesson we will discuss two marks of survival associated with Jesus."

Option: Before class, place in chairs copies of the "Seeing the Lord" word-search activity from the reproducible page, which you can download. Learners can begin working on this as they arrive.

Into the Word

Distribute randomly the following statements on sentence strips, one statement per strip (but without enumeration): 1. On Sunday night, the disciples were together, hiding from the Jewish authorities. 2. Jesus came and stood among the disciples and said, "Peace be with you." 3. After he spoke to the disciples, Jesus showed them his hands and side. 4. The disciples were overjoyed when they saw Jesus. 5. Jesus said to them again, "Peace be with you! As the Father has sent me, I am sending you." 6. Then Jesus breathed on them and gave them the Holy Spirit. 7. Jesus said to them, "If you forgive anyone's sins, their sins are forgiven; if you do not forgive them, they are not forgiven."

Ask those who have strips to stand and read them. After the first person reads, affix his or her strip to the middle of the board. After each subsequent strip is read, ask the class where it should be placed on the board relative to the previous strips in terms of chronology (keep Bibles closed). After all strips are read, ask a volunteer to read today's lesson text aloud, pausing occasionally to allow classmates to correct misplacements of the strips.

Then say, "We can look at a parallel passage to help us gain a fuller understanding of today's text."

Have learners turn to Luke 24:36-49, then pose these questions for discussion: 1. In John 20:20, why would Jesus offer to show the disciples his hands and side (compare Luke 24:38-43)? 2. In verse 21, what is the significance of Jesus' words to the disciples (compare Luke 24:44-47)? 3. In verse 22, what is significant about the bestowal of the Spirit as Jesus breathes on the disciples (compare and contrast with Luke 24:48, 49)? 4. In verse 23, what is the significance of Jesus' words to the disciples about forgiveness of sin? 5. Looking back at how the text opens in verse 19, how does Jesus' bestowal of peace set the tone for the episode as a whole (compare Luke 24:36)? Use the commentary to clarify.

Into Life

Say, "It was easy for the disciples to identify Jesus' physical 'commemorative marks' once he pointed them out; those were the scars on his hands, feet, and side. It may not be as easy to identify the 'commemorative marks' that were not on his body. Can you think of what those might be?"

Allow learners time to process the question and offer suggestions. If no one identifies *the disciples* as those marks, lead them to that realization. Say, "The actions and testimonies of the disciples were to point people to the living Jesus, and those actions and testimonies have done so for centuries. Therefore we also are commemorative marks of Jesus' resurrection."

Invite learners to share specific examples of how they have "made a mark" for Jesus in their community; then lead a discussion of the marks your congregation has made and is making for Christ in the community. Brainstorm other ways your class and/or the church can further do so. End with a prayer of dedication in that regard. *Option:* To enhance your learners' service, distribute copies of the "Where Can I Serve?" activity from the reproducible page as they depart.

THE SON OF DAVID

DEVOTIONAL READING: Isaiah 45:20-25
BACKGROUND SCRIPTURE: Mark 11:1-11

MARK 11:1-11

¹ As they approached Jerusalem and came to Bethphage and Bethany at the Mount of Olives, Jesus sent two of his disciples, ² saying to them, "Go to the village ahead of you, and just as you enter it, you will find a colt tied there, which no one has ever ridden. Untie it and bring it here. ³ If anyone asks you, 'Why are you doing this?' say, 'The Lord needs it and will send it back here shortly.'"

⁴ They went and found a colt outside in the street, tied at a doorway. As they untied it, ⁵ some people standing there asked, "What are you doing, untying that colt?" ⁶ They answered as Jesus had told them to, and the people let them go. ⁷ When they brought the colt to Jesus and threw their cloaks over it, he sat on it. ⁸ Many people spread their cloaks on the road, while others spread branches they had cut in the fields. ⁹ Those who went ahead and those who followed shouted,

"Hosanna!"

"Blessed is he who comes in the name of the Lord!"

¹⁰ "Blessed is the coming kingdom of our father David!"

"Hosanna in the highest heaven!"

¹¹ Jesus entered Jerusalem and went into the temple courts. He looked around at everything, but since it was already late, he went out to Bethany with the Twelve.

Ωσαννα
אושענא
Hosanna!
Hosanna!
Hosanna!
Hosanna!
אושענא
Ωσαννα

KEY VERSE

Those who went ahead and those who followed shouted, "Hosanna!" "Blessed is he who comes in the name of the Lord!" —**Mark 11:9**

THE SPIRIT COMES

Unit 1: The Pledge of God's Presence

LESSONS 1–5

LESSON AIMS

After participating in this lesson, each learner will be able to:

1. Identify elements of the triumphal entry that emphasize Jesus' royal authority and servant humility.

2. Explain how the triumphal entry confirms Jesus' identity as the Messiah.

3. Make or reaffirm a commitment to serving Jesus, the Messiah.

LESSON OUTLINE

Introduction

A. Christmas and Palm Sunday

Christmas reminds us that God does big things in small ways, and that his kingdom extends to everyone—even to (or especially to) those in the most humble circumstances. The same point is made, in a different way, by the story of Jesus' triumphal entry into Jerusalem a few days before his death. The point concerns the nature of the kingdom that Jesus came to establish.

At first glance, the triumphal entry might seem to have been something of a political high point for Jesus, a rare moment when he could revel in the honor and glory rightfully due him. Crowds lined the road, shouted praise, and waved palm branches as he rode into Jerusalem to the acclaim. All this would seem to be a long way from the manger of Bethlehem!

But there are two sides to the story, a fact that makes Palm Sunday one of the most symbolically significant occasions on the Christian calendar. While Jesus offered a glimpse here of his kingly identity, he also made very clear that God's kingdom is not like Caesar's kingdom. In this respect, Jesus' journey to Jerusalem became a fitting introduction to his death on a cross that was soon to follow.

B. Lesson Background

The significance of Jesus' triumphal entry is stressed by the fact that this is one of the few events from his life to be recorded in all four Gospels. Each evangelist reports Jesus' coming to Jerusalem to celebrate Passover a week before his death, and each says that his arrival was marked by popular acclaim.

The triumphal entry was indeed a high point in Jesus' public ministry. Up to that point in Mark's account, Jesus had spent his time moving from village to village in areas north of Judea, ministering primarily in Galilee with occasional forays into Gentile territories. He focused his ministry primarily on rural peasants who lived in and around the villages across Galilee.

Mark 10:1 reveals a transition as Jesus moved from Capernaum in Galilee (9:30, 33) into Perea, the area east of the Jordan River. Jesus was taking his message to Jerusalem (10:32), the center of Jewish faith and the seat of the powerful high priests, who controlled the temple and managed the Jewish population in collaboration with the Romans. Christ's subsequent movement westward from Perea into Judea found him accompanied by a large number of pilgrims who were headed to Jerusalem for the Passover observance.

Having seen Jesus' miracles and having heard his teachings about the coming kingdom of God, many who came to Jerusalem for the festival must have expected him to do something big. Perhaps he would finally declare war on the Romans or demand that the corrupt priests resign from office. Jesus, however, had a very different kind of kingdom in mind, and he had already stressed to his closest followers that he was going to Jerusalem not to conquer but to die (Mark 8:31; 9:31).

Mark's story line by itself can give the impression that the Jewish and Roman leadership in Jerusalem had had little prior exposure to Jesus. But the Gospel of John provides a fuller picture that is helpful for understanding the events of the final week of Jesus' life.

In John's account, Jesus immediately headed to Jerusalem after calling his first disciples. There he criticized the temple leadership for operating a marketplace (John 2:13-17). Jesus left Judea and returned to Galilee (4:3), but over the years made several trips back to Jerusalem to attend major religious festivals. In so doing, he provoked the Pharisees and priests by healing people on the Sabbath (5:1-16; 9:1-16) and by explicitly challenging their teachings and authority.

Tensions mounted to a point where it was not safe for Jesus to be in the city (John 10:30-40). The priests reached the end of their rope when Jesus came to Bethany (just outside Jerusalem) and raised Lazarus from the dead. After this remarkable event, the Sanhedrin (the Jewish high council) decided that if Jesus were not stopped, the masses would flock to him, leading to outright rebellion against Rome and themselves (11:45-57).

Viewed against this backdrop, John makes clear what Mark assumes: when Jesus entered Jerusalem for the final time, to the applause of a massive Passover crowd, a great many people thought that he was coming as a king to claim his rightful throne.

I. The King Prepares
(MARK 11:1-6)
A. Instructions Given (vv. 1-3)

1. As they approached Jerusalem and came to Bethphage and Bethany at the Mount of Olives, Jesus sent two of his disciples,

While Mark draws little attention to the staging area for Jesus' entry into Jerusalem, the places he mentions signal the importance of what is about to happen. *Bethany*, a village about two miles east of Jerusalem, is the home of Lazarus and the site of the resurrection miracle that had led the Jewish authorities to plot Jesus' arrest (John 12:1; see the Lesson Background). Jesus probably goes back and forth between Bethany and Jerusalem each day during the final week of his life (Mark 11:11, 12, 19), perhaps to lodge in Lazarus's home nightly.

The village of *Bethphage* is less well known, probably very near Bethany. Of greater significance is *the Mount of Olives*. Named after the ancient olive groves that occupy the fertile hillside, it is just east of Jerusalem, across the Kidron Valley. The fact that this hill is some 200 feet higher than Jerusalem gives it a commanding view of the temple complex. Five centuries before Jesus' birth, a prophet had predicted that the Lord would one day appear on the Mount of Olives to drive invading armies out of Jerusalem (Zechariah 14:1-9).

HOW TO SAY IT

Bethany	*Beth*-uh-nee.
Bethphage	*Beth*-fuh-gee.
Capernaum	Kuh-*per*-nay-um.
Galilee	*Gal*-uh-lee.
Judea	Joo-*dee*-uh.
Kidron	*Kid*-ron.
Maccabees	*Mack*-uh-bees.
Odysseus	Oh-*dih*-see-us or Oh-*dih*-shus.
Perea	Peh-*ree*-uh.
Pharisees	*Fair*-ih-seez.
Sanhedrin	*San*-huh-drun or San-*heed*-run.

This prediction caused many Jews by Jesus' day to believe that the Messiah would one day muster troops on this hill to lead God's people in a revolt against Rome. This would purify the temple of foreign influences and reestablish Jerusalem as the capital of God's kingdom as in the days of King David. Considering this larger context, Jesus' followers must sense that something big is in the works for this particular Passover observance.

2. . . . saying to them, "Go to the village ahead of you, and just as you enter it, you will find a colt tied there, which no one has ever ridden. Untie it and bring it here.

We normally think of *a colt* as a young horse, but the animal's parentage noted in Matthew 21:5 clarifies that this is a donkey (see also John 12:14). Matthew reminds us of the prophecy that the Messiah would enter Jerusalem riding such an animal (Matthew 21:4, 5; Zechariah 9:9). That prediction surely must be in Jesus' mind as well: this is the only instance in the four Gospels where Jesus rides an animal anywhere, a fact suggesting that he is about to do so now in order to draw attention to this prophecy.

Jesus' instruction that the colt will not have been ridden by anyone is an important detail. One doesn't just get on an animal that has never been mounted and calmly ride into town! But the fact that Jesus will be able to do so will indicate his power and authority as the one who created donkeys and everything else. The one who can command the forces of nature (Mark 4:39) and raise the dead (John 11:38-44) also has the ability to control the potential reactions of a beast of burden that is not accustomed to having a rider.

3. "If anyone asks you, 'Why are you doing this?' say, 'The Lord needs it and will send it back here shortly.'"

Jesus' knowledge of what is about to unfold has been explained in two ways. Some suggest that Jesus' use of the donkey has been prearranged by him. Others propose that Jesus' prophetic awareness of the situation is indicated: Jesus has divine foreknowledge that the colt will be tied to a post in a certain village, that bystanders will question what the disciples are doing, that his authority will be recognized, etc. In either case, a willingness to

part with an expensive animal without objection will be an act of submission to Jesus.

B. Instructions Followed (vv. 4-6)

4. They went and found a colt outside in the street, tied at a doorway. As they untied it,

The disciples proceed to do as Jesus commands. As a result, they find the animal in plain sight, ready to be used.

> **What Do You Think?**
> When have you obeyed a trusted person without knowing the bigger picture first? What did you learn from this experience?
>
> *Talking Points for Your Discussion*
> - Instructions from a friend
> - Instructions from a subject-matter expert
> - Instructions from a spouse
> - Other

5, 6. . . . some people standing there asked, "What are you doing, untying that colt?" They answered as Jesus had told them to, and the people let them go.

The scenario unfolds just as Jesus has said it would. The disciples' action in untying the animal can give the impression that they are stealing it, thus the challenge of the bystanders (*some people*) is understandable. But challenges cease immediately at the response, "The Lord needs it" (v. 3).

❧ THE LORD NEEDS . . . WHAT? ❧

I had a newspaper route when I was about 10 years old, and I made about $1.50 per week. The kids on my block played softball virtually every day all summer, so I spent $7.20 of my hard-earned money to buy a baseball glove.

One afternoon my brother showed up while we were playing baseball in a neighbor's backyard. He was 10 years older than I was, obviously much bigger. He didn't have a baseball glove, so he demanded mine. I refused, but he took it anyway and went off to play with some of his friends. I was furious, but I could do nothing.

We usually have to give in when those with more power (muscles, guns, etc.) make demands. When Jesus sent disciples after the colt, they didn't make demands. When bystanders asked why they were taking the colt, they simply replied, "The Lord needs it." Perhaps those bystanders were also Jesus' followers and accepted his leadership. In any case, it was sufficient for the two disciples merely to state the Lord's need; there was no argument. Do we yield as easily today when the Lord says, "I have need of you"? —J. B. N.

> **What Do You Think?**
> When was a time you resisted making available something that the Lord needed? How did you grow spiritually from this experience?
> *Talking Points for Your Discussion*
> - Regarding your time
> - Regarding your money
> - Regarding a nonmonetary asset

II. The King Arrives
(MARK 11:7-11)
A. Fulfilling a Prophecy (v. 7)

7. When they brought the colt to Jesus and threw their cloaks over it, he sat on it.

As noted above, Matthew 21:4 establishes Jesus' journey into Jerusalem on a colt to be the fulfillment of prophecy. We may wonder why the Messiah is portrayed, both by prophecy and by the Gospels, as riding on a donkey. The donkey is not a particularly prestigious beast! Would not one expect the proper claimant to David's throne, the Lord's Messiah, to appear on a mighty warhorse? Jesus' second coming is portrayed in exactly this way in Revelation 19:11-16.

The explanation for Jesus' actions is found within the ancient prophecy. After predicting that Israel's enemies will be violently overthrown, the prophet says that the conquering Messiah will be different from other rulers: "See, your king comes to you, righteous and victorious, lowly and riding on a donkey, on a colt, the foal of a donkey" (Zechariah 9:9). Viewed in context, the prophecy stresses the humility and compassion of the Lord's Messiah, who is to bring justice and salvation not by force or with terror but in gentle humility. Therefore a donkey fits this picture much more than would a war stallion.

Jesus' choice of transportation is therefore significant on two levels. First, and perhaps most obviously, the donkey shows that Jesus is consciously acting in ways that highlight his fulfillment of the ancient prophecy about the Messiah. Second, and perhaps most significantly, Jesus' actions are in sharp contrast with Roman imperial power (compare Matthew 26:51-54).

The disciples are unwilling to let Jesus ride bareback, which would be undignified. So they use their outer garments to make an impromptu pad upon which the Lord can sit.

B. Praising the Messiah (vv. 8-10)

8a. Many people spread their cloaks on the road,

Many in the crowd express their enthusiasm for Jesus by casting their outer garments on the unpaved roadway on which the donkey will walk. Some students see a connection here with making "the rugged places a plain" (Isaiah 40:4) for the Lord's arrival. Even if that connection is a bit of a stretch, 2 Kings 9:13 offers a precedent for acknowledging a new king in a similar way.

> **What Do You Think?**
> How does being part of a group embolden people to do things they normally would not do? When can this be a good thing? a bad thing?
> *Talking Points for Your Discussion*
> - Peer pressure
> - Moral support
> - Mob mentality
> - Exodus 23:2; 1 Kings 22:13; Ezra 10:1; John 6:14, 15; 18:40; Acts 14:11, 19
> - Other

8b. . . . while others spread branches they had cut in the fields.

This half verse, along with Matthew 21:8 and John 12:13, explains the modern designation of the Sunday before Easter as Palm Sunday. Leviticus 23:40 requires the Israelites to take "branches . . . from palms" and "rejoice before the Lord your God," but that requirement is for the Festival of Tabernacles. That observance is six months distant from Passover, which is in view here. A precedent for using palm branches in contexts other than the Festival of Tabernacles is found in the nonbiblical 1 Maccabees 13:51, where the liberation of Jerusalem from foreign control in 141 BC was celebrated with such branches, among other things. Palm branches are easy to obtain, since date palms are abundant in this area.

Exactly what is the crowd expecting by their enthusiastic display? The next two verses provide the answer.

9. Those who went ahead and those who followed shouted,

"Hosanna!"

"Blessed is he who comes in the name of the Lord!"

The exuberant crowd that accompanies Jesus is shouting, and perhaps singing, praise from Psalm 118. This psalm is part of a collection known as "Egyptian Hallel," which collection is Psalms 113–118. The word *hallel* means "praise," and psalms in this collection are sung by pilgrims traveling to and participating in the Passover observance. The lyrics recall events associated with the exodus, emphasizing the theme of God's deliverance and redemption.

> **What Do You Think?**
> When do you find the energy of a crowd most contagious? Why?
> *Talking Points for Your Discussion*
> - Sporting events
> - Evangelistic crusades
> - Worship events
> - Patriotic observances
> - Other

Hosanna is a Hebrew term, quoted from Psalm 118:25, that means "Save us!" The line *blessed is he who comes in the name of the Lord*, from Psalm 118:26, invokes a blessing on the righteous leader who has defeated Israel's enemies with the help of the Lord (compare Psalm 118:10-16). Overall, Psalm 118 tells the story of a victory parade for a conquering king who has just returned to Jerusalem.

The crowds that recite these lines while accompanying Jesus into the city can scarcely be ignorant of the implications of their song! This conclusion is reinforced by the crowd's words we see next.

10. "Blessed is the coming kingdom of our father David!"

"Hosanna in the highest heaven!"

"He who comes in the name of the Lord" (v. 9) is now identified as the one anticipated to restore the *kingdom of our father David*. That man's reign was a high point in Israel's history, both politically and spiritually. It was an era when unified Israel enjoyed prosperity under a popular king who was famously faithful to God (most of the time). God had promised David that his house, kingdom, and throne would be established forever (2 Samuel 7:16), and nationalistic expectations concerning Jesus are running high in this regard (compare John 6:15). The crowd's acclamations for Jesus can arouse only the deepest concern among the Jewish authorities (John 12:19; compare 7:45-49).

C. Viewing the Temple (v. 11)

11. Jesus entered Jerusalem and went into the temple courts. He looked around at everything, but since it was already late, he went out to Bethany with the Twelve.

Jerusalem, the holy city, is the place where the Messiah is to rule, and the temple is the heart of the city and the focal point of Israel's worship. By concluding the triumphal entry at the temple rather than anywhere else, some commentators see Jesus to be making an important point about the spiritual nature of God's kingdom. That kingdom will not come about at the point of the sword, but with a humble zeal for the purity of God's worship. This humility is climaxed by the cross. And so Jesus' momentous final week has begun.

> **What Do You Think?**
> How is Jesus' kingship and kingdom misunderstood today? What can we do to correct this?
> *Talking Points for Your Discussion*
> - By popular Christian writers
> - By some Christians
> - By unbelievers
> - Other

We had a parade every Memorial Day—the only parade we had all year—in the community where I grew up. It began at the grade school and ended at the Community Center, about a mile away. There was always a color guard in the lead, followed by the high school marching band, fire trucks (we had two), and other entrants. At the Community Center, the color guard fired three volleys from their rifles, an area minister offered a prayer, and some official gave a short speech. The parade had a beginning point and an ending point, where there was always a brief official function.

In the intervening years, every parade I have witnessed has followed this pattern. It probably would seem a bit silly and pointless to have a parade where each element simply disbands as soon as it gets to the end point, with no official function to tie it all together.

The triumphal entry of Jesus looked like a parade. It had a beginning point, it had joyous people along the route that affirmed the central figure in the procession, but . . . where was the official function at the end, the climax of the parade?

There was indeed a climax, but it occurred several weeks later. That climax was the ascension of Jesus to Heaven after his resurrection. That was an official function of divine nature, the event where the one in charge (Jesus) made it clear that what had happened and was happening was not an end but a beginning. See Acts 1:8.   —J. B. N.

Conclusion

A. A Hero's (Un)Welcome

All of us have witnessed at one time or another —in person, on television, etc.—some form of victory parade. The most common seems to be that for members of sports teams, who are paraded through the streets of their city in open cars following a championship season. The heroes deliver speeches before their cheering fans, etc. Scenes of this kind capture to varying degrees the excitement of the Passover crowd that welcomed Jesus into Jerusalem.

Yet in one key respect, Jesus' triumphal entry bears more similarity to the story of Odysseus

Blessed is he that cometh in the name of the Lord! —MARK 11:9

Visual for
Lesson 5

Point to this visual as you ask, "How can we model the enthusiasm of this verse today?"

(also known as Ulysses), a legendary Greek warrior who fought in the Trojan War. After being delayed by many perils in his journey home from the battlefield, Odysseus finally arrived at his estate in the guise of a poor beggar. Everyone there assumed he was dead, and on his return he discovered that several men were courting his wife to gain her hand in marriage. Odysseus' appearance had changed so much that he was recognized only by his old faithful dog.

As a result of all this, Odysseus had to sneak into his own house and fight to reclaim what was rightfully his own. Something similar was true of Jesus. He had come incognito as the baby in Bethlehem to reclaim a world that was rightly his all along (John 1:3). The people who acclaimed him during his triumphal entry did not recognize his true identity. Those crowds would turn against him shortly to demand his death. But that was exactly what Jesus had in mind: to establish a kingdom with a cross, not a sword.

B. Prayer

Father, as we prepare to celebrate your Son's resurrection, help us be mindful of the fact that he is not only our Savior but also our king. May we allow him to enter our hearts triumphantly each and every day. In Jesus' name, amen.

C. Thought to Remember

Jesus is the king triumphant.

INVOLVEMENT LEARNING

Enhance your lesson with NIV® Bible Student (from your curriculum supplier) and the reproducible activity page (at www.standardlesson.com or in the back of the NIV® Standard Lesson Commentary Deluxe Edition).

Into the Lesson

Begin by sharing a memory of the most exciting celebration or parade you've ever attended or witnessed. Identify what it was for, what made it so memorable, and how it made you feel. Ask learners to share similar memories (but don't let this drag out). Make a transition by saying, "A celebration or parade like those we've described often signify honor being bestowed on one or more people. In today's lesson, we will see how a celebration for Jesus signified not only his royal authority but also his servant humility."

Into the Word

Before class, prepare nine index cards with the following words or phrases, one each: *Mount of Olives / Jesus riding the colt / the Lord needs it / found the colt tied by the door as Jesus had said / palm branches / Jesus sitting on garments / many in the crowd spreading their cloaks / Hosanna / Jerusalem.* Create two columns on the board, with column headings of *Authority* and *Humility.* Then have a volunteer read the lesson text aloud. Distribute the index cards following the reading, and ask learners to decide whether the words or phrases on their cards speak to Jesus' divine, royal, and/or messianic authority or to his humility.

After each card is read and the decision made, take the card and affix it to the board in the column chosen. Anticipated responses: **Authority**— *Mount of Olives* (Zechariah 14:1-9 predicts this site to be where the Messiah begins the overthrow of Israel's enemies); *the Lord needs it* (the term *the Lord* is authoritative); *found the colt tied by the door as Jesus had said* (possible prophetic awareness would indicate divine authority); *palm branches* (see commentary on Mark 11:8b); *many in the crowd spreading their cloaks* (a sign of submission to one of greater position); *Hosanna* (see commentary on Mark 11:9); *Jerusalem* (the city of David, the place where the king rules; see 2 Sam-

uel 7:11b-16). **Humility**—*Jesus sitting on garments* (he apparently was willing to ride bareback until the disciples intervened). **Both columns**—*Jesus riding the colt* (Zechariah 9:9 speaks of a coming king who will be lowly in riding a donkey). Use this last one to discuss the concept of *false choice,* which requires one to choose an answer only from a given set of options (either *authority* or *humility*) when an unstated third choice may be available— in this case, both *authority* and *humility.*

Discuss reasons for learners' choices, especially those that don't match the above.

Option: For a review of the entirety of the text, announce a closed-Bible exercise as you distribute copies of the "Triumphing Over the Mix-Up" activity from the reproducible page, which you can download. Have learners check their own results when finished.

Into Life

Explain the meaning of *hallel* as "praise" (see the commentary) if you haven't already; then say, "Jesus' entry into Jerusalem was reminiscent of the victory parade described in the psalms designated as *hallel.* Let's conclude our time together by conducting a choral reading of Psalm 118, from which the crowds quoted in today's lesson."

Have learners pair off as you assign the psalm in three-verse segments. Since there are 29 verses, assign the final three-verse segment to be verses 28, 29, and 1 (v. 1 therefore being read twice). If you have exactly 10 pairs of learners, each pair will have one reading. For smaller classes, give some pairs more than one three-verse segment. Instruct the pairs to have one person read the first verse, the other to read the second verse, and both together read the third verse of the assigned segment.

Option: If you used the "Where Can I Serve?" activity from last week, distribute copies of the "A Commitment to Serve" activity from the reproducible page as a follow-up.

BELIEVE IN THE RESURRECTION

DEVOTIONAL READING: John 11:20-27
BACKGROUND SCRIPTURE: 1 Corinthians 15:1-22

1 CORINTHIANS 15:1-11, 20-22

¹ Now, brothers and sisters, I want to remind you of the gospel I preached to you, which you received and on which you have taken your stand. ² By this gospel you are saved, if you hold firmly to the word I preached to you. Otherwise, you have believed in vain.

³ For what I received I passed on to you as of first importance: that Christ died for our sins according to the Scriptures, ⁴ that he was buried, that he was raised on the third day according to the Scriptures, ⁵ and that he appeared to Cephas, and then to the Twelve. ⁶ After that, he appeared to more than five hundred of the

brothers and sisters at the same time, most of whom are still living, though some have fallen asleep. ⁷ Then he appeared to James, then to all the apostles, ⁸ and last of all he appeared to me also, as to one abnormally born.

⁹ For I am the least of the apostles and do not even deserve to be called an apostle, because I persecuted the church of God. ¹⁰ But by the grace of God I am what I am, and his grace to me was not without effect. No, I worked harder than all of them—yet not I, but the grace of God that was with me. ¹¹ Whether, then, it is I or they, this is what we preach, and this is what you believed.

. . . .

²⁰ But Christ has indeed been raised from the dead, the firstfruits of those who have fallen asleep. ²¹ For since death came through a man, the resurrection of the dead comes also through a man. ²² For as in Adam all die, so in Christ all will be made alive.

KEY VERSE

As in Adam all die, so in Christ all will be made alive. —1 Corinthians 15:22

THE SPIRIT COMES

Unit 2: The Community of Beloved Disciples

LESSONS 6–10

LESSON AIMS

After participating in this lesson, each learner will be able to:

1. List the evidence Paul cites for the resurrection of Christ.

2. Tell the significance of Christ's being the firstfruits of the resurrection.

3. Sing a hymn or song of praise for the resurrected Christ.

LESSON OUTLINE

Introduction

A. What Did He See?

Some Christians claim having had visions of angels, the risen Christ, etc. One of the more spectacular of these was that of a well-known televangelist in the 1970s who claimed to have had a vision of Jesus unlike any previously reported. It was not a vision of the humble carpenter with nail prints in his hands, but of a 900-foot colossus!

The televangelist reported that this giant Jesus had given him a task: to found a faith-based medical center. This the man did, but the medical facility ended up financially unviable and closed within eight years of its completion. Examining all this in hindsight makes one wonder what the televangelist really saw. Did he fabricate the whole thing? Did he see Satan masquerading as Jesus? Did he hallucinate? We simply don't know.

Paul records in today's lesson that many in his day had seen the risen Christ. These appearances were to individuals, small groups, and at least one group of over 500. What was the nature of Jesus' appearance? Did he look like the human he was of some 33 years? the Christ on the Mount of Transfiguration (Mark 9:2, 3)? as he appeared on the first resurrection Sunday (John 20:19-23, last week's lesson)? as he appeared to John on the island of Patmos (Revelation 1:13-16)? Paul's account in today's lesson is not long on details, but his purpose is clear: Christ appeared to show his followers that he was risen from the dead.

B. Lesson Background

Paul had a long and lively relationship with the church in the city of Corinth. He began his work there in a synagogue, but moved to the home of a nearby Gentile when many Jews rejected his message (Acts 18:1-7). Some Jews believed Paul's claim that Jesus was their promised Messiah, and the church in Corinth was thereby composed of both Jews and Gentiles (18:8). All this happened during Paul's second missionary journey, when he spent 18 months in Corinth during the early AD 50s.

Corinth was a nexus of commerce between the eastern and western halves of the Roman Empire. This was because of its *diolkos,* an ingenious system of cranes, stone tracks, and carriage carts that allowed small boats to be lifted from the Aegean Sea to the east, hauled across the Corinthian isthmus (about 5 miles), and deposited in the calm waters of the Gulf of Corinth in the west (or the reverse from west to east). This process allowed shipping to avoid the dangerous voyage around the rocky coastline of the Peloponnese. The tolls charged were the economic engine of Corinth.

The many nationalities represented in this Greek city made it a melting pot of ideas. The issue of life after death was widely debated in the ancient world, and the various theories of immortality (or the lack of such) would have been represented in Corinth. The theories boiled down to three options, although there were many variations.

First, some believed there was no life of any kind after death. A second viewpoint held that the life force or soul of a person was immortal, surviving death of the body. Some holding this view believed the soul of a dead person would be implanted into a new body, whether human or animal (what we call *reincarnation* today), thus creating a cycle of lives. The third viewpoint was that the human body would be reconstituted at some point after death to be rejoined with the soul to enter a new type of existence. This is the doctrine of resurrection, a view held by most Jews of Paul's day (Acts 23:8).

In the end, these three views are mutually exclusive and incompatible—they cannot all be true. Today's study considers one of the most important sections of Scripture that points in the right direction. Paul wrote his first letter to the Corinthians in about AD 56, while he was in Ephesus.

HOW TO SAY IT

Aegean	A-*jee*-un.
Cephas	*See*-fus.
Corinth	*Kor*-inth.
Corinthians	Ko-*rin*-thee-unz (*th* as in *thin*).
diolkos (Greek)	*dih*-all-kos (*o* as in *cost*).
Ephesus	*Ef*-uh-sus.
Matthias	Muh-*thigh*-us (*th* as in *thin*).
Patmos	*Pat*-muss.
Peloponnese	**Pell**-uh-puh-*neez*.

I. Vital Gospel
(1 CORINTHIANS 15:1-4)
A. Why Paul Preaches (vv. 1, 2)

1. Now, brothers and sisters, I want to remind you of the gospel I preached to you, which you received and on which you have taken your stand.

By the time we reach chapter 15, Paul has addressed many problems in the Corinthian church, including factionalism, abuses at the Lord's Supper, and misuse of speaking in tongues. He reserves the most important topic for chapter 15, a doctrine so central that to deny it is to make the church a fraud. This is the doctrine of the resurrection.

Paul begins his reminder on this subject by reviewing the gospel message that he had proclaimed while in Corinth a few years earlier. He emphasizes the vital importance of the gospel message in four ways. First, it was *preached*. Christian action and lifestyle are important (see 1 Peter 2:12), but attempts to spread the gospel through those alone will not suffice. There is no substitute for the bold, public proclamation of the gospel.

Second, the gospel message was *received*. There was an audience that heard and believed (contrast Acts 28:27; Romans 11:8). Third, the gospel is where the Corinthians have taken their *stand*. The gospel is the basis of everything in the church. Without it, the church has no sure foundation.

2. By this gospel you are saved, if you hold firmly to the word I preached to you. Otherwise, you have believed in vain.

Fourth, the gospel is the message whereby the Corinthians *are saved*. The whole of the church's ministry is represented here: saving people from the judgmental wrath of God that is to come (see Luke 3:7). We are to care compassionately for the physical needs of the suffering; but if we do not care about their eternal souls, then we have missed Paul's central claims in these two verses.

Paul touches on the problem of believing *in vain*. This sets the table for this chapter, for if the resurrection of Christ is a fiction, then the gospel and the church are houses of cards that will collapse. Absolutely everything is at stake here regarding the truth of Christianity!

B. What Paul Preaches (vv. 3, 4)

3. For what I received I passed on to you as of first importance: that Christ died for our sins according to the Scriptures,

Paul is careful to remind the Corinthians that the gospel message did not originate with him; he received it from someone else. Galatians 1:12 clarifies that that someone was Jesus Christ himself.

Paul's gospel preaching at Corinth had stressed the reason and importance of Christ's death. We can learn from reading the Gospels that this was a cruel and unjust death. But what separates it from the millions of cruel and unjust deaths in history?

Paul's answer is twofold. First, the death of Jesus was *for our sins*. This is the doctrine of the substitutionary atonement, the process that allows our sins to be forgiven as the result of the sacrifice of another being (compare Leviticus 4:20). In the Jewish system of sacrifices, such beings were animals: bulls, goats, lambs, birds. Jesus was the true Lamb of God, by whose death the sins of the world can be atoned (see John 1:29; 1 John 2:2).

The second way Jesus' death was uniquely significant concerns its fulfillment *according to the Scriptures* (Isaiah 53:8, 9, etc.). This fact gives Paul and the other apostles a way of convincing their fellow Jews that Jesus was and is the prophesied Messiah of their own sacred Scriptures (see Acts 17:1-4, 11; 28:17-23). The prophets of old had painted a composite picture of the coming Savior, and Jesus fits that portrait in detail.

❧ TRADITION, GOOD AND BAD ❧

The word *tradition* in a religious sense often carries a rather negative connotation. The reasons for this are varied, but I suppose most of us think in terms of traditions that have come down through medieval Catholicism. In that context, skepticism is wise. The word *tradition* and its plural are often used in a very negative sense in the pages of the New Testament (example: Mark 7:9).

In a neutral sense, the word means "something that is handed down, passed on from one person to another." This can refer to doctrinal teaching in religious contexts. It is not the "handing down" in and of itself that makes tradition either positive or negative, but rather *what* is handed down or passed along that is either beneficial or detrimental.

We see the positive aspect in 1 Corinthians 11:2, where Paul wants his readers to continue "holding to the traditions just as I passed them on to you." This same word *traditions* is used in negative contexts elsewhere.

We further see this positive handing-down aspect in the vital teaching about the resurrection of Christ that Paul had "received" and subsequently "passed on to" the Corinthian believers. This is something that must be handed down to every generation!   —J. B. N.

4a. . . . that he was buried,

Christ's burial is a valuable historical detail, for it demonstrates that his followers knew he was really dead (Matthew 27:57-61; Mark 15:42-47; Luke 23:50-56; John 19:38-42). The enemies of Jesus confirmed this fact by placing a guard at the tomb to ensure that the body could not be stolen for a pretend resurrection (Matthew 27:62-66).

We note that Paul sees no need to cite eyewitness accounts of Christ's death as he does for Christ's resurrection in verses 5-8, below. The death of Christ is "a given" by both friend and foe of the gospel in Paul's day.

4b. . . . that he was raised on the third day according to the Scriptures,

This is another element of Paul's core gospel message. The resurrection of Jesus *on the third day* counts each full and partial day he spent in the tomb to be a day. He was placed there on Friday before sundown (Luke 23:53, 54; John 19:41, 42), remained there all day Saturday (the Sabbath), and rose on Sunday morning (the first day of the week: Matthew 28:1; Mark 16:1; Luke 24:1; John 20:1). Even though this totaled less than 72 hours, it was nonetheless three days by the reckoning of Paul's culture.

Paul notes both the resurrection and the detail of the third day as being *according to the Scriptures*, but we are unsure of his specific reference. A likely way to understand this is to see the three days Jonah spent in the belly of the fish (Jonah 1:17) as a prophetic foreshadowing of Jesus' three days in the tomb, following that application by Jesus himself (Matthew 12:40). Hosea 6:2 may also be in view: "On the third day he will restore us, that we may live in his presence."

What Do You Think?
How does the reality of Christ's resurrection aid you in daily living? How could it?
Talking Points for Your Discussion
- With regard to finances
- With regard to priorities
- With regard to family life
- With regard to vocation
- Other

II. Dramatic Evidence
(1 CORINTHIANS 15:5-11)

A. Christ Appears to Many (vv. 5-7)

5. . . . and that he appeared to Cephas, and then to the Twelve.

Paul now sets forth a historical basis for preaching that Jesus rose from the dead. He notes first an appearance *to Cephas,* better known to us as Simon Peter (Luke 24:34; John 1:42). This apostle is seen as a leader among the original band of disciples and a pillar of the church in Jerusalem (Galatians 1:18; 2:9; 1 Corinthians 1:12; 3:22; 9:5). If the risen Christ had not been seen by Peter, the claim of Jesus' resurrection would be highly suspect.

Paul's mention of *the Twelve* is shorthand for the group of apostles initially chosen by Jesus, even though their actual number was 11 at the time of Jesus' resurrection, Judas Iscariot having committed suicide (Matthew 27:3-10; Acts 1:15-20). Paul may intend to include Matthias, Judas' replacement, in the enumeration even before that man's selection because he too is a witness to the resurrected Christ (Acts 1:21-26).

6. After that, he appeared to more than five hundred of the brothers and sisters at the same time, most of whom are still living, though some have fallen asleep.

We do not know what precise event is in view when the risen Jesus appeared to more than *five hundred . . . at the same time.* Some speculate that this appearance is recorded in Matthew 28:10, 16, 17, although that account mentions only "the eleven disciples." Paul's point, though, is that an appearance to so many sweeps aside any claim of a hoax.

This appearance would have been about 25 years earlier, thus many of those eyewitnesses are still living. Perhaps some have even visited the Corinthian church. The statement *some have fallen asleep* refers to the fact that a minority of that large group have died (compare Acts 7:60; 13:36).

7. Then he appeared to James, then to all the apostles,

This particular *James* is the half-brother of Jesus (Matthew 13:55). This James became a leader of the Jerusalem church (see Acts 15:13; Galatians 1:19; 2:9). The specifics of this appearance of Jesus are unknown, but it does help explain the remarkable shift from unbelief (John 7:5) to belief (Acts 1:14).

The distinction, if any, between "the Twelve" (v. 5, above) and *all the apostles* here may be that the latter grouping includes Barnabas (Acts 14:14) and others (Romans 16:7; 1 Thessalonians 1:1; 2:6). A broader category that includes the leaders of the Jerusalem church in general is possible (Acts 15:4).

What Do You Think?
Why is it that some who come to Christ later in life (perhaps after strongly opposing the gospel) end up being so much on fire for him?
Talking Points for Your Discussion
- The role of guilt
- The role of gratitude
- The role of urgency
- Other

B. Christ Appears to Paul (vv. 8-11)

8. . . . and last of all he appeared to me also, as to one abnormally born.

The final appearance of the risen Christ in the listing was to Paul himself. This is certainly

Death is **SWALLOWED UP** in **VICTORY!**

1 Corinthians 15:54

Visual for Lesson 6. *Start a discussion by pointing to this visual as you ask, "How will this fact influence the way you live this week?"*

a reference to Paul's experience on the road to Damascus. This account is related three times in Acts (see 9:3-6; 22:6-10; 26:12-18) and surely retold many times by Paul himself to groups like the believers in Corinth. In describing his situation as *one abnormally born,* Paul uses language of the premature arrival of a baby. This is both an expression of Paul's deep humility at being chosen to see the risen Christ and affirmation that he is the most unlikely of candidates to have been chosen to be an apostle (compare 1 Corinthians 9:1).

9. For I am the least of the apostles and do not even deserve to be called an apostle, because I persecuted the church of God.

Paul expands on the unlikely nature of his apostolic commission given that he had *persecuted the church of God* (compare Ephesians 3:8; 1 Timothy 1:15). Paul (as Saul) had been a ruthless and zealous opponent of the Christians (see Acts 8:3; 9:1, 2; Galatians 1:13). What changed him was the appearance of the risen Christ. This makes the discussion of the resurrection deeply personal to Paul. To deny the resurrection, as some false teachers in Corinth are doing (1 Corinthians 15:12, not in today's text), is to make Paul out to be a liar and his entire apostolic work a sham and a scam (15:15).

10. But by the grace of God I am what I am, and his grace to me was not without effect. No, I worked harder than all of them—yet not I, but the grace of God that was with me.

Paul does not wear well the potential charge of being a fraud. His ministry is *not without effect* (compare 2 Corinthians 6:1). Hundreds, maybe thousands, have believed his testimony about Jesus. Paul does not want the prize for being thought of as the greatest apostle, but he does want to be included in the discussion of who works the hardest (compare 2 Corinthians 11:23-27). Even so, Paul does not attribute his work ethic to himself but to *the grace of God.* God, through Christ, has both called him to ministry and given him the power to persevere (see 2 Corinthians 12:9, 10).

11. Whether, then, it is I or they, this is what we preach, and this is what you believed.

Paul closes this line of thought by affirming that he is not interested in statistics for who has won the most converts. He doesn't care who does the preaching, only that the gospel is preached and that hearers believe. While Paul will defend the validity and integrity of his ministry, he does not see his efforts in terms of rivalry. In the end, God alone deserves credit because preachers like Paul are working as his servants (see 1 Corinthians 3:6-9).

What Do You Think?
What role, if any, should the use of statistics play in evaluating a church's effectiveness? Why?
Talking Points for Your Discussion
- Acts 2:41 vis-à-vis 1 Corinthians 1:16
- Numbers 1:1, 2 vis-à-vis 2 Samuel 24:1-17
- "It's not that we're counting numbers, but that numbers count"
- Other

III. Living Hope
(1 Corinthians 15:20-22)
A. Christ Conquers Death (v. 20)

20a. But Christ has indeed been raised from the dead,

Paul describes in verses 12-19 (not in today's text) the dire effects of a Christianity where Christ has not been resurrected. But none of these effects prevail because *Christ has indeed been raised from the dead.* The facts of history establish this. Most of the apostles will die as martyrs, and rational people are not willing to die for a lie that they know to be a lie!

I have been trained as a historian. As such, I have looked at the evidence for the resurrection, and I find the evidence compelling. The only conclusion that can explain all the evidence is that Christ did indeed rise from the dead. That is the rock core of my faith as it is of Christianity in general.

Times of doubt and uncertainty still come occasionally. I sometimes ask "Why?" about life's experiences. I can't always come up with a good explanation. But one thing I know: Jesus rose from the dead. As a result, his teachings have credibility. And if God raised Jesus from the dead, then it is obvious that God has the power to do anything he desires.

God is in control, no matter what. The apostle John saw God still on his throne (Revelation 4:2), and with him was the living Lamb that had been slain (5:6). Christ is risen, and all else will happen as God wills or allows it. When life becomes confused, remember the resurrection! —J. B. N.

20b. . . . the firstfruits of those who have fallen asleep.

Paul moves from fact to result by drawing on Old Testament imagery of *firstfruits* (Leviticus 23:17, 20; etc.). The idea of Jesus' being a pioneer in the matter of life after death is found in many places in the New Testament (Acts 26:23; Revelation 1:5; etc.). The appearance of firstfruits indicates that the remainder of the harvest is on the way; since Christ has conquered death, his followers will too (see Philippians 3:10, 11).

B. Christ Makes Us Alive (vv. 21, 22)

21, 22. For since death came through a man, the resurrection of the dead comes also through a man. For as in Adam all die, so in Christ all will be made alive.

The resurrection of Christ creates a new reality. The sin in the Garden of Eden brought death to all (Genesis 3:17-19; Romans 5:12) despite the serpent's lying assurance to the contrary (Genesis 3:4). But sin's consequence of death, introduced by "the first man Adam" has been cancelled by Jesus, "the last Adam" (1 Corinthians 15:45). The resurrection of the dead that is to come will not be temporary, such as that of Lazarus (John 11:38-44), but permanent (11:24-26). The resurrection to come will be for everyone since *all will be made alive.* This does not mean that all will be saved but that all will be raised (compare Daniel 12:2).

> *What Do You Think?*
> What are some ways to celebrate Christ's victory over death?
> *Talking Points for Your Discussion*
> ▪ In corporate worship
> ▪ In personal devotional life
> ▪ In seemingly mundane daily events
> ▪ Other

Conclusion

A. Death Is Not the End

Having died, Jesus' body was placed in a nearby tomb, a cave carved out of rock (John 19:38-42). This cave-tomb featured a rock carved so as to be rolled in front of the entrance to close it (Matthew 27:60; Mark 15:46; Luke 23:53; John 19:41). The chief priests and Pharisees sealed the tomb and stationed soldiers to guard it (Matthew 27:66). Jesus was dead; and as far as anyone knew, that was the end of the story.

But something beyond dramatic happened on Sunday morning. There was an earthquake, the stone was rolled away from the entrance to the tomb (Matthew 28:2), *and Jesus walked out of the tomb, alive!* God had raised him from the dead. In so doing, God showed us that he had accepted Jesus' death as the sacrifice for our sins.

We can be forgiven and not have to pay God's penalty for our sins because Jesus has already done so. We can know that death is not the end of the story. Beyond death is life eternal.

B. Prayer

Father, your Son is risen indeed! Because of him, we trust in you to give us resurrection on that great day. In the name of the resurrected Jesus, amen.

C. Thought to Remember

Christ's triumph over death is ours as well.

INVOLVEMENT LEARNING

Enhance your lesson with NIV® Bible Student (from your curriculum supplier) and the reproducible activity page (at www.standardlesson.com or in the back of the NIV® Standard Lesson Commentary Deluxe Edition).

Into the Lesson

Ask the class as a whole to brainstorm some "famous firsts," biblical and otherwise. Maintain a rapid-fire pace by saying "OK, name another" as you jot each response on the board. If someone disagrees with a response, say, "We'll get back to that in a minute," then continue soliciting responses.

Stop after two minutes. Ask for explanations and resolve, in a good-natured way, any disagreements. Possible firsts to be mentioned (among many) are in Genesis 1:5; 1 Samuel 10:9-25; Mark 12:29; Luke 2:7; and Colossians 1:18. Make a transition by noting that two important "firsts" are part of today's study: the priority of the gospel message and the risen Christ as firstfruits (1 Corinthians 15:3, 20).

Alternative: Give each learner a copy of the "Firsts, Important and Otherwise" activity from the reproducible page, which you can download. Divide your class in half in some way—down the middle of the room, men vs. women (if the competition can be kept lighthearted), etc. Assign the odd-numbered questions to one group and the even-numbered to the other. Ask groups to huddle, choose their answers, and select a spokesperson. Alternate asking spokespersons for the answers. If an answer is wrong, give the other group a chance to "steal" by providing the correct answer. Use questions 9 and 10 as the transition to Into the Word.

Into the Word

Form learners into pairs, then distribute the following incorrect statements on index cards, one statement per card: A. The Corinthians were noncommittal regarding the message of Christ's resurrection. B. Paul attributed his status as an apostle to having been a faithful Sadducee. C. There's nothing in the Old Testament that should have caused anyone to expect the Messiah's death and resurrection. D. It's possible that Jesus was entombed while still alive, and the coolness of the tomb revived him. E. None of the people who testified about Jesus' being resurrected really knew him all that well. F. Paul was the first to see the risen Jesus. G. The doctrine of the resurrection is based only on the eyewitness testimony of the original 12 apostles. H. Keeping the Sabbath was Paul's most important task. I. The apostles Matthew and John worked harder than Paul. J. The work of Paul is the firstfruits of those who have died.

Say, "The statements on your cards contradict what Paul says in 1 Corinthians 15:1-21. Your task is to find which verse or verses there provide the corrective to the wrong statement on your card." After a few minutes, ask the pair with card A to have one person read it and then the other to read the corrective from the text. Repeat this for all the other cards. (Anticipated corrections from the lesson text are *A, v. 1; B, v. 10; C, vv. 3, 4; D, vv. 3, 4; E, v. 5; F, v. 8; G, vv. 6-8; H, v. 3; I, v. 10; J, v. 20.*)

Into Life

Ask learners to suggest ways they would use the reality of Jesus' resurrection to help the people in the following situations: 1. Kara can't seem to pull out of her depression over her mother's death. Her mother was a believer, but Kara thinks that death is the end of human existence. 2. As a long-time Christian, Frank believes in life after death. But the older he gets, the more aware he is of his sin, and he's afraid he won't get into Heaven.

Alternative: Distribute copies of the "What Adam Ruined, Jesus Restored" activity from the reproducible page. After learners have unscrambled the words, ask them to name hymns and/or songs that celebrate Jesus' resurrection. Some possible responses are "Christ the Lord Is Risen Today," "One Day," "Wounded for Me," "Resurrection Song," "Rise Again," and "Because He Lives." Ask a musically gifted learner to lead the class in singing one or two of these.

Love One Another

DEVOTIONAL READING: John 13:31-35
BACKGROUND SCRIPTURE: 1 John 3:11-24

1 JOHN 3:11-24

[11] For this is the message you heard from the beginning: We should love one another. [12] Do not be like Cain, who belonged to the evil one and murdered his brother. And why did he murder him? Because his own actions were evil and his brother's were righteous. [13] Do not be surprised, my brothers and sisters, if the world hates you. [14] We know that we have passed from death to life, because we love each other. Anyone who does not love remains in death. [15] Anyone who hates a brother or sister is a murderer, and you know that no murderer has eternal life residing in him.

[16] This is how we know what love is: Jesus Christ laid down his life for us. And we ought to lay down our lives for our brothers and sisters. [17] If anyone has material possessions and sees a brother or sister in need but has no pity on them, how can the love of God be in that person? [18] Dear children, let us not love with words or speech but with actions and in truth.

[19] This is how we know that we belong to the truth and how we set our hearts at rest in his presence: [20] If our hearts condemn us, we know that God is greater than our hearts, and he knows everything. [21] Dear friends, if our hearts do not condemn us, we have confidence before God [22] and receive from him anything we ask, because we keep his commands and do what pleases him. [23] And this is his command: to believe in the name of his Son, Jesus Christ, and to love one another as he commanded us. [24] The one who keeps God's commands lives in him, and he in them. And this is how we know that he lives in us: We know it by the Spirit he gave us.

KEY VERSE

This is the message you heard from the beginning: We should love one another. —1 John 3:11

Photo: Jupiterimages / Photos.com / Thinkstock

THE SPIRIT COMES

Unit 2: The Community of Beloved Disciples

LESSONS 6–10

LESSON AIMS

After participating in this lesson, each learner will be able to:

1. Summarize John's message about loving one another.

2. Explain the connection between Christ's love for us and our love for others.

3. Perform one act of Christian love to another believer in the week ahead.

LESSON OUTLINE

Introduction
  A. Giving Love Away
  B. Lesson Background
I. Love as Action (1 JOHN 3:11-18)
  A. Imperative (v. 11)
  B. Challenges (vv. 12, 13)
  C. Status (vv. 14, 15)
    What Love for Others Does
  D. Model (vv. 16-18)
II. Love as Truth (1 JOHN 3:19-24)
  A. Confident Assurance (vv. 19-21)
  B. Clear Command (vv. 22-24)
    Doing What Pleases Him
Conclusion
  A. Of Sculptures and Action
  B. Prayer
  C. Thought to Remember

Introduction

A. Giving Love Away

Perhaps the most beloved Broadway musical of all time is *The Sound of Music*. It was made into a motion picture that is now part of the DVD collection of many American households. It has been staged countless times in high school, college, and community theater productions, living on in frequent revivals in New York or London. It is a lovely story of family, patriotism, and courage set against the backdrop of the horrors of Nazi Europe during World War II.

Oscar Hammerstein II wrote the words to the songs for *The Sound of Music*. Even more than 50 years after it was first staged on Broadway, many of those song lyrics are still quite familiar. One of the most engaging lines (found in the stage plays, but not in the movie) comes during a reprise sung by Maria and Liesl. The sentiment of the line is that love can't be kept to oneself but must be given away.

Hammerstein could have taken this thought from today's lesson. Love must be expressed actively. Love isn't just words; it is self-giving actions. In teaching this, the apostle John echoes things he learned from Jesus and from the teachings of the Old Testament.

B. Lesson Background

There are five books in our New Testament that we attribute to the apostle John, who was one of the original 12 disciples (see Matthew 4:21; 10:2). Three of the five books are epistles (letters)—the ones we designate 1 John, 2 John, and 3 John. Church history strongly associates John with the church in Ephesus; tradition says he died in this great Greek metropolis in the AD 90s. The three letters were probably written in the region of Ephesus for churches in the area, and they date from the AD 80s or 90s. John would have been an elderly man at that time. The dignity of his age peeks through in 1 John, where he addresses his readers as his "little children" numerous times.

The letter of 1 John addresses several problems within the original readers' church or churches. These problems included a denial of Jesus' bodily existence, a denial of sin in the lives of some, and a general lack of love for one another. False teachers were so bold that John referred to them as having "the spirit of the antichrist" (1 John 4:3; compare 2:18, 22); John wanted their influence eliminated.

It was with a spirit of watchfulness combined with an overarching attitude of love that the apostle wrote 1 John. Its short message still speaks powerfully today.

I. Love as Action
(1 JOHN 3:11-18)
A. Imperative (v. 11)

11. For this is the message you heard from the beginning: We should love one another.

The message of love for one another does not originate with John; it was taught to him by the Lord Jesus. John had been present at the last supper when Jesus said, "A new commandment I give you: *Love one another*" (John 13:34). Digging a little deeper, we can find a similar form of this imperative in the Law of Moses, which Jesus declared to be one of the two greatest commandments (see Leviticus 19:18; Matthew 22:37-40). The commandment to love one another is ancient but ever new.

Life is hard, complicated, and full of conflict, but we should never forget this imperative. John's challenge to the believers at Ephesus to *love one another* is no less our challenge as well.

B. Challenges (vv. 12, 13)

12. Do not be like Cain, who belonged to the evil one and murdered his brother. And why did he murder him? Because his own actions were evil and his brother's were righteous.

Not content merely to exhort his readers to love one another, John warns of the other side of the coin, the danger of failing to love. His contrast is stark, equating a lack of love with murder, a most

HOW TO SAY IT

Augustine	*Aw*-gus-*teen* or Aw-*gus*-tin.
Ephesus	*Ef*-uh-sus.
epistle	ee-*pis*-ul.

heinous crime. Cain, the firstborn of Adam and Eve, *murdered his brother* Abel (Genesis 4), and the Greek verb that is translated *murdered* is not the common word for murder as we see, for example, in Matthew 5:21; 23:31. The word John uses is more intense, carrying the sense of "butcher" or "slaughter" (see Revelation 5:12).

John attributes Cain's crime to two factors. First, Cain *belonged to the evil one.* Lack of love is pleasing to Satan, our adversary. Second, Cain killed because *his own actions were evil,* meaning somehow insincere and inferior, thus unacceptable to God. Hebrews 11:4 adds to our understanding here: "By faith Abel brought God a better offering than Cain did." Abel's offering was somehow *righteous*—probably because it came from his worshipful heart—so God found it to be acceptable where Cain's was not.

Evil thoughts desire the other person to fail and begrudge the other's accomplishments. It is impossible to combine godly love with evil.

What Do You Think?

What consequences other than literal murder can result from having Cain's mind-set today? How does our text help us guard against these?

Talking Points for Your Discussion
- At home
- At work or school
- In the church
- Other

---

13. Do not be surprised, my brothers and sisters, if the world hates you.

John again passes along what he has heard from Jesus personally (see John 15:18, 19; 17:14). The hatred in view can be a murderous hatred, something that the churches near John experience (see Revelation 2:13). The murderous hatred that drove Cain to kill is found in the enemies of Christianity in both John's day and ours. Too often Christians futilely try to be loved by the corrupt culture within which they live. We may occasionally be honored by the world or sometimes just left alone. But either way there is a deep, enduring hostility in society toward those who stand for truth and give of themselves selflessly to it. Our mission is

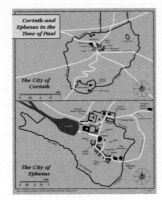

This map can be a useful reference as you discuss the settings of this quarter's lessons.

to bring everyone under the lordship of Jesus. But many will resist and fight this to a bitter end. We are not to be amazed when that happens.

C. Status (vv. 14, 15)

14. We know that we have passed from death to life, because we love each other. Anyone who does not love remains in death.

The one who lives without love—the one living in a personal world of hatred—*remains in death.* We might say that the life of hate is a zombielike existence, cut off from the life-giving presence of God. In this aspect, hating others is suicidal. We are diminished by our own hatred to the point of the death of our souls (see 1 John 2:9-11). The one who hates foregoes all the benefits of the kind of love John is talking about, the kind of love that makes life worthwhile.

❧ WHAT LOVE FOR OTHERS DOES ❧

Love for others can be shown in various ways, from benevolent giving to literally taking a bullet for someone. In the 1999 film *Jakob the Liar,* the main figure does the latter. Jakob lives in the ghetto of Warsaw under Nazi occupation in World War II. Once while being questioned in the office of the local commandant, Jakob hears a German radio broadcast about the approaching Russian armies. Jakob later relays this news to a friend who is getting depressed about remaining under German control. Jakob goes on to invent

additional news clips in order to shore up hope and expectation among other residents that the Nazi occupation is soon to end.

This becomes the talk of the ghetto, and the Germans learn of it. They are convinced that someone is listening to a hidden radio, and they threaten to kill hostages unless this person confesses. To save his friends, Jakob admits that the whole thing is a fabrication, based on that radio report he had heard in the commandant's office. Jakob is put on public display to confess his lie, but he refuses to take away the hopes of his friends. He is shot as a result.

Jakob the Liar is a fictional story, but it addresses a truth: people have been known to show love to the point of sacrificing their lives for the benefit of others. You may never be called to do so. But what *can* you do?   —J. B. N.

15. Anyone who hates a brother or sister is a murderer, and you know that no murderer has eternal life residing in him.

Jesus himself drew a connection between hatred and murder (see Matthew 5:21, 22). Jesus also tied together Satan, murder, and denial of the truth (John 8:44), a subject John will address in a few verses. John's conclusion here is that the murderous, hating heart has no room for life and is cut off from *eternal life.* This is the kind of life that only Christians have, a justified hope of life after death. Paul includes love as a "fruit of the Spirit" while hatred is one of "the acts of the flesh" (Galatians 5:19-26).

D. Model (vv. 16-18)

16. This is how we know what love is: Jesus Christ laid down his life for us. And we ought to lay down our lives for our brothers and sisters.

If Cain is the original pattern (archetype) of one whose hatred drove him to commit murder, then Christ is the ultimate example of one whose love compelled him to lay *down his life for us* so that we can live eternally. The polar opposite of taking another's life (Cain) is to give one's own life (Christ).

Many have enjoyed the verse before us as "the other great 3:16," a parallel to its more famous counterpart of John 3:16. That both verses are enumerated 3:16 is only a coincidence, since John did not include chapter or verse numbers when he wrote either book. Yet the two verses make an interesting commentary on each other. John 3:16 speaks of the great love of God in giving his precious Son so that life may be obtained through faith. First John 3:16 takes this greatest example of God's love and challenges the readers to emulate it.

Jesus taught his disciples that the willing sacrifice of one's life is the greatest expression of love possible (John 15:13). This teaching has never been forgotten by John, and now he teaches it anew to his readers some 50 years later. John does not expect everyone who reads this to die as a martyr, although some will indeed find themselves on that path. *To lay down our lives for our brothers and sisters* can also be the sacrificial giving of one's time, wealth, and attention on behalf of others in love on a consistent basis (compare Philippians 2:17; 1 Thessalonians 2:8).

> *What Do You Think?*
> What are some ways that Christians can lay down their lives for each other? How will you do so in the week ahead?
> *Talking Points for Your Discussion*
> ▪ Giving of one's time
> ▪ Giving of one's wealth
> ▪ Giving of one's attention
> ▪ Other

17. If anyone has material possessions and sees a brother or sister in need but has no pity on them, how can the love of God be in that person?

John gets practical and specific. *Material possessions* refer to one's assets that can be used for the relief of suffering. In this context, for a fellow Christian to be in need is a picture of real misery. John has in mind primarily the suffering of those within the community of faith (compare Deuteronomy 15:7, 8). While it is wonderful for the church to be involved in worldwide disaster relief or global humanitarian projects (compare 2 Corinthians 8, 9), there are always needs within the local body of Christ to be addressed.

Churches sometimes fail in being aware of these needs and in moving to relieve the suffering. Why do we find it easier to write a check for an overseas project than to be closely involved in helping someone who sits in the pew with us? John cautions that those who truly love will move quickly to help those who are near and in need.

18. Dear children, let us not love with words or speech but with actions and in truth.

John sums up this section by contrasting merely talking about love with actively performing deeds motivated by love. Love must be more than words, no matter how kind or heartfelt those words may be. James admonishes his readers to do what the Word says (James 1:22); one's profession of faith is questionable if there is no evidence from works (2:14-17). Likewise for John, one's claims of love are hollow if there are no loving actions flowing from the believer's life to match that profession.

James and John are practical men, raised in the gritty working villages of Galilee. They are not fooled by high rhetoric and lofty language. For them, if you love people, then you help them when they are in need. If you do not step up when a friend is in trouble, then you are not really a friend. This ethic of action is still to guide us today.

> *What Do You Think?*
> How do we avoid thinking that just because our church has a benevolence ministry, we've "done our part" in exhibiting love through deeds?
> *Talking Points for Your Discussion*
> ▪ Regarding physical needs
> ▪ Regarding psychological and emotional needs
> ▪ Regarding relational needs
> ▪ Others

II. Love as Truth
(1 JOHN 3:19-24)

A. Confident Assurance (vv. 19-21)

19. This is how we know that we belong to the truth and how we set our hearts at rest in his presence:

The opening word *This* presents us with a challenge of interpretation: Does this word introduce a summary of what John has just said, or does it introduce what he is about to say next? The paragraph breaks and punctuation of the 1984 NIV point to what was just said, but that of the 2011 NIV point to what comes next. The way to resolve the question is (1) determine where the author uses the same phrasing (in Greek) elsewhere, then (2) compare and contrast those occurrences in their contexts to see if a distinctive pattern emerges.

John uses the same phrasing in John 13:35; 15:8; 16:30; 1 John 2:5; 3:10, 16, 24; 4:2, 9; 5:2. But comparing and contrasting these yield no conclusive answer. The context in some cases points to what has just been said while other contexts point to what is about to be said—and some seem to point both ways! For our text, the safest approach is to see the phrasing as pointing both ways; this will keep John's points from becoming disconnected.

Deeds of love are to be sincere and genuine, not for show or motivated by self-interest. Such deeds are not those of a politician who dishes out meals at a homeless shelter as a photo op. On the other hand, such actions may be those of a public figure who visits a shelter to raise awareness of the need, then privately writes a large check in support.

The motives behind our deeds of love may always be a little muddled, for the sin of pride and the craving for attention may be part of the mix in the most noble of people. True acts of love are pretty simple though: we become aware of a need, realize we can help, and then do so. This is acting in truth, doing the truth (see John 3:21).

20, 21. If our hearts condemn us, we know that God is greater than our hearts, and he knows everything. Dear friends, if our hearts do not condemn us, we have confidence before God

Why would *our hearts condemn us*? This is a difficult verse, and many students see *hearts* as a synonym for *consciences* here. This is unlikely, though, for the human heart is not a guide to righteous decisions, but is the center of one's innermost thoughts. The heart may be fickle and selfish. The idea of condemning here is when a rationalizing heart decides, "I don't really need to help that suffering person because someone else will do so."

A selfish heart does not excuse one from a God-given and God-expected responsibility to help others. *God is greater than our hearts*, and he will never ignore the needs of his children. God's knowledge is absolute, so he knows both the needs of our fellow Christians and our potential to help. *If our hearts condemn us*, it means we are guilty of being hard-hearted toward a fellow Christian in need.

If our hearts do not condemn us, it means that we have not been persuaded or betrayed by our inner selfishness. We act with confidence, seeing needs and lovingly moving to help. We stand before God uncondemned, agents of his will and doers of his deeds in a needy, suffering world.

B. Clear Command (vv. 22-24)

22. . . . and receive from him anything we ask, because we keep his commands and do what pleases him.

The "confidence before God" of verse 21 is shown in our prayers. As Jesus taught, *we ask* and thereby *receive* (Matthew 7:7; 21:22). This should not be taken as a blanket statement or an absolute promise without context. It is teaching us that when we are in the center of God's will—that is, when *we keep his commands* in demonstrating love in actions—then our prayers will line up with our actions. Our perspective will be correctly aligned with God's expectations.

Prayer, then, is part of our loving-life of truth. Our prayers must not be motivated by inner selfishness that attempts to use God as a cosmic Santa Claus. Prayer is to be grounded in the fact that God is the senior partner and guide in our lives of service.

> **What Do You Think?**
> What adjustments should you make to your prayer life regarding the nature of what you ask God to grant you personally?
> *Talking Points for Your Discussion*
> - Psalm 90:17
> - Matthew 6:33
> - James 1:5; 4:3
> - Other

❧ DOING WHAT PLEASES HIM ❧

Augustine of Hippo (354–430) has been considered the greatest theologian of the early church (that is, before the year AD 600). After living dissolutely as a youth, he converted to Christianity in the year 387, going on to write numerous books on doctrine. The effects of his work are still felt today, and one of my professors in divinity school once said, "Of all that the church believes today, 85 percent of it comes from Augustine." That is probably true, as long as one remembers that Augustine got much of his understanding from the apostle Paul!

One of Augustine's famous statements is, "Love God and do what you want." At first glance, that seems to be a license for anarchy, doesn't it? To say that you love God and then live like a hell-bound seeker of pleasure because that is what you want to do—what kind of Christian doctrine is that?

But this is to misunderstand Augustine, because the key phrase here is "Love God." If a person really loves God, then what that person wants will be what God wants. Such a person will not be focused on self-gratification. When love for God is the dominating principle, the only thing to want to do is to please him.   —J. B. N.

23. And this is his command: to believe in the name of his Son, Jesus Christ, and to love one another as he commanded us.

To *believe in the name of his Son, Jesus Christ* (compare John 6:29) and to *love one another* cannot be disconnected from each other. True believers in Jesus Christ will practice mutual love always. Jesus mentioned this repeatedly on the final night he spent with his disciples in the upper room (see John 13:34; 15:12, 17). Many decades later, John shows us that he has not forgotten his master's words of that night. Despite the many problems and challenges of the church(es) John is addressing, this controlling ethic never loses its power or authority.

24. The one who keeps God's commands lives in him, and he in them. And this is how we know that he lives in us: We know it by the Spirit he gave us.

John brings it all together by appealing to our spiritual unity with Christ and with each other (compare 1 John 4:13). Again we are reminded of Jesus' powerful words in the upper room, in this case his promise of "the Spirit of truth," who now abides in the hearts and lives of Christians (John 14:17; compare 15:26). The presence of the Holy Spirit is Christ's guarantee that we belong to him. And so we have all things in unity: love, truth, obedience, and the Holy Spirit. This is Christ's design for his church.

> **What Do You Think?**
> At what times is "head knowledge" of the Spirit's presence in your life more valuable than a "feeling" of the Spirit's presence?
> *Talking Points for Your Discussion*
> - Concerning negative circumstances
> - Concerning positive circumstances

Conclusion
A. Of Sculptures and Action

In the 1960s, artist Robert Indiana created a rendering of the word *LOVE* that has become iconic in America. He took the four letters of that word and put them in two rows, creating a square of letters in the process. To add visual interest, Indiana tilted the letter *O*. This representation has been crafted into three-dimensional sculptures that have become public art in various cities (see picture on page 273).

That is both clever and inspirational, but a sculpture of the word *love* doesn't really help anyone in need. Such a sculpture may coexist in cities with homeless folks who live in daily need. These people are not helped by massive and lifeless works of art; they need active compassion.

May we not be guilty of elevating *love* to statue status while neglecting our duty to help those in need in our families, churches, and communities.

B. Prayer

Loving God, we can never love as fully as you did when you sent your Son to die for our sins. But may we take his ultimate example as our guide to show loving-kindness to our brothers and sisters in need. We pray this in the name of your loving Son, amen.

C. Thought to Remember
Practice active compassion.

INVOLVEMENT LEARNING

Enhance your lesson with NIV® Bible Student (from your curriculum supplier) and the reproducible activity page (at www.standardlesson.com or in the back of the NIV® Standard Lesson Commentary Deluxe Edition).

Into the Lesson

Ask a musically talented individual to come prepared to play on a keyboard or other instrument the first five or six notes of the following songs: "What the World Needs Now," "All You Need Is Love," "Love Me Tender," "Love Will Keep Us Together," "I'll Be There," "Have I Told You Lately." (Feel free to substitute other songs that are more familiar to your class.)

Divide the class into two teams and alternate between them to see if they can "name that tune." If the teams are tied after three songs each, use "Jesus Loves Me" as the tiebreaker, with a few seconds of delay between notes. Conclude: "Some of these songs do a better job than others in telling us what love is all about. The apostle John has a message about love in today's lesson that gets to the true meaning of love from God's viewpoint."

Alternative: Place in chairs copies of the "Right Way/Wrong Way" word-search activity from the reproducible page, which you can download, for learners to begin working on as they arrive. After a few minutes, encourage learners to watch for the words and concepts they have found as they occur in today's lesson on the right way to love.

Into the Word

Divide your class into three groups and distribute the following sets of questions, one per group.

Death by Murder Group: What was Cain notorious for doing? Why did he do it? How was Cain's action the exact opposite of what John teaches us? How can someone become a murderer without actually killing anyone? How can hatred keep a person from inheriting eternal life?" (See Genesis 4:1-16; Hebrews 11:4; 1 John 3:11-15.)

Life Through Loving Group: What's the best example of what love is? What should that example make us want to do? If we can help a fellow Christian but don't do anything, what does that say about us? Why are loving words themselves not enough? What should we do in addition to what we say? (See 1 John 3:16-18.)

Truth in Loving Group: For what reasons might a person perform loving actions without having a loving heart? How does helping a needy person via genuine love give us confidence toward God? What promise do we have from God if we keep his commands and live to please him? What two commandments does John name that are central to the Christian life? What guarantee do we have that God lives in us? (See 1 John 3:19-24.)

Have each group select one person to read the questions and another to give the group's responses. Use the commentary to clarify as necessary.

Write the names *Cain* and *Jesus* on the board as column headers. Say, "These two are examples of the extremes between hating and loving. How many opposite actions and characteristics can you name for each?"

Jot responses on the board. These can include (1) Cain's taking the life of his brother, and Jesus' laying down his life to save others; (2) Cain's motivation of envy and bitterness, and Jesus' motivation of love; and (3) Cain's belonging to "the evil one," and Jesus' being sent by God. The question "What can we learn from Cain's bad example?" can be your transition to Into Life.

Into Life

Ask class members to share personal experiences of receiving tangible expressions of Christian love when they went through a hard time. After each story, ask, "How did that affect your life?" Make the point that when we are on the receiving end of love from a Christian brother or sister, it should cause us to be better able and willing to show love to others.

Option. Distribute copies of the "Helping the Hurting" activity from the reproducible page. Either allow time for students to complete it in class or encourage them to complete it at home.

TRUST IN GOD'S LOVE

DEVOTIONAL READING: Romans 8:31-39
BACKGROUND SCRIPTURE: 1 John 4, 5

1 JOHN 4:13-21

¹³ This is how we know that we live in him and he in us: He has given us of his Spirit. ¹⁴ And we have seen and testify that the Father has sent his Son to be the Savior of the world. ¹⁵ If anyone acknowledges that Jesus is the Son of God, God lives in them and they in God. ¹⁶ And so we know and rely on the love God has for us.

God is love. Whoever lives in love lives in God, and God in them. ¹⁷ This is how love is made complete among us so that we will have confidence on the day of judgment: In this world we are like Jesus. ¹⁸ There is no fear in love. But perfect love drives out fear, because fear has to do with punishment. The one who fears is not made perfect in love.

¹⁹ We love because he first loved us. ²⁰ Whoever claims to love God yet hates a brother or sister is a liar. For whoever does not love their brother and sister, whom they have seen, cannot love God, whom they have not seen. ²¹ And he has given us this command: Anyone who loves God must also love their brother and sister.

1 JOHN 5:1-5

¹ Everyone who believes that Jesus is the Christ is born of God, and everyone who loves the father loves his child as well. ² This is how we know that we love the children of God: by loving God and carrying out his commands. ³ In fact, this is love for God: to keep his commands. And his commands are not burdensome, ⁴ for everyone born of God overcomes the world. This is the victory that has overcome the world, even our faith. ⁵ Who is it that overcomes the world? Only the one who believes that Jesus is the Son of God.

KEY VERSE

Everyone who believes that Jesus is the Christ is born of God, and everyone who loves the father loves his child as well. —**1 John 5:1**

Graphic: iStockphoto / Thinkstock

THE SPIRIT COMES

Unit 2: The Community of Beloved Disciples

LESSONS 6–10

LESSON AIMS

After participating in this lesson, each learner will be able to:

1. List three characteristics of Christian love.

2. Explain why "there is no fear in love" (v. 18).

3. Identify one fear in his or her life that must give way to love, and make a plan to do so.

LESSON OUTLINE

Introduction
A. Et tu, . . . ?
B. Lesson Background
I. Trust in the World's Savior (1 JOHN 4:13-16)
A. Sent by the Father (vv. 13, 14)
B. Confessed by the Believer (vv. 15, 16)
Where Do You Live?
II. Trust in Perfect Love (1 JOHN 4:17-21)
A. No Fear (vv. 17-19)
B. No Deceit (vv. 20, 21)
III. Trust in God's Victory (1 JOHN 5:1-5)
A. Joyfully Obeying (vv. 1-3)
B. Faithfully Overcoming (vv. 4, 5)
The Miracle Worker
Conclusion
A. Fearless Love
B. Prayer
C. Thought to Remember

Introduction

A. Et tu, . . . ?

One of the most memorable scenes in theater comes from William Shakespeare's tragic drama *Julius Caesar.* In the climactic scene of Caesar's murder by a gang of Roman senators, the final blade is plunged into him by Marcus Brutus, a person whom Caesar believed to be his friend. As Caesar suffers this personal betrayal, he speaks these famous words to Brutus: "Et tu, Brute?"

That phrase means, "You too, Brutus?" Shakespeare, the dramatic master, used the Latin wording to transport the English-speaking audience back to Latin-speaking Rome. The fuller, implied meaning is something like, "You, my friend Brutus —have you turned traitor as well?"

There seems to be a regular parade of public figures in the news who have betrayed the public trust in one way or another. In my blog, I often comment on these failures under the title, "*Et tu,* _____?*" as I fill in the blank with the name of the latest offender. We are shown all too often whom we cannot trust. Whether they exhibit dishonesty, pride, or sloth, our heroes often have feet of clay. Whom can we trust in a world of Brutuses? Where can we place our trust and not worry about having an *Et tu?* moment? (Compare Psalm 41:9.)

Christian faith is a system of trust, and today's lesson shows us several aspects of the nature of this trust. God is no Brutus, and we will never have an *Et tu?* moment with our Savior, Jesus Christ. Instead, we can have confidence that leads to fearless and victorious living.

B. Lesson Background

In the writings of John, the word *world* is used in a specific way. The Greek word behind that translation is *kosmos*; this is the source of our English word *cosmos.* We combine it with other roots to make various words. An example is *cosmopolitan,* one meaning of which is "having worldwide rather than limited scope."

The ancient Greeks did not think of *kosmos* in geographical terms; they would not have equated it with planet Earth in a physical way. For them, *the kosmos* was the ordered world, the society and culture that had been built by humanity. This was the framework within which people lived in cities and villages, farmed the land, spoke common languages, and engaged in commerce. Their *kosmos* included government structures and religious institutions. Perhaps the closest equivalent for us today would be the concept of civilization.

For the apostle John, the world (*kosmos*) is a hostile, dangerous place that is in rebellion against God. It has rejected God's standards and embraced sin instead. To use John's metaphors, the world is a place where people love darkness rather than light (John 3:19). This is not the world God created, but the world that has strayed far from its Creator.

God loves the world despite this rebellion (John 3:16; compare 13:1). God's created children have rejected his kingly reign, but he seeks to save them from their chosen fate of eternal death nonetheless. God's plan for this is centered on the sending of his beloved Son, Jesus, to be a sacrifice for sin and to call people to lives of love and holiness. Rather than crushing ungrateful humanity like a bug, God seeks to rescue it from its self-created pit of rebellious sin.

Last week's lesson addressed the world's hatred of Christ's disciples, which should be an understandable state of affairs given the world's hostility toward God himself. But God's victory (and ours) in this great cosmic battle is assured.

I. Trust in the World's Savior
(1 JOHN 4:13-16)
A. Sent by the Father (vv. 13, 14)

13. This is how we know that we live in him and he in us: He has given us of his Spirit.

This week's lesson begins where last week's left off: with the promise of God's Spirit in the life of the believer. A careful reading here might surprise us, because John speaks not only of the Spirit living in the heart of the believer (*he in us*) but also *that we live in him*. God gives his Spirit not only to live in our hearts but also to make it possible that we live in the heart of the Father.

This is similar to Jesus' saying, "Remain in me, as I also remain in you" (John 15:4). Our rela-

tionship with God is not a one-way street. As God gives us his Spirit, we give God ourselves—*we live in him*. Paul, in addressing the Athenians, quoted a pagan philosopher as saying correctly that "in him we live and move and have our being" (Acts 17:28).

14. And we have seen and testify that the Father has sent his Son to be the Savior of the world.

John sometimes uses the word *we* in an apostolic sense, *we [the apostles]*. This is what we find at the beginning of this letter, where those included in the *we* are ones who saw and touched Jesus physically (1 John 1:1). That usage is what we have in the verse before us. Of the original apostolic band, John is likely the only one still living as he writes in the AD 80s or 90s. He knows that his time is short, so he feels compelled to testify yet again before the grave takes him as well.

Jesus has revealed the Father to sinful humanity as a loving God who has never given up on his lost children, the world (*kosmos*; see the Lesson Background) in rebellion against him (John 3:17). There was nothing accidental or incidental about Jesus' mission; he was sent to save. Nothing is more important or central than that for John.

What Do You Think?
In what ways do you testify that the Father has sent the Son to save the world?
Talking Points for Your Discussion
- When in the company of fellow Christians
- When in the company of unbelievers

B. Confessed by the Believer (vv. 15, 16)

15. If anyone acknowledges that Jesus is the Son of God, God lives in them and they in God.

A purpose running throughout this letter is to answer the implied question, "How do I know I am in a true, saving fellowship with God?" (see 1 John 2:5, 6). John answers this in several ways, and the verse before us provides one of those answers.

The confession *Jesus is the Son of God* has substantial implications for the confessor. To acknowledge Jesus this way is to embrace him as the authoritative Lord of one's life, to live for him, and to follow his teachings. To confess Jesus is to be his follower in a trusting relationship of faith and service. It is also to be one who lives in the presence of God and allows God's Spirit to live in his or her life at the deepest level.

16. And so we know and rely on the love God has for us.

God is love. Whoever lives in love lives in God, and God in them.

John's writings are well known for their *God is* _____ statements. His Gospel records Jesus teaching that "God is truthful" (John 3:33) and "God is spirit" (4:24). This letter teaches us that "God is light" (1 John 1:5) and that *God is love* (here and 4:8). These are not contradictory statements but complementary descriptions. God is all of these (and more).

In the verse before us, the love of God is used to explain more fully how we dwell in him. This is not physical habitation but a description of relationship. When we understand and accept the love God has for us (as shown by the gift of his Son), our relationship is determined. It is a relationship of loving trust, so much so that John can say we live in God and he in us.

This cannot be separated from the thought of the previous verse, which conditions our relationship to God with our acknowledgment of Christ as his Son. We cannot accept Jesus as the Son

HOW TO SAY IT

apostolic	ap-uh-*stahl*-ick.
Athenians	Uh-*thin*-e-unz.
Et tu, Brute	Et too, *Brew*-teh.
kosmos *(Greek)*	*kahss*-moss.

of God without understanding the loving sacrifice he represents, a defining expression of God's love. John's point is that when we understand and receive the love of God, it makes us into persons of love as well.

❧   *WHERE DO YOU LIVE?*   ❧

"Where do you live?" is a common question between people. It might be asked by Americans or Canadians of each other when their paths cross while on vacation in Europe. Or it could be Europeans asking the question of each other as they visit Death Valley National Park, a very popular tourist destination for those from Germany, France, and the United Kingdom. But one does not have to be on foreign soil; the same question might be part of the conversation between two residents of the same town.

Where we live is important; it is part of our identity. Revealing that information can give others some hints about "who we are." Of course, it's possible to misjudge others in that respect because of prejudices one may have about those who live "on the other side of the tracks," as the old saying goes.

Now think about this: Have you ever heard anyone answer the question, "Where do you live?" with "I live in Christ"? Whether we answer that way or not, the apostle John encourages us to think about the implications of that fact. How might your life change if you were to ask of yourself "Where will I live today?" each morning as you arise?

—C. R. B.

II. Trust in Perfect Love
(1 JOHN 4:17-21)

A. No Fear (vv. 17-19)

17, 18. This is how love is made complete among us so that we will have confidence on the day of judgment: In this world we are like Jesus. There is no fear in love. But perfect love drives out fear, because fear has to do with punishment. The one who fears is not made perfect in love.

We should not fear those we love if we are convinced they love us back. John reminds his readers that Christians have nothing to fear about *the day of judgment* because the judge has already proven his love for us. This is *perfect love*, a relationship that does not fear punishment because a negative judgment in the future is not going to happen. God will not reverse course and punish those upon whom he has lavished his love.

The test of this is to ask whether we still have fear in our relationship with God. If so, we are *not made perfect in love*—our relationship is fearfully flawed, dangerously imperfect. It will be fixed by loving fearlessly, loving without reservation. We don't quench our fears by reckless courage but by confident love. This is the life of no fear, for we are in fellowship with God (see Psalm 27:1).

> **What Do You Think?**
> How does Satan use fear to hinder our relationship with God? How do we counteract this?
> *Talking Points for Your Discussion*
> - Regarding how we view God
> - Regarding how we view ourselves
> - Regarding how we view the world
> - Other

19. We love because he first loved us.

Christian love is possible because God has made the first move. Our love for God is not the fearful groping for elusive and hidden gods as in paganism; rather, it is a response to a loving Creator God who has revealed himself to us and proven his love for us in his Son, Jesus Christ.

B. No Deceit (vv. 20, 21)

20. Whoever claims to love God yet hates a brother or sister is a liar. For whoever does not love their brother and sister, whom they have seen, cannot love God, whom they have not seen.

Godly love is to be a chain reaction from God to us and from us to others. It is inconsistent to hate others while confessing *I love God*. To do both is to be *a liar*, a very strong statement for John (compare 1 John 2:4). We demonstrate our love for God by more than mere words; we show it by our loving actions toward others. For John, it makes no sense—and is in fact quite self-contradictory—to

claim God's love and not live it out in our relationships with others (compare 1 John 3:11-18, last week's lesson).

> **What Do You Think?**
> What can we do to avoid rationalizing our failure to love as God expects?
> *Talking Points for Your Discussion*
> - Role of prayer
> - Role of Scripture
> - Role of confession and accountability
> - Role of repentance
> - Other

21. And he has given us this command: Anyone who loves God must also love their brother and sister.

A minor problem here is identifying to whom the word *he* refers. Have we received *this command* from God the Father or from Jesus the Son? The flow of thought from verse 20 would seem to indicate that the Father is the source, while Mark 12:29-31 suggests that the command comes from Jesus.

Since Jesus speaks on behalf of the Father (John 12:49, 50), it makes no real difference. Either way, the command *anyone who loves God must also love their brother and sister* is of divine origin, and it reflects the instructions Jesus gave to his disciples in the upper room during the last supper (see John 13:34; compare 15:12, 17).

This speaks directly to those in churches under John's oversight whose members are causing division and strife (compare 3 John 9, 10; lesson 10). It also stands as an appropriate reminder for today's churches where the presence of fussing and fighting makes us wonder whether the combatants really love God when they seem to dislike each other so much.

III. Trust in God's Victory
(1 John 5:1-5)
A. Joyfully Obeying (vv. 1-3)

1. Everyone who believes that Jesus is the Christ is born of God, and everyone who loves the father loves his child as well.

This verse pushes beyond identifying God's children by their love to their identification in terms of being *born of God*. The intersection of "being born" and "love" is most famously found in older translations of John 3:16, which speak to the unique relationship between the Father and the "only begotten" Son. (NIV has "one and only" instead of "only begotten.") As we see in the verse before us, if we have placed faith in the Son, then we are part of God's extended family (compare 1 John 4:7).

John illustrates the expectation of mutual love among the members of that extended family by noting a custom of society: affection for someone who is a father is normally extended to that man's child as well. If I have a dear friend whose child needs my assistance, I will be very inclined to help. Love is a natural experience between members of different families who are close. In a spiritual context, if I love the Father, then I will trust the Son and love all who are bound by this common faith.

2, 3. This is how we know that we love the children of God: by loving God and carrying out his commands. In fact, this is love for God: to keep his commands. And his commands are not burdensome,

As often happens in this letter, John repeats his earlier points as a basis for moving to a new teaching. Where John pushes a little further here is in pointing out that God's expectations *are not burdensome* (compare Matthew 11:30). While the Bible is much more than an instruction manual for teaching us how the Creator intends for us to live, it does have important commands in that regard. Many folks purchase a new tool or gadget but neglect to read the instruction manual, resulting in frustration, damage to the item, or even personal injury. How much better to use a tool the way it is designed to be used!

Following God's commands as he intends will not result in oppressive impositions on our freedom. We are designed to love God and love others. Failure to do either brings disaster. A failure to maintain loving relationships does not merely hurt those we spurn, it also hurts us. Love for God is reciprocal as God loves us in return. Love for others may be a one-way street if our love is not returned, but may we love nevertheless.

B. Faithfully Overcoming (vv. 4, 5)

4, 5. . . . for everyone born of God overcomes the world. This is the victory that has overcome the world, even our faith. Who is it that overcomes the world? Only the one who believes that Jesus is the Son of God.

It is not a crushing victory over the citizens of the world that we seek; rather, it is to overcome the flawed principles by which the world lives (Colossians 2:8, 20-23). The outworking of such principles may be expressed in many categories (see Mark 7:20-23; Romans 1:29-31; Galatians 5:19-21; 1 Peter 2:1). However, we can sum these up by saying that the world's values are polar opposites to God's command to love one another.

Would we have wars if we all loved one another? Would grinding poverty be possible in a world where everyone loved each other? Would crimes be committed in a world where all people loved one another? When we practice love, we may join with Jesus in saying, "I have overcome the world" (John 16:33).

> *What Do You Think?*
> What would you say are the three most important victories that a Christian needs to win in overcoming the world? How does love factor in?
> *Talking Points for Your Discussion*
> - Regarding issues of the body
> - Regarding issues of the spirit
> - Regarding issues of the intellect
> - Other

❧ *The Miracle Worker* ❧

The story of Helen Keller's life was presented dramatically in the 1962 film *The Miracle Worker*. The original stage play of the same name, the film that followed, and later adaptations for TV were based on Keller's 1902 autobiography *The Story of My Life*. She had become blind and deaf in infancy as a result of scarlet fever. Frustrated by the irreversible effects of her illness, she became uncontrollable.

Anne Sullivan came to the Keller home to tutor the youngster. In a fascinating portrayal of the battle of wills between the two, the film shows the power of Anne's love for Helen and a persistent faith that the obstinate child could overcome the huge challenges she was facing. As a result of the discipline Helen learned through Anne's work, she grew up to become the first person who was deaf and blind to earn a Bachelor of Arts degree.

Jesus offered this sobering assessment of those who rejected him: "They hardly hear with their ears, and they have closed their eyes" (Matthew 13:15). Lest we think that we as Christians are exempt from such criticism, we should remember that Jesus offered a similar assessment of his own disciples: "Do you have eyes but fail to see, and ears but fail to hear?" (Mark 8:18). But fear not —Jesus, the ultimate miracle worker, can break through our stubbornness in these areas if we surrender to him. This is part of our faith. To develop spiritual hearing and sight for the things of Jesus is to overcome the things of the world.   —C. R. B.

Visual for Lesson 8. *Point to this visual as you introduce the discussion question that is associated with verses 4, 5.*

Conclusion

A. Fearless Love

Romantic relationships can be sabotaged by fear. What begins as an exploratory friendship may blossom into a committed relationship, but then one or both persons in that relationship may become wary. Perhaps there has been a crushing betrayal in a past relationship. Perhaps there are clues to personality quirks that seem undesirable. Perhaps there is a natural reticence, with an unwillingness to disclose oneself to the other.

What if there could be relationships without reserve, without protective tactics, without fear? What if there could be a giving of oneself without holding anything back, a fearless love? Today's lesson features the memorable line "perfect love drives out fear." As we analyze this truth, we understand why our relationships are imperfect: we fear. If we were to love without limits, there would be no fear. If we could lay our fears aside, we would have full, rich relationships of love.

This might be too much to ask for human relationships, but not for our relationship with God. It is difficult if not impossible to imagine God being afraid of anything, and there was nothing held back in his plan to redeem sinful and rebellious humanity. God sent his Son, his only Son, his beloved Son, into the enemy camp to die in order to save us from certain death, eternal death. It is this God-like, fearless love that we are called to in today's lesson.

Are there fearful things in your relationship with God? Are there hidden closets you don't want him to see into? Fear not, he already knows what is in those places! He knows every nook and cranny of your heart. He knows, but he loves you anyway.

Your relationship with God will always be stunted if you hold back. Today may be the day when your love for your loving God overwhelms those fears. When that happens, you will begin to overcome the world.

B. Prayer

Heavenly Father, we confess that our sin and our tendency to sin cause us to fear. Grant us strength to lay our fears aside as we come to you in loving trust. We can never match your love, but may we strive nevertheless to love you with all of our hearts, souls, minds, and strength. In Jesus' name we pray, amen.

C. Thought to Remember

Love drives out fear.

INVOLVEMENT LEARNING

Enhance your lesson with NIV® Bible Student (from your curriculum supplier) and the reproducible activity page (at www.standardlesson.com or in the back of the NIV® *Standard Lesson Commentary Deluxe Edition).*

Into the Lesson

Write the following list on the board before learners arrive: *Pretending to be something one is not / Being obsessive about one's physical appearance / Being aloof and keeping the other person guessing / Being possessive and controlling.* To begin class, point to the first entry as you ask, "What fears might cause people to act this way in a dating relationship?" Do the same for the other three. Possible responses, respectively, include fear of not being accepted for who they are, fear of not being attractive to the other person, fear of commitment, fear of losing the other person.

Then ask, "Why should none of these be relevant to our having a loving relationship with God?" Responses should include the facts that God already knows everything about us and that he will never abandon us. After some discussion say, "The apostle John tells us that perfect love drives out fear. We'll learn more about the *how* and *why* of God's perfect love in today's lesson."

Into the Word

Form the class into four groups and distribute handouts of the following assignments (one group assignment per handout, one handout per group):

Confidence Group—Four facts: received God's Spirit / Jesus is Savior / confession of faith in Jesus / God's nature. Read 1 John 4:13-16. How do each of the four facts give us the confidence to love others as John says we should?

Fearlessness Group—Four facts: no fear on Judgment Day / we're like Jesus / perfection in love is the goal / God went first. Read 1 John 4:17-19. What do the four facts tell us about why we can be fearless in our love for others?

Caring Group—Four facts: loving God = loving others / hating a fellow Christian = not loving God / we can see others / others are God's children. Read 1 John 4:20, 21; 5:1, 2. In what ways do the four facts motivate us to be caring toward others?

Victory Group—Four facts: to love God is to obey him / his commands are doable / we are faithful overcomers / we are believers in Jesus. Read 1 John 5:3-5. How do the four facts give us confidence that we will be victorious in our efforts to love others?

As the groups work, write the four facts of each on the board. Call for conclusions after an appropriate amount of time. Point to each fact in turn as the groups address them.

Option. To reinforce the lesson, distribute copies of the true/false activity "The Truth About Love" from the reproducible page, which you can download. You can also use this as a pretest to the lesson; in that case, make it a closed-Bible exercise in which learners will only indicate true or false, not chapter and verse numbers. Assure learners that they will score their own work; you will not collect the tests.

Into Life

Either in their small groups or with the class as a whole, ask learners to come up with responses to the following Christians who are having difficulty understanding John's message properly from today's lesson.

Fearful Freddie: "My love for others is far from perfect. What if I come up short in the 'loving others' department on the Day of Judgment?"

Judging Julie: "I do my best to put up with everyone. But some of the people at our church just aren't keeping God's commands the way they should, so it's hard for me to like them, let alone love them!"

Option. Distribute copies of "The Fear Factor" activity from the reproducible page and have learners complete it as a self-evaluation on how fear interferes with their loving expressions of help to fellow Christians. Depending on the nature of your class, you may wish to assign this as a take-home exercise.

WATCH OUT FOR DECEIVERS

DEVOTIONAL READING: Galatians 6:6-10
BACKGROUND SCRIPTURE: 1 John 5:6-12, 18-20; 2 John

2 JOHN

¹ The elder,

To the lady chosen by God and to her children, whom I love in the truth—and not I only, but also all who know the truth—² because of the truth, which lives in us and will be with us forever:

³ Grace, mercy and peace from God the Father and from Jesus Christ, the Father's Son, will be with us in truth and love.

⁴ It has given me great joy to find some of your children walking in the truth, just as the Father commanded us. ⁵ And now, dear lady, I am not writing you a new command but one we have had from the beginning. I ask that we love one another. ⁶ And this is love: that we walk in obedience to his commands. As you have heard from the beginning, his command is that you walk in love.

⁷ I say this because many deceivers, who do not acknowledge Jesus Christ as coming in the flesh, have gone out into the world. Any such person is the deceiver and the antichrist. ⁸ Watch out that you do not lose what we have worked for, but that you may be rewarded fully. ⁹ Anyone who runs ahead and does not continue in the teaching of Christ does not have God; whoever continues in the teaching has both the Father and the Son. ¹⁰ If anyone comes to you and does not bring this teaching, do not take them into your house or welcome them. ¹¹ Anyone who welcomes them shares in their wicked work.

¹² I have much to write to you, but I do not want to use paper and ink. Instead, I hope to visit you and talk with you face to face, so that our joy may be complete.

¹³ The children of your sister, who is chosen by God, send their greetings.

KEY VERSE

Watch out that you do not lose what we have worked for, but that you may be rewarded fully. —2 John 8

THE SPIRIT COMES

Unit 2: The Community of Beloved Disciples

LESSONS 6–10

LESSON AIMS

After participating in this lesson, each learner will be able to:

1. Contrast John's concept of walking in truth with the behavior of the deceivers he warns against.

2. Describe how Christians are to relate to deceivers who attempt to infiltrate the church.

3. Identify a popular philosophy that comes from deceivers and explain how to confront it.

LESSON OUTLINE

Introduction

A. Absolute Truth

Allan Bloom (1930–1992) wrote his bestselling book *The Closing of the American Mind* nearly 30 years ago. Some consider it to be the first intellectual broadside in the so-called culture wars that are still with us today. The book's premise is that the modern university has rejected the concept of absolute truth, teaching instead that all truth is relative. As a result, students are taught that it is possible for our perceptions of truth to evolve and adapt to changing situations. Your truth might not be my truth, for each person is claimed to have the ability to create his or her own truth.

This is sometimes called *a systemic view of truth* or *truth within a particular system*. The effect of this is to see Christian claims of truth as being true for Christians only. In this way of thinking, it is perfectly OK for Christians to believe that Jesus rose from the dead; but for atheists this is not true—it's nonsense. The atheist system and the Christian system have different sets of truths, and it is not necessary to have agreement. Truth, according to this defective philosophy, should never be foisted upon society in an absolute sense, for individuals will not only decide for themselves what is true but will even create their own truths to suit their own lives.

The Bible does not teach that truth is changing and elusive. Scripture does not simply present itself as one set of truths alongside others. The Bible authors believed they were presenting absolute truths. Our lesson text for today has a great deal to say about truth.

B. Lesson Background

We have three epistles that were written by the apostle John, the former Galilean fisherman (see Mark 1:16-20). We do not know the order in which these were written; they are simply arranged by length in the New Testament.

There are connections among all three as well as with the Gospel of John (and, to a lesser extent, with the book of Revelation, also written by John). Early tradition associates all five works by John with the churches in and around the great city of Ephesus, a leading metropolitan center of the Roman Empire of the first century AD.

John probably wrote his letters in the AD 80s or early 90s. Therefore the recipients included the second generation of believers since Paul's time in the area (see Acts 19). Troubling things had happened since then. Toward the end of his life, Paul wrote two letters in this regard to his younger colleague Timothy, who was in Ephesus to help the church with doctrinal and organizational matters. Thus the battle for truth was already being waged there in the AD 60s.

It is after this period that Ephesus seems to have become a center for a burgeoning Christian heresy called *gnosticism*. This movement claimed to have special knowledge of Christ (the word *gnosis* means "knowledge"). The gnostics taught that Jesus had not been fully human but was a divine visitation of deity to earth, something like in the legends of the Greek gods.

Since a nonhuman, immortal Jesus could not really die on the cross, the gnostics did not teach that Jesus' death was an atoning sacrifice for sins. Instead, they taught that salvation came from secret knowledge, from being enlightened to esoteric truths that Jesus had taught only to the innermost circle of his disciples. Gnosticism seems not to have developed fully as a rival version of Christianity until after the end of the first century AD, but its seeds were being sown in John's day. Thus his need to address in his letters gnostic-type falsehoods.

I. Basis of Unity
(2 JOHN 1-3)
A. Loving in Truth (v. 1)

1a. The elder,
To the lady chosen by God and to her children,

John identifies himself merely as *the elder*. This may be a title by which he is known because of both his age and the esteem in which he is held (compare 1 Peter 5:1). Some see the letter's address *to the lady chosen by God* as a symbolic reference to a church, partly because the Greek word for *church* is a feminine noun. But it is more likely that the addressee is a particular woman, perhaps

someone who hosts a church in her home (compare Colossians 4:15; Philemon 2).

She is *chosen* in the sense of being counted among the saved, a believer in Christ (see John 20:31; 1 John 5:13). *Her children* could be a reference to the woman's literal sons and/or daughters, or it may be a symbolic way of referring to the other believers in the congregation.

1b. . . . whom I love in the truth—and not I only, but also all who know the truth—

John, known as "the apostle of love," begins by reminding his readers that he loves them. The phrase *in the truth* has an adverbial sense: he truly loves them. It is equivalent to our idea of *genuine*, as in *I genuinely love you*. Truth refers to reality, and that is the nature of John's affection for the letter's recipients—it is real.

Second, John speaks of truth as something that can be known. Knowing the truth is a path to freedom: "You will know the truth, and the truth will set you free" (John 8:32). Truth is readily accessible, in contrast with the gnostic idea of "secret truth" (see the Lesson Background).

What Do You Think?
How should we converse with someone who denies the existence of absolute truth?
Talking Points for Your Discussion
▪ Questions to ask and not ask
▪ Affirmations to make and avoid
▪ Illustrations to use and avoid
▪ Other

B. Living in Truth (vv. 2, 3)

2a. . . . because of the truth, which lives in us

The fact that truth is something *which lives in us* gives a personal sense to truth as an indwelling power, probably tying truth to the person of Jesus in the process. We have access to Jesus as "the way and the truth and the life" (John 14:6) when we follow his instructions to remain in him as he remains in us (15:4).

2b. . . . and will be with us forever:

Truth is not temporary or situational, but is something that *will be with us forever*. As noted in the Introduction, today's culture has rejected the concept of absolute truth. While John does not use the phrase *absolute truth,* the concept of eternal (*forever*) truth comes close and may even be stronger. Truth is truth whether we recognize it or not. Truth does not require our permission.

3. Grace, mercy and peace from God the Father and from Jesus Christ, the Father's Son, will be with us in truth and love.

John concludes his salutation with a threefold blessing: *grace, mercy,* and *peace* (compare 1 Timothy 1:2; 2 Timothy 1:2). These are gifts from both *God the Father* and *the Father's Son.* In this context, *grace* is the special favor of God (compare 1 Corinthians 15:10), *mercy* is the kindness and compassion of God in light of our shortcomings (compare Luke 1:50), and *peace* is both a lack of personal turmoil and the presence of personal well-being (compare John 14:27).

These things from God are offered by John *in truth and love,* which gives us another aspect to truth. God's ways are true, but for the believer they are accompanied by love. When we are captives to sin, God's truths about right living and holiness may seem harsh, even unreasonable. But there is always a loving Father behind those truths, a Creator who desires the best for us.

II. Threat from Deceivers
(2 John 4-11)
A. Truth (vv. 4-6)

4. It has given me great joy to find some of your children walking in the truth, just as the Father commanded us.

We find in this verse yet another aspect to John's understanding of *truth:* it is something we can walk in. To fail to do so is to "walk in the darkness" (1 John 1:6). *Walking* in this sense is

HOW TO SAY IT

epistles	ee-*pis*-uls.
Galilean	Gal-uh-*lee*-un.
gnosticism	**nahss**-tih-*sizz*-um.
gnostics	*nahss*-ticks.
heresies	*hair*-uh-seez.
heretics	**hair**-uh-*tiks*.
Philemon	Fih-*lee*-mun or Fye-*lee*-mun.

not physical exercise but the manner of one's life. This is the counterpart to John's earlier teaching that truth lives within the believer (v. 2, above).

In both cases, we live truth. We don't just study truth in the way we might study a famous poem to find its meaning. We actually practice truth in words and actions. Our words and actions are to coincide perfectly as guided by God's standards. The concept of walking-as-living has an Old Testament background (see Genesis 17:1; 1 Kings 2:4; 11:33; 2 Kings 20:3; Micah 4:5).

> **What Do You Think?**
> What things bring joy to your life that are different from what brings joy to unbelievers?
> *Talking Points for Your Discussion*
> - Regarding achievements
> - Regarding milestones of life
> - Regarding possessions
> - Other

5. And now, dear lady, I am not writing you a new command but one we have had from the beginning. I ask that we love one another.

John likes to boil things down to a single commandment (see John 15:12; 1 John 4:21, lesson 8): the old but ever-new commandment to *love one another* (John 13:34; 1 John 3:11, lesson 7). John is repeating what he remembers well from Jesus, what John has taught throughout his lengthy ministry.

> **What Do You Think?**
> Why is love for one another so vital among the people of God?
> *Talking Points for Your Discussion*
> - Considering who God is and what he has done
> - Considering what Christ has called his church to be and do
> - Other

6. And this is love: that we walk in obedience to his commands. As you have heard from the beginning, his command is that you walk in love.

Having just discussed the commandment to "love one another," John now adjusts the flow of thought by noting that *this is love: that we walk in obedience to his commands.* We love as we live (*walk*) by God's directions, of which a vitally important one is to live a life of love. The ideas are so tightly bound together as to be inseparable.

Such love is not the same as blanket toleration of false teachers (something John addresses in the second half of the letter). Rather, it is a demonstration of a heart that truly loves God and overflows with tender compassion. God did not create us in such a way that we can love him and hate others. After all, our example in this is Jesus, whose love crosses every ethnic, racial, economic, cultural, and language barrier ever used by humans to justify separation or animosity. Perhaps we can modify the cultural expression "shoot first and ask questions later" to be "love first and ask questions later."

B. Untruth (vv. 7, 8)

7. I say this because many deceivers, who do not acknowledge Jesus Christ as coming in the flesh, have gone out into the world. Any such person is the deceiver and the antichrist.

John now turns his attention to the *many deceivers* who are troubling his people (compare Matthew 7:15; 1 John 4:1). He wants his readers to be loving, but this does not mean they should ignore errors among their teachers, especially errors that undermine the historical basis of the Christian faith.

The false teaching John targets is a denial of the fact that Jesus had come *in the flesh.* This is a denial of the humanity of Jesus, making him into a god similar to the deities of the Greek myths. This is the error of gnosticism (see the Lesson Background). If Jesus were not human, then he could not have died; if he had not died, there would be no atoning sacrifice for our sins (see 1 John 2:2).

This type of deceiver is *the antichrist.* For John, *antichrist* is not simply a singular figure prophesied to emerge at the end of time, but a spirit of falsehood that infiltrates the church (see 1 John 2:18; 4:1-3).

Before moving on, we should not miss the importance of the opening *I say this because.* This phrase ties the previous thoughts to those of the verse before us. Walking in the command to love

will be a vital method to protect oneself from deceivers.

> **What Do You Think?**
> How do we stay on the alert for deceivers?
> *Talking Points for Your Discussion*
> - Regarding their audience (2 Timothy 3:6; etc.)
> - Regarding their goals (1 Timothy 6:3-5; etc.)
> - Regarding their message (2 Timothy 2:18; etc.)
> - Regarding their tactics (Romans 16:18; etc.)
> - Regarding their "proofs" (Mark 13:22; etc.)
> - Regarding their lifestyle (Jude 4; etc.)

8. Watch out that you do not lose what we have worked for, but that you may be rewarded fully.

Watch out is John's way of saying, "Pay attention, this is important!" Those who follow deception may not *be rewarded fully.* John does not say specifically what this potential loss of reward would entail. Some think it refers to loss of salvation (a forfeiture of eternal life), particularly in light of what verse 9 (next) says. Others propose, less severely, that it refers to a diminished recompense in the hereafter (compare Matthew 5:12; Mark 9:41; 1 Corinthians 3:8-15; Revelation 11:18; 22:12).

We can at least say that John is including the loss of spiritual rewards in the here and now: the blessings of grace, mercy, and peace that we saw in the letter's salutation. Following false teaching is not without consequence.

❧ DECEIVING THE GULLIBLE ❧

Who among us hasn't returned home from a vacation with a souvenir of the trip? Such souvenirs are often little more than inexpensive trinkets that "say something" about the location we visited. Often they make nice refrigerator magnets!

But deceivers are everywhere, even in the souvenir business. For example, visitors to Niagara Falls have sometimes purchased worn pieces of wood on the basis of deceitful testimony that the wood was from barrels in which daredevils had gone over the falls. In the early 1900s, gullible visitors bought jewelry made from pieces of white gypsum stones found in the bed of the Niagara River, said souvenir-seekers having been led to believe that the stones were "petrified mist" from the falls!

Much more serious is the kind of deceit about which John warns: false views of Christ. Today, as in John's time, false teachers make a name for themselves—and sometimes accrue a small fortune—by teaching doctrines that contradict the truths God has revealed to us in his Word. People today may go to great lengths to avoid being deceived into buying fake antiques, used cars with falsified titles, etc. Are we as careful to ensure that we are not being deceived spiritually? See Acts 17:11.   —C. R. B.

C. Admonition (vv. 9-11)

9. Anyone who runs ahead and does not continue in the teaching of Christ does not have God; whoever continues in the teaching has both the Father and the Son.

John describes in stark terms the problem of following the false teaching at issue. The one *who runs ahead* goes beyond the boundaries of sound teaching. To do so is to move away from *the teaching of Christ*, the things John has taught about Jesus. To travel such a path causes a person not to have God, since wrong teaching about Christ denies God's rightful place in teaching and life (compare 1 John 2:22, 23).

By contrast, continuing *in the teaching* of Christ is to reject deceptions and therefore to have *both the Father and the Son* (compare 1 John 4:15, lesson 8). John's urgent and heartfelt desire is for his readers to reject dangerous false doctrines about the nature of Christ and thereby remain in fellowship with God and with his people, the church.

10, 11. If anyone comes to you and does not bring this teaching, do not take them into your house or welcome them. Anyone who welcomes them shares in their wicked work.

John is not merely speaking hypothetically in this letter. The false teachers are a real and present danger, and they have visited the churches of the region to spew their heresies. John probably can name names but chooses not to. These deceivers pose such a danger that John instructs "the lady chosen by God and . . . her children"

(v. 1) to deny them any sort of hospitality. Since the churches of this time mostly meet in private homes, the prohibition *do not take them into your house* implies barring the false teachers from the fellowship meeting.

John forbids even welcoming the heretics. The heresies are so dangerous that their advocates do not deserve even a hint of acceptance (although this is not to suggest rudeness instead). The false teacher must be rejected as an act of self-preservation (compare Romans 16:17; Ephesians 5:11; 2 Thessalonians 3:6). To fail in this regard will result in sharing *in their wicked work.*

> **What Do You Think?**
> Under what circumstances, if any, do you invite itinerant missionaries of cults "into your house" when they knock on your door? Why?
> *Talking Points for Your Discussion*
> - Considering opportunities for evangelizing
> - Considering your own spiritual maturity to resist their false teaching
> - Other

III. Complete in Joy
(2 John 12, 13)

A. Anticipation (v. 12)

12. I have much to write to you, but I do not want to use paper and ink. Instead, I hope to visit you and talk with you face to face, so that our joy may be complete.

Now we learn the reason for the brevity of the letter: John expects to visit the lady and her church in the near future. Communication that is *face to face* allows for greater and more immediate clarity than does the writing of letters, texting, or sending e-mails (compare 3 John 13, 14; next week's lesson). John's letter may leave unanswered some questions regarding the false teachers and their message. In-person dialogue will allow all questions to be brought out in the open and answered, and misunderstandings can be corrected in a timely manner.

This is the preferable way, so much so that John speaks of its being a *joy.* He won't come to scold or berate, but to encourage and enjoy their company.

Some of us can remember when a long-distance phone call was an occasional luxury. Instead of a written letter, such a call offered the opportunity to hear a loved one's voice, even if only briefly (because of the cost). Missionaries in foreign countries had to schedule their calls back to their families and supporters, and the costs seemed astronomical.

How times have changed! Now a call across the country is no more expensive than a call across the street—and we carry the phone in our pocket or purse! From that phone we can send a text message around the world almost instantly. We can talk face-to-face, in a sense, with overseas missionaries by using certain audiovisual software free of connection charges! In spite of this, most of us would still rather talk face-to-face in the actual (not virtual) presence of a loved one.

In New Testament times, communication methods other than the face-to-face kind were very much slower than those of today, a fact that accentuates John's strong desire to talk personally with his letter's recipient(s). Do you feel no need to talk with people personally about Christ because you post Scripture verses on your Facebook page? If so, do you see a problem with this? —C. R. B.

B. Greeting (v. 13)

13. The children of your sister, who is chosen by God, send their greetings.

The lady of verse 1 being addressed has a sister. This may be a sister church, but is more likely her literal sibling. The lady's nephews and/or nieces apparently are the current companions of John. We can be sure there is an interesting story here, but John does not tell it. Perhaps he is saving the telling for his reunion with "the lady chosen by God," a beloved sister in Christ.

Conclusion

A. Daily Deceptions

We live in a world of instant media saturation regarding the most trivial of things. We are given information about celebrities beyond any healthy need to know. Some of these reports are so bizarre

Visual for Lesson 9. *Point to this visual as you ask, "How is the classic 'shell game' similar to what deceivers in the church try to do?"*

that they strain credibility, but they are accepted as truth by fascinated fans. In politics, unsubstantiated rumors are started on blogs and sometimes repeated enough so that a lie gains credibility, becoming almost impossible to quash. These are examples of daily deceptions that we must sift through in order to protect ourselves from untruth.

Whom should we believe? Whom should we trust? These are questions we should not have to ask within the church. We should have leaders who teach correct doctrine, not deceptive heresies. The church should be a place of truth, not a place for deceivers to roam freely. This is why John advises such severe tactics when it comes to those who would distort the gospel by denying Christ's true humanity, atoning death, etc. Such teachers must themselves be denied any place of influence within the church. This applies whether they are on speaking tours, writing books, or hosting television shows. May our leaders guard us from error so that our gatherings are times of joy, not dangerous indulgences of falsehood.

B. Prayer

Lord God, may you guard our hearts from those who would deceive us about your Son. May we be lovers of truth and true lovers of you and your children. In Jesus' name, amen.

C. Thought to Remember

Never abandon the truth.

INVOLVEMENT LEARNING

Enhance your lesson with NIV® Bible Student (from your curriculum supplier) and the reproducible activity page (at www.standardlesson.com or in the back of the NIV® Standard Lesson Commentary Deluxe Edition).

Into the Lesson

Wear a mask of a notable person to class. (Or simply wear a brown paper bag with eyeholes cut out and other features crudely drawn on.) Ask, "Why do people wear masks?" Anticipate learners to respond that masks are worn to conceal one's identity in some way. Say, "Masks are designed to deceive. Often this is in harmless fun, such as at a costume party. Today's lesson is about a harmful kind of deception."

Into the Word

Ask volunteers to read the text aloud, changing readers with each verse. Say, "Note the two key words *truth* and *love* that conclude verse 3. Now count the number of times each of those words occurs in the first six verses." (Results: five for *truth*; five for *love*.) Draw learners' attention to verses 7-11 and ask who can identify the one key truth the deceivers are denying. (The answer is in verse 7: denying that Jesus came in the flesh.)

Then ask, "How does the truth of the incarnation relate to the concept of God's love?" If no one suggests John 1:14 and 3:16, do that yourself. The truth of Jesus' incarnation in those verses will allow you to emphasize John's strong affirmation of it, the reason for it, and its role in his writings.

Continue: "John's concern for the ones he addresses—including us by extension—compels him to offer godly counsel about *truth* and *love*. I'm going to state a resolution to see if we can discern the existence of these two ideas side by side. After you hear the resolution, scan the lesson text to determine (1) where the two ideas (not necessarily the words themselves) *truth* and *love* intersect and (2) why." Then say, "Be It Resolved: We should deny hospitality to those who spread false doctrine."

*Expected response: 2 John 10, 11—**truth** is implied by the existence of wrong teaching; **love** is implied by a desire to protect the church from wrong*

teaching and teachers. Use the resulting discussion as a transition into the next activity.

Into Life

Divide learners into pairs or small groups of no more than three. Designate half the groups/pairs to be *Truth Proclaimers*; their assignment is to describe a church that proclaims truth at the expense of promoting love. Designate the other half of the groups/pairs to be *Love Promoters*; their assignment is to describe a church that promotes love at the expense of proclaiming truth. After a few minutes, have pairs/groups present their descriptions for whole-class discussion.

Alternative. Instead of the above, distribute copies of the "Truth Is . . ." and "Love Is . . ." activities from the reproducible page, which you can download. Have learners complete as directed; this can be a small-group exercise.

Following either activity, write the following quotes on the board. Pause after you write each to give learners time to react.

1. "There are no whole truths; all truths are half truths. It is trying to treat them as whole truths that plays the devil" (Alfred North Whitehead).

2. "The victor will never be asked if he told the truth" (Adolf Hitler).

3. "Truth—what we think it is at any given moment of time" (Luigi Pirandello).

If learners need a bit of prompting, challenge them to consider the underlying belief or basis of each quote (the presupposition) and how Christians can confront these. *Possible how-to-confront responses:* 1. By its own declaration, the statement itself must be a half-truth; so which part are we not to believe? 2. Untrue—it happens all the time, especially when today's victor becomes tomorrow's vanquished. 3. People once believed the world was flat. It was not for that reason "true"!

Option. For a take-home exercise, distribute copies of the "Face-to-Face Joy" activity.

WORK TOGETHER FOR THE TRUTH

DEVOTIONAL READING: **2 Timothy 2:14-19**
BACKGROUND SCRIPTURE: **3 John**

3 JOHN

¹ The elder,

To my dear friend Gaius, whom I love in the truth.

² Dear friend, I pray that you may enjoy good health and that all may go well with you, even as your soul is getting along well. ³ It gave me great joy when some believers came and testified about your faithfulness to the truth, telling how you continue to walk in it. ⁴ I have no greater joy than to hear that my children are walking in the truth.

⁵ Dear friend, you are faithful in what you are doing for the brothers and sisters, even though they are strangers to you. ⁶ They have told the church about your love. Please send them on their way in a manner that honors God. ⁷ It was for the sake of the Name that they went out, receiving no help from the pagans. ⁸ We ought therefore to show hospitality to such people so that we may work together for the truth.

⁹ I wrote to the church, but Diotrephes, who loves to be first, will not welcome us. ¹⁰ So when I come, I will call attention to what he is doing, spreading malicious nonsense about us. Not satisfied with that, he even refuses to welcome other believers. He also stops those who want to do so and puts them out of the church.

¹¹ Dear friend, do not imitate what is evil but what is good. Anyone who does what is good is from God. Anyone who does what is evil has not seen God. ¹² Demetrius is well spoken of by everyone—and even by the truth itself. We also speak well of him, and you know that our testimony is true.

¹³ I have much to write you, but I do not want to do so with pen and ink. ¹⁴ I hope to see you soon, and we will talk face to face.

Peace to you. The friends here send their greetings. Greet the friends there by name.

KEY VERSE

We ought therefore to show hospitality to such people so that we may work together for the truth.

—3 John 8

THE SPIRIT COMES

Unit 2: The Community of Beloved Disciples

LESSONS 6–10

LESSON AIMS

After participating in this lesson, each learner will be able to:

1. Summarize the work of Gaius, Diotrephes, and Demetrius.

2. Suggest some modern activities these men might be involved in if they were living today.

3. Identify one faithful worker in the church and tell how he or she can partner with this worker.

LESSON OUTLINE

Introduction

A. The Prosperity Gospel

One peculiarly American distortion of the gospel is known as *the health and wealth gospel* or *the gospel of prosperity.* Religion columnist Cathleen Falsani has put this teaching in her category of "The Worst Ideas of the Decade," so this is not a false teaching hidden behind closed doors.

There are many variations to this teaching, but essentially it ties together physical, material, and spiritual health. Those who preach this doctrine tell their listeners that God wants them to be wealthy and healthy. To prosper in these ways requires strong faith, so the lack of a large bank account and/or a healthy body is a sign of spiritual failure. Sometimes this is tied to a teaching that faithfulness is measured by how much you give to a ministry and that God will multiply your monetary offering many times over in your personal life. This message has funded some very large ministries.

The gospel of prosperity has been picked up by preachers outside North America and delivered with gusto to the poor of Africa, Asia, and particularly Latin America. Christianity is proclaimed not so much as a message of reconciliation with God but as investment wisdom, a path to wealth. How all this will play out has yet to be seen, but the empty promises of this distorted gospel have already alienated many seekers of truth.

One Bible text used by prosperity preachers comes from 3 John, the focus of today's study. We will look at the entire book to see what John really intended his friend Gaius to know in this area, among other things.

B. Lesson Background

We do not know the order in which 1, 2, and 3 John were written; they are simply arranged in our Bibles by length. It is likely, though, that 2 John (lesson 9) and 3 John were written at approximately the same time because of similarity in content. Therefore the background for the two is the same, so that information from lesson 9 need not be repeated here. We can add that 3 John is the shortest book in the Bible, containing a mere 211 words in the Greek; by comparison, 2 John has 245 words and Philemon has 337. The little book of 3 John has many points of similarity with 2 John, but differs in being more specific regarding those addressed.

Both 2 and 3 John deal with the issue of hospitality in the first-century church. Nothing like our modern network of motels, hotels, and bed-and-breakfast lodging existed at the time. Therefore itinerant teachers needed to be hosted by families within a congregation. In 2 John, the apostle forbade extending hospitality to false teachers; this included denial of room and board as well as not allowing them to attend congregational meetings, which likely took place within the homes of believers. The opposite issue is addressed in 3 John.

I. Salutation
(3 John 1)
A. Name of Addressee (v. 1a)
1a. The elder,
To my dear friend Gaius,

As in 2 John 1, the author only identifies himself as *the elder*. This signifies that John enjoys a relationship of respect as a teacher and mentor with a certain *Gaius*. There are several men named Gaius in the New Testament (see Acts 19:29; 20:4; Romans 16:23; 1 Corinthians 1:14). Given that Gaius is a very common name in the Roman Empire, we do not know which, if any, of these men are in view here.

This letter has the tone of communication between two who are very close, with Gaius being addressed as John's *dear friend*. The same expression is also used in verses 2, 5, and 11 (below). John addresses many of his readers this way (see 1 John 2:7; 3:2, 21; 4:1, 7, 11).

HOW TO SAY IT

Ceres	*Sir*-eez.
Demetrius	De-*mee*-tree-us.
Diotrephes	Die-*ot*-rih-feez.
Gaius	*Gay*-us.
Philemon	Fih-*lee*-mun or Fye-*lee*-mun.
Telemachus	Taw-*leh*-maw-kuss.

B. Status of Relationship (v. 1b)
1b. . . . whom I love in the truth.

For John to love Gaius *in the truth* communicates the nature of the author's affection (compare 2 John 1, lesson 9). The warmth of this letter is striking, and we can see that John and Gaius must be very close.

II. Message
(3 John 2-12)
A. Commendation (vv. 2-8)
2. Dear friend, I pray that you may enjoy good health and that all may go well with you, even as your soul is getting along well.

Translated very literally, this verse says, "Dear friend, I am praying that in every way you have a good journey and be healthy, just as your soul has a good journey." To "have a good journey" carries the resultant meaning of doing well or prospering, which we see here. John's twofold desire for Gaius are not separate things, but connected. John seems to be saying, "I'm praying that you might do well materially and have good health, in coordination with your spiritual health."

This verse has served as a proof text for promoters of the gospel of prosperity (see the lesson Introduction). There is no promise here, however, that spiritual health will result in physical and financial health. John is praying these things *for* Gaius, just as we have prayed for our sick brothers and sisters or for fellow Christians in financial distress.

3. It gave me great joy when some believers came and testified about your faithfulness to the truth, telling how you continue to walk in it.

As in 1 and 2 John, the issue of *truth* is of paramount importance for the author. John commends Gaius in regard to truth in two ways. First, other believers have reported that Gaius is indeed one of whom it can be said that the truth is in him. This means that Gaius is demonstrating the truth of the Christian faith in his teaching.

Second, John's commendation of Gaius as being one who walks in the truth means that his life is an acted-out demonstration of what he teaches. True Christian teaching must have an impact that way. It is truth we live.

4. I have no greater joy than to hear that my children are walking in the truth.

To be one of John's *children* means to be a student who listens to his lessons on the truths of the gospel, and Gaius is one such. There is nothing more satisfying than for elderly teachers to see that what they have taught over the years has made a lasting impact on their students. This brings *joy* to any teacher of the gospel, and such is the case here.

What Do You Think?
  What are some ways to walk in truth daily?
Talking Points for Your Discussion
  - In the workplace
  - In relationships with neighbors
  - In church involvement
  - In caring for the marginalized of society
  - Other

5, 6. Dear friend, you are faithful in what you are doing for the brothers and sisters, even though they are strangers to you. They have told the church about your love. Please send them on their way in a manner that honors God.

As we review John's commendation of Gaius regarding his faithful behavior toward *the brothers and sisters*, who *are strangers* to him, we assume this group includes teachers from other congregations. They have sent back a report on how Gaius has helped them.

The fact that John encourages Gaius to send these teachers *on their way* adequately provisioned (compare Titus 3:13) seems to speak to Gaius's regular practice. Gaius should keep doing what he is already doing! This means ensuring that the visitors are well rested, have food in their packs, etc., as they depart to resume their travels. This demonstrates *love* in the best sense.

In the cultural setting of 3 John, strangers in town are seen as threats unless someone welcomes them into his or her home (compare Acts 16:15, 34, 40). Such a welcome changes the strangers' status from *outsider* to *guest*. For Gaius to welcome traveling Christian teachers into his home involves more than provision for immediate needs of food and lodging. It also allows them to operate as temporary residents of the city. Such hospitality, then, is the reception of strangers who become members of the household as long as they are in town.

What Do You Think?
  What does your church do to make Christian *outsiders* feel like welcome *guests*? What can you do personally to enhance this ministry?
Talking Points for Your Discussion
  - Regarding initial greeting
  - Regarding meal invitations
  - Regarding guest-friendly facilities
  - Other

7. It was for the sake of the Name that they went out, receiving no help from the pagans.

The Name in view is that of Jesus Christ, a symbol of the Christian faith and the church. The visitors are not traveling so that they might be personally enriched or honored. They come and go as servants of the Lord, traveling in faith that they will be received by congregations that both accept their teaching and tend to their physical needs.

The traveling teachers do not expect assistance *from the pagans* in the cities they visit. The travelers might be able to utilize their own network of friends, relatives, or business contacts to meet their food and lodging needs regardless of whether such folks are believers. But since the travelers represent Christ, they choose not to do that; instead, they depend on Christians like Gaius to receive them into their homes.

What Do You Think?
  Does this verse have anything to say about soliciting or accepting help from unbelievers today? Why, or why not?
Talking Points for Your Discussion
  - Church fund-raisers that involve selling a product (bake sales, etc.)
  - Church fund-raisers that involve providing a service (youth-group car washes, etc.)
  - Requests for donations
  - Other

8. We ought therefore to show hospitality to such people so that we may work together for the truth.

John closes this section with a broad principle: when Christian leaders travel to teach and encourage other congregations, they should be received warmly. When congregations do this, they *work together for the truth.*

B. Contrast (vv. 9-12)

9. I wrote to the church, but Diotrephes, who loves to be first, will not welcome us.

The church to which John has written is probably the one Gaius attends, but that is not certain. In stark contrast with the gracious Gaius is the inhospitable *Diotrephes,* who also attends there. He is a man who fancies himself to be a leader in the church, but he is actually more of a bully and a control freak. This is the opposite of the kind of leader that Jesus talks about in Mark 9:33-37; 10:35-44. The fact that Diotrephes *will not welcome us* is at least an indication of inhospitality and probably more (next verse).

> **What Do You Think?**
> How do we recognize that what seems to be a legitimate desire to be a church leader (1 Timothy 3:1) is actually an unholy desire for preeminence? What do we do in such cases?
> *Talking Points for Your Discussion*
> ▪ Before an individual becomes a church leader
> ▪ After an individual has become a church leader

10. So when I come, I will call attention to what he is doing, spreading malicious nonsense about us. Not satisfied with that, he even refuses to welcome other believers. He also stops those who want to do so and puts them out of the church.

John has plans to visit personally. We presume that he will be staying with Gaius, not Diotrephes! This is an opponent with whom John has tangled in the past, and John intends to confront him concerning his unacceptable behavior at three levels.

First, Diotrephes has maliciously defamed certain people; the *us* includes the traveling teachers, John himself, and perhaps even Gaius. Diotrephes has attacked either their teaching or their character (or perhaps both).

Second, Diotrephes has refused to *welcome other believers* and render the expected hospitality. From the perspective of his culture, Diotrephes might be within his rights to do this, but from a Christian perspective, he is without justification. Third, Diotrephes has warned others in his congregation not to receive such visitors, even going so far as to disfellowship those who do.

Whether or not the church of Gaius and the church of Diotrephes are the same church, these two men seem to be acquainted. John uses this connection to draw a vivid contrast between them. Gaius, unlike Diotrephes, is a man of faithful love and hospitality. He receives teachers from John because of his desire to benefit from their ministry and his deep love for fellow Christians. Gaius acts in such a way that both the visitors and his congregation will benefit from the interaction that results. Gaius does not feel threatened by the itinerant teachers.

Diotrephes, on the other hand, sees the outsiders as a threat. They remain strangers to him, never becoming guests. It may well be that their message would undermine various false ideas that Diotrephes has been propagating, teachings that perhaps accrue benefits for him personally. In behaving as he does, this man rejects the authority of the apostle John.

❧ THE DESIRE TO BE "SOMEBODY" ❧

President Calvin Coolidge once said, "It is a great advantage to a president, and a major source of safety to the country, for him to know he is not a great man." By this Coolidge was calling attention to the danger of thinking more highly of ourselves than we ought, something the apostle Paul warned about in Romans 12:3. What is true for presidents and others who have climbed to the top of the ladder of earthly success is just as true for those who are anywhere else on that ladder.

Those who aspire to do good in a spiritual sense are also in danger in this regard. As Allen Wheelis has observed, "The greater evil is wrought by those who intend good, and are convinced they know how to bring it about; and the greater their power to bring it about, the greater the evil they achieve while trying to do it."

Both President Coolidge and Dr. Wheelis could have been speaking about Diotrephes. It is possible that his desire to be "somebody" in the church was prompted by the belief that he was doing good, but the apostle John's inspired insight saw through the man's self-deception.

Jesus showed us the way to true significance. It is found in serving others, as John makes clear in his critique of Diotrephes's conduct. "Anyone who wants to be first must be the very last, and the servant of all" (Mark 9:35).   —C. R. B.

11. Dear friend, do not imitate what is evil but what is good. Anyone who does what is good is from God. Anyone who does what is evil has not seen God.

As John brings us back to his dear friend Gaius, we see the marked contrast between that man and Diotrephes. Gaius is the good example who is to be imitated, while Diotrephes is the evil example not to be followed. Gaius *is from God*, a true brother in Christ. Diotrephes *has not seen God* and is a false brother (compare 1 John 3:10).

Character is revealed in deeds. Gaius and Diotrephes act the ways they do because of what is in their hearts. Gaius truly loves God, so hospitality for visiting Christians comes naturally for him. But Diotrephes sees such visitors as threats to his personal empire, the domain of his control; this reveals a lack of relationship with God.

12. Demetrius is well spoken of by everyone —and even by the truth itself. We also speak well of him, and you know that our testimony is true.

The exhortation of verse 11 to pattern oneself after "what is good" is immediately followed by an example of someone who can serve as such a pattern: a certain *Demetrius*. It is very possible that he is the one who ends up carrying this letter to Gaius. One theory holds that this Demetrius is the silversmith of the same name who led the riot against Paul and Silas in Ephesus (Acts 19:23-41). If so, this would be a remarkable conversion story! But ultimately this proposal is speculative.

In any case, the Demetrius in view embodies the things John emphasizes in the letter: spiritual health, walking in truth, faithful actions, and avoidance of evil. We expect that Gaius will receive Demetrius with all the hospitality he shows to the other teachers and that Gaius will welcome with anticipation the coming of John himself.

❧ FOLLOWING A PATTERN ❧

Telemachus, who died in about AD 404, was a monk who was credited with being instrumental in stopping the gladiatorial games in Rome. Theodoret of Cyrus tells us how this happened:

> A certain man of the name of Telemachus had embraced the ascetic life. He had set out from the East and for this reason had repaired to Rome. There, when the abominable spectacle [of gladiatorial combats] was being exhibited, he went himself into the stadium, and stepping down into the arena, endeavoured to stop the men who were wielding their weapons against one another. The spectators of the slaughter were indignant, and inspired by the triad fury of the demon who delights in those bloody deeds, stoned the peacemaker to death.
>
> When the admirable emperor was informed of this he numbered Telemachus in the number of victorious martyrs, and put an end to that impious spectacle.

To walk faithfully in the path of truth can be costly, indeed! But we are to walk that path wherever it leads. Although our ultimate pattern in this regard is Jesus, it helps to have contemporary models who walk in truth. For Gaius, the apostle John says the model can be Demetrius. For some who lived in the fifth century AD, it could have been Telemachus. For those who live today, could it be you?   —C. R. B.

What Do You Think?

What are some traits and behaviors that result in a person having a reputation that is worthy of emulating in the church?

Talking Points for Your Discussion
- Regarding personal practices
- Regarding relationships with other believers
- Regarding reputation among unbelievers (1 Timothy 3:7)
- Other

III. Closing
(3 JOHN 13, 14)
A. Desire (vv. 13, 14a)

13, 14a. I have much to write you, but I do not want to do so with pen and ink. I hope to see you soon, and we will talk face to face.

John expresses the same desire as in 2 John 12: he prefers *face to face* communication over that of a letter. John has much more to say to both Gaius and Diotrephes!

B. Blessing (v. 14b)

14b. Peace to you. The friends here send their greetings. Greet the friends there by name.

John ends the letter with personal touches. The desire for *peace* is the traditional Jewish blessing for health and well-being (see v. 2).

The writer also passes greetings for friends on both sides of the letter; Gaius has friends in John's church and these folks have friends in the church of Gaius. We can imagine that John and Gaius have stayed in some of their homes in the past. This is a long-standing relationship joined in faith, bound together in mutual hospitality, and maintained by love.

Conclusion
A. Spiritual Health and Hospitality

If we are spiritually healthy, we will more easily bend our lives to the needs of others. This may result in extending hospitality to folks we barely know, with many applications in churches today. I have been a guest teacher or preacher in numerous churches over the years. Sometimes it has been necessary for me to stay in a hotel; but, when possible, I have always enjoyed staying with one of the church families. I get great meals, have a clean bed, and make new friends. I especially enjoy it when there are children in the household (since my children are adults), so I can again experience the world through the eyes of a child.

Such hospitality makes my time of teaching and preaching all the more meaningful and precious to me and to the congregation. I come as a stranger, become a guest, and leave as a friend.

Churches may also live this out when they support field missionaries. I have always thought that a church should have at least one missionary family for whom it provides at least partial funding, so that a long-term, fulfilling relationship may be developed with these folks. When the member of a missionary family is home on furlough, he or she should be given proper hospitality while visiting the church. This is more than money. It is friendship, encouragement, and acceptance.

That may be reciprocated if members of the church take the time and expense to visit the missionary family on the field, something that was unthinkable 30 or 40 years ago. Hospitality between Christians builds a bond that strengthens ministry and contributes to the mission of spreading the truth of the gospel to all. The need to extend hospitality endures, and the words of 3 John on this topic continue to be of great value for us.

B. Prayer

God of peace and truth, may we love our fellow Christians as you would have us! May we open wallets, homes, and lives to them. In so doing, may you prosper our souls in the grace of your abundant love. In the name of Jesus, amen.

C. Thought to Remember
Measure prosperity by your relationship with God.

Visual for Lesson 10. *Start a discussion by pointing to this visual as you ask, "How can we better promote teamwork in our church?"*

INVOLVEMENT LEARNING

Enhance your lesson with NIV® Bible Student (from your curriculum supplier) and the reproducible activity page (at www.standardlesson.com or in the back of the NIV® Standard Lesson Commentary Deluxe Edition).

Into the Lesson

Have on display the invitation *GET RICH QUICK!* in big, bold letters as class begins. Ask, "What thoughts come to mind when you see such an enticement?" Though most will probably affirm that they "run the other way," some may honestly say, "Well, I'd probably give it a look!"

Say, "John has words of encouragement for a friend in Christ, and one of those is John's desire that his friend prosper. But that desire is not in order to sell the friend on how to get rich quickly! To find out what John intends, we will need to see John's stated desire in context. What one deeply desires for others is certainly affected by the presence or absence of a Christian motive."

Alternative. Display the state seal of the state of New Jersey (easy to find on the Internet). Point out that above the word *prosperity* on the seal is the image Ceres, the Roman goddess of grain, who holds an overflowing cornucopia. Discuss how that image does and does not reflect secular and Christian concepts of prosperity. Move quickly to the next activity, which will examine John's discussion of prosperity in the Christian worldview.

Into the Word

Call for four volunteers to read the text aloud, switching readers whenever the word *friend* is encountered (beginnings of vv. 2, 5, 11). Point to verse 2 and note that John's prayer for his friend's well-being is stated in terms of desire that Gaius "may enjoy good health and that all may go well with you, even as your soul is getting along well."

Establish three groups of two to five, designating them *Prosperity Group, Physical Health Group,* and *Spiritual Health Group* (larger classes can form additional groups with duplicate designations). Distribute handouts of the following stimulus questions to each group: 1. How does the Christian understanding of what your group's designation implies differ from the cultural understanding,

if at all? 2. How should a believer's approach to attaining what your group's designation implies differ from that of an unbeliever? 3. What do you see as the "success rate" of each approach?

Ask someone from each group to report conclusions. Encourage those from other groups to question and comment at each presentation.

Next, write the name *Gaius* in the upper left corner of the board. Ask learners to use the previous discussion and the lesson text to summarize (1) what Gaius had been doing and (2) what John wanted him yet to do. Jot learner responses in those two categories under the name Gaius. Follow by writing the name *Diotrephes* in the upper middle of the board and ask for summaries in the same two categories regarding that man. Finally, write the name *Demetrius* in the upper right corner of the board and do the same (not as much can be said about him).

Option. For a bigger-picture discussion on the topic of hospitality as this week's lesson interrelates with last week's, distribute copies of the "John + John = ?" activity from the reproducible page, which you can download. Have learners complete in pairs or small groups.

Into Life

Introduce a time of quiet, personal reflection as you distribute this challenge on handouts:

Not mentioning a name aloud, think of someone in our congregation who models a Christian approach to service. How can you encourage and/or assist that person in his or her ministry?

After a few minutes, close with prayers for learners to do so in the week ahead.

Option. Distribute copies of the "Thriving, Body and Soul" activity from the reproducible page. This exercise will help learners communicate encouragement to others. If time is short, this can be a take-home activity.

GIFTS OF
THE SPIRIT

DEVOTIONAL READING: Romans 12:1-8
BACKGROUND SCRIPTURE: 1 Corinthians 12:1-11

1 CORINTHIANS 12:1-11

[1] Now about the gifts of the Spirit, brothers and sisters, I do not want you to be uninformed. [2] You know that when you were pagans, somehow or other you were influenced and led astray to mute idols. [3] Therefore I want you to know that no one who is speaking by the Spirit of God says, "Jesus be cursed," and no one can say, "Jesus is Lord," except by the Holy Spirit.

[4] There are different kinds of gifts, but the same Spirit distributes them. [5] There are different kinds of service, but the same Lord. [6] There are different kinds of working, but in all of them and in everyone it is the same God at work.

[7] Now to each one the manifestation of the Spirit is given for the common good. [8] To one there is given through the Spirit a message of wisdom, to another a message of knowledge by means of the same Spirit, [9] to another faith by the same Spirit, to another gifts of healing by that one Spirit, [10] to another miraculous powers, to another prophecy, to another distinguishing between spirits, to another speaking in different kinds of tongues, and to still another the interpretation of tongues. [11] All these are the work of one and the same Spirit, and he distributes them to each one, just as he determines.

KEY VERSE

Now to each one the manifestation of the Spirit is given for the common good. —1 Corinthians 12:7

Graphic: Zoonar / Thinkstock

THE SPIRIT COMES

Unit 3: One in the Bond of Love
LESSONS 11–14

LESSON AIMS

After participating in this lesson, each learner will be able to:

1. List the spiritual gifts cited in today's passage.

2. Compare and contrast miraculous spiritual gifts with non-miraculous ones.

3. Express esteem for others' gifts and commit to using his or her own gifts to serve others.

LESSON OUTLINE

Introduction
A. A Team of Quarterbacks?

The best-known player on an American football team is usually the quarterback, the player who leads the team's offense. Successful quarterbacks must demonstrate many skills: judgment, passing ability, speed, dexterity, courage, resilience, etc. That is why good quarterbacks become famous. And that is why young football players long to play quarterback.

But we know how unsuccessful a football team would be if it had players only with the abilities and desire to play quarterback. Football, as other team sports, requires different talents and abilities at the various positions to be played, so coaches assign players to positions that match their varied abilities. If everyone were the same, the team would suffer.

Today's text reflects that fact. If God's people did not demonstrate a variety of gifts for service, they would be unable to help each other meet the challenges of following Jesus and winning others to do so.

B. Lesson Background

Corinth was a major city in ancient Greece. Paul spent eighteen months in the city on his second missionary journey, despite much opposition there (Acts 18:1-11). Writing 1 Corinthians from Ephesus in about AD 56 while on his third missionary journey, Paul addressed a variety of issues and problems that had arisen in the Corinthian church in his absence.

That church's many problems seemed to have been rooted in pride, which went hand in hand with airs of spiritual superiority. Some thought themselves to be superior because they identified with a particular leader (1 Corinthians 1–4). Some thought themselves to be exempt from moral expectations (chap. 5–7). Some thought themselves to be superior because of the foods they ate or refused to eat (chap. 8–10). Some thought that they were so superior to other Christians that they could neglect the needs of others (chap. 11). The issue of spiritual gifts was no less a problem at Corinth in this context.

I. Unity in Christ
(1 CORINTHIANS 12:1-3)

A. Addressing a Knowledge Deficit (v. 1)

1. Now about the gifts of the Spirit, brothers and sisters, I do not want you to be uninformed.

Members of the church at Corinth have written to Paul on a variety of subjects (1 Corinthians 7:1). The phrase *now about* signals a shift in topics regarding Paul's response to those.

The topic of *gifts of the Spirit* is complicated and touchy in both Paul's day and ours. One issue to acknowledge at the outset is that the word *gifts* does not occur in Paul's original writing of this verse. It has been added for smoother reading. Paul literally writes, "Now about the spiritual." Given what he has to say in the verses to follow, the word *gifts* is a good insertion.

Such gifts are endowments by the Holy Spirit to followers of Christ. Through such gifts the Spirit empowers believers to fulfill their mission of Matthew 28:19, 20. Paul does not distinguish the Spirit's gifts from our natural abilities. All human abilities are gifts of God. For the Christian, old abilities are dedicated to Christ and directed by the Holy Spirit, while the Spirit imparts new abilities or enables Christians to discover abilities that they did not recognize before.

B. Acknowledging a Sinful Past (v. 2)

2. You know that when you were pagans, somehow or other you were influenced and led astray to mute idols.

One's present status is often best viewed against the backdrop of one's past. In this light, Paul reminds the Corinthians of their past as *pagans.* That word as used here refers especially to worshippers of idols. Idols are *mute,* of course (com-

HOW TO SAY IT

Colossians	Kuh-*losh*-unz.
Corinth	*Kor*-inth.
Corinthians	Ko-*rin*-thee-unz (*th* as in *thin*).
Ephesians	Ee-*fee*-zhunz.
Ephesus	*Ef*-uh-sus.
Habakkuk	Huh-*back*-kuk.

pare Habakkuk 2:18). Certainly such gods have no ability to empower people to speak truth since they themselves cannot make a sound!

Paul's readers certainly can remember when they *were influenced* in their enthusiasm for such gods. They had participated in the pagan celebrations, sometimes even uttering words thought to be inspired by pagan gods. Did such actions make them spiritual? Of course not! Only the true Spirit of God can impart true gifts of the Spirit.

What Do You Think?
How does your experience in being delivered from modern idols compare and contrast with experiences of others in the class?
Talking Points for Your Discussion
- Regarding idols of a physical nature (what money can buy, etc.)
- Regarding idols of the mind (priority of self, etc.)
- Other

C. Describing a Present Fact (v. 3)

3. Therefore I want you to know that no one who is speaking by the Spirit of God says, "Jesus be cursed," and no one can say, "Jesus is Lord," except by the Holy Spirit.

So who, then, are the truly spiritual people, those empowered by God's Spirit and not something else? Paul poses a two-sided test to determine the answer. First, we can be sure *that no one who is speaking by the Spirit of God says, "Jesus be cursed."* This holds true regardless of any amazing power that one who rejects Jesus might display (compare Acts 8:9-11; 16:16-18). Such people not truly spiritual, are not empowered by the Holy Spirit. The flip side of the test is that *no one can say, "Jesus is Lord," except by the Holy Spirit.* Only those who are empowered by the Spirit can make such a confession (compare 1 John 4:2, 3).

Does the Spirit empower you? The two-sided test applies to you as well as to the Corinthians. If you affirm *Jesus is Lord*, both by word and by a life lived in submission to scriptural precepts, then there is no doubt! Christians need not worry about whether the Holy Spirit is present in their lives (compare Acts 2:38; Romans 8:9).

II. Variety of Gifts

(1 CORINTHIANS 12:4-11)

A. From the Triune God (vv. 4-6)

4. There are different kinds of gifts, but the same Spirit distributes them.

The differences in the ways that the Holy Spirit empowers people are obvious (compare Romans 12:6). Do those differences indicate that some people are spiritually superior? Paul's answer is a resounding *no* because *the same Spirit* is the source of all giftedness. All the ways that God empowers his people are, in fact, utterly equal precisely because all these gifts are God's gifts.

Recognizing the fact that there are indeed *different kinds of gifts,* we might say that there are as many different gifts as there are people who receive them (see 1 Corinthians 7:7). Because all gifts come from the Spirit of God, they are all of the highest spiritual order. None can be higher or more valuable than any other, for God's Spirit does not give second-tier gifts. (On "the greater gifts" in 1 Corinthians 12:31, see next week's lesson.)

> **What Do You Think?**
> Why is it important to view God as the source of our giftedness?
> **Talking Points for Your Discussion**
> * What can happen when we do (John 17:23; Ephesians 4:11-13; 1 Peter 2:5; etc.)
> * What may happen if we don't (Daniel 4:29-33; Acts 12:21-23; James 3:16; etc.)

5. There are different kinds of service, but the same Lord.

To drive that point home, Paul repeats it with two variations. Instead of "gifts" (v. 4), he uses a different word to refer to what his readers have received. That word, translated *service,* is also translated "ministry" in 2 Corinthians 4:1; 5:18; 6:3.

The concept of ministry emphasizes not status but lowliness, not what one receives for self but what one does for others. Paul is beginning to make his crucial point: gifts of the Spirit are not for the benefit of the one who has the gift but for the benefit of those to whom the gifted person ministers.

Paul goes on to ascribe the giving of such ministry differences as focused on *the same Lord,* meaning the Lord Jesus. We are reminded that Christ entered the world as a human not for his own benefit but to serve others (Mark 10:45; Philippians 2:5-8). Any gift that Christ gives must therefore be used in the same way: to serve others. There can be no assuming of a superior position on the basis of having a particular gift for ministry from such a Lord.

> **What Do You Think?**
> In what ways do you believe that you are gifted by the Spirit for Christian service? How have your conclusions changed over the years? Why?
> **Talking Points for Your Discussion**
> * Regarding spiritual gifts that primarily have to do with interacting with others
> * Regarding spiritual gifts that do not primarily deal with interacting with others

6. There are different kinds of working, but in all of them and in everyone it is the same God at work.

Paul repeats his point yet again, also with variations. Using three different Greek words, what were called "gifts" (v. 4) and "service" (v. 5) are now called *working.* The Greek for the latter also is translated "powers" in verse 10a (below), both of which help us get the sense. Spiritual gifts are the means by which God works through the faithful. Again, there can be no claiming superiority because of a particular gift: the work is God's, not ours.

Notice what Paul is doing in verses 4-6: he refers to the Holy Spirit, to the Lord Jesus, and to God the Father in turn. Each person of the trinity—or if you will, the tri-unity of God—is the source of the gifts. Among Father, Son, and Spirit, there is no claiming of superiority, no bragging, no one-upmanship. Father, Son, and Spirit live in perfect love and harmony. The Son submits to the Father not because the Son is less than the Father but willingly, to serve unworthy humanity. The Spirit likewise submits willingly to both the Father and the Son, again to serve unworthy humanity. Yet Father, Son, and Holy Spirit are equal. God is love and service (John 3:16). If

Paul's readers are to honor such a God, they cannot seek to use his gifts to gain advantage over one another.

B. For the Common Benefit (v. 7)

7. Now to each one the manifestation of the Spirit is given for the common good.

Any gift that the Spirit gives can be called a *manifestation of the Spirit.* That is, the gift when exercised draws attention not to the one who exercises it but to the one who gives it. The Holy Spirit is made manifest, visible, clear to those who witness the gift at work.

Paul also states directly the purpose of these spiritual gifts at work: the triune God grants them so that they may be exercised for the benefit of all. Paul introduced this idea earlier (1 Corinthians 10:23, 24), will hit the topic again later (14:26), and will remind the Ephesians of these same things (Ephesians 4:12).

The status-seeking Corinthians need to learn a lesson of the cross: God's people are called not to exalt themselves but to serve others. In so doing, they exalt the Christ who died and rose in service of them. Only by using their gifts for beneficial service can the Corinthians truly say that their gifts manifest the presence of God's Spirit.

> **What Do You Think?**
> What are some ways to use one's giftedness for the common benefit of the church?
> *Talking Points for Your Discussion*
> - Regarding abilities (teaching, musical, etc.)
> - Regarding personal reputation
> - Regarding personal assets
> - Other

❧ ONE FOR ALL, ALL FOR ONE ❧

"One for all, all for one" is the unofficial motto of Switzerland. The Swiss cantons united to become a federal state in 1848, and the occasion for the motto was widespread flooding that occurred in the Alps some 20 years later. Government officials used "One for all, all for one" as the rallying cry for donations to aid the flood victims. Newspapers ran the slogan to publicize the need.

Citizens responded dramatically, both from a sense of duty and as a display of national unity. The motto has since become connected in the popular mind with the stories of the nation's founding. Although unofficial, the motto is inscribed in the cupola of the Swiss Federal Palace.

Paul's treatment of spiritual gifts follows a similar theme. The Holy Spirit bestows the gifts so that recipients may serve the greater, godly good of the church as a whole. This never changes. How well are you doing in this regard?   —C. R. B.

C. In Diverse Expressions (vv. 8-11)

8. To one there is given through the Spirit a message of wisdom, to another a message of knowledge by means of the same Spirit,

Paul proceeds to illustrate the variety of Spirit-giftedness by offering a representative list of gifts. It is vital to realize that this is not an exhaustive list of the ways that the Holy Spirit empowers Christians. Even combining the list here with those in Romans 12:6-8 and Ephesians 4:11, 12 will not name every kind of service for which the Spirit bestows gifts. Paul's purpose is not to describe every gift but to suggest the broad range —some would say unlimited range—of spiritual gifts.

Likewise, we cannot tell the precise kind of ministry Paul is referring to with each term. Some of the terms are very close to others in their general sense, and some of the terms are quite broad, capable of encompassing all kinds of beneficial acts of ministry. Some interpreters indicate with great confidence that this term or that term refers to a very specific kind of activity among believers. But we should be careful not to go beyond the evidence with conjectures and speculations.

For example, consider *a message of wisdom* and *a message of knowledge* here. What exactly do these activities look like, and how are they different from one another? We cannot be too exacting in our conclusion. *Wisdom* and *knowledge* both are reflections of God's truth (compare Romans 11:33; Colossians 2:2, 3), especially as that truth speaks into our lives and directs our thoughts and actions. These gifts involve *a message*, so the one with either gift is to speak God's truth to others.

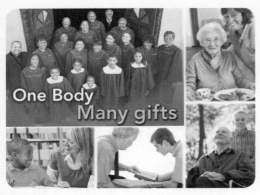

Visual for Lessons 11 & 12. *Point to this visual as you introduce the discussion question that is associated with verse 7.*

Beyond that, we cannot easily distinguish *wisdom* from *knowledge* in their application here.

Even so, Paul's point is clear enough. He is emphasizing the Spirit's work in enabling God's people to speak God's truth meaningfully into their lives. Such a gift is surely for the good of all, as lives that receive God's truth are lived out for his purposes. Such gifts represent the principle of verse 7: they are gifts that serve and benefit others.

9a. . . . to another faith by the same Spirit,

Paul names *faith* as a gift received by some followers of Christ and not by others. Clearly, then, he is not referring to the faith in Christ that brings us to salvation. The apostle must be referring to some demonstration of faith beyond that.

Perhaps he means those who demonstrate exceptional faith in hard times. Some commentaries propose that Paul refers to those who call on God to act in miraculous ways and see those prayers answered. Again, we cannot specify too closely. But we can affirm that any exceptional manifestation of faith is a reflection of the Spirit's power, not the spiritual superiority of the individual.

9b. . . . to another gifts of healing by that one Spirit,

The Gospels show Jesus healing people of all kinds of maladies. In the book of Acts, the apostles perform similar miracles. These are impressive demonstrations of Christ's power to bless where there is suffering. We cannot determine with confident precision how often such healings are experienced in the first-century church and how many people are empowered to perform them. But we can certainly affirm that the exercise of such a gift brings great benefit to those healed and, in certain cases, pain and persecution to those through whom the healings come (Acts 5:12-18).

10a. . . . to another miraculous powers,

We see further the broad range of the Spirit's gifts as Paul continues his listing. Certainly it is divine power that is in view when we compare "God at work" in verse 6 with *miraculous powers* in the verse before us. Without doubt, God's acts that defy the usual pattern of cause and effect (miracles) are included in this category. Yet the emphasis is not on the miraculous nature of the acts as such but on the power of God.

God can wield his power in spectacular and unusual ways but also in ways that seem small and unassuming to us. Since the wide spectrum of such power certainly includes "gifts of healing" in verse 9, Paul is therefore not providing distinct, airtight categories so much as offering a descriptive range of the Spirit's gifts.

10b. . . . to another prophecy,

Prophecy is another term that may confuse us. We may tend to think of prophecy narrowly as predicting the future by God's power. In fact, biblical prophecy includes more than that. It is the forthright speaking of God's message, inspired by him, to people in the situations of their time. Like those gifted for wisdom or knowledge, the prophet speaks God's message by God's power to strengthen other believers. Paul is stressing not the authority of the one speaking but that person's role in serving others with God's Word.

10c. . . . to another distinguishing between spirits,

Distinguishing between spirits is difficult. Paul may have in mind those who discern true works of God's Spirit from those falsely claimed to be done in his name. Or Paul may be referring to those able to call attention to what the Spirit is doing that others might overlook. Either way, some are specially gifted for such a ministry, although all must be properly discerning (compare Hebrews 5:14).

10d. . . . to another speaking in different kinds of tongues,

Opinions also differ regarding the nature of this gift. If the Holy Spirit's gift *of tongues* at Corinth is like that on the Day of Pentecost (Acts 2:4-11), then some are empowered to speak in known human languages that they have not studied.

But some think the gift of tongues in Corinth to be the Spirit's enabling of a person to express deep feelings of devotion to God with utterances that belong to no human language (1 Corinthians 13:1; 14:2). Whatever the precise nature of the gift, Paul's message is the same: the Holy Spirit empowers Christians not for their own benefit but for the service of others, for the good of all.

10e. . . . and to still another the interpretation of tongues.

Whatever the specific action that is called tongues at Corinth, it cannot be understood by most of those who hear it. Thus the need for *interpretation.* Paul later emphasizes that for the gift of tongues to be used properly in the church's assembly, what is said in tongues must be interpreted for all to understand so they can be built up (1 Corinthians 14:5, 26-28). Those who speak in tongues are in no way superior. In fact, their gift depends on others gifted to interpret.

❧ PERFORMANCE ART? ❧

An avant-garde exhibit titled "Ecstatic Alphabets/Heaps of Language" opened on May 6, 2012, at New York's Museum of Modern Art. Presented in conjunction was a performance-art program called "Words in the World." In this segment, performers took positions in the shapes of letters and numerals, signifying that "words, signs, and numbers can also have an independent life, liberated from their conventional forms and meanings."

When reading that last statement, one wonders if the writer would object to readers interpreting it in wildly different ways as they exercise their freedom to "liberate" its words from their conventional meanings! And it seems quite likely that no two responses would be the same to the question "What did that mean?" if posed to audience members.

Unintelligible use of tongues, whether of men or of angels (1 Corinthians 13:1), was a problem in Corinth. The solution, then as now, is to look at the bigger picture. Use of tongues, whatever the exact nature of that gift, is not to be some kind of performance art subject to multiple interpretations. The message of the church must be unambiguous. That's probably why Paul follows "different kinds of tongues" immediately with "interpretation of tongues." Is there ambiguity in the way your church presents the gospel?   —C. R. B.

11. All these are the work of one and the same Spirit, and he distributes them to each one, just as he determines.

The diversity of gifts has but one source: *one and the same Spirit.* Whether we list a few gifts or hundreds, he gives them all. All are therefore equal, for all come from the same source. There is no room for boasting (Romans 12:3), but there is enormous scope for serving!

> *What Do You Think?*
> How might you counsel someone who is gifted in
>   a way that he or she feels is inferior to others?
> *Talking Points for Your Discussion*
> ▪ In establishing common ground
> ▪ In exploring misunderstandings of Scripture
> ▪ In exploring past use or misuse of giftedness
> ▪ Other

Conclusion
A. Are You "Spiritual"?

What is the real proof that a person is "spiritual"? It is not the gift or ability that the person demonstrates. It is, rather, whether the person lives in Christ to serve and build up others. Spirituality is not a competitive event; it is a cooperative venture. The Spirit distributes his gifts so that believers are compelled to rely on each other in unity, not to contend with each other in selfishness. The Spirit of Christ compels us to become like Christ.

B. Prayer

Father, may we work for unity as we exercise our diverse giftedness. May all traces of spiritual pride disappear as we do. In Jesus' name, amen!

C. Thought to Remember

Use your spiritual giftedness to benefit others.

INVOLVEMENT LEARNING

Enhance your lesson with NIV® *Bible Student (from your curriculum supplier) and the reproducible activity page (at www.standardlesson.com or in the back of the* NIV® *Standard Lesson Commentary Deluxe Edition).*

Into the Lesson

Gift-wrap five small boxes in various ways: one fancifully done, one in tattered scrap paper, some with and some without bows, etc. To each box attach a tag that has one of the following wordings: *Do not open until you are ready to serve / Not your gift! / Utilitarian purposes only; not for decoration / Must be used in conjunction with other gifts / To: You; From: God.*

Have these on display as learners arrive. Distribute the boxes randomly as you say, "Do not open." Ask for the tags to be read aloud. To those not having a box, ask, "As you look at these gifts, is there one you wish you had received, just based on its appearance and tag? Is there one you are glad you did not?" Allow brief reactions.

Transition by saying, "Today's lesson is about gifts—gifts of the Spirit. As we study, think about three things: (1) the outward appearances of the gift boxes, (2) the manner in which the gift boxes were distributed, and (3) how the information on their tags can be related to the truths Paul writes."

Into the Word

Review the historical context of the church at Corinth (see the Lesson Background of this and the next three lessons). *Option:* for deeper study, have learners contrast the idol-gods of the first-century environment with the real God by completing the "The Manifest God" activity from the reproducible page, which you can download.

Next, distribute handouts measuring 4¼" x 11" with the heading "Gift List." (*Option:* have the handouts decorated with a picture of a wrapped gift with a "From: God" tag.) Say, "For those of you whose birthdays fall on even-numbered days, make a quick list of miraculous gifts Paul notes in today's text. For those of you whose birthdays fall on odd-numbered days, make a quick list of personality and skill gifts that may be considered non-miraculous." Allow no more than five min-utes. Have learners work either individually or as two groups. If those of the odd numbers seem to be working slowly, offer this hint: "Think of people in our congregation who demonstrate gifts of service in life and worship."

Call for entries from both listings and jot them on the board in two columns. After all discoveries are mentioned, ask, "What do these gifts have in common?" Anticipate responses such as, "When spiritual gifts are used properly, they are a blessing to God's people," and "When spiritual gifts are abused, they create jealousies and envy."

Ask learners to look at the text again and propose one or more key principles that Paul expresses or implies to keep the Corinthians from being "ignorant" in matters of the gifts of the Spirit. Learners may suggest a general principle, such as, "The gifts of the Spirit are just that: they are gifts in that they are not of ourselves," or, "Spiritual gifts, both miraculous and non-miraculous, are revealed as they are exercised." Encourage learners to question or comment on statements offered. Confirm the textual basis for each affirmation.

Option. Check comprehension by distributing copies of the "Tools, Not Toys" activity from the reproducible page. After completing individually or in small groups, compare conclusions.

Option. Return to your instructions in the last paragraph of Into the Lesson. Ask learners for their conclusions regarding your three challenges.

Into Life

Distribute index cards, each having this double-commitment statement: *Because I know that God gives gifts to his children and that his gifts are for the benefit of all, I affirm my commitment to (1) value others in their giftedness, and (2) use my own giftedness to serve others as God intends.* Include two "Sign Here" lines to stress the double commitment. Suggest learners post cards to be seen daily as self-reminders in the week ahead.

ONE BODY;
MANY MEMBERS

DEVOTIONAL READING: Galatians 3:23-29
BACKGROUND SCRIPTURE: 1 Corinthians 12:12-31

1 CORINTHIANS 12:12-31

¹² Just as a body, though one, has many parts, but all its many parts form one body, so it is with Christ. ¹³ For we were all baptized by one Spirit so as to form one body—whether Jews or Gentiles, slave or free—and we were all given the one Spirit to drink. ¹⁴ Even so the body is not made up of one part but of many.

¹⁵ Now if the foot should say, "Because I am not a hand, I do not belong to the body," it would not for that reason stop being part of the body. ¹⁶ And if the ear should say, "Because I am not an eye, I do not belong to the body," it would not for that reason stop being part of the body. ¹⁷ If the whole body were an eye, where would the sense of hearing be? If the whole body were an ear, where would the sense of smell be? ¹⁸ But in fact God has placed the parts in the body, every one of them, just as he wanted them to be. ¹⁹ If they were all one part, where would the body be? ²⁰ As it is, there are many parts, but one body.

²¹ The eye cannot say to the hand, "I don't need you!" And the head cannot say to the feet, "I don't need you!" ²² On the contrary, those

parts of the body that seem to be weaker are indispensable, ²³ and the parts that we think are less honorable we treat with special honor. And the parts that are unpresentable are treated with special modesty, ²⁴ while our presentable parts need no special treatment. But God has put the body together, giving greater honor to the parts that lacked it, ²⁵ so that there should be no division in the body, but that its parts should have equal concern for each other. ²⁶ If one part suffers, every part suffers with it; if one part is honored, every part rejoices with it.

²⁷ Now you are the body of Christ, and each one of you is a part of it. ²⁸ And God has placed in the church first of all apostles, second prophets, third teachers, then miracles, then gifts of healing, of helping, of guidance, and of different kinds of tongues. ²⁹ Are all apostles? Are all prophets? Are all teachers? Do all work miracles? ³⁰ Do all have gifts of healing? Do all speak in tongues? Do all interpret? ³¹ Now eagerly desire the greater gifts.

And yet I will show you the most excellent way.

KEY VERSE

We were all baptized by one Spirit so as to form one body—whether Jews or Gentiles, slave or free—and we were all given the one Spirit to drink. —**1 Corinthians 12:13**

THE SPIRIT COMES

Unit 3: One in the Bond of Love
LESSONS 11–14

LESSON AIMS

After participating in this lesson, each learner will be able to:

1. Summarize Paul's illustration of the church as a body.

2. Illustrate the church's unity in diversity with examples from the Bible and the present day.

3. Write a note of appreciation to a fellow believer whose spiritual giftedness differs from his or hers.

LESSON OUTLINE

Introduction
  A. "My Hair Hurts"
  B. Lesson Background
 I. Unity Stated (1 CORINTHIANS 12:12-14)
  A. Many Formed into One (v. 12)
  B. One Formed from Many (vv. 13, 14)
    E Pluribus Unum
 II. Unity Illustrated (1 CORINTHIANS 12:15-26)
  A. No Part Inferior (vv. 15-17)
  B. All Parts Designed by God (vv. 18-20)
  C. No Part Superior (vv. 21-24)
  D. All Care for Each (vv. 25, 26)
 III. Unity Practiced (1 CORINTHIANS 12:27-31)
  A. Many Gifts (vv. 27, 28)
  B. Seven Questions (vv. 29, 30)
  C. One Imperative (v. 31)
    Maximizers
Conclusion
  A. Strength in Variety
  B. Prayer
  C. Thought to Remember

Introduction
A. "My Hair Hurts"

We all know what it is to feel tired and sore. We spend a day working hard and later experience the sore muscles, aching joints, and blistered skin. If asked, "Where does it hurt?" some might respond, "I hurt everywhere. Even my hair hurts."

Of course, no one's hair hurts. But the pain in one part of the body disturbs every part of the body. Our bodies, fearfully and wonderfully made (Psalm 139:14), function as many parts in harmony. Each part is designed to do something that complements the other parts. Each part shares the experience of the other parts. In functions and feelings, the human body is a remarkable unity.

Today's text uses the God-designed unity of the human body to illustrate God's intention for the church. Like the human body, the church consists of many distinct parts—its people, each different from the other. Like the human body, each part exists to complement the whole. Like the human body, the church can do amazing things when all parts are working together as designed.

B. Lesson Background

This week's lesson picks up right where last week's ended. The background for this lesson is therefore the same as last week's, so that information need not be repeated here.

What is different this week is Paul's use of the human body as an illustration of unity. Such an illustration was widely used in Paul's day to describe the functioning of a city or organization. The parts of the body are different, like the people of a city or organization, but their differences are necessary to carry out all the functions needed to thrive. To that image Paul adds the unique perspective of the gospel.

I. Unity Stated
(1 CORINTHIANS 12:12-14)
A. Many Formed into One (v. 12)

12. Just as a body, though one, has many parts, but all its many parts form one body, so it is with Christ.

The human body is complex. Its many and varied parts work together for the good of the whole. Such an image forms the basis for Paul's discussion that follows. The oneness of the body, the consistent unity in its functioning, is the reason for the existence of its various parts. *So it is with Christ*, referring to the followers of Christ who stand in union with him (also Romans 12:4, 5; 1 Corinthians 10:17; Ephesians 5:30).

B. One Formed from Many (vv. 13, 14)

13. For we were all baptized by one Spirit so as to form one body—whether Jews or Gentiles, slave or free—and we were all given the one Spirit to drink.

The Corinthians need to be reminded of the body's essential unity. To do so, Paul appeals to their common experience of baptism and reception of the Holy Spirit. Some students think that the phrase *we were all baptized by one Spirit* refers only to Spirit baptism, not water baptism. But the two cannot be separated (Acts 2:38; Titus 3:5). In the New Testament, the dipping of the repentant sinner into water to ask Christ for his cleansing forgiveness is the experience of all who come to faith in him. Whatever distinctives make the Corinthians different from one another is subordinate to the fact that they are made one by receiving God's Spirit by faith in baptism (compare Galatians 3:28).

The clause *we were all given the one Spirit to drink* is a figure of speech noting that all Christians are empowered by the same Holy Spirit. Though some Corinthians may try to make the Spirit's work a reason to think themselves superior, the Spirit in fact makes them utterly one with others.

What Do You Think?
What distinctions does the church at large seem to have the most trouble overcoming? Why?
Talking Points for Your Discussion
- Racial
- Cultural
- Gender
- Other

---

14. Even so the body is not made up of one part but of many.

We do not want to stress the oneness of the body to the point of denying the individual parts, however. Having stressed the unity of the body, Paul now asserts its variety. No functioning body is a single part. A body requires countless parts to work as it is designed.

❧ *E Pluribus Unum* ❧

The phrase *E Pluribus Unum* appears on various coins and currency of the U.S. It is a Latin phrase that means "out of many, one." That is an ideal that America has struggled with since its founding. Much of the tension is traced to the reality of having 50 states, each of which resists Federal laws and regulations that are seen to be contrary to the freedom of the state's citizens.

A similar tension exists in the life of the church, and Paul was well aware of this (see 1 Corinthians 8; Galatians 5:13; etc.). At what point does the exercise of our many parts' freedom in Christ begin to harm the functional unity? Going the other way, at what point does a stress on church unity become an undue expectation of uniformity, where the diverse functions of the individual parts are unduly minimized and Christian liberty overly restricted?

Paul expended much energy to address this issue (see especially 1 Corinthians 13, lesson 14). But half the battle is making sure that we ask ourselves those two questions frequently. Do we?—C. R. B.

II. Unity Illustrated
(1 CORINTHIANS 12:15-26)

A. No Part Inferior (vv. 15-17)

15. Now if the foot should say, "Because I am not a hand, I do not belong to the body," it would not for that reason stop being part of the body.

The parts of the body have differing functions, but no function makes one part less a *part of the body* than any other. We can imagine that *the foot*, always on the ground doing the "dirty work," may seem inferior to *a hand*, which receives glory for its feats of dexterity. But without the presence of feet, the hands would be hampered in moving efficiently from one place to another. Both feet and hands are part of a fully able body.

16. And if the ear should say, "Because I am not an eye, I do not belong to the body," it would not for that reason stop being part of the body.

What is true of hand and foot is also true of *ear* and *eye*. We rely so much on eyesight that we might imagine hearing to be less important. But both are important for the body's fullest functionality. Neither can be treated as less a part of the body on the basis that it is not the other.

17. If the whole body were an eye, where would the sense of hearing be? If the whole body were an ear, where would the sense of smell be?

Paul's illustration ridicules those who act as if their function in Christ's body is the most important. Body parts obviously do not vie with one another for supremacy. Hands do not argue with feet nor eyes with ears or noses. The parts of the body work together naturally. The same must be the case for the church if it is to reflect its ideal unity and carry out its Christ-commissioned work.

> *What Do You Think?*
> Other than churches, what examples can you give of failures attributable to a spirit of disunity?
> *Talking Points for Your Discussion*
> - A sports team
> - A business
> - A military unit
> - Other

B. All Parts Designed by God (vv. 18-20)

18. But in fact God has placed the parts in the body, every one of them, just as he wanted them to be.

Diversity within unity is God's design. The human body's intricate and varied design enables us to adapt to all kinds of circumstances. Likewise, God grants the church a wide array of abilities, empowered by his Spirit, so that together we can adapt and thrive as Christ's servants.

Those who insist that their abilities are more important are denying the design that God has for his church. Since it pleases God to give different gifts to his people (last week's lesson), it profoundly displeases him for any to show disrespect to others who are part of his church.

19. If they were all one part, where would the body be?

Paul asks a rhetorical question to establish the absurdity of treating one gift as superior to others. To claim that one function is superior is to say that it would be better for that one function alone to exist. But what would result? A monstrosity —something far from the elegant design of the Creator. Sadly, those claiming superiority in the Corinthian church are trying to turn the church into just such a monstrosity.

> *What Do You Think?*
> What are some ways that differing giftedness helps the church fulfill its mission?
> *Talking Points for Your Discussion*
> - In evangelism
> - In discipleship
> - In worship
> - Other

20. As it is, there are many parts, but one body.

But the body is not just one part, one function. It consists of thousands of parts, each doing its distinct work. Only as each part does its work does the body perform as God designed it. The true unity of the body is seen not when every part tries to do the same thing but when each part does what God designed it to do, working together in harmony for the common good and for his purpose.

C. No Part Superior (vv. 21-24)

21. The eye cannot say to the hand, "I don't need you!" And the head cannot say to the feet, "I don't need you!"

The diverse parts of the body all depend on each other, so none can claim to be independent or more important. The eye can see, but it cannot take hold of what it sees. The eye needs the hand and vice versa. The head registers all of our senses, but it needs the feet to carry it wherever the senses direct.

In the same way, the church needs every "part," every believer, to function for the good of the entire body. We deny this obvious truth if we imagine our own gifts to be more important. We also deny it if we imagine that we have nothing to contribute to the life of the body.

22. On the contrary, those parts of the body that seem to be weaker are indispensable,

Paul now points out a great irony about our bodies, applying it to the church. Some parts of the body seem to us to be less important. But in fact, those less-important parts are utterly vital. We deny their importance at our peril, for we would not want to try to function without them.

The *weaker* parts of the body can remind us that Christ took the position of weakness to die for our sakes (1 Corinthians 1:23-25). We do not reflect Christ's glory when we pretend to be strong. Rather, we reflect his glory when we admit that we are all weak, rejoicing that Christ has joined us in our weakness and made his strength our strength.

23. . . . and the parts that we think are less honorable we treat with special honor. And the parts that are unpresentable are treated with special modesty,

The story of strength and weakness is also the story of honor and dishonor. The parts of the body that we cover with clothing are those that *we think are less honorable*. Yet they have to do with vital functions. Our sense that it would be shameful to expose those parts leads us to show them a special kind of honor: the adornment of clothing.

24. . . . while our presentable parts need no special treatment. But God has put the body together, giving greater honor to the parts that lacked it,

In God's plan, the lowly are exalted and the high are brought low. The *presentable parts*, which seem honorable, need no covering. The parts that seem to be less honorable, even shameful, receive greater prestige because they are clothed.

So it should be with the church. Those who seem less important ought to receive greater honor, while those who seem more important already have their honor. Thus each member of the church will be affirmed and cherished by all others, and the body as a whole will function in God's design (compare Romans 12:10; 1 Timothy 5:17). Those who claim a superior position for themselves merely show how little they understand God's plan.

D. All Care for Each (vv. 25, 26)

25. . . . so that there should be no division in the body, but that its parts should have equal concern for each other.

God's grand design for the church has a specific result. Because the weaker and less honorable receive greater honor, because each part depends on every other part, then all are compelled to work together, never seeking superiority over others.

Putting that outlook into practice prevents division, the very thing that has infected the Corinthian church. That church has divided over all kinds of issues—to which apostle they are loyal, which foods they may eat, etc. They have even divided over which Holy Spirit–granted gifts are most important!

But the Corinthians will not divide and splinter if they perceive the parts of Christ's body for what they truly are. When that happens, they will practice the same care for one another that they do for themselves. Like parts of the body that work in concert to serve the whole, they will learn to love each other as they love themselves, just as Jesus taught (Luke 10:27).

26. If one part suffers, every part suffers with it; if one part is honored, every part rejoices with it.

HOW TO SAY IT

Corinthians	Ko-*rin*-thee-unz (*th* as in *thin*).
Ephesians	Ee-*fee*-zhunz.
E Pluribus Unum (*Latin*)	*Ee Plur*-uh-bas **You**-num (*u* in *Plur* and *num* as in *pull*).

What the Corinthians currently have is the opposite of a properly functioning body. Everyone knows by experience that when a part of a human body hurts, the rest of the body is not indifferent to the pain. Only one part may be injured, but all parts share the suffering. Likewise, when one part of the body is honored or praised, the entire body, the person as a whole, shares that honor. Since the parts exist to serve the whole, seeking preeminence in the church is at odds with both the plan of God and common sense.

III. Unity Practiced
(1 CORINTHIANS 12:27-31)
A. Many Gifts (vv. 27, 28)

27. Now you are the body of Christ, and each one of you is a part of it.

Paul sums up and applies the lesson of the previous verses. The church is *the body of Christ,* unified by its relationship with him, empowered by the Holy Spirit to accomplish Christ's work. Within that body, each *is a part of it,* a distinct body part with a distinct function.

What Do You Think?
How should the image of the church as the body of Christ affect our relationships?
Talking Points for Your Discussion
- With fellow church members
- With Christians of other congregations

28a. And God has placed in the church first of all apostles, second prophets, third teachers,

Paul proceeds with a short, representative list of gifts and gifted functions in the church. This listing is aimed not at describing each and every gift but at reminding the Corinthians of the vital nature of all the Spirit's gifts.

Apostles are the church's authoritative messengers of the first century, those who are both eyewitnesses of Christ and chosen by him to share their authoritative witness to the gospel message. Their function is vital. Even so, they constitute but one part of the church, and they work together as Christ's servants, not for their own prestige. Paul's use of the terms *first . . ., second . . . , third* should

not be taken as a rank-ordering of importance since in Paul's experience "God has put us apostles on display at the end of the procession, like those condemned to die in the arena. We have been made a spectacle to the whole universe" (1 Corinthians 4:9). It's better to see these terms as indicating a chronological ordering (see Ephesians 2:20).

The work of New Testament *prophets* is that of gifted, inspired spokesmen of the Word (Acts 11:27; 13:1; 15:32; 21:10). The church is built on the foundation of apostles and prophets (again, Ephesians 2:20). As spokesmen for God and not for themselves, prophets do not seek their own glory.

Teachers round out the first part of the listing that focuses on the service of God's Word. They instruct others in it, explaining its basis, meaning, and application. As above, they function for the good of all in Christ's body.

It is interesting to compare and contrast Paul's listing of the gifted functions here with that of Ephesians 4:11: "Christ himself gave the apostles, the prophets, the evangelists, the pastors and teachers." The differences between the two listings indicate that neither is exhaustive but representational.

28b. . . . then miracles, then gifts of healing,

Miracles and *gifts of healing* are mighty works of God's power that demonstrate the truth of the Christian message and the power of Christ to bless his people. As these gifts support the ministry of the Word, they depend on the gifted positions listed above. Miracles and healings have no meaning apart from the Word of God and those who proclaim it. (See further discussion in last week's lesson on 1 Corinthians 12:9b, 10a.)

28c. . . . of helping, of guidance,

These two are a bit difficult to translate since Paul uses two nouns that are found nowhere else in the New Testament. Elsewhere, the first is used in contexts of giving aid. Therefore *helping* probably refers to the backstage tasks of carrying out a range of contributory functions needed in the church.

The second noun is found in contexts involving navigation, steering, and pilotage. Thus the translation *guidance* refers to various leadership tasks such as devising strategies and working with others to see that plans are carried out. The work of those captured in verse 28a and b would have little lasting effect if not for those exercising gifts of helping and guidance.

28d. . . . and of different kinds of tongues.

This is the gift that some in the Corinthian church are promoting as most important (see last week's lesson and 1 Corinthians 14:1-28). Although Paul does not rank-order the gifts, putting this one last may indicate his intent to suggest a different perspective. Like any gift, it must be used to build up the body.

B. Seven Questions (vv. 29, 30)

29, 30. Are all apostles? Are all prophets? Are all teachers? Do all work miracles? Do all have gifts of healing? Do all speak in tongues? Do all interpret?

Obviously, not all are gifted the same. Obviously, a gift would not have the impact God intends were all to have the same giftedness. God's people are interdependent as are the gifts he grants.

To the listing of verse 28, Paul adds that of interpretation. See discussion of this in last week's lesson on 1 Corinthians 12:10e.

C. One Imperative (v. 31)

31. Now eagerly desire the greater gifts. And yet I will show you the most excellent way.

So how should the Corinthians approach the differences in their gifts? Paul answers by using irony when he speaks of *the greater gifts.* Those are the gifts each already has, not those others have! The Corinthians imagine some gifts to be better than others. In truth, all gifts are valuable when exercised in humility and interdependence. That is what the Corinthians should seek zealously. That is *the most excellent way,* the way of love that honors Christ.

❧ *MAXIMIZERS* ❧

Maximizer is a designation used to describe a restless person who is always searching for something better. One problem with being a maximizer is that such a person can be plagued with self-doubt, always wondering if such and such a choice was or is the *best* choice. And if a certain choice is indeed the best for the moment, the max-

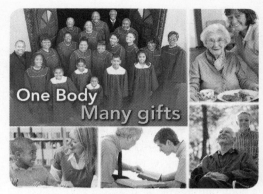

Visual for Lessons 11 & 12. *Point to this visual as you introduce the discussion question that is associated with either verse 19 (p. 316) or 21 (p. 317).*

imizer has the mentally exhausting need to stay on the alert should something better come along.

When it comes to spiritual gifts, we can relax in the assurance that the Holy Spirit is making the best choice for us. We do not choose our spiritual gifts, he does. As Paul discusses these gifts, he helps us see "the most excellent way" in this regard. That is a fitting introduction to what follows: Paul's discussion on the priority of love (see lesson 14). As we adopt that priority as our own, we maximize in the best way possible!—C. R. B.

Conclusion

A. Strength in Variety

As we contemplate creation, we see that God establishes variety. This is no less true in the church. As members of Christ's body, we learn to treasure differences among us, to rely on those unlike ourselves, to celebrate what God can do when we unite in the power of his Spirit and in the name of his Son. How are you doing in this regard?

B. Prayer

Father, we confess our pride and envy. Change us so that we may become humble servants, united in faith to honor one another, exercising our gifts to honor you. In your Son's name, amen.

C. Thought to Remember

There are many gifts, but just one body.

INVOLVEMENT LEARNING

Enhance your lesson with NIV® Bible Student *(from your curriculum supplier) and the reproducible activity page (at www.standardlesson.com or in the back of the* NIV® Standard Lesson Commentary Deluxe Edition*).*

Into the Lesson

Distribute copies of a simple outline of the human body. As you mention a body part, ask learners to note on their outlines how the function of that part has a parallel in the church body. Give *shoulders* as an example as you write that word on a body outline you have sketched on the board. Two possible responses are "to keep the arms and hands connected to the body—that is, to encourage a close relationship among members" and "to be the place for bearing heavy burdens."

Some body parts you can mention are *arms, ears, toes, lips, fingers, spine,* and *legs.* Pause after each for learners to consider it silently and note their response. (To keep this segment from dragging out, reduce the number of parts mentioned.)

After the final part, ask for volunteers to share their thoughts as you go back over the list. Expect both humorous and serious responses. Make a transition as you say, "A body is a unified whole with parts that are interdependent by design. Let's take a deeper look at how that fact applies to the church."

Into the Word

Have learners take turns reading the text aloud. Then ask who can recall from last week's lesson the foundational premise behind the gifting of Christians in various ways. (Expected responses should draw on 1 Corinthians 12:7—diversity of giftedness for the common good.) Then ask, "As you look at Paul's thoughts about various parts of the physical body as his illustration of the church, how do you see that same idea of 'for the common good'?" (Expected response: it takes all parts working in harmony to create an effective whole.)

Write the word *body* on the board. Ask learners to count silently the number of times that word occurs in today's lesson text, jot the total on the handout, but do not voice the answer aloud until requested. Allow a minute for silent counting, then call for the total. (There are 17 occurrences in the *New International Version.*) Follow by forming small groups to determine how many of the occurrences of *body* are speaking of the church as such. As you call for voiced conclusions, disagreements will promote comprehension as learners struggle to explain differences in their counts.

Next, lead a discussion regarding the interplay between the text's 12 uses of the singular *one* and the 11 occurrences of the plurals *many, parts,* and *many parts.* Pose these questions: 1. Is it possible to emphasize the *one* to the point that the *many* are inadequately considered? If so, how do we prevent this? 2. Is it possible to emphasize the *many* to the point that the *one* is inadequately considered? If so, how do we prevent this?

Option. To reinforce the lesson, have learners complete the "Parts of the Whole" activity from the reproducible page, which you can download.

Into Life

Give each learner a copy of the template below for composing a note to send to another church member who serves in a way that is as different as possible from the learner's own giftedness.

> Dear _____,
> I am so glad you are a part of our church body! Your service in the area of _____ blesses all, especially those of us not gifted as you are. We thank God for enabling you the way he has!
> Your fellow "body part" (1 Corinthians 12:12-31),
> _____

Caution! If learners choose to send the above on paper (letter or note), they should **not** simply copy the template and fill in the blanks with handwriting, as that will create the appearance of a rather thoughtless form letter. The note should be personalized to the greatest extent possible!

As learners depart, distribute copies of the "A Bit of Self-Counseling" activity from the reproducible page. This should be a take-home activity due to its highly personal nature.

Gift of
Languages

DEVOTIONAL READING: Deuteronomy 4:32-40
BACKGROUND SCRIPTURE: Acts 2:1-21; 1 Corinthians 14:1-25

ACTS 2:1-7, 12

¹ When the day of Pentecost came, they were all together in one place. ² Suddenly a sound like the blowing of a violent wind came from heaven and filled the whole house where they were sitting. ³ They saw what seemed to be tongues of fire that separated and came to rest on each of them. ⁴ All of them were filled with the Holy Spirit and began to speak in other tongues as the Spirit enabled them.

⁵ Now there were staying in Jerusalem God-fearing Jews from every nation under heaven. ⁶ When they heard this sound, a crowd came together in bewilderment, because each one heard their own language being spoken. ⁷ Utterly amazed, they asked: "Aren't all these who are speaking Galileans?

· ·

¹² Amazed and perplexed, they asked one another, "What does this mean?"

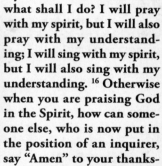

1 CORINTHIANS 14:13-19

¹³ For this reason the one who speaks in a tongue should pray that they may interpret what they say. ¹⁴ For if I pray in a tongue, my spirit prays, but my mind is unfruitful. ¹⁵ So what shall I do? I will pray with my spirit, but I will also pray with my understanding; I will sing with my spirit, but I will also sing with my understanding. ¹⁶ Otherwise when you are praising God in the Spirit, how can someone else, who is now put in the position of an inquirer, say "Amen" to your thanksgiving, since they do not know what you are saying? ¹⁷ You are giving thanks well enough, but no one else is edified.

¹⁸ I thank God that I speak in tongues more than all of you. ¹⁹ But in the church I would rather speak five intelligible words to instruct others than ten thousand words in a tongue.

KEY VERSE

So what shall I do? I will pray with my spirit, but I will also pray with my understanding; I will sing with my spirit, but I will also sing with my understanding. —**1 Corinthians 14:15**

Graphic: Hemera / Thinkstock

THE SPIRIT COMES

Unit 3: One in the Bond of Love
LESSONS 11–14

LESSON AIMS

After participating in this lesson, each learner will be able to:

1. Describe the purpose of speaking in tongues in the New Testament church.

2. Suggest some modern innovations in communication that enhance the transmission of the message as the gift of tongues did in the first-century church.

3. Identify one barrier to communication within his or her church and offer assistance to change the situation.

LESSON OUTLINE

Introduction
A. Understanding Means Belonging

What makes you feel like you really belong with a group of people? We appreciate a warm welcome, the offer of a place to sit, etc. But what we need most is to understand what is going on around us. We want to listen to conversation that we can understand, and we want to be understood when we speak. Without such understanding, we easily feel that we do not belong. We can make an effort to relate with gestures or facial expressions, but words are our best means of making a connection.

Today's text is about an extraordinary way that God enabled some followers of Christ in the first century to make a connection with language. But that enabling was a double-edged sword, and Paul needed to issue special instructions to the believers in Corinth in that regard.

B. Lesson Background

The issue of language in human relationships has deep roots in the Bible. It tells of the tower of Babel, where people of one language banded together to build a tower "that reaches to the heavens" so that they could "make a name" for themselves (Genesis 11:4). In response to their unholy ambitions, God caused their language to be confused as he scattered them across the earth (11:6-9). In doing so, God restrained peoples' ability to work together for evil.

The story of Babel becomes foundational to the rest of the biblical worldview. The division and resulting conflict between tribes and nations, epitomized in the multiplying of languages, is rooted in human pride and rebellion against God.

But God promised to bring blessings to the plurality of nations that resulted from his judgment on human pride. He promised a blessing on Abram, to make his descendants a great nation so that "all peoples on earth will be blessed" (Genesis 12:3) through him. As the nation of Israel grew, God sent prophets who repeated that promise. Sometimes those prophets delivered the promise with an image of people of many languages coming to know the true God (Isaiah 66:18; Zechariah 8:23; etc.).

With Christ's death and resurrection, God brought to the point of fulfillment his promise to bless the nations. The risen Christ commanded his followers to wait for power from on high, the Holy Spirit, who would enable them to be witnesses to the entire earth (Luke 24:45-49; Acts 1:4-8). The Spirit would enable the worldwide triumph of God, the fulfillment of his promise to Abram and a reversal of the judgment of Babel. That enabling began on the Day of Pentecost, about seven weeks after Christ's crucifixion.

What Do You Think?

What lessons have you learned from situations in which a time of waiting on God was followed by a surprising blessing?

Talking Points for Your Discussion

- Inside the church
- Outside the church

Pentecost is known in the Old Testament variously as the Festival of Weeks, day of firstfruits, and Festival of Harvest (Exodus 23:16a; 34:22a; Leviticus 23:15-21; Numbers 28:26-31; Deuteronomy 16:9-12, 16). Meaning "50 days," Pentecost came seven weeks after Passover to celebrate and dedicate the grain harvest of spring (Deuteronomy 16:9, 10). By the first century AD, Jewish tradition had come to associate Pentecost with God's giving of the law to Moses at Mount Sinai 50 days after the exodus, although there is no trace of such a time line in the Bible.

I. Tongues at the Church's Birth
(ACTS 2:1-7, 12)

A. Event (vv. 1-4)

1. When the day of Pentecost came, they were all together in one place.

The word *they* refers to Jesus' apostles, who are gathered in Jerusalem (Acts 1:26). This is according to Jesus' instructions as they await the promised Holy Spirit (1:4, 5). They are about to participate in one of the great demonstrations of God's saving power, greater even than the giving of the law that they celebrate on *the day of Pentecost* (see the Lesson Background).

2. Suddenly a sound like the blowing of a violent wind came from heaven and filled the whole house where they were sitting.

That which is about to take place unfolds with a great demonstration of power. The details serve to underline the significance. In both Greek (the common language of the New Testament world) and Hebrew (the ancient language of Israel), the word for *wind* sounds much like the word for "spirit" (compare John 3:8). So *a sound like the blowing of a violent wind* can easily suggest the idea of God's Spirit. The fact that the sound comes *from heaven* indicates that what is about to be given originates with God himself.

We note that the text does not say an actual wind is present, only the sound of one. The particular house mentioned is not identified.

3. They saw what seemed to be tongues of fire that separated and came to rest on each of them.

Added to the sound is a visible sign of *tongues of fire*, which appears *on each* of the gathered apostles. John the Baptist prophesied of the one who would baptize with the Holy Spirit and fire (Matthew 3:11; Luke 3:16); the image of fire may be intended to recall that promise.

4. All of them were filled with the Holy Spirit and began to speak in other tongues as the Spirit enabled them.

The sound and sight are followed by an act of empowerment as *the Holy Spirit* fills the followers of Jesus. The Holy Spirit was active in Old Testament days, but only with a few of God's people, primarily to empower prophets to speak (Numbers 11:25-29; 1 Samuel 10:6, 10; 19:20, 23; Nehemiah 9:30). But now the promise of God is coming to fulfillment, the promise that he will pour his Spirit on his people (Isaiah 44:3-5; 32:15; Ezekiel 36:27; 37:14; Joel 2:28).

The Holy Spirit at this point empowers a gift of speech as he did for the prophets. But this event is distinct: Jesus' apostles *speak in other tongues* or known human languages (Acts 2:6, below). It is as if Babel is happening again (see the Lesson Background), but this time in reverse—a sign that God is now blessing all nations as he had promised so many centuries before.

B. Reaction (vv. 5-7, 12)

5. Now there were staying in Jerusalem God-fearing Jews from every nation under heaven.

For centuries the Jewish people have been scattered across the Near East and around the Mediterranean Sea. The Assyrians had taken many Israelites into exile in 722 BC. The Babylonians had finalized their conquest of Judah in 586 BC and taken its people as captives to Babylon. Those exiled there were allowed to return decades later, but most chose to remain where they were (Ezra 2:1-65; 8:1-20). Jews continued to migrate in later generations—sometimes willingly, sometimes not. The result is called the Diaspora, the scattering of Israel (compare John 7:35; James 1:1).

But Jerusalem remains the center of Jewish life and hope nonetheless. Diaspora Jews often abandon homes elsewhere to return to Jerusalem to settle there. Others visit the city periodically for the three annual pilgrimage festivals (Deuteronomy 16:16; Exodus 23:14-17). A crowd of such people is gathered on this occasion. They are from so many places that the text describes them as *from every nation under heaven* (further defined in Acts 2:9-11).

> ### What Do You Think?
> What are some good ways for a church to use cultural observances and celebrations to spread the gospel? What are some dangers to this?
> *Talking Points for Your Discussion*
> - Regarding observances having religious overtones (Thanksgiving, etc.)
> - Regarding observances not having religious overtones (Labor Day, etc.)
> - Regarding cultural celebrations not connected with a holiday

6. When they heard this sound, a crowd came together in bewilderment, because each one heard their own language being spoken.

The unfolding miracle draws a crowd! What they witness is utterly unlike anything previously experienced. The wording of this verse and the six that follow suggests not a quiet state of confusion and murmuring but open consternation, with plenty of talking and questioning. It is an uproar.

What causes amazement is hearing people speaking many languages. Individuals in the crowd gathered for Pentecost can hear their native languages being spoken as they detect familiar sounds from among the other languages that they cannot understand. What causes a group of people to be able to speak so many languages?

7. Utterly amazed, they asked: "Aren't all these who are speaking Galileans?"

Perhaps by their dress, perhaps by their accents, the speakers are clearly identified as being from Galilee (compare Matthew 26:73; Acts 1:11). This is a key part of the amazement. One does not expect a group from one region to speak the languages of so many places at once!

> ### What Do You Think?
> How can we exercise of our giftedness to draw attention to God rather than to ourselves?
> *Talking Points for Your Discussion*
> - Regarding leadership skills
> - Regarding musical talents
> - Regarding ability for public speaking
> - Other

12. Amazed and perplexed, they asked one another, "What does this mean?"

An event so spectacular must mean something! So the crowd asks that question, which leads to Peter's sermon to provide the answer. Jesus has risen from the dead and ascended to God's right hand. From there he has poured out the promised Holy Spirit on his followers. This means that God's promises are being fulfilled. He is now making himself known to all the nations. The gift of tongues represents the global impact of Christ's work and the global scope of the church's mission.

❧ ATTENTION GRABBERS ❧

You may have heard the old story of the man who lived by a railroad track for most of his life. Like clockwork, a freight train would come roaring by at 2:00 a.m. daily, rattling the windows of the man's house. He became so used to the sound that eventually it no longer awakened him. However, the train didn't come one morning. So exactly at 2:00 a.m., the man awoke with a start and exclaimed, "What was that?"

The crowd gathered in Jerusalem at Pentecost seems to have reacted in a similar way. The noise created by the mass of people crowding the city was expected. Sudden quiet would have caused everyone to look around to see why. But sudden quiet isn't what grabbed everyone's attention; rather, it was the distinctive, unexpected hearing of native languages being spoken by Galileans (compare Acts 22:2).

In the pages of the Bible, God sometimes uses quietness to command attention (example: 1 Kings 19:11-13); sometimes he uses the opposite (example: Job 38:1, 2); sometimes he uses something in between but distinctive, as at Pentecost. What does God have to do to get your attention? —C. R. B.

II. Tongues in the Church's Life
(1 CORINTHIANS 14:13-19)
A. Interpreting for Others (vv. 13-17)

13. For this reason the one who speaks in a tongue should pray that they may interpret what they say.

There is controversy today over what exactly the gift of speaking in tongues is. In the text from Acts just considered, to be able to speak in tongues obviously is miraculous empowerment to speak human languages otherwise unknown to the speaker. The same may be the case in Corinth. However, some interpreters believe that the *tongue* at issue is empowerment to speak not in human languages but in an ecstatic expression of deep connection to God (with reference to 1 Corinthians 13:1; 14:2).

HOW TO SAY IT

Assyrians	Uh-*sear*-e-unz.
Babel	*Bay*-bul.
Babylon	*Bab*-uh-lun.
Babylonians	Bab-ih-*low*-nee-unz.
Diaspora	Dee-*as*-puh-ruh.
Mediterranean	*Med*-uh-tuh-*ray*-nee-un.
Pentecost	*Pent*-ih-kost.
Zechariah	*Zek*-uh-*rye*-uh.

We cannot settle that debate here, but we can certainly pay close attention to the gift's significance. We dare not neglect Paul's instructions because of controversy. Whatever abilities God's Spirit gives to his people, then or now, all those abilities must be used to serve God's purpose, not to boost our own positions.

Some in the Corinthian church apparently are empowered by the Holy Spirit to have the gift of tongues (however construed), and at least some of them choose to exercise the gift when the church is gathered. Paul criticizes this practice because those who so exercise their gift are less concerned for others' benefit than for their own prestige (1 Corinthians 14:4). Others cannot understand what those speaking in tongues are saying, but the speakers want attention and prominence for their spectacular exercise of this gift.

Paul corrects this behavior by putting the emphasis on understanding. At Pentecost, God's gift enables many to hear him praised in their most familiar language; at Corinth, the same breadth of understanding is not present (1 Corinthians 14:2). So Paul insists that those who are gifted to speak in tongues should pray that God will enable them also to *interpret what they* are saying. Without interpretation, others are left out. A gift intended to show that God seeks everyone must not be used in a way that excludes anyone.

> *What Do You Think?*
> Which church activities, parts of worship, etc., are most in need of "interpretation" today in terms of meaning and significance? Why?
> *Talking Points for Your Discussion*
> - For believers
> - For unbelievers who are seeking
> - For the culture at large
> - Other

14. For if I pray in a tongue, my spirit prays, but my mind is unfruitful.

The gift of speaking in tongues has limits. The person who so speaks may be expressing deep feelings to God, things of that person's inmost being or spirit. But is that person able to put those feelings into words that the mind can genuinely

Visual for
Lesson 13

UNDERSTANDING

Ask, "Which of the six areas at the top of this visual need the most work to promote understanding?"

grasp? Paul's implication is clear: it would be far better for that person, let alone for those listening, if that which is expressed through tongues is shared by means of interpretation. Then everyone, including the speaker, can understand, and all will be strengthened.

15. So what shall I do? I will pray with my spirit, but I will also pray with my understanding; I will sing with my spirit, but I will also sing with my understanding.

The Holy Spirit does not seek a display of deep feelings that cannot be expressed in words. But neither does the Spirit seek a faith that we articulate but cannot feel. Both heart and mind are the Spirit's territory, and both should express themselves together in the life of the Spirit-filled person.

Some in Corinth imagine that their mode of expression—the "heart mode" expressed in speaking in tongues—is spiritually superior. Paul says otherwise. But neither is the "mind mode" superior. Both are needed. Each depends on the other. Whether singing or praying, both heart and mind can submit to God's Spirit and come to expression.

16. Otherwise when you are praising God in the Spirit, how can someone else, who is now put in the position of an inquirer, say "Amen" to your thanksgiving, since they do not know what you are saying?

To this point Paul has been considering the effect that uninterpreted tongues primarily has on the individual doing the speaking. Now he turns outward. If the individual speaking cannot understand or articulate the meaning of the utterance, then how will others be expected to do so?

Imagine, Paul says, another person (*an inquirer*) who is unfamiliar with this gift. Such a person might be an unbeliever, but could just as well be a Christian. What good does the tongues-utterance do for such a person? He or she cannot understand what is being said, and so cannot give the deep agreement and affirmation of an *Amen*. The experience thus belongs only to the speaker, with limited benefit, and not to anyone else. Others do not understand, so they are excluded from the event. They become (or remain) outsiders.

17. You are giving thanks well enough, but no one else is edified.

The one who praises God with utterances that others do not understand is acting selfishly, without respect for the benefit of the others. Such a speaker is able to give *thanks well enough* to God, but what of everyone else? They are not at all built up (*edified*).

Elsewhere Paul pictures the church as a building constructed of many, varied people to be a dwelling of God (Ephesians 2:19-22). To use the Spirit's gifts in ways that do not edify (build up) other believers is rank abuse of those gifts.

B. Speaking for Others (vv. 18, 19)

18. I thank God that I speak in tongues more than all of you.

Paul's criticism of those who abuse their gifts is sharp. But is he saying that they should not exercise their gifts at all? By no means! All gifts of the Spirit have legitimate, vital uses. Paul affirms that truth by revealing that he too exercises the gift of speaking in tongues. In fact, he says he does so more than any of them! For this he thanks God.

But as Paul noted before, it is useless to thank God in the presence of others if they cannot comprehend and share in that thanks. What the Corinthians must do is focus their exercise of spiritual gifts on others, not on themselves.

"I'M ONE OF YOU"

U.S. President John F. Kennedy gave an important speech in West Berlin on June 26, 1963. That was at the height of the Cold War and some 22 months after the Communists had erected the Berlin Wall. Kennedy's intent was to warn the Soviets against further belligerence and to reassure the West German people that he stood with them.

In what is considered one of his best speeches, Kennedy declared "Ich bin ein Berliner!" Translated, that means "I am a Berliner!" In identifying himself (in German) with the residents of Berlin, President Kennedy was declaring his solidarity with a people in distress.

Paul did something similar when he said, "I thank God that I speak in tongues more than all of you" (compare Acts 22:3; 23:6). What an important declaration! Having made this statement, no one could say, "Well, he's limiting our tongues-speaking because he isn't familiar with the gift."

This is an important principle in Christian communication. Before we pontificate on who should do what and why, have we taken time to identify ourselves with the situation of the other person? Have we done so in such a way that he or she accepts that identification as realistic? —C. R. B.

19. But in the church I would rather speak five intelligible words to instruct others than ten thousand words in a tongue.

Paul's own exercise of the Spirit's gifts is focused on building others up. That requires that his mind be fully engaged so that others' minds can also be engaged with him. Just a few words from the mind are therefore far more valuable to all than is a great volume of words that no one, not even the speaker, can understand. The words spoken with the gift of tongues may be deeply felt, but they cannot communicate without the engagement of the mind.

What Do You Think?
What have you found effective in protecting yourself from self-seeking motives in service to Christ? What has been less effective? Why?
Talking Points for Your Discussion
- Spiritual disciplines practiced alone
- Spiritual disciplines practiced in group settings
- Other

Conclusion
A. Everyone Fully Welcomed

At Pentecost the Holy Spirit enabled the apostles to do something amazing: speak in languages understood by an international multitude. God declared by that act that his promise to bless the nations was coming to fulfillment. The doors of his sanctuary were thus opened to those who had been previously excluded. Understanding was the first step to belonging.

How tragic it was, then, when the Corinthians used a gift that should signal the inclusion of all in a way that excluded! By using their gifts inappropriately, seeking their own prestige rather than others' benefit, they sent a bitter, haughty message to those around them. In effect they said, "You do not belong; you are not important." Lack of understanding meant exclusion.

Clearly, we all need to consider how we use the abilities that God's Spirit has given us. We need to look past the controversy about speaking in tongues in our day and instead give careful thought to whether we act in the name of Christ in ways that make others feel second-rate or left out altogether.

What do we say or do in the church that is hard for others to understand? Do we ever speak or act in ways that put others in the position of outsiders? What should we do to assure that everyone is fully welcomed, fully engaged, fully a part of the life of Christ's church? How do we tell every person for whom Christ died that he or she is at home among Christ's people? Is our church more like the Day of Pentecost or the tower of Babel? Is our church more like the church at Corinth as corrected or as uncorrected?

B. Prayer

Father, we thank you for creating us with such variety! But we confess that instead of celebrating that variety, we often create barriers. Empower us to remove those barriers as we build one another up as your holy temple. In Jesus' name, amen!

C. Thought to Remember
Use spiritual gifts to include and edify.

INVOLVEMENT LEARNING

Enhance your lesson with NIV® Bible Student (from your curriculum supplier) and the reproducible activity page (at www.standardlesson.com or in the back of the NIV® Standard Lesson Commentary Deluxe Edition).

Into the Lesson

Display this list in the order given: *be / be / built / church / done / Everything / may / must / so / that / the / up.* Say, "These words are listed in alphabetical order, which is not a helpful arrangement! By putting the words in the correct order, you will have the foundational principle taught in the two texts of today's lesson. Note the capitalization!" Allow a minute for learners to come up with the solution. Reveal the principle if no one else does: "Everything must be done so that the church may be built up." Note that all the Spirit's gifts are given to that end.

Alternative. Distribute copies of the "Clarifying" activity from the reproducible page, which you can download. Have learners work individually; allow no more than five minutes. Discuss the frustration of lack of comprehension and/or the relief at eventual understanding as a transition.

Into the Word

Say, "Before we examine our texts, we need to see the issue of languages and tongues in a broader context." Deliver a mini-lecture on the Lesson Background, then distribute handouts featuring two columns, one headed *Expected* and the other headed *Unexpected.* Have listed down the left side of the handout individual references to the eight verses of Acts 2:1-7, 12. Say, "As you read the verses, note on your handout what each reveals explicitly or implies to be expected and/or unexpected."

Have learners work individually, in pairs, or in groups of three. Call for responses after an appropriate amount of time; write learner responses on the board as they are offered. Possible observations: *verse 1*—for the apostles to be gathered in Jerusalem was expected due to Jesus' instruction (Luke 24:49; Acts 1:4); some think that the apostles were celebrating Pentecost along with other observant Jews in the city, although the text does not say that; *verses 2, 3*—the apostles expected to receive "power from on high" (Luke

24:49), but the sound of wind and appearance of fire were probably unexpected; *verse 4*—the apostles expected power of the Holy Spirit to come (Acts 1:8), but the ability to speak in tongues was probably unexpected; *verse 5*—the diverse gathering was expected because Pentecost was a pilgrimage festival; *verses 6, 7, 12*—the amazement of the diverse crowd was expected given the unexpected ability of the apostles to speak in tongues.

Shift to 1 Corinthians 14:13-19 by having that text read aloud. Then write the following on the board (from the commentary on verse 13): "A gift intended to show that God seeks everyone must not be used in a way that excludes anyone." After writing, face the class but say nothing until a learner does. If 15 seconds of awkward silence elapse with no reaction, simply say, "Well, . . ." as you gesture to invite responses. After each reaction, say only "Hmmm . . . that's interesting."

Use reactions to determine where to probe deeper. Work the following sequence of questions into this exploration: 1. What does Paul desire for anyone having the gift of tongues, however that gift may be construed? *(interpretation, v. 13)* 2. When interpretation of tongues is present, what positive element is added as one praises "in the Spirit"? *(edification, vv. 16, 17)* 3. How does the idea of edification connect with what Paul says in verse 19? *(edification results from teaching)*

Into Life

Say, "Complete this sentence: 'Our church has an opportunity to improve its edifying communication to her members regarding _____.'" As follow up to each response, ask, "What are barriers to improving in that area?" Wrap up by asking, "What can we do as a class to eliminate these barriers to edification?" Push for practical ideas that learners are willing to help initiate.

Alternative. Use the "Edifying" activity from the reproducible page instead of the above.

THE GREATEST IS LOVE

DEVOTIONAL READING: Ephesians 3:14-21
BACKGROUND SCRIPTURE: 1 Corinthians 13

1 CORINTHIANS 13

¹ If I speak in the tongues of men or of angels, but do not have love, I am only a resounding gong or a clanging cymbal. ² If I have the gift of prophecy and can fathom all mysteries and all knowledge, and if I have a faith that can move mountains, but do not have love, I am nothing. ³ If I give all I possess to the poor and give over my body to hardship that I may boast, but do not have love, I gain nothing.

⁴ Love is patient, love is kind. It does not envy, it does not boast, it is not proud. ⁵ It does not dishonor others, it is not self-seeking, it is not easily angered, it keeps no record of wrongs. ⁶ Love does not delight in evil but rejoices with the truth. ⁷ It always protects, always trusts, always hopes, always perseveres.

⁸ Love never fails. But where there are prophecies, they will cease; where there are tongues, they will be stilled; where there is knowledge, it will pass away. ⁹ For we know in part and we prophesy in part, ¹⁰ but when completeness comes, what is in part disappears. ¹¹ When I was a child, I talked like a child, I thought like a child, I reasoned like a child. When I became a man, I put the ways of childhood behind me. ¹² For now we see only a reflection as in a mirror; then we shall see face to face. Now I know in part; then I shall know fully, even as I am fully known.

¹³ And now these three remain: faith, hope and love. But the greatest of these is love.

KEY VERSE

Now these three remain: faith, hope and love. But the greatest of these is love. —**1 Corinthians 13:13**

THE SPIRIT COMES

Unit 3: One in the Bond of Love
LESSONS 11–14

LESSON AIMS

After participating in this lesson, each learner will be able to:

1. List the characteristics of godly, self-giving love.

2. Explain why godly love is the defining feature of the truly spiritual life.

3. Propose one way that his or her class can express love as a group in a tangible way to another class or individual in the church.

LESSON OUTLINE

Introduction
A. Authentic Spirituality

Our world chatters about spirituality. While *religion* has negative connotations for many, *spirituality* is widely seen in positive terms. "I'm not religious, but I am very spiritual," say many. If we were to accept such a distinction for the sake of argument, we would still have to ask how we can distinguish authentic spirituality from the inauthentic kind. What makes a person truly spiritual?

To get the answer to that question, we need to begin with a conceptualization of spirituality. The apostle Paul has done just that for us. His conceptualization is grounded in a most essential expression of God's character: *love.*

B. Lesson Background

The Christians to whom Paul wrote the letter we call 1 Corinthians had come to equate knowledge with spirituality (1 Corinthians 8:1-3). They also had associated certain Holy Spirit–given abilities, such as the ability to speak in tongues, with spirituality (14:1-5). Do such things make a person spiritual? Paul's answer is a qualified *no.* Things such as knowledge or the ability to speak in other languages are indeed gifts from the Holy Spirit (12:8, 10), but these gifts by themselves do not make a person spiritually superior. In fact, the very idea of being spiritually superior is unspiritual!

In the midst of that discussion of spiritual gifts —but really in the midst of all the discussions of church problems at Corinth—Paul offered an extended, lyrical discourse on godly love. This text, our lesson for today, is in many respects the climax of 1 Corinthians. The Corinthian church was rife with problems and divisions. With God's kind of love, Paul said, the rivalries infecting the Corinthian church would disappear.

I. Supremacy of Love
(1 CORINTHIANS 13:1-3)
A. Regarding the Tongue (v. 1)

1. If I speak in the tongues of men or of angels, but do not have love, I am only a resounding gong or a clanging cymbal.

Some in the Corinthian church exalt the ability to speak in other languages by the Holy Spirit's power. Paul began to address that issue in the preceding chapter (lesson 12), and he finishes his discussion in the chapter that follows this one (lesson 13). In the verse before us, he launches an extended discussion of the use of that gift (and others) in the context of godly love.

The Greek noun being translated *love* throughout this chapter is *agapē*. Many of us are familiar with this word from its inclusion in the names of parachurch organizations and Sunday school classes. Contrary to some lines of thinking, this word in and of itself does not refer to some kind of "distinctively Christian love." For example, the verb form of *agapē* takes a negative object in 2 Timothy 4:10: "Demas, because he loved this world, has deserted me." As Douglas Moo notes, the early Christians may have chosen to use this word "because of unwanted nuances in other words for 'love' in Greek."

To speak various human languages by God's power is quite impressive. It appears that some Corinthians think, without Paul's approval of their view, that their Spirit-enabled languages are heavenly, angelic languages. "Surely such a gift has to come from God, showing thereby that a person is truly favored by God" they may be thinking.

But if such an impressive gift is exercised to exalt the person who is speaking, then it is done without God's kind of love. In that case, the gift is no longer reflective of God or expressive of his will. It is no longer "spiritual."

The person who would *speak in the tongues of men or of angels* in a loveless manner becomes like an inanimate object that makes repetitive sounds. A *resounding gong* is an instrument that is struck to make a loud noise; it also may be a large bronze vessel that is put in the corner of a public building to vibrate and so amplify the sound when someone delivers a speech. The *clanging cymbal* is one of a small pair of metal pieces that are struck together, like castanets or finger cymbals, making a monotonous, meaningless sound in the process.

Any gift of the Holy Spirit is genuinely spiritual only when exercised with God's kind of love. God's gifts are wasted when they are used for purposes that do not reflect who God is.

❦ ON BEING MULTILINGUAL ❦

Alice Lapuerta, editor of *Multilingual Living Magazine,* grew up in a home where German, Korean, and English were spoken. She, her husband from Ecuador, and her three children now live in Austria. As a result, their children are being brought up in a trilingual environment of German, Spanish, and English.

Lapuerta notes the various challenges of being multilingual. One challenge is the spirit of elitism that can characterize some who are able to speak more than one language. Such folks may view themselves as superior to those who speak fewer languages.

A similar feeling of superiority seems to have infected some (or many) in Corinth. The tongues-speakers perhaps projected an aura that provoked envy on the part of those who lacked the gift. To cast a broader perspective, Paul noted other gifts that could result in similar airs of superiority and envy: the gifts of prophecy, knowledge, extraordinary faith, unusual benevolence, and extreme self-sacrifice (see the next two verses below).

To counteract prideful multilingualism, etc., Paul informed the Corinthians that they needed to learn one more language: the language of love. That is the language that must always be spoken!

—C. R. B.

HOW TO SAY IT

agape (Greek)	Uh-*gah*-pay.
Corinth	*Kor*-inth.
Corinthians	Ko-*rin*-thee-unz (*th* as in *thin*).
Demas	*Dee*-mus.
Philippians	Fih-*lip*-ee-unz.

B. Regarding Spirituality (v. 2)

2. If I have the gift of prophecy and can fathom all mysteries and all knowledge, and if I have a faith that can move mountains, but do not have love, I am nothing.

The gift of prophecy is being able to speak God's message by the Spirit's power (1 Corinthians 12:10, lesson 11). Paul has already noted that the Spirit equips some with exceptional gifts of *knowledge*—the ability to know or understand the things of God (12:8, lesson 11). No gift enables a person to know everything of God or all the *mysteries* that he might reveal. But try to imagine someone to be so gifted as to know everything. Such giftedness would not make that person anything unless exercised with godly love.

The same is true for those gifted with exceptional *faith*. Here Paul speaks as he does earlier —not about the faith in Christ that saves but about an exceptionally firm faith in difficult circumstances. Such a gift is from the Holy Spirit (1 Corinthians 12:9, lesson 11). Jesus told his disciples that with even small faith they could move mountains (Matthew 17:20; 21:21), and that assurance is echoed here. In the day of Jesus and Paul, to "move mountains" is a figurative expression meaning to do something very difficult or extraordinary. But even such a gift of faith makes the person nothing without godly love.

C. Regarding Personal Sacrifice (v. 3)

3. If I give all I possess to the poor and give over my body to hardship that I may boast, but do not have love, I gain nothing.

Now imagine someone so generous as to give away everything to those in need. That generosity certainly would be honored by all who see it. But if such benevolence is done for selfish motives (notoriety, etc.) rather than for the selfless good of others and love for Christ, it brings no benefit to the person who does the great act. Motive and attitude are vital (see Matthew 6:2)!

The same may be said for anyone who would go so far as to give his or her body; Paul's *give over my body to hardship* may be referring to surrendering faithfully even to the point of death in martyrdom. Any act of service and sacrifice —even martyrdom—can be twisted into something self-serving. Even acts that mimic God's self-sacrificial gift in Jesus are invalidated when we do them to exalt ourselves rather than to bless others. Paul is one who dedicates himself completely to the Lord's service, suffering great physical distress in the process (2 Corinthians 11:23-27). But what he knows about bodily suffering, he must communicate: it means nothing if not done out of love for others.

II. Behaviors of Love
(1 CORINTHIANS 13:4-7)
A. Patient, Kind, Helpful (v. 4)

4a. Love is patient,

The person who loves like God exercises the kind of patience that is willing to undergo lengthy hardship. How long? For as long as necessary, just as God exercises long-standing patience with us.

4b. . . . love is kind.

Godly love practices kindness. This means thinking first of the other person's needs rather than one's own. This is exactly what God has done for us in Christ (Titus 3:4-7).

4c. It does not envy,

Envy is deadly (Romans 1:29; 1 Timothy 6:3-5). The person who loves is not jealous of those who have more honor or possessions. Rather, they are as glad for others' blessings as they are for their own.

4d. . . . it does not boast,

Godly love and bragging are incompatible. Loving people do not praise themselves or seek the praises of others. In love there is no need to be greater than others. The cure for bragging is to reflect on God's love in Christ, who went to his death for us despite the ridicule and insults that he received. No good works we do in Christ leave room for boasting (Ephesians 2:8, 9).

4e. . . . it is not proud.

Paul visits this problem several times in this letter (1 Corinthians 4:6, 18, 19; 5:2), but with special emphasis in 8:1: "Knowledge puffs up while love builds up." Posturing oneself to appear better than others is being *proud*. Love, on the other hand, seeks to build up others. Paul wants the Corinthians to use their spiritual gifts not in order to appear important but to build up (edify) those around them. That is the true way of love like Christ's.

B. Concerned, Unselfish, Forgiving (v. 5)

5a. It does not dishonor others,

Love does not act in a way that brings shame or embarrassment to others. Godly concern for others means that even in small, incidental ways, followers of Christ will show unselfish respect.

5b. . . . it is not self-seeking,

Because the essence of God's love is concern for others, godly love is not self-centered. As such, love does not focus on amassing possessions, honors, or status for oneself. Love's focus is on giving, not receiving (Acts 20:35; Philippians 2:4).

5c. . . . it is not easily angered,

Imagine someone being poked with a pointed stick. The natural reaction is to get riled up and poke back. But love does not respond in that way. It does not return evil for evil (Romans 12:17). Rather, love does what Christ did when he prayed for the forgiveness of those who crucified him (Luke 23:34).

What Do You Think?

When was a time that love kept you from reacting to a provocation? How did things turn out?

Talking Points for Your Discussion

- A family situation
- A work or school situation
- A church situation
- Other

5d. . . . it keeps no record of wrongs.

This expression refers to keeping an account of evil things that others do to oneself. Love forgives, and true forgiveness means treating the other person as if nothing had happened. Keeping a mental *record of wrongs* that others have done to us serves no purpose except to justify taking revenge on that person at some time in the future. For one who loves, such a record is pointless (compare Hebrews 8:12; 10:17).

C. Truthful, Faithful, Hopeful (vv. 6, 7)

6. Love does not delight in evil but rejoices with the truth.

When we focus on ourselves, we resent other people's blessings and are happy when others experience hardships. But when the godly person *rejoices with the truth,* he or she sets aside the self-interest that deceives us into being glad when others suffer. The loving person is free and ready to celebrate when others rejoice and to mourn sincerely when others mourn (Romans 12:15).

7. It always protects, always trusts, always hopes, always perseveres.

What are the boundaries of godly love? Peter asked Jesus whether he was to forgive up to seven times, and Jesus replied "I tell you, not seven times, but seventy-seven times" (Matthew 18:21, 22). Just as God is willing to wait a lifetime for wayward people to turn back to him, so those who love as God loves are prepared to undergo what may seem to be an endless line of hardships for the sake of others. They never give up supporting others, never cease in believing in others, never run out of hope for others, and always endure whatever happens because of their commitment to others.

If this kind of love seems unreasonable, remember God's own boundless love. As those who have received his love, we are compelled to love others in the same way. With Paul, let us "put up with anything rather than hinder the gospel of Christ" (1 Corinthians 9:12).

❧ SECOND PLACE? ❧

Time magazine featured President Obama as its 2012 Person of the Year. Tim Cook, the successor to Steve Jobs at Apple, was the runner-up. One commentator said, "There's absolutely no shame in finishing second, especially when you're going up against the President of the United States." On the other hand, some propose that first place is everything and second place is nothing. Perhaps you remember this Nike™ advertising slogan from the 1996 Olympics: "You don't win silver; you lose gold." Third place? Don't bother to ask!

So which philosophy above reflects the Christian life? Neither one! Both assume that (1) there is only one first-place finisher just by definition and (2) there is also a second-place, silver-medal position. But in Christ everyone can be awarded the gold medal of eternal life. A silver medal does not exist in Christianity, only gold.

Earlier in this letter, Paul draws a parallel between the Christian life and the athletic contests of running and boxing (1 Corinthians 9:24-27; compare Galatians 5:7; 2 Timothy 4:7). There is indeed an opponent to defeat, but that opponent is Satan and his influences, not our fellow Christian. Instead of competing against others, we extend loving hands of patience, kindness, humility, etc., to help them cross the finish line with us. —C. R. B.

III. Priority of Love
(1 CORINTHIANS 13:8-13)

A. Temporary Gifts vs. Perfect Love (vv. 8-10)

8. Love never fails. But where there are prophecies, they will cease; where there are tongues, they will be stilled; where there is knowledge, it will pass away.

Summing up the previous section, Paul affirms that godly love will never give up or give out. That observation leads to a comparison. The gifts that the Corinthians are emphasizing are of lesser significance than godly love because unlike love, they will not endure forever. When God's purpose is fulfilled at Christ's return, there will be no need for *prophecies* (the Spirit-empowered declaration of God's message), for God's truth will reign supreme. The gift of *tongues* will cease as it gives way to perfect, face-to-face communication between God and his people. Special gifts of *knowledge* will no longer be needed as all God's people will learn directly from the Lord, as his truth is fully revealed to all.

Such gifts, important as they are, lack the eternal priority that characterizes love. They will no longer be exercised, but in God's eternal presence

his people will love him and love each other forever in perfect harmony.

9, 10. For we know in part and we prophesy in part, but when completeness comes, what is in part disappears.

Paul has already affirmed the importance of knowledge and prophecy for building up believers (1 Corinthians 12:8, 10; see lesson 11). Rightly exercised, those gifts provide the understanding that the Corinthians need to put their faith into practice. But presently their knowledge of God's message comes to them step by step, piece by piece. The gifts that contribute to their growth are important, but only as long as their condition is partial, still being added to.

Things change *when completeness comes*, and there are different proposals on what this *completeness* refers to. Some think it refers to the day of Christ's return, when the partial, step-by-step growth in Christian knowledge we experience now shall give way to full knowledge of God's will for his people. Others think that the *completeness* refers to the completion of the New Testament. When that happens, the readers will have no need for further divine revelation to supplement what they currently receive piecemeal (as Paul writes his letters, etc.).

Either way, the stress is on the contrast between that which is temporary and that which is permanent. Love is in the latter category. It will remain as the eternal foundation of God's relationship with his people.

B. Childhood vs. Adulthood (v. 11)

11. When I was a child, I talked like a child, I thought like a child, I reasoned like a child. When I became a man, I put the ways of childhood behind me.

Paul now uses a person's developmental stages to illustrate Christian growth. A child's view of the world is partial, growing by steps. Each child requires special supports for nurture and growth. So it is with God's people regarding spiritual growth (compare 1 Corinthians 3:2). God is nurturing us, growing us, through the Spirit's gifts.

In adulthood, however, one can set aside the means by which one was nurtured as a child. So it is, Paul says, with the Spirit's gifts. On the day they are set aside, God's love continues still.

> **What Do You Think?**
> How has the hope of Heaven changed your perspective on worldly things? How does this relate to issues of childhood to be left behind?
> *Talking Points for Your Discussion*
> - Regarding material possessions
> - Regarding personal talents and abilities
> - Regarding personal accomplishments
> - Regarding personal goals
> - Other

C. Present vs. Future (vv. 12, 13)

12. For now we see only a reflection as in a mirror; then we shall see face to face. Now I know in part; then I shall know fully, even as I am fully known.

Paul uses his readers' experience with mirrors to move his arguments to their conclusion. An ancient mirror, unlike a modern mirror, is made of polished bronze. This yields a reasonable image, but an image that is not as clear as viewing something directly. So it is in the Corinthians' current experience: they see truly, but only via the imperfect image of *a reflection* that polished bronze can yield.

Full knowledge, on the other hand, is like seeing *face to face*—much clearer! The goal is to know God as he already knows us. When that goal is achieved, the need for the Spirit's gifts will be ended. Even so, love will continue (next verse).

13. And now these three remain: faith, hope and love. But the greatest of these is love.

Elsewhere Paul presents faith, love, and hope as the chief virtues of the Christian life (see 1 Thessalonians 1:3; 5:8). *Faith* is fundamental; it is the attitude of trust and confidence in God. *Hope* is that confident trust focused on the future; it is believing with assurance that God will fulfill his promises for us. *Love* is the commitment to the other person's good at whatever cost to ourselves.

In eternity, faith will be transformed as it yields to sight. Hope will be transformed as God's promises are fulfilled for us. But love, *the greatest of these* three, will become only greater.

> **What Do You Think?**
> Why is a proper understanding of *love* critical to genuine biblical faith?
> *Talking Points for Your Discussion*
> - In terms of how God is to be viewed
> - In terms of how other people are to be viewed
> - In terms of how we are to view ourselves

Conclusion

A. Learning to Love Now

God the Father, God the Son, and God the Holy Spirit have shared love eternally, without beginning. Christians will join in that eternal love without end.

But the challenge is not in eternity. The challenge is in the present. We need to see each other as God sees us: of great worth despite the way we fail and disappoint. In loving others as God loves us, we gain a glimpse of what life, what eternal life, is all about.

B. Prayer

O God, your everlasting, all-enduring, gracious, merciful love is beyond comprehension! Teach us how you love us so that we can love one another. In the name of the loving Christ, amen.

C. Thought to Remember

To give love, first give in to love.

Visual for Lesson 14. *Point to this visual as you ask, "In what ways can expressions of love within a marriage be modeled on today's text?"*

INVOLVEMENT LEARNING

Enhance your lesson with NIV® Bible Student *(from your curriculum supplier) and the reproducible activity page (at www.standardlesson.com or in the back of the* NIV® Standard Lesson Commentary Deluxe Edition*).*

Into the Lesson

Write the phrase *Even though* _____, *so what unless* _____? on the board in large letters. Ask learners to suggest possible completions. If you want to give an example, say, "Even though I am a teacher of this class, so what unless I show up to teach?"

After several proposals, say, "We could call this the conclusion to today's text: Even though one has impressive God-given gifts, so what if there is no love shown?"

Into the Word

Give two good readers a copy of the following dialogue to deliver to your class. Inform Reader 2 not to read the verse designations at the end of his or her segments.

Reader 1: I can speak six languages!
Reader 2: But you don't love others! So what? *(v. 1)*
Reader 1: God has given me the ability to speak like the angels Gabriel and Michael!
Reader 2: So? You're not using that ability to bless others. *(v. 1)*
Reader 1: I can predict the future!
Reader 2: But your communication is hindered because of your lack of love. *(v. 2a)*
Reader 1: I have degrees from the best universities. My understanding of the human condition is the envy of scholars!
Reader 2: But it's only fodder for your ego since you're not using your knowledge to benefit others. *(v. 2b)*
Reader 1: My faith is so profound, I can move mountains!
Reader 2: But why aren't you helping others deepen their faith? *(v. 2b)*
Reader 1: I may give the fortune I have accumulated in the stock market to a foundation to benefit the poor!
Reader 2: If you do, will you be caring about the poor or the accolades of others? *(v. 3a)*

Reader 1: I'm even thinking about donating a kidney for someone who needs one!
Reader 2: But what would be your motive? *(v. 3b)*
Reader 1: Look! I have all the attributes of a good person: I'm kind and self-controlled; I don't anger easily; I am always glad to see truth triumphant; etc. Look at me!
Reader 2: That is certainly what you want. But you do not love others. And that is why it will all come to nothing. Love is everything! *(vv. 4-7)*

When the dialogue ends, go back over its segments with learners to note the parallels and inadequacies of the paraphrase as you compare and contrast it with the actual text. (Giving each learner a copy of the dialogue before you do so, or projecting it on a screen, will make it easier to follow along.) When you are ready to consider verses 8-13 (not covered by the dialogue), lead a discussion as you ask, "What parallels, summations, and enhancements do you see in verses 8-13 in relation to verses 1-7?"

Option. Distribute copies of the "If I . . ." activity from the reproducible page, which you can download, for learners to work on individually for a few minutes. This will serve as a good transition to Into Life.

Into Life

Say, "Note that Reader 1 in the dialogue was ready and eager to talk about his [or her] abilities and contemplated sacrifices, but was hesitant to examine motives behind those. What are some things we could do as a class to serve an individual or our church as a whole while maintaining love as our only motive?" Encourage brainstorming, jot ideas on the board, and select one to initiate.

Option. Distribute copies of the "Love Is . . ." activity from the reproducible page as a take-home exercise. This will enhance your learners' understanding of the Bible's concept of love and encourage individual action in that regard.

GOD'S PROPHETS
DEMAND JUSTICE

Special Features

Lessons

Unit 1: Amos Rails Against Injustice

Unit 2: Micah Calls for Justice Among Unjust People

Unit 3: Advocates of Justice for All

QUARTERLY QUIZ

Use these questions as a pretest or as a review. The answers are on page iv of This Quarter in the Word.

Lesson 1

1. What does the Lord threaten to send on Judah? (flood, fire, lightning?) *Amos 2:5*

2. Amos condemns the people of Israel for selling the needy for a pair of _____. *Amos 2:6*

Lesson 2

1. The day of the Lord will be like a man who escapes a lion only to be met by a ____. *Amos 5:19*

2. The Lord wants justice to roll on like a river. T/F. *Amos 5:24*

Lesson 3

1. The beds of the rich in Israel were adorned with what? (gold, silver, ivory?) *Amos 6:4*

2. The rich of Israel drank _____ out of bowls. *Amos 6:6*

Lesson 4

1. Amos used a basket of what as an illustration? (fruit, dirt, old clothes?) *Amos 8:1*

2. Amos prophesied a day when the Lord would make the sun go down at _____. *Amos 8:9*

Lesson 5

1. Micah says the people have risen up like a(n) what? (festering boil, flood, enemy?) *Micah 2:8*

2. The land was undefiled by sin in Micah's day. T/F. *Micah 2:10*

Lesson 6

1. According to Micah, Jerusalem was being built with wickedness. T/F. *Micah 3:10*

2. Micah commended the priests for not teaching merely for a price. T/F. *Micah 3:11*

Lesson 7

1. Balak had been king of what nation? (Israel, Egypt, Moab?) *Micah 6:5*

2. The three things the Lord requires are justice, mercy, and _____. *Micah 6:8*

Lesson 8

1. The "nations" would end up licking dust like a(n) what? (snake, ant, dog?) *Micah 7:16, 17*

2. God's forgiveness is like casting iniquities into the depths of the _____. *Micah 7:19*

Lesson 9

1. Isaiah noted that the one who shuns evil was hunted like prey. T/F. *Isaiah 59:15*

2. Isaiah pictured the Lord putting on a helmet of what? (iron, salvation, victory?) *Isaiah 59:17*

Lesson 10

1. To what false god did Jeremiah's people burn incense? (Zeus, Poseidon, Baal?) *Jeremiah 7:9*

2. The temple had been made into a den of _____. *Jeremiah 7:11*

3. Shiloh was an example of a place that had escaped God's judgment. T/F. *Jeremiah 7:12*

Lesson 11

1. God claimed all souls to be his. T/F. *Ezekiel 18:4*

2. Ezekiel pointed out the vile sin of defiling the _____ of one's neighbor. *Ezekiel 18:6*

Lesson 12

1. God expected his people not to oppress "the foreigner." T/F. *Zechariah 7:10*

2. Zechariah denounced hearts that were hard like what? (flint, wood, ice?) *Zechariah 7:12*

3. A time came when God wouldn't listen when the Israelites cried out to him. T/F. *Zechariah 7:13*

Lesson 13

1. God would send his messenger to prepare the _____ of the Lord. *Malachi 3:1*

2. *Sorcerers* are on the list of those condemned by Malachi. T/F. *Malachi 3:5*

3. The Israelites robbed God when they withheld what? (singing, prayers, tithes?) *Malachi 3:8*

QUARTER AT A GLANCE

by Douglas Redford

MANY ASSOCIATE the Old Testament prophets with stern, unyielding "turn or burn" proclamations of judgment. While the judgment of God on a wayward people is certainly an inescapable part of the prophets' language, one could also summarize their message with the phrase "turn and burn": God's people must both turn from their selfish, sinful ways and burn with a passion for justice. The lessons for this quarter highlight some of the Old Testament prophets' most notable calls to just living.

The Roots of Justice

The demand for justice is frequently voiced in modern society. In some cases, Old Testament prophets are quoted to support such a demand. However, many of today's advocates of justice have divorced their pleas from any sense of obedience to the God for whom the prophets spoke.

For the prophets, justice is defined by the sovereign God who has revealed standards of right and wrong. He expects those standards to be reflected in the lives of his people, and he requires that they demonstrate the mercy they have received.

Amos, for example, challenges his hearers to "hate evil, love good; maintain justice in the courts" (Amos 5:15, lesson 2). Micah points out that God "has shown you, O mortal, what is good . . . to act justly and to love mercy and to walk humbly with your God" (Micah 6:8, lesson 7). The people already knew what God expected; they had chosen to ignore those expectations to their own peril.

The prophets' cries against injustice often include equally passionate cries against idolatry and those who perverted God's truth (lessons 2, 6, and 11). Without the roots of revealed truth from the real God, justice has no firm foundation, becoming instead subject to the personal whims and desires of whoever may be in power at any given time (lesson 6).

The Fruits of Justice

Many are familiar with the statue of Lady Justice, who is depicted wearing a blindfold. This is to illustrate that justice must be administered without any hint of favoritism. The Bible clearly teaches this (Leviticus 19:15; etc.). But justice in the sense of viewing others as God views them means keeping one's eyes wide open to the plight of others. Specific groups noted by the prophets include the most neglected and vulnerable: the poor (lessons 1, 4), and the foreigner, the fatherless, and the widow (lessons 10, 12).

The problem was that God's people eventually became more enamored with the privilege of being chosen than with the purpose that accompanied such a status. Jeremiah confronted this attitude among those who had chosen to trust in lies (lesson 10). These self-deceived people preferred to drown out his unpleasant (but truthful) words with a false mantra.

It is fairly easy for modern Christians to read the prophets' words and think of how they apply to the sins of contemporary society. Even though the prophets' audience was the people of God in the Old Testament period (Israel) while Christians are the people of God in the New Testament era,

> *Without the roots of revealed truth from the real God, justice has no firm foundation.*

we recall that part of James's definition of pure religion is "to look after orphans and widows in their distress" (James 1:27). These are the same groups that the prophets told God's people they were neglecting.

We must not read the prophets' words and scathingly point a finger at society; we must see each prophet's finger pointed directly at us. We who are God's people today must give their words a hearing. And we must obey.

GET THE SETTING

by Lloyd Pelfrey

THE LESSONS FOR this quarter's study include prophecies delivered from about 760 to 430 BC. Three of the world's first empires rose during those years. Each had a role in the plan of God, and each was replaced when its task was completed. The three empires were Assyria, Babylon, and Persia.

These nations served as agents for God's justice, and they became objects of that same justice when they were overcome by sins that often signal the end of a nation. The wars and conquests fulfilled God's purposes to shape his people so that the Messiah could come just when everything was ready.

The Assyrian Empire

Amos began thundering his judgments against Israel, Judah, and six nearby nations and cities in about 760 BC. The agent to punish them would be Assyria. The Assyrian Empire became a reality a few years later, in 745 BC. The conquests began, and Samaria, the capital of Israel, fell in 722 BC. The northern nation of Israel was no more.

Judah also experienced the might of Assyria, but the Assyrians made mistakes: they insulted God (2 Kings 19:10-13) and became arrogant (Isaiah 10:5-12). King Sennacherib of Assyria brought the campaign against Judah, and in his *Annals* he boasts of having captured 46 cities and shutting up Hezekiah in Jerusalem "like a caged bird." Sennacherib never captured Jerusalem, however, for the angel of the Lord struck down 185,000 of his army in 701 BC (2 Kings 19:35, 36).

The year was 612 BC when Nebuchadnezzar, the young crown prince of Babylon, combined with the Medes to destroy Nineveh, Assyria's capital city (prophesied in Zephaniah 2:13-15). Assyria had fulfilled its part in God's plan.

The Babylonian Empire

Nebuchadnezzar became king of Babylon when his father died in 605 BC. Judah became sub-servient immediately (2 Kings 24:1; Daniel 1:1, 2). God's purposes for Babylon were to punish Assyria (Isaiah 30:31) and to take the people of Judah into captivity (Jeremiah 32:28).

The kings of Judah were not good subjects. They rebelled each time they thought they could get away with it, such as when the Babylonians were off quelling rebellions in other areas. When Nebuchadnezzar finally had had enough, his forces destroyed Jerusalem and the temple in 586 BC.

The Jews in Babylonian exile finally understood that God meant what he said; as a result, idolatry was never again a serious problem. But could a nation that had lost its king, its people, its capital, and its temple be restored? The answer is *yes*, but only when God is in the equation.

The Persian Empire

The Babylonian Empire lasted less than a century. It was brought to an unexpected end by Cyrus the Great, a king about whom Isaiah had prophesied specifically by name (Isaiah 44:28; 45:1). He captured Babylon in 539 BC.

Cyrus proclaimed that all captive groups in the empire could go home and they could take their gods with them. His proclamation is in the last verses of 2 Chronicles and the first verses of Ezra. The generic form is on the famous Cyrus Cylinder that is in the British Museum. The Persian Empire lasted a little over 200 years, until the time of Alexander the Great and his successors (Daniel 8:5-7).

Preparations Complete

Alexander's empire became fragmented after his death, eventually being replaced by that of Rome. Finally, at just the right time, the Messiah came (Galatians 4:4). Our task is to learn from the past and to be ready when he returns. He is indeed coming again—at just the right time.

THIS QUARTER IN THE WORD

Mon, June 1	I Will Judge with Equity	Psalm 75
Tue, June 2	No Escape	Amos 2:9-16
Wed, June 3	I Will Punish Your Iniquities	Amos 3:1-8
Thu, June 4	I Will Punish Your Transgressions	Amos 3:9-15
Fri, June 5	Judgment Is Surely Coming	Amos 4:1-6
Sat, June 6	You Did Not Return to Me	Amos 4:7-13
Sun, June 7	I Will Not Revoke Punishment	Amos 2:4-8
Mon, June 8	Fools Say, "There Is No God"	Psalm 14
Tue, June 9	Can You Deceive God?	Job 13:7-12
Wed, June 10	Full of Hypocrisy and Wickedness	Matthew 23:23-28
Thu, June 11	To Obey Is Better than Sacrifice	1 Samuel 15:17-23
Fri, June 12	Seek the Lord and Live	Amos 5:1-6
Sat, June 13	I Know Your Transgressions and Sins	Amos 5:7-13
Sun, June 14	Love Good and Establish Justice	Amos 5:14, 15, 18-27
Mon, June 15	Full of Greed Inside	Luke 11:37-42
Tue, June 16	A Large Income with Injustice	Proverbs 16:1-11
Wed, June 17	Preaching Christ Out of Selfish Ambition	Philippians 1:12-20
Thu, June 18	Guard Against All Kinds of Greed	Luke 12:15-21
Fri, June 19	Turn My Heart from Selfish Gain	Psalm 119:31-38
Sat, June 20	The Righteous Are Generous	Psalm 37:14-22
Sun, June 21	The Idle Rich	Amos 6:4-8, 11-14

Mon, Aug. 17	You Sinned Worse than Your Ancestors	Jeremiah 16:9-13
Tue, Aug. 18	I Call upon the Lord	2 Samuel 22:1-7
Wed, Aug. 19	Hope in God's Unfailing Love	Psalm 147:1-11
Thu, Aug. 20	Walking in the Way	Judges 2:16-23
Fri, Aug. 21	Pursue Justice and Only Justice	Deuteronomy 16:16-20
Sat, Aug. 22	The Lord Waits to Be Gracious	Isaiah 30:18-26
Sun, Aug. 23	The Results of Not Listening	Zechariah 7:8-14
Mon, Aug. 24	Teach Me Your Paths, O Lord	Psalm 25
Tue, Aug. 25	How Shall We Treat Others?	Matthew 7:7-14
Wed, Aug. 26	How Have We Spoken Against You?	Malachi 3:11-18
Thu, Aug. 27	The Valley of Decision	Joel 3:9-16
Fri, Aug. 28	Repentance or Rejection	Jeremiah 6:26-30
Sat, Aug. 29	The Contrite and Humble in Spirit	Isaiah 57:10-21
Sun, Aug. 30	How Shall We Return?	Malachi 3:1-10

Answers to the Quarterly Quiz on page 338

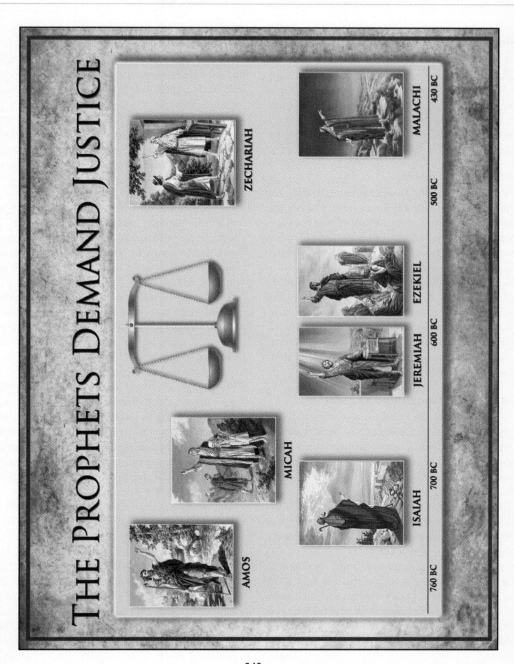

THE PROPHETS DEMAND JUSTICE

AMOS — 760 BC

MICAH

ISAIAH — 700 BC

JEREMIAH — 600 BC

EZEKIEL

ZECHARIAH — 500 BC

MALACHI — 430 BC

COMMUNITY IN SERVICE

Teacher Tips by Wendy Guthrie

I N THE FIRST THREE installments of this four-part series, we looked at the importance of building community and how that happens through classroom engagement and shared responsibility. But for a community of learners to achieve the ultimate purpose of fellowship, its members must also engage in serving one another and those outside of their community.

What Is Service?

Service is identifying what needs to be done for others and then doing it. Jesus spent a lot of time developing and modeling this concept in the Gospels (see Matthew 20:25-28; John 13:4-15; etc.); he placed a high emphasis on service throughout his earthly ministry.

The apostle Paul identified *serving* as a spiritual gift (Romans 12:7). This was a necessary aspect in the building up of the first-century church. So vital was service to the church's health that the 12 apostles decided that the needy widows in Jerusalem had to be served by men "known to be full of the Spirit and wisdom" (Acts 6:3).

Serving the Household of Faith

Many uses of the word *fellowship* in the New Testament occur in the context of mutual service within the body of Christ (example: Acts 2:42-45; 4:32). Paul noted to those in the church at Rome that others had made "a contribution for the poor among the Lord's people in Jerusalem" (Romans 15:26). He also challenged the Corinthians with the example of others' desire to participate in "sharing in this service to the Lord's people" (2 Corinthians 8:4).

A teacher who is intent on building community will encourage class members to find areas of need within their congregation and plan ways to meet those needs. These acts of service do not have to be monumental feats. Some possibilities are tasks such as organizing a car-service day for single or widowed women, providing transportation to the grocery store or doctor's office for senior citizens, or paying for a babysitter so a couple with a special-needs child can go out on a date night.

Putting hands and feet to the Bible is a vital aspect of building community! "As we have opportunity, let us do good to all people, especially to those who belong to the family of believers" (Galatians 6:10).

Serving Outside the Fellowship

While focusing on the "especially to" in the passage just cited, we must not overlook the other part that urges us to "do good to all." That was not a new imperative in Paul's day. When God established his law for Israel, he charged his people that provisions were to be made for "the foreigner" (that is, non-Israelites) who lived among them (Leviticus 19:9, 10). He rebuked his people time and again for not adhering to this law (see lessons 10, 12, and 13).

God himself serves unbelievers by having the "sun to rise on the evil and the good" and sending "rain on the righteous and the unrighteous" (Matthew 5:45). A teacher who wants to build a class into a community will follow the examples set in Scripture and find ways to engage learners in meeting the physical needs of those outside the church. Volunteering at a homeless shelter, delivering meals to shut-ins, organizing a coat drive, or helping residents at the local nursing home are all ways of serving those whose ability to help themselves is limited in some way.

To serve others is to share the love of God with them. But more than that, serving others creates a bond among the members of your class; it creates this bond by extending beyond the classroom walls the purpose for meeting together. If you're teaching to your learners' heads but not to their hands and feet, are you really teaching?

God Passes Judgment

DEVOTIONAL READING: Psalm 75
BACKGROUND SCRIPTURE: Amos 2:4-16

Amos 2:4-8

4 This is what the LORD says:

"For three sins of Judah,
  even for four, I will not relent.
Because they have rejected the law of the
  LORD
  and have not kept his decrees,
because they have been led astray by false
  gods,
  the gods their ancestors followed,
5 I will send fire on Judah
  that will consume the fortresses of
  Jerusalem."

6 This is what the LORD says:

"For three sins of Israel,
  even for four, I will not relent.
They sell the innocent for silver,
  and the needy for a pair of sandals.
7 They trample on the heads of the poor
  as on the dust of the ground
  and deny justice to the oppressed.
Father and son use the same girl
  and so profane my holy name.
8 They lie down beside every altar
  on garments taken in pledge.
In the house of their god
  they drink wine taken as fines."

KEY VERSE

This is what the LORD says: "For three sins of Judah, even for four, I will not relent. Because they have rejected the law of the LORD and have not kept his decrees, because they have been led astray by false gods, the gods their ancestors followed." —Amos 2:4

GOD'S PROPHETS DEMAND JUSTICE

Unit 1: Amos Rails Against Injustice

LESSONS 1–4

LESSON AIMS

After participating in this lesson, each learner will be able to:

1. List the sins of Israel and Judah that the Lord condemned through his prophet Amos.

2. Write a modern parallel for each sin listed in the text.

3. Write a prayer of confession for at least one of the sins identified as a parallel to the sins of Israel and Judah.

LESSON OUTLINE

Introduction
   A. A Line in the Sand
   B. Lesson Background: God's People
   C. Lesson Background: God's Prophecies
I. Indicting Judah (AMOS 2:4, 5)
   A. Introductory Formula (v. 4a)
   B. Iniquities Indicated (v. 4b)
      "Functional Saviors"?
   C. Incendiary Promise (v. 5)
II. Indicting Israel (AMOS 2:6-8)
   A. Introductory Formula (v. 6a)
   B. Iniquities Indicated (v. 6b-8)
      What's at the Root?
Conclusion
   A. What You Deserve!
   B. Prayer
   C. Thought to Remember

Introduction

A. A Line in the Sand

The expression "a line in the sand" may originate from an event that took place in Egypt in 168 BC. Antiochus IV, a king of Syria, had attacked Egypt two years earlier to take advantage of perceived weaknesses there. As a result, he had conquered all of Egypt except the city of Alexandria. He was on his way to finish the task when his entire army was halted by one man: Gaius Popillius Laenas.

Popillius had been a consul in the Roman Republic, the highest elected office. The king and the former consul knew each other, and Antiochus extended his hand in greeting. Instead of receiving a hand in return, Antiochus was given a message from the Roman Senate. The message said that Rome did not want Syrian forces in Egypt. Antiochus told Popillius that he and his officers would consider it. The former consul reacted by drawing a circle in the sand, with the king in its center. Popillius then ordered Antiochus not to step outside the circle until he had made his decision.

Antiochus had been a political hostage in Rome in his early years, and he knew the might of the Roman army. The one man Popillius could be pushed aside easily, but he represented Rome. The king finally gave his answer: "I will do what the Senate thinks right." Only at that point did Popillius extend his own hand in friendship.

Actions have consequences, and Antiochus knew it. How much more serious it is when a person or nation violates God's expectations! To cross God's "line in the sand" is to invite divine judgment. The nation of Israel had crossed that line in pursuit of unrighteousness. As a result, Amos was God's messenger to announce the end of Israel.

B. Lesson Background: God's People

Solomon was the last king of united Israel. When he died in about 930 BC, his son Rehoboam, his successor, refused a request to reduce the tax load, so the 10 northern tribes seceded. In so doing, they established a separate nation and retained the name *Israel*. The southern kingdom had only the tribes of Judah and Benjamin. Judah was the larger, so that became the kingdom's name.

The first king of the northern nation was Jeroboam. He quickly realized that he would lose the allegiance of his people if they continued to go to Jerusalem to worship (1 Kings 12:26, 27). His remedy was to build two centers of worship to rival the temple in Jerusalem. One such was at Dan to the north; the other was at Bethel to the south, only 10 miles from Jerusalem itself. He made a golden calf for each place, and he encouraged idolatrous devotion to the calf-gods (12:28-30). He appointed unqualified people to be priests, and he established an alternative festival (12:31-33).

These actions are shocking to us, but the people of Israel had become fascinated by idols. The time had come for emphatic warnings of judgment. God's first messenger to Israel for this purpose was Amos.

Amos 1:1 identifies the time period as being during the concurrent reigns of King Uzziah in Judah and King Jeroboam II in Israel. Their reigns overlapped from about 790 to 753 BC, and it is usually suggested that Amos prophesied about 760 BC.

C. Lesson Background: God's Prophecies

The book of Amos is third in the arrangement of the 12 Minor Prophets. The author identifies himself as a shepherd from Tekoa (Amos 1:1), which was about 10 miles south of Jerusalem. By one count, Amos mentions 38 cities or districts, so he was well informed about current events.

God sent Amos from his home in Judah to prophesy in Israel. His purpose was to announce that judgment was coming not only on Israel but on surrounding nations. Amos began his ministry by proclaiming that "the Lord roars from Zion" (Amos 1:2). The roar of a lion may be heard up to five miles away. It announces to all that this is *his* territory!

The order of the locations cited by Amos begins at the more distant points. The first cities or nations to receive his thundering condemnations were (or were in) Aram/Syria, Philistia, and Phoenicia. Amos was aware of the atrocities of Syria against Israelites who lived east of the Jordan River. Philistine cities and Tyre were accused of selling captured peoples to the Edomites, and this suggests a thriving slave trade (Amos 1:6-10).

The formula "for three sins . . . even for four" is used to indict each. This figure of speech is generally regarded to mean "sin after sin." The transgressing nations and cities had reached the limit, and God was ready to act. One specific sin is mentioned in each case, and fire was promised as judgment. Each indictment affirmed that God would not revoke the punishment. The overall context suggests that the crimes had been committed against Israel or Judah.

The next three nations (Amos 1:7–2:3) had historical connections via Jacob or Lot. Edom was another name for Jacob's twin brother, Esau (Genesis 25:29, 30). Inhabitants of Ammon and Moab were descended from Lot, Abraham's nephew (Genesis 13; 19:30-38). An examination of the listed transgressions leads to this conclusion: God expects all nations to maintain standards of decency in the treatment of others. The nations cited by Amos were being brutal for the sake of being brutal, not because defensive measures demanded it.

The people of Israel may have been very enthusiastic about the first parts of Amos's sermon. He condemned nations on every side, and his credentials as a prophet of God were strengthened as he listed past crimes and the predicted punishments. These nations were going to receive what they deserved. Some Israelites may have been aware that God often works with the number *seven* to signify completeness. So after hearing a series of six "for three sins . . . , even for four" (Amos 1:3, 6, 9, 11, 13; 2:1), they may have wondered which nation would be the seventh.

Surprise! The seventh nation was Judah, where Amos lived. He was condemning his own nation! (Note: the Lesson Backgrounds for lessons 2–4 also apply to this lesson.)

I. Indicting Judah
(Amos 2:4, 5)

A. Introductory Formula (v. 4a)

4a. This is what the Lord says:
"For three sins of Judah,
 even for four, I will not relent.

Judah is indicted with the same *for three . . . for four* formula that is used for the previous six cities or nations (see the Lesson Background). This formula indicates that there have been many occasions when the nation of Judah sinned against God's law. Even the people of Judah have crossed God's figurative line in the sand. The judgment from God is definitely going to take place!

God had announced judgments in the past. Examples include those on humanity in general in the days of Noah, on Sodom and Gomorrah in the time of Abraham, and on Nineveh when Jonah was sent there with a message of destruction. The last of this trilogy did not take place as prophesied, and Jesus gives the reason: the citizens of Nineveh repented (Matthew 12:41). God's warnings are motivated by love, for he does not wish that any should perish, but that all should come to repentance (2 Peter 3:9).

If a nation abandons God and does not repent, even after (or especially after) hearing the warnings, then judgment is inevitable—in God's time. Righteousness exalts a nation, but sin will lead to God's condemnation (Proverbs 14:34).

> **What Do You Think?**
> What factors shape your response when someone accuses you of improper behavior?
> *Talking Points for Your Discussion*
> * Considering the source
> * Considering the timing
> * Considering the justification
> * Other

B. Iniquities Indicated (v. 4b)

4b. "Because they have rejected the law of the Lord
and have not kept his decrees,
because they have been led astray by false gods,
the gods their ancestors followed,

Here we see that the accusation against Judah is different from that of the six nations and cities condemned thus far by the "for three . . . for four" formula. Instead of citing physical atrocities between peoples, the heart of the indictment involves *the law of the Lord*. Judah is guilty not of violating international covenants but of violating the covenant between the Lord and his people.

The people of Judah have the privilege of worship in Jerusalem, and the temple is a constant reminder of God's special relationship to them. Self-deluding lies cause people to go after other gods, and this happens while going through the habitual rituals at the temple. By spurning the statutes of the Lord, the people choose to believe that God's warnings can be ignored (Deuteronomy 28:15-68). *Their ancestors* had to learn the foolishness thereof the hard way (Judges 6:1; 10:7; 13:1; etc.).

> **What Do You Think?**
> What are some ways to follow God's law in the midst of a culture that is hostile to it?
> *Talking Points for Your Discussion*
> * When moral purity is mocked as outdated
> * When faith is mocked as ignorance
> * When honesty is mocked as simplistic
> * Other

❧ *"Functional Saviors"?* ❧

In February 2012, the director of counseling at a nonprofit organization in Houston, Texas, confessed to lying about his military record. He had claimed to have received a Silver Star and to have served in multiple combat missions in Iraq, Afghanistan, Africa, and South America. He supposedly had recovered from posttraumatic stress disorder.

When pressed by a reporter to produce evidence of his claims, he confessed to fabricating most of the stories. The result was a shameful resignation, crushing in the process the spirits of those who had come to think of him as a hero.

Idolatry isn't just an interesting cultural manifestation of ancient history. Modern people create idols as well. Such idols are not necessarily gods as traditionally conceived; they may instead be people in whom trust is placed as "functional saviors." But when lies are exposed, idols of all kinds crash to the ground. Let's not dismiss the idea that we may have idols in our own lives. Is there anyone other than Jesus whom you can't imagine life without? Any thing? Beware of idolizing, lest you too walk after lies.　　　　　　—D. C. S.

C. Incendiary Promise (v. 5)

**5. "I will send fire on Judah
that will consume the fortresses of
Jerusalem."**

By this time (mid eighth-century BC) it is not a new thing for Judah or Jerusalem to be victimized by nations that conquer and plunder. The Philistines, Arabs, Egyptians, and even the northern nation of Israel had previously subjugated Judah in these ways. The book of Amos begins with a statement that Uzziah is the king of Judah when Amos prophesies, and Uzziah's father had been taken as a prisoner by the northern nation of Israel. Concurrently, the walls of Jerusalem were broken to humiliate and weaken the city.

All this is recorded in the parallel passages of 2 Kings 14:11-13 and 2 Chronicles 25:20-23. The latter adds that "God so worked that he might deliver them into the hands of Jehoash, because they sought the gods of Edom" (v. 20).

This time, however, a more ominous punishment is in view. It is generally agreed that the predicted *fire on Judah* refers to the coming destruction of Jerusalem by the forces of Nebuchadnezzar in the summer of 586 BC, almost 175 years after this prophecy is delivered. In the same century as Amos, the prophet Micah (see lessons 5–8) bluntly affirms that Zion will be plowed, Jerusalem will be a ruin, and Judeans will go to Babylon (Micah 3:12; 4:10).

HOW TO SAY IT

Antiochus	An-*tie*-oh-kus.
Bethel	*Beth*-ul.
Canaanite	*Kay*-nun-ite.
Gomorrah	Guh-*more*-uh.
Jehoash	Jeh-*hoe*-ash.
Jeroboam	Jair-uh-*boe*-um.
Nebuchadnezzar	*Neb*-yuh-kud-***nez***-er.
Nineveh	*Nin*-uh-vuh.
Philistia	Fuh-*liss*-tee-uh.
Phoenicia	Fuh-*nish*-uh.
Rehoboam	Ree-huh-*boe*-um.
Sodom	*Sod*-um.
Tekoa	Tih-*ko*-uh.
Uzziah	Uh-*zye*-uh.

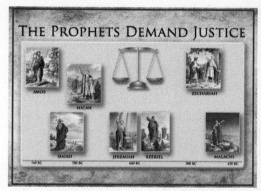

Visual for Lesson 1. *Keep this chart posted throughout the quarter to give your learners a chronological perspective on the lessons.*

Fire is also a promised judgment in each of the other six condemnations to this point in the prophecies of Amos (see Amos 1:4, 7, 10, 12, 14; 2:2). Through the centuries, God has used fire to punish (examples: Genesis 19:24; Leviticus 10:1, 2; Numbers 11:1; 16:35; Joshua 6:24). And so it shall be again (see 2 Kings 25:8, 9).

II. Indicting Israel
(AMOS 2:6-8)

A. Introductory Formula (v. 6a)

**6a. This is what the LORD says:
"For three sins of Israel,
even for four, I will not relent.**

Following his surprise prophecy against Judah, Amos continues with the unexpected. He does not stop after the seventh nation, but adds one more by prophesying against Israel—a seven-plus-one approach. This is a dangerous thing to do for Amos personally, because he, a Judean, is in Israelite territory at the time (see Amos 7:10-13).

The half-verse before us repeats the same *for three . . . for four* formula used the seven previous times. But that marks the end of the similarities because many more points of indictment are in store for this particular audience. Amos is just getting started, and his approach uses a pattern of repeated phrases that help organize and bind together all that he says. The eventual outcome is that Amos will be told to go home to Judah and prophesy there (Amos 7:12). The proverbial statement sometimes applied to situations like this is that Amos has "quit preaching and gone to meddling."

B. Iniquities Indicated (vv. 6b-8)
6b. "They sell the innocent for silver, and the needy for a pair of sandals.

It is important to note that the charges against the northern nation of Israel are different from what is said about the southern kingdom of Judah. Yes, Israel too despises the law of God, but the violations in this case involve social injustices against fellow Israelites. The rich take advantage of those who are in no position to resist, and Amos is ready to announce God's displeasure in this regard.

Impoverished people who are being sold have done nothing wrong. These people are simply betrayed by others who take advantage of them. The greed of the wealthy seems to know no limitations. Some commentators view this as corruption in the courts—that the men who sit in the city gates to render judgments are not honest. They are for sale to the highest bidders.

7a. "They trample on the heads of the poor as on the dust of the ground

Verse 7 gives three additional situations that violate what God has ordained for the care of the poor (see Deuteronomy 15:7-18). The first one is quite startling: the oppressors treat the poor no differently than the dirt upon which everyone walks! A very similar charge is seen in Amos 8:4 (see lesson 4).

What Do You Think?
How are the needy taken advantage of today? How can we intercede on their behalf when we see this happening?
Talking Points for Your Discussion
- Regarding monetary lending practices
- Regarding employment policies
- Other

7b. ". . . and deny justice to the oppressed.

The second situation involves taking advantage of the person who may not have the means to pursue a case with the elders holding court at the city gate. The result is justice denied—no one cares.

7c. "Father and son use the same girl and so profane my holy name.

The third indictment has drawn different interpretations. One view is that Amos is condemning religious prostitution. The worship of Canaanite deities combines that degradation with an emphasis on fertility; what would otherwise be called *adultery* is deemed acceptable because it is an act of worship. It is unclear whether the profaning of the Lord's *holy name* is the intention of such acts or simply a result that occurs under this interpretation. In any case, God has forbidden his people to participate in such rituals (Deuteronomy 23:17, 18).

The other major view contends that the victim is a young woman who is not a prostitute. Amos knows the word for "prostitute" (see Amos 7:17), but he does not use it here. This suggests that two men in the same household take advantage of a servant or someone else who does not have the ability to resist.

What Do You Think?
How can Christians better hallow the holy name that we bear?
Talking Points for Your Discussion
- In worship (1 Chronicles 16:29; Revelation 15:4)
- In sexuality (Romans 1:24-27; Hebrews 13:4)
- In treatment of the disadvantaged (Isaiah 58:5-8; James 1:27)
- Other

8a. "They lie down beside every altar on garments taken in pledge.

The northern nation of Israel has sanctuaries at Dan and Bethel (see Lesson Background: God's People). But true worship is to be restricted to the place of God's choice—at the tabernacle at first, and then at the temple in Jerusalem after that structure was built by Solomon.

Wrongdoing in this regard is compounded by worshippers taking with them the clothing of the poor to unauthorized places of worship. Such clothing comes into possession of those who are better off when surrendered to them as collateral for loans. But the law is emphatic that such clothing must be returned by sundown, when it will be needed for one to keep warm (Deuteronomy 24:10-13). That ordinance is being violated.

8b. "In the house of their god they drink wine taken as fines."

A corrupt system can condemn an innocent person (contra Psalm 82:3) and require payment of a fine with whatever the victim has available. In this case such payment is made in wine. The guilty compound their guilt by drinking such confiscated wine *in the house of their god.* Thus sin multiplies as the first of the Ten Commandments, about having no other gods before the Lord, is violated (Exodus 20:3).

Amos came to pronounce God's judgment on these people, and what we see here is only the beginning of a lengthy indictment.

❦ WHAT'S AT THE ROOT? ❦

Did you know that when you look at a group of aspen trees, you're looking at only "one" tree? Somewhere in the center of the group is a core tree from which a complex root system extends, sometimes for miles. From those roots sprout the other trees. So what looks like several aspen trees above ground is really only one below ground. Because of this shared root system, a grove of aspens is difficult to remove permanently as long as the root system remains intact underneath the ground.

That's the way it seems to be with sin as well. Amos described a variety of sins among the nations of Judah and Israel. But this variety could be traced back to a single root system: a disregard for God and his law. That disregard resulted in a focus on fulfilling fleshly desires without moral restriction.

We may find it fairly easy to admit that we're sinners in a general sense and even be able to iden-

tify sins that need to go. But when it comes to identifying the singular, root motive that sustains them, we may be a bit more hesitant! What does your root system for sin look like? What will have to happen for you to eliminate that root system?
—D. C. S.

Conclusion
A. What You Deserve!

As descendants of Jacob, the people of Israel and Judah were the special covenant people of God. But this resulted in an attitude problem —the attitude that they deserved the blessings that they enjoyed because of who they were. God worked through these people to bring the Messiah into the world at just the right time, but moral failures and social injustices along the way were not ignored. The guilty got what they deserved.

But what does any person deserve? Commercials and politicians today use the word *deserve* to sell goods or to secure votes. But every person is a sinner, and what everyone deserves in that regard is far different from what can be received through an obedient trust in Jesus Christ as the Son of God. Christians are the people of the new covenant. By the grace of God, we don't get what we deserve! May our attitudes and actions always be that of humility in light of this fact.

B. Prayer

Almighty God, thank you for the reminders that your people are accountable for the ways that they treat others. May others see Christ in me, as I pray in his name, amen.

C. Thought to Remember
May our attitudes and actions reflect our covenant status.

VISUALS FOR THESE LESSONS

INVOLVEMENT LEARNING

Enhance your lesson with NIV® Bible Student (from your curriculum supplier) and the reproducible activity page (at www.standardlesson.com or in the back of the NIV® Standard Lesson Commentary Deluxe Edition).

Into the Lesson

Prepare nine cards featuring the following nine words, one word per card: *a / any / BUT / condemns / exalts / nation / people / righteousness / sin.* Keep the *BUT* card for yourself and distribute the other eight cards randomly to learners. Say, "The eight word-cards I have just distributed will make two affirmations of four words each when put in the correct order."

Have the eight words read aloud randomly. Ask for a volunteer to collect four of the cards that he or she believes can be assembled for one statement and read them in statement order. Ask a second volunteer to collect the other four cards and read them likewise. When assembled correctly, the two statements will read "righteousness exalts a nation" and "sin condemns any people." If the two leaners have not come up with these, ask a third learner what adjustments should be made; repeat as necessary. Then have your two volunteers affix their statements to the board in proper order.

Say, "I have a significant word to add" as you affix the *BUT* card between the two statements. Explain: "There is a *but* because you can't have both righteousness *and* sin. Thus God warns of the need to forsake sin and commit to righteousness. This truth is from Proverbs 14:34. It is also a message of the book of Amos. Let's take a look."

Alternative. Distribute copies of the "A Foundational Truth" activity from the reproducible page, which you can download. After learners complete as indicated, say, "God desires all to forsake sin and commit to righteousness, as we will see in today's text."

Into the Word

Set the context by reviewing the two sections of the Lesson Background. (*Option:* You can also include material from the Lesson Backgrounds of lessons 2–4.) Then give each learner a copy of a two-column handout that features the five verses of today's lesson reproduced down the left-hand side and the following Scripture references down the right-hand side: A. Deuteronomy 24:10-13; B. 2 Peter 3:12; C. 2 Kings 22:13; D. Amos 5:11, 12; 8:4; E. Joel 3:3; Amos 8:6.

Say, "Take a few minutes to see what the passages on the right have to say, then match them with the verses from today's text on the left. Choose the single best match in each case." (*Option:* You may wish to reproduce the full texts of the passages on the right instead of just their references. This will allow the exercise to be completed faster, but will not yield the learning experience of looking up passages personally.)

Allow several minutes for learners to complete the matching exercise individually; then discuss results as a class. (*Expected matches: A, verse 8; B, verse 5; C, verse 4; D, verse 7; E, verse 6.*) Learners' matches that differ from those expected will allow opportunity for discussion and explanation. As you draw the discussion to a close, point out that Amos 8:6, which is part of answer E, will be addressed again in lesson 4.

Option. The activity "Sin: Then and Now," from the reproducible page, can be used at this point to bridge this segment with the next. Have learners complete this as indicated either in pairs or in groups of three. Discuss as a class; ask learners to defend differences of opinion.

Into Life

Give each learner a sticky note that is at least 3" x 3" in size. Ask each to write on it the heading *Watch Out For.* Then ask learners to write below the heading a short list of sins that are typically committed today that relate to today's text. (These can be copied from the "Sin: Then and Now" activity, if you used it.) Say, "Post your note where you will see it often in the week ahead. Each time you are tempted by any of the sins, say a brief prayer to ask God for strength to resist."

GOD IS NOT FOOLED

DEVOTIONAL READING: Psalm 14
BACKGROUND SCRIPTURE: Amos 5

AMOS 5:14, 15, 18-27

¹⁴ Seek good, not evil,
　that you may live.
Then the LORD God Almighty will be with
　　you,
　just as you say he is.
¹⁵ Hate evil, love good;
　maintain justice in the courts.
Perhaps the LORD God Almighty will have
　　mercy
　on the remnant of Joseph.

· ·

¹⁸ Woe to you who long
　for the day of the LORD!
Why do you long for the day of the LORD?
　That day will be darkness, not light.
¹⁹ It will be as though a man fled from a lion
　only to meet a bear,
as though he entered his house
　and rested his hand on the wall
　only to have a snake bite him.
²⁰ Will not the day of the LORD be darkness,
　　not light—
　pitch-dark, without a ray of brightness?

²¹ "I hate, I despise your religious festivals;
　your assemblies are a stench to me.
²² Even though you bring me burnt offer-
　　ings and grain offerings,
　I will not accept them.
Though you bring choice fellowship
　　offerings,
　I will have no regard for them.
²³ Away with the noise of your songs!
　I will not listen to the music of your
　　harps.
²⁴ But let justice roll on like a river,
　righteousness like a never-failing stream!
²⁵ "Did you bring me sacrifices and offerings
　forty years in the wilderness, people of
　　Israel?
²⁶ You have lifted up the shrine of your king,
　the pedestal of your idols,
　the star of your god—
　which you made for yourselves.
²⁷ Therefore I will send you into exile
　　beyond Damascus,"
　says the LORD, whose name is God
　　Almighty.

KEY VERSE

Let justice roll on like a river, righteousness like a never-failing stream! —**Amos 5:24**

GOD'S PROPHETS DEMAND JUSTICE

Unit 1: Amos Rails Against Injustice

LESSONS 1–4

LESSON AIMS

After participating in this lesson, each learner will be able to:

1. Describe the kind of justice Amos pleads for.

2. Compare and contrast the injustices Amos condemns with modern injustices.

3. Describe one way he or she can work to achieve the justice God desires and make a plan to do so.

LESSON OUTLINE

Introduction

A. How Did She Know?

The son was confident that he could get away with what was forbidden. The secret joy was suddenly interrupted by his mother's stern command: "Stop jumping on the furniture!" How did she know? She was not in the room, and she could not see what he was doing.

The fun-loving boy decided to turn it into a game. The object was for him to undertake an action in one room, and his mother, in a different room, was to try to guess what he was doing. He was impressed: time after time she guessed correctly.

Similar accounts have given rise to the statement that "a mother has eyes in the back of her head," or so it seems to children who are apprehended while being happily disobedient. Mothers do not need to see jam on faces or catch hands in cookie jars to be aware of wrongdoing.

Even so, fooling a parent is possible, and confessions in family gatherings many years later make for good entertainment. To attempt to fool God, however, is another matter. It makes no difference whether the inappropriate action is undertaken in the dark, on vacation, or when no one seems to be watching—because God always is.

The nation of Israel was infamous for the times throughout its history when the covenant was renewed and then broken—again and again. God knew, and from his heavenly courts he sent messages through his prophets to tell the covenant people as much. Perhaps they thought God did not know or did not really care. But he did.

B. Lesson Background

The year was about 760 BC when God sent Amos from Judah to the northern nation of Israel to proclaim a warning. The previous study showed how Amos pronounced God's judgment on nation after nation, and then he came to the eighth nation: Israel. Amos reminded the people there that God had chosen them from among all the nations of the earth (Amos 3:2), but their actions did not demonstrate gratitude for this divine favor.

In the seven centuries since the time of Moses, Israel had violated often its commitment to God. The pattern that emerged was for God to discipline his people because he loved them, and for the nation to repent when the situation became critical (see the book of Judges for examples). Although God punished, he would always forgive, wouldn't he?

Amos's mission included challenging the distorted views of the people in that regard. They regularly performed the religious rituals that were prescribed in their covenant with God, but they also worshipped other gods. This violated the first of the Ten Commandments (Exodus 20:3). In addition, the high standards of morality that the Lord had established gave way to gross immorality. The people's arrogance about their favored status caused virtue to vanish from private and public lives.

The opening words of the Charles Dickens classic *A Tale of Two Cities* accurately describe the situation in Israel:

> It was the best of times, it was the worst of times, it was the age of wisdom, it was the age of foolishness, it was the epoch of belief, it was the epoch of incredulity, it was the season of Light, it was the season of Darkness, it was the spring of hope, it was the winter of despair, we had everything before us, we had nothing before us, we were all going direct to Heaven, we were all going direct the other way.

What the people saw as "the best of times" God saw as "the worst of times." He was making his final appeal to a favored nation. Historical hindsight tells us that captivity at the hands of the Assyrians was less than 40 years away by the time Amos preached.

HOW TO SAY IT

Amos	*Ay*-mus.
Damascus	Duh-*mass*-kus.
Deuteronomy	Due-ter-*ahn*-uh-me.
Ephraim	*Ee*-fray-im.
Judah	*Joo*-duh.
Leviticus	Leh-*vit*-ih-kus.
Manasseh	Muh-*nass*-uh.
Molek	*Mo*-lek.

I. Desires of God
(AMOS 5:14, 15)

A. What to Seek and Not Seek (v. 14)

14. Seek good, not evil,
that you may live.
Then the LORD God Almighty will be with you,
just as you say he is.

The command to *seek good* is in the plural, so it is for everyone. The Hebrew command translated as *seek* is used four times in this chapter (vv. 4, 5, 6, 14). The objectives of this command are both positive (vv. 4, 6, 14) and negative (vv. 5, 14). The positive objective has the same goal each time: to *live*. An extra blessing in this verse is that the Lord promises to be with his people. The Israelites already have the concept that the Lord is with them (*just as you say he is*), but they tend to take for granted that God will always say, "I forgive."

B. What to Hate, Love, and Establish (v. 15)

15. Hate evil, love good;
maintain justice in the courts.
Perhaps the LORD God Almighty will have mercy
on the remnant of Joseph.

Amos continues with three imperatives regarding what to *hate,* what to *love,* and what to *maintain.* The third one is particularly confrontational, for it is the opposite of what the prophet has just described as being the current state of affairs in Israel (Amos 5:10-12). The people are guilty of taking advantage of the poor, receiving bribes, and becoming rich by doing so (5:11, 12). They have abandoned righteousness, and they hate anyone who rebukes them (5:10).

⅍ *No Courtroom Needed* ⅍

Mitch Torbett was applying for a construction permit in Signal Mountain, Tennessee, when he suddenly found himself in handcuffs. He was under arrest for a federal crime that his identical twin brother had allegedly committed. Mitch protested the mistaken identity, but the arresting officers would have none of it. They had heard wild stories in the past, and they weren't buying this one!

So Mitch spent 36 hours in jail, waiting for extradition. That process eventually revealed, however, that the wrong guy was behind bars. Identical twins do not have identical fingerprints, and Mitch's didn't match those of his brother's from the crime scene. The FBI admitted the mistaken identity, a judge released Mitch, and "wrong person" was entered on his legal documents.

We can be grateful for having a justice system with built-in safeguards to correct instances of false accusation. God had created Israel's justice system with safeguards as well (Deuteronomy 16:18-20; etc.). By the time of Amos, however, the safeguards had been abandoned. Those responsible to "maintain justice in the courts" were notorious for tolerating, even encouraging, bribery. They served themselves rather than the cause of justice.

We do not need to be in a courtroom to address injustice. "See something, say something" applies! God simply requires this of us.   —D. C. S.

Most of the prophets have messages that condemn sin and promise doom, but offer hope if there is repentance. The last part of the verse before us does offer the possibility of hope that God *will have mercy on the remnant of Joseph,* but that hope is very problematic! Taken narrowly, *the remnant of Joseph* refers to the two tribes that bear the names of that man's sons, Manasseh and Ephraim (Genesis 46:20). Those two tribes are part of the 10 that constitute the northern nation Israel; in context, *the remnant of Joseph* should be taken to refer to that nation broadly. We see an interesting connection in the fact that the competing (idolatrous) center of worship in Bethel (1 Kings 12:28-30; Amos 3:14; 4:4; 5:5, 6) is located within the territory of Manasseh.

What Do You Think?
How can you help create a more just society?
Talking Points for Your Discussion
- Regarding civic duties or opportunities
- Regarding personal conduct
- Regarding the church as the conscience of the community
- Other

II. Day of the Lord
(Amos 5:18-23)
A. Fact of Darkness (vv. 18-20)

18. Woe to you who long
     for the day of the Lord!
Why do you long for the day of the Lord?
     That day will be darkness, not light.

Amos repeats various phrases to demonstrate the arrangement of his messages. This is especially true in the middle portion of the book. For example, the phrase "Hear this word" begins each of chapters 3, 4, and 5. The two messages that follow in Amos 5:18 (here) and 6:1 are woe oracles, for the word *woe* is used to begin them. We may safely presume that the progression of thought in this regard is not what the people of Israel want to hear!

In this particular woe oracle, Amos declares that people have a wrong understanding of *the day of the Lord.* They believe that it will be a glorious time when they will have the proverbial peace, prosperity, and progress. They believe that God will use his power to give other nations what they deserve. Amos shatters this delusion by saying that the day of the Lord is a day of *darkness, not light.* The imagery of darkness is very ominous to ancient people, who do not have streetlights, flashlights, etc., to dispel darkness as we do so easily today.

What Do You Think?
What similarities and differences do you see between "the day of the Lord" Amos discussed and the one to come in 2 Peter 3:10-13?
Talking Points for Your Discussion
- Recipients of rewards and punishment
- Nature of rewards and punishment
- Basis of rewards and punishment
- Other

19. It will be as though a man fled from a
     lion
          only to meet a bear,
as though he entered his house
          and rested his hand on the wall
          only to have a snake bite him.

Amos begins illustrating the nature of the day of the Lord by using two of the most ferocious animals with which the people are familiar: the lion and the bear. David used the same two when he described to Saul how the Lord had been with him (1 Samuel 17:34-37). The illustration this time is different, almost humorous. To be running *from a lion only to meet a bear* is not a desirable situation (compare Lamentations 3:10, 11; Hosea 13:8)!

The second illustration draws on the supposed security that is found by entering a house, only to be bitten by *a snake*. The intensity of the illustration indicates that the bite is of the poisonous kind. Antivenin shots are not available, so death from such bites is typical (compare Acts 28:3-6).

When the illustrations are combined, they teach that God's judgment cannot be avoided. It is not possible to hide from him. Jonah is an excellent example of one who attempted to hide from God, but his scheme did not work.

20. Will not the day of the LORD be darkness, not light—
pitch-dark, without a ray of brightness?

Amos uses a question to continue his description of *the day of the Lord*; the question implies that it is only reasonable for a day of judgment to *be darkness*. A tour of caverns today often includes a segment when the guide turns off all lights. This is a moment of panic for some people, since absolutely nothing can be seen. One of the judgmental plagues in Egypt in the days of Moses was total darkness (Exodus 10:22). Other prophets also describe the day of the Lord as a day of darkness (Isaiah 13:6-10; Joel 2:1, 2; 3:14, 15).

❧ *A Matter of Perspective* ❧

World War II has been aptly described as a time when darkness fell across Europe. But Nazi leaders saw their conquests as bringing about a "new order"; they called their propaganda "public enlightenment." But what their twisted minds saw as enlightenment turned very dark for them personally as Russian forces closed in on Berlin in 1945. For example, Joseph Goebbels (Hitler's minister of propaganda) spent his final days with his wife and six children underground for safety. When it became obvious that the Russians would capture their bunker complex, the children were poisoned and their parents committed suicide.

Whether or not that was some kind of "interim" day of the Lord for Goebbels and other Nazi leaders can be a matter of debate. What is certain, however, is the promise of an ultimate day of the Lord (2 Peter 3:10). It will be "the great day of . . . wrath" (Revelation 6:17). It will be the darkest of dark days for those who remain unrepentant.

God's perspective is the one that counts: he is "not wanting anyone to perish, but everyone to come to repentance" (2 Peter 3:9). Rather than harbor thoughts of revenge, we ponder the fact that no one is beyond redemption. We keep God's perspective as we pray for their repentance and our ability to forgive. May God, by the power of his Holy Spirit, give us the ability to do just that.—D. C. S.

B. Causes of Darkness (vv. 21-23)

21. "I hate, I despise your religious festivals;
your assemblies are a stench to me.

Amos has no hesitation about criticizing religious practices that are an abomination to God. It is always risky to challenge the sincerity of religious practices, but Amos takes that risk and thunders a reason as to why the day of the Lord will be darkness: it is because the rituals have become a sham. God despises what the people are doing, and he will have no regard for their observances of *religious festivals* (Exodus 23:15-18; 34:22-25; etc.) and their *assemblies* (Leviticus 23:36; Numbers 29:35; Deuteronomy 16:8).

Moses had frequently described the genuine sacrifices of Israel as being a "pleasing aroma" to God (Exodus 29:18; Leviticus 1:9, 13; etc.), but these have become *a stench* to him. Leviticus 26:31 connects this change with dire consequences: "I will turn your cities into ruins . . . , and I will take no delight in the pleasing aroma of your offerings."

22. "Even though you bring me burnt
offerings and grain offerings,
I will not accept them.
Though you bring choice fellowship offerings,
I will have no regard for them.

God is not fooled with what can be termed "gifts of conscience"—trying to buy his approval. The various offerings that the Lord has ordained for worship at the temple are being imitated in the northern nation of Israel, but "to do what is right and just is more acceptable to the Lord than sacrifice" (Proverbs 21:3; compare Isaiah 1:11-14).

23. "Away with the noise of your songs! I will not listen to the music of your harps.

The book of Psalms establishes that singing and use of musical instruments may be included in ancient Israel's worship (example: Psalm 150). The Lord authorized such instruments in the days of David (2 Chronicles 29:25). When the heart and conduct are not right, however, God cannot bear to hear any musical expressions of worship. These mean less than nothing to him.

> *What Do You Think?*
> What adjustments in attitudes and actions toward others can we make to ensure our worship is acceptable to God?
> *Talking Points for Your Discussion*
> - Toward the poor
> - Toward those in the community who do not attend church
> - Toward fellow believers with whom we disagree
> - Other

III. Demand for Justice
(Amos 5:24)

24. "But let justice roll on like a river, righteousness like a never-failing stream!

This verse is an example of Hebrew parallelism, where a single thought is expressed using synonyms or near-synonyms. *Justice* and *righteousness* are the same thing (see Job 29:14; Psalm 36:6; 72:1; Proverbs 8:20; Isaiah 28:17; 32:16; etc.). Religion without this is worthless in the sight of God. One teacher said that God does not want merely a trickle but a Niagara Falls of justice. What a contrast!

The verses in the previous lesson show how the rich in Israel are taking advantage of the poor. This lack of social justice is not the way God had instructed his people to live! They are to remember that they had been slaves in Egypt, and they are to have compassion for the underprivileged.

It is sad to see pictures of suffering and starvation, especially when children are innocent victims of what adults have done. It is especially disturbing to see such things while living in a land that has plenty. Although the gospel is not to be twisted so that it is only a social gospel that meets physical needs, the gospel does include societal obligations that must be met.

> *What Do You Think?*
> What injustices do you see in your community? What can you do as an individual and as part of a church to fix these?
> *Talking Points for Your Discussion*
> - Regarding various kinds of exploitation
> - Regarding various kinds of discrimination
> - Regarding indifference
> - Other

IV. Declaration of Penalties
(Amos 5:25-27)
A. Issue: Idolatry (vv. 25, 26)

25. "Did you bring me sacrifices and offerings forty years in the wilderness, people of Israel?

God now poses a rhetorical question through his prophet. To this question one might initially expect a *yes* answer, given the fact that the books of Exodus through Deuteronomy list examples regarding *sacrifices and offerings forty years in the wilderness*. But deeper probing reveals that the answer is actually *no*. Since much of that worship was not to God, it was not genuine. Religious leaders easily fall into the trap of being concerned with doing the procedures correctly while losing sight of the real significance of each act of worship; the next verse shows where much of Israel's worship was actually directed.

26. "You have lifted up the shrine of your king, the pedestal of your idols, the star of your god— which you made for yourselves.

The phrase *you have lifted up* indicates a continuation of thought from the previous verse— that there has been a persistent disobedience of Israel since its beginning as a nation. However, the Hebrew behind the verb *lifted* may also be understood to refer to a future event, as it is translated in Isaiah 14:4 ("you will take up"). A future reference here would make this verse part of the prophecy of what will happen when northern Israel goes into exile, never to return. Either sense indicates a big problem on the part of the Israelites!

The identities of the gods is another area of uncertainty, since the Hebrew consonants for the words *king* and *Molek* are the same (compare Acts 7:43). Without digging into all the intricacies of this issue, the main point is that God's own people worship other gods. The use of the word *star* may point to a fascination with worshipping the points of light in the night sky (compare Deuteronomy 4:19). Whether the reference is to a past or future trespass, Israel bears the guilt of worshipping other gods alongside the Lord, a violation of the first of the Ten Commandments. This is totally unacceptable!

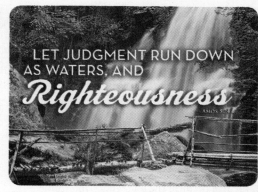

Visual for Lesson 2. *Point to this visual as you pose the discussion question that is associated with Amos 5:24.*

> **What Do You Think?**
> How do we recognize idolatry today? What can we do to avoid it?
> *Talking Points for Your Discussion*
> - Regarding things and achievements currently possessed
> - Regarding things and achievements desired
> - Other

B. Consequence: Exile (v. 27)

27. "Therefore I will send you into exile beyond Damascus,"
says the LORD, whose name is God Almighty.

The conclusion of this message is ominous as punishment is pronounced in view of all that Israel has done and failed to do. The prophecy indeed comes to pass as Amos says. He prophesies around 760 BC, and the northern nation of Israel is overthrown completely by the Assyrians in about 722 BC. The nation that is so prosperous will disappear in less than 40 years as the people go *into exile beyond Damascus*. Details and causes are given in 2 Kings 17.

An interesting footnote is that Stephen quotes Amos 5:25-27 in Acts 7:42, 43 to show that Israel has always been in rebellion against what God has ordained. The rebellion goes so far as to reject Jesus as the Son of God.

Conclusion

A. Fool Me Once?

Perhaps you've heard this old saying: *Fool me once, shame on you; fool me twice, shame on me.* That's often a good axiom to adopt regarding our dealings with others. But God does not take such a position toward us, since he cannot be fooled even once. How amazing to see, then, people living as if God can be fooled or at least not caring about what they are doing.

Taking advantage of others is nothing new; it happens often today. Elaborate rationalizations are created to justify such behavior. Such rationalizing may fool others, but it never fools God. The genuine follower of Christ pursues good for all, loves to do so, and actively seeks opportunities in that regard. Considering all that God has done for us, how can it be otherwise?

B. Prayer

Thank you, Lord, for these admonitions that remind us of our obligations to others. May we see the opportunities that are around us in times like these. In Jesus' name, amen.

C. Thought to Remember

Seek the good—always.

INVOLVEMENT LEARNING

Enhance your lesson with NIV® Bible Student (from your curriculum supplier) and the reproducible activity page (at www.standardlesson.com or in the back of the NIV® Standard Lesson Commentary Deluxe Edition).

Into the Lesson

Have ready to play the sounds of a roaring lion, a growling bear, and a hissing snake. The Internet can provide the sounds, or you can simply ask someone to simulate them. Recruit in advance two learners to assist; one will read Amos 5:19 on cue, and the other will perform the following pantomime:

Walk along casually until the roar is heard, then react appropriately. When the growl is heard, run with fear into a pretend house, open the door, enter, and slam it shut behind you. Lean against the wall in obvious relief. React appropriately when you hear the hiss of a snake.

When the pantomime concludes, ask, "Do you know how bad it was going to get in Israel? It would get so bad that [point to the other learner as the cue to read Amos 5:19]." Say, "Although there is some humor in the image of that verse, there is no humor in its truth: the unrepentant cannot and will not avoid God's justice."

Into the Word

Next, display these phrases to be completed:

_____ good, _____ evil;
_____ evil, _____ good!

Ask learners to help you fill in the blanks to complete the two phrases. A variety of good responses may be offered, but the ones you should end up with are found in Amos 5:14, 15. Allow learners the chance to discover that source on their own (perhaps after some hints from you). For discussion, ask, "What are some ways the Israelites could have sought and loved good while hating evil?"

Next, post a sign that reads *Wishes and Reality.* Say, "Let's take a look at what the people hoped for in contrast with the way things really were in God's sight." Distribute to five learners the following statements on strips of paper, one each: A. "I, for one, plan to jump for joy when the Lord cracks down on all the nonsense in our world!" B. "I am

sure the Lord will reward me for my diligence in attending worship!" C. "God will, of course, take into account the contributions my family makes to support his work." D. "I have a feeling that God loves our singing as much as I do!" E. "Who cares about the past—that was then, this is now!"

Say, "Let's listen to five statements that might have been heard among the ancient Israelites." Proceed through the statements, requesting that learners stand and read with dramatic emphasis. Pause for discussion after each. Ask, "Where in today's text does God express a reality that contrasts with the wish you just heard?" *(Expected responses: A, verses 18, 20; B, verse 21; C, verse 22; D, verse 23; E, verses 25-27.)* Wrap up by noting how important it is to distinguish between wishful thinking and God's view of reality.

Make a transition by asking, "Which verse in today's text has not been given the attention it deserves so far?" After receiving the expected answer "verse 24" (the key verse), say, "Let's explore the application of that verse now."

Option. Begin the Into the Word segment by distributing copies of the "Why, God?" activity from the reproducible page, which you can download. This exercise will explore the background that prompted God's judgment. Have learners work in pairs or groups of three to complete as indicated.

Into Life

Write this statement on the board and ask for completions: "The biggest injustice I see in our community is _____." After several responses say, "Of course, the next question is, 'What can I do about that?'" Encourage discussion that involves practical actions, not simply wishful thinking.

Option. Distribute copies of the "A Worship Principle" activity from the reproducible page. Have learners work in pairs to complete as indicated.

GOD ABHORS SELFISHNESS

DEVOTIONAL READING: Psalm 119:31-38

BACKGROUND SCRIPTURE: Amos 6

AMOS 6:4-8, 11-14

4 You lie on beds adorned with ivory
and lounge on your couches.
You dine on choice lambs
and fattened calves.
5 You strum away on your harps like David
and improvise on musical instruments.
6 You drink wine by the bowlful
and use the finest lotions,
but you do not grieve over the ruin of
Joseph.
7 Therefore you will be among the first to go
into exile;
your feasting and lounging will end.

8 The Sovereign LORD has sworn by himself
—the LORD God Almighty declares:

"I abhor the pride of Jacob
and detest his fortresses;
I will deliver up the city
and everything in it."

. . . .

11 For the LORD has given the command,
and he will smash the great house into
pieces
and the small house into bits.
12 Do horses run on the rocky crags?
Does one plow the sea with oxen?
But you have turned justice into poison
and the fruit of righteousness into
bitterness—
13 you who rejoice in the conquest of Lo
Debar
and say, "Did we not take Karnaim by
our own strength?"

14 For the LORD God Almighty declares,
"I will stir up a nation against you,
Israel,
that will oppress you all the way
from Lebo Hamath to the valley of the
Arabah."

KEY VERSE

Do horses run on the rocky crags? Does one plow the sea with oxen? But you have turned justice into poison and the fruit of righteousness into bitterness.. —**Amos 6:12**

Graphic: iStockphoto / Thinkstock

GOD'S PROPHETS DEMAND JUSTICE

Unit 1: Amos Rails Against Injustice

LESSONS 1–4

LESSON AIMS

After participating in this lesson, each learner will be able to:

1. Describe ways that the people of Israel abused their privileges and blessings.

2. Explain why selfishness, greed, and pride are antithetical to a godly lifestyle.

3. Identify one area of selfishness, greed, or pride in his or her life and make a plan to correct it.

LESSON OUTLINE

Introduction

A. A Little Rebellious

It was just "girl talk" in the youth group at the church. They were discussing things of importance to those in high school—classes, clothes, teachers, diets, sports, boys, and the latest dating couples. The daughter of the preacher interjected a new thought when she said, "I feel like doing something a little rebellious!"

The room became reflectively quiet as the statement was processed by all present. Was she inviting suggestions of something that the girls could all do together, or was she speaking only for herself? Was it just an idle comment? After all, she was the preacher's daughter, and she had just made a proposal that was different from the expectations that her friends had for her.

The response by another girl demonstrated a maturity that many never reach. Her reply was almost Solomonic: "A little rebellion often leads to another that is even more rebellious." At that point the conversations paused again, and then reverted to the usual things—classes, clothes, etc.

The principle expressed characterizes the life that is ungodly. One falsehood leads to another. One sin may be followed by something progressively rebellious in the attempt to recreate the same level of excitement. Some people in the entertainment world behave in ways that are increasingly bizarre in order to hold their audiences and maintain coverage by the media. The slippery slope of being "a little rebellious" is nothing new, however. It was also a problem for Israel in the days of Amos.

B. Lesson Background

The background for this lesson is the same as last week's, so that information need not be repeated here. We can add the fact that Amos traveled from Judah to Israel to deliver his oracles from God during what has been called Israel's "Indian Summer."

That expression is used to describe a weather phenomenon in the fall of the year—a period of pleasant warmth and sunshine after the first frost. When Amos preached, Israel was enjoying a period of peace that it had not experienced for many years. There was no oppressing nation at that time, and the nations of Israel and Judah were not at war with each other.

This situation allowed Israel to expand its boundaries to such an extent that they approached what they had been in the days of Kings David and Solomon. Jonah had prophesied that this would happen (see 2 Kings 14:25); it is assumed his prophecy was made in the early days of King Jeroboam II, who reigned about 793–753 BC. The 790–739 BC reign of King Azariah (also called Uzziah) of Judah overlapped much of Jeroboam's reign in the north. The descriptions for Judah's parallel prosperity are given in 2 Chronicles 26:1-15. Outwardly, the reigns of these two kings were characterized by success in military expansion, economic recovery, and sustained peace.

But spiritual apostasy had been the norm in the northern nation of Israel for decades, beginning with King Jeroboam I, who created rival centers of worship shortly after Solomon's death in 930 BC (1 Kings 12:25-33). Jeroboam II is assessed as one who "did evil in the eyes of the Lord and did not turn away from any of the sins of Jeroboam son of Nebat, which he had caused Israel to commit" (2 Kings 14:24). To the south, King Uzziah became proud in his accomplishments, and he acted corruptly by attempting to function as a priest. His penalty was to be stricken with leprosy for the rest of his life (2 Chronicles 26:16-21).

Then Amos came to Israel from Judah. His first "woe oracle" was the study for last week's lesson. A second such oracle begins at Amos 6:1, addressed to the arrogant of Zion (Jerusalem, capital of Judah) and Samaria (capital of Israel). The leaders of these two nations were challenged to tour areas to the north and south; in so doing, they should conclude that their own nations were no better off that those they visited (6:2). But those leaders will continue in their blindness to coming judgment (6:3a) as they oppress the vulnerable (6:3b).

Peace, prosperity, and progress—those factors are the background when Amos came from Judah to preach in Israel. He was ready to ridicule the attempts of the wealthy to find happiness and fulfillment by excesses of sinful indulgences and mistreatment of the poor.

I. Excesses Described
(Amos 6:4-6)
A. Indulgent Dining (v. 4)
**4. You lie on beds adorned with ivory
and lounge on your couches.
You dine on choice lambs
and fattened calves.**

The indulgent people being described here are identified in Amos 6:1 (see the Lesson Background). The verbs *lie* and *dine* are actually participles in Hebrew. In using these, Amos is employing a literary device that repeats a structure to create a greater impact. These two participles can be understood as "the ones who are lying on" and "the ones who are dining on."

The picture is one of extravagant luxury on the part of wealthy people. They are rich enough to own beds having decorative inlays of ivory. Amos has already referred to "houses adorned with ivory" that are to perish, along with the summer homes and the winter homes (Amos 3:15), so the use of ivory is widespread. Archaeologists working at Samaria about a century ago discovered ivory inlays in over 500 fragments. The source for the ivory was probably the tusks of Syrian elephants, today extinct, which were a subspecies of Asian elephants.

HOW TO SAY IT

Amos	*Ay*-mus.
Arabah	*Air*-ah-bah.
Azariah	Az-uh-*rye*-uh.
Ephraim	*Ee*-fray-im.
Jeroboam	Jair-uh-*boe*-um.
Karnaim	Car-*nay*-im.
Lebo Hamath	Leh-*bow Hay*-math.
Lo Debar	Low *Dee*-bar.
Manasseh	Muh-*nass*-uh.
Nebat	*Nee*-bat.
Samaria	Suh-*mare*-ee-uh.
Sargon	*Sar*-gon.
Shalmaneser	Shal-mun-*ee*-zer.
Tiglath-Pileser	*Tig*-lath-Pih-*lee*-zer.
Uzziah	Uh-*zye*-uh.
Zion	*Zi*-un.

In addition to those lounging on beds and couches, Amos also indicts those—most likely the same people—who eat choice, tender lambs and calves. Meat is not an ordinary staple of diet at the time, being reserved for special occasions or feasts. Thus Amos is describing what is considered to be a life of luxury. Previously, the Bible noted that people sat down to eat (Genesis 37:25; Judges 19:6; 1 Samuel 20:24); the verse before us seems to be the first reference in the Bible (chronologically) of lying down (reclining) while eating.

Amos hurls one accusation after another against the guilty. He certainly knows how to lose friends and irritate audiences!

❧ THE PET SPA ❧

A few years ago, our family was blessed to host five Ugandans in our home: two boys, their mothers, and an interpreter. The boys had been selected through Samaritan's Purse Children's Heart Project to come to America for surgical procedures that were not available in their home nation. The interpreter helped bridge the cultural and language gap.

One mother and her son were from a poor village, and they were completely overwhelmed by the wealth of our community. The other mother and son had had more exposure to different lifestyles because they lived near Kampala, Uganda's capital city. Even so, they too were amazed by the ready availability of almost every type of material goods at various stores.

As I was showing my guests around town, I also pointed out where I had my dogs groomed, which was right next door to where I bought groceries. "Are you kidding?!" exclaimed the more savvy of the two African mothers. While she could understand much of what she had seen, the idea of beauty parlors for animals blew her away.

I was surprised and amused that someone would think of my lifestyle as extreme or lavish. But as more material resources become ours, we easily adjust our standards upwards, don't we? I will always remember this outside perspective, lest I become so engulfed in the comforts of my life that I neglect to notice the needs of others.

—V. E.

B. Drunken Revelry (vv. 5, 6a)

**5, 6a. You strum away on your harps like David
and improvise on musical instruments.
You drink wine by the bowlful
and use the finest lotions,**

Amos continues using participles as a literary device to create greater impact; this time the Hebrew participles are behind the words translated *strum* and *drink*. The word behind *strum* is used only here in the Old Testament, and the exact meaning is uncertain as a result. Even so, the context of a party atmosphere is clear.

Ordinary drinking goblets are not considered adequate for the kind of carousing in view. Participants choose instead to drink their wine from much larger containers, bowl after bowl. We don't know exactly what *lotions* are in use, but the word *finest* indicates the most expensive types.

> **What Do You Think?**
> To what extent does Amos's condemnation of the Israelites apply to us? Why?
> *Talking Points for Your Discussion*
> - Regarding our housing (and mortgage) choices given the reality of homelessness
> - Regarding our dietary choices given the reality of those lacking adequate food
> - Other

C. Selfish Indifference (v. 6b)

6b. . . . but you do not grieve over the ruin of Joseph.

The two tribes of the northern nation of Israel having the largest territories are Ephraim and Manasseh, and both were sons *of Joseph* (see discussion on Amos 5:15 in lesson 2). Therefore to refer to Joseph is another way of referring to the entire nation. A further example is that Hosea, the prophet who succeeds Amos in Israel, refers to the northern nation as "Ephraim" (Hosea 6:4; compare Isaiah 7:17; Jeremiah 7:15; etc.).

The selfish preoccupation of the wealthy leaders blinds them from being concerned about *the ruin of* their people. The forthcoming collapse, mentioned often to this point in this book, has drawn different interpretations. Some think it refers to an economic disaster to be inflicted by God because of the disparity that is produced by taking advantage of the poor (see Leviticus 19:10, 15; Deuteronomy 15:7, 8).

An alternative view is that the disaster to come will be destruction at the hands of the Assyrians. Those invaders will first take captives from the region of Galilee in about 733 BC (2 Kings 15:29). That will be only the beginning, and the conquest of the northern nation of Israel will culminate in 722 BC. Those whose behavior Amos condemns will see his prophecy come to pass in stages, but they will not change their ways as they continue on their way to oblivion. Our next verse supports this interpretation.

What Do You Think?

How can we become more sensitive to the afflictions of those around us?

Talking Points for Your Discussion

- Regarding ways to increase our awareness of the problems of poverty, discrimination, chronic illness, etc.
- Regarding how we submit ourselves to be accountable to address problems of poverty, discrimination, chronic illness, etc.
- Other

II. Exile Determined
(Amos 6:7, 8)

A. Captivity for the Calloused (v. 7)

**7. Therefore you will be among the first to go into exile;
your feasting and lounging will end.**

With the charges against Israel now finished, God's messenger is ready to confirm the judgment that will come on this nation that thinks itself to be so strong and secure. The previous listing of sinful act after sinful act is followed not by a pleading for repentance but by a promise. Amos has already described what will happen—that "hooks" and "fishhooks" will be used to take the captives away (Amos 4:2). Such hooks are often placed through the lower lips to keep captives in line. Amos prophesies that the leading citizens who are so self-indulgent *will be among the first to go into exile.* Conquerors customarily remove the leaders of the conquered nation to diminish the possibility of later resistance.

Amos's prophecy comes to pass when Samaria succumbs to a three-year siege that is placed on the city in 725 BC by King Shalmaneser V of Assyria (2 Kings 17:5). Historical records reveal that King Sargon II, his successor, claims that he led away 27,290 captives when the siege concluded in 722 BC. He also states in Assyrian records that he restored the city and made it better than before. His additional claim to have brought peoples from other lands to Samaria is confirmed by 2 Kings 17:24.

❧ Heart Condition ❧

My family lived in Louisiana in the 1980s. Our community was comprised mainly of low- to moderate-income households, and our fairly large church reflected that demographic. The one notable exception was a local millionaire by the name of Alton Howard (1925–2006).

Alton, along with his brother Jack, started a chain of discount stores in 1959. Howard Brothers Discount eventually expanded into several states, peaking at 87 stores before the brothers sold out in 1986. Business success brought wealth to that family, and our church stressed a healthy, biblical doctrine regarding money. I recall two points from one sermon in particular: it is not a sin to succeed financially in the process of providing for

GOD HATES SELFISHNESS

Visual for Lesson 3. *Point to this visual as you ask, "Does the fact that God hates selfishness mean that he also hates the selfish person? Why, or why not?"*

one's family; it is a sin, however, to revere money since that attitude is accompanied by selfishness and greed.

Alton Howard was neither selfish nor greedy. Instead, he was known for his hospitality and for helping to fund various international ministries to spread the gospel and aid those affected by disasters. The text for today's lesson warns not against wealth as such but against the selfish attitude of pride that can accompany a full wallet so easily. The heart condition that would spend all of one's resources on self is easy to see and condemn in others. How do we go about checking our own heart condition in this regard?　　　—V. E.

B. Confirmed by an Oath (v. 8)

**8. The Sovereign LORD has sworn by himself
　　—the LORD God Almighty declares:
"I abhor the pride of Jacob
　　and detest his fortresses;
I will deliver up the city
　　and everything in it."**

The strongest of all oaths is when the Lord swears *by himself*. The fulfillment is a guaranteed certainty. The word *fortresses* occurs numerous times in this book (compare Amos 1:4, 7, 10, 12, 14; 2:2, 5; 3:11), and the Lord detests the prideful attitude and confidence that the people place in these security structures. Thus his promise that he *will deliver up the city and everything in it.*

In politics it is often said that "to the victors belong the spoils," and throughout history this has also served as an axiom for the victors in war. The promise of God is that another nation will become the possessor of what the haughty leaders of Israel now use as part of their spiritual corruption.

What Do You Think?

How can we show that we trust God rather than the security structures our culture has created?

Talking Points for Your Discussion

- Regarding confidence in national defense (1 Thessalonians 5:3; etc.)
- Regarding confidence in retirement planning (Luke 12:16-21; etc.)
- Other

III. Extent of Destruction
(AMOS 6:11-14)

A. Houses Demolished (v. 11)

**11. For the LORD has given the command,
　　and he will smash the great house into
　　　　pieces
　　and the small house into bits.**

The plan for destruction of houses both *great* and *small* is already firm in the mind of God. It will become an accomplished fact, for the Lord is decreeing it. The timing is not as important as the certainty. All homes in Samaria—from the largest of the wealthy to the smallest of the poor, whether made of quarried stone or clay bricks—are subject to destruction. King Sargon thus will use something of a "scorched earth" policy as he carries off 27,290 Israelite captives (see comments on v. 7, above). The Lord has commanded, and the houses will be razed. No home will be exempt.

B. Arrogance Confronted (vv. 12, 13)

**12. Do horses run on the rocky crags?
　　Does one plow the sea with oxen?
But you have turned justice into poison
　　and the fruit of righteousness into
　　　　bitterness—**

Two rhetorical questions, preposterous in their imagery, are asked. They expect negative answers. It is not reasonable for horses to run on rocks, and it is even more unreasonable to attempt to plow what cannot by nature be plowed. Figuratively, this is what the arrogant Israelites have done by their actions, which result in turning *justice into poison and the fruit of righteousness into bitterness.*

**13. . . . . you who rejoice in the conquest of
　　　　Lo Debar
　　and say, "Did we not take Karnaim by
　　　　our own strength?"**

The Hebrew language is one in which names and proper nouns have meanings. This verse is an excellent example of one where such words may be translated either (1) for what they actually mean or (2) as the names of places. Either choice shows the arrogant Israelites to be rejoicing about the wrong things. The background seems to be recent military successes by Israel, including *the conquest of Lo*

Debar, a town east of the Jordan River (see 2 Samuel 9:4, 5; 17:27). The place name *Lo Debar* can be translated literally as "nothing"; thus we seem to have a sarcastic play on words: the Israelite victory actually doesn't amount to anything.

Similar is the victory in taking *Karnaim,* another insignificant place east of the Jordan. For Israel to boast of its *own strength* about capturing such places is not all that impressive. Israel has problems of attitude that manifest themselves in self-centered national activities and personal living.

> **What Do You Think?**
> What can Christians do to avoid being labeled as selfish and self-centered?
> *Talking Points for Your Discussion*
> - Before such labeling occurs
> - After being unjustly labeled that way
> - After behaving in a way that justifies such a label

C. Oppressor Promised (v. 14)

14. For the Lord God Almighty declares,
"I will stir up a nation against you,
Israel,
that will oppress you all the way
from Lebo Hamath to the valley of the
Arabah."

Although not mentioned by name in the book of Amos, the nation that will come against Israel is Assyria. This nation has been in existence for centuries, but within a few years after the time of Amos it will develop into what is sometimes called the first world-empire. The important factor in the verse before us is not Assyria, however. It is, rather, the fact that the Lord is the one who will cause Assyria to become such a superpower. Its primary purpose will be to take Israel into captivity. Tiglath-Pileser III will become the new king of Assyria in 745 BC, and he will lead his nation to a dominant position in that part of the world (compare 2 Kings 15:29; 16:7, 10).

Assyria will approach Israel from the north, and the oppression will expand southward. The extent is described as being *all the way from Lebo Hamath,* which is near Mount Hor (Numbers 34:8), *to the valley of the Arabah,* which is near the Dead Sea. These represent Israel's northernmost and southernmost boundaries, respectively (2 Kings 14:25). Thus the destruction will be that extensive!

Israel has become smug, sinful, and selfish. And God abhors selfishness, whether by ancient Israel or by any nation in any century.

> **What Do You Think?**
> Why is it sometimes hard to accept the idea that God should and will inflict punishment?
> *Talking Points for Your Discussion*
> - Regarding our willingness to recognize wrath as part of God's nature
> - Regarding failure to take sin seriously
> - Regarding refusal to accept that a disbelieving loved one is lost
> - Other

Conclusion
A. What About Selfishness?

The word *selfish* occurs only eight times in the *New International Version.* The concept is also present, however, in words such as *greedy, ill-gotten,* etc. Foundational to all these is the concept of *covetousness,* the concern of the Tenth Commandment as given in Exodus 20:17; the idea of selfishness is dominant when one covets what belongs to another.

Someone proposed recently that selfishness is at the root of all sin. It means putting self ahead of God and all that he has commanded his people to do or not do. There is some validity to that observation, especially when it is combined with the affirmation in Colossians 3:5 that greed is idolatry.

God hates selfishness, and selfishness can manifest itself in many ways. The world may use other terms to disguise it, but in the end it is still sin.

B. Prayer

Almighty God, grant me wisdom today to discern the different ways that selfishness disguises itself, for it is my desire to make the right choices in my service for you. In Jesus' name, amen.

C. Thought to Remember
Abhor what God abhors.

INVOLVEMENT LEARNING

Enhance your lesson with NIV® Bible Student *(from your curriculum supplier) and the reproducible activity page (at www.standardlesson.com or in the back of the* NIV® Standard Lesson Commentary Deluxe Edition*).*

Into the Lesson

As learners arrive, give each a large capital letter *I* cut from ordinary blank paper. Say, "These represent an exaggerated sense of self-importance and entitlement. On your *I* summarize one act of selfishness you became aware of this past week." If learners seem stuck, say, "You might write about the report of a traffic accident that involved someone who was driving as if he 'owned the road,' etc."

Collect the summaries after a couple of minutes. Select one or more at random to read aloud. Then ask, "What is the title of today's study?" After the answer "God Abhors Selfishness" is voiced, say, "It is time to get our *I* down to the right size." Pull out a pair of scissors and trim an *I* down for dramatic effect.

Next, write *The Life of Luxury* on the board. Ask, "What characterizes such a life?" As responses are forthcoming, jot them on a very large capital letter *I* that you have cut from poster board beforehand. Responses may include the following: living in lavish homes, eating gourmet foods, spending excessive amounts of time in leisure activities, owning season tickets to the most expensive box seats at a sports stadium or arena, having a cabinet stocked with expensive beverages, availing oneself of the finest beauty treatments, etc. Leave the responses on the board for the next segment.

Into the Word

After you have a sizable *Life of Luxury* list above, ask, "Where do you see matches between our list and the list in verses 4-7 of today's text?" Depending on the nature of your class, this comparison can be a whole-class exercise or done in small groups. Discuss how self-aggrandizement often leads to destruction, either in terms of natural consequences or God-ordained consequences.

Next, remind learners of the 1980s marketing slogan that proclaimed, "When E. F. Hutton talks, people listen." Affirm that when God

speaks, everyone should listen! Say, "In the remainder of today's text, let's stay alert for what God says he is going to do, particularly in terms of his *I will* statements."

Read aloud Amos 6:7, 8, 11-14. After learners identify "I will" in verses 8 and 14, ask, "What other Scriptures can you cite where God states what he will do to sinners?" Discuss responses, which may include Matthew 7:23; 10:33; 1 Corinthians 1:19; Hebrews 10:30; and Revelation 2:22, 23; 3:9. Responses may also include statements of God's intent (though not specifically *I will*) such as in Hebrews 10:31; 1 Peter 4:17, 18; 2 Peter 2:4-12; and Revelation 19:1-3.

Option. Distribute copies of the "No Concern? No Comfort!" activity from the reproducible page, which you can download. This exercise will reinforce what has been learned from study of the text. Form learners into pairs or groups of three to complete.

Into Life

Display the word *Selfishness.* For open-ended discussion, ask simply, "Any thoughts on a cure for this?" After several comments, circle the letter *i* and say, "Today's study is not simply a lesson about ancient Israel. It is fundamentally about each 'I' here. Each of us needs to ponder our own tendency toward selfishness. What are we going to do about it, with God's help?" Note that God's depiction of the self-centered lifestyle of Amos's day can apply to many segments of twenty-first-century western culture, but do not allow the discussion to become one of political solutions. Keep the focus on the Christian's responsibility to be selfless.

Option. To reinforce the need for personal application, distribute copies of the "Comfortable or Concerned?" activity from the reproducible page, to be completed individually. If appropriate for the nature of your class, be prepared to share your own results; do not put anyone on the spot to do so.

GOD WILL NEVER FORGET

DEVOTIONAL READING: Hosea 11:1-7
BACKGROUND SCRIPTURE: Amos 8

AMOS 8:1-6, 9, 10

¹ This is what the Sovereign LORD showed me: a basket of ripe fruit. ² "What do you see, Amos?" he asked.

"A basket of ripe fruit," I answered.

Then the LORD said to me, "The time is ripe for my people Israel; I will spare them no longer.

³ "In that day," declares the Sovereign LORD, "the songs in the temple will turn to wailing. Many, many bodies—flung everywhere! Silence!"

⁴ Hear this, you who trample the needy
  and do away with the poor of the land,
⁵ saying,

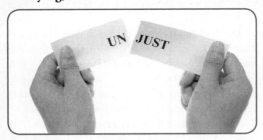

"When will the New Moon be over
  that we may sell grain,
and the Sabbath be ended
  that we may market wheat?"—
skimping on the measure,
  boosting the price
  and cheating with dishonest scales,
⁶ buying the poor with silver
  and the needy for a pair of sandals,
  selling even the sweepings with the
    wheat.

. . . .

⁹ "In that day," declares the Sovereign LORD,

"I will make the sun go down at noon
  and darken the earth in broad daylight.
¹⁰ I will turn your religious festivals into
    mourning
  and all your singing into weeping.
I will make all of you wear sackcloth
  and shave your heads.
I will make that time like mourning for an
    only son
  and the end of it like a bitter day."

KEY VERSE

Then the LORD said to me, "The time is ripe for my people Israel; I will spare them no longer."

—Amos 8:2

GOD'S PROPHETS DEMAND JUSTICE

Unit 1: Amos Rails Against Injustice

LESSONS 1–4

LESSON AIMS

After participating in this lesson, each learner will be able to:

1. List reasons for God's condemnation of Israel.

2. Compare and contrast the behaviors and attitudes of the Israelites with those of people today.

3. Resolve to lead or encourage in correcting social abuses that are harmful to the needy.

LESSON OUTLINE

Introduction
  A. Exploiting Others
  B. Lesson Background: Amos the Man
  C. Lesson Background: Amos the Book
 I. Basket of Fruit (AMOS 8:1-3)
  A. Vision Seen (vv. 1, 2a)
  B. Verdict Pronounced (vv. 2b, 3)
    Choosing the Path
 II. Sins of Israel (AMOS 8:4-6)
  A. Abuse of the Poor (v. 4)
  B. Abuse of Righteousness (vv. 5, 6)
 III. Punishment for Israel (AMOS 8:9, 10)
  A. Darkness (v. 9)
    God's View
  B. Suffering (v. 10)
Conclusion
  A. Accentuate the Positive!
  B. Thought to Remember
  C. Prayer

Introduction

A. Exploiting Others

An unemployed man was able to find a job, but he needed a car to fulfill travel needs that were part of the new employment. One dealer seemed eager to help, and the payments proposed were reasonable. Not mentioned verbally was the fact that the payments were to be made semimonthly, and the buyer discovered this fact too late. Making two payments per month was impossible for the purchaser if he were also to provide basic necessities for his family. The results were that he had to return the car, he lost his new job, and he forfeited his down payment.

Many Old Testament issues and practices seem far removed from our twenty-first-century experience, but not that of exploitation of others. It still happens—often. Acts of greedy exploitation make themselves known by both individuals and corporations. Such acts are committed by the rich, the poor, and those in between; the victims are in the same categories.

It is all too easy to wring our hands and develop a mere "Isn't it awful!" outlook when we see exploitation. Today's lesson helps us move beyond that.

B. Lesson Background: Amos the Man

Since we are still in the book of Amos, the Lesson Backgrounds of the three previous lessons still apply, and that information need not be repeated here. Even so, a bit more can be said about Amos the man himself.

The opening words of the book of Amos reveal only a few facts about him. No ancestors are named, but the prophet stated his residence to be Tekoa, a town about 10 miles south of Jerusalem. Tekoa's elevation of 2,280 feet above sea level is a factor regarding one of his three occupations.

Amos 1:1 states that he was a shepherd, but it is not the usual Hebrew word for that occupation. The word indicates that he cared for a special type of sheep, smaller animals that produced excellent wool. There is evidence that this type of wool was desired by royalty. Mesha, a king of Moab, paid his annual tax or tribute to the kings of Israel with wool from such sheep (2 Kings 3:4).

God Will Never Forget

The dry season each summer caused Amos to move his sheep west, toward the Mediterranean Sea, in order to have pasture for his flocks in the lower regions. This relates to his second occupation involving sycamore trees, which produce figs (Amos 7:14). Such trees grow only in lower areas. Amos may have been a seasonal worker who gathered the figs; or he may have worked to cut, pierce, or pinch the ends of the figs, which hastened ripening, added to the sweetness, and allowed an insect in it to escape. These figs grew in "the western foothills" of Judah (1 Chronicles 27:28), but also in Egypt and southern Africa.

Amos 7:14 also mentions his career as "shepherd," but a different word is used from that translated the same way in Amos 1:1. The word in 7:14 may refer to caring for cattle or oxen. A similar word is used for the oxen cited in 6:12 (lesson 3), so it is sometimes assumed that Amos cared for such animals as well as sheep.

Opinions are divided on whether Amos owned these enterprises, or if he scrambled among all three as a laborer to make a living. By going annually to the west where a major trade route existed, he had opportunities to talk with travelers and other shepherds, thereby learning about the conditions in other nations. This enhanced his ability to speak authoritatively about them.

C. Lesson Background: Amos the Book

A suggested outline of the book of Amos is that of three major sections: chapters 1, 2; chapters 3–6; and chapters 7–9. The first section features eight messages to eight nations and cities (see lesson 1). The second section has five sermons that announce God's pending judgments on Israel; these are marked by the phrases "Hear this word" (Amos 3:1; 4:1; 5:1) and "Woe" (5:18; 6:1). The third section contains five scenes of divine revelation to Amos (7:1-3; 7:4-6; 7:7-9; 8:1-3; 9:1-4); we might call these *visions,* although that specific word is not used. In addition, there is a dramatic, historical interlude in the last part of chapter 7.

Each of the first three visions features a promise of destruction for Israel. The first vision is that of an invasion of locusts; Amos besought God that this would not happen, and God relented.

The second vision was that of a ravaging fire; again Amos prayed that it might not come to pass, and the judgment was averted. The third vision was that of testing Israel against God's plumb line, and Amos was convinced: God's judgment was just. The destruction of Israel would reach to the palaces and the sanctuaries of Israel. It was at that point in Amos's prophesying that "Amaziah the priest of Bethel" told him to shut up and go home, back to Judah (Amos 7:10, 12, 13).

In response, Amos protested that he was not a prophet in any professional way. He then listed the ways he made a living (see above). Amos also responded with prophecies about Amaziah: he would die in a foreign land, his children would die by the sword, and his wife would become a prostitute in order to survive (Amos 7:14-17).

Whether staying in Israel or leaving for Judah, Amos had two visions yet to be received. Today's lesson takes us to the first of those remaining two.

I. Basket of Fruit
(AMOS 8:1-3)

A. Vision Seen (vv. 1, 2a)

1. This is what the Sovereign LORD showed me: a basket of ripe fruit.

To illustrate his intentions, *the Sovereign Lord* uses imagery common to people of the day: locusts (Amos 7:1), fire (7:4), a plumb line (7:7), and, in the verse before us, *a basket of ripe fruit.* Amos is about to discover that the meaning is not in the basket but in the fruit. The ancients enjoy fruit as a source of something sweet, but this vision does not have an enjoyable outcome.

> *What Do You Think?*
> What has God used to get your attention? What has been the result when he has done so?
> *Talking Points for Your Discussion*
> - A sermon
> - A lesson from nature
> - A setback
> - Other

2a. "What do you see, Amos?" he asked. "A basket of ripe fruit," I answered.

The purpose of the Lord's question is to focus Amos's attention. This follows the same question-and-answer approach of the third vision (Amos 7:8). This is not a parable that has to be explained. It is a direct question, and Amos gives the obvious answer.

B. Verdict Pronounced (vv. 2b, 3)

2b. Then the LORD said to me, "The time is ripe for my people Israel; I will spare them no longer.

The Lord's declaration features a play on the Hebrew words for "ripe fruit" of the first half of verse 2 and *the time is ripe* here. The original words look very similar when written and sound identical (or nearly so) when spoken. As the fruit in the basket is ripe, so the time is ripe for the end of Israel.

The declaration *I will spare them no longer* signals no reprieve for those whom God calls *my people*. A few years later, the prophet Hosea will prefix a negative word to the latter phrase and use it as the name of his child: *Lo-Ammi,* meaning "not my people" (Hosea 1:9). The approaching calamity for Israel is definite and intended. Later there will be prophecies about the southern nation of Judah and its own forthcoming captivity, but the focus here is the northern nation of Israel. For Israel, this is the end. There is to be no reprieve. There is a limit in testing God's patience, and Israel has reached it.

HOW TO SAY IT

Amaziah	Am-uh-*zye*-uh.
Assyrian	Uh-*sear*-e-un.
caveat emptor	*kah*-vee-ought *emp*-tur.
Ezekiel	Ee-*zeek*-ee-ul or Ee-*zeek*-yul.
Hammurabi	*Ham*-muh-**rah**-bee.
Hosea	Ho-*zay*-uh.
Judah	*Joo*-duh.
Lamentations	Lam-en-*tay*-shunz.
Lo-Ammi	Lo-*Am*-my.
Mesha	*Me*-shuh.
Micah	*My*-kuh.
Moab	*Mo*-ab.
Tekoa	Tih-*ko*-uh.

❧ CHOOSING THE PATH ❧

She whispered to me with intrigue about how the associate minister had flirted with her. Her—a happily married woman! He also was married, yet found her compelling. She confessed that she found him attractive. They had set a time and place to meet privately. On the way, her well-maintained car failed. She knew in her spirit that the Lord had prevented the meeting. Although firmly believing the car malfunction to have been divine intervention, she asked me to keep her accountable as she planned again to meet in private with this man—for the purpose of explaining to him why they could never be together!

Questions bombarded my mind: How was it that this bright woman was not hearing her own conflict? How was my Christian friend not able to sense the dangers of her secret plan? I pointed out that although the Lord in his mercy had prevented the first rendezvous, future determined planning to continue down that path would eventually succeed. I encouraged her to share the whole account with her husband, and thankfully she did. That's not necessarily the best solution in all such cases, but it was for her.

God is so good! He warns and waits and withholds judgment time and time again. But if we are set on rebellion, consequences are inevitable. God's greatest plans for us are delayed or derailed altogether when we choose the path of sin.

—V. E.

3. "In that day," declares the Sovereign LORD, "the songs in the temple will turn to wail-

ing. Many, many bodies—flung everywhere! Silence!"

Last week's lesson depicted the people of Israel as idly singing and making music on instruments while drinking bowl after bowl of wine (Amos 6:5, 6). That is going to change, and such songs will become loud lamentations (*wailing*). The cause for such grievous sounds is given: *many, many bodies—flung everywhere!*

As the realities of death and desolation register on the survivors, the final sound—if we can call it that—will be silence (see also 6:10). Since this prophecy is against northern Israel, *the temple* in view is not the one in Jerusalem but in Bethel (Amos 7:13).

II. Sins of Israel
(AMOS 8:4-6)

A. Abuse of the Poor (v. 4)

**4. Hear this, you who trample the needy
   and do away with the poor of the land,**

The Lord continues by making general accusations (through Amos) against people who are smug as they exploit *the needy* in Israel. The Lord has already condemned such viciousness (Amos 2:6, 7; 4:1; 5:11, 12), but now he adds that this oppression is producing a sobering outcome: *the poor of the land* are perishing (which is the idea of *do away with*). The violation of the Law of Moses is quite brazen in this regard (see Deuteronomy 15:7-11; 24:14; etc.).

What Do You Think?
What is being done right now to prevent injustice to the most vulnerable? Why is such prevention ours to address?
Talking Points for Your Discussion
- Regarding my church
- Regarding my Bible-study group
- Regarding my family
- Regarding myself

B. Abuse of Righteousness (vv. 5, 6)

**5, 6. . . . saying,
"When will the New Moon be over
   that we may sell grain,**

**and the Sabbath be ended
   that we may market wheat?"—
skimping on the measure,
   boosting the price
   and cheating with dishonest scales,
buying the poor with silver
   and the needy for a pair of sandals,
   selling even the sweepings with the
      wheat.**

The recitation of sins continues with an exposure of the false piety of the Israelites. *The New Moon* celebration at the beginning of each month seems to be observed carefully (Numbers 10:10; 28:11), but it is also resented because it interferes with acquiring wealth. The people have the same attitude toward *the Sabbath,* the mandatory day of rest (Exodus 20:8; 23:12; 34:21). They would rather sell wheat than honor God's command.

In addition, the merchandising practices are designed to cheat, whether buying or selling. *The measure* (literally, an ephah) should be about three-fifths of a bushel, but the one who sells wheat uses a measure smaller than what it is supposed to be. Neither are the balance-scale weights used in transactions correct. Moses had condemned such practices in his final exhortations (Deuteronomy 25:13-16). He included a blessing if the people obeyed: that their days in the land would be prolonged. But they have not obeyed, and the consequences loom (compare Leviticus 19:35, 36; Proverbs 11:1; 16:11; 20:23; Ezekiel 45:9-12).

The shady practices seen here seem to be universal and constant. One of the codes of law from the time of Hammurabi (about 1750 BC) condemned such actions. The same charges are levied by Hosea, who prophesies in Israel only a few years after Amos (see Hosea 12:7). The same methods for cheating the poor are cited for Judah by Micah in about 740 BC (see Micah 6:11). Such practices continue to this day.

The cheating is not only in terms of quantity but also quality. *The sweepings* refers to the worthless chaff that is left after the winnowing process (compare Matthew 3:12). Instead of being thrown out, some chaff is mixed back in with the wheat that is sold. The treatment of the poor also smacks of a slave trade (compare Deuteronomy 15:12-18).

III. Punishment for Israel
(AMOS 8:9, 10)

A. Darkness (v. 9)

9. "In that day," declares the Sovereign LORD, "I will make the sun go down at noon and darken the earth in broad daylight.

Amos 8:8 (not in today's text) tells of the beginning of God's judgment signs in terms of the land trembling. But his displeasure against Israel is to be demonstrated by signs that are usually taken figuratively. The famous "Assyrian eclipse" of the sun, dated June 15, 763 BC, may have already occurred as Amos prophesies. If so, the people of Israel have experienced a partial eclipse, and this would be in their collective memory. But a literal darkness, such as from an eclipse of the sun, is not in view here.

Moses used darkness imagery in describing one of the curses for Israel's disobedience (Deuteronomy 28:15, 29). Other prophets use the same language to describe punishments from God (see Isaiah 59:10; Jeremiah 13:16; Micah 3:6; etc.). This darkness represents God's judgment.

What Do You Think?

How does God warn people today of the need to repent? What cautions should be acknowledged in drawing conclusions here?

Talking Points for Your Discussion
- Disasters, natural and otherwise (Luke 13:1-5)
- Personal productivity (Luke 13:6-8)
- Personal health (John 9:1-3)
- Timeless Scripture passages (Acts 2:38)
- Other

In her book *Walking on Water,* Christian author Madeleine L'Engle (1918–2007) offered this poignant thought: "I have a point of view. You have a point of view. But *God* has *view*" (emphasis is original). Sadly, many history books and political commentaries that examine the rise and fall of nations are written without consideration of God's view.

Such inquiries are not entirely without merit, however, in that thoughtful secular observers often will uncover valuable threads of truth. In an article on foreignpolicy.com, for example, Daron Acemoglu and James A. Robinson propose 10 reasons why countries fall apart. They attribute the failures of nations to factors such as use of forced labor, blocking of opportunities to people of certain races, and blocking of new technologies that threaten the entrenched status of economic elites. A common thread through much of their findings is that of greed.

The secular observer can condemn greed by concluding that it simply "doesn't work" in pointing to example after example of nations that fail when greed predominates. The Christian should point out, however, that while we may not know God's view regarding any particular nation's rise or fall today (since he has not told us), we know his view in general: his heart is with society's most vulnerable.

God still sees the suffering of the poor, and he still detests abuses by those of power and privilege. God's view doesn't change. —V. E.

B. Suffering (v. 10)

10. "I will turn your religious festivals into mourning and all your singing into weeping. I will make all of you wear sackcloth and shave your heads. I will make that time like mourning for an only son and the end of it like a bitter day."

The three occurrences of *I will* point to emphatic promises. These are promises that a person or a nation does not wish to hear. The Israelites know that their ancestor Joseph became second only to Pharaoh after he (Joseph) experienced dramatic reversals in his life; his status went from bad to good (Genesis 39:1–41:40). The reverse will be true for Israel: they will go from experiencing lives of luxury to nothing.

The Lord pronounces this judgment with vivid examples that contrast with the Israelites' current lifestyle. The sumptuous eating at *religious festivals* (see Amos 6:4, lesson 3) will be turned *into mourning.* The carefree music that accompanies such indulgences (6:5, lesson 3) will become *weeping.* Dressing for the change will mean wearing coarse, crude *sackcloth,* a sign of grief (compare Isaiah 22:12; Joel 1:8, 13; Jonah 3:5). Care of one's hair will change from that of careful grooming to shaving it off, also a sign of grief (compare Job 1:20; Jeremiah 48:37). Mourning will be so intense that it will be like grief expressed at the death of *an only son,* since the loss of such a one imperils family lineage. That will be *a bitter day* indeed (compare Ruth 1:3-5, 20).

Those who ignore or deliberately violate the terms of the covenant will experience all this. God will not forget sin—unless nations and individuals come to him in genuine faith, repentance, and obedience.

Conclusion

A. Accentuate the Positive!

Destruction! Desolation! Doom! These concepts dominate the book of Amos. Would his preaching have produced the desired result of repentance if he had toned down the harshness of his message? That is extremely doubtful, for nothing was going to change the people at that point.

That, however, did not mean that there was no room for a positive aspect to the message. Most prophets blended messages of doom and hope. Amos, for his part, offered a very positive outcome in Amos 9:11-15. Two of these positive verses are cited by James at the famous conference in Jerusalem (Acts 15:16, 17). James made the point that God was concerned that Gentiles be included for honoring his name and that the prophets had foretold that that was to happen. God loves the world, and the prophets revealed that even Gentiles would be included in God's plan.

Visual for Lessons 4 & 10

Point to this as you ask, "How is an hourglass better than a clock for illustrating the coming judgment?"

Amos 8:7 is not included in today's lesson text, but the title for this lesson comes from there: God "will never forget." Yet God *wants* to forget sins! This is affirmed in Isaiah 43:25, a verse that has been termed the high point of grace in the Old Testament. Jeremiah 31:34 also affirms as much. That verse is a part of the promise of the new covenant; included in Hebrews 8:8-12, it forms part of the longest quotation of the Old Testament in the New.

The outcomes of the current ungodly trends and megatrends are important to contemplate. But the Christian must not become so enamored with how bad things are (or can be) that he or she forgets the glorious blessings that God has planned for his people. Thus while we acknowledge the reality of sin, we also accentuate the positive of forgiveness that is available in Christ alone. The church must determine to do what it can to care for the needy, but the spiritual dimensions concerning sin, righteousness, and forgiveness must be shared as primary. May it be so until Christ returns!

B. Prayer

Almighty God, may the ancient words of Amos not fall on deaf ears today! Grant us compassionate lives as examples of faith, hope, and love to an unbelieving world. In Jesus' name, amen.

C. Thought to Remember

God forgets the sins of those
who are in Christ!

INVOLVEMENT LEARNING

Enhance your lesson with NIV® Bible Student (from your curriculum supplier) and the reproducible activity page (at www.standardlesson.com or in the back of the NIV® Standard Lesson Commentary Deluxe Edition).

Into the Lesson

Display a basket having several kinds of ripe fruit. Next to it have a basket with some fruit that is obviously not ripe (green bananas would be a good choice). Ask, "What do you see?" as you gesture toward the baskets. Responses can range from the generalized "baskets of fruit" to naming of the specific fruits present.

If no one mentions the ripe/unripe distinction, lead learners to that observation yourself. As you do, affix on the first basket a sign that reads *Ripe for consumption!* (*Option:* use pictures instead of actual fruit.)

Say, "The people of Israel were becoming ever more sinful by the time of Amos. Finally, God had had enough. His warnings had fallen on deaf ears one too many times, and the time was right for the consuming wrath of his anger to be felt. Turn to Amos 8 and we'll see why."

Option. Before doing the above, place in chairs copies of the "Visions" activity from the reproducible page, which you can download. Learners can begin working on this as they arrive. This will help (1) sketch a wider context of divine revelation to some of God's chosen recipients and (2) distinguish between Bible and modern uses of the term *vision.* Use learners' discoveries to compare and contrast the nature of the divine communication to Amos.

Into the Word

After learners turn to Amos 8, read the first two verses aloud and use the commentary on verse 2 to explain the play on words between "ripe fruit" and "the time is ripe."

Next, distribute 12 pieces of yellow paper that are cut to look like bananas. Each banana is to have written on it one of the following verse references of today's text: 2b, 3a, 3b, 4, 5a, 5b, 6a, 6b, 9, 10a, 10b, 10c. If you have fewer than 12 learners, some will have more than one banana; if you

anticipate having more than 12 learners, use the commentary to determine how best to use smaller segments of the lesson text to create more bananas.

Say to all, "First read to yourself all eight verses of today's text. Then focus on your verse or portion of verse and write either *cause* or *effect* on your banana. You will write *cause* if your segment is talking about a sinful action or attitude on the part of the Israelites; you will write *effect* if your segment is talking about a judgmental action of God that is prompted by sinful actions."

After learners finish, work through the text segment by segment. Disagreements will offer a chance for deeper study. (*Expected identifications:* **cause**—*verses 4, 5a, 5b, 6a, 6b;* **effect**—*verses 2b, 3a, 3b, 9, 10a, 10b, 10c.*)

Into Life

Say, "Let's see if we can find reports of abuses of the most vulnerable that have parallels with those Amos describes." Distribute relevant newspapers and magazines for quick research in that regard; learners who have mobile devices with Internet access can be encouraged to use those instead. Encourage mention of abuses that are both illegal (human trafficking, etc.) and legal (high interest rates on payday loans, etc.).

Ask learners to explain the parallels they discover. Wrap up by asking the class, "What can we as individuals and as a group do to stop these abuses?" Allow free response, but try to focus on one specific activity the class can implement. If learners need a thinking stimulus, ask, "What Christian ministries are already doing this kind of work, and how can we partner with them?" (Come prepared with examples of such ministries.)

Option. If your learners would benefit from a review of this month's four lessons from Amos, distribute copies of the "God's Call and Declaration" activity from the reproducible page. This exercise is ideal for small groups.

NO REST FOR
THE WICKED

DEVOTIONAL READING: Proverbs 11:1-10
BACKGROUND SCRIPTURE: Micah 2

MICAH 2:4-11

4 "In that day people will ridicule you;
    they will taunt you with this mourn-
       ful song:
'We are utterly ruined;
    my people's possession is divided up.
He takes it from me!
    He assigns our fields to traitors.'"
5 Therefore you will have no one in the
      assembly of the LORD
    to divide the land by lot.

6 "Do not prophesy," their prophets say.
    "Do not prophesy about these things;
    disgrace will not overtake us."
7 You descendants of Jacob, should it be said,
    "Does the LORD become impatient?
    Does he do such things?"
"Do not my words do good
    to the one whose ways are upright?
8 Lately my people have risen up
    like an enemy.
You strip off the rich robe
    from those who pass by without a care,
    like men returning from battle.
9 You drive the women of my people
    from their pleasant homes.
You take away my blessing
    from their children forever.
10 Get up, go away!
    For this is not your resting place,
because it is defiled,
    it is ruined, beyond all remedy.
11 If a liar and deceiver comes and says,
    'I will prophesy for you plenty of wine
       and beer,'
    that would be just the prophet for this
       people!"

KEY VERSE

You descendants of Jacob, should it be said, "Does the LORD become impatient? Does he do such things? Do not my words do good to the one whose ways are upright?" —**Micah 2:7**

GOD'S PROPHETS DEMAND JUSTICE

Unit 2: Micah Calls for Justice Among Unjust People

LESSONS 5–8

LESSON AIMS

After participating in this lesson, each learner will be able to:

1. Summarize how the Lord's people acted unjustly, how they had mocked both God and his messengers, and the judgment that awaited them.

2. Tell how God's people today (the church) are sometimes guilty of the attitudes and actions of Micah's hearers.

3. Examine areas of life where he or she has not taken God's Word seriously in daily conduct or treatment of others and make a plan for change.

LESSON OUTLINE

Introduction

A. Cheerleaders or Coaches?

Samuel A. Meier contrasts false prophets with the Lord's true prophets in terms of *cheerleaders* and *coaches*. The false prophets were like cheerleaders during a football game in which the team they root for is getting crushed by an opponent. They continue to cheer and exhort the team to keep playing and giving their best, even though the outlook is hopeless.

The true prophets, however, are more like coaches who take corrective action when they see mistakes and careless play occurring. As these coaches become frustrated with the team's effort (or lack thereof), they call time-out and tell one or more players in no uncertain terms how badly they are playing, even to the point of benching them. Good coaches will tell the truth and not mince words, which is essentially what true prophets of the Lord always did.

Today's lesson continues this quarter's study of some of the Old Testament prophets. These were men who did not hesitate to confront and rebuke God's people when that was called for, and it certainly was called for in the days of the prophet Micah. His book is the source of our next four lessons.

B. Lesson Background

Like Amos (lessons 1–4), the prophet Micah possessed a great passion for justice and for right living among God's chosen people. Micah 6:8 (see lesson 7) includes one of the most compelling statements in all of Scripture of what God requires of his people. The Hebrew name *Micah* means, "Who is like the Lord?" Micah will raise that very question at the conclusion of the book (lesson 8). There are several men of the name *Micah* (or the longer form *Micaiah*) mentioned in the Old Testament, so we take care not to get them mixed up. The man of interest to us is mentioned by name only in two places: Micah 1:1 and Jeremiah 26:18 (see lesson 6).

Amos and Micah may well have been contemporaries. While Amos's ministry is dated during the reign of Uzziah king of Judah (Amos 1:1),

Micah's occurred during the reigns of Jotham (Uzziah's son), Ahaz (Jotham's son), and Hezekiah (Ahaz's son). Jotham's reign overlapped that of his father's since Uzziah had to be confined during the latter years of his reign because of a leprous condition he brought on himself. Jotham ruled in his stead until and after Uzziah's death (2 Chronicles 26:16-23). So Amos and Micah could have carried out a portion of their ministries at the same time.

We know Micah was a contemporary of Isaiah since Isaiah 1:1 mentions the same kings that Micah 1:1 does except for Uzziah. But while Isaiah seems to have been more like a "court prophet," having contact especially with kings Ahaz (Isaiah 7:1-14) and Hezekiah (38:1-6; 39:1-8), it appears that Micah ministered more in the rural areas of Judah. He notes in his book a number of towns in Judah that are mentioned nowhere else in the Bible. He himself was from a village called Moresheth, located about 25 miles southwest of Jerusalem. Of course, the smaller towns needed to hear God's message just as much as the city dwellers in Jerusalem.

There was great turmoil and uncertainty for both Israel (the northern kingdom) and Judah (the southern kingdom) during Micah's time. The Assyrians had become a formidable threat to both Israel and Judah when Micah's ministry began; in fact, they would be the instruments in God's hands to carry out his judgment against the northern kingdom, whose capital Samaria finally fell in 722 BC (2 Kings 17:1-6).

Micah's message was aimed at both Israel and Judah. His book begins with a reference to both capital cities, Samaria and Jerusalem (Micah 1:1), and proceeds to indict both on account of their rebellion against the Lord (1:5-9). As chapter 2 opens, Micah declares a "woe" against those who had become obsessed with doing evil and could think of nothing else, even while lying "on their beds" (2:1).

In their defiance of God, such people had become so arrogant and smug that they were confident the Lord would do nothing to hold them accountable for their actions. Such people are described as those who "covet fields and seize them, and houses, and take them" (Micah 2:2). Such seizure of others' property was strictly forbidden by the Law of Moses. The promised land belonged to the Lord; in recognition of that fact, land was not to be transferred permanently to another party (Leviticus 25:23; Numbers 36:7-9). The fate of the schemers opens today's lesson.

I. Prophecies of the Future
(MICAH 2:4, 5)

A. God's People to Be Jeered (v. 4)

4. "In that day people will ridicule you; they will taunt you with this mournful song:
'We are utterly ruined;
my people's possession is divided up.
He takes it from me!
He assigns our fields to traitors.'"

The Hebrew noun translated as the verb *ridicule* can mean more than to mock someone. It can also designate a parable or something much more concise—a wise saying, or what we could call *a proverb* (that is how this same word is translated in Ecclesiastes 12:9 and Proverbs 10:1). It can also describe a poem, perhaps something as simple as a nursery rhyme, such as many of us learned as children.

In the context of the verse before us, the taunting to come is further described as a *mournful song*. The song that immediately follows will be

HOW TO SAY IT

Ahaz	*Ay*-haz.
Amos	*Ay*-mus.
Hezekiah	Hez-ih-*kye*-uh.
Isaiah	Eye-*zay*-uh.
Jeremiah	Jair-uh-*my*-uh.
Jotham	*Jo*-thum.
Judah	*Joo*-duh.
Micah	*My*-kuh.
Micaiah	My-*kay*-uh.
Moresheth	*Mo*-resh-eth.
Pharisee	*Fair*-ih-see.
Samaria	Suh-*mare*-ee-uh.
Uzziah	Uh-*zye*-uh.

Visual for Lesson 5. *Point to this visual as you ask, "Is changing one's ways the same as repentance? Why, or why not?"*

used sarcastically by enemies to mock God's people following the judgment that he will bring on Israel and Judah because of their passion for pursuing evil.

The statement *my people's possession is divided up* refers to the sections of land that the greedy have seized from others and claimed as their own, since that is the context of Micah 2:1, 2. But the tables will be turned: the oppressors will find themselves to be the oppressed as the seizers suddenly become the seized. The *he* in this verse (two times) most likely refers to the Lord. He is the one to change the way the land has been shamefully reapportioned.

On what basis would the Lord do such a thing? Very simple: it's his land. He had granted it to the nation of Israel, and he can take it from those who have refused to acknowledge him as the giver. He will allow outsiders to take control of the fields over which the greedy think themselves to be in control.

B. God's People to Be Judged (v. 5)

5. Therefore you will have no one in the assembly of the LORD to divide the land by lot.

To determine land boundaries *by lot* recalls the process by which the promised land was originally allocated to the tribes of Israel (see Joshua 18:1-7). Those who are guided by selfish interests have ignored these divisions of the land and have taken

it upon themselves to reassign boundaries in their own favor. But they will be denied any further opportunity to do so; in fact, they will find themselves outside the borders of the promised land altogether—living in exile.

> **What Do You Think?**
> When are we most likely to act selfishly? What can we do to resist this temptation?
> *Talking Points for Your Discussion*
> - In the exercise of authority (at work, in church, etc.)
> - In thinking about and voting on social issues
> - In how we handle money
> - Other

❧ MAKING PRACTICE MATCH PROFESSION ❧

When I was teaching in a certain city a few years ago, some students in the class told me of a recent event in their town. Two men robbed a convenience store on a Sunday morning. The store had a surveillance camera, so the thieves took the video cassette from the camera before they left.

The police had been called, however, and they soon caught the thieves with the video still in their possession. One of the policemen inquired, "I know I shouldn't ask this, but why didn't you dispose of this tape that proves you are the thieves?" Their answer: "We didn't have time, because that would have made us late for church." It is amazing how often people will profess to a particular religious identity—to a religion that has high moral values—but then act in direct opposition to that identification!

Recently my wife was watching a TV program that described the efforts of a charitable organization that was meeting a dire social need. She told me that we should send money to these people. But while doing some research online, I discovered they were under investigation for fraud and financial mismanagement. They were trading on heartrending conditions as a cover for their base dishonesty. Perhaps they had some clever rationalization to justify to themselves the validity of their practice. Jesus had something to say about this in Mark 7:9-13 and elsewhere. —J. B. N.

II. Problems in the Present
(MICAH 2:6-11)

A. The People's View of God (vv. 6, 7a)

6. "Do not prophesy," their prophets say. "Do not prophesy about these things; disgrace will not overtake us."

The evildoers' attitude toward God's appointed messengers (prophets such as Micah) is now exposed. We see in this verse what seems to be the very words the false prophets use to try to counter Micah's message of coming judgment. The false prophets have the audacity to tell someone like Micah, whom the Lord has called and commissioned to speak his word, *do not prophesy*.

The Hebrew verb translated *prophesy* in this verse is interesting in that it is not the usual word used for the action of prophesying. The word used here is literally "to drip" or "to drop" (as in water dripping drop after drop). It appears to be a derogatory way of picturing what prophets like Micah do (the same word occurs in Amos 7:16). When we think of how irritating a constant dripping sound can be, we will have a good mental picture of how the evildoers view Micah and what he stands for. They want his annoying "dripping" to stop!

These selfish, greedy people should feel shame. But as Jeremiah later states it so well, "They have no shame at all; they do not even know how to blush" (Jeremiah 6:15). The evildoers want a message that caters to their self-serving agenda, not one that holds them accountable for the wrongs they have done and are doing. This is why prophets like Micah, who challenge the status quo, are often treated with such contempt (compare Jeremiah 26:7-11; Amos 7:10-13; Acts 7:52).

What Do You Think?

How does culture try to silence the voice of God today? How do we counteract this?

Talking Points for Your Discussion
- Regarding legal (judicial) methods
- Regarding misrepresentation
- Regarding labeling or stigmatizing
- Other

7a. You descendants of Jacob, should it be said,
"Does the LORD become impatient? Does he do such things?"

The prophet now attacks the rhetorical questions that his opponents are using or will use. Micah's opponents are accusing him of being too narrow in his view of God. *Does the Lord become impatient?* and *Does he do such things?* [the acts of judgment that Micah prophesies] they are depicted as asking. "Certainly not!" is the answer they expect.

Those opponents presume that God will never act toward the *descendants of Jacob* in ways like prophets such as Micah predict that he will. These evildoers think that a broader, more tolerant view of God is needed.

❧ IS GOD INTOLERANT? ❧

Our "politically correct" culture discourages people from talking about the realities of immorality. When I was a youngster, people who indulged in certain kinds of immoral behavior were called *perverts*; now they are called *practitioners of alternative lifestyles*. The list of justification-by-renaming grows longer by the day.

Even so, I do not normally listen to the various talk shows that point out such problems. It is not because I disagree with what they say; rather, it is because they often make their points in incendiary and belligerent ways. However, a member of my family often does listen to these programs. One day I was walking through the house and heard a talk-show host speak of a recent survey that indicated 80 percent of Americans think that the country is going downhill morally. The other 20 percent think morals to be improving. The talk-show host was dumbfounded by the latter.

But I thought, *You must pay attention to how that 20 percent defines morality.* To that segment, if governments pass laws allowing same-sex marriage, then that indicates people are becoming more tolerant, abandoning the "narrow-minded" views of the past. Therefore the "moral" levels are improving! To that segment of the population, allowing abortion on demand, etc., means we are forsaking previous intolerance and becoming more "moral."

We dare not mistake God's patience as tolerance or approval of sin. God is just as intolerant of sin as he ever was. Isaiah 5:20 still applies: "Woe to those who call evil good and good evil, who put darkness for light and light for darkness, who put bitter for sweet and sweet for bitter."

—J. B. N.

B. God's View of the People (vv. 7b-11)

7b. "Do not my words do good to the one whose ways are upright?

The rhetorical questions of the enemies (v. 7a) are now answered by a rhetorical question from the Lord. Two can play this game! True, God is good, loving, and merciful. But his goodness should not be used as a means of rationalizing or avoiding responsibility for sinful actions. "Good and upright is the Lord," writes David in Psalm 25:8, "therefore he instructs sinners in his ways." God's goodness is experienced personally and intimately by those *whose ways are upright*—those who receive his instruction and align their ways with his.

Ironically, the evildoers are pictured earlier as walking proudly (Micah 2:3). One gets the picture of people who stand tall in their arrogance and self-assurance. But spiritually they are not *upright* at all; they fall far short of what God finds pleasing.

> **What Do You Think?**
> How is God's Word a source of blessing to the upright today?
> *Talking Points for Your Discussion*
> ▪ Regarding the blessings that come from knowing truth
> ▪ Regarding the blessings that come from following divine guidance
> ▪ Other

8. "Lately my people have risen up like an enemy.

You strip off the rich robe from those who pass by without a care, like men returning from battle.

So far have God's people strayed from his righteous and just standards that he considers them *like an enemy.* He then cites specific examples of their heartless actions. The greedy are pictured as seizing the clothing of others. The phrase *those who pass by without a care* seems to describe their callous attitude: the greedy are *like men returning from battle,* who arrogantly feel they have every right to seize the possessions of others as plunder. Satisfying their own desires is their priority.

> **What Do You Think?**
> How do we resist having an attitude of arrogance that leads to (or results from) greed?
> *Talking Points for Your Discussion*
> ▪ In business
> ▪ In politics
> ▪ In cultural struggles between "the haves" and "the have nots"
> ▪ Other

9. "You drive the women of my people from their pleasant homes.

You take away my blessing from their children forever.

The cruel acts against *the women of my people* illustrate the charges issued earlier in Micah 2:2: "they covet fields and seize them, and houses, and take them." *Their children* are also mentioned, as those from whom God's blessing has been taken away. The Hebrew word for *blessing* signifies something of honor or adornment; perhaps one can think of a legacy or heirloom meant to be passed on from generation to generation. The greedy evildoers are depriving people of land that, by God's design, is meant to be theirs.

The absence of any reference to a husband or father may indicate that these women and children are widows and orphans. As such, they are vulnerable to abuse, having no one to protect them from the scavengers.

10. "Get up, go away! For this is not your resting place, because it is defiled, it is ruined, beyond all remedy.

Now come the words of judgment, decreed through Micah by the righteous judge of all the earth. Those described as having "risen up like an enemy" (v. 8, above) are now commanded to *get up, go away!* from the promised land. They are being evicted.

The promised land is intended to be a place of rest for the people of God (Deuteronomy 12:8, 9; Hebrews 3:18, 19), but the evildoers have defiled that land with their sinful conduct. The severe language here is in keeping with the words of Moses in Leviticus 18:28, where he commands the people to be obedient to God or else the land "will vomit you out as it vomited out the nations that were before you."

**11. "If a liar and deceiver comes and says,
    'I will prophesy for you plenty of wine
    and beer,'
    that would be just the prophet for this
    people!"**

The final verse of our lesson exhibits the use of satire. Earlier (v. 6) Micah had quoted the greedy evildoers who wanted messengers like him to keep quiet and avoid unpleasant topics like God's wrath and judgment. Now Micah offers the Lord's declaration as to what kind of prophet would appeal to *this people.* If someone would *prophesy* (again Micah uses the Hebrew word meaning "to drip" that was noted in verse 6) for them *wine and beer,* he would be just the right kind of prophet for this crowd! Again, the only "prophets" these selfish individuals are interested in listening to are those who will give their stamp of approval to the sins they like to commit.

What Do You Think?
  What kinds of false messages seem most attractive to unbelievers today? How would you rank-order these in terms of temptation-danger?
Talking Points for Your Discussion
  ▪ How wealth is to be gained
  ▪ Where truth is to be found
  ▪ How satisfaction is to be obtained
  ▪ Where the greatest threats lie
  ▪ Other

Micah calls these false prophets liars and deceivers. By contrast, however, Micah claims to be "filled with power, with the Spirit of the Lord" in Micah 3:8, a passage to be considered in lesson 6.

Conclusion
A. "Mercy Me!"

The expression "Mercy Me!" was used by past generations to express amazement at seeing or hearing something unexpected or unusual. Apparently it comes from a prayer asking the Lord to have mercy on an individual who is praying. Perhaps the expression arose from the idea of asking God for mercy to survive or endure some unexpected news, especially of something quite disturbing.

The prayer for God to have mercy is of itself a valid request. One thinks of the tax collector in one of Jesus' parables who was so distraught at his unworthiness to come before God (in contrast with a haughty Pharisee) that he simply but earnestly prayed, "God, have mercy on me, a sinner" (Luke 18:13).

However, the one who prays for God's mercy must recognize that mercy, like any of God's good gifts, is not to be hoarded but to be displayed openly toward others. This is what the wicked in Micah's day failed to understand or refused to accept. Like the unforgiving servant in another of Jesus' parables, those who receive mercy yet fail to extend it to others forfeit whatever mercy has been demonstrated toward them (Matthew 18:21-35). The next time you need God's mercy, ask yourself when was the last time you extended mercy to someone else!

B. Prayer

Father of mercy, be merciful to us sinners. Prompt us, however, to do more than just ask for mercy for ourselves. Help us not to become so proud or spiritually nearsighted that we view mercy as only for us and forget that it is to be extended to others daily. We have so freely received; may we freely give. In Jesus' name, amen.

C. Thought to Remember

Treat others with the mercy you desire God
to extend to you.

INVOLVEMENT LEARNING

Enhance your lesson with NIV® Bible Student *(from your curriculum supplier) and the reproducible activity page (at www.standardlesson.com or in the back of the* NIV® Standard Lesson Commentary Deluxe Edition*).*

Into the Lesson

Hold up (or pass around) pictures of a happy cheerleader and an unhappy coach. Say, "There were both false and true prophets in Old Testament times. One scholar has compared the false prophets to cheerleaders and the true prophets to coaches. To help us understand this analogy, let's assume that a certain football team is losing badly. As I describe an action, tell me if it sounds more like that of a cheerleader or a coach."

Read the following statements and pause for responses: 1. Shouts instructions like "That's OK, that's all right; stay right in there—fight, fight, fight!" (*cheerleader*); 2. Notices mistakes (*coach*); 3. Looks extremely annoyed (*coach*); 4. Celebrates tiny successes (*cheerleader*); 5. Gives only positive reinforcement (*cheerleader*); 6. Singles out players for correction (*coach*); 7. Tells the truth and does not mince words (*coach*); 8. Keeps smiling until the end (*cheerleader*)."

For discussion, ask learners if the analogy comparing prophets to cheerleaders and coaches is a good one and why. After responses say, "Micah was a true prophet of God and noticed many wrong things happening. Let's see what they were."

Into the Word

Give each learner a two-column handout with column headings *Micah's Indictment* and *God's Punishment*. Have the following paraphrases reproduced under the indicated header; leave space for learners to write a verse number from today's text. *Micah's Indictment:* A. You snatch clothing off the backs of others. B. Your false prophets are unashamed and even tell me to shut up. C. You throw women and children out of their homes. D. You mock God by denying that he will do the things that he has told me he will do. *God's Punishment:* E. You will no longer have any right to reside in the promised land. F. You will deserve the false prophets you choose to listen to. G. The

exile to come will deny you any further opportunity to cast lots for deciding how to divide the land. H. After my judgment comes to pass, your enemies will sing mocking songs about you. I. By your sin you have desecrated the land where you now live.

Have learners work in small groups to match the paraphrases with the verses in Micah 2:4-11. To save time you may wish to have half of the groups work on the indictments and the other half on the punishments. (*Correct matches: A, v. 8; B, v. 6; C, v. 9; D, v. 7; E, v. 10a; F, v. 11; G, v. 5; H, v. 4; I, v. 10b.*)

Into Life

Give each learner one index card and say, "Write on your card a favorite biblical imperative, citing book, chapter, and verse. When you finish, fold you card so the verse can't be seen." Then have learners pass cards one person to the right. State this challenge: "Like the Israelites, we are tempted not to take the Scriptures seriously at times, living like we don't believe God means what he says. To accept a challenge to take God at his word, open the card, read the verse, and commit to living it." (*Option:* Have learners keep the verse on the card unseen until they pray about it after they get home.) Follow up next week in asking for volunteers to see how many took the challenge. Allow a time then for sharing how it affected them.

Alternative. Distribute copies of the "Who, Me?" activity from the reproducible page, which you can download. Have learners work in small groups to complete as indicated. Ask for volunteers to share their results.

Option. After discussing the lesson's conclusion ("Mercy Me!"), distribute copies of the "Mercy Received and Practiced" activity for learners to complete in silent reflection during the final two minutes of class. Suggest that they take it home to post where they will see it daily in the week ahead.

NO TOLERANCE FOR CORRUPT OFFICIALS

DEVOTIONAL READING: Matthew 7:15-20
BACKGROUND SCRIPTURE: Micah 3

MICAH 3:5-12

⁵ This is what the LORD says:

"As for the prophets
   who lead my people astray,
they proclaim 'peace'
   if they have something to eat,
but prepare to wage war against anyone
   who refuses to feed them.
⁶ Therefore night will come over you, without visions,
   and darkness, without divination.
The sun will set for the prophets,
   and the day will go dark for them.
⁷ The seers will be ashamed
   and the diviners disgraced.
They will all cover their faces
   because there is no answer from God."
⁸ But as for me, I am filled with power,
   with the Spirit of the LORD,
   and with justice and might,
to declare to Jacob his transgression,
   to Israel his sin.
⁹ Hear this, you leaders of Jacob,
   you rulers of Israel,
who despise justice
   and distort all that is right;

¹⁰ who build Zion with bloodshed,
   and Jerusalem with wickedness.
¹¹ Her leaders judge for a bribe,
   her priests teach for a price,
   and her prophets tell fortunes for
     money.
Yet they look for the LORD's support and say,
   "Is not the LORD among us?
   No disaster will come upon us."
¹² Therefore because of you,
Zion will be plowed like a field,
   Jerusalem will become a heap of rubble,
   the temple hill a mound overgrown
     with thickets.

KEY VERSE

As for me, I am filled with power, with the Spirit of the LORD, and with justice and might, to declare to Jacob his transgression, to Israel his sin.. —**Micah 3:8**

GOD'S PROPHETS DEMAND JUSTICE

Unit 2: Micah Calls for Justice Among Unjust People

LESSONS 5–8

LESSON AIMS

After participating in this lesson, each learner will be able to:

1. List descriptions of the false prophets and of Micah's prophetic office.

2. Explain how greed can influence someone to use a position of power to exploit people.

3. Plan a worship service in which leaders in the church and/or community are honored and in which prayers are offered on their behalf.

LESSON OUTLINE

Introduction

A. Before You Lead Others . . .

Toward the end of his outstanding baseball career, Babe Ruth began to entertain the idea of managing a team. One possibility was the New York Yankees, for whom he had played many great seasons. But Ruth had a reputation for wild and undisciplined behavior off the field. So when he approached Yankees' owner Jacob Ruppert about the manager's job, he was asked, "You can't manage yourself, [Ruth]. How do you expect to manage others?"

Such a problem among those who would be leaders is nothing new. The leaders of God's people in Micah's day had shown no self-discipline in shaping their lives after God's holy standards. These frauds even dared to use the Lord's name to support their agendas, claiming (as did Micah's critics in last week's study) that any threat of disaster or judgment should not be taken seriously. This problem could not go unconfronted.

Leadership is an important topic and receives significant attention in many churches today, as it should. While the New Testament is our primary guide in training and setting standards for church leaders, Old Testament prophets like Micah also have much wisdom to offer concerning leadership.

B. Lesson Background

Micah 3 begins with a verbal "grabbing by the lapel" to get the attention of the leaders of God's people. The prophet describes them as those "who hate good and love evil" (Micah 3:2), a direct contrast with another prophet's command to "hate evil, love good" (Amos 5:15).

Micah didn't stop there. He took his critique a step further, characterizing the leaders as vicious cannibals "who tear the skin from my people and the flesh from their bones; who eat my people's flesh" (Micah 3:2, 3). So savage were these individuals in their callous treatment of others that only a metaphor as gruesome as cannibalism would do.

Lest we become put off by such language or view it as limited to the world of the Old Testament, consider Paul's warning in Galatians 5:15: "If you bite and devour each other, watch out or you will be destroyed by each other." This warning was not addressed to church leaders only but to everyone in the churches in Galatia. Only God himself knows how many churches have been damaged, in some cases irreparably, by such cannibalism.

I. Corrupt Messengers
(MICAH 3:5-7)

A. Selfish Motives (v. 5)

5. This is what the LORD says:
"As for the prophets
    who lead my people astray,
they proclaim 'peace'
    if they have something to eat,
but prepare to wage war against anyone
    who refuses to feed them.

Like last week's lesson from Micah 2, today's text includes an exposure of false prophets, described here as those *who lead my people astray.* This is a sad indictment indeed. Such leaders assure their listeners that they have nothing to fear when in reality they are on a path to judgment. Those leaders prescribe bandages when major surgery is needed (compare Jeremiah 6:14).

What motivates these false prophets more than anything is their selfish desires. As long as *they have something to eat,* they will proclaim a message of peace. In other words, they are more than willing to speak a positive message that fails to hold people accountable for their sinful behavior if the price is right. But *anyone who refuses to feed them* (that is, the one who refuses to pay their price) is treated as the enemy; the false prophets *prepare to wage war against* them.

HOW TO SAY IT

Amos	*Ay*-mus.
Babylon	*Bab*-uh-lun.
Deuteronomy	Due-ter-*ahn*-uh-me.
Isaiah	Eye-*zay*-uh.
Jehoiakim	Jeh-*hoy*-uh-kim.
Jeremiah	Jair-uh-*my*-uh.
Micah	*My*-kuh.
Moresheth	*Mo*-resh-eth.

To such leaders, the prophetic office is nothing more than a source of income. They will do whatever they can do to increase that income. Their approach to ministry is a reversal of what Jesus will later teach and live by; these frauds have come "to be served" and not "to serve" (Matthew 20:28).

❧ *PROPHESYING FOR . . . WHAT?* ❧

I attended several graduate schools in pursuing advanced degrees, and one institution was a very liberal divinity school. Most of the faculty did not take the Bible literally about much of anything. Since I was studying in the field of church history, I was not directly influenced by the professors' views regarding Bible interpretation.

Some of those professors were regarded as experts in their field. But I soon came to realize it was just an academic exercise for them. They had no interest in applying the Bible to their own lives. I read a book written by one of these men that was actually a diary of his travels around Europe. He recorded his activities on many Sundays, but he never mentioned going to church. Teaching theology was a good vocation; it paid him well.

The prophets that Micah describes were like that. They didn't make waves by taking a chance that God's thoughts might disrupt their stream of income. "Peace!" was what the people wanted to hear, so that was the message delivered. We do well to keep in mind Paul's warning: "The time will come when people will not put up with sound doctrine. Instead, to suit their own desires, they will gather around them a great number of teachers to say what their itching ears want to hear" (2 Timothy 4:3).   —J. B. N.

B. Sure Doom (vv. 6, 7)

**6. "Therefore night will come over you,
without visions,
and darkness, without divination.
The sun will set for the prophets,
and the day will go dark for them.**

Micah describes the utter despair that awaits these false harbingers of hope. What lies ahead for them is far removed from the peace that they so glibly predict. Whatever means they use to obtain their messages—*visions, divination,* etc.—will all prove worthless.

┌───┐

What Do You Think?

How can we evaluate possible false prophets today without violating Jesus' prohibition on judging (Matthew 7:1)?

Talking Points for Your Discussion
- Bad vs. good fruit (Matthew 7:15-20)
- False vs. true-but-incomplete preaching (Acts 18:24-26)
- Bad vs. good motives (Philippians 1:15-18)
- Not on our team (Mark 9:38-41)
- Other

└───┘

It appears that Micah is saying that these false spokesmen have actually had visions or received messages of some kind thus far. We can recall that the magicians of Pharaoh were able to duplicate Moses' first two actions of plague by their "secret arts" (Exodus 7:22; 8:7). What this specifically involved is unknown. Some suggest that a Satanic element could have empowered the magicians to do what they did, but the Scriptures do not clearly indicate this. When the third plague (gnats) began, the magicians found themselves unable to duplicate it (8:18, 19).

From Micah's words in the verse before us, it is clear that whatever may be working for these false prophets will no longer be available in the future. Divination, being associated with the practices of the pagan nations surrounding Israel, is strictly forbidden by the Law of Moses (Deuteronomy 18:9-14). This is another reason to view the false prophets with skepticism; not only is the content of their message suspect but also their methods for obtaining that content.

┌───┐

What Do You Think?

How do false prophets and false teachers today compare and contrast with those in Micah's time regarding claimed sources for their messages? How do we handle these?

Talking Points for Your Discussion
- Supernatural source ("God told me," etc.)
- Nonsupernatural source (tradition, etc.)

└───┘

**7. "The seers will be ashamed
and the diviners disgraced.
They will all cover their faces
because there is no answer from God."**

The word *seers* implies the ability to foresee; however, there will be nothing for the false prophets to see, as the previous verse indicates. Darkness will be everywhere. In their humiliation, these ashamed *diviners . . . will all cover their faces.* They may claim to speak for God for the present, but a time is certainly coming when it is apparent to everyone that *there is no answer from God.* Isaiah speaks of a similar judgment in Isaiah 29:10.

II. Courageous Messenger
(MICAH 3:8-12)

A. Empowered by God (v. 8)

**8. But as for me, I am filled with power,
with the Spirit of the LORD,
and with justice and might,
to declare to Jacob his transgression,
to Israel his sin.**

The contrast between Micah and the false prophets is as clear as night and day! As they get no answer from God (v. 7), Micah can declare *I am filled with power, with the Spirit of the Lord.* The pronoun *I* is emphatic in the Hebrew text, as if to say, "*I,* as opposed to *they.*" While Micah's call is not described as are the calls of other prophets (Isaiah 6; Jeremiah 1; etc.), he leaves no doubt that his ministry illustrates Peter's description of "prophets, though human, spoke from God as they were carried along by the Holy Spirit" (2 Peter 1:21).

Micah's empowerment gives him the courage to do what the false prophets will never do: *declare to Jacob his transgression, and to Israel his sin.* Here we see the Hebrew fondness for expressing a single thought with parallel expressions. The patriarch *Jacob* had his name changed to *Israel* (Genesis 32:28), and *transgression* is another word for *sin*. Thus one grouping of people and set of actions is in view, not two (see also v. 9, next).

To speak in the name of God concerning *justice* means speaking openly about his just standards. This includes calling sin what God calls sin. The true prophet does not gloss over the severity of this reality just to gain a more receptive audience.

> **What Do You Think?**
> What is the right proportion between proclaiming God's grace and warning of his judgment?
> *Talking Points for Your Discussion*
> - Considering the practice of Jesus and the apostles
> - Considering factors internal to a church (needs of members, etc.)
> - Considering factors external to the church (cultural trends, etc.)
> - Other factors

❧ *You, on Retainer* ❧

C. G. Finney (1792–1875) was one of the great evangelists of the first half of nineteenth-century America. Initially a lawyer in Adams, New York, Finney eventually decided to search out the question of his salvation. He was uncertain about his spiritual condition even though he was active in a local church and sang in the choir.

His crisis of faith reached its boiling point in the autumn of 1821. In Finney's own words, "I was brought face to face with the question whether I would accept Christ as presented in the Gospel, or pursue a worldly course of life." A short time later, he sensed an inward voice that seemed to ask, "Will you accept it now, today?" His reply: "Yes; I will accept it today, or I will die in the attempt."

But the seeming rashness of the promise only increased Finney's inner turmoil. He was still uncertain. Having sought privacy in the nearby woods for prayer, he was ashamed that someone might find him praying. He yielded to the promises of God's Word that were flooding his mind

when he finally acknowledged the absurdity of his situation. Peaceful at last, he hastened back to his office, where a deacon of the church was waiting for him. The man had hired Finney to argue a case for him in court, but Finney told him, "I am sorry, but I have received a retainer from the Lord Jesus Christ to plead his case, and I cannot plead yours."

Micah too had "received a retainer from the Lord"; thus Micah could represent no "client" but that one. Should the same be true of us?—J. B. N.

B. Exposing Sinful Acts (vv. 9-11)
9. Hear this, you leaders of Jacob,
 you rulers of Israel,
who despise justice
 and distort all that is right;

Having just described his ministry as one that declares the sin of God's people, Micah proceeds to expose that sin, especially the sin of the leadership. The language of this verse is similar to that found at the beginning of the chapter, also addressed to the *leaders* or *rulers* of the people (Micah 3:1). There the prophet asks, "Should you not embrace justice?" These leaders in fact do not promote justice. They hate it! By their actions they *distort all that is right*. They twist what God has declared to be straight or true into something crooked. Isaiah pronounces "woe" on such as these, who "call evil good and good evil" (Isaiah 5:20).

10. . . . who build Zion with bloodshed,
 and Jerusalem with wickedness.

Micah turns his attention to what is happening specifically in the capital city of Judah. Some see mention of *Zion* and *Jerusalem* as another instance of Hebrew parallelism, as in verses 8, 9, just considered. Others see a slight distinction, with Zion referring to the older part of Jerusalem that King David improved (2 Samuel 5:9). Either way, the tragedy here is quite painful to consider. In the very city that is associated with the man after God's own heart (Acts 13:22), the rulers' hearts are about as far from God as possible. They build the city *with bloodshed* and *with wickedness*.

Micah's words bring to mind Jeremiah's later indictment of King Jehoiakim of Judah: "Woe to him who builds his palace by unrighteousness, his upper rooms by injustice, making his own people work for nothing, not paying them for their labor" (Jeremiah 22:13). Jehoiakim will rule in Judah more than 100 years after Micah's ministry. The fact that such corrupt, ungodly leadership continues to plague God's people does nothing to delay the destruction of Jerusalem in 586 BC. Those who build with the methods highlighted by Micah are building structures doomed to collapse.

11. Her leaders judge for a bribe,
her priests teach for a price,
and her prophets tell fortunes for money.
Yet they look for the LORD's support and say,
"Is not the LORD among us?
No disaster will come upon us."

A broad indictment of both civil and religious leadership is in view in the condemnation of the *leaders,* the *priests,* and the *prophets.* One would hope that the latter at least would be sensitive to God's will! But they compromise his righteous standards instead of modeling them. They are in it *for money.* The phrase "follow the money trail" is often cynically used today to explain how certain decisions in business, politics, etc., are made. How sad when this is the case among God's people! Where is the trail of sacrificial service to follow?

An important aspect of the leaders' flawed mind-set is their self-deluding claim of God's presence among them as they participate in the disgusting practices noted here. When these leaders brashly affirm that *no disaster will come upon us,* they are referring to a physical evil, such as the destruction prophesied by Micah (compare Jeremiah 23:16, 17), rather than a moral evil. A deadly and deadening complacency sets in when such twisted thinking characterizes the leaders of God's people. The nation's future is bleak indeed.

> **What Do You Think?**
> How does complacency manifest itself in the church today? How do we guard against this?
> *Talking Points for Your Discussion*
> - Amos 6:1
> - Obadiah 3
> - 1 Corinthians 10:12
> - Revelation 2:4, 5; 3:2, 3
> - Other

C. Expecting Judgment (v. 12)

12. Therefore because of you,
Zion will be plowed like a field,
Jerusalem will become a heap of rubble,
the temple hill a mound overgrown
with thickets.

The leaders' reprehensible conduct is cited by Micah as the reason for the ominous judgment that lies ahead. Zion, "the joy of the whole earth" and "the city of the Great King" (Psalm 48:2), *will be plowed like a field.* Areas where crops are to be planted must first be cleared of debris; the picture is thus one of total destruction as the city of *Jerusalem will become a heap of rubble.*

The designation *the temple hill* refers to the place where the temple is located; this means, naturally, that the forthcoming destruction of Jerusalem also will include that structure. Describing this hill as *a mound overgrown with thickets* brings to mind the height of overgrown thorns or bramble bushes found within a forest. In any case, that which awaits Jerusalem is similar to what Samaria, capital of the northern kingdom, experiences first (Micah 1:6, 7).

It is worth noting that this verse will be quoted in Jerusalem some 100 years in the future. When a mob clamors for Jeremiah's execution, some elders step forward and remind everyone what "Micah of Moresheth prophesied in the days of Hezekiah king of Judah" (Jeremiah 26:8-19). They proceed to quote Micah 3:12 and note that Hezekiah did not put Micah to death for his prediction of doom. Instead, Hezekiah feared the Lord, sought his favor, and the city was spared. The implied plea is to heed Jeremiah as Hezekiah heeded Micah.

Whatever change of heart is to be experienced on that future occasion will be only temporary. In time, the Babylonians will have their way—or more accurately, God's way—with the temple and the city. God's promise of judgment issued through Micah and Jeremiah will come true.

Conclusion
A. Leaders in Society

Micah's words about corrupt, deficient leadership can bring to mind troubling applications to today's society. We see evidence of corruption almost daily on every level—locally, statewide, nationally, and internationally—and in many areas (church, school, and workplace, etc.). How can we as followers of Jesus make a difference? Where do we start? Three suggestions can be offered.

First, *pray*. Paul's instructions to Timothy is the model: "I urge, then, first of all, that petitions, prayers, intercession and thanksgiving be made for all people—for kings and all those in authority, that we may live peaceful and quiet lives in all godliness and holiness" (1 Timothy 2:1, 2). Paul wrote in a time of corruption among government officials. These included the evil Roman emperor Nero, who was likely in power when Paul wrote his letter to Timothy. Even so, Paul encouraged prayer for all in authority that we as Christians may be able to fulfill our God-appointed ministry of living lives pleasing to him. Such lives can witness to others of God's grace and generate questions from those who want to know more about "the reason for the hope that [we] have" (1 Peter 3:15).

Second, *work with them*. It is all too easy to criticize leaders instead of finding creative, constructive ways to build relationships and work with them without compromising Christian principles. Read Daniel 1 and observe how that man and his friends determined a way, without becoming belligerent or obnoxious in the process of doing so, to avoid the king's decree about what food to eat, (Daniel 1:8-16). There is indeed a time to confront leaders who are in the wrong (Daniel 3:16-18; Acts 4:19; 5:29). Knowing when to cooperate and when to confront requires discernment.

Third, *become one of them*. Serving in positions of leadership on a local, state, or national level is not the calling for everyone. But it can be a ministry that some are equipped to carry out to God's glory. Those who see themselves as called to this arena should consider prayerfully what God is leading them to do. Daniel was in a position of very high authority while on foreign soil in Babylon, and yet he maintained a record of unquestioned integrity during his service (Daniel 6:4).

Who will "dare to be a Daniel" today?

B. Leaders in the Church

Consider how the above three suggestions also apply within the church. First, *pray*. If Paul realized the need to request prayers on his behalf, how much more do church leaders in the twenty-first century need prayers as well! They are often faced with very challenging situations. Do you pray regularly for them in that regard? What about those who lead various church-related ministries, such as Bible colleges and Christian service camps?

Second, *work with them*. It is easy to stay on the sidelines and complain about mistakes or oversights by church leaders. Perhaps we can volunteer our services in a particular area of church life where help is needed (see Hebrews 13:17).

Third, *become one of them*. Paul tells Timothy, "Whoever aspires to be an overseer [elder] desires a noble task" (1 Timothy 3:1). Do you have the desire or passion to pursue leadership of the Lord's people? It is indeed a high calling to pursue—challenging but eternally rewarding.

C. Prayer

Father, in a time when your people starve for leadership, use us in ways that bless and empower your church to speak the prophetic voice of your Word anew. In Jesus' name, amen.

D. Thought to Remember

True leadership is not taking control but giving control—to the Lord.

I AM FULL OF POWER BY THE SPIRIT OF THE LORD, AND OF JUDGMENT, AND OF MIGHT, TO DECLARE UNTO JACOB HIS TRANSGRESSION, AND TO ISRAEL HIS SIN. — MICAH 3:8

Visual for Lesson 6. *Point to this visual as you ask, "How does our mission to confront a sinful culture compare and contrast with that of Micah's?"*

INVOLVEMENT LEARNING

Enhance your lesson with NIV® *Bible Student (from your curriculum supplier) and the reproducible activity page (at www.standardlesson.com or in the back of the* NIV® *Standard Lesson Commentary Deluxe Edition).*

Into the Lesson

Come to class wearing a wild tie or a gaudy piece of costume jewelry. Talk with enthusiasm about what a great buy it was. Ask learners what they think of it. After several comments say, "In attempting to spare my feelings, some people may not tell me what they *really* think. So, give me your honest opinion." After several comments, say, "Today we're going to learn about some false prophets who told the people what they wanted to hear. But Micah didn't pull his punches and had some harsh truths to tell these corrupt leaders."

Into the Word

Ask a skillful reader to prepare in advance to read Micah 3:5-12 aloud in the manner of a fire-and-brimstone preacher. Before the reading, say to the class, "Imagine that you were one of the false prophets or corrupt leaders during Micah's day. You've been deceiving the people and raking in money without any punishment from the Lord. What would be your reaction to the following message from Micah?" After the passage is "preached," pause for responses.

Form groups of four or five. Each group is to select someone to be "Micah," who will answer interview questions. Distribute handouts that list the following questions; each group's "Micah" should draw on the verse reference noted after each question to state the response in different words but with the same intent. A. "Micah, why are you so upset with the false prophets?" *(v. 5)*; B. "How is the status of the false prophets going to change?" *(vv. 6, 7)*; C. "In what ways are you a different kind of prophet from the false ones?" *(v. 8a)*; D. "What message do you have the courage to deliver that the false prophets do not?" *(v. 8b)*; E. "Amos says we are to 'hate evil, love good.' How have the Israelite leaders acted on that imperative?" *(vv. 9, 10)*; F. "What are some ways the corrupt leaders demonstrate their greed?"

(v. 11); G. "What do you mean by the colorful phrases you use to describe the coming destruction of Zion, etc.?" *(v. 12)*.

After a time for questions and responses within the groups, pose the first question to the class as a whole and invite one "Micah" to offer a response. Do the same for each succeeding question, rotating among "Micahs" for responses. Invite reactions.

Alternative. Distribute copies of the "What Did Micah Say?" activity from the reproducible page, which you can download. Have learners work in pairs to complete the exercise as indicated. Allow time for whole-class discussion of answers.

Conclude either activity by leading a discussion on the temptations of greedy selfishness faced by leaders then and now. Pose questions such as these: 1. What character flaws cause prophets or preachers to turn from serving God to serving themselves? 2. Why do leaders abandon their intended role of doing good on behalf of people in order to find ways to exploit them?

Into Life

Assist your learners in planning a worship service to honor and pray for a group of leaders from your congregation. First, discuss which group of leaders they would like to honor (ministerial staff, elders and deacons, Sunday school teachers, youth workers, etc.). Then either plan the service together as a class or assign different aspects of the service to small groups. Assignments can include finding Scriptures about leadership, selecting songs for the service, writing prayers for the leaders, preparing a message of appreciation, selecting commemorative gifts, etc. Finally, present the plan to the appropriate church leaders (not the ones to be honored) for approval.

Option. Distribute copies of the "What Will You Say?" activity from the reproducible page. Allow three minutes of silent reflection for learners to complete individually.

WHAT THE LORD REQUIRES

DEVOTIONAL READING: Deuteronomy 10:12-22
BACKGROUND SCRIPTURE: Micah 6

MICAH 6:3-8

3 "My people, what have I done to you?
   How have I burdened you? Answer me.
4 I brought you up out of Egypt
   and redeemed you from the land of
      slavery.
I sent Moses to lead you,
   also Aaron and Miriam.
5 My people, remember
   what Balak king of Moab plotted
   and what Balaam son of Beor answered.
Remember your journey from Shittim to
      Gilgal,
   that you may know the righteous acts of
      the LORD."
6 With what shall I come before the LORD
   and bow down before the exalted God?
Shall I come before him with burnt offerings,
   with calves a year old?
7 Will the LORD be pleased with thousands
      of rams,
   with ten thousand rivers of olive oil?
Shall I offer my firstborn for my transgression,
   the fruit of my body for the sin of my
      soul?

8 He has shown you, O mortal, what is good.
   And what does the LORD require of you?
To act justly and to love mercy
   and to walk humbly with your God.

KEY VERSE

He has shown you, O mortal, what is good. And what does the LORD require of you? To act justly and to love mercy and to walk humbly with your God. —**Micah 6:8**

GOD'S PROPHETS DEMAND JUSTICE

Unit 2: Micah Calls for Justice Among Unjust People

LESSONS 5–8

LESSON AIMS

After participating in this lesson, each learner will be able to:

1. Tell what God reminds his people that He did for them and the response he requires.

2. Give examples of how the three criteria of a God-honoring life of Micah 6:8 are emphasized elsewhere in Scripture.

3. Identify his or her weakest area in acting justly, loving mercy, or walking humbly, and make a plan for change.

LESSON OUTLINE

Introduction

A. More Than Spectators

Christian author Howard Hendricks (1924–2013) used to tell a story about Bud Wilkinson, who was the head football coach at the University of Oklahoma from 1947 to 1963. On one occasion, Wilkinson was in a certain city giving a series of lectures on physical fitness. During an interview, a reporter asked, "Mr. Wilkinson, what would you say is the contribution of football to physical fitness?" The reporter expected a rather lengthy answer, but Wilkinson's reply was surprisingly brief: "Absolutely nothing."

The reporter, somewhat taken aback, responded, "Would you care to elaborate on that?" "Certainly," the coach said. "I define football as 22 men on the field who desperately need rest and 50,000 people in the stands who desperately need exercise."

Today's study is a challenge to be more than spectators—to know what God requires of us all. Our task is to "get out on the field" and do it. But it is easy to drift into the thinking that a calling from God applies only to those in specialized Christian service (preachers, missionaries, etc.). The fact is that all God's people are called to be salt and light in being his instruments of bringing gospel hope to a fallen world (Matthew 5:13-16). It wasn't only Christian leaders whom Paul addressed when he wrote "I urge you to live a life worthy of the calling you have received" (Ephesians 4:1).

Likewise, the calling God issued to his people in Old Testament times was not just to leaders. His covenant addressed all the Israelites as "a kingdom of priests and a holy nation" (Exodus 19:6). Where they failed to be so is our warning.

B. Lesson Background

The previous study concluded with an ominous prophecy of Jerusalem's demise (Micah 3:12). Lest one think that Micah's message was nothing but gloom and doom, the very next verse promised that "the mountain of the Lord's temple," for which destruction was predicted and promised, "will be established as the highest of the mountains; . . . and peoples will stream to it" (4:1).

Micah's prediction (also reflected in Isaiah 2:1-4) is best understood to foreshadow the proclamation of the gospel that began in Jerusalem on the Day of Pentecost (Acts 2) and subsequently to be taken "to the ends of the earth" (Acts 1:8).

Such positive glimpses in the book of Micah are interspersed with painfully honest evaluations of the crisis then engulfing God's people. In a powerful word-picture, the people are told that "pain seizes you like that of a woman in labor" (Micah 4:9). That was a figurative, poignant reminder that pain as a consequence of the first sin (Genesis 3:16) is not limited to women in literal childbirth. Nations, even God's chosen people, can experience similar pains (compare Romans 8:22).

The source of the crisis of Micah's day—the reason why God's people were feeling the "pain" —was not external, but internal. Despite all of the "-ites" that posed threats periodically (Canaanites, etc.), the people who brought the most misery to the Israelites were the Israelites themselves! They were their own worst enemy.

Just before today's text, the Lord began confronting his people as though he were a prosecutor in a courtroom. He challenged the people to plead their case "before the mountains; let the hills hear what you have to say" (Micah 6:1, 2). This language is rooted in the "witness language" used by Moses in Deuteronomy 30:19. The witnesses of Heaven, earth, the mountains, etc., had remained in place since the time of that great leader. Thus they have watched the history of the Israelites through the years. They were commanded in Micah 6:2 to "hear" what the Lord had to say about his people and to verify whether his assessment of them was accurate.

I. The Lord Summons
(MICAH 6:3-5)
A. Challenging the People (v. 3)
3. "My people, what have I done to you? How have I burdened you? Answer me.

The Lord begins his "accusation" (Micah 6:2) against his people in a tender manner, addressing them here as *my people.* These same people have "risen up like an enemy" against the Lord (2:8, lesson 5).

In this light, the Lord asks the two questions we see here. Is there something he has done to cause them to turn against him? Have his expectations been oppressive in some way? A noun form of the Hebrew verb translated *burdened* is used in Numbers 20:14 of Israel's "hardships" during their oppression as slaves in Egypt. Is the Lord guilty of treating his people as they were treated in Egypt?

❧ *"WHAT DID WE DO WRONG?"* ❧

So many parents have asked themselves that very question! It is often prompted by a child's behavior that violates the standards by which the parents have nurtured him or her. The problem behavior may present itself in adolescence, but often it does so after the child has become an adult. Sometimes the son or daughter is intentionally rejecting the parents' values. The rejection may be seen in substance abuse, criminal activity, or turning away from the parents' faith.

The question *What did we do wrong?* is frequently unanswerable. There may be no one action or attitude of the parents that has triggered the problematic behavior. Or there may be many, of which the parents are unaware! Even if the parents know that the question is unanswerable, they may ask it anyway.

In the case of the Israelites, however, the heavenly Father's question "What have I done to you?" is answerable! But God does not ask it because he lacks information. He asks the question for the

HOW TO SAY IT

Aaron	*Air*-un.
Balak	*Bay*-lack.
Beor	*Be*-or.
Canaan	*Kay*-nun.
Egypt	*Ee*-jipt.
Gilgal	*Gil*-gal (*G* as in *get*).
Israelites	*Iz*-ray-el-ites.
Miriam	*Meer*-ee-um.
Micah	*My*-kuh.
Moab	*Mo*-ab.
Shittim	Shih-*teem*.
Sinai	*Sigh*-nye or *Sigh*-nay-eye.

benefit of the Israelites, and the expected answer of *nothing* makes the question an accusation. God had not failed them. On the contrary, he had blessed them abundantly—which made their disrespect all the more ironic! The knowledge that we are all wayward children of God may help us deal productively with our own children, be they sons and daughters of the flesh or in the faith (1 Timothy 1:2).   —C. R. B.

B. Charting History (vv. 4, 5)

4. "I brought you up out of Egypt
and redeemed you from the land of
slavery.
I sent Moses to lead you,
also Aaron and Miriam.

A review of history reveals that the Lord has not "burdened" the Israelites at all! On the contrary, he has removed their burdens by redeeming them *from the land of slavery* in Egypt. Being redeemed implies a ransom's having been paid to secure the people's freedom. That ransom (the death of the Egyptian firstborn) is what is to be commemorated by the yearly celebration of the Passover (Exodus 12:14-17). Has Micah's audience forgotten this?

What Do You Think?

What examples can you offer of God's protection or provision for you in critical times? Why is it important to reflect on these periodically?

Talking Points for Your Discussion
- Times of physical protection or provision
- Times of spiritual protection or provision
- Times of emotional protection or provision

The Lord also highlights *Moses, Aaron,* and *Miriam* as the instruments of his deliverance. They were not perfect; each had flaws. Moses acted rashly at times (Exodus 2:11, 12; Numbers 20:2-12). Aaron yielded to pressure and built the golden calf at Mount Sinai (Exodus 32:1-4). Miriam (along with Aaron) grumbled at one point against Moses, voicing jealousy at his being given prominence (Numbers 12:1, 2). But overall they had served the Lord and his people faithfully some 700 years previously. Their faithful service does not describe the leaders in Micah's day (see last week's study).

5. "My people, remember
what Balak king of Moab plotted
and what Balaam son of Beor answered.
Remember your journey from Shittim to
Gilgal,
that you may know the righteous acts of
the LORD."

The Lord offers more examples of his faithfulness. The incident noted is in Numbers 22–24. *Balak king of Moab* had observed the Israelites on their way to the promised land. Thinking them to be a threat to his kingdom, he contracted for the services of *Balaam son of Beor* to curse the Israelites. But Balaam was guided by the Lord to bless the people instead. This illustrates the Lord's commitment to protect his people from their enemies.

The phrase *from Shittim to Gilgal* highlights something else for the people to remember. Shittim was the final place where the Israelites camped east of the Jordan River before crossing over into Canaan (Joshua 3:1); Gilgal was where the people camped after the crossing (4:19). Between the two locations was where the Lord miraculously parted the river, which was at flood stage. This allowed the people to cross on dry land (3:14-17).

The purpose of this history lesson is so that Micah's audience *may know the righteous acts of the Lord.* Although the people in Micah's day view themselves as having been "burdened" by the Lord's treatment of them (Micah 6:3; compare Malachi 1:13), the Lord's track record paints a much different picture. It is he who has been righteous, not they. Their record, in contrast, is marked with continual failure to obey the Lord. It is they who have burdened him often with their sin and rebellion (compare Isaiah 43:22-24). Even so, God has demonstrated extraordinary patience.

No one in Micah's audience had been brought up out of Egypt and redeemed from slavery personally. None had been led by Moses, Aaron, and Miriam, nor had journeyed from Shittim to Gilgal. But these acts and events are all a part of Israelite history, and the God who provided all that guidance and blessing is now recalled by Micah as still being the God of Israel. No other nation has a history as theirs because no other nation's socalled gods can do the mighty acts that the only real God has done. To forget that glorious past is a sure path to a very inglorious future.

God's righteous acts should inspire a much stronger response of gratitude and obedience than the people have demonstrated to this point. Instead, they seem to think of God as a taskmaster who has mistreated them, an attitude that elicits God's questions of verse 3. The problem, however, does not lie with the Lord; it lies with the people. The need for the people to take a good, hard look at themselves leads to the next portion of our text.

What Do You Think?

Which biblical instances of God's provision for and presence with his people are particularly meaningful to you right now? Why is that?

Talking Points for Your Discussion

- Provision of physical sustenance
- Provision of rescue from enemies
- Provision of divine guidance
- Other

II. The People Speak
(Micah 6:6-8)
A. Pivotal Question (v. 6a)
6a. With what shall I come before the Lord and bow down before the exalted God?

It is time for the people to respond to the Lord's charges. Micah depicts the Lord as questioning the people in verse 3; here the people are pictured as asking questions of themselves. The *I* may refer to Micah himself as one of the respondents, asking the questions raised here and in the verse that follows. The issue is vital: What does God really want from those who should desire to please him?

What Do You Think?

What are ways for us to prepare ourselves to "come before the Lord" in worship? What happens if such preparation is neglected?

Talking Points for Your Discussion

- Negatives to eliminate (Matthew 5:23; 1 Corinthians 11:17-34; etc.)
- Positives to accentuate (Romans 12:1; 1 Corinthians 14:40; etc.)

B. Possible Answers (vv. 6b, 7)
6b. Shall I come before him with burnt offerings, with calves a year old?

With a rhetorical question, the first answer explored is that one should come before the Lord *with burnt offerings*. Such are to be made each morning and evening for all Israel (Exodus 29:38-43; Numbers 28:1-8). The requirement daily is "two lambs a year old without defect" (Numbers 28:3). *Calves a year old* would be even more valuable.

Furthermore, two burnt offerings are to be brought on each Sabbath (Numbers 28:9, 10), and additional burnt offerings are to be made on the special feast days (28:11–29:40). Any Israelite can bring a burnt offering as an expression of devotion to the Lord (Leviticus 1:1-3).

Burnt offerings are the most basic of the offerings commanded by the Lord, the requirements of which are found in Leviticus 1. Therefore it is quite natural for Israelites to think along this line.

7. Will the Lord be pleased with thousands of rams, with ten thousand rivers of olive oil? Shall I offer my firstborn for my transgression, the fruit of my body for the sin of my soul?

The questions continue as offerings of increasing quantity are considered. Is God impressed with numbers? What about *thousands of rams* or even *ten thousand rivers of olive oil*? Such oil accompanies certain offerings (Exodus 29:1, 2; Leviticus 2:1).

Micah reaches the climax of the proposals by putting forth, in typical Hebrew parallelism, a most radical idea: *shall I offer my firstborn for my transgression, the fruit of my body for the sin of my soul?* The horrific practice of child sacrifice is a part of various pagan religions in antiquity. The Old Testament describes the practice as part of the worship of at least two pagan deities (see Leviticus 18:21; 2 Kings 23:10; Jeremiah 19:5; 32:35; etc.). Such a practice is strictly forbidden by God (Deuteronomy 12:31; 18:10), so the proposal here is hypothetical.

After raising these questions, perhaps Micah pauses to let his audience reflect on the matter. What does God really want? The answer is found in the next verse.

C. Plain Response (v. 8)

8. He has shown you, O mortal, what is good. And what does the LORD require of you? To act justly and to love mercy and to walk humbly with your God.

There is no need to speculate about what pleases the Lord. In fact, Micah's audience already knows the answer, since he has shown *you, O mortal, what is good*. People often ask questions about God or his will even though the answer they seek is already revealed in his Word. The problem is that people do not want to consult that Word, or they have preconceived notions that leave them unwilling to investigate what the Word of God really says.

Among Micah's audience, the all-too-common view is that what the Lord desires most of all are the various sacrifices and offerings. Hasn't God specifically stated in the Law of Moses that no one is to come before him empty-handed (Exodus 23:15)? Thus their initial answer to the questions posed beginning with verse 6 includes things within that frame of reference. But these are not (and never have been) the primary requirement from God's people.

Micah's statement of what God ultimately desires is yet today one of the most compelling in all of Scripture: *to act justly and to love mercy and to walk humbly with your God.* (Presidents Harding and Carter used this passage in taking their oaths of office.) The question in verse 6 is posed as if by an individual; the correct answer here addresses the individual. The three qualities mentioned are closely related and are like the legs of a tripod: if one is removed, the stand collapses.

❧ THE COMMON GOOD ❧

"Whatever Happened to the 'Common Good'?" was the title of an article that surprised many people. The article was surprising because of where it appeared: *Time* magazine (April 4, 2013), which is not a religious publication.

Tracing the idea of the *common good* back to the early days of Christianity (and Judaism before that), author Jim Wallis quotes John Chrysostom (lived about AD 347–407): "This is the rule of most perfect Christianity . . . the seeking of the **common good** . . . for nothing can so make a person an imitator of Christ as caring for his neighbors" (emphasis of Wallis). Wallis contends that the problems that beset our society, politically polarized as it is, can be solved by a recommitment to this value.

The *common good* is an idea that runs throughout Scripture. Jesus spoke of it (see Matthew 5:43-45; 22:39; 25:34-40). It's what Micah and other prophets were talking about. Just think: How much better would this world be if we all made it the rule of our lives to seek the common good of justice for neighbors as we extend loving mercy to them while conducting ourselves humbly before God? What specific steps would it take for this to become the practice of your life?   —C. R. B.

Before digging deeper into Micah's answer, we should observe that the requirement here should not be used to justify "salvation by works." The issue under discussion is not salvation; Micah is not addressing the question, "What must I do to be saved?" The issue, rather, is how God's covenant people must conduct themselves in a way that is pleasing to God. Micah's audience is wrong to think that their offerings and rituals alone will please God; Christians today who think the same about their "Sunday only" acts of worship are just as misguided.

To both *act justly* and *love mercy* may appear to be opposite ideas. This is because of the common association of *justice* with *judgment*. At the risk

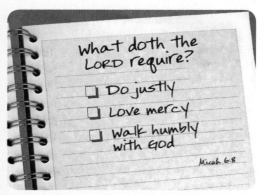

Visual for Lesson 7. *Point to this visual as you ask, "In which of these three areas do you see Christians needing to improve the most? Why?"*

of oversimplification, justice may be thought of as treating people just as God would treat them, and that includes extending mercy. Micah's words address both one's actions (*act justly*) and motivation (*love mercy*). The key to understanding justice and mercy lies in a relationship with God, and that's where the challenge to *walk humbly with* him comes in. Apart from such a walk, true justice and mercy are unattainable.

Many view the Old Testament as concerned primarily with one's outward actions, especially sacrifices and rituals, with little concern for one's heart or motivation. Nothing could be further from the truth! Micah's point is that God has never demanded merely sacrifices, rituals, or offerings. Without the underlying principles of justice, mercy, and humility before God, all acts of worship are in fact devoid of meaning in God's sight and are an offense to him. To use Amos's exceptionally candid language, "I hate, I despise your religious festivals; your assemblies are a stench to me" (Amos 5:21, lesson 2). Amos then calls for righteous living (5:24), just as Micah does.

Isaiah is equally outspoken in voicing God's displeasure with acts of worship that do not translate into a daily life of service: "Your New Moon feasts and your appointed festivals I hate with all my being" (Isaiah 1:14). The prophet then gives the Lord's remedy: "Wash and make yourselves clean. . . . Stop doing wrong. Learn to do right; seek justice. Defend the oppressed. Take up the cause of the fatherless; plead the case of the widow" (1:16, 17). Centuries later, Jesus will have something important to say in this area as well (Matthew 23:23; compare Mark 12:32, 33).

> **What Do You Think?**
> How do the problems Micah addresses compare and contrast with those that Jesus confronted the Pharisees about? Why is this question important for today's church?
> *Talking Points for Your Discussion*
> - Concerning mercy in relation to sacrifice
> - Concerning association with "sinners"
> - Concerning the elevation of tradition over Scripture

It isn't that Micah's audience does not have access to the knowledge of what God wants. They *do* have that knowledge—they have simply chosen to ignore it. Could the same be said of us? While it is true that we are under the new covenant, the essentials of pleasing God remain the same for us as they were in Micah's day.

> **What Do You Think?**
> How can we improve in the areas that Micah addresses? What will be our biggest obstacles in doing so?
> *Talking Points for Your Discussion*
> - Concerning issues of attitude
> - Concerning issues of action
> - Concerning issues of speech

Conclusion
A. Start Here

A television commercial from a few years ago featured a person wondering about how to prepare for retirement. As he pondered, a green pathway appeared magically on the ground. All he had to do was follow it! The dilemma was solved in about 15 seconds of commercial air time!

"What does the Lord require of you?" asks Micah in today's text. His answer, in essence, is this: *You know the answer—God has already shown it to you. Just follow the path of his revealed truth.* It bears repeating that many seek to know God's will in certain areas even though his answer is already available—if they would only take the time to look into his Word.

The oft-quoted advice is still true: "When all else fails, read the instructions"—especially when those instructions come from God!

B. Prayer

Father, may the challenges of Micah 6:8 be more than just a slogan. As we take them to heart, may we bring them to life daily. In Jesus' name, amen.

C. Thought to Remember
To be open to God's desires,
open his Word.

INVOLVEMENT LEARNING

Enhance your lesson with NIV® Bible Student (from your curriculum supplier) and the reproducible activity page (at www.standardlesson.com or in the back of the NIV® Standard Lesson Commentary Deluxe Edition).

Into the Lesson

Divide the class into two groups, designate them *Smith Family* and *Jones Family,* and tell them that they will play a modified version of the TV game show *Family Feud.* Instruct each side to pick a spokesperson. Say that 100 people were *not* interviewed, and answers were chosen on an "it seems right" basis. A family scores a point by getting all answers right before guessing wrong three times. After three wrong guesses, the other family gets one chance to steal the point by providing one correct response for the one or more answers remaining.

To the Smith family say, "Name the top three requirements to attend a prestigious college." The responses you are looking for are (1) a letter of acceptance, (2) a high SAT score, (3) lots of money. Then say to the Jones family, "Name the top three requirements to be the evening news anchor." Look for some form of these answers: (1) physically attractive, (2) good speaking voice, (3) ability to read from a teleprompter.

Lead into the lesson by saying, "While the answers we came up with may or may not be the most important requirements in the situations mentioned, we will learn from Micah three expectations that God has for his people for life."

Into the Word

Write the following on the board: A. What has God not done according to Micah 6:3? B. What has God done according to Micah 6:4, 5? C. What is secondary to God according to Micah 6:6, 7? D. What is primary for God according to Micah 6:8? (*Option:* reproduce the questions on handouts.) Lead the class in discussing the answers, making sure to have the text read aloud. This can be a small-group exercise for larger classes, with each group being assigned all four questions.

Initial responses should be along these lines: A. *God had not given the Israelites any reason to complain.* B. *God delivered the Israelites from bondage*

in Egypt, provided leaders for the journey ahead, and caused Balaam to bless them. C. *Material offerings are secondary to God.* D. *To act justly, love mercy, and walk humbly are primary for God.* Use the commentary to help learners push deeper in each case—beyond the bare facts of what did or did not happen and what should or should not happen.

Option. Say, "As just seen, God reminded the people that they had no reason to complain after all the things he had done for them. But rather than spelling out his past deliverance miracles and provisions in detail, God used various summary phrases to get the people to ponder their history. Let's see if we can recognize the references of those summary phrases." Distribute copies of the "Remembering History" activity from the reproducible page, which you can download. Allow two minutes for learners to work individually.

Into Life

Draw on the board three columns having the following headings, one each: *Act Justly / Love Mercy / Walk Humbly.* Distribute 12 index cards that have the following references, one per card: A. Exodus 23:1, 2; B. Proverbs 16:19; C. Proverbs 18:5; D. Proverbs 29:23; E. Isaiah 1:17; F. Jeremiah 21:12; G. Matthew 5:7; H. Matthew 6:14; I. Luke 14:11; J. Ephesians 4:32; K. Philippians 2:3; L. James 4:6. (If you have fewer than 12 learners, some will end up with more than one card.)

Instruct: "There are many places in the Bible where we are told what God requires. Look up your Scripture and decide which of the three columns it best fits." Have each learner (1) read his or her card(s), (2) affix it to the board in the correct column, and (3) suggest a modern-day application. (*Anticipated responses: Act Justly–A, C, E, F; Love Mercy–G, H, J; Walk Humbly–B, D, I, K, L.*)

Alternative. Distribute copies of the "Just, Merciful, or Humble?" activity from the reproducible page. Have learners complete it as indicated.

GOD'S MATCHLESS MERCY

DEVOTIONAL READING: Psalm 13
BACKGROUND SCRIPTURE: Micah 7:11-20

MICAH 7:14-20

¹⁴ Shepherd your people with your staff,
    the flock of your inheritance,
which lives by itself in a forest,
    in fertile pasturelands.
Let them feed in Bashan and Gilead
    as in days long ago.
¹⁵ "As in the days when you came out of
        Egypt,
    I will show them my wonders."
¹⁶ Nations will see and be ashamed,
    deprived of all their power.
They will put their hands over their mouths
    and their ears will become deaf.
¹⁷ They will lick dust like a snake,
    like creatures that crawl on the ground.
They will come trembling out of their dens;
    they will turn in fear to the LORD our
        God
    and will be afraid of you.
¹⁸ Who is a God like you,
    who pardons sin and forgives the
        transgression
    of the remnant of his inheritance?
You do not stay angry forever
    but delight to show mercy.

¹⁹ You will again have compassion on us;
    you will tread our sins underfoot
    and hurl all our iniquities into the
        depths of the sea.
²⁰ You will be faithful to Jacob,
    and show love to Abraham,
as you pledged on oath to our ancestors
    in days long ago.

KEY VERSE

Who is a God like you, who pardons sin and forgives the transgression of the remnant of his inheritance?
You do not stay angry forever but delight to show mercy. —**Micah 7:18**

GOD'S PROPHETS DEMAND JUSTICE

Unit 2: Micah Calls for Justice Among Unjust People

LESSONS 5–8

LESSON AIMS

After participating in this lesson, each learner will be able to:

1. List some elements of hope for God's people.

2. Rewrite the message of hope using contemporary, nonagrarian language.

3. Write a prayer of thanks to the Lord for Micah's powerful closing words.

LESSON OUTLINE

Introduction
  A. A Matchless Gift
  B. Lesson Background
I. Israel's Shepherd (MICAH 7:14-17)
  A. Helping His People (vv. 14, 15)
    Longing for the "Good Ol' Days"?
  B. Humbling the Nations (vv. 16, 17)
II. Israel's Savior (MICAH 7:18-20)
  A. Filled with Compassion (vv. 18, 19)
  B. Faithful to His Word (v. 20)
    God's Faithfulness and Societal Decay
Conclusion
  A. "Do It Again, Lord!"
  B. Prayer
  C. Thought to Remember

Introduction

A. A Matchless Gift

During the summer of 2012, a Hall of Fame broadcaster for a major league baseball team helped raise $50,000 for the team's Community Fund. A well-known actor, becoming aware of this, then pledged to match that gift personally. Part of the fund's function is to provide opportunities to children with disabilities and to underwrite expenses for inner-city baseball teams. Fans applauded the actor for his generous match.

Generous giving can indeed inspire equally generous, matching giving on a human level. But attempting to match what God has given us is an exercise in futility. The blessings of God, those of the cross and empty tomb of Jesus, can in no way be matched. Paul's declaration "Thanks be to God for his indescribable gift!" (2 Corinthians 9:15) points right to the idea of *matchless*. The Old Testament prophets did not have the advantage of seeing the work of Christ as an accomplished fact of history. Nevertheless, they understood the *matchless* concept regarding God's blessings.

B. Lesson Background

Today's lesson concludes our unit of studies from the Old Testament prophet Micah. The seventh and final chapter of his book, from which today's text comes, presents an interesting mix of prayers and promises from that prophet.

The part of this chapter that comes just before today's lesson text begins on a very distressing note. Micah cried "What misery is mine!" as he seemed overwhelmed by the conditions of the world around him (Micah 7:1). He expressed his frustration in verse 2: "The faithful have been swept from the land; not one upright person remains. Everyone lies in wait to shed blood; they hunt each other with nets."

The evildoers had become so skilled in their wrongdoing that figuratively they had become ambidextrous, willing and able to use "both hands" in carrying out their evil designs (Micah 7:3). The societal breakdown was so bad that one could not trust even a friend or family member, and one had to use words with caution (7:5, 6).

Much later, Jesus used the words of Micah 7:6 to describe how loyalty to him would result in alienation from family members (Matthew 10:35, 36).

In the second part of Micah 7, the prophet addressed his (and Israel's) enemy: those nations that had wreaked havoc among God's people and destroyed their cities. Someday the tables would be turned (7:7-12)! This leads us into the prayer of today's text.

I. Israel's Shepherd
(MICAH 7:14-17)
A. Helping His People (vv. 14, 15)

14. Shepherd your people with your staff, the flock of your inheritance, which lives by itself in a forest, in fertile pasturelands. Let them feed in Bashan and Gilead as in days long ago.

The picture of God as shepherd of his people is used throughout both Old and New Testaments. Probably the most familiar appearances of it are found in Psalm 23 and John 10:1-18. The description of God's people as *the flock of your inheritance* appeals to the special standing of Israel before the Lord; they are his "treasured possession" (Exodus 19:5). On the basis of covenant relationship, Micah pleads for the Lord to care for his people.

Such protection is greatly needed, given what Micah continues to say about their status. For the flock to live *by itself in a forest, in fertile pasturelands* depicts God's people as being all alone, restricted to a heavily forested area while around them is land that is much more attractive and productive. Overall, the picture is one of isolation and poverty while living tantalizingly close to the relief of abundance.

After such a forlorn picture, Micah appeals once more to the Lord: *let them feed in Bashan and Gilead as in days long ago.* Those two territories are east of the Jordan River. Bashan was part of the land allotted to half the tribe of Manasseh, and parts of Gilead were allotted to tribes Manasseh and Gad (Joshua 13:24-31). This land had been known for its abundance and productivity (Deu-

teronomy 32:14; Jeremiah 50:19). But by the time of Micah, some of that territory, such as Ramoth in Gilead, had been seized by the Syrians, or Arameans (1 Kings 22:1-4). Micah's prayer asks that the glorious *days long ago* be restored, when God's people were free from external threats as they lived in Bashan and Gilead.

What Do You Think?

How do the ways the good shepherd cares for his flock today compare and contrast with those of Micah's time?

Talking Points for Your Discussion

- Regarding physical needs
- Regarding spiritual needs
- Other

❧ LONGING FOR THE "GOOD OL' DAYS"? ❧

Think back to a time when everything seemed to be going right for you. Perhaps it was during those summer days when you were a child on vacation from school, with not a care in the world. Or maybe it was in the years when your children were young and the challenges of adolescence had not yet confronted your family. Some of us might ponder the economic brightness that existed before the Great Recession of 2007 and following.

In our tendency to romanticize the past, however, we may forget that even when we had it good, others did not. The circumstances were varied: some lived on poor cropland, some were subject to a segregated society, some shouldered a great burden of student-loan debt as they toiled away at minimum-wage jobs. The "good ol' days" to some are always "bad ol' days" to others.

The same was true of the people to whom Micah ministered. The small minority of wealthy elite were in their good days (or so they thought), while the vast majority experienced the opposite, with no hope in sight. But God answered Micah's plea on behalf of the people with a promise of deliverance. God sees the troubles of his people and responds with abundant mercy when the time is appropriate. May we have faith that he will provide for us as well! —C. R. B.

**15. "As in the days when you came out of Egypt,
I will show them my wonders."**

God is the one who is "able to do immeasurably more than all we ask or imagine," to use Paul's words in Ephesians 3:20. This is no less true in Micah's day. Here the Lord declares that he will do something on a par with the most memorable act in Israel's history: the exodus *out of Egypt*, which ended the cruel bondage there. That event was surrounded by a series of wondrous miracles from the Lord's hand, including the plagues while in Egypt and the deliverance at the Red Sea after departure. The latter miracle served as a kind of exclamation point, ending any efforts by Egypt and the Pharaoh to reverse the exodus and reenslave the Israelites.

Other prophets also draw on the importance of the exodus to declare that God is not through doing great things for his people (Isaiah 11:15, 16; Jeremiah 23:7, 8; etc.). He will one day do something at least as dramatic and awe-inspiring. Those wonders come to pass with the ministry of Jesus, climaxed by his death, resurrection, and ascension.

What Do You Think?
What are some marvelous things of God that unbelievers do not experience or even notice?
Talking Points for Your Discussion
- Concerning creation in general
- Concerning individuals in particular
- Concerning relationships
- Other

Micah has more to say about those coming events. For now, we should consider Luke's description of how Moses and Elijah, at the transfiguration of Jesus, "spoke about his departure, which he was about to bring to fulfillment at Jerusalem" (Luke 9:30, 31). The Greek word translated "departure" is literally the word *exodus* (compare 2 Peter 1:15). It foreshadows the deliverance from spiritual bondage that Jesus will make available for all humanity by means of his death for their sins. That is the mission that he "resolutely set out" to accomplish (Luke 9:51).

B. Humbling the Nations (vv. 16, 17)

**16. Nations will see and be ashamed,
deprived of all their power.
They will put their hands over their mouths
and their ears will become deaf.**

The nations of the world are pictured as reacting to the coming display of God's power much as Edom, Moab, etc., did to the events surrounding the exodus (see Exodus 15:13-16). The nations will be disheartened by how inadequate their resources are to counter the power of God.

The prediction *they will put their hands over their mouths and their ears will become deaf* reminds us of what the false prophets will end up doing according to Micah 3:7 (lesson 6): "they will all cover their faces." The nations will be ashamed to the point of being able neither to speak nor hear. Perhaps the deafness is a consequence of the impact of God's powerful voice (Psalm 29:3-9).

What Do You Think?
Under what circumstances do people exhibit, either individually or collectively, deafness to God's Word? How can we cure such deafness?
Talking Points for Your Discussion
- Outside the church (Acts 7:56, 57; 28:23-28; etc.)
- Within the church (Revelation 2:17, 29; 3:6, 13, 22; etc.)

**17. They will lick dust like a snake,
like creatures that crawl on the ground.
They will come trembling out of their dens;
they will turn in fear to the LORD our God
and will be afraid of you.**

To *lick dust like a snake* is another gesture signifying utter humiliation, as does being reduced to the status of *creatures that crawl on the ground*. The comparison with a snake may equate the opposition of the nations with that of Satan himself, who opposes the plans and purposes of the Lord (compare Genesis 3:14; Revelation 12:9; 20:2).

The reason for behaviors of licking dust and crawling on the ground is stated at the end of the verse: *they will turn in fear to the Lord our God.* And because of the Lord's presence with his people, they *will be afraid of you.* Quite a reversal from the "What misery is mine!" that Micah utters at the beginning of the chapter! But this is what looking to the Lord in faith and hope can do (Micah 7:7). We are to see beyond the despair of this world and recognize that the Lord remains in control even in—or especially in—the bleakest of circumstances.

What Do You Think?
What are some indicators that God is not feared as he should be? What are some causes and solutions for this?
Talking Points for Your Discussion
▪ Regarding individuals
▪ Regarding nations
▪ Other

II. Israel's Savior
(MICAH 7:18-20)

A. Filled with Compassion (vv. 18, 19)

18a. Who is a God like you,
who pardons sin and forgives the transgression
of the remnant of his inheritance?

The question *Who is a God like you?* is noteworthy for two reasons. First, the Hebrew name *Micah* means, "Who is like the Lord?" Micah thus uses his own name in a final tribute of praise to the Lord.

Second, the question calls to mind the language of a portion of the song that Moses and the Israelites sang following God's deliverance at the

HOW TO SAY IT

Arameans	*Ar*-uh-*me*-uns.
Assyria	Uh-*sear*-ee-uh.
Babylon	*Bab*-uh-lun.
Bashan	*Bay*-shan.
Egypt	*Ee*-jipt.
Gilead	*Gil*-ee-ud (*G* as in *get*).
Manasseh	Muh-*nass*-uh.
Micah	*My*-kuh.
Ramoth	*Ray*-muth.
Syrians	*Sear*-ee-unz.

Red Sea: "Who among the gods is like you, Lord? Who is like you—majestic in holiness, awesome in glory, working wonders?" (Exodus 15:11).

Micah has just noted God's promise to do "wonders" that will be at least as dramatic as what he did at the time of the exodus (Micah 7:15). When one considers the marvels of God highlighted by Micah in the text above, before us, and to follow, then recalling Israel's exodus for comparison is more than appropriate. Scarcely to be improved on is the answer to Micah's question provided by Isaiah: "I am God, and there is no other; I am God, and there is none like me" (Isaiah 46:9).

Part of what makes God unlike any other so-called god is his desire (due to his nature) and ability (due to the fact that he actually exists) to pardon and forgive *the transgression of the remnant of his inheritance.* The term *remnant* describes those who remain alive following the exile of God's people from the promised land. God's promise is to release them from their captivity much as he freed his people from bondage in Egypt centuries before (Micah 4:10).

18b. You do not stay angry forever
but delight to show mercy.

Certainly God's anger, or wrath, is a central part of Micah's message: a holy God must judge sinful people. In fact, Micah earlier reprimanded those who are "descendants of Jacob" who questioned whether the Lord would ever exhibit such an emotion against them (Micah 2:7, lesson 5).

Yet as strong as God's anger against sin is, even stronger is his mercy and willingness to forgive. Indeed, it is God's *delight to show mercy!* His holiness requires that he judge sin and sinner, but he prefers to extend mercy.

19. You will again have compassion on us;
you will tread our sins underfoot
and hurl all our iniquities into the depths of the sea.

Micah expresses his deep longing that Israel's sin problem be addressed decisively and thoroughly. After all, the real threat, the real bondage that plagues God's people, has always been internal, not external. It is a bondage that is spiritual in nature—captivity to sin. Such bondage, the ultimate bondage, enslaves not only Israel but all peoples. When those chains are broken, true freedom results.

The word-pictures employed by Micah to describe the forgiveness of sins are among the most insightful in the entire Bible. The word translated *tread . . . underfoot* is often used to describe the conquest of enemies (examples: Numbers 32:20-22; Joshua 18:1; 2 Samuel 8:11; 1 Chronicles 22:18). A word-picture such as this underlines the important truth that the real enemy of God's people has never been nations such as Egypt, Assyria, or Babylon. The real enemy has always been sin. That is the enemy that must be subdued and rendered powerless.

The word-picture of casting *iniquities into the depths of the sea* also has an important usage elsewhere in Scripture. The Egyptians who pursued the Israelites with the intent of making them slaves again were "hurled into the sea . . . the deep waters have covered them; they sank to the depths like a stone" (Exodus 15:4, 5; compare Isaiah 51:10). Thus sin, the most odious taskmaster of God's people, is to be treated as the Egyptians were dealt with at the Red Sea.

Consider once more God's promise in Micah 7:15: "As in the days when you came out of Egypt, I will show them my wonders." Wondrous indeed will be the work of Jesus Christ, who will bring about the conquest of sin that is described in Micah's picturesque language.

Some have expanded on Micah's portrayal by adding that when God casts *iniquities into the depths of the sea* he also puts up a sign that says, "No fishing!" In other words, those who have accepted Jesus' sacrifice on their behalf should view their sins the way God sees them: forgiven, forgotten, forever.

B. Faithful to His Word (v. 20)

20. You will be faithful to Jacob,
and show love to Abraham,
as you pledged on oath to our ancestors
in days long ago.

In concluding his striking description of the Lord's mercy, Micah draws additional links to Israel's past. These take the reader back to the *days long ago* that preceded the exodus: *Jacob,* a grandson of Abraham, had his name changed to *Israel* (Genesis 32:28), and the names of his sons designate the tribes of Israel. Abraham, of course, is acknowledged as the father of the Israelite nation (Luke 1:73; John 8:53; Acts 7:2; Romans 4:12). His journey of faith in answer to God's call brought him to Canaan, the land God promised to his descendants.

But there were promises to Abraham and Jacob that involved much more than just land. God had also declared to Abraham, "All peoples on earth will be blessed through you" (Genesis 12:3). The New Testament reveals to us how this promise has come to pass (see Romans 4:9-25; Galatians 3:8, 26-29). If Micah can exclaim, "Who is a God like you, who pardons sin?" (Micah 7:18, above) without living to see this fulfillment in Christ, how much more should we be able to do so—we who *know* that such promises have come to pass! Matchless mercy indeed!

Centuries after Micah, Mary, the mother of Jesus, will speak in very Micah-like language as she describes what God will do through her son: "He has helped his servant Israel, remembering to be merciful to Abraham and his descendants forever, just as he promised our ancestors" (Luke 1:54, 55). How Jesus, the seed of Abraham, makes it possible for anyone to be a descendant of Abraham by faith is an important New Testament theme (Romans 4:12; Galatians 3:7-9; etc.).

❧ GOD'S FAITHFULNESS AND SOCIETAL DECAY ❧

In June 2013, the U.S. Supreme Court declared a key section of the Defense of Marriage Act of 1996 to be unconstitutional. Concurrently, the court declined to overturn a decision by a lower court that had ruled the California Marriage Protection Act of 2008 (also known as "Proposition 8") to be unconstitutional. Both rulings undermined "one man, one woman" marriage as an established foundation of society.

Those approving the two decisions rejoiced at what they interpreted to be the court's rejection of attempts to deny civil rights. Many Christians responded in anger and/or dismay in recognizing America's continuing rejection of God's standards.

Micah reminded Israel of God's abundant mercy and forgiveness, but spoke also of God's faithfulness to his Word from ancient times. That Word contained promises of both blessing for obedience and punishment for sin. Today the most important question Christians face in a world intent on going its own way may well be, "How can we most effectively proclaim the realities of God's blessings that are available in Christ and certain punishment for those who reject him?"   —C. R. B.

Conclusion

A. "Do It Again, Lord!"

A few days after the attacks of 9/11, Max Lucado prepared a prayer to offer encouragement and perspective at a time of great distress throughout the U.S. He entitled the prayer, "Do It Again, Lord!" The following is an excerpt:

> And so we come to you. We don't ask you for help; we beg you for it. We don't request it; we implore it. We know what you can do. We've read the accounts. We've pondered the stories and now we plead, "Do it again, Lord. Do it again."
>
> Remember Joseph? You rescued him from the pit. You can do the same for us. Do it again, Lord.
>
> Remember the Hebrews in Egypt? You protected their children from the angel of death. We have children too, Lord. Do it again.
>
> And Sarah? Remember her prayers? You heard them. Joshua? Remember his fears? You inspired him. The women at the tomb? You resurrected their hope. The doubts of Thomas? You took them away. Do it again, Lord. Do it again.
>
> You changed Daniel from a captive into a king's counselor. You took Peter the fisherman

Visual for Lesson 8. *Start a discussion by pointing to this visual as you ask, "After this happens, what is our responsibility?"*

and made him Peter an apostle. Because of you, David went from leading sheep to leading armies. Do it again, Lord, for we need counselors today, Lord. We need leaders. Do it again, dear Lord.

While Micah did not utter such a specific prayer in his book, today's text reveals the Lord's promise that declares in essence, "I will do it again!" The prophet spoke clearly of coming judgment on both Israel and Judah. But judgment was a comma, not a period; that is, the judgment was to signify a pause, not an end. God was not finished with his people; the mighty arm that had done great works in the past had not weakened.

The God who had the ability to destroy oppressors of the body by drowning them in the sea also has the ability to "hurl all our iniquities into the depths of the sea" (Micah 7:19). And that is the good news that the church bears witness to today: the mercy (v. 18) and compassion (v. 19) that have been demonstrated mightily in Jesus' death, burial, and resurrection. God is not only willing and able to do it again, he has already done so.

B. Prayer

Thank you, Father, for your matchless mercy—prophesied by Micah and demonstrated by Jesus. May we be your instruments in extending that mercy to others. In Jesus' name, amen.

C. Thought to Remember

Proclaim God's matchless mercy in Jesus.

INVOLVEMENT LEARNING

Enhance your lesson with NIV® Bible Student *(from your curriculum supplier) and the reproducible activity page (at www.standardlesson.com or in the back of the* NIV® Standard Lesson Commentary Deluxe Edition*).*

Into the Lesson

Give each learner a sheet of paper and a pencil. Say, "Write very briefly about a concern that is weighing you down at the moment. It can be a personal problem or something in the conditions of the world at large. I will not collect these; no one else will see this." When everyone is finished, ask each person to fold the paper in half and hold it in front of his or her face. Then say, "Suppose you were to walk around all day holding that paper in front of your face. Where would your thoughts be focused?"

After the obvious answer is voiced, say, "In Micah 7, the prophet could see how bad things were in the nation of Israel. But instead of focusing on the evil around him, he decided to lift his gaze to God and focus on hope in him. Let's throw our problems in the trash, and see what Micah can teach us about trusting them to God." Hold up a wastebasket and allow students to wad their papers and throw them in. (*Option:* if you think your learners will hesitate to part with what they've written due to privacy concerns, you can have them use imaginary pencils to write on imaginary pieces of paper at the outset.)

Option. Place in chairs copies of the "Who Is a God Like You?" activity from the reproducible page, which you can download, for learners to begin working on as they arrive.

Into the Word

Form learners into small groups of no more than five each. Distribute handouts featuring the questions below so that half the groups will discuss God's role as shepherd and the other half will discuss God's role as Savior.

Israel's Shepherd Group—Read Micah 7:14-17. 1. How do Micah's thoughts on God-as-shepherd compare and contrast with Jesus' explanation of himself in that regard in John 10:1-18? 2. How do Micah's thoughts on "days long ago" com-

pare and contrast with what Solomon has to say about "the old days" in Ecclesiastes 7:10? 3. How does coming "out of Egypt" compare and contrast with being "called . . . out of darkness into his wonderful light" in 1 Peter 2:9? 4. How do the nations' reaction in putting "their hands over their mouths" compare and contrast with the guarantee that "every tongue [will] acknowledge that Jesus Christ is Lord, to the glory of God the Father" in Philippians 2:11?

Israel's Savior Group—Read Micah 7:18-20. 1. How does Micah's doxology compare and contrast with that of Moses in Exodus 15:11-18? 2. How does Micah's doxology compare and contrast with that of David in 1 Chronicles 29:10-13? 3. How does Micah's rhetorical question and statements that follow it compare and contrast with those in Psalm 77:13-15? 4. How does Micah's use of "the depths of the sea" imagery compare and contrast with the same imagery used by David in Psalm 68:22?

Call for groups to present conclusions to the class as a whole. If you think the group discussions will be too time-consuming given the number and nature of the questions, you can double the number of groups and give each only two questions instead of four.

Into Life

Distribute index cards. Say, "We're going to take a few minutes to allow everyone to write a personal prayer of praise and thanksgiving to God for his mercy and compassion. As you do, be sure to incorporate the themes of Micah 7:18-20. I will not collect the prayers. Instead, you can keep them in your Bibles to use during personal daily devotions in the week ahead."

Alternative. Distribute copies of the "Message of Hope for Today" activity from the reproducible page. Encourage creativity as learners complete as indicated.

A REDEEMER IN ZION

DEVOTIONAL READING: Exodus 6:2-8
BACKGROUND SCRIPTURE: Isaiah 59; Psalm 89:11-18

ISAIAH 59:15-21

¹⁵ Truth is nowhere to be found,
    and whoever shuns evil becomes a prey.
The LORD looked and was displeased
    that there was no justice.
¹⁶ He saw that there was no one,
    he was appalled that there was no one
        to intervene;
so his own arm achieved salvation for him,
    and his own righteousness sustained
        him.
¹⁷ He put on righteousness as his breastplate,
    and the helmet of salvation on his head;
he put on the garments of vengeance
    and wrapped himself in zeal as in a
        cloak.
¹⁸ According to what they have done,
    so will he repay
wrath to his enemies
    and retribution to his foes;
    he will repay the islands their due.
¹⁹ From the west, people will fear the name
        of the LORD,
    and from the rising of the sun, they will
        revere his glory.

For he will come like a pent-up flood
    that the breath of the LORD drives
        along.

²⁰ "The Redeemer will come to Zion,
    to those in Jacob who repent of their
        sins,"

                                        declares the LORD.

²¹ "As for me, this is my covenant with them,"
says the LORD. "My Spirit, who is on you, will
not depart from you, and my words that I have
put in your mouth will always be on your lips,
on the lips of your children and on the lips of
their descendants—from this time on and forever," says the LORD.

KEY VERSE

"The Redeemer will come to Zion, to those in Jacob who repent of their sins," declares the LORD.

—**Isaiah 59:20**

GOD'S PROPHETS DEMAND JUSTICE

Unit 3: Advocates of Justice for All

LESSON AIMS

After participating in this lesson, each learner will be able to:

1. Describe the state of affairs in the Israel of Isaiah's day and God's reaction to it.

2. Explain how and why God's warning of his righteous judgment forms part of his message of redemption.

3. Plan an outreach event to spread the message of the Redeemer in the community.

LESSON OUTLINE

Introduction

A. Are You Angry?

If you aren't angry, you aren't paying attention. Perhaps you have seen this slogan on bumper stickers or billboards. We might object to it. After all, we should control our anger, shouldn't we? And I resent being told that I am not paying attention! I read the bumper sticker, did I not?

But that provocative saying makes a point that Christians should affirm. Injustice and wickedness seem rampant. Everywhere we turn, we see the power of evil. How can a thoughtful person not be angry in a world like this? Our indignant reaction reflects how God made us. As people who bear his image, our response to the world should reflect his own. Our Creator is utterly just, righteous, and holy. He cannot tolerate the evil that mars his creation and victimizes people. God's wrath, his righteous anger against evil, burns against all that is wrong. When we feel indignant anger about the evils we see, we reflect God's own reaction.

But God's intent is not merely to destroy evil. He also intends to enact justice and righteousness as he reasserts his rightful reign over creation. As those who bear his image, we long for his will to be done! Yet if we are honest, we know that we are part of the reason that God's justice does not reign as fully as it should in our world. The righteousness that we desire is the very thing we often reject in our stubborn selfishness. We regularly act in ways that embody evil, not justice. We who long for the solution are part of the problem.

Today's text reflects these realities. Above and beyond that, however, it expresses God's promise to establish his justice despite our failures.

B. Lesson Background

The prophet Isaiah delivered his messages during the turbulent eighth century BC. Judah, the southern kingdom in Israel's divided monarchy, was threatened by the powerful Assyrian empire. Isaiah's generation had witnessed the Assyrians' destruction of the northern kingdom of Israel in 722 BC, and only by God's intervention did Judah and Jerusalem survive that awful time (see 2 Kings 18:13–19:37; Isaiah 36, 37).

But the threat from within was just as great, if not more so. Of the four kings who ruled Judah in Isaiah's day (see Isaiah 1:1), three were relatively "good" and one was quite evil. But the unholiness that had gained a grip continued during the reigns of the good kings (2 Kings 15:4, 35). Temporary repentance would occur (2 Chronicles 32:26), but it was always just that—temporary. Judah was surrounded by violent, ungodly nations, and Judah itself had become such a nation.

How could a holy God tolerate all that unholiness? How could he promise that his people would become a "light for the Gentiles" (Isaiah 42:6; compare 49:6) when the Israelites were as sinful as the pagan nations around them? Our text today is part of a larger context that addresses such questions.

I. Injustice and Righteousness
(ISAIAH 59:15-17)

A. The Lord's Displeasure (vv. 15, 16a)

15. Truth is nowhere to be found,
and whoever shuns evil becomes a prey.
The LORD looked and was displeased
that there was no justice.

As God surveys his world, he sees the utter ruin of his original design. Truth, understanding, and living in accord with God's reality has failed. Isaiah has just compared truth's condition with a person who stumbles and falls helpless in the street (Isaiah 59:14). That image is appropriate for a nation like Judah. Although entrusted with God's law and land, it chooses to seek safety in wealth and political alliances with pagan nations.

Evil runs rampant in settings where truth is ignored. *Whoever shuns evil* is victimized by those who have abandoned truth to embrace evil. Often such victims are society's most vulnerable (see Isaiah 1:17, 23; 10:2). In such an environment, the

HOW TO SAY IT

anthropomorphism	an-thruh-puh-*more-fih*-zum.
Assyrian	Uh-*sear*-e-un.
Isaiah	Eye-*zay*-uh.
Judah	*Joo*-duh.
Sinai	*Sigh*-nye or *Sigh*-nay-eye.

weak are left unprotected and the righteous are abused as the godless, truth-denying people exercise unbridled power.

What Do You Think?
Who has been the greatest influence for you being a truthful person at various stages of life? Why?
Talking Points for Your Discussion
▪ During your preteen years
▪ During your teenage years
▪ During adulthood

But God sees all this. He is not distant and indifferent; he is in fact deeply engaged. What God seeks is *justice,* referring to governance of his world that reflects his character and purpose. This is the responsibility of all who are created in his image. This responsibility involves how to live, how to interact with others, and what to expect from others. For the powerful, it means discretion in their own exercise of power as they yield to God's purposes. For the weak, it means to trust in his way for protection and relief.

But the prophet tells us that God sees *no justice* as he looks at his world. Such a situation is intolerable for him, the holy one.

16a. He saw that there was no one,
he was appalled that there was no one
to intervene;

As God surveys the situation, he sees its hopelessness. His justice is absent because there is no one who practices it! So God is *appalled that there* is also *no one to intervene* to make things right again. This is the issue that confronted Isaiah when he had a vision of the holy God: that man realized himself to be a sinful person, surrounded by sinful people (Isaiah 6:5). Who can be God's instrument in such a dire situation?

B. The Lord's Solution (vv. 16b, 17)

16b. . . . so his own arm achieved salvation
for him,
and his own righteousness sustained him.

The answer! If none but God expresses his justice, then God himself must be the one to establish that justice. Isaiah speaks of God's *arm* as a way of referring to his mighty power, exercised like a warrior who uses his strong arm to wield a sword. That mighty power of God will bring *salvation*, which refers to the entire plan of God to retake his world. As God does so, he will establish justice and rescue his people from the terrible position in which they find themselves by their own doing.

God's *righteousness*—his utter commitment to that which is right and just—is the basis on which he moves to transform his deeply unrighteous and unjust people and the unrighteous and unjust world in which they live. In this sinful world, none but God can do this!

🕊 ACTING ON GOD'S BEHALF 🕊

The Bible sometimes presents God to us in terms of human form, characteristics, or actions. (The technical term for this is *anthropomorphism*.) That's what we see in the verse above and the one following. This technique helps us understand God at a level most familiar to us. The Bible on occasion also presents God to us in terms of animal characteristics (examples: Psalm 91:4; Luke 13:34).

We are grateful for this aid to understanding! But as we ponder what is to be brought about by God's "arm," we should not let the magnificence of this imagery cause us to miss a vital point: *This action was not God's first choice!* His first choice was that a human intercessor would act on his behalf. But since "there was no one" to be found to do so, God decided to take the necessary action himself. We see the same issue in Ezekiel 22:29, 30.

When God looks at the world today, does he see anyone willing to act on his behalf to bring about his justice? Praying for God's justice to prevail is a good thing. Following that prayer with action to make it happen is even better!   —R. L. N.

> **What Do You Think?**
> When was a time you expected someone to act on your behalf but the person failed to do so? What did you learn from this experience?
> *Talking Points for Your Discussion*
> - Regarding a legal issue
> - Regarding an issue at work or school
> - Regarding a family issue
> - Other

17a. He put on righteousness as his breastplate,
and the helmet of salvation on his head;

Seeing the awful, helpless condition of the world, God figuratively arms himself for battle. His armaments of *breastplate* and *helmet* are characterized by the very qualities that he alone can bring to the world, two attributes on which Isaiah has already focused: *righteousness* and *salvation*. No one can be found to have God's righteousness, so he is the one to bring it to the battle. None but God can bring salvation, so he is the one to bring it to the battle as well. There can be no doubt: God, so armed with what the world lacks, will prevail in the battle with evil.

> **What Do You Think?**
> Considering this armament alongside that of Ephesians 6:13-17, where is your preparedness for spiritual battle most in need of improvement? How will that improvement happen?
> *Talking Points for Your Discussion*
> - Regarding offensive functions
> - Regarding defensive functions
> - Other

17b. . . . he put on the garments of vengeance

The picture becomes more intense. God's figurative clothing for battle is *vengeance*. That word may trouble us at some level, but it is a vital expression of God's righteousness and holiness. The God whom Isaiah saw in his vision of chapter 6 is the holy one who cannot tolerate evil. His very nature requires that evil be punished. The crime demands a punishment, and the punishment will fit the crime.

To pay back what evil deserves is to deliver the vengeance of retributive justice. Humans are imperfect agents of doing so. But the God who demands such retribution is capable of delivering it perfectly—and he does! Vengeance belongs only to him (Deuteronomy 32:35; quoted in Romans 12:19). Were it not for God's vengeance, we would have no assurance of justice in the world.

God's vengeance is also part of the framework of his mercy, since the reality of his justified vengeance is what makes his offer of mercy meaningful. Justice demands retribution, and as sinners we all fall under that sentence of death. Without God's mercy, we would all be doomed. As we clamor for justice, we will see our guilt in that regard. In turn, this should make us aware of our utter need for God's mercy.

17c. . . . and wrapped himself in zeal as in a cloak.

At least some in Isaiah's audience doubtless wonder whether God will ever act to bring justice and retribution. They are not alone in that regard (examples: Judges 6:13; Habakkuk 1:2; Revelation 6:10). Has God forgotten the plight of the weak? Has he abandoned the world to evil?

The prophet delivers a ringing assurance to the contrary! God demonstrates a passionate *zeal* for the battle to establish his justice. Figuratively, God's zeal is such an important part of his nature that he wears it as though it were *a cloak*. Even if he seems distant as we toil in the midst of evil, his zeal for righteousness assures us that he will always act on his people's behalf in his time.

II. Repayment and Glory
(Isaiah 59:18, 19)
A. Enemies Defeated (v. 18)

**18. According to what they have done,
so will he repay
wrath to his enemies
and retribution to his foes;
he will repay the islands their due.**

To establish justice, God assures that the punishment fits the crime—the idea of *according to what they have done.* He does not act arbitrarily. Each individual is to receive punishment for what he or she does (compare Revelation 20:12, 13; 22:12). God's judgment is, in effect, repayment: simple and perfect retributive justice. This is the very justice that the oppressed cry out for (Psalm 28:4).

God accomplishes this by unleashing his power on *his enemies.* Wrongdoers are rebels against him; they are subjects of the divine king who plot insurrection. God's judgment brings those enemies to the divine bar of justice. His *wrath* is not an irrational, knee-jerk reaction. Rather, such judgment

is his righteous, holy indignation in response to the evil done by those who rebel against him.

This justice is not merely for the Israelites and their neighbors—it goes worldwide. Isaiah understands that God is Lord not just of a single nation or region but of the whole world. All peoples in all places are subject to his judgment and justice. For the Israelites, a people unaccustomed to seafaring, many such are across the seas; these places are *the islands* beyond the horizon. Isaiah expresses conviction that even those places, usually inaccessible to him and his people, will also be the objects of God's retributive justice.

The holy one of Israel will not let evil continue forever in his world. Were he to do so, he would not be true to himself. The justice that people long for is the justice that he promises ultimately to all.

What Do You Think?
How does belief in God's ultimate justice help when facing injustice in the here and now?
Talking Points for Your Discussion
- When you are wronged
- When a fellow believer is wronged
- When interacting with unbelievers
- Other

B. God Triumphant (v. 19)

**19a. From the west, people will fear the name of the Lord,
and from the rising of the sun, they will revere his glory.**

Isaiah promises that the ultimate result of God's judgment is global submission to his rule. The worldwide scope is seen in Isaiah's pointing to both *the west* and the east (*the rising of the sun*). The fear that people will demonstrate will not be simply a dread of punishment but one of awe and respect that reflects a corrected assessment of God. Such fear is directed especially to *the name of the Lord,* meaning his authority. To fear God's name is to revere him and submit to him as king, being fully aware of his righteousness and power.

❧ Universal Justice ❧

The U.N. Commission on Human Rights was formed in 1948 to be a watchdog over issues of human rights. But the commission came under criticism through the years because many of its member-states had poor records on human rights themselves. A tipping point came in 2004 when the U.S. ambassador declared Sudan's election to the commission an "absurdity" given that country's campaign of ethnic cleansing in its Darfur region.

The commission was replaced in 2006 by the U.N. Human Rights Council for a fresh start at promoting human rights. But achieving justice at the international level is hindered by vested interests that resist change. Further adding to the problem is that there are various kinds of justice to be considered (retributive, distributive, procedural, and restorative) and defined.

This problem is not confined to the international level. What I think is just and right may seem terribly unfair to you. Apart from a divine standard, justice is difficult to imagine and hard to attain. Isaiah gives us hope as he predicts the day when the whole creation will experience God's justice. There is no better kind. —C. R. B.

19b. For he will come like a pent-up flood that the breath of the LORD drives along.

The proper translation of this half-verse is uncertain, and this alternative is offered in a footnote of some editions of the NIV: "When enemies come in like a flood, the Spirit of the Lord will put them to flight." But under either translation, the end result is clear: as God's rule is established, he sweeps away every imaginable threat. The emphasis is on the full accomplishment of God's will in the world. The holy one of Israel will reign as king over all that he has created.

III. Redeemer and Covenant
(ISAIAH 59:20, 21)
A. Future Deliverance (v. 20)

20. "The Redeemer will come to Zion, to those in Jacob who repent of their sins,"

declares the LORD.

When God establishes his global justice, it will mean restoration for his people. As Isaiah writes

this, he addresses an audience that is aware of his earlier warnings that Judah will one day be taken captive as God's judgment on their rebellion (Isaiah 3; 39:6, 7). But God has promised to visit his people beyond that captivity to liberate them as he did in the exodus from Egypt (Deuteronomy 30:1-5; Isaiah 49:8-26), and Isaiah repeats that promise here. God will not abandon his to-be-exiled people. As their Redeemer, he will lead them a second time from enslavement to freedom. This promise is to those *in Jacob*—that is, Jacob's descendants, the people of Israel—*who repent of their sins* (compare Paul's loose quotation of this verse and part of the next in Romans 11:26, 27a).

With the use of the word *Redeemer*, Isaiah embeds God's mercy in the announcement of judgment. Justice requires that rebellion against him be penalized, the penalty here taking the form of exile. But God promises restoration for those who repent and seek his mercy. It is his mercy, not his judgment, that God ultimately seeks for his people. In warning of judgment, God is exercising his mercy as he invites stubborn rebels to be restored to his blessing.

> **What Do You Think?**
> When have you seen a person having to experience the pain of "hitting rock bottom" before finally repenting? What did you learn from this?
> *Talking Points for Your Discussion*
> - A colleague
> - A family member
> - A neighbor
> - Other

B. Eternal Relationship (v. 21)

21. "As for me, this is my covenant with them," says the LORD. "My Spirit, who is on you, will not depart from you, and my words that I have put in your mouth will always be on your lips, on the lips of your children and on the lips of their descendants—from this time on and forever," says the LORD.

To reinforce his promise to restore justice for his people, God recalls his *covenant with them*. This covenant is the statement of obligations and promises that he gave to his people at Mount

Sinai. God's covenant includes both warnings of judgment for disobedience and promises of restored blessing for repentance.

But as God recalls this covenant, an abrupt change takes place as he switches from discussing the plural *them* to begin addressing *you* (twice) and *your* (three times), which are singular in number. This singular individual is endowed with God's Spirit (compare 1 Samuel 10:6). God puts his *words* in the *mouth* of this person, as he does with the prophets (compare Ezra 1:1). His words in this individual's mouth will remain powerful for the *descendants* of generations that extend *from this time on and forever*.

Of whom is God speaking? The concept of one who establishes God's truth forever reminds us of the promise of a great king like David, a forthcoming ruler whose throne God is to establish forever (2 Samuel 7:16). The concept of one who speaks for God by his Spirit reminds us of the promise to send a prophet like Moses (Deuteronomy 18:18, 19). The reference to *descendants* echoes God's promise to Abraham that by his offspring all the nations are to be blessed (Genesis 22:18). Thus we are driven to conclude that Isaiah is voicing God's promise to send the great king, the great prophet, the one who blesses all nations.

Isaiah has already spoken of one to be known as *Immanuel*, meaning "God with us" (Isaiah 7:14), one to have God's authority to bring his peace (9:6, 7), "a Branch" from the roots of King David's father, Jesse, to establish perfect peace (11:1). Knowing what happens some eight centuries after Isaiah's prophecy, we can identify Jesus as the *you* of the verse before us. He is the means by which God restores blessing to people (Matthew 1:23). He is the means by which God brings his perfect justice to the world.

Conclusion
A. God's Justice Brings Hope

Living in a world filled with evil and injustice as we do, it is natural to become angry or discouraged. But we have great hope in hearing of God's commitment to bring justice. Isaiah

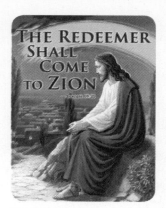

Visual for
Lesson 9

Use this visual as a focal point to discuss the who, what, why, and how of redemption in Christ.

offered a glimpse of what lies beyond the oppression of injustice and certainty of God's judgment: the promise of God's mercy. The prophet reminded the people of his day that the merciful God intended to restore his glorious design to those willing to receive it. That reminder is ours as well.

The fact that we know the climax of the story gives us an advantage over Isaiah and his audience: the Son of God has indeed visited his people! Having given his life as the perfect sacrifice, he has satisfied the requirements of God's justice to punish sin (Isaiah 52:13–53:12), thus enabling his mercy to be poured out. Risen from the dead, Jesus now reigns on high (Hebrews 1:3) as we await his return when he will judge some (Acts 10:42) and redeem others (Mark 13:26, 27).

Knowing how the promises are fulfilled, we have a duty beyond that of Isaiah's audience. Knowing how God exhibits his justice and mercy through Jesus, we have every reason and obligation to reflect those in the way we live.

B. Prayer

Almighty God, we ask that you empower us to be people of justice even as we extend mercy as you have been merciful to us. In the name of Jesus, our just and merciful king, amen!

C. Thought to Remember

Proclaim both God's justice and his mercy.

INVOLVEMENT LEARNING

Enhance your lesson with NIV® Bible Student (from your curriculum supplier) and the reproducible activity page (at www.standardlesson.com or in the back of the NIV® Standard Lesson Commentary Deluxe Edition).

Into the Lesson

Draw two columns on the board; write *Me* at the top of the left column and *God* at the top of the right. Say, "We don't have to look far to realize we live in a fallen world. Let's consider some recent events and compare our responses to them with how we think God might respond."

Summarize some incidents that involve injustice of the past week that you have researched in advance. Pause after each to ask, "What justice would you want to see imposed on the apparent wrongdoer and why?" Jot responses in the column labeled *Me*. (Leave the responses on the board; the *God* column will be filled in later.) Wrap up this segment by saying, "We naturally want wrongdoers to receive the punishment they deserve. God also demands justice, but today we will see that his justice is accompanied by his merciful salvation."

Option. Before class, place in chairs copies of the "Justice and Mercy" activity from the reproducible page, which you can download. Learners can begin working on this as they arrive.

Into the Word

Distribute handouts titled *Kings of Judah in the Time of Isaiah* that feature the following names of kings (column on the left) and associated passages (column on the right): Uzziah (also known as Azariah): 2 Kings 15:1-5; 2 Chronicles 26:16-21 / Jotham: 2 Kings 15:32-35; 2 Chronicles 27:1-4 / Ahaz: 2 Kings 16:1-4; 2 Chronicles 28:1-4 / Hezekiah: 2 Kings 18:1-8; 2 Chronicles 32:24-26.

Say, "Take a couple of minutes to skim through the listed passages and jot down important details about each of the four kings." (*Option:* save time by assigning the kings individually to pairs or small groups.) When you call for conclusions, learners should note that Ahaz was utterly evil. The other three notably "did what was right in the eyes of the Lord," but they each had problems: Hezekiah and Uzziah both had issues of pride,

and the latter tolerated his people's sinful worship practices, as did Jotham. Say, "Even though three of the four kings of Judah in Isaiah's day did what was right, the same could not be said of their people by and large. This is the context of today's study."

Have verses 15, 16 from today's lesson text read aloud. Use the commentary on these two verses to establish further the spiritual condition of Judah at the time. Then write the words *righteousness* and *salvation* on the board. Say, "The remainder of the verses for today's lesson gives us the picture of what God's righteousness and salvation look like. Let's examine these."

As you work through verses 17-21, pause at each image to ask whether it fits better as an image of righteousness or as an image of salvation. The first two images ("righteousness as his breastplate" and "helmet of salvation") are obviously easy in that regard. The third image ("garments of vengeance") fits righteousness, while the fourth image ("wrapped . . . in zeal as in a cloak") can fit both, etc. (If you used the "Justice and Mercy" activity at the outset, refer back to it to show how *justice* connects with *righteousness* and how *mercy* connects with *salvation*.)

Into Life

Say, "We began by identifying what we believed to be 'just' responses to those who acted unjustly. Let's go back to those incidents to think of God's response in terms of both righteousness and offers of salvation." Discuss how an outreach event in the community would incorporate both messages of the justice that the righteous God demands and the merciful salvation that Jesus makes available.

Option. Distribute copies of the "Intercessors Today" activity from the reproducible page for brainstorming as indicated. Come prepared with ideas that you have researched in advance should learners seem at a loss.

A CHOICE
TO BE JUST

DEVOTIONAL READING: Jeremiah 26:8-15
BACKGROUND SCRIPTURE: Ezra 7:1, 6, 21-28; Jeremiah 7:1-15

JEREMIAH 7:1-15

¹ This is the word that came to Jeremiah from the LORD: ² "Stand at the gate of the LORD's house and there proclaim this message:

"'Hear the word of the LORD, all you people of Judah who come through these gates to worship the LORD. ³ This is what the LORD Almighty, the God of Israel, says: Reform your ways and your actions, and I will let you live in this place. ⁴ Do not trust in deceptive words and say, "This is the temple of the LORD, the temple of the LORD, the temple of the LORD!" ⁵ If you really change your ways and your actions and deal with each other justly, ⁶ if you do not oppress the foreigner, the fatherless or the widow and do not shed innocent blood in this place, and if you do not follow other gods to your own harm, ⁷ then I will let you live in this place, in the land I gave your ancestors for ever and ever. ⁸ But look, you are trusting in deceptive words that are worthless.

⁹ "'Will you steal and murder, commit adultery and perjury, burn incense to Baal and follow other gods you have not known, ¹⁰ and then come and stand before me in this house, which bears my Name, and say, "We are safe"—safe to do all these detestable things? ¹¹ Has this house, which bears my Name, become a den of robbers to you? But I have been watching! declares the LORD.

¹² "'Go now to the place in Shiloh where I first made a dwelling for my Name, and see what I did to it because of the wickedness of my people Israel. ¹³ While you were doing all these things, declares the LORD, I spoke to you again and again, but you did not listen; I called you, but you did not answer. ¹⁴ Therefore, what I did to Shiloh I will now do to the house that bears my Name, the temple you trust in, the place I gave to you and your ancestors. ¹⁵ I will thrust you from my presence, just as I did all your fellow Israelites, the people of Ephraim.'"

KEY VERSE

This is what the LORD Almighty, the God of Israel, says: Reform your ways and your actions, and I will let you live in this place. —**Jeremiah 7:3**

GOD'S PROPHETS DEMAND JUSTICE

Unit 3: Advocates of Justice for All

LESSONS 9–13

LESSON AIMS

After participating in this lesson, each learner will be able to:

1. Identify the "deceptive words" that the people of Judah had accepted, and tell how their confidence in those deceptive words had corrupted their behavior.

2. Compare and contrast the "deceptive words" of Jeremiah's day with the "deceptive words" that falsely comfort and corrupt today's society.

3. Select one specific false massage prevalent today and explain how best to refute it with God's truth.

LESSON OUTLINE

Introduction

A. A Godly Good-Luck Charm?

We all know about so-called good-luck charms. The rabbit's foot, the horseshoe, and the four-leaf clover are staples of that ilk, at least in North America. In some cultures, certain insects or animals are seen as bringing good luck.

But skepticism regarding the power of good-luck charms is well advised. If we have a friend who sees no need to fasten a seat belt because a "dream catcher" hangs from the rearview mirror for good luck, we will probably try to persuade that person to put more confidence in the seat belt.

Thoughtfulness in this regard can have a connection with how we view our relationship with God. While probably few Christians see the Christian-themed knickknacks in their houses to be godly good-luck charms, it's easy to treat particular religious routines as such. Danger looms when we perceive our standing with God in light of reliance on such practices. Faithfulness to routine is one thing; having faith *in* the routine is quite another!

We easily note and critique such misplaced faith when displayed in others, don't we? But it may not be so easy to recognize the problem when it is our own. Today's text will help us in that regard.

B. Lesson Background

The prophet Jeremiah ministered in the late seventh and early sixth centuries BC, during the final years of the monarchy of Judah (Jeremiah 1:1-3). That was the southern part of Israel's divided kingdom. In that day, Judah was confronted by the aggressive Babylonian Empire. The Babylonians oppressed Judah over a period of several years, treating it as a vassal kingdom (2 Kings 24). The Babylonians ultimately laid siege to Jerusalem, put it to the sword and torch, destroyed its temple, and took its people into exile (2 Kings 25).

From one perspective, these events could appear to be a simple issue of power politics: Babylon was strong; Judah was not. But from the perspective of Jeremiah, these events fulfilled warnings that God had given his people long ago. As God gave Israel the land of promise, he had warned that they must receive it as a gift, with gratitude reflected in obedience. Submitting to God's law would mean blessing; disobedience would mean return to captivity (Deuteronomy 29:14-29).

That penalty was partially realized as Jeremiah delivered the prophecy of today's lesson, since the territory of Israel's 10 northern tribes had been overrun by the Assyrians about a century before Jeremiah began prophesying (2 Kings 17:5-23). But God had granted Judah a miraculous deliverance in that same era (18:13–19:37). That deliverance had become a source of misplaced confidence by Jeremiah's day. Many believed that God would never allow his temple to fall. It was against such a perspective that Jeremiah directed the warning in our text.

I. Prophetic Message
(JEREMIAH 7:1, 2)
A. From Whom (v. 1)

1. This is the word that came to Jeremiah from the LORD:

This section begins with what is sometimes called *a prophetic formula*. This affirms that the forthcoming message is not that of the messenger but of God, on whose behalf the messenger speaks.

B. For Whom (v. 2)

2. "Stand at the gate of the LORD's house and there proclaim this message:

"'Hear the word of the LORD, all you people of Judah who come through these gates to worship the LORD.

HOW TO SAY IT

Assyrians	Uh-*sear*-e-unz.
Baal	*Bay*-ul.
Babylon	*Bab*-uh-lun.
Babylonians	Bab-ih-*low*-nee-unz.
Eli	*Ee*-lye.
Ephraim	*Ee*-fray-im.
Judah	*Joo*-duh.
Judeans	Joo-*dee*-unz.
Shiloh	*Shy*-low.

God sends Jeremiah to the temple's entrance to announce the message. The temple itself is to provide the visual context of the prophet's words. Those who enter the temple, *the Lord's house*, imagine that structure to be the guarantee of their standing with God, as will be seen. They are about to hear a message that differs sharply from that viewpoint!

II. False Trust
(JEREMIAH 7:3-8)
A. Message of Life (vv. 3-7)

3. "'This is what the LORD Almighty, the God of Israel, says: Reform your ways and your actions, and I will let you live in this place.

The prophet's message begins on a loud, clear note. The people of Judah live where they do by God's permission and God's gift. Their standing is conditional: only by submitting to him can they remain in the land he has given them (see the Lesson Background). Presently they do not submit, as evidenced by the fact that Jeremiah confrontationally says *reform your ways and your actions*. The people must improve their walk with God.

4. "'Do not trust in deceptive words and say, "This is the temple of the LORD, the temple of the LORD, the temple of the LORD!"

Deceptive words are especially powerful and tragic when we are deceiving ourselves! So it is for Jeremiah's audience. They have convinced themselves that the existence of God's temple in their midst provides absolute assurance against disaster. With misunderstanding of their sinful past and misplaced trust in a physical structure, the people of Judah have become like pagans who believe that repeating certain words or creating certain objects provides magical power. The Judeans' trust is empty; their words, trite.

5a. "'If you really change your ways and your actions

In contrast with the people's merely parroting "the temple of the Lord" over and over, Jeremiah proclaims that the people must change their lifestyles completely. Behind the two-word phrase *really change* in the original language is a single word meaning "make good" that is repeated to emphasize the idea.

5b. "'. . . and deal with each other justly,

The kind of duplication for emphasis in verse 5a is also behind the phrase *deal with each other justly* that we see here. God himself is the model for just actions. He demonstrated his just judgment in rescuing the Israelites from their unjust bondage in Egypt. Such action on his part calls for obedience, thankfulness, fairness, generosity, and humility on the part of those so rescued. Such are to be the hallmarks of God's people, not empty reliance on a physical structure.

6a. "'. . . if you do not oppress the foreigner, the fatherless or the widow

Jeremiah proceeds to describe what the people's amended ways, especially in terms of executed justice, should entail. The Israelites' ancestors had been enslaved in Egypt for 400 years (Genesis 15:13; Exodus 12:40, 41; Acts 7:6). God's liberation taught them (or should have taught them) that justice means fair, merciful, and respectful treatment of all (Exodus 22:21; 23:9). Society's most vulnerable are therefore in need of the greatest protection in God's program.

These vulnerable include *the foreigner*, referring to non-Israelites who settle in the promised land. Israel's forefathers knew what it was like to be a stranger in the land (Genesis 23:4), and King David set an example of the attitude to have when he wrote, "Hear my prayer, Lord, listen to my cry for help; do not be deaf to my weeping. I dwell with you as a foreigner, a stranger, as all my ancestors were" (Psalm 39:12).

The fatherless and *the widow* typically have no one to support and protect them in the culture of Jeremiah's day; they depend on the generosity of others. As God provides and protects, so must the Israelites act toward society's most vulnerable. The prophets have to remind the Israelites periodically of their responsibilities in this regard. Particularly strong is the indictment of Ezekiel 22:29.

6b. "'. . . and do not shed innocent blood in this place,

Securing justice for the vulnerable parallels renunciation of violence. Shedding of *innocent blood* (murder) represents the complete denial of God's creation of humans in his image (Genesis 1:26, 27; 9:6). Such violence is driven by radically selfish desires. It represents the ultimate injustice. Jeremiah 22:17 is quite pointed in revealing the people's tendencies in this area.

6c. "'. . . and if you do not follow other gods to your own harm,

The list of transgressions ends with the problem of following *other gods*, prohibited in the First Commandment (Exodus 20:3). Idolatry is an affront to the being and nature of God. Made to suit the desires of the worshipper, idols represent humans' attempts to gather spiritual power for their own uses. Devotion to other gods becomes, in many cases, the justification for all kinds of crimes (example: Psalm 106:38). Ultimately, the one harmed most by idolatry is the idol worshipper because of the eternal consequences.

7. "'. . . then I will let you live in this place, in the land I gave your ancestors for ever and ever.

God's promise is always clear: obedience is the condition for remaining *in the land* that God gave to the forefathers. Jeremiah repeats that promise to his temple-gate audience as a warning: the people must change their ways if they want the promise to remain in effect. What God had done when he rescued Jerusalem by striking down the Assyrians (2 Kings 19:35) he can certainly do again. But the people must repent.

B. Message of Death (v. 8)

8. "'But look, you are trusting in deceptive words that are worthless.'"

The people's confident chant "the temple of the Lord" (v. 4) is an exercise in misplaced trust. This self-delusion will prove to be their undoing. Jeremiah stands before them to announce that this misdirected faith is a fatally dangerous sham. It is time to abandon *deceptive words* and admit the truth.

✢ DIRTY SOCKS ✢

Athletes don't want to break routine when they are playing well. A baseball player on a hitting streak won't risk changing anything—not even his socks—lest his hot streak be jinxed!

Going the other way, athletes may be all too willing to change routine when things aren't going well. Minnie Minoso took an interesting approach in this regard after going hitless in a game in which he played for the Chicago White Sox. Reportedly blaming his uniform for his troubles, he wore it into the shower. The next day he had three hits, so his teammates joined him in the shower afterward with *their* uniforms on! Eccentricities of routine and superstition can be found in virtually any sport. Even fans have "special" shirts or caps they wear so their team will win.

Jeremiah told his people that the superstitious trust they placed in the temple amounted to no more than deceptive words. Their self-deception told them that things were just fine, so they were unwilling to change their "dirty socks." What self-deceptions do we indulge in yet today?—C. R. B.

III. Exposed Injustice
(JEREMIAH 7:9-15)
A. Commandments Broken (v. 9)

9. "'Will you steal and murder, commit adultery and perjury, burn incense to Baal and follow other gods you have not known,

Drawing on offenses just mentioned, Jeremiah now poses a rhetorical question that demonstrates the people's hypocrisy. First he lists sins that remind us of several of the Ten Commandments (Exodus 20:1-17; Deuteronomy 5:7-21). Theft, murder, adultery, falsehood, and idolatry are obvi-

ous violations. In one way or another, such transgressions all involve defrauding the vulnerable.

Another element is the indictment that the people are burning *incense to Baal*. The designation *Baal* means "master" and refers to various gods worshipped by Israel's neighbors; note the plural *Baals* in Jeremiah 2:23; 9:14. Their worshippers believe that these gods control the fertility of people, livestock, and agriculture. Offering incense to Baal is a shorthand way of suggesting all acts of worship offered to these gods, which sometimes include sexual immorality and even infant sacrifice. Idolatry produces atrocities in its adherents.

The Baals are just some of the many gods worshipped in the ancient Near East. Hopeful to receive power from any possible source, idol worshippers are more than happy to add more deities to their sacred shrines. Jeremiah's question implies that his hearers are guilty in this regard.

> *What Do You Think?*
> How can we best confront the modern idolatries that challenge our faithfulness to God?
> *Talking Points for Your Discussion*
> - Regarding the idolatry of "me first"
> - Regarding the idolizing of one's country and its ideals
> - Regarding the idolizing of public figures
> - Other

B. Temple Trusted (vv. 10, 11)

10. "'. . . and then come and stand before me in this house, which bears my Name, and say, "We are safe"—safe to do all these detestable things?

The utter emptiness of the people's misplaced faith becomes clearer still. Habitual evildoers and idolaters, they nevertheless return time and again to God's temple, God's house, to go through the motions of worship. There they offer sacrifices, pray, and sing the psalms. In so doing, the people believe that they *are safe* from enemies such as Babylon. In effect, the Judeans believe that God cares more about the form of worship in his temple, or even the temple structure itself, than he does about his people's submission to him. What a miserable, blasphemous view of the holy God!

A letter to Henry Ford of April 1934 had this to say:

> Dear Sir: --
> While I still have got breath in my lungs I will tell you what a dandy car you make. I have drove Fords exclusively when I could get away with one. . . . [E]ven if my business hasn't been strickly legal it don't hurt anything to tell you what a fine car you got in the V8 --

The (unauthenticated) letter was from Clyde Barrow, of "Bonnie and Clyde" infamy. He apparently found stolen Ford V8s quite to his liking for evading the police, thus prompting the letter of praise. The outlaws died in a police ambush several weeks after the letter was sent.

Such praise was hardly the kind of testimony that Henry Ford could use in advertising or otherwise appreciate! Likewise, the tainted praise offered in the temple by the Judeans was not the praise God could honor. Our sins might not be as gross as theirs, but we need to ask, "Does my life validate the praise I offer to God?"   —C. R. B.

What Do You Think?
In what ways can the nature of our worship gatherings influence and be influenced by our individual lifestyles?
Talking Points for Your Discussion
- Positive influences (Acts 2:44-47; Romans 12:1; etc.)
- Negative influences (1 Corinthians 11:17; James 2:1-4; etc.)

---

11. "'Has this house, which bears my Name, become a den of robbers to you? But I have been watching! declares the LORD.

Trusting in the temple is pointless since Judah's actions have made it into something other than God's house. If it were his house in more than name only, then those who worship there would follow his law and pursue his justice. Instead, it is filled with people who commit all the abominations already noted. The people have turned the temple into a bandits' hideout, *a den of robbers.*

But the evildoers can conceal nothing. They cannot hide. God sees everything they do.

Centuries later, Jesus draws on the imagery of this verse when he takes action in the temple (Matthew 21:13; Mark 11:17; Luke 19:46). At least one issue then is the same as in Jeremiah's day: the corrupt temple leadership takes advantage of the weak for their own gain. Even worse, the temple leaders of Jesus' day plot his death so that they can hold on to their own power (John 11:48).

C. Lesson Unlearned (vv. 12-15)

12. "'Go now to the place in Shiloh where I first made a dwelling for my Name, and see what I did to it because of the wickedness of my people Israel.

The question Jeremiah's audience may be thinking at this point is, *Well, then, what will God do with his temple?* To answer this, Jeremiah offers a real-life illustration from Israel's history.

The tabernacle (the temple's precursor) had been located at Shiloh, about 19 miles north of Jerusalem, for years after Israel's conquest of the land (Joshua 18:1; Judges 18:31; 1 Samuel 1:3). In Samuel's time, over 400 years before the days of Jeremiah, the sons of the high priest Eli turned their ministry at the tabernacle into a personal racket, extracting bribes and sexual favors from worshippers there (1 Samuel 2:12-17, 22-25). To make matters worse, some Israelites decided to treat the tabernacle's ark of the covenant like a magical object by taking it into battle (4:3-5). But Israel lost the battle, the ark was captured, and Eli's wicked sons were killed (4:6-11).

Therefore God "abandoned the tabernacle of Shiloh, the tent he had set up among humans" (Psalm 78:60). Jeremiah's audience need only take a trip to God's *place in Shiloh* to understand what he can do to Jerusalem as well. The ark of the covenant did not serve as an object of magical protection, and neither will the temple.

What Do You Think?
What are some things in your personal past that help you refocus your faith and trust in God?
Talking Points for Your Discussion
- Places, events, relationships of a positive nature
- Places, events, relationships of a negative nature

---

13. "'While you were doing all these things, declares the LORD, I spoke to you again and again, but you did not listen; I called you, but you did not answer.

The people of Judah have been warned many times. They have received the law, which specifies the consequences of disobedience. They have received the message of earlier prophets that reminded them of the same. They have seen judgment fall on their kin in northern Israel for habitual idolatry and injustice. They barely escaped a similar destruction themselves (2 Kings 19). Their disobedience (*all these things*) has continued literally for centuries.

It's not that God hasn't done his part—he has, *again and again*! Yet just as habitually the people ignore him and his messengers. Judah's historical track record in this regard portends little hope of escaping God's judgment.

14. "'Therefore, what I did to Shiloh I will now do to the house that bears my Name, the temple you trust in, the place I gave to you and your ancestors.

Again Jeremiah piles up phrases to stress the enormity of Judah's false trust in the temple. *The house* is God's house, the symbol of his authority. It has been his gift to Israel for generations. It is intended as the place where Israel can stand before God and find forgiveness and instruction. This they have turned into a den of robbers.

So God must destroy the temple and those who corrupt it. As he *did to Shiloh*, he *will now do to the house* bearing his name. Allowing the temple to fall will not bring his name into disrepute, but allowing it to continue to stand as a den of robbers certainly will! The calamity to come will affirm that God is the holy, sovereign king who tolerates no hypocrisy.

15. "'I will thrust you from my presence, just as I did all your fellow Israelites, the people of Ephraim.'"

The second history lesson is more recent: the story of the northern kingdom of Israel—here referred to as *Ephraim*, the name of a leading tribe. The people of Judah know that their *fellow Israelites* to the north had fallen to Assyria by God's decision (2 Kings 17:1-23). God's promise of a similar

Visual for
Lessons 4 & 10

Point to this as you ask, "How do people today convince themselves that this statement is wrong?"

fate for Judah indicates that he sees the sins of both groups as identical. While the Judeans like to think of themselves as more favored than their erstwhile kin to the north, God thinks otherwise. And it is his viewpoint that will prevail.

Conclusion
A. God's Promises Stand

God's message was stern and uncompromising. Yet despite Judah's failure, God's promise was still in force to establish David's throne forever (2 Samuel 7:16). Today we know that we have received the fulfillment of that promise in Jesus. We also should realize that we have a clear responsibility regarding how we are to live before God. As followers of Christ, we are to promote God's justice. We are not to be hypocrites who worship God outwardly while plotting rebellion inwardly. As the God of the temple would not be mocked, neither will the God of the cross—the same God.

B. Prayer

O God, we come to you from our hiding places to confess the sin that you already see. Show us your mercy, not the punishment that we deserve, as we show mercy to others. In Jesus' name, amen.

C. Thought to Remember
Know God's desires, and do them.

INVOLVEMENT LEARNING

Enhance your lesson with NIV® Bible Student (from your curriculum supplier) and the reproducible activity page (at www.standardlesson.com or in the back of the NIV® Standard Lesson Commentary Deluxe Edition).

Into the Lesson

Ask each learner to write two true statements about himself or herself along with one false statement. Let them take turns reading the statements to the class. (Encourage learners to mix the order of their statements so everyone doesn't have the false one in the same place.) Class members can then take turns trying to identify the false statement. Keep track of who identifies the most false statements. Then say, "[Winner's name] has done a good job of ferreting out the 'deceptive words' of fellow class members. Today's text will give us some help in identifying 'deceptive words' within society."

Into the Word

Form learners into four groups. Give each group a piece of poster board that features these headings, one each: *Setting, Characters, Problem, Message.* (The groups receiving the *Setting* and *Characters* poster boards can have fewer members; smaller classes can form three groups and assign both *Setting* and *Characters* to one group.) Ask groups to record the relevant elements from the lesson text onto their poster board according to its heading.

Have groups share their findings with the rest of the class. Findings should include the following: *Setting*—temple gate in Jerusalem (v. 2); *Characters*—God, Jeremiah, people of Judah (vv. 1, 2); *Problem*—trusting in "deceptive words" that the temple was a guarantee of safety (vv. 4, 8), holy lives were not required if worship procedures were followed (vv. 9, 10), the people's idolatry had desecrated the temple (v. 11) and they had stopped listening to God (v. 13); *Message*—God would allow the people to stay in the land if they changed their ways (vv. 3-7), otherwise God would bring judgment as he had on Shiloh and Ephraim/Israel (vv. 12, 14, 15). (Note: the *Setting Group* might include Shiloh in its findings since that is a setting of an illustration; similarly, the *Characters Group* might include Ephraim/Israel.)

After the *Problem* group shares its findings, discuss possible reasons for the people to have believed lies. (Use the lesson commentary to guide this discussion.) Moving to the *Message* presentation, discuss whether this was a new message or one the people had heard before. Refer to the following as previous warnings if learners do not do so: 1 Samuel 7:3; 2 Kings 17:13; 2 Chronicles 7:14; Isaiah 55:6, 7; and Jeremiah 3:14-18.

Discuss what God expected (vv. 4-6) and what would happen if the people did not comply. Discuss also what happened at and to Shiloh (1 Samuel 2:12-17, 22-25; Psalm 78:60), what happened to Ephraim/Israel (2 Kings 17), and how these served as illustrative warnings. Connect the results to the message God had given throughout the existence of the Israelites as a people.

Alternative. Distribute copies of the "The Power of Words" activity from the reproducible page, which you can download. Have learners work in small groups to complete. Compare group results in whole-class discussion.

Into Life

Say, "The people of Judah chose to listen to deceptive words rather than to God's Word. Let's compare and contrast their decision with what people choose today." Draw two columns on the board, the left one headed *Jeremiah's Day* and the right one headed *Today.*

Review the lies the Judeans listened to, either expressed or implied in the text, and jot them in the left column. Then brainstorm lies that people heed today; jot those in the other column. (Possible responses: "There are many paths to God." "Surely a loving God would not . . ." etc.) Discuss similarities and differences between entries in the two columns. Ask how to refute the lies.

Alternative. Distribute copies of the "Start with Truth" activity from the reproducible page, to be completed in small groups as indicated.

A CALL FOR
REPENTANCE

DEVOTIONAL READING: Hosea 14
BACKGROUND SCRIPTURE: Ezekiel 18; Proverbs 21:2-15

EZEKIEL 18:1-13, 30-32

[1] The word of the LORD came to me: [2] "What do you people mean by quoting this proverb about the land of Israel:

"'The parents eat sour grapes,
and the children's teeth are set on edge'?

[3] "As surely as I live, declares the Sovereign LORD, you will no longer quote this proverb in Israel. [4] For everyone belongs to me, the parent as well as the child—both alike belong to me. The one who sins is the one who will die.

[5] "Suppose there is a righteous man
who does what is just and right.
[6] He does not eat at the mountain shrines
or look to the idols of Israel.
He does not defile his neighbor's wife
or have sexual relations with a woman during her period.
[7] He does not oppress anyone,
but returns what he took in pledge for a loan.
He does not commit robbery
but gives his food to the hungry
and provides clothing for the naked.
[8] He does not lend to them at interest
or take a profit from them.
He withholds his hand from doing wrong
and judges fairly between two parties.
[9] He follows my decrees
and faithfully keeps my laws.

That man is righteous;
he will surely live,
declares the Sovereign LORD.

[10] "Suppose he has a violent son, who sheds blood or does any of these other things [11] (though the father has done none of them):

"He eats at the mountain shrines.
He defiles his neighbor's wife.
[12] He oppresses the poor and needy.
He commits robbery.
He does not return what he took in pledge.
He looks to the idols.
He does detestable things.
[13] He lends at interest and takes a profit.

Will such a man live? He will not! Because he has done all these detestable things, he is to be put to death; his blood will be on his own head."

. . . .

[30] "Therefore, you Israelites, I will judge each of you according to your own ways, declares the Sovereign LORD. Repent! Turn away from all your offenses; then sin will not be your downfall. [31] Rid yourselves of all the offenses you have committed, and get a new heart and a new spirit. Why will you die, people of Israel? [32] For I take no pleasure in the death of anyone, declares the Sovereign LORD. Repent and live!"

KEY VERSES

Therefore, you Israelites, I will judge each of you according to your own ways, declares the Sovereign LORD. Repent! Turn away from all your offenses; then sin will not be your downfall. Rid yourselves of all the offenses you have committed, and get a new heart and a new spirit. Why will you die, people of Israel? —**Ezekiel 18:30, 31**

GOD'S PROPHETS DEMAND JUSTICE

Unit 3: Advocates of Justice for All

LESSONS 9–13

LESSON AIMS

After participating in this lesson, each learner will be able to:

1. Describe how God refuted the Israelites' belief that they suffered unjustly for the sins of earlier generations.

2. Explain the importance of personal responsibility and culpability in the context of the new covenant of grace.

3. Identify an area of blame-shifting in his or her life and make a plan for change.

LESSON OUTLINE

Introduction
  A. Pass the Blame
  B. Lesson Background
I. Self-Delusion Exposed (Ezekiel 18:1-4)
  A. Proverb Used (vv. 1, 2)
  B. Proverb Forbidden (vv. 3, 4)
    Sour Grapes
II. Who Will Live? (Ezekiel 18:5-9)
  A. Example Introduced (v. 5)
  B. Behavior Described (vv. 6-8)
  C. Innocence Affirmed (v. 9)
III. Who Will Die? (Ezekiel 18:10-13)
  A. Counterexample Introduced (vv. 10, 11a)
  B. Behavior Contrasted (vv. 11b-13a)
  C. Guilt Affirmed (v. 13b)
IV. Choice Offered (Ezekiel 18:30-32)
  A. God's Promise (v. 30a)
  B. God's Call (vv. 30b, 31)
    A New Heart and a New Spirit
  C. God's Desires (v. 32)
Conclusion
  A. The Community and the Individual
  B. Prayer
  C. Thought to Remember

Introduction

A. Pass the Blame

I was sitting on a bench in a mall the first time I saw the saying printed on a T-shirt worn by a young man. It simply read, "Blame my parents."

That witticism is both appealing and appalling at the same time. It has a certain appeal because there is some truth in it: the young man is who he is in large part because of the inherited characteristics (heredity) and upbringing (environment) of and by his parents. It is also appealing when one considers the psychological comfort that results when people use it to relieve themselves of responsibility for who they are and what they have done.

On the other hand, the slogan is appalling because it expresses attitudes of fatalism and irresponsibility by implying that the young man is completely controlled by genetics (nature) and/or upbringing (nurture). Having had no control over either, the slogan proposes that he isn't responsible for who he is and what he does. What a miserable condition all people would be in if this were true!

The young man's T-shirt expresses a popular view today that our bad behavior is not our fault. It is the fault of others. Although the people of Ezekiel's day did not know about genes and probably did not engage in the "nature vs. nurture" debate, they too found comfort by passing the blame back to their ancestors. They did so in the form of a proverb condemned in today's lesson.

B. Lesson Background

Ezekiel, a contemporary of Jeremiah, prophesied during and after the final chaotic years of the kingdom of Judah. King Jehoiakim, whose reign in Judah ended in 597 BC, was succeeded by his son Jehoiachin. He reigned only three months before the Babylonians conquered Jerusalem and took him, along with thousands of the most prominent and skilled people of Judah, to Babylon (2 Kings 24:14). This group of deportees included the prophet Ezekiel (Ezekiel 1:1-3).

The Babylonians placed Zedekiah, Jehoiachin's uncle, on the throne in Jerusalem to implement the will of the Babylonian government (2 Kings 24:17). Zedekiah eventually conspired with other nations to revolt, but this did not succeed. The Babylonians put down the rebellion and destroyed Jerusalem and the temple in 586 BC.

While Jeremiah was preaching in Jerusalem before its destruction, Ezekiel lived with a community of fellow exiles in Babylon. He ministered to a people who had been torn from the land that God had promised them, away from the temple where he promised his presence to be, away from all that was familiar. As they pondered and grieved their situation, what lessons would they learn?

I. Self-Delusion Exposed
(Ezekiel 18:1-4)
A. Proverb Used (vv. 1, 2)

1, 2. The word of the Lord came to me: "What do you people mean by quoting this proverb about the land of Israel:

**"'The parents eat sour grapes,
and the children's teeth are set on edge'?**

As the exiles wallow in the misery of their situation, now in its sixth or seventh year (Ezekiel 8:1; 20:1), they naturally try to come to grips with the reason for it. In so doing, they land on a proverb that becomes popular. A proverb is a short, pithy statement used to express a general truth in a memorable way. The proverb that seems best to explain the situation is the one we see here. The prophet Jeremiah is also confronted with this proverb in his situation back in Judea (Jeremiah 31:29, 30).

The Targum, an ancient Aramaic paraphrase of the Hebrew, gives the meaning of the proverb: "The fathers sin, the children suffer." Therefore,

HOW TO SAY IT

Aramaic	*Air*-uh-*may*-ik.
Aesop	*Ee*-sop.
Babylon	*Bab*-uh-lun.
Babylonians	Bab-ih-*low*-nee-unz.
Ezekiel	Ee-*zeek*-ee-ul or Ee-*zeek*-yul.
Jehoiachin	Jeh-*hoy*-uh-kin.
Jehoiakim	Jeh-*hoy*-uh-kim.
Judah	*Joo*-duh.
Judea	Joo-*dee*-uh.
Zedekiah	Zed-uh-*kye*-uh.

The parents eat sour grapes, and the children's teeth are set on edge expresses the belief that those in exile (the children) are unjustly bearing the punishment for the sins of earlier generations (the parents). Claiming that their problem is inherited, the exiles deny responsibility or guilt on their part.

> ### What Do You Think?
> What are some excuses you have heard used to shift blame? How should we react when we hear these?
> ### Talking Points for Your Discussion
> ▪ Regarding coworkers
> ▪ Regarding fellow church members
> ▪ Regarding family members
> ▪ Other

B. Proverb Forbidden (vv. 3, 4)

3. "As surely as I live, declares the Sovereign Lord, you will no longer quote this proverb in Israel.

The proverb being used has some truth to it in that the sins of one generation can have a serious and lasting effect on the next. We may think of how children suffer today when a breadwinning parent is sent to jail for a crime. Ezekiel himself points out that the exile is the result of covenant unfaithfulness by many generations of Israelites (Ezekiel 16). The Ten Commandments witness to the concept of intergenerational consequences for sin (Exodus 20:5). However, the fact that the sins of one generation have consequences for another is not the same as saying that God punishes an innocent group for the sins of a guilty group.

Israelite history offers instances of children dying as a consequence of the sins of their parents (see Numbers 16:23-33; Joshua 7:24, 25; 2 Samuel 11:1–12:19; 21:1-9). Although there are times when the all-knowing and sovereign God deems this to be fitting, it is rare and certainly not the norm. The problem in today's text is that the exiles specifically apply their proverb to disavow any culpability for their situation. In so doing, they can claim that God is unjust in his dealings with them (Ezekiel 18:25-29; 33:17-20). God corrects their faulty thinking in the examples below.

4. "For everyone belongs to me, the parent as well as the child—both alike belong to me. The one who sins is the one who will die.

Everyone belongs to God since he is the sovereign Creator. Therefore he has the right to declare *the one who sins is the one who will die.* Each person is responsible to God for his or her own sin, and he will deal with each person individually. In giving the Israelites his law, God commanded that "parents are not to be put to death for their children, nor children put to death for their parents; each will die for their own sin" (Deuteronomy 24:16). This principle applies to how God deals with the exiles. His judgments are fair and true.

❧ Sour Grapes ❧

Aesop was the legendary Greek slave who may have lived between 620 and 560 BC. Fables attributed to him live on to this day. One such is "The Fox and the Grapes." It tells of a fox that wants grapes he sees growing on a vine high above him. Unable to reach them, he eventually walks away saying, "The grapes were probably sour anyway."

We still speak of "sour grapes" when a person expresses disdain for something he or she would like to have but cannot possess. For example, one might envy another's expensive sports car but feign lack of desire by saying, "It only holds two people and probably gets terrible gas mileage besides."

The "sour grapes" of which Ezekiel spoke, however, had a different context: a context of blame-shifting to avoid accountability for sin. We may try to comfort ourselves with either the fox's or the Israelites' sour-grapes reasoning, but both are self-delusional. What modern examples of Israelite sour-grapes thinking have you seen?—C. R. B.

II. Who Will Live?
(Ezekiel 18:5-9)

A. Example Introduced (v. 5)

5. "Suppose there is a righteous man who does what is just and right.

The first example the Lord sets forth to illustrate his decree is that of a man who is just. Such a man's desire is to do *what is just and right* in the sight of God and humanity. Specifics follow.

B. Behavior Described (vv. 6-8)

6a. "He does not eat at the mountain shrines or look to the idols of Israel.

The first and arguably most important characteristic of a just or righteous man is that he worships the one and only true God according to the way that God says is proper. To *eat at the mountain shrines* is to participate in sacrifices and religious feasts in places other than the location ordained by the Lord (Deuteronomy 12:13, 14). To *look to the idols of Israel* is to worship and seek help from false gods or to make an image of the true God for worship (5:7, 8). The righteous man is careful first and foremost to remain religiously pure.

6b. "He does not defile his neighbor's wife or have sexual relations with a woman during her period.

The just man also is careful to stay morally pure. The law prohibits both adultery (Exodus 20:14) and intercourse during a woman's menstrual period (Leviticus 15:19-33). The Bible does not explain the latter except to say that a violator "has exposed the source of her flow, and she has also uncovered it" (Leviticus 20:18). Some suggest that this may speak to the special role of blood in atoning for sins, respecting certain rights of women, or to maintain ceremonial purity. Whatever the reason, the righteous man observes this statute.

7, 8. "He does not oppress anyone, but returns what he took in pledge for a loan.

He does not commit robbery but gives his food to the hungry and provides clothing for the naked.

"He does not lend to them at interest or take a profit from them.

**He withholds his hand from doing wrong
and judges fairly between two parties.**

The righteous man also exhibits godly love toward others. It is important to note that all the positive and negative actions addressed here are covered in the Law of Moses. Regarding oppression of a fellow Israelite or a resident non-Israelite, see Exodus 21:2; 22:21. On restoring what a debtor had pledged for security, see Exodus 22:26, 27. *Robbery* is addressed in Exodus 20:15. Meeting the needs of *the hungry* and *the naked* is dealt with in Deuteronomy 15:7-11. Lending to those in need without trying to profit by charging interest is covered in Deuteronomy 23:19, 20.

What Do You Think?

What helps you decide how best to assist those in need when you are overwhelmed with opportunities to do so?

Talking Points for Your Discussion

- Regarding needs within your church family
- Regarding needs within your extended family
- Regarding needs in your larger community
- Other

The righteous man never lies about or wrongs a neighbor for any reason, in careful obedience to Deuteronomy 5:20, 21. Rather, he keeps his distance from evil and all forms of judicial corruption (16:19). In short, such a man puts God's law above any opportunity to gain at the expense of another.

C. Innocence Affirmed (v. 9)

**9. "He follows my decrees
and faithfully keeps my laws.
That man is righteous;
he will surely live,
declares the Sovereign LORD.**

Here we have a sparkling example of the parallelism that is a hallmark of Hebrew poetry: *follows* is another way of saying *faithfully keeps*. Likewise, God's *decrees* are the same as his *laws*. Comprehensively, the righteous man does not follow the selfish, sinful ways of others; he is instead committed to doing what is right and just. God therefore declares *he will surely live*. God will not judge or punish him for the sins of others.

III. Who Will Die?
(EZEKIEL 18:10-13)

A. Counterexample Introduced (vv. 10, 11a)

10, 11a. "Suppose he has a violent son, who sheds blood or does any of these other things (though the father has done none of them):

In a counterexample, the hypothetical righteous man has a wicked son who does not embrace his father's values and lifestyle. Indeed, the wicked son is the exact opposite of his father. In committing robbery and murder, the son acts in ways his father would never countenance. While the father no doubt has taught and modeled the ways of the Lord to his son, the son has the freedom to choose what type of man he will be. He will also be solely responsible to the Lord for the path he chooses.

B. Behavior Contrasted (vv. 11b-13a)

**11b-13a. "He eats at the mountain shrines.
He defiles his neighbor's wife.
He oppresses the poor and needy.
He commits robbery.
He does not return what he took in pledge.
He looks to the idols.
He does detestable things.
He lends at interest and takes a profit.
Will such a man live?**

It's almost like the son is thinking, *Whatever dad does, I'm going to do the opposite!* The son does not worship the one true God in the way that God prescribes. He takes (or creates) every possible opportunity to exploit others. As he *looks to the idols*, he attributes to them the abilities to provide blessings that can come only from the one true God. In so doing, the son follows the example of other nations rather than the law that God has given to the Israelites.

A person who does not love God and is not loyal to him will not love other people or be loyal to them either. The reason is that love for one's neighbor grows out of a love for God. The wicked son uses people to fulfill his own lust and greed. He has no concern for the needs of others. He has no moral reservations about committing adultery, oppressing the most vulnerable, practicing violence, etc., when there is personal gain to be had in doing so.

C. Guilt Affirmed (v. 13b)

13b. "He will not! Because he has done all these detestable things, he is to be put to death; his blood will be on his own head."

The wicked son who walks contrary to the righteous requirements of God is the one to die. He will die for his own sins despite the fact that his father is righteous. Verses 14-20 (not in today's text) establish that if this wicked man has a righteous son who does not commit the abominations of his father but follows the righteous path of his grandfather, then that righteous man will live. These examples demonstrate the fallacy of the proverb that the exiles are using. God replaces that proverb with the truth that "the one who sins is the one who will die" (v. 4, above).

IV. Choice Offered
(EZEKIEL 18:30-32)
A. God's Promise (v. 30a)

30a. "Therefore, you Israelites, I will judge each of you according to your own ways, declares the Sovereign LORD.

Each Israelite decides how he or she lives, and God judges each based on that choice. Although every person is responsible for his or her own guilt before the Lord, individual decisions do indeed affect the community as a whole. God says he will judge *you Israelites* [plural], *each of you* [singular]. The plural *you Israelites* shows that the covenant God has with Israel is corporate; it includes all Israel as a whole. The singular *each of you* shows that the overall moral tone of the community is formed on the collective choices of individuals.

B. God's Call (vv. 30b, 31)

30b, 31. "Repent! Turn away from all your offenses; then sin will not be your downfall. Rid yourselves of all the offenses you have committed, and get a new heart and a new spirit. Why will you die, people of Israel?

After correcting the Israelites' thinking concerning their situation, God calls them to return to him. The Israelites are to look not at the conduct of their ancestors but to their own. The people are to rid themselves of any and all personal sin. To repent is to avoid the judgment of death that sin brings. God is gracious and forgives all who turn to him in repentance and faith. The result of that turn will be *a new heart and a new spirit* that loves the Lord and lives according to his Word. When that happens, the *people of Israel* as a whole will experience new life.

Again, God asks a rhetorical question: *Why will you die?* The sentence of death is not inevitable since God extends an offer of forgiveness through repentance. Each individual has the freedom to choose life or death. If people did not have free will, then they would not be responsible. People are capable of knowing right from wrong, and God deals with them on that basis. The blame for one's sin and judgment cannot be shifted to God, Satan, nature, nurture, parents, or circumstances.

❧ *A NEW HEART AND A NEW SPIRIT* ❧

As a member of the New York Colombo crime syndicate, Michael Franzese created fraudulent schemes that brought him millions of dollars. His biggest illegal profits came from a scam that stole $1 billion in gasoline excise taxes in the 1980s.

Franzese eventually got involved in the movie business. On a movie set in 1984, he met dancer Cammy Garcia. He was attracted to her because she seemed "different" from others he met in the industry. Cammy didn't know what kind of business Michael was in, but she started talking to him about God. Love blossomed, and Michael and Cammy were married in 1985.

But that was also the year the law caught up with Michael, and he spent 43 months in prison. Although having accepted Jesus as Savior just before the marriage, it took some time for Michael to realize his need for radical life-change. It was during a second incarceration, of 29 months for violating parole, that he says he "ate, drank, and slept the Bible." Since release from prison in 1994, Michael has become a Christian motivational speaker.

Repentance does indeed bring a new heart and a new spirit. With it comes a new life that builds and heals, and Michael Franzese's story demonstrates that God still has the power to do exactly that! And so it is for all of us. —C. R. B.

What Do You Think?

What is the most startling example of lifestyle change you know of that resulted from having received "a new heart and a new spirit"?

Talking Points for Your Discussion

- A public figure
- A colleague at work or school
- A personal friend
- Other

C. God's Desires (v. 32)

32. "For I take no pleasure in the death of anyone, declares the Sovereign LORD. Repent and live!"

God wants everyone to live. He desires to deliver people from their unfaithfulness and the death that it brings. He never enjoys condemning the wicked (also Ezekiel 33:11). Even so, he is righteous in dispensing judgment. He will bring judgment if necessary, but will not take pleasure in it.

Therefore, God issues an invitation to repent and live, as he has done so many times before. He demonstrates love by his willingness to set people free from their sinful past and the punishment they deserve. He demonstrates his holiness and justice by not allowing them to continue in sin forever. God is still patient today, not wishing any to perish but to come to repentance (2 Peter 3:9).

Conclusion

A. The Community and the Individual

Ezekiel teaches us how a person is to respond to the condition of a community. It is true that each generation influences the next, but none controls what its successor does. A generation is not predetermined for blessings or judgments by actions of the previous one. The individual and the generation of which he or she is part of have freedom to choose how to live: either walking the path of God or the path of rebellion. Those who keep God's Word will live; those who rebel will die. Each will bear his or her own iniquity. Even if a person lives in a grossly immoral society, that is not to be an excuse for sin. Rather, living in such a society is all the more reason to do what is just, right, and true.

Visual for Lesson 11

Point to this visual as you introduce the discussion question associated with verse 31.

Ezekiel also teaches us that individuals form the overall tone of communities. The choices of individuals determine the spiritual and moral condition of the whole. God desires that each individual turn to him and thus help build strong and righteous communities. The choices each person makes today will have more impact on determining the condition of the community than either heredity or environment.

B. Prayer

Lord, forgive us for passing off the guilt for our sins! Help us take responsibility for our own actions as a foundation for building holy communities. We praise you for the eternal life that we have in Jesus Christ, who bore the penalty for sins that were not his. In his name, amen.

C. Thought to Remember

Each person is responsible before God.

INVOLVEMENT LEARNING

Enhance your lesson with NIV® Bible Student (from your curriculum supplier) and the reproducible activity page (at www.standardlesson.com or in the back of the NIV® Standard Lesson Commentary Deluxe Edition).

Into the Lesson

As learners arrive, give each an index card with a well-known proverb written on it. The following are possibilities; many more are easy to find on the Internet:

> *A bird in the hand is worth two in the bush.*
> *A little learning is a dangerous thing.*
> *Well begun is half done.*

Say, "One definition is that a proverb is 'a short, pithy statement of a general truth.' With that definition in mind, take a minute to write the meaning of your proverb on the card." When you call time, have learners take turns reading their proverbs aloud for others to discuss meanings. Make a transition by saying, "Our lesson text centers on a familiar proverb of Ezekiel's day. But God's opinion of it as 'a general truth' didn't match the popular understanding. Let's see why."

Into the Word

Display a sentence strip, prepared in advance with very large lettering, featuring the proverb in Ezekiel 18:2b. Briefly discuss what learners think it means. Record proposals on the board, but do not evaluate the correctness of the responses. Then have a volunteer read verses 3 and 4 aloud. Ask learners what they believe to be the connection between these verses and the proverb in verse 2.

Wrap that discussion up by noting that the meaning of the proverb is "The fathers sin, the children suffer." Guide your learners to understand that the exiles from Judah living in Babylon used this proverb to explain their circumstances and, in the process, deny their culpability. Say, "The rest of our lesson text this morning is God's refutation of that belief."

Divide the class into at least two groups. Assign one group verses 5-9 and the other group verses 10-13. (Give duplicate assignments if you form more that two groups.) Ask each group to record the behaviors listed for the hypothetical individual listed and the consequences of those behaviors. After groups finish, create two columns on the board, headed *Righteous Man* and *Wicked Son.* Record the behaviors and consequences in each column, as summarized in group presentations.

Say, "We need to understand the difference between a generation's (1) suffering the effects of the sins of previous generations and (2) being held accountable for those sins. The Israelites were trying to shift the blame for their situation and thereby excuse themselves from any responsibility concerning that status. But God judges each person according to personal behavior."

Read verses 30-32 aloud. Have learners brainstorm how the thoughts in these verses are reflected in the New Testament. Learners may mention Luke 3:8; Romans 8:13; 10:5; and Galatians 3:10-12, among others.

Option. Begin this segment by distributing copies of "A Scrambled Mess" from the reproducible page, which you can download. Without looking in their Bibles, have learners work in pairs to see who can complete it the fastest (or who can complete the most within a time limit). Console all nonwinning pairs with this proverb: "The race is not to the swift or the battle to the strong" (Ecclesiastes 9:11). Expect humorous reactions!

Into Life

Ask learners to brainstorm some common proverbial excuses they have used (or heard others use) to rationalize their misbehavior or failure to follow God's Word. (Some possible responses: "well, nobody's perfect," "to err is human," "the devil made me do it," and "I'm not as bad as I used to be.") Close with a minute of silent prayer of confession and recommitment in this regard.

Alternative. Distribute copies of the "Start from Scratch" activity from the reproducible page. Allow two minutes for learners to complete as indicated.

A DEMAND
FOR JUSTICE

DEVOTIONAL READING: Psalm 147:1-11
BACKGROUND SCRIPTURE: Zechariah 7; Isaiah 30:18-26

ZECHARIAH 7:8-14

⁸ And the word of the LORD came again to Zechariah: ⁹ "This is what the LORD Almighty said: 'Administer true justice; show mercy and compassion to one another. ¹⁰ Do not oppress the widow or the fatherless, the foreigner or the poor. Do not plot evil against each other.'

¹¹ "But they refused to pay attention; stubbornly they turned their backs and covered their ears. ¹² They made their hearts as hard as flint and would not listen to the law or to the words that the LORD Almighty had sent by his Spirit through the earlier prophets. So the LORD Almighty was very angry.

¹³ "'When I called, they did not listen; so when they called, I would not listen,' says the LORD Almighty. ¹⁴ 'I scattered them with a whirlwind among all the nations, where they were strangers. The land they left behind them was so desolate that no one traveled through it. This is how they made the pleasant land desolate.'"

KEY VERSES

"This is what the LORD Almighty said: 'Administer true justice; show mercy and compassion to one another. Do not oppress the widow or the fatherless, the foreigner or the poor. Do not plot evil against each other.'"
—**Zechariah 7:9, 10**

GOD'S PROPHETS DEMAND JUSTICE

Unit 3: Advocates of Justice for All

LESSONS 9–13

LESSON AIMS

After participating in this lesson, each learner will be able to:

1. Summarize Zechariah's message of judgment against Israel.

2. Compare and contrast the stated consequences of Israel's sin with modern situations and afflictions that might be said to be consequences of sin.

3. Identify one area of hardness in his or her heart and write a prayer for change.

LESSON OUTLINE

Introduction

Introduction

A. When Is It Too Late?

Not long ago, my wife and I were celebrating an anniversary with an overnight stay in a nearby resort town. As we perused the shops, she found a nice top she liked, and we went to the cashier to purchase it. That's when I remembered I had a gift card for $50 in my wallet, received from my cellphone company for plan renewal. I thought this would be an excellent time to use the gift card, since I was low on cash.

I was surprised when the card was rejected. The clerk looked at it and said, "Sorry, this card is expired." What?! I had no idea that such a card had an expiration date! Without realizing it, I had waited too long. It was too late, and the value of the card had been reclaimed by the phone company.

This causes me to reflect on other "too lates." For instance, think about relationships. Ministers often counsel alienated family members who wish there had been reconciliation before an untimely death. There is not much comfort or satisfaction in saying, "Sorry, please forgive me" while standing at a casket or a grave. It is too late.

More importantly, we may hear someone ask, "Is it ever too late to repair a relationship with God?" Our first impulse may be to reply, "Of course not! God is gracious and loving and will always welcome back his wandering children." But our lesson text for today may cause us to rethink that response.

B. Lesson Background

By one count, there are 31 men by the name of *Zechariah* in the Bible, so we take care not to get them mixed up. The Zechariah who delivered the message of today's text was a post-exilic prophet, having ministered in the period after some of the people of Israel had returned from their forced relocation to Babylon.

That exile was the result of the crushing of the nation of Judah by the Babylonian army at God's decree (Jeremiah 20:4-6; 21:4-10). This disaster included destruction of the temple in Jerusalem in 586 BC. Many Israelites were killed, and many were deported some 880 miles to the east to serve their conquerors. The powerful emotions accompanying all this were captured by a psalmist: "By the rivers of Babylon we sat and wept when we remembered Zion" (Psalm 137:1).

Zechariah was one of those who returned to Jerusalem in 538 BC to rebuild the temple after release from captivity (Ezra 6:14). But rebuilding a physical structure wouldn't do any good without a proper spiritual framework to go with it. Zechariah's focus was on constructing just such a framework.

Zechariah is careful to date his prophecies and give some context. Chapter 7 of his book, from which today's lesson text comes, begins by specifying a date that computes to December 7, 518 BC. Temple reconstruction had begun in the spring of 536 BC, but was halted shortly thereafter due to opposition (Ezra 3:8; 4:24). After work resumed on September 21, 520 BC (Ezra 4:24; Haggai 1:14, 15), rebuilding was finished on March 12, 515 BC (Ezra 6:15). Therefore the prophecy in today's text occurred about halfway between the resumption of that construction project and its completion.

The occasion for Zechariah's teaching was a question raised by a delegation from Bethel, a town about 12 miles north of Jerusalem (Zechariah 7:2). They wanted to know whether it was still necessary or appropriate to fast in the fifth month each year (7:3). That custom was probably begun as a remembrance of Jerusalem's destruction by the armies of King Nebuchadnezzar, which occurred in the fifth month of the Jewish year (see 2 Kings 25:8-10). The context of the question, which includes progress on rebuilding city and temple, indicates a desire to discontinue the fast (also observed in the seventh month per Zechariah 7:5).

HOW TO SAY IT

Amos	*Ay*-mus.
Babylon	*Bab*-uh-lun.
Babylonian	Bab-ih-*low*-nee-un.
Ezra	*Ez*-ruh.
Isaiah	Eye-*zay*-uh.
Jeremiah	Jair-uh-*my*-uh.
Nebuchadnezzar	*Neb*-yuh-kud-**nez**-er.
Zechariah	Zek-uh-**rye**-uh.

God's four responses to this question, delivered through Zechariah, address the underlying heart-condition of the people. The first response questioned the sincerity of the fasting (Zechariah 7:4-7). The second response is the text of this week's lesson.

I. God's Requirements
(ZECHARIAH 7:8-10)
A. What to Do (vv. 8, 9)

8, 9a. And the word of the LORD came again to Zechariah: "This is what the LORD Almighty said:

We see here a characteristic introduction of a prophecy from Zechariah. First, he announces that *the word of the Lord* has come to him personally (also in Zechariah 1:1, 7; 4:6, 8; 6:9; 7:1, 4; 8:1, 18). The prophet does not explain how this happened, whether as an audible voice, a message imprinted on his consciousness in some way, or something else. Second, he proceeds to verbalize this word to the people. In so doing, he speaks on behalf of *the Lord Almighty,* delivering a message of power and authority to the people of Jerusalem.

9b. "'Administer true justice; show mercy and compassion to one another.

Remember that the question on the floor is about the necessity to continue certain fasting, as posed by a delegation from Bethel (see the Lesson Background). Zechariah brushes aside this seemingly sincere query to get to a more important issue: What is the condition of the heart of the people as evidenced by their keeping of God's commandments?

There is no biblical record that the Lord had instituted a requirement for the fasting about which the delegation asks; it seems to have been a human initiative. Such a practice may serve a good purpose, but it means nothing if the people are not concerned about the Lord's expressed requirements for a just, merciful, and compassionate society. Are the people concerned about *true justice,* meaning fair and impartial legal proceedings in their courts (compare Isaiah 1:17)? Are they showing *mercy and compassion* in their interpersonal dealings (compare Micah 6:8)?

❧ THE ULTRA-WEALTHY AND THE REST OF US ❧

In 1871, Mark Twain asked, "What is the chief end of man? To get rich. In what way? Dishonestly if we can; honestly if we must." Twain was satirizing the beginning of the Gilded Age in America, a period from about 1870 to 1900. That was the era of the notorious "robber barons" such as John D. Rockefeller, whose net worth has been estimated at nearly $200 billion in today's money. The ultra-wealthy were known for flaunting their wealth at a time when the average annual family income was about $9,000 in today's money.

A class of ultra-wealthy exists today, but perhaps with a difference. In 2010, Warren Buffett and Bill Gates challenged the richest people in America to commit to giving 50 percent of their net worth to charity, either while alive or in their estates. By one estimate, that could total $600 billion!

It's easy to condemn the robber barons of the 1800s and look with skepticism at the giving motives of today's ultra-wealthy. But before we go down that path, consider this: a recent study reveals that those in the bottom 10 percent of income in the U.S. are in the upper 30 percent income bracket of the world as a whole! When we realize that we are quite well off in a global context, any fingers we point at the ultra-wealthy may end up pointing right back at ourselves.   —C. R. B.

B. What Not to Do (v. 10)

10. "'Do not oppress the widow or the father-less, the foreigner or the poor. Do not plot evil against each other.'"

Zechariah continues with pointed reminders about behavior toward the most vulnerable. Death of a husband and father leaves behind *the widow* and *the fatherless*, who usually have little means to take care of themselves. There are no government assistance programs to provide food stamps or community housing. Unless the extended families of these unfortunate folks step up to help, their options are grim—as horrible as the widow prostituting herself or selling her children as servant-slaves so they can at least be clothed and fed. They need helpful neighbors and impartial courts, not ruthless masters who will steal what little they have. Widows and orphans have a special place in God's heart (see Exodus 22:22-24), and he will not forget those who abuse them (compare Luke 20:47; James 1:27).

Another category of the most vulnerable is *the foreigner*. This is the non-Israelite who lives among the people of Israel. Such a person is not a wealthy expatriate, but a refugee who has fled oppression and/or poverty back in his or her homeland to seek opportunities among the Israelites (the reverse of which is seen in Ruth 1:1). These non-citizens constitute an underclass that is susceptible to exploitation. Although they may observe Israel's laws (Exodus 12:48; etc.), they are still an underclass, a fact that leaves them vulnerable to unjust court judgments.

God had taught Israel long before that widows, orphans, and strangers are under his special protection (see Deuteronomy 10:18; Psalm 146:9). Provision must be made for their livelihoods (Deuteronomy 24:20, 21; etc.).

Zechariah's last group is *the poor*. Widows, orphans, and foreigners can, of course, be included in this designation. But as an umbrella term, *the poor* includes others as well—anyone who needs assistance for the basics of food, clothing, and shelter. There is no excuse for starvation in a city where resources are available to help.

This verse ends with a blanket statement of a controlling ethic: stop planning evil against others. Don't plot how you may exploit the powerless and gullible; seek to protect them instead. This gives a broad-stroke backward glance of the tone of society before the destruction of Jerusalem in

586 BC: a selfish, ruthless culture that dishonored God by oppressing the most vulnerable.

II. Israel's Refusal
(ZECHARIAH 7:11, 12a)
A. Unhearing Ears (v. 11)

11. "But they refused to pay attention; stubbornly they turned their backs and covered their ears.

Verses 13, 14 (below) indicate that the prophet is describing the refusal of the Israelites to listen to God prior to the Babylonian exile. This is an indictment of Israel's active neglect of his demands for social justice. Simply put, *they refused to pay attention.* God's plea through his prophets for Israel to reform was ignored with contempt.

Two vivid word-pictures illustrate this. First, the fact that they *turned their backs* means they faced away from God and his messengers. This is body language of disrespect and scorn. Second, the fact that they *covered their ears* indicates an intentional refusal to listen. We easily imagine a child who turns his back and puts his hands over his ears while being given a stern talk by a parent. This is more than a mere failure to listen; it is an actively defiant way of saying, "I have no interest in even hearing what you say, so you might as well be quiet" (compare Acts 7:57).

B. Unresponsive Hearts (v. 12a)

12a. "They made their hearts as hard as flint and would not listen to the law or to the words that the LORD Almighty had sent by his Spirit through the earlier prophets."

With one of the starkest word-pictures in the Bible, Zechariah goes on to describe this defi-

ant unresponsiveness of the ancestors of his audience. The word translated *flint* suggests the idea of "absolute, unyielding stubbornness" (see also Jeremiah 17:1; Ezekiel 3:9).

The hardened heart is a sad part of the Bible's story line (see Deuteronomy 15:7). This condition is more severe than that of a cold heart, which indicates lack of emotional response. It is, rather, the heart that has aligned itself against God. Such hardening is the stubborn refusal to submit to God, the illusion that one can make his or her own way in this world without God, that the mercy of God is unnecessary in one's life.

That had been the intolerable spiritual condition of the Israelites, God's people, before the exile. They had willfully chosen to rebel against their Lord despite his repeated warnings through prophets such as Amos, Isaiah, and Jeremiah. The implied question to Zechariah's audience is whether that heart condition has changed.

III. God's Response
(ZECHARIAH 7:12b-14)
A. Rising Anger (v. 12b)

12b. "So the LORD Almighty was very angry.

We have no way of knowing exactly when the Lord reached the end of his patience, the point of no return. One hint from the prophet Jeremiah indicates that things were so bad under King Manasseh (ruled Judah 697–643 BC) that it was during that man's reign when sin reached its tipping point for God (Jeremiah 15:4; compare 2 Kings 21:11-16; 23:25-27; 24:2-4). Punishment could be delayed (2 Kings 22:19, 20; etc.), but the great judgmental wrath of God was certain nonetheless (compare Revelation 6:15-17).

B. Unflinching Determination (v. 13)

13. "'When I called, they did not listen; so when they called, I would not listen,' says the LORD Almighty.

In a passage dripping with irony, Zechariah presents how the tables turned completely. For many generations, God's prophets had begged Israel to repent of patterns of social oppression and injustice, warning of the consequences that awaited if they failed to do so. They did not listen, and things only got worse.

Finally, the day came for the fury of God's wrath to be unleashed on Jerusalem through the devastating siege by the Babylonian army. The people undoubtedly cried out to God to show mercy and deliver them. But that time God was the one not listening. His plan to punish was not to be diverted, delayed, or softened. It was too late. All chances to repent and reform had been ignored and used up.

What Do You Think?

Under what circumstances might God refuse to listen to people today? How do we prevent this?

Talking Points for Your Discussion

- Job 35:12, 13
- Lamentations 3:44
- Isaiah 1:15
- James 4:3
- 1 Peter 3:7
- Other

C. Sobering Result (v. 14)

14. "'I scattered them with a whirlwind among all the nations, where they were strangers. The land they left behind them was so desolate that no one traveled through it. This is how they made the pleasant land desolate.'"

We can only imagine what Jerusalem and its surrounding villages looked like after the Babylonian army had devastated the area (compare Jeremiah 52:13, 14). Most Judeans were scattered to Babylon as prisoners; some found temporary refuge in Egypt (44:12-14, 24-28) and other foreign nations. Truly, *the land they left behind them was . . . desolate.* It was nearly depopulated, with only the poorest of the poor being left behind (52:16). The villages were looted and burned (19:15). The great city of Jerusalem was laid waste, its walls and temple merely piles of rubble. Orchards, vineyards, and groves of olive trees undoubtedly were destroyed. The Babylonian army probably had confiscated for food all the flocks of animals in the surrounding countryside.

Zechariah describes this ruination as being so complete *that no one traveled through* the area. There was no reason to go there except to mock (compare Lamentations 2:15), and we get the picture that even the infrastructure of roads was destroyed. *The pleasant land* that once flowed "with milk and honey" (Ezekiel 20:6) was a desolation. The beloved temple of Solomon was destroyed. The royal city of Jerusalem was no more. In our own times, we can compare this with images of bombed-out cities where every building is flattened, the few remaining people living in makeshift hovels constructed from whatever can be scrounged.

The divine anger behind this destruction was not like a human rage that rumbles out of control. God's wrath was a righteous punishment for rebellion. It flowed from his holy nature. The wrath of the Lord was complete, and the hard lessons of the consequences for disobedience were to be seared into the collective memory of the nation of Israel.

❧ WASTELANDS, THEN AND NOW ❧

T. S. Eliot's *The Waste Land*, published in 1922, has been called one of the most important poems of the twentieth century. A casual reader might wonder why, since it is quite long and very difficult to understand. The voices that speak in the poem change frequently and abruptly. *The Waste Land* is filled with references to obscure sections of classic literature.

Literary critics speculate that these characteristics of the poem were Eliot's way of showing the reader that he or she was a contributing factor to the "dumbing down" of Western culture in not being able to recognize the references. Eliot was pessimistic about the future, believing the culture was becoming an intellectual and spiritual wasteland. Now, nearly 100 years later, some observers believe what Eliot dreaded has become reality.

Eliot's concern somewhat parallels that of Zechariah's regarding the wasteland that Judah had become. Everything about the culture pointed to the sad reality of a desolation. This wasteland did not result from natural disasters such as droughts or floods, but from rejection of spiritual heritage and identity. The result of such rejection was to face God's wrath. How do you think God views the status of our nation in the twenty-first century?   —C. R. B.

What Do You Think?

What could be some consequences for neglecting justice and mercy today? How would we know whether those consequences were divine or natural in origin, or would it matter?

Talking Points for Your Discussion
- For individuals
- For families
- For churches
- For nations

Conclusion

A. "Give Me Thy Heart"

Eliza Edmunds Hewitt (1851–1920) taught in the tough public schools of Philadelphia in the latter half of the nineteenth century. Along the way, she suffered a tragic back injury that caused her to be confined to her bed for many years. As she was recovering, she did not allow herself to wallow in self-pity or bitterness. Instead, she turned to writing hymns. Among the dozens of her compositions are "More About Jesus" and "When We All Get to Heaven," still sung today.

As an invalid, Eliza Hewitt developed deep insights into the nature of God. One of her most powerful hymns reinforces the message of Zechariah in today's lesson. This hymn, "Give Me Thy Heart," expresses the sentiment this way:

"Give me thy heart," says the Father above,
No gift so precious to him as our love;
Softly he whispers wherever thou art,
"Gratefully trust me, and give my thy heart."
"Give me thy heart, Give me thy heart,"

Visual for Lesson 12. *Start a discussion by pointing to this visual as you ask, "Is 'failing to help' a form of oppression? Why, or why not?"*

Hear the soft whisper, wherever thou art,
From this dark world he would draw thee apart,
Speaking so tenderly, "Give me thy heart."

That was the Lord's message to his chosen people for centuries: *Give me your hearts! Don't let them be hard! Don't let selfishness and disobedience rule your lives! Give me your hearts!*

But they didn't. History records that even as the Babylonians threatened their land and their beloved Jerusalem, the people continued in their stubborn ways.

What about us? Our disobedience and lack of compassion try God's heart today as well. Have you really given him your heart, or do you guard it for yourself? Do you assume that God will wait forever for you to finally turn to him with all your heart, all your soul, all your mind, and all your strength (Mark 12:30)? Don't wait, don't make excuses, don't dawdle. Heed the lesson of Israel. Give him your heart!

B. Prayer

Father, you loved us so much that you gave your Son for us. Yet we have often turned our backs on you. We have covered our ears. We have treated your expectations as optional. Today, may we fully give you our hearts. We pray for this in Jesus' name; amen.

C. Thought to Remember

God wants full commitment to him.

INVOLVEMENT LEARNING

Enhance your lesson with NIV® Bible Student *(from your curriculum supplier) and the reproducible activity page (at www.standardlesson.com or in the back of the* NIV® Standard Lesson Commentary Deluxe Edition*).*

Into the Lesson

Ask learners to recall a time when they were "too late" for something (using a gift card, catching a plane, etc.), and let a few share stories with the class (but don't let this drag out). Ask, "Is it ever too late to repair one's relationship with God?" After reactions say, "Today's lesson text tells us of a time when God's people prayed, but God refused to hear them because it was too late. We see the result also in Psalm 137."

Ask a volunteer to read Psalm 137:1-6. Explain that this psalm was written as a response to the reality of the Babylonian exile. Then say, "In today's lesson, we find that some exiles had returned to Jerusalem, and the prophet Zechariah was ministering to them. Sidestepping a question concerning fasting, he relayed God's perspective on why Israel has suffered as a nation."

Into the Word

Divide the class into three groups of no more than four each. Assign verses 8-10 of the lesson text to the *God's Requirements Group* to summarize God's original message to the Israelites. Assign verses 11, 12a (ending with the word *prophets*) to the *Israel's Refusal Group* to summarize Israel's response to God's message. Assign verses 12b-14 (beginning with the word *So*) to the *God's Reaction Group* to summarize God's rejoinder. (Larger classes can form more groups and be given duplicate assignments.) After a few minutes, ask groups to share their summaries with the rest of the class. Be sure to note any issues the groups overlook.

Next, ask learners to call out short phrases that summarize the Israelites' patterns of behavior that have revealed themselves over the past three weeks of study (lessons 9–11). Jot responses on the board as they are voiced. (Expected responses: *injustice, oppression, idolatry, murder, adultery, temple misused, people shifted blame.*)

Next, ask learners to call out short phrases that summarize God's reactions to those patterns of behavior as studied over the past three weeks. Again, jot responses on the board. (Expected responses: *a Redeemer would come, the unrepentant would be expelled from the land, the obedient would live, the disobedient would die.*) Be sure to mention any that learners do not.

Tie those summaries to today's lesson as you ask, "How are the Israelites' patterns of behavior and God's reactions just mentioned reflected in today's text?" Following open discussion, say, "Some propose that the disastrous consequences wrought by God on the Israelites for sin have parallels with the modern calamities of terrorist attacks, natural disasters, governmental persecution, etc. How would we know whether such events are God's judgment or just random consequences of living in a fallen world?" Use Luke 13:1-5 and John 9:1-3 to clarify the discussion.

Into Life

Say, "Today's lesson notes the determining factor regarding God's response to Israel's behavior: the people had hardened their hearts against God's Word. Let's take a few minutes to identify some reasons why people do the same thing today." Brainstorm some reasons in that regard. (Possible responses: *extreme sorrow, anger at God, sense of self-sufficiency, "what kind of God would allow . . . ," etc.*). End with a time of silent prayer for those within the community and the church who may have hardened their hearts against God.

Alternative. Distribute copies of the "Justice, Mercy, Compassion" activity from the reproducible page, which you can download. Have learners complete it in pairs or groups of three.

Option. Distribute copies of the "Don't Be a Pharaoh" activity from the reproducible page. Save time at the end of class for learners to complete it in silent reflection.

A PLEA TO RETURN TO GOD

DEVOTIONAL READING: Psalm 25:4-11
BACKGROUND SCRIPTURE: Malachi 3:1-12; Matthew 7:12

MALACHI 3:1-10

¹ "I will send my messenger, who will prepare the way before me. Then suddenly the Lord you are seeking will come to his temple; the messenger of the covenant, whom you desire, will come," says the LORD Almighty.

² But who can endure the day of his coming? Who can stand when he appears? For he will be like a refiner's fire or a launderer's soap. ³ He will sit as a refiner and purifier of silver; he will purify the Levites and refine them like gold and silver. Then the LORD will have men who will bring offerings in righteousness, ⁴ and the offerings of Judah and Jerusalem will be acceptable to the LORD, as in days gone by, as in former years.

⁵ "So I will come to put you on trial. I will be quick to testify against sorcerers, adulterers and perjurers, against those who defraud laborers of their wages, who oppress the widows and the fatherless, and deprive the foreigners among you of justice, but do not fear me," says the LORD Almighty.

⁶ "I the LORD do not change. So you, the descendants of Jacob, are not destroyed. ⁷ Ever since the time of your ancestors you have turned away from my decrees and have not kept them. Return to me, and I will return to you," says the LORD Almighty.

"But you ask, 'How are we to return?'

⁸ "Will a mere mortal rob God? Yet you rob me.

"But you ask, 'How are we robbing you?'

"In tithes and offerings. ⁹ You are under a curse—your whole nation—because you are robbing me. ¹⁰ Bring the whole tithe into the storehouse, that there may be food in my house. Test me in this," says the LORD Almighty, "and see if I will not throw open the floodgates of heaven and pour out so much blessing that there will not be room enough to store it."

KEY VERSE

So in everything, do to others what you would have them do to you, for this sums up the Law and the Prophets. —**Matthew 7:12**

GOD'S PROPHETS DEMAND JUSTICE

Unit 3: Advocates of Justice for All

LESSONS 9–13

LESSON AIMS

After participating in this lesson, each learner will be able to:

1. List some indicators that the people of Malachi's day had broken God's covenant.

2. Explain Malachi's rebuke of the people's breach of the covenant in the context of the coming day of the Lord.

3. Examine his or her fidelity to the new covenant and commit to greater faithfulness.

LESSON OUTLINE

Introduction

A. Tithing Today

While visiting Ely Cathedral in England, I also saw a former home of Oliver Cromwell (1599–1658), who became the Lord Protector of the commonwealth of England, Scotland, and Ireland. This structure, dating to the thirteenth century, had been the cathedral's "tithing house." Cromwell lived there for about a decade as he served as the agent to collect tithes from local farmers and store them in the nearby "tithing barn."

This tithe was a levy of 10 percent on farmers' produce, the most practical way to receive tithes in a largely cashless society. Not only was tithing obligatory in those days, it was enforced by a quasi-governmental system. This seems very foreign to us today, yet the issue of tithing has been a source of controversy in several churches I have served. Should the church expect all members to tithe (give 10 percent)? Should the church *require* this? If so, how should it be enforced? Should the tithe be on gross or net income? Should all the tithe go to the local church, or does money given to other charitable organizations count as part of the tithe? So many questions!

Despite the system of Cromwell's England and traditions of many churches today, there is no direct New Testament teaching that requires tithing. Paul taught the Corinthians to give willingly, generously, and cheerfully (2 Corinthians 9:5-7) in proportion to what one has (1 Corinthians 16:2), but he did not specify a percentage.

Any biblical doctrine of tithing is therefore based on Old Testament passages, and many Christians do not see these as binding in the church. However, Old Testament teachings about tithing are important for they reveal how God views the purposes of giving. Perhaps the most famous passage about tithing is found in the book of Malachi, the source of this week's lesson.

B. Lesson Background

The name *Malachi* means "my messenger." It may be that this is a title rather than a personal name, for essentially the same Hebrew word occurs both in Malachi 1:1 (translated "Malachi") and 3:1 (translated "my messenger"). We have little definitive knowledge about this man or his prophetic ministry. The issues he addressed seem to parallel those of Ezra and Nehemiah, which would place Malachi in the mid-fifth century BC. For context, this dating means that the rebuilt temple had been in operation for over half a century and that most of Malachi's audience had grown up with this institution being fully functional.

Malachi addressed a variety of issues, but his core complaint was that the people no longer honored or respected the Lord (see Malachi 1:6a). The worst offenders seem to have been the temple priests themselves, who were guilty of using defective animals as sacrifices (1:6b-8). Malachi told them that it would be better to shut down the temple than to operate in such a shameful manner (1:10). He prophesied terrible judgment for the priests, a curse to span generations (2:2, 3).

But the future was not entirely bleak for Malachi, and he promised a renewed presence of the Lord. It is the fulfillment of that promise that is especially important for us today.

I. What to Expect

(MALACHI 3:1-5)

A. My Messenger and the Lord (v. 1)

1. "I will send my messenger, who will prepare the way before me. Then suddenly the Lord you are seeking will come to his temple; the messenger of the covenant, whom you desire, will come," says the LORD Almighty.

This can be a confusing verse, because at first glance it may seem to refer to four individuals: (1) *my messenger,* (2) *the Lord you are seeking,* (3) *the messenger of the covenant,* and (4) *the Lord Almighty.* The first refers to a specially designated future messenger of the Lord. The last three are different ways to refer to the God of Israel.

Let's break this down a bit further. The given purpose of the first individual is to *prepare the way before* the Lord. The nature of this preparation is not explained. But presuming that the preparation is not conducted in secret, we can safely assume that it includes at least an announcement of the Lord's coming, whose arrival at and appearance in *his temple* will be sudden.

The word *suddenly* may include the idea of "unexpectedly" (as in Numbers 6:9; Isaiah 47:11) for those who don't pay attention to the preparations to be made by the messenger. Malachi's audience is in for an unwanted surprise if they don't repent (see the Lesson Background).

On the other hand, the Lord's arrival will be a welcome time for those who anticipate his coming. Malachi pictures the Lord as a messenger concerned with his covenant with Israel; thus the second and third individuals are one and the same. Since this prophecy originates directly from the *Lord Almighty,* its fulfillment is guaranteed. The Lord God Almighty (compare Revelation 4:8) is the author of Israel's covenant, the one whose glory has filled the temple in the past (1 Kings 8:11).

The facts of history establish Malachi's words to be predictive of John the Baptist as the messenger of the Lord, and Jesus Christ as the Lord who comes to his people. Jesus quotes Malachi 3:1 in identifying the role of John the Baptist as Jesus' forerunner (Matthew 11:10; Luke 7:27).

What Do You Think?

How did others help "prepare the way" for you to receive Christ? How can you do so for others?

Talking Points for Your Discussion

- Regarding lifestyle modeled
- Regarding conversational patterns
- Regarding informal teaching opportunities
- Other

❧ THE LORD IS RETURNING! ❧

With the Lord's first coming now a fact of history, focus rightfully shifts to his promised return (Acts 1:11; etc.). Even so, most Christians know all too well the pitfalls of being obsessive about signs and calculations in this regard.

But some never seem to learn! Some prognosticators saw proof of the end approaching when a giant meteor exploded in the sky over eastern Russia on February 15, 2013, the same day asteroid 2012 DA14 passed very close to Earth. End-time significance was also seen in the names of the constellations through which comet C/2012 S1 passed in the fall of 2013.

Unlike modern false prophets, Malachi left the timing up to God. Far more important than ascertaining the time of the Lord's coming—whether of the first instance in Malachi's prophecy or the second in our day—is letting the world know that it *will* happen! Do we need to spend our time more wisely in that regard?　　　—C. R. B.

B. Fire and Soap (vv. 2, 3a)

2. But who can endure the day of his coming? Who can stand when he appears? For he will be like a refiner's fire or a launderer's soap.

Malachi prophesies the coming of the Lord in terms of judgment. The implied answer to his two rhetorical questions is "no one," meaning that all are subject to judgment. The effect of the judgment to come *will be like a refiner's fire*, which burns away the impurities in the ore of a precious metal (see more on this in v. 3, below).

> *What Do You Think?*
> How have life experiences served as "a refiner's fire" regarding your commitment to Christ?
> *Talking Points for Your Discussion*
> - Health problems (illnesses, accidents, etc.)
> - Financial setbacks
> - Loss of loved ones
> - Other

Malachi also compares this judgment with *launderer's soap.* The Hebrew phrasing behind this occurs only here and in Jeremiah 2:22. A launderer is one who dresses cloth. The soap used in such a trade is not the gentle soap for washing clothes as we use today, but is strong lye soap. It can turn linen or wool from brownish to intensely white (see Mark 9:3). Jeremiah 2:22 notes the impossibility of sinful Israel's using such cleansing powder to purge itself from sin. But here in Malachi, such cleansing is possible from the Lord.

3a. He will sit as a refiner and purifier of silver; he will purify the Levites and refine them like gold and silver.

Refining fire purifies *gold and silver* in a brutal process that separates the metal from con-

taminants. As applied to people, this happens in terms of three distinctives. First, the Lord *will sit* as he refines, intending perhaps a double image of a judge seated on a judgment throne as well as a metallurgist at work in a forge. Second, the special objects of refining judgment are *the Levites,* the priestly class that is corrupting the temple (Malachi 1:6; 2:1-9). Third, the intent of this judgment is not annihilation but purity (see the next verse).

C. Good and Bad (vv. 3b-5)

3b. Then the Lord will have men who will bring offerings in righteousness,

The result of the purification is that these sons of Levi will be able to give *offerings in righteousness.* The correction in the temple's sacrificial practices will be a sign that the covenant is restored, but we must not understand this apart from the sacrifice of Jesus Christ. His crucifixion in close proximity to the temple was the perfect, righteous sacrifice for all time, making an eternal covenant (see Hebrews 13:11, 12, 20).

4. . . . and the offerings of Judah and Jerusalem will be acceptable to the Lord, as in days gone by, as in former years.

Having looked to the future, Malachi takes a glance at the past. Proper sacrifice will not be a new development but a return to *days gone by.* The priestly system of sacrifices has been part of Israel's history for perhaps a thousand years by Malachi's day. That system has been defiled often over the centuries, but the future renewal *will be acceptable to the Lord.* This indicates reconciliation between God and his people.

> *What Do You Think?*
> How has your understanding of giving grown over the years? What or who influenced that growth?
> *Talking Points for Your Discussion*
> - During various stages of childhood
> - During various stages of adulthood

5. "So I will come to put you on trial. I will be quick to testify against sorcerers, adulterers and perjurers, against those who defraud laborers of their wages, who oppress the wid-

ows and the fatherless, and deprive the foreigners among you of justice, but do not fear me," says the LORD Almighty.

Now we learn that the judgment of God is not just against the corrupt and cynical Levites. It is also against a long list of those whose sins are being tolerated in Malachi's day, perhaps as such people are favored by the priestly class ("the Levites," v. 3). Malachi's list of evildoers, one of the most comprehensive in the prophets, identifies *sorcerers* (those engaging in occult practices), who are condemned in Isaiah 47:9, 12; *adulterers* (those breaking the Seventh Commandment), who are condemned in Malachi 2:14; *perjurers* (those violating the Ninth Commandment), who are condemned in Leviticus 6:1-6; and those who oppress the most vulnerable, oppressors condemned in Zechariah 7:10 (last week's lesson).

The blanket description of all these folks is that they *do not fear* the Lord. They view the requirements of God as irrelevant. The Lord *will be quick to testify against* these wrongdoers! The perversion of justice in Malachi's society is abhorrent and intolerable to the Lord. Such injustice is a frequent target of his prophets (see Isaiah 59:15, lesson 9; Jeremiah 7:5-11, lesson 10; Amos 5:7, 24, lesson 2; Micah 3:9, lesson 6; etc.). If humans do not enact God's justice, then God himself will act to do so.

What Do You Think?
How can Malachi's words help form a Christian viewpoint on various social issues today?
Talking Points for Your Discussion
- Regarding aid from the government vs. aid by the church vs. seeing giving of aid as "enabling"
- Regarding governmental economic policies
- Regarding immigration policy
- Other

II. How to Prepare
(MALACHI 3:6-10)
A. Problem (vv. 6-9)

6. "I the LORD do not change. So you, the descendants of Jacob, are not destroyed.

With injustice and evil rampant, where is the justice of the Lord? Malachi answers this implied question with a brief but profound assertion from God: *I the Lord do not change.* In other words, God is not subject to human expectations. That was God's reply to Job when that man demanded answers of the Lord for his suffering (Job 38:4). God is not answerable to us or to our questions about his plans. It is his decision for the present that *the descendants of Jacob, are not destroyed.*

7a. "Ever since the time of your ancestors you have turned away from my decrees and have not kept them. Return to me, and I will return to you," says the LORD Almighty.

To stray from the covenant is not a new thing for Israel, the covenant people. They have sinned willfully from the earliest days (example: the notorious golden-calf incident of Exodus 32).

The invitation *return to me* means repenting—rededicating hearts to the Lord while renouncing a sinful path. *Return* is a directional word, recognizing that a course must be reversed. A picture found often in the Bible is that of the heavenly Father waiting and longing for people to return to him (compare Luke 15:20). The act and response *Return to me, and I will return to you* reminds us of James 4:8: "Come near to God and he will come near to you."

7b. "But you ask, 'How are we to return?'

The question Malachi anticipates from his audience may imply a rebellious state of mind as the people respond, "We don't need to turn to God. We are just fine. Go away and leave us alone." On the other hand, the question Malachi anticipates may imply sincere bewilderment as in, "We're already *with* God. How can we return to him when we're already there?" Either way, Malachi is about to describe something specific that the people must do to begin their return to the Lord.

8. "Will a mere mortal rob God? Yet you rob me.
But you ask, 'How are we robbing you?'
"In tithes and offerings.

The chosen issue has to do with one of the covenant obligations of the people, the matter of *tithes and offerings.* The Law of Moses features extensive regulations concerning tithes. Studying these yields an important principle: the tithe belongs to the Lord. In a flock of sheep, for example, every tenth animal is God's (Leviticus 27:32). This is not a matter of the flock's owner being generous by giving valuable sheep to the temple. Rather, it is yielding to the Lord an asset under one's oversight as one realizes that the asset is already the Lord's by right.

When we give an offering at church today, we may be tempted to view it like a parent giving a child an allowance, or like a taxpayer dutifully writing a check to the government. Malachi's understanding flows in the opposite direction: all the sheep are God's to begin with, yet he claims only one-tenth. For an ancient Israelite to tithe was God's permission for them to keep the other nine-tenths. Therefore, to withhold the tithe was not a lack of generosity but outright thievery—a taking of that which belonged to another.

What Do You Think?
What can one's giving practices say about the condition of his or her relationship with God?
Talking Points for Your Discussion
- Regarding consistency in giving
- Regarding preparations to give
- Regarding reasons for giving
- Other

❧ ROBBING GOD TODAY ❧

By one estimate, the average churchgoer puts only about 3 percent of his or her income in the offering plate. Another study claims that if this would rise to 10 percent, then American Christians "could evangelize the world, stop the daily deaths of 29,000 children younger than 5 worldwide, provide elementary education across the globe and tackle domestic poverty—and have $150 billion left over annually."

How those figures were calculated is not clear, but the claimed outcomes would indeed be impressive! More conservatively, however, think what would happen if that 3 percent level of giving increased only to 4 percent: funding for ministry would go up by a whopping one-third!

But all this talk of percentages may be missing a key element of the bigger picture: God is interested in much more than a formulaic relationship

with his people. His call for purity of life indicates there is more to being godly than giving a specified percentage of one's income.

Are there ways we rob God other than by being stingy when the offering plate is passed? Perhaps the time and effort I pour into furthering my career is robbing God of my service for his kingdom. Perhaps my leisure activities are robbing God of the attention he wants me to give to my family on his behalf. What other areas of potential robbery come to mind?   —C. R. B.

9. "You are under a curse—your whole nation —because you are robbing me.

Stealing from God? Bad. Very bad. It is so bad that Malachi portrays it as *a curse,* something that affects the prosperity of the *whole nation.* The miserly, thieving heart misses out on the blessings of God. If the love of money and possessions is so consuming that a person chooses not to release even a small percentage of them, there will be strong motivation for the social injustices already condemned (Malachi 3:5). The result will be a society where wages are withheld without cause, where widows and orphans will be destitute, and where foreigners will be denied basic human rights. Such is the bitter yield of selfishness!

B. Solution (v. 10)

10. "Bring the whole tithe into the storehouse, that there may be food in my house. Test me in this," says the LORD Almighty, "and see if I will not throw open the floodgates of heaven and pour out so much blessing that there will not be room enough to store it."

God promises to bless those who give freely and in full measure. This verse, used in countless offering meditations for decades, does not have the mechanical, legalistic application for Christians and churches that it is sometimes given. But it does establish at least two wonderful and important principles.

First, God promises that when the community is a giving community, there is *food in my house.* Under the old covenant, tithes and offerings go to Levites as their livelihood for their work in ministry (Numbers 18; Nehemiah 10:36-39). Failure to provide for Levites in this way results in decreased functioning of the temple (Nehemiah 13:10-13). The needs of the family of God are being met by the generosity of its members.

Giving in free and full measure today means that the necessary budget of the church is met by the church membership. Our contributions provide for and maintain church facilities as well as salary for church staff members who devote themselves to ministry as a vocation. In the context of Malachi, generosity also includes assistance for the needy, and this obligation is ours today as well (2 Corinthians 8:1-15; etc.).

Second, the giver will be blessed. In a beloved word-picture, Malachi promises that *the floodgates of heaven* will be opened for generous people. Normally, we are not to tempt or test God (Deuteronomy 6:16; Matthew 4:7). But here God invites his people to *test me in this*. The blessings of God will far exceed the sacrificial giving of the generous person.

We should not necessarily anticipate these blessings in tangible ways, although that may be part of it. Generosity is its own reward as our hearts are warmed when we know our gifts make a difference in the lives of others. Whether those gifts mean providing for our minister, supporting a homeless shelter, or helping purchase a cow for subsistence farmers in Africa, there is satisfaction in having done as God desires.

Conclusion

A. Leaving a Legacy

Not long ago, I spoke with an elderly friend who had a vexing problem. He had spent most of his life

Visual for
Lesson 13

Use this visual as a backdrop for discussing how returning, repenting, and giving are interrelated.

becoming rich. He had done this by sacrificial saving, careful investing, frugal living, and hard work. At the end of his life, he had far more money than he would ever use. What should he do with all his money? He was reluctant to leave it to his children, because they were all doing well themselves.

I had suggestions for him, but the situation also made me ponder what plans we Christians should make for our assets. We are motivated to save for the future and often warned that we can never save too much. But it seems to me that we are missing a blessing if we do not begin to release our assets before we die. Wouldn't I enjoy increasing my support for my favorite Christian ministry *now* rather than designate a substantial gift in my will?

The answer to this sort of question will depend on one's financial position, needs for retirement, etc. Perhaps, though, the teachings of Malachi may spur us to giving generously so that the floodgates of Heaven will open for blessings long before we are actually *in* Heaven!

B. Prayer

Father, help us to be more like you as we seek to live lives of generosity. We thank you for the blessings we have received from your bounty and for those you have planned for our future. We pray this in the name of your generous Son, Jesus; amen.

C. Thought to Remember

God still blesses generosity.

HOW TO SAY IT

Asa	*Ay*-zuh.
Ezra	*Ez*-ruh.
Isaiah	Eye-*zay*-uh.
Jeremiah	Jair-uh-*my*-uh.
Malachi	*Mal*-uh-kye.
Moses	*Mo*-zes or *Mo*-zez.
Nehemiah	*Nee*-huh-**my**-uh.
Zechariah	Zek-uh-**rye**-uh.

INVOLVEMENT LEARNING

Enhance your lesson with NIV® Bible Student (from your curriculum supplier) and the reproducible activity page (at www.standardlesson.com or in the back of the NIV® Standard Lesson Commentary Deluxe Edition).

Into the Lesson

Form learners into four groups or pairs. Give each group/pair an index card that features one of the following four Scripture references: Leviticus 27:30-33; 1 Corinthians 16:1, 2; 2 Corinthians 9:5-8; 2 Corinthians 8:10-12. (Smaller classes can form fewer groups/pairs to receive more than one card.) Ask each group/pair to study the Scripture indicated to discern principles of giving, then share their conclusions with the class as a whole.

Say, "God specified an amount to give under the old covenant but not under the new. But under either covenant, he is concerned primarily with the attitude of the giver. Notice, for example, the wording 'no one may pick out the good from the bad' in Leviticus 27:33 and 'what you have decided in your heart to give' in 2 Corinthians 9:7. The prophet Malachi addressed this heart issue with the Israelites after they had resettled in Jerusalem and rebuilt the temple. Let's see how his thoughts still challenge us today."

Into the Word

Divide the board into four quadrants labeled *Messenger(s) / Israel's Sin / God's Rebuke / God's Promise*, one label each. Have a learner read Malachi 3:1-4 aloud. Ask, "Are the phrases 'my messenger' and 'the messenger of the covenant' referring to one and the same person? Why, or why not?" Use the commentary to correct misperceptions as you lead a discussion of the Messianic nature of these verses. Jot responses and clarifications in the *Messenger(s)* quadrant, making sure to cover the purposes of the two messengers and Jesus' quote of Malachi 3:1 in Matthew 11:10 (also Luke 7:27).

Next, have a volunteer read verse 5, then write the following references in the *Israel's Sin* quadrant: Leviticus 6:1-6; Isaiah 47:9, 12; Zechariah 7:10; Malachi 2:14. For each reference, have a learner look it up, read it, and match it to a sin or sinner in Malachi 3:5. Ask learners how the Isra-elites' behavior in each area revealed the intent of their hearts.

Move to verses 6-9 of the lesson text and ask a learner to read them. Call for a summary of God's rebuke, and jot responses in that quadrant. For discussion, ask, "How is it possible to 'rob God' since he himself has said, 'Every animal of the forest is mine, and the cattle on a thousand hills' in Psalm 50:10?" If responses do not address the issue of the condition of the people's hearts, be sure to lead the discussion in that direction.

Immediately after you read verse 10 to the class, write "If _____, then _____" in the *God's Promise* quadrant. Call for suggestions regarding what should go in the blanks as verse 10 indicates. After each set of suggestions, ask, "Can anyone do better?" Continue until there are no more suggestions. If learners do not do so, be sure to propose how this statement should be completed in light of the two principles that verse 10 establishes, per the lesson commentary.

Into Life

Say, "Handel's *Messiah* contains two segments taken from parts of today's lesson text. As we listen, let us reflect on the ways God refines us to be vessels that are appropriate to bear his image and message." Play "But Who May Abide the Day of His Coming?" (about five minutes) and "And He Shall Purify" (about two and a half minutes) from a CD or, if you have Internet access, YouTube®. Encourage learners to follow along in verses 2 and 3 of the lesson text, which constitute the lyrics of the two pieces of music, respectively. When the pieces finish, conclude with a prayer drawn from those verses.

Alternative. Distribute copies of the choral reading "My Offering of Praise," from the reproducible page, which you can download. Divide the class into two groups and perform the reading as indicated.